Botanica's

ANNUALS &
PERENNIALS

D1057662

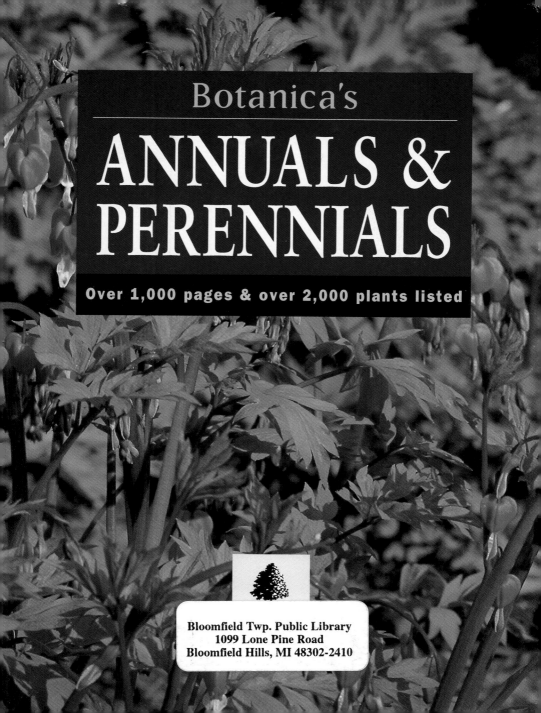

Botanica's

ANNUALS & PERENNIALS

Over 1,000 pages & over 2,000 plants listed

First published in the United States by
Laurel Glen Publishing
5880 Oberlin Drive, Suite 400
San Diego, CA 92121-4794

ISBN 1-57145-648-1
Library of Congress Cataloging-in-Publication Data available
upon request.

1 2 3 4 5 99 00 01 02 03

Consultants: Geoff Bryant, Tony Rodd and Dr Gerlinde von Berg

Publisher: **Gordon Cheers**

Associate Publisher: **Margaret Olds**

Managing Editor: **James Young**

Editors: **Anna Cheifetz, Clare Double, Loretta Barnard and
Denise Imwold**

Design: **Stan Lamond**

Cover Design: **Bob Mitchell**

Photolibrarian: **Susan Page**

Assembly: **Paula Kelly and James Young**

Typesetting: **Dee Rogers**

Index: **Glenda Browne**

Production Manager: **Linda Watchorn**

Publishing Coordinator: **Sarah Sherlock**

Printed by Sing Cheong Printing Co. Ltd, Hong Kong

Film separation: Pica Colour Separation, Singapore

PHOTOGRAPHS, PRELIMINARY PAGES AND CHAPTER OPENINGS

Contents

Introduction

People often think of annuals and perennials simply as a way to provide quick garden color. However, they should not be underestimated; they encompass an enormous diversity of foliage forms, textures and growth habits. Certainly, they can be short lived and sometimes they become untidy well before the end of the growing season, but unlike more permanent plants, they are relatively cheap, easily propagated, tough, adaptable and above all, versatile.

Trees and shrubs will probably remain the framework of your garden, yet on their own they can seem staid and uninteresting. Annuals and perennials brighten the garden and provide continuous variety of flower, foliage and form. Think of them as the color palette for your garden, to be used to fill in the broad lines of the more permanent features. Use the pastel shades of *Impatiens* in broad washes as you would watercolors, or the vivid oil paint colors of marigolds for intense spots of brightness.

Whatever the design of your garden and regardless of the climate it experiences, there is such a wide range of annuals and perennials in this book that you need never be short of choice. However, ornamental grasses and bulbs, corms and tubers are not included here.

What are annuals and perennials?

The difference between annuals, biennials and perennials relates to the life cycles of the plants. Annuals grow from seed to full maturity within one growing season. Marigolds, ageratums and zinnias are

Anticlockwise from bottom left:
Lychnis coronaria, Salvia nemorosa 'Primavera', *Phlomis russeliana* and a *Verbascum* cultivar

Ajania 'Bess' and 'Benny' make a striking pot planting

typical annuals. They flower, set seed and die, all within a single year. Biennials, such as Canterbury bells and some foxgloves, complete their life cycles over two years, sometimes producing a few flowers in the first season, but most often just making foliage growth and establishing their root systems. Perennials live longer than two seasons and may outlive many shrubs. In fact, strictly speaking, shrubs and trees are perennials, but when gardeners talk of perennials they generally mean plants that don't develop permanent woody stems.

Perennials occur in several types. Some, such as *Acanthus*, are evergreen and don't have a period of total dormancy, though few flower continually except in very mild climates. Herbaceous perennials—those most common in temperate climate gardens—usually have a period of dormancy when they die back to a permanent rootstock. Most commonly this is during winter, but plants from hot dry areas may be dormant in summer or during periods of very low rainfall.

Some herbaceous perennials have developed the ability to use their roots or stems as food storage organs to enable them to survive extended periods of dormancy. Known as rhizomes and tubers, these storage roots can often be separated from the parent plant and grown on as new plants, in much the same way as bulbs and corms. Dahlias and alstroemerias are well-known tuberous plants, while bearded irises are probably the most widely grown rhizomatous plants. Some plants have specialized rhizomes known as stolons, which spread across the surface of the ground, or just below the surface, taking root as they spread.

Some perennials are treated as annuals, either because they cease to be attractive as they age, or because they are incapable of surviving cold winters. Petunias and impatiens, for example, may live for several seasons if protected from frost, but they become leggy and untidy, so they are usually replaced annually.

It is not uncommon for a genus to contain both annual and perennial species, such as the annual and perennial cosmos, or species with differing growth habits, like the fibrous and tuberous rooted irises and begonias. In cultivation, the differences between annuals, biennials and the various types of perennials tend to become blurred. The important thing is how you use the plants, and with annuals and perennials you can give free rein to your imagination.

Obtaining plants

When first establishing a perennial garden you will probably buy all of your plants from a nursery or garden center. However, one of the great advantages of perennials is their ease of propagation. By the end of the first season you will have quite a few large plants ready for dividing. Some, such as peonies, will grow for many years without needing to be divided, and may not recover quickly once broken up, but to maintain their

Anticlockwise from left:

Raising annuals from seed: Fill the seed tray with a good soil mix; lightly sprinkle the seed over the surface; cover the seeds with a little seed-raising mixture; cover with clear plastic or glass; remove the cover once the seedlings have germinated and grow on until large enough to transplant

Anticlockwise from left:

Transplanting seedlings: Makes holes with an old pencil or 'dibble'; loosen soil around the seedling and separate the roots; place the seedling in the hole, firm the soil down and water immediately

vigor most perennials need dividing at least every three years. Many can also be grown from cuttings, usually of the fast-growing spring shoots.

Annuals must be raised from seed. You can do this yourself or buy ready-to-plant seedlings from a garden center. For small quantities, raising your own seed is seldom cheaper than buying seedlings, but if you have large beds to plant out, raising your own plants often represents a considerable saving. If you need large quantities of seedlings it's best to find a nursery that will order for you from commercial growers' seed catalogs. Not only will you make greater financial savings this way, you'll also find that the commercial seed selection is usually better than garden center stock in range, quality and price.

Seed sowing and germination are usually very straightforward procedures.

In many cases the seed may be sown directly where it is to grow, although it is more common to sow in trays and then plant out. The only complication is timing: you don't want to sow too early as your seed may fail to germinate or the seedlings may be frost damaged; too late and they may not mature before cold stops their growth.

Climate adaptability

Most of the traditional garden perennials are hardy and very adaptable. However, those from southern Africa, Central and South America and parts of Australia tend to be less cold-tolerant and may not be suited to frosty areas, especially where late frosts can be expected.

If you live in a cool-temperate climate you may still be able to grow these plants. Often the problem is not so much the cold, but a combination of cold and wet

Annuals such as this *Gerbera jamesonii* cultivar can be brought indoors during the flowering period

conditions. Plants such as *Gerbera* will tolerate quite hard frosts if they are kept dry but will rot when cold and wet. Most gardens have a few areas that are protected and remain dry in winter; these are the places to plant the Southern African daisies and the tender novelties like *Alonsoa*. Some tender perennials, such as *Heliotrope* and the 'Butterfly' *Impatiens*, demand complete frost protection. Treat them as annuals, grow them in containers that can be moved under cover for the winter, or take cuttings in the autumn and keep them indoors until spring.

Annuals are usually grown to provide color. Because they are only temporary plants and always treated as such they succeed everywhere. They permit gardeners in cold areas to briefly ignore the prospect of winter bleakness and inject a touch of tropical summer color into their gardens.

Annuals are subject to all the normal climatic considerations—wind, salt spray and summer heat—but they are remarkably resilient plants that carry on flowering under most conditions, except severe cold.

Tender annuals must be planted in spring, after the last frosts, with a view to summer and autumn flowering. However, the so-called hardy annuals are often planted in the autumn and left to over-winter for spring flowering. Pansies, sweet William and Iceland poppies are among the best known hardy annuals. With careful planning it is possible to have bloom almost all year round.

Garden design

Although annuals allow far more scope for design changes and mixing and matching than permanent plants, many people prefer to work to some sort of garden design. If you're keen on cottage gardens, perennials may make up the bulk of your planting; conversely if large rose beds are your preference you may need just a few annuals as fillers. Every garden has a place for annuals and perennials and there are many ways to use them.

Below: This garden makes good use of water, trees, shrubs and annuals and perennials: *Papaver orientale, Stachys macrantha* and a *Hemerocallis* cultivar

Below: A semi-formal garden of petunias, pelargoniums, roses, lavender, potato vine and clipped *Buxus*

Annual flower bed

Think of annuals and the chances are you'll think of vivid flower beds. While the massed plantings seen in botanic gardens and large private gardens are beyond most of us, a bed or two of annuals does not look out of place, even in a small garden. Of course, lawns and flower beds go well together. A velvety green sward is offset to perfection by a bed of riotous color, and the flower beds are easy to view and walk around when surrounded by lawn. It's hard not to be impressed by the effect of all that color in such a small space. However, massed bedding demands a considerable amount of time and effort for a fairly brief display, and the effort has to be repeated at least twice a year. This eventually loses its novelty for all but the most dedicated gardeners, which is why really impressive flower beds tend to be restricted to botanic or corporate gardens and private show gardens.

Making a good flower bed requires that the soil be worked to a fine tilth and regularly fertilized. To keep up the color as long as possible may mean replanting up to three times a year. The main summer display must be planted by mid-spring and removed by late summer, to be replaced by an autumn selection; this is then replaced in early winter by hardy annuals that will flower from late winter to mid-spring.

The bold display we expect from massed annuals allows the gardener to get away with some pretty unusual color combinations. Beds composed of many clashing colors certainly create an immediate impact, but they can be hard to live with. Careful color planning and consideration of height will result in a bed that is just as colorful, but far more harmonious and relaxing.

Massed bedding doesn't have to be rigidly planned. The readily available wildflower seed mixes offer an easier alternative: just scatter the seed, rake it in lightly and wait. Provided the seed bed has been well prepared and you keep the weeds down, the plants will do the

Helichrysum petiolare 'Goring Silver', *Verbena* 'Temari Scarlet' and *Argyranthemum frutescens* 'Summer Melody'

An herbaceous border featuring *Lychnis coronaria* and *Salvia* × *sylvestris* cultivars

rest. The seed companies have done all the color mixing and size gradation for you, although there's nothing to stop you making up your own seed mixtures and scattering them to the wind. Quite often the effects of such random sowing are better than anything you could have planned—which just goes to show that nature is still the best gardener!

Beds of annuals are not just about flowers; some very interesting effects can be created by foliage alone. Silverleaf, bloodleaf, *Coleus* and many other bedding plants don't need flowers to make an impact. Others, such as *Celosia* and the red leaf begonias, combine interesting foliage with bright flowers.

Herbaceous border

Perennials too, are often best grown in large beds, which provide bold impact when planted in color groups, and allow the plants to be viewed from all angles, often emphasizing the foliage forms. Because these perennial beds are often used as an edging to a lawn, driveway or wall, they are usually called herbaceous borders, even when they are not really borders.

Herbaceous perennials blend well with other garden plants, especially annuals, but because they are regularly lifted and divided, it's often more convenient to cultivate them separately in large beds. Lifting the plants and dividing and removing the waste is greatly simplified when there are no permanent shrubs or trees in the way.

The herbaceous border requires no special construction techniques: it is just a large garden bed. It can be edged with a low hedge or some form of retainer, such as bricks, or it may just be cut from a lawn. The soil should be thoroughly prepared by digging in plenty of compost and applying supplementary fertilizers. Beds cut from lawns will benefit from a light dressing of lime, otherwise a general garden fertilizer will be adequate. Most large perennials grow rapidly, and with their fairly deep roots they feed heavily; the more you can loosen the soil to allow the roots to spread, the better they will grow. It's not possible to add too much compost, provided it's well rotted down.

The skill in developing a herbaceous border is in the planting. A good planting is the peak of garden excellence; a poor one is just an assortment of mismatched plants. Decide on an overall theme before you begin. There should be some sense of direction or emphasis, for example plantings within a restricted color range; groups of compatible foliage, such as all silver-leafed plants; or plants with similar flower types, such as a bed composed entirely of daisies. Remember to consider the varying heights of the plants, keeping the taller ones to the back and making sure they don't hide one another in a jumble of foliage. You can also use variations in size to highlight particular plants by exposing their best features. Less attractive parts can be strategically hidden.

This may seem a rather rigid way of planting, and indeed it can be. The best gardeners know when to break the rules with effects like brightly contrasting colors or foliage, and they know when to hold back too. Growing a successful herbaceous border demands that you know your plants.

Ornamental grasses can be combined with annuals and perennials to great effect. *Festuca mairei, Lychnis coronaria, Coreopsis verticillata* and *Achillea millefolium* are featured here.

Cottage garden

The cottage garden aims for seemingly natural randomness and attractive plant associations. By planting simple flowers and rambling old fashioned shrubs, particularly roses and others with fragrance, it's possible to create a charming effect. A cottage garden should make you want to explore; it should be filled with interesting little novelties waiting to be found. Night-scented stocks, small pansies, cornflowers and larkspur are annuals that are perfect for the cottage look. Among the biennials and perennials, consider foxgloves, *Coreopsis*, *Scabiosa*, *Dianthus*, all the various primulas, and peonies.

If your aim is to create a garden reminiscent of the past, avoid using too many plants with large double flowers and vibrant colors. If the semi-wild look is what you're after, any color is acceptable, but once again avoid flowers that look 'overdeveloped'. Cottage and semi-wild gardens should have a light, airy feel; single flowers on rather open bushes are often more appropriate than compact bushes with large double blooms.

Cottage gardens and semi-wild gardens are often promoted as an easy-care alternative, but don't be fooled. They require just as much planning as any other garden style and probably more maintenance. Planning a cottage garden depends largely on the layout of your site. Large open areas lend themselves to extensive beds and drifts of plants, the wildflower seed mixes are very useful here. If large beds don't appeal, dividing up a big garden into several small theme

A classic cottage garden at Great Dixter in Kent, UK

The gray foliage of *Artemisia* makes a pleasnt foil for peonies and penstemons

gardens is a good way to maintain interest. Try to design the garden so there's always something new around every corner; the prospect of a pleasant surprise keeps people looking and adds to your own pleasure. Compact gardens are usually better suited to small pockets of flowers and containers full of color.

Woodland garden

Recreating a natural effect is the prime aim of the woodland garden, and the closely associated bog garden. However, such freedom doesn't mean that you can ignore the rules: the natural look and the randomness are only apparent, not real. The great paradox of gardening is that the more natural the effect, the more planning it requires. However, making mistakes is one of the best ways to learn, so accept occasional setbacks by putting your new-found knowledge to work.

Of course, you can't plant a woodland from scratch—first you need trees. Initial appearances may suggest that foliage dominates in the woodland garden (think of all those hostas and ferns) but careful study will reveal a subtle blend of foliage and flowers, and give you an idea of the proportions of the plants. Novice gardeners are inclined to think that a woodland garden must be absolutely full of plants, when in reality a better understanding of plant sizes and growth forms enables the gardener to create an illusion of abundance even with relatively few plants.

The advantage of not cramming everything in is that you have room for little treasures: those plants that you forget about for most of the year, then all of a sudden, much to your delight, they're there again. Woodlands tend to be spring gardens, but there are enough late-flowering small perennials and shrubs to maintain year-round interest. It's also acceptable to plant a few shade-loving summer annuals, such as impatiens and mimulus, to add a dash of color. However, be discreet, tranquillity is important in the woodland garden.

Rock gardens

Rock gardens, more than most other garden styles, attempt to recreate natural features in the garden and as is often the case, the more natural and simple the finished product appears, the more difficult it is to create. It should therefore come as no surprise that rockeries are one of the most difficult areas of garden design. Indeed, they are often viewed as the height of the gardener's art.

The secret lies in creating a sense of scale. The plants must be in proportion to size of the rocks and the garden as a whole. A large rock garden with sizeable rocks allows larger plants to be used; creating a successful small rock garden demands more skill as it is difficult to maintain realistic proportions on a small scale. It requires a knowledgeable gardener with an artistic touch.

Before building your rock garden, visit some of the natural rockeries that

Above right: **Pulsatilla halleri** subsp. *slavica*
Right: **Calceolaria**, Herbeohybrida Group cultivar

can be found in hills and mountains. Look at how time and the forces of nature have acted on the rocks. In stable areas where the rocks have settled and plants have started to grow, you will usually find that the rocks are well embedded and their grain tends to run in the same direction. Jumbled piles of loose rocks are unstable and liable to move, and few plants will be found there. Keep these natural variations in mind when designing your rockery and you will be able to create changes of mood in the design. You will also be better able to cater for the particular needs of the plants.

Rockeries are all about slopes and changes in level, so they are an excellent way of developing a naturally sloping site. On flat ground there are no natural slopes, so positioning the rockery becomes critical. A small rockery in the middle of a flat expanse of lawn is bound to look unnatural. Flat sites require large rocks or extensive contouring to provide the necessary variations in level.

Ground cover plants

Ground covers are not just ornamental, they also serve to bind the soil with their roots, preventing erosion by heavy rains. By covering the surface of soil they also prevent the sun drying the ground and stop the wind blowing away the topsoil. They are, in effect, living mulches.

Some ground covers, such as *Dichondra*, can be used as lawn substitutes while others are an easy way of adding quick color or foliage variation. Massed annuals and many perennials may be used as ground covers even if they are not usually grown for the purpose.

Lysimachia nummularia (yellow) intertwined with *Duchesnia indica*

Clockwise from top: ***Chrysanthemum*** 'Dreamstar Deborah', *Salvia officinalis* 'Ictarina', a *Hedera helix* cultivar and *Heuchera* 'Rachel' in a striking container planting

Container growing

Annuals and perennials often make excellent container plants because they provide plenty of color, yet don't take up a lot of room. Many, such as pelargoniums and *Portulaca* are also drought tolerant, which can be a lifesaver when you forget to water.

Use window boxes and tubs planted with vivid annuals to brighten up dark areas in summer, then replace them with polyanthus and violas for winter color. If you have a greenhouse, conservatory or covered patio, you can grow your tender perennials in containers and move them under cover for the winter.

Always use a good potting mix in containers and remember to add some slow-release fertilizer. Add a wetting agent too, or you may find the mix very difficult to re-wet if it dries out completely. Your potting mix will probably contain fertilizers, but regular watering leaches them out. Container plants demand regular feeding—liquid fertilizers are usually the most convenient to apply.

Don't be afraid to innovate and improvise with shocking color combinations or novelty containers, such as boots, teapots and old commodes. There are endless ways of using annuals and perennials in containers.

Soil and planting

The plant and the climate in which it evolves are inextricably entwined. Everything about a plant—its soil preference, flower type, flowering time, pollination strategy, germination requirements and even its lifespan—are determined by its natural environment. With few exceptions, these things usually remain the same even when the plant is growing in garden conditions that are nothing like

Tulips and
Aubrietia ×
cultorum (purple edge)
seen through an
arbor covered in
Mahonia species

its natural environment. You may experience cool moist summers but that will not make the belladonnas bloom in mid-summer. You may experience mild winters but the hellebores will not germinate in autumn. Once evolved it usually takes many generations for a successful survival characteristic to be adapted or bred out.

Generally, plants perform better if the garden conditions are slightly easier than those they may experience in the wild. A little extra water, slightly richer soil and more shelter usually result in better growth, but there are limits. When in doubt, you can't go too far wrong by trying to emulate the plant's natural conditions.

When growing plants from arid regions, bear in mind that in the wild these plants usually start life as tiny seedlings. They often develop large tap roots or storage organs below ground before much above-ground growth is apparent. When you plant one of these species, it will most likely have been container-grown under good conditions and may not have the root system or reserves necessary to allow it to immediately cope with drought or other adversity. In such cases you will need to provide ample moisture to establish new plants, even though they will ultimately be very drought tolerant.

Most large herbaceous perennials thrive on soil with ample humus, as do woodland plants. When growing such plants, incorporate as much compost as possible. Genuine leaf mold from around deciduous trees is best, but well-rotted garden composts and commercially available soil conditioners are satisfactory.

Alpine plants are more likely to prefer a scree soil. Scree is a term that is often misunderstood—it does not mean pure shingle. That may be the dictionary definition, but in a gardening sense it means a soil composed of fine gritty stone chips and organic matter, as if you had mixed potting soil with shingle.

This type of soil is free draining but fairly moisture retentive at depth. Most surface hugging alpines will rot if the soil surface remains wet for long periods; a scree soil helps prevent this problem, as does a thin layer of fine stone chips around the crown of the plant.

Scree soils are usually suitable for dry climate plants too. Very few plants, even those that are very drought tolerant, actually demand a sandy soil. In most cases additional humus is beneficial but some plants, particularly those from dry winter climates, require very sharp drainage. To achieve this add stone chips rather than sand. Sand drains well but results in soils that can be hard to re-wet once dry; shingle improves the soil porosity and drainage while remaining easy to dampen.

Most annuals and perennial are planted either when very small or as divisions of larger plants. There is nothing very tricky about the planting. Simply plant seedlings at the same level as they were in their seed trays and avoid burying the

crowns of herbaceous perennials too deeply. The top of a perennial's crown usually sits at or just below soil level.

Care and cultivation
FEEDING
Annuals and perennials pack a lot of growth into a short period of time and consequently often have high nutrient demands. Thorough preparation with plenty of compost and supplementary fertilizer is preferable to trying to correct problems later. Additional fertilizers incorporated in mulches, or in organic, powdered chemical or liquid forms can be used to keep the plants growing steadily, but they can't make up for inadequate preparation.

The vivid orange calyces that surround the ripening fruit of *Physalis alkekengi*

Precise nutrient requirements vary depending on the plant, but the conditions under which they grow in the wild should give you some idea. However, don't take the native conditions as the final guide—many garden plants are far removed from the wild species and often require more care and attention to feeding and watering.

Avoid using very high nitrogen fertilizers or you may find that you get plenty of foliage but few flowers. A balanced fertilizer with a little extra potash is usually best. Some perennials, notably the southern African daisies, prefer fairly poor soils, so yet again it pays to know your plants.

When establishing large flower beds and herbaceous borders take the time to work in plenty of nutrient-rich humus. Your own garden compost is the best choice but well-rotted stable manure and other farmyard residues will also be beneficial. Rotted sawdust, peat and bark-based soil conditioners will help to improve the structure of the soil but as they contain few nutrients, you will need to add fertilizers to supplement them.

Whatever you use, make sure it is thoroughly decomposed. If it has to break down further after incorporation it will inevitably rob the soil of nitrogen.

If you have areas that are regularly used for flower beds repeat the composting every year, several weeks prior to planting. Likewise, whenever you lift your perennials for division incorporate plenty of compost before replanting.

Inevitably some experimentation will be necessary until you become familiar with your plants' requirements but don't neglect fertilizing simply because you're a bit worried about over-doing it. It is better to kill a few plants with kindness (and learn from your mistakes) than to stunt them all through neglect.

Pink phlox, white lilies, white erigeron daisies and dark blue delphiniums in an herbaceous border

Another herbaceous border featuring *Canna* species, *Dahlia* 'Bishop of Landaff', *Salvia microphylla*, *Miscanthus* species and *Cortaderia* species

WATERING

Regular watering is also important. It's no good having great soil if the plants are too wilted to use it.

Watering annuals and perennials from above with sprinklers can damage the flowers and beat the plants down to the ground. It also causes puddling, which can result in the development of a hard crust on the soil surface. Perforated soak hoses and drip lines are preferable, as well as being more water-efficient. If you must use sprinklers, choose the finest mist you can get. Containers demand regular watering, often daily in summer, and hanging baskets dry out particularly quickly.

Annuals should be watered as often as is necessary to ensure steady growth and flowering. On the whole you should err on the dry side. Most annuals will tolerate short dry periods but few will tolerate excess moisture without rotting or developing fungus diseases.

The establishment period, immediately after the planting out of seedlings, is when water is most needed. Seedlings grown *in situ* develop at a rate determined by the growing conditions, but young plants transplanted into new conditions need assistance to get established.

Ensure the young plants are moist before taking them out of their seedling trays and handle them carefully to lessen any root disturbance or transplant shock. This is particularly important with plants such as larkspur that resent any root disturbance. They may struggle on for quite some time but they rarely recover fully after an initial setback.

When to water perennials largely depends on their growing and flowering seasons. Those that bloom in early spring can usually get by with natural rainfall unless the spring weather is very dry. As the summer heats up they can be left to dry off naturally. Summer flowering perennials need even moisture throughout the growing season to be at their best.

Maintenance

Routine maintenance will keep your plants blooming longer. Remove any spent flowers and developing seed heads (unless you want the plants to self-sow), as once a plant sets seed it may cease flowering. Remove any damaged foliage or stems and stake tall plants, such as delphiniums. If producing the largest flowers is important, it pays to disbud plants like chrysanthemums, dahlias and tuberous begonias. This means removing the small lateral flower buds to produce larger terminal buds. You will need to consult specialist publications for the precise methods for each genus.

Provided they are kept growing steadily, annuals and perennials are remarkably free of pests and diseases. Of course, they can fall foul of all the regular pests, such as aphids, mites and various caterpillars, but these problems can usually be traced back to the growing conditions. Established plants in good growing conditions can cope with minor pests and diseases, but those in poor growing conditions will succumb.

The annual and perennial borders curve through lush lawn to create an inviting garden retreat

Above: Tip pruning encourages bushiness and greater flower production
Right: Annuals and perennials in this very formal garden provide year-round color and variation

Young seedlings are far more vulnerable regardless of the conditions. They are likely to be attacked by slugs, snails, cutworms, earwigs, slaters and birds, although losses from anything other than slugs and snails are seldom significant. Seedlings are also prone to the fungal disease known as damping off. Damping off rots the seed leaves and stems, causing the seedling to collapse. Good hygiene lessens the problem but damping off can occur at any time, so it's a good idea to regularly drench young seedlings with a fungicide solution.

Because the range of pests and diseases varies depending on your climate and location, only general advice is offered here. Consult your nursery or garden center for specialized information.

At the end of the summer season you will need to remove the spent annuals and tidy up dead growth on the perennials. If you intend to replant with overwintering hardy annuals remove the summer plants when they show noticeable signs of deterioration, otherwise leave them for some late color. Getting your winter and spring annuals planted early ensures they are well established before the really cold weather arrives.

Success with annuals and perennials requires more gardening effort than growing shrubs and trees, but this is repaid by a garden with more seasonal change and greater interest and color.

Top 20 annuals and perennials for special purposes

FOR COASTAL GARDENS

Arctotis (many)
Armeria maritima
Aurinia saxatilis
Centaurea cyanus
Cerastium tomentosum
Convolvulus cneorum
Crambe maritima
Dorotheanthus bellidiformis
Erysimum (many)
Eschscholzia californica
Felicia amelloides
Euryops (many)
Gazania (many)
Hesperis matrionalis
Limonium perezii
Lobularia maritima
Pelargonium (many)
Silene uniflora
Tanacetum coccineum
Xeronema callistemon

FOR ROCK GARDENS

Aethionema grandiflorum
Anagallis monellii
Androsace sarmentosa
Arabis caucasica
Aubrieta deltoidea
Campanula (many)
Dianthus (many)
Eschscholzia californica
Gazania (many)
Gentiana (many)
Iberis sempervirens
Lewisia cotyledon
Papaver alpinum
Phlox (ground covers)
Primula (many)
Pulsatilla vulgaris
Saxifraga (many)
Soldanella montana
Thymus (many)
Veronica austriaca and cultivars

FOR SHADY SITUATIONS

Acanthus mollis
Aconitum napellus
Ajuga reptans and cultivars
Anemone nemorosa
Aquilegia (many)
Bergenia cordifolia
Campanula (many)
Clivia miniata
Convallaria majalis
Dicentra (many)
Epimedium (many)
Helleborus (many)
Hosta (many)
Meconopsis betonicifolia
Myosotis sylvatica
Primula (many)
Rodgersia (many)
Streptocarpus capensis
Tricyrtis (many)
Trillium (many)

FOR DROUGHT TOLERANCE

Achillea (many)
Arctotis (many)
Baptisia australis
Coreopsis verticillata
Cosmos bipinnatus
Dorotheanthus bellidiformis
Eryngium (many)
Eschscholzia californica
Euphorbia (many)
Gazania (many)
Limonium perezii
Pelargonium (many)
Portulaca grandiflora
Romneya coulteri
Sedum (many)
Sempervivum (many)
Tithonia rotundifolia
Verbena (most)
Yucca (many)
Zauschneria (many)

FOR FRAGRANCE

Convallaria majalis
Dianthus (many)
Galium odoratum
Gypsophila paniculata
Hedychium gardnerianum
Heliotropium arborescens
Hesperis matrionalis
Hosta plantaginea
Iberis amara
Lathyrus odorata
Lobularia maritima
Matthiola incana
Melissa officinalis
Mentha (many)
Nicotiana sylvestris
Paeonia lactiflora hybrids (several)
Phlox paniculata cultivars
Reseda odorata
Thymus (many)
Viola odorata

Clockwise from top: Papaver orientale 'China Boy', Paeonia officinalis cultivar, Tanacetum coccineum cultivar, Papaver orientale cultivar

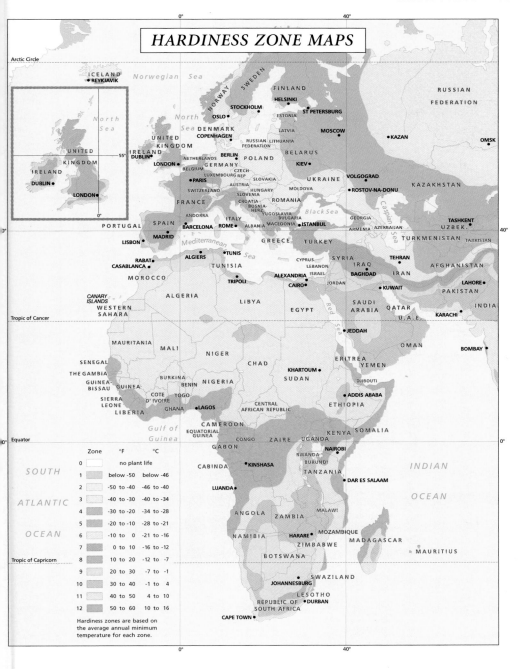

HARDINESS ZONE MAPS

Zone	°F	°C
0	no plant life	
1	below -50	below -46
2	-50 to -40	-46 to -40
3	-40 to -30	-40 to -34
4	-30 to -20	-34 to -28
5	-20 to -10	-28 to -21
6	-10 to 0	-21 to -16
7	0 to 10	-16 to -12
8	10 to 20	-12 to -7
9	20 to 30	-7 to -1
10	30 to 40	-1 to 4
11	40 to 50	4 to 10
12	50 to 60	10 to 16

Hardiness zones are based on
the average annual minimum
temperature for each zone.

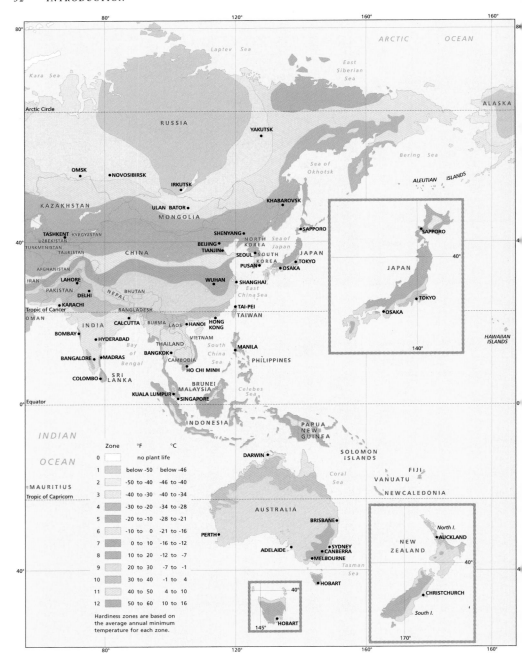

Zone	°F	°C
0		no plant life
1		below -50	below -46
2		-50 to -40	-46 to -40
3		-40 to -30	-40 to -34
4		-30 to -20	-34 to -28
5		-20 to -10	-28 to -21
6		-10 to 0	-21 to -16
7		0 to 10	-16 to -12
8		10 to 20	-12 to -7
9		20 to 30	-7 to -1
10		30 to 40	-1 to 4
11		40 to 50	4 to 10
12		50 to 60	10 to 16

Hardiness zones are based on
the average annual minimum
temperature for each zone.

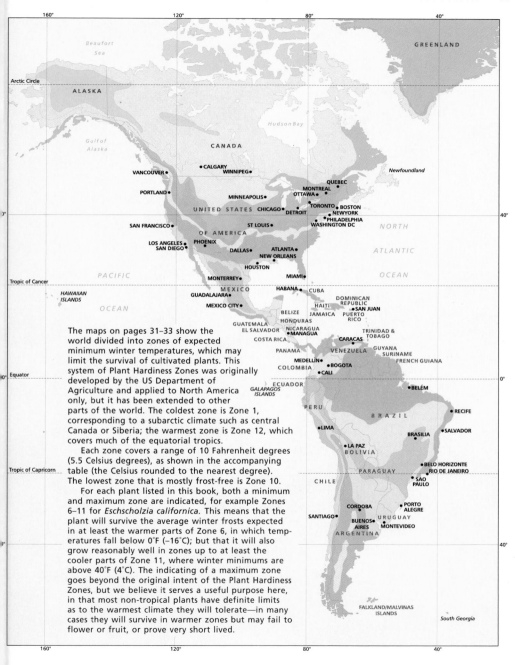

The maps on pages 31–33 show the world divided into zones of expected minimum winter temperatures, which may limit the survival of cultivated plants. This system of Plant Hardiness Zones was originally developed by the US Department of Agriculture and applied to North America only, but it has been extended to other parts of the world. The coldest zone is Zone 1, corresponding to a subarctic climate such as central Canada or Siberia; the warmest zone is Zone 12, which covers much of the equatorial tropics.

Each zone covers a range of 10 Fahrenheit degrees (5.5 Celsius degrees), as shown in the accompanying table (the Celsius rounded to the nearest degree). The lowest zone that is mostly frost-free is Zone 10.

For each plant listed in this book, both a minimum and maximum zone are indicated, for example Zones 6–11 for *Eschscholzia californica*. This means that the plant will survive the average winter frosts expected in at least the warmer parts of Zone 6, in which temperatures fall below 0°F (–16°C); but that it will also grow reasonably well in zones up to at least the cooler parts of Zone 11, where winter minimums are above 40°F (4°C). The indicating of a maximum zone goes beyond the original intent of the Plant Hardiness Zones, but we believe it serves a useful purpose here, in that most non-tropical plants have definite limits as to the warmest climate they will tolerate—in many cases they will survive in warmer zones but may fail to flower or fruit, or prove very short lived.

A

ABELMOSCHUS

This genus of around 15 species is from tropical Africa and Asia. In older books all the species were included in the larger genus *Hibiscus*. They are annuals, biennials or short-lived perennials with tough bark (sometimes used for fiber) and maple-like leaves. Some species die back to a large tuber in the tropical dry season. The hibiscus-like flowers occur in shades of yellow, pink, orange or red. Several species make attractive ornamentals and the vegetable okra or gumbo *(Abelmoschus esculentus)* is grown for its edible young pods.

CULTIVATION

They are mostly grown as summer annuals, requiring fertile, well-drained soil, a sheltered position in full sun, and plentiful water. Propagate from seed in spring. Rust disease can be a problem: spray with a fungicide.

Abelmoschus moschatus
MUSK MALLOW

This tropical Asian species is very variable, with many wild and cultivated races. Some are used for fiber and the seeds (musk seeds) yield oils and fats (ambrette) used medicinally and in perfumery. The whole plant has a slight musky smell. The hairs on the leaves are often bristly and the large flowers are typically pale yellow with a purple eye. Ornamental cultivars have a range of flower colors. The compact cultivar **'Mischief'** grows well in pots or can be naturalized in a sunny sheltered position; red, pink or white flowers are borne in summer and autumn. **'Pacific Light Pink'** is an 18 in (45 cm) dwarf cultivar with 2-tone pink flowers up to 4 in (10 cm) wide. **'Pacific Orange Scarlet'** (syn. 'Oriental Red') is also very popular. ZONES 8–12.

Abelmoschus moschatus 'Pacific Orange Scarlet' *(below)*

Acaena argentea
(right)

This species from Peru and Chile has prostrate stems that spread to form a 24 in (60 cm) wide mat. The leaves, which are up to 6 in (15 cm) long, are pinnate with 9 to 15 leaflets, blue-gray above with silvery undersides. The flower and seed heads are purple. **ZONES 7–10.**

ACAENA

Around 100 species make up this genus of low-growing evergreen perennials. Those grown in gardens all have thin, creeping stems or buried rhizomes that bear, at intervals, tufts of small pinnate leaves with toothed margins. Flowers are rather insignificant, green or purple-brown, in dense stalked heads or spikes, but are followed by small dry fruit with barbed hooks that cling to socks at the slightest touch. Acaenas are grown as rock garden plants or sometimes as ground covers, valued for their pretty, intricate foliage. Some more vigorous species are regarded as weeds, even in their native countries.

CULTIVATION
They are tough little plants, thriving in exposed places and poor soil, but do demand good drainage and summer moisture. Propagate from seed or by division.

Acaena novae-zelandiae *(above)*

This species from New Zealand, southeast Australia and New Guinea may be prostrate or mounding with wiry stems from 6–24 in (15–60 cm) long. The bright green leaves (sometimes tinted red) are up to 4 in (10 cm) long and composed of 9 to 15 leaflets. The flowerhead is cream and the immature fruiting heads have bright red spines on the burrs. It is a vigorous grower, sometimes becoming a nuisance. **ZONES 5–10.**

A

ACANTHUS
BEAR'S BREECHES

Around 30 species of perennials and shrubs from tropical Africa and Asia as well as Mediterranean Europe make up this genus. The genus name goes back to ancient Greek, and the large and colorful family Acanthaceae (mainly tropical) takes its name from the genus. The deeply lobed and toothed leaves of *Acanthus mollis* and *A. spinosus* have lent their shape to the carved motifs used to decorate the capitals of Corinthian columns. It is only the more temperate perennial species that have been much cultivated, valued for their erect spikes of bracted, curiously shaped flowers, as well as their handsome foliage. The flowers appear in spring and early summer, after which the leaves may die back but sprout again before winter.

CULTIVATION
Frost hardy, they do best in full sun or light shade. They prefer a rich, well-drained soil with adequate moisture in winter and spring. Spent flower stems and leaves can be removed if they offend. Snails and caterpillars can damage the new leaves. Propagate by division in autumn, or from seed.

Acanthus mollis
(below left)

Occurring on both sides of the Mediterranean, this well-known species is somewhat variable, the form grown in gardens having broader, softer leaves and taller flowering stems than most wild plants. It is more of a woodland plant than other acanthuses, appreciating shelter and deep, moist soil. The large leaves are a deep, glossy green and rather soft, inclined to droop in hot dry weather. Flower spikes can be over 6 ft (1.8 m) tall, the purple-pink bracts contrasting sharply with the crinkled white flowers. Spreading by deeply buried rhizomes, it can be hard to eradicate once established. **'Candelabrus'** is one of several cultivars of *Acanthus mollis*. ZONES 7–10.

Acanthus hungaricus *(above)*
syn. *Acanthus balcanicus*

Despite its species name, this plant does not occur wild in present-day Hungary, though some of the Balkan countries to which it is native were once part of the Austro-Hungarian Empire. It forms dense tufts of pinnately divided, soft, rather narrow leaves. The flower spikes may be up to 5 ft (1.5 m) tall, with vertical rows of white flowers almost hidden beneath dull pinkish bracts. It prefers a hot sunny position. **ZONES 7–10.**

Acanthus mollis **'Candelabrus'** *(above)*

Acanthus spinosus
(left)

This eastern Mediterranean species has large leaves that are deeply divided, the segments having coarse, spine-tipped teeth. In summer it sends up flower spikes to about 4 ft (1.2 m) high, the individual flowers and bracts being very similar to those of *Acanthus mollis.* **ZONES 7–10.**

Achillea 'Coronation Gold'
(left & below)

This vigorous hybrid cultivar originated as a cross between *Achillea clypeolata* and *A. filipendulina*. It has luxuriant grayish green foliage and flowering stems up to 3 ft (1 m) tall with large heads of deep golden yellow in summer and early autumn. **ZONES 4–10.**

ACHILLEA
YARROW, MILFOIL, SNEEZEWORT

There are about 85 species of *Achillea*, most native to Europe and temperate Asia, with a handful in North America. Foliage is fern-like, aromatic and often hairy. Most species bear masses of large, flat heads of tiny daisy flowers from late spring to autumn in shades of white, yellow, orange, pink or red. They are suitable for massed border planting and rockeries. The flowerheads can be dried and retain their color for winter decoration.

CULTIVATION

These hardy perennials are easily grown and tolerant of poor soils, but they do best in sunny, well-drained sites in temperate climates. They multiply rapidly by deep rhizomes and are easily propagated by division in late winter or from cuttings in early summer. Flowering stems may be cut when spent or left to die down naturally in winter, when the clumps should be pruned to stimulate strong spring growth. Fertilize in spring.

Achillea filipendulina

This species, native to the Caucasus, bears brilliant, deep yellow flowers over a long summer season. It grows to 4 ft (1.2 m) with flowerheads up to 6 in (15 cm) wide and is one of the most drought resistant of summer flowers. **'Gold Plate'**, a strong-growing, erect cultivar reaching 4 ft (1.2 m), has aromatic, bright green foliage, and flat, rounded heads of golden yellow flowers, 4–6 in (10–15 cm) wide. **'Parker's Variety'** has yellow flowers. ZONES 3–10.

Achillea 'Great Expectations' *(left)*
syn. *Achillea* 'Hoffnung'

Often listed as a cultivar of *A. millefolium*, 'Great Expectations' is a hybrid between *A. millefolium* and *A.* 'Taygetea', a cultivar of uncertain origin. 'Great Expectations' is a vigorous 30 in (75 cm) high plant that produces a prolific display of butter yellow flowerheads. ZONES 2–10.

Achillea filipendulina
'Cloth of Gold' *(below)*

Achillea filipendulina
'Gold Plate' *(right)*

Achillea × *kellereri*
(right)

This unusual achillea
is a hybrid between
Achillea clypeolata and
the rarely cultivated *A.
ageratifolia*. It is a mat-
forming plant, no more
than 8 in (20 cm) tall
even when flowering.
It has massed rosettes
of narrow gray-green
leaves with comb-like
toothing. In summer
it produces on loosely
branched stems daisy-
like cream flowerheads
³⁄₄ in (18 mm) across,
with a darker disc.
ZONES 5–10.

Achillea 'Lachsschönheit'
(right)
syn. *Achillea* 'Salmon
Beauty'

This is one of the re-
cently developed Gal-
axy hybrids. A cross
between *Achillea
millefolium* and *A.*
'Taygetea', this cultivar
resembles the former in
growth habit. In sum-
mer it produces masses
of salmon pink heads
which fade to paler
pink, then almost to
white. **ZONES 3–10.**

Achillea millefolium *(left)*
MILFOIL, YARROW

Widely distributed in
Europe and temperate
Asia, this common spe-
cies is hardy and vigor-
ous to the point of
weediness, and natural-
izes freely. It grows to
24 in (60 cm) tall with
soft, feathery, dark
green foliage and white
to pink flowers in sum-
mer. Cultivars include
'Cerise Queen', cherry

Achillea millefolium
'**Apfelblüte**' *(above)*

Achillea millefolium
'**Red Beauty**' *(right)*

red with pale colors;
'**Fanal**' (syn. 'The Beacon'), bright red; '**Red
Beauty**', silvery leaves
and rose red flowers;
the pink '**Rosea**'; and
'**Apfelblüte**', which is
deep rose pink. Once
established, plants can
be difficult to eradicate.
Most *Achillea* hybrids
have this species as one
parent. '**Paprika**' has
orange-red flowerheads
that fade with age.
ZONES 3–10.

Achillea millefolium
'**Fanal**' *(right)*

A

Achillea 'Moonshine' *(above)*

A cultivar of hybrid origin, this plant bears pretty flattened heads of pale sulfur yellow to bright yellow flowers throughout summer. It is a good species for cut flowers. It has delicate, feathery, silvery gray leaves and an upright habit, reaching a height of 24 in (60 cm). It should be divided regularly in spring to promote strong growth. **ZONES 3–10.**

Achillea ptarmica 'The Pearl' *(right)*

Achillea ptarmica

SNEEZEWORT

This plant has upright stems springing from long-running rhizomes and in spring bears large heads of small white flowers among the dark green leaves which are unusual among achilleas, not being dissected, but merely toothed. It reaches a height of 30 in (75 cm), providing a quick-growing cover in a sunny situation. **'The Pearl'** is a double cultivar, widely grown. **ZONES 3–10.**

Achillea 'Taygetea' (above)

This popular achillea is known by the above for want of a better name. The true *Achillea taygetea* is a little known species from southern Greece (Taygetos Mountains), now treated as a synonym of *A. aegyptiaca*, whereas our *A.* 'Taygetea' is now thought to be a garden hybrid, its parents possibly *A. millefolium* and *A. clypeolata*. It is a vigorous grower with flowering stems about 24 in (60 cm) tall, the flowerheads pale creamy yellow in large flat plates. **ZONES 4–10.**

Achillea tomentosa (below)
WOOLLY YARROW

Native to southwestern Europe, this is a low, spreading plant with woolly or silky-haired, finely divided gray-green leaves and flowerheads of bright yellow on 12 in (30 cm) stems. Tolerating dry conditions and hot sun, it is excellent in the rock garden or as an edging plant. **ZONES 4–10.**

Achillea 'Schwellenberg'
(right)

A distinctive hybrid cultivar of spreading habit and grayish foliage, the leaf divisions are broad and overlapping. Tight heads of yellow flowers appear on short stalks through summer and into autumn. **ZONES 3–10.**

A

ACINOS
CALAMINT

This genus of 10 species of annuals and woody, evergreen perennials gets its name from the Greek word *akinos*, the name of a small aromatic plant. Usually small, tufted, bushy or spreading plants growing to 8 in (20 cm), they come from central and southern Europe and western Asia. The 2-lipped, tubular flowers are borne on erect spikes in mid-summer.

CULTIVATION
Mostly quite frost hardy, they will grow in poor soil as long as it is well drained (they do not like wet conditions) and need full sun. Propagate from seed or cuttings in spring.

Acinos alpinus
syn. *Calamintha alpina* (above)
ALPINE CALAMINT

Spikes of violet flowers 1 in (25 mm) wide and with white marks on the lower lips are borne on this spreading, short-lived perennial, a native of central and southern Europe. Growing from 4–8 in (10–20 cm) in height, it has rounded leaves with either pointed or blunt tips. ZONES 6–9.

ACIPHYLLA
SPEARGRASS, SPANIARD

This genus consists of 40 or so species of stiff-leafed perennials in the carrot family, mainly native to New Zealand with a few species in Australia. They are found primarily in alpine areas or wind-swept open grasslands at lower altitudes. Despite the common name speargrass, they are quite unrelated to grasses. They have deep tap roots that give rise to clusters of deeply divided basal leaves with long, narrow leaflets, often ochre in color with vicious spines at their tips. Strong, long-spined flower stems develop in summer and extend beyond the foliage clump. They carry masses of small white or yellow-green flowers. There are separate male and female flower stems.

CULTIVATION
The small to medium-sized species are not too difficult to cultivate but the larger species are liable to sudden collapse outside their natural environment. Plant in full sun with moist, well-drained soil deep enough to allow the tap root to develop. Do not remove the insulating thatch of dead leaves. Propagate from seed, or small suckers used as cuttings, or by division.

A

Aciphylla aurea
(below)

GOLDEN SPANIARD, TARAMEA

Found in drier conditions than most, this species from New Zealand's South Island forms a foliage clump around 3 ft (1 m) tall by 5 ft (1.5 m) wide. Its golden fan-shaped leaves have narrow 24 in (60 cm) long leaflets. The flower stems grow to around 4 ft (1.2 m) tall. ZONES 7–9.

A

Aciphylla montana (left)

Found in the southern half of the South Island of New Zealand, this species forms a clump of finely divided olive green leaves about 12 in (45 cm) high by 18 in (45 cm) wide. The flower stems, which are up to 18 in (45 cm) tall, are topped with a branched head of pale yellow flowers. Conspicuous sheath-like bracts surround the base of the flowerhead. ZONES 7–9.

Aciphylla hectori (above)

A tiny species found in the southwest of the South Island of New Zealand, this plant consists of a tuft of stiff olive green foliage up to 4 in (10 cm) high and wide. The flower stem is up to 10 in (25 cm) tall; flowers are pale yellow to white. ZONES 7–9.

A

Aconitum carmichaelii *(above)*
syn. *Aconitum fischeri*

A native of northern and western China, this has become one of the most popular monkshoods by virtue of the rich violet-blue flowers, which are densely packed on the spikes in late summer. The leaves, thick, glossy and deeply veined, grow on rather woody stems. Several races and selections are cultivated, varying in stature from 3–6 ft (1–1.8 m). These include the **Wilsonii Group**, which contains, among others, the award-winning '**Kelmscott**'; '**Arendsii**' (syn. 'Arends') is another striking blue-flowered cultivar. ZONES 4–9.

ACONITUM
ACONITE, MONKSHOOD, WOLFSBANE

Consisting of around 100 species of perennials scattered across temperate regions of the northern hemisphere, this genus is renowned for the virulent poisons contained in the sap of many. From ancient times until quite recently they were widely employed for deliberate poisoning, from execution of criminals to baiting wolves, or placing in an enemy's water supply. The poison has also been used medicinally in carefully controlled doses and continues to attract the interest of pharmaceutical

Aconitum carmichaelii
'Arendsii' *(above)*

researchers. The plants themselves are instantly recognizable by their flowers, mostly in shades of deep blue or purple or less commonly white, pink or yellow, with 5 petals of which the upper one bulges up into a prominent helmet-like shape. In growth habit and leaves, the monkshoods show a strong resemblance to their relatives the delphiniums.

CULTIVATION
Monkshoods make attractive additions to herbaceous borders and woodland gardens. They prefer deep, moist soil and a sheltered position, partly shaded if summers are hot and dry. Propagate by division after the leaves die back in autumn, or from seed.

A

Aconitum napellus
(right)

ACONITE, MONKSHOOD

Of wide distribution in Europe and temperate Asia, this is also the monkshood species most widely grown in gardens and is as handsome as any when well grown. The stems are erect, to 4 ft (1.2 m) high, with large leaves divided into very narrow segments and a tall, open spike of deep blue to purplish blooms. A vigorous grower, it likes damp woodland or stream bank conditions. ZONES 5–9.

Aconitum 'Ivorine'
(below)

This hybrid cultivar grows to about 3 ft (1 m) tall with dense foliage. The many spikes of pale ivory-yellow flowers rise a short distance above the foliage. ZONES 4–9.

Aconitum vulparia *(left)*
syn. *Aconitum lycoctonum* subsp. *vulparia*

WOLFSBANE

Growing to over 3 ft (1 m) in height, this species has tall, erect stems and rounded, hairy leaves that are 6–8 in (15–20 cm) wide. Rather open spikes of pale yellow flowers, longer and narrower than those of most other species, are borne in summer. It is native to central and southern Europe. ZONES 4–9.

ACORUS
SWEET FLAG

This unusual genus consists of only 2 species of grass-like ever-green perennials from stream banks and marshes in the northern hemisphere. They are in fact highly atypical members of the arum family, lacking the large bract (spathe) that characteristically encloses the fleshy spike (spadix) of minute flowers. The flower spikes are inconspicuous and the plants are grown mainly for their foliage. The leaves are in flattened fans like those of irises, crowded along short rhizomes. Both leaves and rhizomes are sweet-scented, most noticeably as they dry, and have been used in folk medicine, perfumery and food flavorings.

CULTIVATION
Sweet flags are easily grown in any boggy spot or in shallow water at pond edges, needing no maintenance except cutting back to limit their spread. They are fully frost hardy. Propagate by division.

A

Acorus gramineus
Native to Japan, this species has soft, curved leaves under 12 in (30 cm) long and about $1/4$ in (6 mm) wide. The flower spikes are about 1 in (25 mm) long and emerge in spring and summer. **'Pusillus'**, popular in aquariums, is only about 4 in (10 cm) high; **'Variegatus'** has cream-striped leaves; **'Ogon'**, more recently introduced from Japan, has chartreuse and cream variegated leaves. ZONES 3–11.

Acorus gramineus
'Ogon' *(above)*

A

ACTAEA
BANEBERRY

Only 8 species of frost-hardy perennials belong to this genus, which occurs in Europe, temperate Asia and North America, mostly in damp woodlands and on limestone outcrops. They are attractive plants with large compound leaves springing from a root-crown, the leaflets thin and broad with strong veining and sharp teeth. Flowers are in short, feathery spikes or heads, the individual flowers smallish with many white stamens among which the narrow petals are hardly detectable. The fruits are white, red or black berries, often on a stalk of contrasting color. All parts of the plants are very poisonous but particularly the berries, which may be attractive to small children.

CULTIVATION
Requiring a cool, moist climate, these plants grow best in sheltered woodland conditions or in a damp, cool spot in a rock garden. Propagate from seed or by division.

Actaea alba (below)
WHITE BANEBERRY

From eastern USA, this summer-flowering perennial is most notable for its handsome berries, though its flowers and foliage are also attractive. It forms a clump of fresh green, divided leaves with a spread of 18 in (45 cm), from which rise the fluffy white flowers on stems up to 3 ft (1 m) high. By late summer they have developed into spires of small, gleaming white berries on red stalks. **ZONES 3–9.**

Actaea rubra (above)
RED BANEBERRY, SNAKEBERRY

This North American species grows to 24–30 in (60–75 cm) tall and wide and its leaves are 6–18 in (15–45 cm) wide. The mauve-tinted white flowers are about $^1/_4$ in (6 mm) in diameter and clustered in round heads on wiry stems. The berries are bright red. **Actaea rubra f. neglecta** is a taller growing form with white berries. **ZONES 3–9.**

Actinotus helianthi
(left)

FLANNEL FLOWER

This biennial or short-lived, evergreen perennial grows 12 in–3 ft (30–90 cm) high with a spread of 24 in (60 cm). It has deeply divided gray-green foliage. Furry erect stems appear in spring and summer, topped by star-like flowerheads which consist of a cluster of pink-stamened, greenish florets surrounded by flannel-textured dull white bracts with grayish green tips. Flannel flowers prefer a well-drained soil in full sun and grow especially well in arid situations. **ZONES 9–10.**

ACTINOTUS

There are 11 species in the Australian genus *Actinotus*, of which the best known is *Actinotus helianthi*—a favorite wild-flower native to the open woodlands of the sandstone country around Sydney where it makes a great display in late spring and summer. In the structure of their flowerheads, members of this genus mimic those of the daisy (composite) family, but in fact they belong to the carrot (umbellifer) family. The leaves and flowerheads are both felted with dense hairs which help *Actinotus* species reduce moisture loss in a dry climate and grow in poor, scarcely water-retentive soils.

CULTIVATION
They demand light shade, a mild climate and very good drainage. Plants are usually treated as biennials. Propagate from seed or stem cuttings in spring or summer.

A

ADENOPHORA

A genus of around 40 species of herbaceous perennials closely related to
Campanula, in fact distinguished from it
only by an internal feature of flower structure. Most are native to eastern Asia but 2
species occur wild in Europe. One species
is grown in Japan for its edible roots.

CULTIVATION
Cultivation requirements and mode of
propagation are the same as for
Campanula.

Adenophora
uehatae (below)

Native to eastern Asia,
this is a charming
dwarf species with
large, pendulous pale
mauve-blue bells borne
on short leafy stems. It
makes a fine rock gar-
den subject. **ZONES 5–9.**

A

Adonis annua
(right)

PHEASANT'S EYE

Quite different from most species, this is a summer-flowering annual with finely divided foliage and branching stems 12–15 in (30–38 cm) tall. The bright red, 5 to 8-petalled flowers are about 1 in (25 mm) wide with black centers. It occurs naturally in southern Europe and southwest Asia. **ZONES 6–9.**

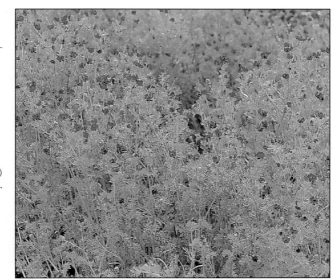

ADONIS

This genus consists of 20 species of annuals and perennials from Europe and cooler parts of Asia, with brightly colored flowers similar to *Anemone*, to which it is closely related. The Greek god Adonis, beloved of Aphrodite, gave his name to the original annual species; its red flowers were said to have sprung from drops of his blood when he was killed by a boar. The leaves are mostly finely divided, the uppermost ones on each stem forming a sort of 'nest' on which the single bowl-shaped flower rests. It is only the perennial species that are much cultivated, used in herbaceous borders and rock gardens.

CULTIVATION

Adonis require a cool climate with warm dry summers. They are best grown in a sheltered spot in full sun, and in moist, fertile soil with a high humus content. Propagate from fresh seed or by division of clumps.

Adonis vernalis *(above)*

This European perennial species has very narrow, almost needle-like, finely divided leaflets. Its 12- to 20-petalled, bright yellow flowers are large, up to 3 in (8 cm) across, and open in early spring. Both this species and *A. annua* have been used medicinally, but are now regarded as too toxic for general use. **ZONES 3–9.**

A

AECHMEA

Take your pick in pronouncing this name, which is of
Greek origin. Regardless of whether you call it ike-
maya, eek-mee-a, aitch-mee-a, ak-mee-a, or ek-
mee-a, you will have company! It is one of the
largest and most diverse bromeliad genera, as well
as being one of the most popular among indoor
plant growers. *Aechmea* consists of over 170 species
from Central and South America. Most are epiphytes or rock-dwellers, conserving water in the
vase-like structure formed by the rosette of stiff
leaves, which may be barred, striped or otherwise
patterned, and prickly margined in some such as
Aechmea agavifolia. The flowers are small but often intensely colored, in dense spikes that vary
greatly in size and structure but always with numerous overlapping bracts that usually contrast in
color with the flowers: a typical example is ***Aechmea* 'Mary Brett'**.
The berry-like fruits that follow are often colorful as well.

Aechmea agavifolia
(above)

CULTIVATION

How aechmeas are treated depends very much on the climate.
In the humid tropics and subtropics they grow happily outdoors,
most preferring filtered sun. Despite being epiphytes, they will
grow on the ground as long as soil is open and high in humus,

Aechmea 'Mary Brett'
(below)

and the bed is raised
slightly. Some tolerate
surprisingly cool condi-
tions and can be grown
outdoors well into the
temperate zones, so long
as frost is absent. In
more severe climates
they are grown as in-
door or conservatory
plants, potted in a
coarse medium just
like many orchids.
Propagate by division
(separating 'pups' with
a sharp knife), or
from seed.

A

Aechmea fasciata
(right)

SILVER VASE

Reminiscent of a formal flower arrangement, this Brazilian species has a 'vase' of silvery gray leaves irregularly barred green, from which emerges in summer a short, broad cluster of violet-blue flowers among crowded, spiky bracts of a most delicate clear pink. The rosettes, up to about 18 in (45 cm) high, do not clump up much. **ZONES 10–12.**

Aechmea chantinii *(left)*

Known as the Queen of the Aechmeas, this species from northwestern South America has vivid red and yellow flowers rising above long, drooping, salmon-orange bracts. The rosettes consist of olive green leaves often with silvery gray dark green or almost black banding. The flowers appear in summer, followed by blue or white berries. It has an upright, urn-like habit and reaches a height and spread of 12–24 in (30–60 cm). **'Black'** is one of several cultivars of *Aechmea chantinii.* Ensure that growing conditions are not too moist in winter. This species is very cold sensitive. **ZONES 11–12.**

Aechmea chantinii
'Black' *(right)*

A

Aechmea nidularioides *(left)*

This species has strap-like leaves about 24 in (60 cm) long; the flowering stalk terminates in a rosette of red bracts at the center of which sit yellow flowers in an eye-catching display. **ZONES 10–12.**

Aechmea 'Shining Light' *(left)*

This hybrid cultivar has a broad rosette of leaves that are glossy, pale green above and wine red on the under-sides. It produces a large, about 24 in (60 cm) high, much-branched panicle, with bright red bracts and numerous small red flowers in summer. **ZONES 11–12.**

Aechmea pineliana *(above)*

Attractive grown in bright light or full sun where the foliage takes on a deep rose color, this south Brazilian species grows to a height and spread of 12–15 in (30–38 cm). It has a dense upright habit with stiff, pointed gray-green leaves edged with red spines. The yellow flowers form a short, cylindrical head and are borne above the scarlet stems and bracts from winter through to spring. On maturity the flowers turn black. It is sun and cold toler-ant and adapts well to outdoor conditions. **ZONES 10–12.**

Aechmea 'Royal Wine' *(below)*

This popular hybrid cultivar, well adapted to indoor culture, has strap-like, bronze-green leaves with red bases and a slightly branched, pendent inflores-cence with dark blue petals. The fruits that follow the flowers are scarlet. **ZONES 11–12.**

AEGOPODIUM

Consisting of 5 species of perennials in the carrot family, native to Europe and Asia, this genus is known in cool-temperate gardens only in the form of the common ground elder or goutweed—admittedly a moderately handsome plant, but detested by most for its rampant spread by underground rhizomes and the virtual impossibility of eradicating it. Resembling a lower-growing version of parsnip, it has compound leaves with large, toothed leaflets and rounded umbels of white flowers. Ground elder was for a long time used in herbal medicine, once thought effective against gout, and its young shoots can be used as a green vegetable.

CULTIVATION

Growing ground elder is far easier than stopping it, and it is difficult to see why anyone would wish to do so. However, it is undoubtedly an effective ground cover where space allows, smothering other weeds. It does best in moist soil and partial shade. Any piece of root will grow.

Aegopodium podagraria
GROUND ELDER, GOUTWEED

Spreading to an indefinite width, and up to 3 ft (1 m) high, ground elder sends up its pure white umbels of bloom during summer. **'Variegatum'** is sometimes grown as a ground cover: its leaflets are neatly edged white and it is slightly smaller and less aggressive than the normal green form. ZONES 3–9.

Aegopodium podagraria 'Variegata' *(below)*

***Aethionema
grandiflorum*** *(left)*
syn. ***Aethionema
pulchellum***
PERSIAN STONE CRESS

Grown for its sprays
of dainty, phlox-like,
pale pink to rose pink
flowers in spring, this
Middle Eastern species
is a short-lived peren-
nial. It has a loose
habit, narrow, bluish
green leaves and
reaches a height of
12 in (30 cm). It makes
a good rock garden
specimen. **ZONES 7–9.**

AETHIONEMA

Ranging through the Mediterranean region and into western
Asia, the 30 or more species of this genus include evergreen perennials, subshrubs and low shrubs, all with small, narrow leaves
and producing spikes or clusters of 4-petalled pink to white
flowers in spring and summer. The genus belongs to the
mustard family, falling into the same tribe as *Arabis* and
Alyssum. A number of species are cultivated, prized mainly by
rock garden enthusiasts for their compact habit and profuse display of blooms such as the mauve-pink
cultivar **'Mavis Holmes'**.

Aethionema 'Mavis
Holmes' *(below)*

CULTIVATION

Aethionemas thrive best in a climate with
cool, moist winter and a warm, dry summer. They should be grown in raised beds
or rockeries in gritty, free-draining soil and
exposed to full sun. Propagate from seed
or cuttings.

AGAPANTHUS
AFRICAN LILY, AGAPANTHUS, LILY-OF-THE-NILE

A

Native to southern Africa, these strong-growing perennials are popular for their fine foliage and showy flowers produced in abundance over summer. Arching, strap-shaped leaves spring from short rhizomes with dense, fleshy roots. Flowers are various shades of blue (white in some cultivars) in many flowered umbels, borne on a long erect stem, often 3 ft (1 m) or more tall. Agapanthus are ideal for background plants or for edging along a wall, fence or driveway. Some hybrid examples are '**Irving Cantor**' and '**Storm Cloud**'. **Headbourne Hybrids** are especially vigorous and hardy. They grow to 3 ft (1 m) and come in a range of bright colors.

CULTIVATION

Agapanthus can thrive in conditions of neglect, on sites such as dry slopes and near the coast. They enjoy full sun but will tolerate some shade, and will grow in any soil as long as they get water in spring and summer. They naturalize readily, soon forming large clumps; they also make excellent tub and container specimens. Remove spent flower stems and dead leaves at the end of winter. Agapanthus are frost hardy to marginally frost hardy. Propagate by division in late winter, or from seed in spring or autumn.

Agapanthus africanus *(above)*

This species from western Cape Province is moderately frost tolerant, but is not common in gardens. Often plants sold under this name turn out to be *Agapanthus praecox*. It produces blue flowers on 18 in (45 cm) stems from mid-summer to early autumn; each flowerhead contains 20 to 50 individual blossoms, the color varying from pale to deep blue. The leaves are shorter than on *A. praecox*. **ZONES 8–10.**

Agapanthus 'Irving Cantor' *(left)*

A

Agapanthus campanulatus *(left)*

Native to Natal in South Africa, this species makes a large clump of narrow, grayish leaves that die back in autumn. In mid- to late summer, crowded umbels of pale blue flowers with broadly spreading petals are borne on 3 ft (1 m) stems. It is the most frost-hardy agapanthus. ***Agapanthus campanulatus* var. *patens*,** smaller and more slender, is one of the daintiest of all the agapanthus. **ZONES 7–11.**

Agapanthus praecox

This is the most popular agapanthus. Its glorious starbursts of lavender blue flowers appear in summer, and its densely clumped evergreen foliage is handsome in the garden all year round. It is also available in white. **Agapanthus praecox subsp.** *orientalis* has large dense umbels of blue flowers. It prefers full sun, moist soil and is marginally frost hardy. **ZONES 9–11.**

Agapanthus 'Loch Hope' *(above)*

A late-flowering agapanthus, this cultivar grows to a height of 4 ft (1.2 m) and has abundant, large dark violet blue flowerheads. **ZONES 9–11.**

Agapanthus praecox subsp. *orientalis (left)*

AGASTACHE

This is a genus of some 20 species of perennials found in China, Japan and North
America. Most species are upright with
stiff, angular stems clothed in toothed-
edged, lance-shaped leaves from ½–6 in
(1.2–15 cm) long depending on the species.
Heights range from 18 in–6 ft (45 cm–1.8 m)
tall. Upright spikes of tubular, 2-lipped
flowers develop at the stem tips in summer. The flower color is usually white,
pink, mauve or purple with the bracts that
back the flowers being of the same or a
slightly contrasting color.

CULTIVATION

Species are easily grown in moist, well-
drained soil and prefer a sunny position.
Hardiness varies, but most species will tolerate occasional frosts down to 20°F (–7°C).
Propagate from seed or cuttings.

Agastache rugosa (above)

This species from China and Japan grows to 4 ft
(1.2 m) tall with branching stems that make it
more shrubby than most species. The leaves are
around 3 in (8 cm) long and rather sticky. The
flower spikes are up to 4 in (10 cm) long with
small pink or mauve flowers that have white
lobes. ZONES 8–10.

Agastache
foeniculum (right)
syn. *Agastache*
anethiodora

ANISE HYSSOP

This 18 in–4 ft
(45 cm–1.2 m) tall,
soft-stemmed North
American species
makes a clump of up-
right stems with 3 in
(8 cm) leaves. Often
treated as an annual, it
is primarily grown for
the ornamental value
of its purple flower
spikes. The anise-
scented and flavored
foliage is used to make
a herbal tea or as a
flavoring. ZONES 8–10.

A

AGERATINA

This is just one of many genera, predominantly American, that has been split off the large and unwieldy *Eupatorium*. Although composites, that is, members of the daisy family, they have inflorescences consisting of many small fluffy heads without ray florets, and hence are quite un-daisy-like in appearance. *Ageratina* consists of over 200 species from warmer parts of the Americas, a small number extending to somewhat cooler parts of eastern USA. Two Mexican species have become bad weeds in parts of Australia. The genus includes annuals, perennials and soft-wooded shrubs. Leaves are in opposite pairs on the cane-like stems and have a musky, slightly unpleasant smell. The small, soft flowerheads are in terminal panicles and are either white or pale pink.

CULTIVATION

They are easily grown in any sheltered spot in moist soil. The species from the USA are fairly frost hardy, others hardly at all. Propagate from seed, cuttings or by division.

Ageratina altissima (below) syn. *Eupatorium altissimum*

Native over a wide area of eastern and central USA, this perennial is one of the taller species, growing to about 8 ft (2.4 m) high. Its leaves are up to 5 in (12 cm) long, toothed in the upper part, and the numerous small white flowerheads appear in late summer. ZONES 6–9.

Ageratina ligustrina *(right)*
syn. *Eupatorium ligustrinum*

A very distinctive shrubby species native to Central America, *Ageratina ligustrina* can reach as much as 15 ft (4.5 m) tall, with densely massed branches and glossy evergreen leaves reminiscent of privet leaves (hence *ligustrina*, 'privet-like'). The white flowerheads with pinkish enclosing bracts are borne in large panicles in autumn. **ZONES 9–11.**

Ageratina occidentalis *(left)*
syn. *Eupatorium occidentale*

Native to the north-western states of the USA, this is a many-stemmed perennial about 30 in (75 cm) high, with small almost triangular leaves. The fluffy flowerheads, borne in late summer in numerous small panicles, vary in color from white to pink or purple. **ZONES 6–9.**

A

**Ageratum
houstonianum** *(left)*

Native to Central
America and the West
Indies, this annual
ageratum is popular as
a summer bedding
plant. Available in tall
(12 in [30 cm]), me-
dium (8 in [20 cm])
and dwarf (6 in [15 cm])
sizes, they form clumps
of foliage with fluffy
flowers in an unusual
dusky blue that blends
effectively with many
other bedding plants.
Also available are pink
and white forms.
ZONES 9–12.

AGERATUM
FLOSS FLOWER

While undoubtedly best known for the annual bedding plants
that are derived from *Ageratum houstonianum,* this genus includes some 43 species of annuals and perennials mostly native
to warmer regions of the Americas. They are clump-forming or
mounding plants up to 30 in (75 cm) tall with felted or hairy,
roughly oval to heart-shaped leaves with shallowly toothed or
serrated edges. Flowerheads are a mass of fine filaments, usually
dusky blue, lavender or pink and crowded in terminal clusters.

CULTIVATION
Best grown in full sun in moist, well-drained soil. Regular
deadheading is essential to prolong the flowering. Propagate by
spring-sown seed, either raised indoors in containers or sown
directly in the garden.

AGLAONEMA

This genus of about 20 species of perennial subshrubs comes from the humid tropics of Southeast Asia. In growth form they are the old world counterparts of the tropical American *Dieffenbachia* and can be used for indoor decoration in a similar way. Some species are renowned for their tenacious hold on life and ability to grow in conditions of poor light and soil. The somewhat fleshy stems branch from the base and may root where they touch the ground. The broad, oblong leaves are often mottled or barred with cream. Tiny flowers are borne in a short fleshy spike within a furled spathe, an arrangement typical of the arum family. The spikes are more conspicuous in the fruiting stage, displaying oval berries that can be quite colorful.

CULTIVATION

In the tropics aglaonemas are easily grown in any moist, shady area beneath trees but in temperate regions they are grown indoors in containers. Propagation is normally by cuttings or offsets, which are easily rooted.

Aglaonema 'Silver Queen' *(above)*

This *A. nitidum* 'Curtisii' × *A. pictum* 'Tricolor' hybrid branches freely from the base, eventually forming a large clump of foliage. It has narrow, 12 in (30 cm) long leaves marbled and flecked with silvery white. **ZONES** 11–12.

Aglaonema 'Parrot Jungle' *(right)*

This hybrid has *A. nitidum* as one of its parents; the other is unknown. It is an upright, 3 ft (1 m) high plant with 18 in (45 cm) long, leathery dull green, lance-shaped leaves with silvery markings on the upper surfaces. The spathes are creamy white. **ZONES** 11–12.

A

AGRIMONIA
AGRIMONY

About 15 species of perennials belong in this genus, occurring in temperate regions of the northern hemisphere. It is related to *Potentilla* but has its small yellow flowers in elongated spikes, opening progressively from the base, and its fruits are small spiny burrs. The pinnate leaves with thin, toothed leaflets are mainly basal. Agrimonias are plants of woodland verges and meadows and have little ornamental value, but they have a long history of medicinal use, the leaves and flowers making an infusion with astringent and diuretic properties due to their tannin content. They also yield a yellow dye.

CULTIVATION
They are very easily grown in any moist fertile soil, in full sun or light shade. Seed is difficult to germinate so propagation is usually by division of the rhizome.

Agrimonia eupatoria (below)
COMMON AGRIMONY

Native to Europe, western Asia and North Africa, this species makes a sparse clump of foliage from a deeply buried rhizome; leaves consist of up to 13 leaflets, white-haired on the undersides, and the weak flowering stem is up to about 24 in (60 cm) tall. ZONES 6–10.

***Agrostemma
githago*** *(right)*
CORN COCKLE

This fast-growing
showy annual reaches
a height of 24–36 in
(60–90 cm), making it
ideal for planting at the
back of an annual bor-
der. It has a slender,
few-branched, willowy
habit with long narrow
leaves in opposite pairs.
Broadly funnel-shaped
pink flowers about 2 in
(5 cm) in diameter
appear on long hairy
stalks from late spring
to early autumn. The
tiny dark brown seeds
are poisonous.
ZONES 8–10.

AGROSTEMMA

Two or possibly more species of slender annuals from the Mediterranean region belong to this genus, related to *Lychnis* and
Silene. One of them is well known as a weed of crops in Europe,
but is still a pretty plant with large rose-pink flowers and is
sometimes used in meadow plantings and cottage gardens. Distinctive features of the genus are the long silky hairs on the leaves
and the calyx consisting of 5 very long, leaf-like sepals radiating
well beyond the petals.

CULTIVATION

They are very frost hardy, growing best in full sun in a well-
drained soil. Young plants should be thinned to about 10 in
(25 cm) spacing and may need light staking if growing in exposed
areas. Propagate from seed sown in early spring or autumn.

A

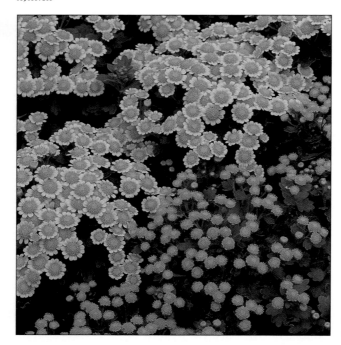

Ajania 'Bess' and
A. 'Benny' *(left)*

AJANIA

This genus, consisting of 30 or so species from eastern and central Asia, is one of a number of genera now recognized in place of
Chrysanthemum in its older, broader sense. *Ajania* is closest to
Dendranthema and its species have similar bluntly lobed leaves
usually with whitish woolly hairs on the undersides. Flowerheads
are small and button-like, lacking ray florets and arranged in flattish panicles at the branch tips. The plants have extensively
branching underground rhizomes, sending up numerous tough,
wiry stems. Only *Ajania pacifica* is widely cultivated for ornament in gardens and parks. *Ajania* 'Bess' differs in having small
white ray florets on the flowers and *A.* 'Benny' has flowers typical of the genus.

CULTIVATION
The plants are very hardy and easily grown in a wide range of
situations, thriving in both poor and fertile soils, though preferring good drainage and full sun. If not cut back hard after
flowering, including the rhizome, they may rapidly smother
adjacent plants. Propagate from rhizome divisions.

Ajania pacifica (right)
syns *Chrysanthemum pacificum,*
Dendranthema pacificum

An attractive plant, occurring wild
in far eastern Asia, this species
makes a spreading, loose mound of
evergreen foliage up to about 18 in
(45 cm) high. The leaves are deep
green on the upper side and clothed
in dense white hairs beneath; the
white shows at the coarsely scalloped edges, making a striking contrast with the green. Sprays of
brilliant gold flowerheads in autumn
further enhance the effect. **Ajania**
pacifica 'Silver and Gold' has silver-
edged leaves and bright golden yellow
button-like flowers. **ZONES 4–10.**

Ajania pacifica 'Silver and Gold' *(below)*

AJUGA
BUGLE

About 50 species of low-growing annuals and perennials make up this genus, which ranges through Europe, Asia, Africa and Australia, mainly in cooler regions. Although belonging to the mint family, their foliage is hardly aromatic. Rosettes of soft, spatulate leaves lengthen into spikes of blue, purple or pink (rarely yellow) 2-lipped flowers. In most perennial species the plants spread by runners or underground rhizomes, some forming extensive carpets. They make attractive ground covers, especially for shady places such as corners of courtyards.

Ajuga pyramidalis
'Metallica Crispa'
(below)

CULTIVATION
These are frost-hardy, trouble-free plants requiring little but moist soil and shelter from strong sun, though the bronze and variegated forms develop best color in sun. The commonly grown species thrive in a range of climates, from severe cold to subtropical. Snails and slugs can damage foliage. Propagate by division.

Ajuga pyramidalis (left)
PYRAMIDAL BUGLE

Widely distributed in Europe including parts of the UK, this attractive species makes a compact mat of rosettes, spreading by short underground rhizomes. The hairy dark green rosette leaves grade into the broad leafy bracts of the flowering stem to give it a narrowly pyramidal form, usually about 8 in (20 cm) tall. Flowers are mostly blue or mauve, and open from spring to midsummer. **'Metallica Crispa'** is a curious miniature form, with rounded and somewhat contorted leaves showing a metallic purple sheen.
ZONES 5–9.

Ajuga reptans
(bottom)

EUROPEAN BUGLE,
COMMON BUGLE, BLUE BUGLE

The commonly grown ajuga, native to Europe, spreads by surface runners like a strawberry plant, making a mat of leafy rosettes only 2–3 in (5–8 cm) high and indefinite spread. In spring it sends up spikes of deep blue flowers, up to 8 in (20 cm) high in some cultivars. The most familiar versions are: **'Atropurpurea'** (syn. 'Purpurea'), which has dull purple to bronzy green leaves; **'Burgundy Glow'**, with cream and maroon variegated leaves; **'Multicolor'**, with white, pink and purple leaves; and **'Variegata'**, with light green and cream leaves. Rather different is **'Jungle Beauty'**, which is much larger, spreads more rapidly, and has dark green leaves tinged with purple. **'Catlin's Giant'** has much larger leaves and longer, to 8 in (20 cm), inflorescences. **'Pink Elf'** is a compact form with dark pink flowers. ZONES 3–10.

Ajuga reptans
'Atropurpurea' *(above)*

Ajuga reptans
'Jungle Beauty' *(right)*

ALCEA
HOLLYHOCK

The botanical name *Alcea* is the old Roman one; Linnaeus adopted it although he also used the name *Althaea,* from the Greek *altheo,* to cure, in allusion to the plant's use in traditional medicine. Native to the eastern Mediterranean, hollyhocks were originally called holy hock or holy mallow; it is said that plants were taken to England from the Holy Land during the Crusades. There are about 60 species in the genus, all from western and central Asia. They bear flowers on spikes which may be 6 ft (1.8 m) or more high, making them far too tall for the average flowerbed; even 'dwarf' cultivars grow to 3 ft (1 m) tall.

CULTIVATION
Hollyhocks are quite frost hardy but need shelter from wind, benefiting from staking in exposed positions. They prefer sun, a rich, heavy well-drained soil and frequent watering in dry weather. Propagate from seed in late summer or spring. Rust disease can be a problem; spray with fungicide.

Alcea rosea (above & above right)
syn. *Althaea rosea*
HOLLYHOCK

This biennial, believed originally to have come from Turkey or Palestine, is popular for its tall spikes of flowers which appear in summer and early autumn, and come in a range of colors including pink, purple, cream and yellow; they can be either single, flat circles of color 4 in (10 cm) across, or so lavishly double that they are like spheres of ruffled petals. Foliage is roundish and rough and the plants may be as much as 10 ft (3 m) tall, erect and generally unbranched. The **Chater's Double Group** of cultivars have peony-shaped, double flowers that may be any color from purple-blue, purple, red, yellow and white to pink or apricot. There are many other cultivars and series, which include **Pinafore Mixed** and **Majorette Mixed** with lacy, semi-double flowers in pastel shades. ZONES 4–10.

ALCHEMILLA

LADY'S MANTLE

A

There are around 300 species of herbaceous perennials in this Eurasian genus. There are also a few alpine species in Australia and New Zealand, but it is not clear if they are natives or naturalized introductions. They form clumps of palmate (hand-shaped) or rounded, lobed, gray-green leaves often covered with fine hairs. Their spreading stems often root as they grow. Branched inflorescences of tiny yellow-green flowers develop in summer. Their sizes range from 6–30 in (15–75 cm) tall and wide. Many species have styptic and other medicinal properties.

CULTIVATION

They are very hardy and easily grown in any well-drained soil in afternoon shade. They may be grown in sun but the foliage will deteriorate in the summer heat. Propagate from seed or division in late winter to early spring.

Alchemilla conjuncta (below)

Native to the French and Swiss Alps, this 12 in (30 cm) tall species has 7 to 9 lobed, pale green leaves with toothed edges and a dense covering of silvery hairs on the undersides. The flowering stems are up to 15 in (38 cm) tall. ZONES 5–9.

Alchemilla rohdii
(left)

One of the numerous European species that have at times been included under the name *Alchemilla vulgaris*, this makes a low spreading plant less than 8 in (20 cm) high with fresh green leaves, their short rounded lobes finely toothed. The greenish yellow flowers are not very showy. **ZONES 6–9.**

Alchemilla mollis
(center left)

LADY'S MANTLE

Sometimes sold as *Alchemilla vulgaris,* this is the most widely cultivated species in the genus. It is a low-growing perennial ideal for ground cover, the front of borders or for rock gardens. It is clump forming, growing to a height and spread of 16 in (40 cm). It has decorative, wavy edged leaves which hold dew or raindrops to give a sparkling effect. In summer, it bears masses of small sprays of greenish yellow flowers, similar to *Gypsophila*. **Alchemilla speciosa** is very like *A. mollis* except that its leaves are more deeply lobed and the leaf stems have a covering of fine hairs. **ZONES 4–9.**

Alchemilla speciosa
(right)

Very similar in general appearance to the commonly grown *Alchemilla mollis*, this Caucasian species has slightly more deeply divided leaves with narrower, sharper teeth. It also differs in minor floral details. **ZONES 6–10.**

A

ALONSOA
MASK FLOWER

This genus consists of some 12 species of perennials and subshrubs found in tropical western America from Mexico to Peru. Named for Alonzo Zanoni, an eighteenth-century Colombian Secretary of State, they are commonly known as mask flowers because the shape of the flower bears a fancied resemblance to a carnival mask. The flowers are usually small, but often vividly colored and open through most of the year.

CULTIVATION
Provided they receive some sun, mask flowers are very easily grown in any free-draining soil. They are propagated from seed, cuttings or by layering the stems. Only very light frosts are tolerated, though young plants can be propagated in autumn and overwintered under cover.

Alonsoa warscewiczii (above)

An evergreen perennial that in some climates (zones 5–9) is short-lived and treated as an annual, this native of Peru can form a 24 in (60 cm) high subshrub in a frost-free climate. Named after Joseph Warscewicz (1812–66), a botanist who collected in South America, it bears clusters of small, vivid orange-red flowers. In suitably mild conditions these appear throughout the year. There are several cultivars with flowers in various shades of pink and orange. ZONES 9–11.

A

ALPINIA
ORNAMENTAL GINGER

Of Asian and Pacific origin, these plants are widely cultivated in tropical and subtropical gardens, for their showy blooms, some as commercial cut flowers. They grow from fleshy rhizomes to form large clumps. The aboveground shoots are in fact pseudostems consisting of tightly furled leaf bases as in cannas and bananas. The large thin leaves form 2 rows. Although strictly speaking perennials, they do not die back and can be used in the garden like a shrub.

CULTIVATION

Although frost tender, many will tolerate winter temperatures just above freezing as long as summers are warm and humid. They like part-shade, a warm, moist atmosphere and rich soil. Propagate by division.

Alpinia galanga
(left)
GALANGAL, THAI GINGER

Although most alpinias are grown for ornament and are not regarded as edible, this Southeast Asian species is the source of an important spice, a vital ingredient of Thai cooking in particular. It is the thick, white-fleshed rhizome that is used, either freshly grated, dried or powdered ('laos powder'), to add a subtle piquancy to dishes such as curries. The plant makes a clump of leafy stems 6 ft (1.8 m) high. The flowers, white with pink markings, are not very showy. ZONES 11–12.

Alpinia zerumbet *(above)*

syns *Alpinia nutans, A. speciosa*

SHELL GINGER

This evergreen, clump-forming perennial grows
to around 10 ft (3 m) with a spread of 5–10 ft
(1.5–3 m). It has long, densely massed stems with
broad, green leaves. The drooping sprays of flowers
appear in spring and intermittently in other seasons, starting as waxy white or ivory buds, opening one at a time to reveal yellow lips with pink-
or red-marked throats. **'Variegata'** has leaves irregularly striped yellow; it tends to be lower
growing. **ZONES 10–12.**

Alpinia purpurata *(right)*

RED GINGER

This Pacific Islands species produces showy spikes
of small white flowers among vivid scarlet bracts
throughout the year. The glossy leaves are narrow
and lance-shaped. New plantlets sprout among
the flower bracts and take root when the dying
flower stems fall to the ground under the weight
of the growing plantlets. The plants grow to 10 ft
(3 m) tall. **ZONES 11–12.**

ALSTROEMERIA
PERUVIAN LILY

Native to South America where they occur mostly in the Andes, these tuberous and rhizomatous plants with about 50 species are among the finest perennials for cutting, but they do drop their petals. Erect, wiry stems bear scattered, thin, twisted leaves concentrated on the upper half, and terminate in umbels of outward-facing flowers, usually with flaring petals that are variously spotted or streaked. They flower profusely from spring to summer.

CULTIVATION

All grow well in sun or light shade in a well-enriched, well-drained acidic soil. They soon form large clumps, bearing dozens of flowerheads. Propagate from seed or by division in early spring. They are frost hardy, but in cold winters protect the dormant tubers by covering with loose peat or dry bracken. They are best left un-disturbed when established, but one-year-old seedlings transplant well. They do well naturalized under trees or on sloping banks.

Alstroemeria aurea
(left)
syn. *Alstroemeria aurantiaca*

Native to Chile, this is the most common and easily grown species of *Alstroemeria*. It has heads of orange flowers, tipped with green and streaked with maroon. The leaves are twisted, narrow and lance-shaped. Several cultivars exist, which include '**Majestic**' and '**Bronze Beauty**'. Both have deep orange or bronzy orange flowers; they grow to 2–3 ft (0.6–1 m) with a similar spread. ZONES 7–9.

Alstroemeria, Dr Salter's Hybrids

This group of hybrid cultivars includes a wide range of colors. The flowerheads are more compact than in the Ligtu Hybrids, the flowers open more widely, and the 3 inner petals are more heavily marked. '**Walter Fleming**' has flowering stems up to 3 ft (1 m) tall and cream and gold flowers tinged with purple, the inner petals spotted red-purple. ZONES 7–9.

Alstroemeria, Dr Salter's Hybrid, 'Walter Fleming' *(left)*

Alstroemeria, Dutch Hybrid,
'Yellow Friendship' *(above)*

Alstroemeria, Dutch Hybrid
cultivar *(right)*

Alstroemeria, Dutch Hybrids

These are the alstroemerias
that now dominate the cut-
flower trade in many countries. They are bred mainly
by one Dutch firm, and
some of the newer
cultivars are only made
available to commercial
cut-flower growers, who
grow them under glass to
avoid any rain damage to
the blooms. The flowers,
in compact umbels, are
broad petalled and have
heavily marked upper pet-
als often in strongly contrasting colors. **'Yellow
Friendship'** and **'Mirella'**
are examples of this type
of hybrid. ZONES 8–10.

Alstroemeria, Dutch
Hybrid, 'Mirella' *(right)*

A

Alstroemeria psittacina *(right)*
syn. *Alstroemeria pulchella*
NEW ZEALAND CHRISTMAS BELL

Though native to Brazil, *Alstroemeria psittacina* gets its common name from its popularity in New Zealand, where its narrow, crimson and green flowers are borne at Christmas. The well-spaced stems, about 24 in (60 cm) high, spring from tuberous roots. Easily grown in warm-temperate climates, it can spread rapidly and prove difficult to eradicate. **ZONES 8–10.**

Alstroemeria haemantha *(left)*
HERB LILY

This Chilean species has green leaves with a slightly hairy margin. The stiff flower stems up to 3 ft (1 m) tall carry up to 15 orange to dull red flowers during early summer, their upper petals splashed with yellow. The plants can spread by their fleshy rhizomes to form quite large patches. **ZONES 7–9.**

Alstroemeria, Ligtu Hybrids

The well-known Ligtu Hybrids first appeared in Britain in the late 1920s, when *Alstroemeria ligtu* was crossed with *A. haemantha*. They come in a range of colors from cream to orange, red and yellow, but have been overshadowed in recent years as cut flowers by other hybrid strains derived from *A. aurea*. The plants die down soon after flowering. **ZONES 7–9.**

Alstroemeria, Ligtu
Hybrid cultivar *(left)*

ALYSSUM
MADWORT

The commonly grown bedding alyssum is now classified under *Lobularia*, but there are still some 170 species of annuals, perennials and subshrubs in this genus and many of them are superb rockery plants. They are mainly low spreaders with small elliptical leaves. In spring and early summer they are smothered in heads of tiny white, cream, yellow or pink flowers. Most are less than 8 in (20 cm) tall with a few of the shrubbier species reaching 24 in (60 cm).

CULTIVATION
Plant in full sun with gritty, well-drained soil. Alyssums are ideal for growing in rock crevices and as dry-stone wall plants, though it is important that they are given an occasional soaking in spring and summer. Most species are fairly frost hardy and are propagated from seed or small cuttings.

Alyssum chalcidicum (above)

Considered by some authorities to be simply a form of *A. murale*, this Turkish perennial forms a tufted gray-green mound up to 15 in (45 cm) high. The individual leaves are around $^1/_2$ in (12 mm) long and are very densely packed. From mid-spring the mound is covered in tiny yellow flowers. ZONES 7–10.

Alyssum murale (above)
YELLOW TUFT

One of the taller species, this native of southeastern Europe grows to around 18 in (45 cm) tall. Its leaves are gray-green and $^1/_2$–1 in (12–25 mm) long. The flowers are yellow. ZONES 7–9.

A

AMARANTHUS

The 60 or so species of annuals and short-lived perennials that make up this genus range through most warmer parts of the world and include weeds, leaf vegetables and grain crops as well as a few ornamentals, grown for their brilliant foliage, curious flowers and adaptability to hot, dry conditions. They are popular bedding plants, with large and attractively colored leaves and minute flowers borne in drooping tassel-like spikes.

CULTIVATION

A sunny, dry position with protection from strong winds is essential, and they enjoy a fertile, well-drained soil, mulched during hot weather. They are marginally frost hardy and in cool climates are usually brought on under glass before planting out in late spring. Prune when young to thicken growth. Prepare soil for planting with plenty of manure, and water seedlings regularly. Protect from snails when young and watch for caterpillars and aphids. Propagate from seed.

Amaranthus caudatus (left)

LOVE-LIES-BLEEDING, TASSEL FLOWER

This species, growing to 4 ft (1.2 m) or more high, has oval, dull green leaves and dark red flowers in long, drooping cords, their ends often touching the ground. Flowers appear in summer through to autumn. In many old gardens this plant was used to give height in the center of circular beds. ZONES 8–11.

Amaranthus tricolor

Native to tropical Africa and Asia, this quick-growing annual has given rise to many cultivated strains, some used as leaf vegetables (Chinese spinach), others as bedding plants with brilliantly colored leaves. They are bushy and reach about 3 ft (1 m) high and 18 in (45 cm) wide. Tiny red flowers appear in summer. **'Flaming Fountain'** has leaves that are deep green at the base, bronze tinted higher up, and entirely blood red at the top. **'Joseph's Coat',** has brilliant bronze, gold, orange and red variegated 8 in (20 cm) long leaves which retain their coloring into late autumn. **ZONES 8–11.**

Amaranthus tricolor
'Flaming Fountain'
(above)

Amaranthus tricolor
'Joseph's Coat' *(left)*

A

AMMI

Six species of carrot-like perennials belong to this genus, occurring wild in the Mediterranean region, western Asia and the Canary Islands. They are fairly typical umbellifers with large, ferny basal leaves and flowering stems bearing large umbels of numerous small white flowers. One species *(Ammi majus)* is sometimes grown for cut flowers or as a 'cottage garden' plant, and a second *(A. visnaga)* has long been used medicinally in the Middle East. *Ammi* was the classical Greek and Latin name for a plant of this type, though its exact identity is uncertain.

CULTIVATION

Usually treated as annuals, they are easily grown in a sheltered but sunny position in any reasonable garden soil, kept fairly moist. Propagate from seed in spring. They will usually self-seed once established.

Ammi majus (above)
BISHOP'S WEED

Native to the Mediterranean region and western Asia, this species has become widely naturalized in other continents. It grows to about 24–36 in (60–90 cm) tall, producing a succession of large, lacy flowering heads in summer and autumn. The cut flowers are sometimes sold in florists' shops. ZONES 6–10.

AMSONIA
BLUE STAR

A

A genus of around 20 species of perennials and subshrubs native to southern Europe, western Asia, Japan and North America. They grow to around 3 ft (1 m) tall and have bright to deep green, narrow, lance-shaped leaves. Stems and leaves bleed milky sap when cut. The flowers, borne mainly in summer, are tubular with widely flared mouths. They are carried in phlox-like heads at the stem tips.

CULTIVATION
Amsonias are easily grown in any moist, well-drained soil that does not dry out in summer. Plant in full sun or part-shade. They are moderately to very frost hardy and generally die back to the rootstock in winter. Propagation is from seed, early summer cuttings or by division in late winter.

Amsonia tabernaemontana
(right)

BLUE STAR, BLUE DOGBANE

Amsonia tabernaemontana is a delightful perennial from northeastern and central USA. Stiff stems, 24–36 in (60–90 cm) tall, are topped by pyramidal clusters of small, star-shaped flowers of pale blue from late spring to summer, flowering along with peonies and irises. The leaves are narrow to elliptical and about 2½ in (6 cm) long. This species needs minimal care if given a moist, fertile soil in full sun to light shade. It is good in the perennial border or in a damp wildflower meadow. The species name commemorates a famous sixteenth-century German herbalist, who latinized his name as Tabernaemontanus. ZONES 3–9.

A

Anagallis tenella
(left)

BOG PIMPERNEL

Found in western Europe, this prostrate perennial has stems up to 6 in (15 cm) long that root as they grow. It is seldom over 1 in (25 mm) high and has a spread of around 12 in (30 cm). The funnel-shaped flowers are soft pink, occasionally white, and are borne in summer. Growing in boggy spots in the wild, it is best suited to the edges of ponds and other damp, sheltered spots. **'Studland'** has scented, deeper pink flowers. ZONES 8–10.

ANAGALLIS
PIMPERNEL

These are low-growing, often mat-forming annuals and perennials with small, heart-shaped to elliptical, bright green leaves arranged in opposite pairs. In spring and summer small, 5-petalled flowers appear in profusion on short stems. The flowers usually arise from the leaf axils or occasionally in small racemes at the stem tips. They come in a variety of colors including pink, orange, red, blue and white.

CULTIVATION
Plant in full sun in any well-drained soil that does not dry out entirely in summer. The more attractive, less vigorous species are excellent rockery plants. Propagate annuals from seed; perennials from seed, by division or from small tip cuttings. Some of the weedy species self-sow only too readily.

Anagallis monellii (below)
syns Anagallis linifolia, A. collina

This charming little plant is grown for its brilliant blue or scarlet flowers of ½ in (12 mm) diameter, which appear during summer. This species grows to under 18 in (45 cm), with a spread of 6 in (15 cm) or more. ZONES 7–10.

ANAPHALIS
PEARLY EVERLASTING

A genus of around 100 species of gray-foliaged perennials. They occur over most of the northern temperate regions and at high altitudes in the tropics. The narrow, lance-shaped leaves are often clothed in cobwebby hairs attached directly to upright stems. Panicles on clusters of papery white flowerheads terminate the stems in summer or autumn. The flowerheads may be small, resembling some achilleas, or large, with large papery bracts resembling helichrysums. Heights range from 6–30 in (15–75 cm) depending on the species. Like other everlastings they are useful for cut flowers, and the foliage and flowers are just as decorative when dried.

CULTIVATION
Plant in light, gritty, well-drained soil in full sun. They do not like being wet but when in active growth the soil should not be allowed to dry out completely. Prune back hard in winter. Propagate from seed or division.

Anaphalis triplinervis (above)

This is a Himalayan species that grows to 30 in (75 cm) tall. It has daisy-like white bracts and leaves that are pale green above with felted undersides, broader towards the apex and usually with 3 prominent veins diverging from the base. 'Sommerschnee' ('Summer Snow') grows only to a height of 12 in (30 cm) and has shorter, more heavily felted leaves. It may be, in fact, a hybrid with *Anaphalis nepalensis*. ZONES 5–9.

Anaphalis javanica (above)

From higher mountains of the Malay archipelago, this is a somewhat shrubby, evergreen species with a very dense coating of silver-gray hairs on the narrow leaves. It grows to about 18 in (45 cm) high and bears clusters of small, white flowerheads in summer. ZONES 9–10.

Anaphalis triplinervis
'Sommerschnee' (above)

A

Anchusa azurea
'Loddon Royalist' *(left)*

ANCHUSA
ALKANET, SUMMER FORGET-ME-NOT

This genus consists of about 50 species of annuals, biennials and perennials occurring in Europe, North and South Africa and western Asia. Many have a rather weedy habit and undistinguished foliage, but they bear flowers of a wonderful sapphire blue. Though individually not large, they are carried in clusters over a long spring and early summer season and do not fade easily. They are popular with bees, and are suitable for beds, borders and containers. The dwarf perennials are at home in a rock garden.

CULTIVATION

Frost hardy, they grow best in a sunny position in deep, rich, well-drained soil. In very hot areas, planting in part-shade helps maintain the flower color. Feed sparingly and water generously. Taller species benefit from staking and the plants require plenty of room as they make large root systems. Cut flower stalks back after blooming to promote new growth. Propagate perennials by division in winter, annuals and biennials from seed in autumn or spring. Transplant perennials when dormant in winter.

A

Anchusa azurea
(center right)
syn. *Anchusa italica*

ITALIAN ALKANET

Native to the Mediterranean and Black Sea areas, this species is an upright perennial 3–4 ft (1–1.2 m) high and 24 in (60 cm) wide. It has coarse, hairy leaves and an erect habit with tiers of brilliant blue flowers borne in spring to summer. Its several cultivars differ in their precise shade of blue: deep blue, tinted purple **'Dropmore'**; purple **'Dropmore Purple'**; rich blue **'Morning Glory'**; light blue **'Opal'**; and the intense deep blue of **'Loddon Royalist'**. ZONES 3–9.

Anchusa azurea
'Dropmore Purple' *(above)*

Anchusa azurea
'Dropmore' *(below)*

Anchusa capensis
'Blue Angel' *(left)*

Anchusa capensis
(center left)
CAPE FORGET-ME-NOT

This southern African
species is biennial in
cool climates, but in
warm-temperate gar-
dens it can be sown very
early in spring to bear
intense blue flowers in
summer. It grows to
15 in (40 cm) tall and
wide. As an annual,
'Blue Angel' reaches a
height and spread of
8 in (20 cm), and forms
a compact pyramid of
shallow, bowl-shaped,
sky blue flowers in
early summer. **'Blue
Bird'** is taller, 24 in
(60 cm), but equally
striking. **ZONES 8–10.**

Anchusa granatensis (below)

This low-growing spe-
cies from southwestern
Europe is unusual in
having flowers of a
bright purplish red
rather than the usual
blue of other anchusas.
The epithet *granatensis*
means 'of Granada' re-
ferring in this case to
the southern Spanish
city. **ZONES 6–9.**

Androsace sarmentosa
'Brilliant' *(right)*

Androsace
sarmentosa
(below)

This is another
Himalayan perennial
species that spreads
by runners. It forms
patches of rosettes of
small, oval leaves with
a covering of fine sil-
very hairs. Large heads
of yellow-centered,
pink flowers on 4 in
(10 cm) stalks are
borne in spring.
'Brilliant' has darker
mauve-pink flowers.
ZONES 3–8.

ANDROSACE
ROCK JASMINE

This genus consists of around 100 species of annuals and perennials from cooler regions of the northern hemisphere. It is mainly
the low-growing perennials that are valued as garden plants, forming dense mats or cushions no more than 4 in (10 cm) high.
Favorites for rock garden planting, they are rarely spectacular but
are appealing. Most species have light green or silvery gray, loose
rosettes of foliage crowded along prostrate stems, topped with
umbels of small, white or pink, 5-petalled flowers in spring
and summer.

CULTIVATION
They grow best in sunny, well-drained
scree or rockery conditions with free-
draining, gravel-based soil and additional
humus. Most are quite frost hardy, but
some may require alpine-house conditions
in areas subject to heavy winter rains.
Propagate from seed, cuttings or self-
rooted layers.

A

ANEMONE
WINDFLOWER

This genus of over 100 species of perennials occurs widely in the northern hemisphere, but with the majority in temperate Asia. Species include a diverse range of woodland plants as well as the common florist's anemone *(Anemone coronaria)*. All have tufts of basal leaves that are divided in palmate fashion into few to many leaflets. The starry or bowl-shaped flowers have 5 or more petals, their colors covering almost the whole range of flower colors. Anemones can be divided into the autumn flowering species with fibrous roots, such as *A. hupehensis* and *A.* × *hybrida,* and the tuberous and rhizomatous types, usually spring flowering, which include the ground-hugging *A. blanda* and *A. nemorosa.* There are other rhizomatous species which tolerate less moisture and more open conditions. Given the right conditions and left undisturbed for many years, many of these will form wonderful carpets of both leaf texture and color through their delicate flowers. The tuberous-rooted types, of which *A. coronaria* is best known, flower in spring and are best replaced every 1–2 years.

CULTIVATION

Most woodland species are very frost hardy and do well in rich, moist yet well-drained soil in a lightly shaded position. Propagate from seed planted in summer or divide established clumps in early winter when the plant is dormant. The tuberous-rooted types appreciate full sun and well-drained soil, and welcome a dry dormancy period. However, they are more prone to frost damage and the tubers tend to become weakened after blooming. For this reason, they are often treated as annuals.

Anemone appenina
(left)

A 6 in (15 cm) tall, rhizomatous species from southern Europe, it has a clump of basal leaves, each divided into 3 segments which are themselves further divided. Pinkish flowers about 1 in (25 mm) wide on short stems open in spring. **'Petrovac'** is a vigorous cultivar with many-petalled, deep blue flowers. **'Purpurea'** has pinkish purple flowers, while ***Anemone appenina*** var. *albiflora* has all-white flowers. ZONES 6–9.

Anemone blanda
'Radar' *(right)*

Anemone hupehensis

JAPANESE WIND FLOWER

A perennial with fi-
brous roots, this species
from central and
western China (long
cultivated in Japan),
can be almost evergreen
in milder climates
where, if conditions are
to its liking, it may
spread and provide
good ground cover,
producing its single
white to mauve flowers
on tall, openly
branched stems during
the early autumn. The
cultivar **'Hadspen
Abundance'** has deep
pink petals edged with
pale pink to almost
white. **'September
Charm'** has large pale
pink flowers with 5 to 6
petals, while *Anemone
hupehensis* var.
japonica is the Japa-
nese cultivated race,
taller and with more
petals than the wild
Chinese plants. It in-
cludes **'Prinz Heinrich'**
('Prince Henry') with
10 or more deep rose
pink petals, paler on the
undersides. Most of the
cultivars ascribed to
this species are now
placed under *Anemone
× hybrida*. ZONES 6–10.

Anemone hupehensis
'Hadspen Abundance'
(right)

Anemone blanda

This delicate-looking
tuberous species is frost
hardy. Native to Greece
and Turkey, it grows to
8 in (20 cm) with
crowded tufts of ferny
leaves. White, pink or
blue star-shaped flowers,
1½ in (35 mm) wide,
appear in spring. It self-
seeds freely and, given
moist, slightly shaded
conditions, should
spread into a beautiful
display of flowers.
Popular cultivars in-
clude the large-flowered
'White Splendour';
'Atrocaerulea', with
deep blue flowers;
'Blue Star', with pale
blue flowers; and
'Radar' with white-
centered magenta
flowers. ZONES 6–9.

Anemone blanda
'White Splendour' *(left)*

A

Anemone × *hybrida* 'Honorine Jobert' *(above)*

Anemone × hybrida

These popular hybrids are believed to have arisen as crosses between *Anemone hupehensis* and its close relative the Himalayan *A. vitifolia*, the latter distinguished by the dense woolly hair on its leaf undersides and usually white flowers. The hybrids generally have leaves that are hairier beneath than in *A. hupehensis*, and flowers in all shades from white to deepest rose, the petals numbering from 5 to over 30. They generally lack fertile pollen. The robust plants may reach heights of 5 ft (1.5 m) in flower. There are over 30 cultivars, among the most common being **'Honorine Jobert'** with pure white, 6–9-petalled flowers and very dark green leaves. Most nurseries do not list cultivar names but just sell the plants in flower, when they are easy to select both for color and flower type. **ZONES 6–10.**

Anemone × *hybrida* cultivar *(left)*

Anemone nemorosa
(below)

WOOD ANEMONE

As its common name
implies, this European
species is happiest in a
moist, shaded position
where its delicate
creamy white early
spring flowers delight
the passer by. Usually
under 4 in (10 cm)
high, it has fine creep-
ing rhizomes that will
quickly cover a wanted
area if conditions are
suitable. Many named
cultivars exist includ-
ing **'Allenii'**, a rich lilac
blue on the outside of
the petals and pale lilac
on the insides;
'Robinsoniana', with
lavender-blue petals;
and **'Vestal'**, a late-
blooming white vari-
ety. ZONES 5–9.

Anemone nemorosa 'Robinsoniana' *(above)*

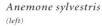

Anemone sylvestris
(left)

SNOWDROP ANEMONE

From Europe, this fibrous-rooted species is usually about 8 in (20 cm) tall, with deeply dissected glossy dark green leaves. The solitary, fragrant, single white flowers have prominent yellow stamens and are borne over a long season in spring and early summer. Cultivars include **'Grandiflora'**, with large nodding flowers and **'Elisa Fellmann'**, with semi-double flowers. ZONES 4–9.

Anemone rivularis
(right)

Ranging from India to western China and flowering in late to mid summer, this fibrous-rooted species has leaves with broader, more rounded divisions than most anemones. It grows to around 24 in (60 cm) tall, with white cup-shaped flowers tinted blue on the outside, and purple stamens. ZONES 6–9.

Anemone trullifolia *(right)*

Originating from the eastern Himalayas and western China, this fibrous-rooted anemone grows to around 12 in (30 cm) high with broadly lobed basal leaves. Delicate, long-stalked bluish, white or yellow flowers appear in summer. ZONES 5–9.

ANEMONELLA
RUE ANEMONE

The name is a diminutive of *Anemone* and in fact the sole species of this North American genus is a more diminutive plant than most anemones, but in foliage and flowers it is more reminiscent of a *Thalictrum*. It is a tuberous-rooted perennial forming a small, dense clump of foliage, the compound leaves with few but rather large leaflets. The flowers are large for the size of the plant and few to each short flowering stem, with a variable number of overlapping petals in shades of white to pale mauve.

CULTIVATION

It makes a charming rock garden plant but also adapts to moist, undisturbed spots in a woodland garden. It requires moist but very well-drained, humus-rich soil, and a semi-shaded position. Growth is slow and skilful management is needed to keep plants healthy for many years. Propagate by careful division of mature plants in autumn or from seed in spring.

Anemonella thalictroides (below)

This beautiful plant occurs wild in eastern USA and southeastern Canada, in mountain woodlands. Usually 8 in (20 cm) or less in height, it has smooth blue-green leaves. In spring and early summer it bears delicate bowl-shaped flowers about ¾ in (18 mm) wide with 5 to 10 petals. ZONES 4–9.

ANEMOPSIS
YERBA MANSA

Although its name means 'anemone-like', this genus of a single species from western USA and Mexico is quite unrelated to anemones, but related rather to the lizard's-tail genera *Saururus* and *Houttuynia*. The 'flowers' that look like those of some of the anemones with elongated receptacles are in fact inflorescences, with a group of petal-like white bracts at the base of a spike of tiny, fleshy greenish flowers. It is a creeping evergreen perennial that spreads both by thick underground rhizomes and surface runners that develop rosettes of leaves at intervals. The rhizome is used medicinally by Native Americans, who also use the small, hard fruits for beadwork.

CULTIVATION
It will grow equally well in boggy ground or in a well-drained raised bed or rockery, preferably in full sun. Although quite ornamental and unusual, it is a vigorous grower and can quickly become invasive, and is difficult to eradicate due to its tenacious rhizomes. A boggy stream or pond edge is perhaps its most appropriate placement. Propagate by division or from cuttings.

Anemopsis californica (above)
YERBA MANSA

Occurring wild in the southwestern states of the USA and adjacent Baja, California (Mexico), yerba mansa can rapidly spread over a very large area when conditions suit it, mounding sometimes to about 18 in (45 cm) high. The spoon-shaped leaves become purple-tinged in the sun, and the curious white-bracted flower spikes develop over a long season in spring, summer and autumn. ZONES 8–11.

Angelica sylvestris
(right)

WILD ANGELICA, WOOD ANGELICA

This 7 ft (2 m) tall biennial is a European native found in woods and damp meadows. It has bipinnate or tripinnate leaves up to 2 ft (60cm) long, each segment of which can be 3 in (8 cm) long). The leaves are covered with small bristly hairs and have serrated edges. The flowers may be white or pink. This species is seldom used for culinary or herbal purposes. ZONES 7–10.

ANGELICA

This genus of 50 or so species is mainly indigenous to the cooler parts of the northern hemisphere. They are valued for the bold palm-like structure of their leaves, the bunches of pale green flowers on tall stems and the pleasant aroma.

CULTIVATION

They prefer moist, well-drained, rich soil in sun or shade. Plants die after flowering and setting seed and should then be removed. Angelica will self-sow or can be propagated from seed.

Angelica pachycarpa *(right)*

A species that has recently come into cultivation as an ornamental, this is semi-evergreen and remarkable for the succulence and glossiness of its compact foliage. The flowering branches barely rise above the foliage and rapidly develop clusters of small thick fruits. ZONES 8–10.

A

ANIGOZANTHOS
KANGAROO PAW

Native to southwestern Australia, these evergreen perennials are noted for their unique bird-attracting tubular flowers, the outsides coated with dense shaggy hairs and opening at the apex into 6 'claws', the whole resembling an animal's paw. Foliage is somewhat grass-like, and the various species can range in height from 1–6 ft (0.3–1.8 m). Flowers come in many colors including green, gold, deep red and orange-red; some species and hybrids are bicolored. In recent years many hybrids have been produced, meeting the demands of the cut-flower industry and the florists' trade in potted flowers, although most will grow outdoors equally well. An example is *Anigozanthos* 'Red Cross'.

Anigozanthos
'Red Cross' *(below)*

CULTIVATION
They prefer warm, very well-drained sandy or gravelly soil and a hot, sunny, open position. Water well during dry seasons. Most will tolerate very light frosts and do well in coastal regions. Most tolerate drought, although flowering will be prolonged with summer water. Propagate by division in spring or from fresh seed. Plants are often affected by ink disease, a fungus which blackens the foliage. Watch for snails which can shred younger leaves overnight.

Anigozanthos, Bush Gems Series

The best of the kangaroo paws for their resistance to ink disease, the Bush Gems hybrids are mostly of compact size, with flowers ranging from yellow, gold and green through to orange, red and burgundy. **'Bush Heritage'** is a small cultivar of 12–20 in (30–50 cm) in height with flowers of burnt terracotta and olive green. **'Bush Twilight'** grows 8–15 in (20–40 cm) tall. Its prolific flowers in muted orange, yellow and green tones appear mainly in spring above the dull green, very narrow leaves. Other popular cultivars in the series are **'Bush Glow'**, sunset red, and **'Bush Gold'**, golden yellow. ZONES 9–11.

Anigozanthos,
Bush Gems Series, 'Bush Heritage' *(below)*

Anigozanthos,
Bush Gems Series, 'Bush Glow' *(left)*

Anigozanthos flavidus *(center)*

YELLOW KANGAROO PAW

Regarded as the hardiest of the kangaroo paws, this species has a vigorous clumping growth habit to 3 ft (1 m) across. With long, dull green leaves, flowering stems 3–5 ft (1–1.5 m) tall, and flowers in green, yellow or soft red tones, this species has proved adaptable to a range of soils and climates. Native to the far southwestern corner of Australia, where it is attractive to native birds, it is used extensively in hybridization programs. ZONES 9–11.

Anigozanthos,
Bush Gems Series, 'Bush Twilight' *(below)*

A

Anigozanthos humilis *(left)*

This is a low, clumping perennial, growing no taller than 15 in (40 cm) but spreading anything up to 3 ft (1 m) if conditions are favorable. It can die back in summer and autumn, so should be positioned so that it will not be overgrown while dormant. The flowering stems, often twice the height of the foliage, carry blooms in a wide range of colors from cream through dull orange to red. It prefers full sun. ZONES 9–11.

Anigozanthos 'Regal Claw' *(right)*

One of the many striking cultivars with parents listed as *Anigozanthos preissii* and *A. flavidus*, 'Regal Claw' is a dwarf plant with flowers of orange with a red felted overlay. ZONES 9–11.

Anigozanthos manglesii *(right)*

RED-AND-GREEN KANGAROO PAW

This striking plant has blue-green, strap-like leaves. The deep green flowers contrast vividly with a red base and stem, and appear mainly in spring. Flowering stems are 18–36 in (45–90 cm) in height and the plant has a spread at the base of about 18 in (45 cm). Unfortunately this spectacular species is one of the most difficult to cultivate, being very susceptible to ink disease as well as summer root rot. ZONES 9–10.

A

Antennaria dioica
(below right)
CATSFOOT

Antennaria dioica
'Australis' *(above)*

ANTENNARIA
CAT'S EARS, LADIES' TOBACCO

A genus of around 45 species of evergreen to near-evergreen perennials of the daisy family from temperate regions of the northern hemisphere, most species form dense mats of leaf rosettes that root as they spread; a few are mounding and up to 15 in (38 cm) tall. The narrow, crowded leaves are usually silver gray and hairy. The summer-borne flowerheads are of the 'everlasting' type with dry, papery bracts surrounding a disc of petal-less florets, the heads clustered on short stems that hold them clear of the foliage mat.

CULTIVATION
Most species are very frost hardy and are best grown in moist, well-drained soil in full sun or morning shade. They can be used in perennial borders or as rockery plants. Propagate from seed or division.

A stoloniferous perennial occurring wild in the colder parts of the northern hemisphere. It forms a mat of rosettes of narrow spatula- to lance-shaped leaves, dark green above but white-woolly on the undersides. In summer, strong 8 in (20 cm) tall flower stems develop bearing clusters of white, pink or yellow flowerheads. Catsfoot is unusual among composites (daisies) in having different sexes on different plants (dioecious), the female flowerheads larger than the male. An attractive ground cover or rock garden plant, it also has some medicinal uses. *Antennaria dioica* **'Rosea'** has deep pink flowerheads; and **'Australis'** silvery gray stems topped with clusters of white flowers. ZONES 5–9.

Anthemis 'Moonlight' *(above)*

ANTHEMIS

In suitable conditions the 100 or so species of this genus of annuals and perennials from Mediterranean regions and western Asia flower prolifically, and this is what prompted the name, from the Greek *anthemon*. Belonging to the larger daisy family, the flowerheads have the typical daisy shape and are generally white, cream or yellow with distinctive contrasting disc florets; a typical example is *Anthemis* 'Moonlight'. Even when not in flower most species have somewhat aromatic, finely dissected foliage in shades of green or silver gray, which can be used to advantage in the mixed border or rockery. Formerly *Anthemis* was taken in a broader sense to include the herb chamomile, which belongs to the genus *Chamaemelum*.

CULTIVATION

These plants flower best in full sun and like well-drained soil. The perennials can be short-lived and often become untidy, but cutting back after flowering in the autumn ensures a more shapely plant. They are easily replaced by cuttings taken in the warmer months or by division in autumn or spring. Annual species can be grown from seed.

Anthemis cretica (below)

A mound-forming perennial from southern Europe and Turkey, often with a gray down on its leaves, this species has white flowerheads with yellow discs held on solitary stems up to 12 in (30 cm) high during the spring and summer months. ZONES 5–9.

Anthemis tinctoria (below)
DYER'S CHAMOMILE, GOLDEN MARGUERITE

Native to Europe and western Asia, this is a very hardy, easily grown perennial that is covered in late spring and summer with a dazzling display of daisy flowers above fern-like, crinkled green leaves. The plant mounds to as much as 3 ft (1 m) high if supported on a rockery or a bank. The epithet *tinctoria* signifies a dye plant, and indeed the flowers of this species were once used to make a yellow dye. The typical form with bright golden flowers is now less popular than some of the cultivars, notably '**E. C. Buxton**' with subtle soft yellow blooms blending beautifully with the fine foliage. ZONES 4–10.

ANTHERICUM
SPIDER PLANT

A genus of some 50 species of fleshy-rooted perennial lilies that form clumps of narrow, grass-like leaves. The flower stems are wiry and up to 3 ft (1 m) tall and by mid-summer are bearing their small, starry, 6-petalled, white flowers. They are natives of Europe, northern Africa and Asia Minor.

CULTIVATION
Plant in moist, well-drained soil in full sun or morning shade. Moderately frost hardy, they are propagated by sowing fresh seed or by division in late winter to early spring.

Anthericum liliago
'Major' *(below)*

Anthericum liliago
(right)
ST BERNARD'S LILY

This European species has 15 in (38 cm) long, gray-green leaves and in summer develops 3 ft (1 m) tall spikes of narrow-petalled, 1 in (25 mm) wide white flowers, each petal with a greenish mid-vein. **'Major'** has larger, pure white flowers.
ZONES 7–10.

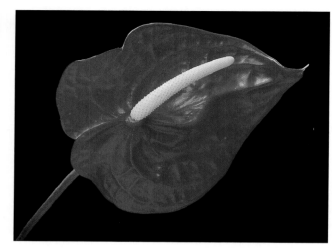

ANTHURIUM
FLAMINGO FLOWER

This is a huge and diverse genus of ever-green, clumping or climbing epiphytes in the arum family, all from tropical America. Familiar as florists' plants and cut flowers are 2 to 3 species with typically brilliant red, flat spathes held above broad leathery leaves; selection and breeding has broadened the range of colors to include white, pink and orange. The actual flowers are the tiny bumps gathered around the central spadix.

CULTIVATION
Anthuriums are easy to grow in a tropical climate but elsewhere they are more likely to flourish in a greenhouse or indoors in containers. Indoors, they need bright light, high humidity and constant warmth and moisture to flower. Plant outdoors in a humid position, in well-drained, peaty soil in full or part-shade out of the wind. Keep soil moist but not soggy. Daytime temperatures should not fall below about 60°F (15°C). Propagate from rhizomes in early spring. Potted plants need dividing and repotting every few years.

Anthurium andraeanum (left)

Grown for its large, brilliantly colored spathe with raised vein-ing, this species grows to about 24 in (60 cm) high, with large heart-shaped leaves. The plants only produce one or two flowers at a time but they bloom all year. The spathes, so glossy they appear var-nished, are typically bright red, but other colors have been bred including pink, and green marbled with red. ZONES 11–12.

Anthurium scherzerianum (above)
FLAMINGO FLOWER

Growing to 24–30 in (60–75 cm) this species typi-cally has red spathes, with curled spadices but cultivars vary from white to pink to very dark red, sometimes with paler spots. The elongated, rather dull green leaves are very thick and leathery. Al-though this is one of the more cold-hardy species, it must be protected from frost. ZONES 10–12.

ANTHYLLIS

This is a genus of around 25 species of annuals, perennials and small shrubs. The leaves are pinnate but the leaflets are often small and closely crowded, creating the appearance of coarsely serrated leaves. The individual flowers are small and pea-like but borne abundantly in dense, rounded heads from spring to summer. Flower colors include yellows, reds and pinks.

CULTIVATION

Easily grown in any well-drained soil in full sun. Cold hardiness varies with the species but most will tolerate moderate frosts. Propagate from seed or small cuttings.

Anthyllis montana
'Atrorubens' *(above right)*

Anthyllis vulneraria
var. *alpestris (below)*

Anthyllis vulneraria
KIDNEY VETCH, LADIES' FINGERS

This spreading, short-lived perennial ground cover is native to Europe and North Africa. It forms crowded rosettes of silky-haired foliage and may sometimes mound up to about 18 in (45 cm) tall. The flowers, in ½ in (12 mm) wide heads, are cream and yellow, often with red or purple tints. The species is used medicinally as an astringent, laxative and cough remedy. It is also dried for use in flower arrangements. *Anthyllis vulneraria* var. *alpestris* is a variety from mountainous areas. ZONES 7–9.

Anthyllis montana

This perennial species from the mountains of southern Europe has ferny pinnate leaves and spreads to form a mat of foliage up to 10 in (25 cm) tall and 3 ft (1 m) wide. From late spring the plant is studded with profuse ½ in (12 mm) wide heads of pink and white flowers that from a distance resemble pink clover. **'Atrorubens'** has deeper pink to purplish flowers. ZONES 7–9.

A

ANTIRRHINUM
SNAPDRAGON

The resemblance of snapdragon flowers to the face of a beast was noted by the ancient Greeks, who called them Antirrhinon, nose-like. In French they are gueule de loup, wolf's mouth, and in German and Italian the name means lion's mouth. Closely related to the toadflaxes *(Linaria)*, the genus consists of about 40 species, most from the western Mediterranean region but with a few from western North America. They are annuals, perennials and evergreen subshrubs. The common snapdragon *(Antirrhinum majus)* is a perennial but it is normally treated as an annual in gardens.

CULTIVATION
They prefer fertile, well-drained soil in full sun. Propagate the garden snapdragon from seed in spring or early autumn.

Antirrhinum hispanicum (left)

This short-lived perennial from Spain is a very pretty miniature species, 10 in (25 cm) tall with flowers about half the size of the garden snapdragon. Mauve-pink is its only color. ZONES 7–10.

A

Antirrhinum majus *(above)*

GARDEN SNAPDRAGON

This bushy, short-lived perennial is valued for its showy flowers, borne over a long period from spring to autumn. The many named cultivars, usually grown as annuals, spread 12–18 in (30–45 cm) and may be tall, 30 in (75 cm); medium, 18 in (45 cm); or dwarf, 10 in (25 cm). Plant breeders have developed snapdragons with wide open or double flowers, but none have the charm of the traditional form, as exemplified by the strain called **Liberty**. Treat these garden snapdragons as annuals—they rarely flower well after the first year, and old plants are apt to succumb to the fungus, antirrhinum rust. Deadhead to prolong flowering and pinch out early buds to increase branching. The **Coronette Series** of F1 hybrids, bred as bedding plants, exemplifies some of the qualities plant geneticists are injecting into their breeding programs. These include tolerance of bad weather, extra large blooms on heavy spikes and uniformity from seedling stage. They can grow to 24 in (60 cm) or more tall and a number of individual colors are available, from bronze through shades of pink to deep red to yellows and white. Two popular cultivars are **'Flower Carpet'** and **'Madame Butterfly'**. ZONES 6–10.

Antirrhinum majus, Liberty Series cultivar *(above)*

A

APONOGETON
WATER HAWTHORN

This genus of aquatic plants consists of 40-odd species, found wild in streams and lakes through tropical and subtropical regions of Africa, Asia and Australasia, but with the greatest concentration in Madagascar. The leaves are long-stalked, oval to narrowly oblong, with a close network of veining; they may be fully submerged, or most of the leaves may float on the surface. Long-stalked flowering heads emerge just above water, branched into short fleshy spikes of curious small white, pink or purplish flowers. The tuberous roots and flower buds are sometimes eaten in their native countries.

CULTIVATION

Aponogetons fall into 2 groups as far as cultivation is concerned. The larger group consists of choice subjects for the tropical aquarium, notably the magnificent Madagascar lace plant (*Aponogeton madagascariensis*) with its large lattice-like submerged leaves. Although not quite typical of this group, its requirements are very specialized. This group requires a fairly deep tank, the water kept to at least 60°F (16°C) in winter, higher in summer. The smaller group, typified by *A. distachyos*, is more cold hardy and vigorous. These plants can be grown outdoors in temperate climates so long as the water has no more than a thin crust of ice from time to time in winter. They are easily grown, planted into the bottom mud or sand. Propagate by division of the tubers, or from seed.

Aponogeton distachyos *(below left)*
WATER HAWTHORN

From southern Africa, this plant makes an interesting ornamental for garden ponds, but is best not grown too close to waterlilies (*Nymphaea*), as its densely massed foliage tends to smother them. Hawthorn-scented white flower spikes, 2–4 in (5–10 cm) long and of a curious Y-shape, are produced from late spring to autumn and sometimes into winter, turning green as they age and bend into the water, where the fruit ripens. It will grow in temperate climates provided the water does not freeze. ZONES 8–10.

Aquilegia caerulea (right)

BLUE COLUMBINE, ROCKY MOUNTAIN COLUMBINE

This short-lived, upright, alpine species from the Rocky Mountains grows to 24 in (60 cm) or more in height with a rather narrow growth habit. It is Colorado's state flower and arguably the finest of the wild columbines. Large, powdery blue and white nodding flowers on branching stems appear in late spring and early summer. It sometimes produces a few blooms in autumn. It does best in rich soil. ZONES 3–9.

Aquilegia atrata (above)

DARK COLUMBINE

Native to the alpine woodlands of Europe but tolerant of milder conditions, this species closely resembles the common columbine *(Aquilegia vulgaris)* but has dark violet-purple flowers with protruding yellow stamens, borne in late spring and early summer. Preferring part-shade in warmer areas, it grows to around 18 in (45 cm) tall. ZONES 3–9.

AQUILEGIA

COLUMBINE

The common name comes from the Latin for dove, as the flowers were thought to resemble a cluster of doves. Native to Europe, North America and temperate regions of Asia, these graceful, clump-forming perennials are grown for their spurred, bell-shaped—single and double forms—flowers in a varied color range, and for their fern-like foliage. Some are also useful as cut flowers, and the dwarf and alpine species make good rock garden plants. They flower mostly in late spring and early summer, and look best in bold clumps with a foreground planting of annuals.

CULTIVATION

Frost hardy, they prefer well-drained light soil, enriched with manure, and a sunny site protected from strong winds and with some shade in hot areas. In cold climates columbines are perennials and need to be cut to the ground in late winter, but growing larger-flowered cultivars as annuals usually gives best results. Propagate by division or from seed in autumn and spring; many of them self-seed readily.

Aquilegia 'Crimson Star' *(left)*

These long-spurred aquilegias usually face their flowers upwards to the viewer, in contrast to the pendent flowers of the short-spurred granny's bonnets. The nectar spurs, which in other aquilegias normally match the color of the petals of which they are a prolongation, match the crimson of the sepals in this cultivar. **ZONES 3–10.**

Aquilegia chrysantha *(below)*

GOLDEN COLUMBINE

This is among the showiest of the North American columbines, with large, long-spurred, fragrant yellow flowers on stems often exceeding 3 ft (1 m) in height. Native to southwestern North America, it is more tolerant of sun and heat than most. White and double-flowered cultivars are available. **ZONES 3–10.**

Aquilegia elegantula *(below)*

This species from the Rocky Mountains and northern Mexico is closely allied to *Aquilegia formosa* but is smaller, to 24 in (60 cm), and the pale orange or yellow flowers are slightly longer-spurred. **ZONES 5–9.**

Aquilegia canadensis *(right)*

AMERICAN WILD COLUMBINE

This native of eastern North America produces masses of nodding, red and yellow flowers with medium-length spurs, on 18–24 in (45–60 cm) stems in late spring and early summer. It is tolerant of full sun, provided there is plenty of moisture. It will also tolerate heat if some shade is provided. Hummingbirds love the nectar-rich flowers. **ZONES 3–9.**

Aquilegia flabellata *(right)*

This hardy alpine species from Japan and Korea has soft, blue-green, ferny leaves and nodding, blue-purple flowers with short hooked spurs. A summer-flowering species, it grows to about 18 in (45 cm) high. ZONE 5.

Aquilegia, McKana Hybrid cultivar *(below)*

Aquilegia, McKana Hybrids

This best-known strain of long-spurred columbines is derived from North American species, chiefly *Aquilegia caerulea, A. chrysantha* and *A. formosa.* They bear flowers in a wide range of colors in late spring and early summer. Whatever the color of the sepals, the 5 petals that carry the spurs are usually white or yellow. Pinching off spent flowers will prolong the season. The plants grow to 3 ft (1 m) or more. ZONES 3–10.

Aquilegia formosa *(left)*

WESTERN COLUMBINE

This attractive species with long-spurred, nodding, pale scarlet flowers and protruding stamens comes from the Pacific Northwest of North America and is the parent of many popular garden cultivars. The flowering stems reach up to 3 ft (1 m) and are held above ferny leaflets. Its main flowering season is late spring and early summer. ZONES 5–9.

A

Aquilegia vulgaris
GRANNY'S BONNETS, COLUMBINE

This is the true columbine of
Europe, one of the parents of many
hybrids. It grows to 3 ft (1 m) high
with a spread of 18 in (45 cm) or
more. On long stems from the
center of a loose rosette of gray-
green foliage, it bears funnel-
shaped, short-spurred flowers,
typically dull blue in wild plants
but ranging through pink, crimson,
white and purple in garden varieties. The cultivar **'Nora Barlow'** has
double flowers of a curious form,
with many narrow, greenish sepals
and pink petals that lack spurs.
ZONES 3–10.

Aquilegia vulgaris,
double form *(left)*

Aquilegia vulgaris
'Nora Barlow' *(below left)*

Aquilegia vulgaris
cultivar *(below)*

A

ARABIS
ROCK CRESS

Over 120 species make up this northern hemisphere genus of annuals and perennials, the latter mostly evergreen. Although some can reach as much as 3 ft (1 m) in height, species grown in gardens are dwarf, often mat-forming perennials suited to the rock garden, dry walls and crevices. They spread by short rhizomes, producing crowded tufts of spatula-shaped leaves. Short sprays of delicate, 4-petalled flowers are held above the foliage in spring and summer.

CULTIVATION

They grow best in very well-drained soil in a sunny position. Propagation is from seed or from cuttings taken in summer, or by division.

Arabis blepharophylla (above)
CALIFORNIA ROCK CRESS

This moderately frost-hardy Californian native, which grows at low altitudes, forms a compact clump 4–6 in (10–15 cm) high. It has tufts of toothed green leaves that extend into short, leafy spikes of pink to purple flowers during spring. It is best in a rockery or crevice where it will not be overrun. The most available cultivar is **'Frühlingzauber'** (syn. 'Spring Charm'), with rich rose purple flowers. **ZONES 7–10.**

Arabis caucasica var. *brevifolia* (right)

Arabis caucasica
(below right)
syn. *Arabis albida*
WALL ROCK CRESS

This tough, evergreen perennial is sometimes used to overplant spring-flowering bulbs. Easily grown, it forms dense clusters of thick foliage up to 6 in (15 cm) high and 18 in (45 cm) wide. In spring it has white flowers on loose racemes above gray-green leaf rosettes. There are various forms of *Arabis caucasica* such as **'Pinkie'**, *A. c.* var. *brevifolia* and double-flowered forms such as **'Flore Pleno'** (syn. 'Plena'). **ZONES 4–10.**

A

ARCTOTHECA

This is a South African genus composed of 5 species of rosette-forming perennials, some with prostrate short stems, others lacking any aboveground stem. The growth form is dandelion-like, with flower stems emerging from the center of the foliage rosette. The toothed or lobed leaves are densely coated in downy, white hairs, on the undersides only in some species and on both sides in others. The daisy-like flowerheads are borne singly on short stems. They are usually pale yellow or brownish yellow. In warmer temperate climates some species naturalize freely, in places becoming troublesome weeds.

CULTIVATION

Arctotheca species are very easily grown in any well-drained soil in full sun. They are marginally frost hardy and are propagated from seed or by removing small offset rosettes from established clumps.

Arctotheca calendula (right)
CAPE DANDELION, CAPE WEED

A short-lived species that often pops up in lawns, Cape dandelion can be cultivated as a ground cover. In some parts of the world it is regarded as a trouble-some weed, choking vegetable crops and tainting cows' milk. Its leaves are around 6 in (15 cm) long and the light yellow flower-heads, about 2 in (5 cm) in diameter, appear in continuous succession on short stems from the center of the rosette from spring to autumn. Plants that are sub-jected to frequent mowing are far smaller than those that are left to develop naturally.
ZONES 8–11.

Arctotheca populifolia (below)

This species occurs naturally on beaches and coastal dunes, its prostrate stems becom-ing buried by loose sand. It has become natural-ized along coasts of southern Australia. Its 3 in (8 cm) long leaves are often elliptical in shape and unlobed with a dense felty coat-ing of white hairs on both sides. The yellow flowerheads are small, ½–1 in (12–25 mm) in diameter on very short stalks, and appear from summer to autumn.
ZONES 9–11.

Arctotis cumbletonii
(right)

Arctotis fastuosa
(below)
syn. *Venidium fastuosum*
CAPE DAISY, MONARCH OF THE VELD

A perennial from the open veld in South Africa's western Cape Province, this is an adaptable plant and can be treated as an annual in colder regions. It will grow 24 in (60 cm) high, with silvery green, lobed leaves and glistening orange flowerheads with purple zones at the base of each of the many ray petals and a black central disc. It is a colorful choice for a sunny position in the garden. ZONES 9–11.

ARCTOTIS

syns *Venidium*, × *Venidioarctotis*
AFRICAN DAISY

This genus consists of about 50 species of annuals and evergreen perennials from South Africa. The stems and leaves are to varying degrees coated in matted downy hairs, giving them a gray-green or silvery gray color. The showy flowers are typical of the daisy family. They rely on the sun to open fully and come in a range of colors from creamy yellow often through orange to deep pinks and claret reds. Many hybrids are now available, their blooms with rings of darker color towards the center. Growth habit varies from compact and shrubby to quite prostrate, plants of the latter type making a faster-spreading and colorful ground cover. Some of the more distinctive *Arctotis* species include *A. arctotoides,* with narrow, deeply lobed leaves, and *A. cumbletonii* with narrow disc florets.

CULTIVATION
Given plenty of space in full sun and well-drained, sandy soil, arctotises may be used as bedding plants or to cover a large area of dry bank. Flowering can be prolonged if blooms are deadheaded after the first flush in early summer. Propagate from seed or cuttings, which can be rooted at any time of year.

A

Arctotis hirsuta
(left)

This annual species of *Arctotis* has lobed, hairy, gray-green leaves. The flowers, in shades of orange and yellow to white, are borne in spring to mid-summer. *Arctotis hirsuta* is best propagated from seeds sown in early autumn. **ZONES 9–11.**

Arctotis Hybrid, 'Apricot' *(left)*

Arctotis Hybrid, 'Dream Coat' *(below)*

Arctotis Hybrids

These plants were known until recently as × *Venidioarctotis* hybrids, one of the main parent species having being placed in the genus *Venidium* (now combined with *Arctotis*). They are grown as annual bedding plants in frost-prone areas but will overwinter in milder climates. Growing to a height and spread of around 18 in (45 cm), they have gray, lobed leaves that are quite downy beneath. In summer and autumn they produce a long succession of showy blooms, to 3 in (8 cm) across in a very wide range of colors, often 2-toned. **'Gold Bi-Color'**, **'Apricot'**, **'Flame'**, **'Dream Coat'** and **'Wine'** are among the more popular named hybrids. **ZONES 9–11.**

Arctotis Hybrid,
'Flame' *(right)*

Arctotis Hybrid,
'Wine' *(right)*

Arctotis Hybrid,
'Gold Bi-Color' *(below)*

ARENARIA
SANDWORT

This genus is composed of around 160 species of mainly mound-forming or ground cover perennials, some of which become shrubby with age. They are widespread in the northern hemisphere, with a few southern hemisphere species too. The plants commonly develop a dense mass of fine stems clothed with tiny, deep green or gray-green leaves and small, usually white, flowers in spring or summer. The flowers may be borne singly or in small clusters.

CULTIVATION
They are easily grown in any moist, well-drained soil in full sun. They are ideal rockery or tub plants and are generally very frost hardy. Propagate from seed, self-rooted layers or small tip cuttings.

Arenaria balearica
(left)

Native to the islands of the western Mediterranean, this miniature species forms a mat of stems that root as they spread. The shiny, bright green leaves are less than ¼ in (6 mm) long and are almost circular. The plant is dotted profusely with ¼ in (6 mm) wide, green-centered, white flowers in spring and summer. **ZONES 7–9.**

Arenaria montana
(below)

This species from southwest Europe is larger than most arenarias in both leaves and flowers. It has gray-green leaves up to 1½ in (35 mm) long and mounds to about 6 in (15 cm) tall. Its flowering stems tend to be rather upright and extend slightly above the foliage clump. The abundant flowers are nearly 1 in (25 mm) in diameter, pure white with yellow-green centers. **ZONES 4–9.**

Arenaria tetraquetra (below)

This is a densely foliaged, 1–2 in (2.5–5 cm) high, cushion plant from the mountains of southwest Europe. It has tiny overlapping leaves that give it a heather-like appearance. Small, white flowers are massed at the stem tips in spring. **ZONES 6–9.**

ARGEMONE
PRICKLY POPPY

This is a genus of 29 species of poppy-like plants native to the Americas, occurring mostly in drier subtropical regions. Most are annuals or perennials, but one is a shrub. They tend to be upright growers, many reaching 4 ft (1.2 m) or more tall, with strong stems and lobed leaves. In many species the stems, leaves and flowerbuds are a pale blue-gray and are covered in sharp prickles. The flowers, mainly yellow or orange, are from 2–6 in (5–15 cm) in diameter, usually 6-petalled and appearing throughout the warmer months. Several species, first grown as ornamentals, have become troublesome weeds of crops and waste places. They are all poisonous.

CULTIVATION
They are very easily grown in any well-drained soil in full sun. Hardiness varies with the species, though most will tolerate moderate frosts. Propagate from seed. Some species self-sow and become invasive.

Argemone mexicana (below)

This annual species is native to Mexico and nearby areas of the Caribbean but has spread widely through warmer parts of the world as a weed of crops and waste ground. It has prickly, white-marked, grayish green leaves and fragrant, yellow, poppy-like flowers about 2 in (5 cm) wide appearing in summer. It has an erect habit, growing to 3 ft (1 m) high. ZONES 8–11.

A

Aristea ecklonii
(left)

This vigorous, ever-
green from southeast-
ern Africa is 18–24 in
(45–60 cm) tall. It
forms tangled clumps
of long, lanceolate
green leaves, above
which starry, deep blue
flowers appear rather
sparsely in summer.
ZONES 9–11.

ARISTEA

This genus contains around 50 species of mainly evergreen,
rhizomatous, iris-like perennials from tropical and southern
Africa and Madagascar. They form clumps of sword-shaped
leaves from 8–36 in (20–90 cm) tall depending on the species.
The ½–1 in (12–25 mm) wide, 6-petalled flowers are clustered
along erect, cane-like stems and are usually in shades of blue or
purple. The flowering season ranges from late winter to summer.

CULTIVATION

Aristeas thrive on stream banks, in moist, sandy, humus-rich soil
in full sun or light shade. Most species are hardy to about 25°F
(−4°C) but are damaged if subjected to frequent frosts. Older
plants do not transplant well, so division may not always be
successful. Propagation from seed in autumn or spring usually
produces an abundance.

ARISTOLOCHIA
DUTCHMAN'S PIPE, BIRTHWORT

This large genus of over 500 species comprises evergreen and deciduous, twining climbers and some herbaceous perennials, native to many different climatic regions. The climbers are most often cultivated, chosen for their heart-shaped leaves and unusually shaped tubular flowers, which have a swelling at the base and a hood above, usually with a sharply bent tube between them. Insects are attracted into the mouth of the flowers by a strong scent, and pollen is scattered over their bodies. The fruit are also curiously shaped, dangling from slender stalks and splitting at maturity to spill fine seed as they rock in the breeze.

CULTIVATION
The plants require well-drained, humus-rich soil in a sunny position with some shade in summer, and support for their climbing habit. Many have some degree of frost tolerance and will grow vigorously in warm-temperate climates. In spring, prune the previous year's growth to 2 to 3 nodes. Propagate from seed in spring or from cuttings in summer. Watch out for spider mites.

Aristolochia clematitis (below)
BIRTHWORT

Now seldom grown in gardens, this European species was used by medieval midwives, following the medieval Doctrine of Signatures—a belief that the Creator had marked plants in such a way that doctors could recognize diseases they were intended to cure. The womb-like shape of the birthwort flower indicated that the plant would help in problems of childbirth. ZONES 5–9.

A

ARMERIA

THRIFT, SEA PINK

This genus of about 35 species of low-growing, tufted, early summer-flowering perennials grows in a wide variety of environments in the temperate zones of Eurasia, Africa and the Americas—from salt marshes and storm-swept headlands to alpine meadows. The crowded, narrow, mostly evergreen leaves usually form a dense mound, and atop each slender stalk are small flowers crowded into globular heads.

CULTIVATION

They are suitable for rock gardens or borders and prefer exposed, sunny positions and rather dry soil with good drainage. They are generally frost hardy. Propagate from seed or cuttings in spring or autumn.

Armeria alliacea
(left)

Occurring widely in the western half of Europe, this is one of the more robust species, with large tufts of long, soft, flat, deep green leaves and numerous bright reddish purple flowerheads on stems up to 18 in (45 cm) tall. ZONES 5–9.

A

Armeria leucocephala 'Corsica' *(right)*

Armeria leucocephala

A dwarf, densely mound-forming
perennial from the Mediterranean
islands of Corsica and Sardinia, this
attractive species has tangled, fine,
linear leaves up to 4 in (10 cm) long,
often finely hairy, as are the fine
flower stalks, up to 15 in (38 cm) tall.
The small flowerheads vary in color;
it is usually **'Corsica'** with brick-red
summer flowers that is seen in gardens.
ZONES 7–9.

Armeria maritima *(below)*
COMMON THRIFT, SEA PINK

Native around much of the northern
hemisphere, thrift grows to 4 in
(10 cm) high and to 8 in (20 cm) wide,
and forms a mound-like mass of narrow, dark green leaves. Dense flowerheads of small, white to pink flowers
are produced in spring and summer.
Most *Armeria* cultivars are derived
from this species. **'Vindictive'** has
vibrant rose pink flowers. **'Alba'** has
small white flowers. ZONES 4–9.

ARTEMISIA
WORMWOOD

This large genus of evergreen and deciduous perennials and shrubs from temperate regions of the northern hemisphere has many species from arid and semi-arid environments. They are grown for their decorative foliage, which is often aromatic, sometimes repellent to insects and may be coated with whitish hairs. Attractive in a flower border, the feathery foliage provides year-round interest. The small yellowish flowerheads are not showy.

CULTIVATION
Mostly quite frost hardy, they prefer an open, sunny situation with light, well-drained soil. Prune back lightly in spring to stimulate growth. Propagate from cuttings in summer or by division in spring. Transplant during winter.

Artemisia arborescens *(below)*

This spreading, evergreen perennial from the Mediterranean region reaches a height of 4 ft (1.2 m) with a rounded habit and lacy, silver-gray foliage. Small, yellowish blooms are borne in summer and early autumn. Only moderately frost hardy, it is a good plant for the back of a border. ZONES 8–11.

Artemisia absinthium *(left)*
COMMON WORMWOOD, ABSINTHE

Of wide natural occurrence in Europe and temperate Asia, common wormwood grows to 3 ft (1 m) though often rather lower, with much divided, dull gray foliage. It is a perennial that spreads by rhizomes, the tangled, flopping stems also rooting as they spread. Inconspicuous, dull yellow flowerheads are borne in late summer. Trim after flowering to keep neat. '**Lambrook Silver**', with its tidy habit is considered one of the better silver-leaved shrubs, and provides a restful contrast to brightly colored flowers in a herbaceous border. ZONES 4–10.

A

Artemisia caucasica *(right)*
syns *Artemisia lanata, A. pedemontana*

Widely distributed through southern European mountains from Spain to the Ukraine and the Caucasus, this is a semi-deciduous or evergreen perennial less than 12 in (30 cm) high and of spreading habit, with soft, silvery grayish leaves divided into very narrow lobes. In summer it produces short spikes of dull yellow flowerheads. **ZONES 5–9.**

Artemisia dracunculus *(left)*
TARRAGON

Native to central and eastern Europe and grown for its narrow, aromatic, green leaves which have a delicate, peppery aniseed flavor, tarragon grows up to 3 ft (1 m) in the warmer months, dying back to a perennial rootstock over winter. As it does not produce seed, propagate by division in early spring. The tarragon seed sometimes offered is the flavorless *Artemisia dracunculoides*, known as Russian tarragon. **ZONES 6–9.**

Artemisia ludoviciana
syn. *Artemisia purshiana*
WESTERN MUGWORT, WHITE SAGE

Native to western North America and Mexico, this rhizomatous species is grown for its lance-shaped, sometimes coarsely toothed leaves, which are densely white-felted beneath and gray- to white-haired above. Bell-shaped, grayish flowerheads are produced in summer. A spreading, invasive species, it reaches 4 ft (1.2 m) high and is very frost hardy. **'Valerie Finnis'**, with its jagged leaf margins, together with **'Silver Queen'** are 2 of several popular cultivars. **ZONES 4–10.**

Artemisia ludoviciana
'Silver Queen' *(right)*

A

Arthropodium cirratum (left)

RENGA RENGA LILY

This New Zealand species bears graceful sprays of starry white flowers on a 24 in (60 cm) stem above tufts of broad, handsome leaves in late spring. It looks a little like a hosta and is a good substitute in the hot-summer climates in which hostas languish. The Maoris used the fleshy roots in medicine. **ZONES 8–10.**

ARTHROPODIUM

The ungainly name *Arthropodium* is from the Greek and means having a jointed foot, referring to the way the footstalk of each flower has a joint in the middle. Of this genus of a dozen or so perennials from Australasia, only 2 or 3 are seen in gardens, the most ornamental being the New Zealand renga renga, *A. cirratum.*

CULTIVATION

Essentially warm-temperate plants, in cool areas they need a sheltered spot in fertile, well-drained soil. Propagate from seed or by division.

Arthropodium milleflorum (right)

Native to Australia, this deciduous species with tuberous roots has long, narrow leaves and in late spring bears numerous, small, pale lilac flowers on 24 in (60 cm) tall stems. The effect is rather like an ornamental grass and it would be a good choice for this role in warm-temperate flowerbeds. The species name means 'thousand-flowers', which is perhaps an exaggeration. **ZONES 8–11.**

ARUNCUS
GOAT'S BEARD

There are 3 species in this genus of rhizomatous perennials, occurring widely over temperate and subarctic regions of the northern hemisphere. Their appearance is very much that of a giant astilbe, with ferny basal leaves up to 3 ft (1 m) long and summer plumes of tiny cream flowers in 8–18 in (20–45 cm) long, pyramidal panicles carried on wiry stems that hold them well above the foliage.

CULTIVATION

They are best grown in sun or part-shade in moist, humus-rich, well-drained soil around edges of ponds. Goat's beard is very frost hardy and is propagated from seed or by division.

Aruncus dioicus
'Kneiffii' *(below)*

Aruncus dioicus
(above)
syns *Aruncus sylvestris,*
Spiraea aruncus

A graceful, woodland perennial, this clump-forming plant produces a mass of rich green, fern-like foliage and arching plumes of tiny, greenish or creamy white flowers in summer. It grows 6 ft (1.8 m) tall and 4 ft (1.2 m) wide. Cut flowering stems back hard in autumn. **'Kneiffii'** reaches about 3 ft (1 m) and has cream-colored flowers. **ZONES 3–9.**

Asarum arifolium
(left)

This is a variable, ever-green species from southeastern USA with large, elongated, heart-shaped leaves up to about 6 in (15 cm) long, marked with lighter green between the prominent veins. **ZONES 7–9.**

ASARUM
WILD GINGER

This genus, belonging to the same family as *Aristolochia* (Dutch-man's pipe), consists of over 70 species of rhizomatous perenni-als, both evergreen and deciduous, distributed widely through temperate areas of the northern hemisphere but most numerous in Japan and the USA. They are better known for their use in traditional medicine than as ornamental plants, though the foliage can make an attractive ground cover in shaded woodland gardens. The leaves are either kidney- or heart-shaped, and the small, bell-shaped flowers, which are usually hidden below the leaves, are mostly dull brownish or purplish and open at the mouth into 3 sharply reflexed sepals. Some examples include *Asarum chinense, A. maximum, A. muramatui* and *A. sieboldii.* All 4 species have very attractive foliage.

CULTIVATION
These plants prefer a shady site in moist, well-drained soil and can be planted out any time between autumn and spring. They spread rapidly; divide the clumps every few years in spring. They can also be propagated from seed. They are prone to attack from slugs and snails.

Asarum muramatui
(below)

A

Asarum canadense (right)
CANADIAN SNAKEROOT

This deciduous perennial native to the woodlands of eastern North America forms tufted mats with fleshy, creeping rhizomes and coarse-textured, heart-shaped leaves, 2–3 in (5–8 cm) wide rising on hairy stalks to 8 in (20 cm) high. Hidden beneath in spring are inconspicuous, brown, bell-shaped flowers. Decoctions of the rhizomes were used medicinally by Native Americans and white settlers. ZONES 3–8.

Asarum caudatum (left)
BRITISH COLUMBIA WILD GINGER

Native to the coastal mountains of western North America, this ground-hugging, evergreen perennial grows in relatively deep shade on the forest floor. Spreading by rhizomes, it forms irregular, open patches and flowers from late spring into summer. Large, 6 in (15 cm) long, kidney-shaped leaves rise to 8 in (20 cm) above ground, hiding the brownish purple blooms. ZONES 6–9.

Asarum europaeum (right)
ASARABACCA

Widely distributed in European woodlands, this species has conspicuous shaggy hairs on both the creeping rhizomes and the 4–6 in (10–15 cm) long leaf stalks. The deep-green, glossy leaves are kidney-shaped to almost circular, up to 3 in (8 cm) wide. The dull purplish flowers, hidden under the leaves, are insignificant, only about ½ in (12 mm) long. Asarabacca was formerly used medicinally and as an ingredient of snuff powders, but is moderately toxic. ZONES 6–9.

Asarum maximum (left)

Native to China, this species has the heart-shaped leaves typical of many within the genus, but they are characterized by gray mottling, which contrasts well with the dark green base color. In spring it produces 2 in (5 cm) wide pear-shaped red-purple flowers with white or yellow markings. ZONES 7–10.

A

ASCLEPIAS
MILKWEED

Found naturally in the Americas, this genus consists of over 100 species of perennials, subshrubs and (rarely) shrubs and includes both evergreen and deciduous plants. Most have narrow, pointed elliptical to lance-shaped leaves and all have milky white sap. The flowers are borne in stalked clusters arising from the upper leaf axils. They are small, with 5 reflexed petals below a waxy corona, a feature characteristic of the milkwood family (see also *Hoya*). Elongated seed pods follow; the seeds have silky plumes and are dispersed on the breeze. Their sap is acrid and poisonous, and the butterfly larvae that feed on them are toxic to predators such as birds. A few species have become widespread weeds of warmer regions. Some African species with inflated, prickly pods are now placed in the genus *Physocarpus*.

Asclepias speciosa
(below)

A 3 ft (1 m) tall perennial from eastern North America, this species has oval leaves up to 6 in (15 cm) long. The flowers are dull pinkish red and white and up to 1 in (25 mm) in diameter. The fruit have soft spines. ZONES 2–9.

CULTIVATION
They are easily grown in any well-drained soil in full sun. Hardiness varies considerably with the species. Some of the shorter-lived perennials may be treated as annuals, and are usually raised from seed. Some hardier North American species require a cool climate and will not survive in the dormant state where winters are too warm. Propagate from seed or semi-ripe cuttings.

Asperula setosa
(right)

Native to Turkey, this annual species grows to about 12 in (30 cm) high with very narrow, small leaves and lilac flowers arranged in dense clusters at the branch tips. **ZONES 5–9.**

ASPERULA
WOODRUFF

There are around 100 species of annuals, perennials and small, twiggy subshrubs in this genus, distinguished from the closely related *Galium* by the generally longer tube of the small flowers. They occur mainly in temperate regions of Europe, Asia and Australasia. Most are densely foliaged mat- or tuft-forming perennials with tiny, narrow leaves arranged in whorls of 4 or more on the fine stems. In spring and summer the plants may be smothered in tiny flowers, usually white, pale pink or occasionally yellow. Most species spread by underground runners and a few of the woodland species grow to around 24 in (60 cm) high, with larger, bright green leaves. Like galiums, asperulas often develop fragrance as the cut foliage dries and some were once used as strewing herbs; at least one species yields a dye.

CULTIVATION
The small species generally do best in rockery conditions with gritty, well-drained soil in full sun. They can be raised from seed, from small rooted pieces removed from the clump, or by division.

Asperula
arcadiensis *(below)*

This perennial Greek species makes a woody based tuft of foliage to 6 in (15 cm) high. The narrow leaves are gray and downy, about ½ in (12 mm) long. The tiny flowers are pink to pale purple. **ZONES 5–9.**

A

Asphodeline lutea
(left)
ASPHODEL, KING'S SPEAR

A native of the Mediterranean region eastward from Italy, this fragrant, frost-hardy plant can grow to 5 ft (1.5 m), though usually rather less so. Tufts of narrow, glossy leaves appear below spear-like stems bearing spikes of yellow, star-shaped flowers, some 1¼ in (30 mm) wide. The plants should be kept moist before the flowering period in spring. ZONES 6–10.

ASPHODELINE
JACOB'S ROD

This is a genus of some 20 species of biennial and perennial lilies, native to the Mediterranean region and Asia Minor. The name indicates their close similarity to *Asphodelus*. They have thick, fleshy roots, from which sprout narrow, grassy to spear-shaped leaves that are usually bright green, sometimes with a bluish tint. Stiffly upright flower spikes up to 5 ft (1.5 m) tall develop in summer. They carry large numbers of star-shaped yellow, white or pale pink flowers on the upper half of the stem.

CULTIVATION
These plants are very frost hardy and easily grown in any well-drained soil in full sun. Propagate from seed or by division in winter or early spring. Try to avoid damaging the roots or they may rot.

A

ASPHODELUS

When Tennyson's lotus eaters 'rested weary limbs at last on beds of asphodel', it was the plant now known as *Asphodelus albus* on which they probably reclined—the name *asphodelos* goes back to the ancient Greeks. The genus consists of 12 species of fleshy-rooted annual and perennial lilies, native to the Mediterranean region and to western Asia as far as the Himalayas. They have basal tufts of narrow, grass-like leaves and 6-petalled, starry, white, green or pink flowers borne along stiff, upright stems, which may be branched. Spring and summer are the main flowering seasons.

CULTIVATION

Hardiness varies with the species, though most will tolerate moderate frosts. They require reasonably sunny, warm, dry summer conditions to flower well and prefer a light, sandy, humus-rich soil with good drainage. Propagate by division immediately after flowering or from seed.

Asphodelus aestivus *(left)*

Widely distributed around the Mediterranean, this species grows to a height of about 3 ft (1 m), with broad, leathery basal leaves. The branched panicles, elongating in spring, bear white to very pale pink flowers as much as 3 in (8 cm) across, the petals with darker mid-lines. **ZONES 6–10.**

Asphodelus albus *(above)*

Native to Europe and North Africa, *Asphodelus albus* is probably the most commonly cultivated species in the genus. It has thick, fleshy roots and sword-shaped leaves up to 24 in (60 cm) long. The 12–36 in (30–90 cm) tall flower stems bear pinkish brown striped, white flowers along most of their length in spring, those at the base opening first. The variable bracts—white or brown—are especially noticeable before the star-shaped flowers open. **ZONES 5–10.**

ASTELIA

This genus of some 25 species of rhizomatous, evergreen perennials has a scattered distribution around the southern hemisphere including the Falkland Islands, Mauritius and Réunion, southeastern Australia and New Zealand, the latter being the richest in species. The bold, sword-shaped leaves are arranged in rosettes or tufts and the plants vary in stature from about 2 in (5 cm) to 8 ft (2.4 m) or even more. Most have a silvery coating of fine, silky hairs on the leaves, though this may be confined to the undersides. Habitats vary from alpine bogs to temperate rainforests, the larger-growing species generally in the latter, sometimes as epiphytes. Inconspicuous flowers are often hidden by the foliage but in many species are followed by showy clusters of brightly colored berries. There are separate male and female flowers, on the same plant in some species, on separate plants in others.

CULTIVATION

They are easily grown in moist, peaty, well-drained soil in full sun or part-shade; a few species will grow in boggy soil. Hardiness varies, though most species will tolerate light frosts. Propagate from seed or by division.

Astelia nervosa
(above)
KAKAHA

Spreading 6 ft (1.8 m) or more and up to 36 in (90 cm) high, this vigorously clumping, New Zealand species is valued for its narrow arching leaves thinly coated with silvery hairs and growing 2–6 ft (0.6–1.8 m) long. In summer, starry, light brown fragrant flowers form in clusters on the ends of long, slender stems. These are followed by small green fruit, which turn orange-red when ripe. ZONES 9–10.

A

Aster 'Coombe's Violet'
(right)

ASTER
MICHAELMAS OR EASTER DAISY, ASTER

Native to temperate regions of the northern hemisphere (most numerous in North America), this large genus of perennials and deciduous or evergreen subshrubs has over 250 species, ranging from miniatures suitable for rock gardens to 6 ft (1.8 m) giants. The simple leaves are mostly smooth edged, sometimes hairy, often quite small. Showy, daisy-like flowerheads are usually produced in late summer or autumn in a wide range of colors, including blue, violet, purple, pink, red and white, all with a central disc of yellow or purple. There are many aster cultivars once listed under the parent species, but this has become too complex and many now stand alone. A typical example is *Aster* 'Coombe's Violet'. The 'China asters' grown as bedding annuals are now placed in the genus *Callistephus*.

CULTIVATION
Easily grown, they prefer sun (or part-shade in hot areas) in a well-drained soil, preferably enriched with compost. Keep moist at all times and shelter from strong winds and stake the taller species. Cut the long stems down to ground level and tidy the clumps when the flowers have faded. Propagate by division in spring or late autumn, or from softwood cuttings in spring. Divide plants every 2 to 3 years, using the most vigorous outer part. Powdery mildew, rust, aphids and snails can be a problem.

Aster alpinus *(below)*

From the higher mountains of Europe, this clump-forming plant, usually about 6–12 in (15–30 cm) high and 18 in (45 cm) wide, bears large, violet-blue, daisy flowers with yellow centers from late spring until mid-summer; the foliage is dark green. It is a popular rock garden plant and is fully frost hardy. There are a number of named cultivars. 'Trimix' grows to 8 in (20 cm) and has flowers that are a tricolor mix of pink, blue and white.
ZONES 3–9.

Aster amellus 'Breslau'
(left)

Aster amellus
'Blutendecke' *(below)*

Aster amellus
ITALIAN ASTER

The Italian aster, actually a native of the eastern half of Europe and also Turkey, is usually represented in gardens by its many cultivars. In its typical form it grows to 18–24 in (45–60 cm) with oblong basal leaves that can be somewhat hairy and erect stems which can become floppy if grown in too much shade. Although spreading by underground rhizomes, it is not considered invasive and is especially disease resistant. The large, fragrant flowerheads are pink and purple-blue, while popular cultivars are stronger in color and include **'King George'**, a deep violet, **'Violet Queen'**, somewhat paler, and the bright pink **'Sonia'**. **'Blutendecke'** is a German Foerster selection dating from 1950. It grows to 18 in (45 cm) tall with silvery violet-blue flowers. **'Breslau'** was introduced by Kock of Germany in 1960 and is 18 in (45 cm) tall with violet-blue flowers. **'Sternkugel'** has paler flowers. ZONES 4–9.

Aster amellus
'Violet Queen'
(left)

Aster amellus
'Sternkugel' *(above)*

Aster amellus 'Sonia'
(below)

Aster amellus 'King
George' *(above)*

Aster divaricatus *(right)*
WHITE WOOD ASTER

Also from eastern North America, this is a distinctive species with slender, wiry, dark mahogany stems to about 24 in (60 cm) tall that tend to twist and wander, broad-based leaves tapering to fine points, and delicate, open sprays of small, white flowerheads. Spreading by rhizomes to form loose clumps, it is essentially a plant for the woodland garden. Some forms are taller and more robust. **ZONES 3–9.**

Aster ericoides *(left)*
HEATH ASTER

The specific name means 'with leaves like those of *Erica*', the heath genus, and indeed this species from eastern and central USA and northern Mexico has very small, narrow leaves, at least on the upper stems. With flowering stems rising up to 3 ft (1 m) high from tufted basal shoots towards mid-summer and into autumn, it provides a wonderful display of massed, small, white flowerheads as does one of its more compact cultivars, **'White Heather'**. There are a number of cultivars of varied heights, mostly with pale pinkish or yellowish blooms. The cut flowers are popular with florists. **ZONES 4–10.**

Aster ericoides
'White Heather'
(right)

Aster novae-angliae
'Andenken an Alma
Pötschke' *(left)*

Aster novae-angliae
NEW ENGLAND ASTER

Originally native over a
wide area of the eastern
and central USA, this
species is represented
in cultivation by many
cultivars, showing
much variation in form
and color of blooms.
Vigorous clumps of
mostly vertical, 3–5 ft
(1–1.5 m) stems may
lean with the weight of
large, loose clusters of
daisies, making staking
necessary. Cultivars
include the late-
blooming, clear pink
'Harrington's Pink';
the rose pink, mildew-
resistant **'Barr's Pink'**;
the cerise **'September
Ruby'**; and **'Hella
Lacy'**. **'Andenken an
Alma Pötschke'**, often
shortened to **'Alma
Pötschke'**, is a compact-
growing, though 4 ft
(1.2 m) tall plant
with bright rose pink
blooms. **'Dauerblau'**
was introduced in
1950 by Foerster of
Germany. Its flowers
open late and it grows
to 4 ft (1.2 m) tall.
They all prefer moist,
rich soil in full sun.
ZONES 4–9.

Aster linosyris × *A.
sedifolius (right)*

Aster linosyris
GOLDILOCKS ASTER

Very different from the
usual concept of an
aster, this species from
Europe, North Africa
and western Asia is a
rather insignificant
plant, but good for
areas where summers
are hot and dry.
Goldilocks aster grows
to 24 in (60 cm) in
height with very fine,
dull gray-green foliage
and erect sprays of
small yellow flower-
heads in late summer.
The heads lack the
usual ray florets—this
trait has dominated in
its hybrid with *Aster
sedifolius (A. linosyris* ×
A. sedifolius).
ZONES 4–10.

Aster novae-angliae
cultivar *(left)*

A

Aster novae-angliae
'Dauerblau' *(left)*

Aster novae-angliae
'Barr's Pink' *(below)*

Aster novi-belgii
NEW YORK ASTER

Novi-belgii is Linnaeus' attempt to translate New Amsterdam (now New York) into Latin; the Belgii were the tribe encountered by Julius Caesar in the Low Countries. The New York aster in its wild form is native to the east coast, from Newfoundland to Georgia. It has given rise to innumerable garden forms in colors ranging from the palest mauve to violet and deep pink, and with varying degrees of 'doubling' of the flowerheads. They are among the most useful plants for the perennial border in cooler-temperate climates, responding to generous feeding and watering in spring and summer. Watch for mildew. Cultivars include **'Court Herald'**; **'Mulberry'** has large, semi-double, rich mulberry red blooms. **'Ernest Ballard'**, named for a leading aster breeder, grows to 3 ft (1 m) with large, purple-red blooms. **'Audrey'** grows to a compact 12 in (30 cm) with double, lavender blue autumn flowers. **'Schone von Dietlikon'** has deep violet-blue flowers and grows to 4 ft (1.2 m) tall. **ZONES 3–9.**

Aster novi-belgii
'Ernest Ballard'
(above right)

Aster novi-belgii
'Audrey' *(right)*

Aster novi-belgii
'Court Herald' *(below)*

A

Aster umbellatus *(below)*

FLAT-TOPPED ASTER

From eastern USA, this robust aster can grow up to 4 ft
(1.2 m). By flowering time
its rather broad basal leaves
have withered, leaving only
the smaller stem leaves. In
summer it produces densely
clustered white flowerheads
$\frac{3}{4}$–1 in (18–25 mm) in
diameter. ZONES 3–9.

Aster novi-belgii
'Schone von Dietlikon'
(above)

Aster sedifolius
(right)

Native to central and
southern Europe, this
vigorous, spreading
perennial, sometimes
treated as an annual,
grows to 3 ft (1 m)
high. It has tiny leaves
and masses of pink,
violet-blue or purple
flowerheads over a
long flowering season
that can extend from
late spring through
summer to autumn.
ZONES 5–9.

A

Astilbe, Arendsii Hybrid, 'Europa' *(above)*

Astilbe, Arendsii Hybrid, 'Brautschleier' *(above)*

Astilbe, Arendsii Hybrids
(above & right)

This hybrid group, derived from four east Asian species, *Astilbe astilboides, A. japonica, A. davidii* and *A. thunbergii*, is named after German horticulturalist Georg Arends (1863–1952) to whom many of the finest cultivars are credited. Heights vary from 18–48 in (0.45–1.2 m), with a spread of 18–30 in (45–75 cm). They produce feathery spikes from late spring to early summer. Cultivars are available in a range of colors from red through pink to white and include **'Amethyst'**, with pale purple to pink flowers; **'Fanal'** with long-lasting scarlet flowers; **'Brautschleier'** ('Bridal Veil'), white; **'Professor van der Wielen'**, white; **'Rheinland'**, deep rose; and **'Europa'**, pale pink flowers. ZONES 6–10.

ASTILBE
FALSE SPIRAEA

This genus of 14 species of pretty, early to late summer perennials comes mostly from eastern Asia, where they grow in the moist ground beside woodland streams though there are also 2 species occurring in the eastern USA. All astilbes have basal tufts of ferny, compound leaves, the leaflets usually sharply toothed. Pointed, plume-like panicles of tiny, white to pink or red flowers rise well above the foliage. Most usual in cultivation are the hybrids grouped under the name *Astilbe × arendsii*, though there are many recent hybrid cultivars of different parentage. The name 'spiraea' was mistakenly attached to this genus when they were introduced to England in the 1820s.

CULTIVATION
They need a lightly shaded place with rich, leafy soil that never dries out, though they do not like being actually flooded, especially in winter. Cooler climates suit them best; in hot summers they need constant watering to keep their roots cool. Good cut flowers, they also make pretty pot plants for bringing indoors for a while when the blooms are at their best. In a heated greenhouse they will flower early. Propagate by division in winter.

Astilbe, Arendsii Hybrid,
'Professor van der Wielen'
(above)

Astilbe 'Betsy
Cuperus' *(above)*

One of the larger hy-
brid cultivars, this
plant grows to over 3 ft
(1 m) and has deep
green foliage and arch-
ing sprays of pale
peachy pink flowers.
ZONES 6–10.

Astilbe, Arendsii
Hybrid, 'Fanal' *(left)*

Astilbe chinensis

A late-summer-flowering species native to China, Korea and eastern Siberia, this attractive, clump-forming plant reaches 24 in (60 cm) with toothed, hairy, dark green leaflets and dense, fluffy flower spikes of tiny, star-shaped, white, flushed with pink blooms. **'Pumila'**, a dwarf form growing to 12 in (30 cm) with pinkish mauve flowers, will tolerate heavier clay soils and will spread quickly if conditions are to its liking. **Astilbe chinensis var. davidii**, to 6 ft (1.8 m) with purple-pink flowers crowded on long, slender panicles, has the added interest of bronze-toned new foliage. **A. c. var. taquetti** has lavender-pink flowers on a plant about 3 ft (1 m) tall. **ZONES 6–10.**

Astilbe chinensis 'Pumila' *(above)*

Astilbe chinensis var. *davidii (left)*

A

Astilbe 'Straussenfeder'
(right)

Bred in Germany, 'Straussenfeder' grows to 3 ft (1 m) tall, with decorative leaves and distinctive flowering panicles with drooping branches, the blooms rose pink. The name is German for 'ostrich feather'. **ZONES 6–10.**

Astilbe 'Serenade'
(below)

Often listed under *Astilbe chinensis*, but probably a hybrid, 'Serenade' has pinkish red flowers on stems up to 15 in (40 cm) high. Otherwise, it is very similar to *A. chinensis*. **ZONES 5–10.**

ASTRAGALUS
MILK VETCH

There are some 2,000 species of annuals, perennials and shrubs in this legume genus and they are found over much of the temperate zone of the northern hemisphere. The leaves are usually pinnate with up to 45 leaflets. A few have trifoliate leaves. Size varies considerably, from small cushion plants through to plants 5 ft (1.5 m) tall. The flowers are pea-like and are carried in spikes or racemes in the leaf axils near the top of the plant. A number of the west Asian species including *Astragalus gummifer* are the traditional source of gum tragacanth, a gelatinous gum used in cosmetics, pharmaceutical products and ice-creams, among other uses.

CULTIVATION
Plant in moist, well-drained soil in full sun. Most species will tolerate moderate to severe frosts. Propagate the annuals from seed, the perennials and shrubs from seed or small cuttings.

Astragalus angustifolius (above)

A native of Greece and the Middle East, this species is an 18 in (45 cm) high, cushion-forming shrub with spiny stems. The leaves are pinnate with 5 to 12 pairs of leaflets. Racemes of 1 in (25 mm), cream to light purple flowers open in summer.
ZONES 7–9.

A

ASTRANTIA
MASTERWORT

All 10 species of this genus, an unusual member of the carrot family, are herbaceous perennials that occur in mountain meadows and woodlands of Europe and western Asia. Gardeners delight in their delicate flowerheads surrounded by a collar of pointed bracts, carried on wiry stems above clumps of deeply toothed, lobed foliage of soft mid-green.

CULTIVATION
Keeping in mind their natural habitat, these plants are best suited to moist, fertile, woodland conditions, or near the edges of streams or ponds where the soil is always moist. As long as the roots are kept moist they will tolerate full sun, indeed the variegated species color much better in such a position. In a suitable situation they will build up clumps. Propagate by division in early spring or from seed.

Astrantia major
(above)

Astrantia major
‘Sunningdale
Variegated’ *(below)*

Native to central and eastern Europe, this species has deeply lobed, palmate leaves forming a loose mound of foliage 18 in (45 cm) tall from which rise nearly bare stems to 24 in (60 cm) or more, each topped by intricately formed, soft pink or white, daisy-like flowerheads, surrounded by petal-like bracts in the same colors. The flowers are produced almost throughout summer. **‘Rosea’** is slightly taller, with blooms of rich rose pink. **‘Sunningdale Variegated’** is grown for the rich tapestry of its large yellow- and cream-marked leaves and for its delicate, pink-flushed white blooms. **ZONES 6–9.**

A

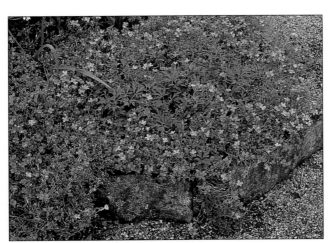

AUBRIETA
ROCK CRESS

Although mountain flowers, aubrietas are not diminutive and temperamental as are many alpine plants. Rather they make carpets of color at the front of flowerbeds, or down retaining walls. Not very tall—6 in (15 cm) or so at most—they will happily sprawl to several times their height and in spring cover themselves with 4-petalled flowers, mainly in shades of purple. About a dozen species are native to stony hillsides and mountains from the Mediterranean area to as far east as Iran. The plants most often seen in gardens are hybrids mainly derived from *Aubrieta deltoidea*. The genus name honors the French botanical painter Claude Aubriet (1668–1743); it has sometimes been spelt *Aubrietia*.

CULTIVATION

They are easy to grow in cool-temperate climates (flowering is erratic in warm ones), asking only for sunshine or a little shade and fertile, well-drained soil. They are short lived and it is wise to take a few cuttings in summer every 3 or 4 years; they are readily propagated also by division of the rhizomatous rootstock.

Aubrieta × *cultorum*
'Cobalt Violet' *(left)*

Aubrieta × *cultorum*

There are many garden hybrids that come under this heading, plants with unknown parentage and with a wide range of growth and flowering habit. The flower color varies from white through pinks and purples to almost violet, some double, and some with variegated foliage. Some examples include **'Cobalt Violet'**, **'Purple Gem'** and **'Doctor Mules'**, which has rich blue-violet flowers. ZONES 4–9.

Aubrieta deltoidea
(below left)

Native to southeastern Europe and Turkey, this compact, mat-forming perennial has greenish gray leaves and masses of starry, mauve-pink flowers borne over a long period in spring. The species is now rare in gardens, most cultivated aubrietas being hybrids now known collectively as *Aubrieta* × *cultorum*, though they are commonly listed as *A. deltoidea*. ZONES 4–9.

A

Aubrieta gracilis
(right)

A delicate species form-
ing thin mats, *Aubrieta
gracilis* comes from
Greece and Albania.
The leaves are tiny and
narrow and the slender
3–4 in (8–10 cm)
flowering stems bear
½–¾ in (12–18 mm)
wide purple flowers in
summer. **A. *macedonica***
is a very similar species.
ZONES 5–9.

Aubrieta macedonica
(below)

Aurinia saxatilis
(right)
syn. *Alyssum saxatile*

BASKET OF GOLD,
YELLOW ALYSSUM

This native of central and southeastern Europe is the only commonly grown species. It has hairy, gray-green leaves, forms rather loose mounds to 10 in (25 cm) high and is smothered in bright yellow flowers in spring and early summer. It is very popular as a rockery or wall plant. There are a number of cultivars, including **'Argentea'** with very silvery leaves; **'Citrina'** with lemon yellow flowers; **'Gold Dust'**, up to 12 in (30 cm) mounds with deep golden yellow flowers; **'Sulphurea'** with glowing yellow flowers; and **'Tom Thumb'**, a 4 in (10 cm) high dwarf with small leaves. ZONES 4–9.

AURINIA

This is a genus of 7 species of biennials and evergreen perennials, formerly included in *Alyssum*, found from central and southern Europe to the Ukraine and Turkey. They are mainly small, spreading, mound-forming plants. The leaves are initially in basal rosettes, mostly fairly narrow. They bear elongated sprays of tiny yellow or white flowers in spring and early summer.

CULTIVATION

Plant in light, gritty, well-drained soil in full sun. They are ideal for rockeries, rock crevices or dry-stone walls. Most species are very frost hardy and are propagated from seed or small tip cuttings; they will self-sow in suitable locations.

B

BAPTISIA
FALSE INDIGO

Baptisia is a genus of 20–30 species of pea-flowered perennials that grow naturally among the tall grasses of the prairies and woodlands of eastern and central USA. The common name arises from the former use of some species by dyers as a substitute for true indigo *(Indigofera)*. Few of the species are grown much in gardens. Most are somewhat shrubby in habit, and the leaves are divided into 3 leaflets like a clover or a medic. The blue, purple, yellow or white pea-flowers are borne in terminal spikes over a fairly long summer season.

CULTIVATION

The plants prefer full sun and neutral, well-drained soil. They are not bothered by frost, nor do they resent very dry conditions in summer. As they have a deep root system they should not be transplanted or disturbed. Propagation is best done from seed in autumn or by division.

Baptisia alba *(above)*

This bushy, upright species grows to around 5 ft (1.5 m). Its bluish green foliage provides a backdrop to the sprays of pea-like blooms, white sometimes streaked with purple, borne during early summer. ZONES 7–10.

Baptisia australis
(left)
FALSE INDIGO

This summer-flowering perennial is attractive in both flower and foliage. The leaves are blue-green and form a loose mound up to about 4 ft (1.2 m) high and 3 ft (1 m) across. The lupin-like flowers are borne on erect spikes from early to mid-summer and are an unusual shade of purplish blue. The seed pods can be dried for indoor decoration. ZONES 3–10.

Begonia
'Cleopatra' *(right)*

This rhizomatous begonia is a popular, easy-to-grow plant with a dense mass of shortly creeping rhizomes that support crowded, sharply lobed, yellow-green and purplish brown leaves. Profuse, long-stalked sprays of pale pink flowers bloom in early spring. In warm climates it is a popular balcony plant, thriving in hot sun.
ZONES 10–12.

B

BEGONIA
BEGONIA

Begonias are native to moist tropical and subtropical regions of all continents except Australia, and are most diverse in South America. There are over 1500 known species, ranging from rhizomatous perennials a few inches (centimeters) high to 10 ft (3 m) shrubs. Many are grown indoors, prized for their beautifully colored and textured foliage or showy flowers, sometimes both present on the one species or cultivar. Mostly evergreen, their broad, usually asymmetrical leaves have a rather brittle and waxy texture. Female flowers, as distinct from male flowers that are on the same plant, have broad, colored flanges on the ovaries, which develop into winged fruits. Begonia enthusiasts divide the species and cultivars into a number of classes depending on growth habit and type of rootstock. The **cane-stemmed** begonias are erect growers, sometimes quite tall, with straight stems, fibrous roots, and usually pendent clusters of showy flowers; somewhat similar are some **shrubby** begonias, with a more closely branched habit (the bedding begonias belong here); another similar group but with lower, softer stems are known as the **winter-flowering** begonias, grown for their profuse and colorful flowers that peak in winter; the **rhizomatous** begonias are a large and varied class, with leaves arising directly from creeping, knotty rhizomes—they include the **Rex** begonias with colorfully variegated leaves and many others grown for foliage; finally the **tuberous** begonias, now largely represented by hybrids of the **Tuberhybrida Group**, which die back to tubers in winter and bear large, showy, often double flowers in summer, for example, '**Mandy Henscke**'.

B

Begonia fuchsioides
'Vesuv' *(left)*

Begonia fuchsioides

Native to Venezuela, this shrubby begonia has small, crowded, oval leaves, flushed pink on new growths. Small coral red to pale pink flowers are borne in numerous short sprays over a long season from autumn to spring. Suitable for outdoor use, it grows to 3 ft (1 m) tall with an erect, closely branched habit and gracefully drooping branchlets. It prefers good light. The cultivar **'Vesuv'** is a good example.
ZONES 10–12.

CULTIVATION

Many of the cane-stemmed, winter-flowering, shrubby and rhizomatous types can be grown outdoors in frost-free climates and make fine garden plants, though rhizomatous kinds in particular are prone to slug and snail attack. As indoor plants they do well in standard potting mix with peat moss or leafmold added to increase acidity. Grow in bright to moderate light, with good ventilation and above-average humidity, which can be maintained by standing pots on a tray of pebbles and water. Pinch back young plants of the shrubby type to keep them compact and to encourage flowers. Tuberous begonias require special treatment: tubers must be forced into growth in early spring at a temperature of 65°F (18°C) in peat moss or sphagnum, and kept in a cool, well-ventilated greenhouse for the summer flowering season. After flowering, plants die back and tubers are lifted in mid-autumn and stored dry. Propagate from tubers in the case of tuberous begonias. Other begonias may be propagated from stem or leaf cuttings (laying the cut leaf blades flat on damp sand and weighing them down with pebbles), or by division of rhizomes, or from seed. Begonias are susceptible to gray mold, powdery mildew and botrytis in the warmer part of the year if conditions are too damp.

Begonia × *hiemalis* *(above)*
syn. *Begonia* × *elatior*
WINTER-FLOWERING BEGONIA

This name applies to a group of winter-flowering hybrid cultivars originating from crosses between *Begonia socotrana* and Tuberhybrida Group begonias, resulting in a range of easily grown plants with single or double blooms in subtle colors from white through yellow and orange to red and pink. They have fibrous rather than tuberous root systems and tend to die after flowering, though some newer cultivars have overcome this drawback. **ZONES 10–11.**

Begonia, Semperflorens-cultorum Group
(right & center)

BEDDING BEGONIA, WAX BEGONIA

Derived largely from the Brazilian ***Begonia semperflorens,*** the dwarf, shrubby begonias of this group are often grown as bedding annuals, for example, '**Ernst Benary**', or for borders in shaded gardens. They are also popular as potted plants for window boxes or patio tubs. Freely branching with soft, succulent stems, their rounded, glossy green (bronze or variegated in some cultivars) leaves are about 2 in (5 cm) long. The flowers are profuse, opening progressively at the branch tips over a long summer and early autumn season (most of the year in warmer climates). The numerous cultivars include singles and doubles in colors of bright rose pink, light pink, white or red; they are generally released as a series, with mixed colors. They are grown from seed or stem cuttings and planted out in late spring in cooler climates; pinch out growing tips to encourage bushy growth. **Cocktail Series** are bushy miniatures with bronzy foliage and single flowers: '**Gin**' has metallic black-green leaves and deep pink flowers; '**Vodka**' produces deep red flowers against very dark green leaves; and the pale bronze leaves of '**Whiskey**' are offset by white flowers. **Thousand Wonders** is an older series consisting of compact, sun-hardy plants in mixed shades of pink and white. **ZONES 9–11.**

Begonia 'Pink Shasta' *(above)*

One of the 'angel-wing' type of cane-stemmed begonias, 'Pink Shasta' grows to 3–4 ft (1–1.2 m) high with branching stems and leaves slightly silver spotted. It produces pendulous panicles of light salmon-pink flowers through spring, summer and autumn. It originated as a seedling of '**Shasta**', which is derived from *Begonia coccinea*. **ZONES 10–12.**

Begonia, Semperflorens-cultorum Group, 'Ernst Benary' used as a border *(left)*

B

Belamcanda chinensis *(left)*
LEOPARD LILY, BLACKBERRY LILY

This 24–36 in (60–90 cm) tall plant has something of the habit of an iris but the summer flowers are quite un-iris-like in appearance. Up to 2 in (5 cm) across, they come in a range of colors from cream to yellow, apricot or deep orange-red, usually with darker spotting, hence the common name leopard lily. The seed pods open to reveal tight clusters of seeds resembling the fruitlets of a blackberry, hence their other common name. ZONES 8–11.

BELAMCANDA

This genus, native to southern and eastern Asia and belonging to the iris family, contains only 2 species. The plants are perennials but of weak growth and tending to be short lived, with flattened fans of thin-textured leaves arising from thin rhizomes. Slender flowering stems terminate in a few rather small flowers with 6 narrow petals; these are followed by seed pods which split widely to reveal rows of shiny black seeds, like small berries—these are popular for dried flower arrangements.

CULTIVATION
These are warm-temperate plants that require sunshine and rich, well-drained soil. Water well in summer. In a cold climate the dormant plants will need protection from heavy frosts. Propagate by division or from seed, which should be sown every second or third year to ensure the plants' survival.

BELLIS
DAISY

The little white flower that spangles lawns in spring is one of the best loved of European wildflowers. These, the true daisies, consist of 15 species of small perennials that occur wild in Europe, North Africa and Turkey. *Bellis* is from the Latin *bellus* which means 'pretty' or 'charming', while the English 'daisy' is a corruption of 'day's eye', arising from the way the flower closes up at night, opening again to greet the sunrise. The plants form rosettes with small oval to spoon-shaped leaves; each rosette produces a succession of flowerheads on individual stalks in shades of white, pink, blue or crimson. Only one of the species is widely cultivated, mostly in the form of improved strains.

CULTIVATION
Daisies are favorite flowers for edging flowerbeds in spring and, while they are perennial in cool-temperate climates, it is usual to treat them as annuals or biennials, sowing seed in autumn. They thrive in any good garden soil in sun or part-shade; keep soil moist in winter and spring. Propagate from seed or by division.

Bellis perennis
'Medici's White' *(below)*

Bellis perennis,
Pomponette Series cultivar *(above)*

Bellis perennis *(below)*
ENGLISH DAISY, COMMON DAISY

This daisy has become widely naturalized in temperate parts of most continents. The wild plants are small, forming carpets of crowded rosettes that spread through lawns by runners. The 1 in (25 mm) wide flowerheads, appearing from late winter to early summer, are white with golden centers and pale purplish undersides. **'Medici's White'** is a white cultivar. The garden strains mostly have double flowerheads of red, crimson, pink or white, all with a gold center. **'Alba Plena'** is an old double white cultivar, very different from the **Pomponette Series** daisies now popular as bedding plants and cut flowers; these are a far cry from the wild flowers, making neat hemispherical flowerheads 1½ in (35 mm) wide with curled petals, on stems up to 10 in (25 cm) high, in mixed colors. ZONES 3–10.

B

BELLIUM

This is a genus of 3 species of annual and perennial, trailing or mounding daisies native to southern Europe. The botanical name was intended to indicate their close similarity to *Bellis*, though in fine details of floral structure they are quite distinct. They are delightful miniature plants with very small, crowded, spatula-shaped leaves and tiny white flowerheads borne in profusion.

CULTIVATION

They prefer a sunnier, drier position than English daisies and thrive in well-drained rockeries. They should be mulched with fine gravel to prevent the foliage becoming mud-splashed during rain. All species will tolerate light to moderate frosts. Propagate from seed or by division.

Bellium minutum *(above)*

A summer-flowering annual from the islands of the Mediterranean, this species has leaves that are slightly over ¼ in (6 mm) long. Its white flowerheads, which are carried on 2 in (5 cm) stems, are equally tiny, just over ½ in (12 mm) wide with purplish undersides. ZONES 6–9.

B

Bergenia cordifolia (right)
HEARTLEAF SAXIFRAGE

Native to Siberia's Altai Mountains, this tough perennial has
crinkly edged, more or less heart-
shaped leaves up to 8 in (20 cm)
wide, and produces panicles of
drooping purple-pink flowers on
12–15 in (30–38 cm) stems in
late winter and early spring. It is
long flowering and leaves remain
green in winter. **'Purpurea'** has
magenta-pink flowers and leaves
tinged purple. **ZONES 3–9.**

BERGENIA

Consisting of 6 or 7 species of
rhizomatous, semi-evergreen perennials in
the saxifrage family from eastern and central Asia, this genus is characterized by
large, handsome, paddle-shaped leaves,
arising from the ground on short stalks to
form loose clumps. There are also many
garden hybrids that have been developed
over the last 100 years or so. Large clusters
of flowers—mostly pale pink, but also
white and dark pink—are borne on short,
stout stems in winter and spring. An example is **'Eroica'**, with deep pink flowers.
The foliage often develops attractive red
tints in winter.

Bergenia 'Eroica'
(below)

CULTIVATION

Bergenias make excellent rockery plants,
thriving in sun or shade and tolerant of
exposed sites as well as moist ground beside streams or ponds, but leaves color
most strongly when plants are grown
under drier conditions. Some are good as
ground cover when planted *en masse.*
Water well in hot weather and remove
spent flowerheads to prolong flowering.
Propagate by division in spring after
flowering, when plants become crowded.

B

Bergenia 'Morgenröte' *(left)*
syn. *Bergenia* 'Morning Red'

This small-growing cultivar has plain green leaves under 6 in (15 cm) and produces dense small clusters of largish orchid pink flowers on deep red stalks in late spring, sometimes blooming again in the summer. **ZONES 4–9.**

Bergenia purpurascens *(below)*
syn. *Bergenia beesiana*

The large fleshy, oval, purple-tinted leaves of this species develop a deeper color in winter, especially in a cold climate where frost occurs. Bright pink to reddish purple flowers are borne in late winter and spring on stems up to 18 in (45 cm) tall. **ZONES 5–9.**

Bergenia × schmidtii *(left)*

Arguably the most vigorous and most widely planted bergenia, this old hybrid between *Bergenia ciliata* and *B. crassifolia* has large, rounded, fleshy, dull green leaves. Set among the foliage are rose pink blooms on stalks up to 12 in (30 cm) long. The main flush of flowers occurs in late winter and early spring; frosts may damage blooms, but it often flowers sporadically at other times. The plant spreads to make a fine ground cover, and adapts well to warm-temperate humid climates. **ZONES 5–10.**

B

Bergenia 'Silberlicht' *(above)*
syn. *Bergenia* 'Silver Light'

This hybrid cultivar forms compact clumps of glossy green leaves up to 8 in (20 cm) long with scalloped margins. The large, pure white to palest pink flowers appear in late spring in compact clusters on a succession of flower stalks up to 18 in (45 cm) high. **ZONES 5–9.**

Bergenia stracheyi *(right)*
syn. *Bergenia milesii*

This species has relatively small leaves with hairs lining the edges and wedge-shaped at the base. Forming extensive clumps with age, it produces tight clusters of nodding, cup-shaped, deep pink to white flowers in early spring on stalks 10 in (25 cm) high. **ZONES 6–9.**

B

Bidens ferulifolia 'Gold Marie' *(above)*

Bidens ferulifolia

Native to Mexico and Arizona, *Bidens ferulifolia* is a bushy, evergreen perennial 18–24 in (45–60 cm) tall, usually short lived. The leaves are small and fern-like, divided into narrow segments, and it bears golden-yellow, few-rayed flowerheads 1–1½ in (25–35 mm) wide in a long succession from late spring to autumn. Cultivars available include '**Arizona**', '**Gold Marie**', '**Golden Goddess**' and '**Peter's Goldteppich**'. ZONES 8–10.

Bidens aequisquamea (below)

BIDENS
TICKSEED, BEGGAR'S TICKS, BURR-MARIGOLD

This is a genus of around 200 species of annuals, perennials, subshrubs and shrubs that is closely related to *Cosmos* and occurs in most parts of the world except very cold regions. In most countries this genus is represented only by a weedy species. The majority are native to Mexico and adjacent regions of the Americas. The plants have erect leafy stems, usually much branched, with opposite pairs of leaves that are generally compound or deeply divided. Yellow daisy flowers (occasionally red to purple, for example, the purplish pink *Bidens aequisquamea*), mostly with very few but broad ray florets, open in a long succession and are followed by burr-like seed heads containing narrow seeds, each tipped with 2-barbed bristles (*Bidens* means '2-toothed') that can stick to clothing and fur.

CULTIVATION

These plants are very easily grown in any well-drained soil. Plant in full sun or morning shade, and water well in summer. Although hardiness varies with the species, most will withstand moderate frosts. Propagate from seed or cuttings, or by division, depending on the growth form.

Bidens ferulifolia 'Peter's Goldteppich' *(below)*

Billbergia amoena *(left)*

The species name is Latin for 'delightful to the eye' and this Brazilian bromeliad is eye-catching when well grown. Its loosely clustered leaf rosettes consist of rather few, broad leaves up to 24 in (60 cm) long, making large 'tanks', and may be pale gray-green or various shades of purple with cream or green spotting. The flower spikes may rise as high as 3 ft (1 m) with very large dark pink bracts and a few chalky blue-green flowers about 2 in (5 cm) long. ZONES 11–12.

Billbergia nutans *(left)*

QUEEN'S TEARS, FRIENDSHIP PLANT

This popular species from southern Brazil and Argentina can be grown outdoors in sheltered rockeries or tubs, even in full sun and in places with occasional light frosts. Indoors it likes coarse potting mix and good light. Reaching a height of 24 in (60 cm) and spreading to make large dense clumps, its pale olive green leaves are grass-like, tapering into long thread-like, recurving tips, and pendent clusters of flowers appear in spring on long arching spikes. The curled-back petals are pale green and navy blue, but the long pink bracts are more eye-catching. ZONES 10–12.

BILLBERGIA

VASE PLANT

This genus of bromeliads consists of around 50 species of evergreen perennials from Central and South America. Most species are 'tank epiphytes', plants that perch on trees with the bases of their broad, strap-like leaves tightly overlapping around a central hollow that fills with rainwater, providing a reservoir for the plant between rainfalls. The horny-textured leaves, often edged with small teeth, in many species have a coating of mealy, grayish white scales interrupted by greener bands. Showy, stalked flower clusters appear at any time of year from the centers of the leaf rosettes, with pink or red bracts often more conspicuous than the tubular flowers.

CULTIVATION

Easy to grow, they make ideal indoor plants, or can be planted outdoors in subtropical or tropical climates in sheltered, humid spots. A porous, fast-draining soil mix suits them, or plant them on a mound of stones. Some species soon form quite large clumps and can be propagated by division after flowering; propagate the slower-growing ones by cutting off the basal 'pups' and treat as cuttings. Scale insects and mealybugs can be a problem; brown leaves may result from too much sun.

B

Blandfordia grandiflora (left)
syn. *Blandfordia flammea*

This is the most colorful species and the one most prized for cut flowers. Its leaves are very narrow and rather rigid, and flowering stems are 24–36 in (60–90 cm) tall, carrying 3 to 10 flowers; these are up to 2½ in (6 cm) long, flared toward the mouth, and vary from deep pinkish red to red with yellow tips or sometimes pure yellow, always with a thin waxy bloom.
ZONES 9–11.

BLANDFORDIA
CHRISTMAS BELLS

This is an eastern Australian genus of 4 species of grassy leaved perennials with deeply buried corm-like rhizomes. They are prized for their beautiful, waxy red or red-and-yellow flowers that appear around Christmas in the southern hemisphere. The plants are long lived, with tough, narrow basal leaves in sparse to dense tufts, from which arise one to several stiff flowering stems, bearing near the top semi-pendent flowers; these are bell-shaped and up to 3 in (8 cm) long, the 6 petals fused for most of their length.

CULTIVATION
Coming mainly from peaty coastal swamps in the wild, these are not easy plants to maintain in cultivation—they are prone to root-rot and are sensitive to nutrient imbalances. Plant in moist, peaty soil in full sun or light shade. Keep consistently moist. They tolerate light frosts and may be propagated by division or raised from seed. Both develop slowly.

BOLTONIA
FALSE CHAMOMILE

B

This is a genus of 8 species of perennial daisies, all from eastern and central USA except for one species which comes from temperate East Asia. Very much like tall asters, they have in recent years become popular as background plants for perennial borders and as cut flowers. Over winter they die back to a clump of simple, narrow leaves. In late spring, tall flowering stems begin to develop and by late summer they carry hundreds of small daisies in shades of white, pink, lilac, violet or purple.

CULTIVATION
They are very easily grown in moist, well-drained soil in any sunny position. However, like many of the asters, they are prone to mildew from late summer, which cuts short the flower display. Frost hardy, they are propagated from seed or cuttings or by division.

Boltonia asteroides
(below)

This is the best known boltonia in gardens. It is widely distributed in northeastern USA. The flowering stems may be as much as 8 ft (2.4 m) tall, with the ¾ in (20 mm) flowerheads ranging in color from white through pale pink to mauve. **'Snowbank'** is a white-flowered selection with stems growing up to 6 ft (1.8 m) tall. ***Boltonia asteroides* var. *latisquama*** differs in its larger flowerheads, which are up to 1¼ in (3 cm) across in shades of mauve or purple. ZONES 4–9.

B

BORAGO

This is a European genus of 3 species of annuals and short-lived perennials. The plants are generally erect with rather coarse growth and are covered with bristly hairs. They form clumps of lance-shaped basal leaves that rapidly develop in spring into branched, leafy flowering stems. By late spring the plants bear semi-pendulous, starry purple-blue or white flowers, which are quite ornamental. The flowers are a rich source of nectar and are popular with beekeepers.

CULTIVATION

These plants are easily grown in any light, moist, well-drained soil in full sun. Usually they are propagated from seed, which often self-sows, so plants may become slightly invasive. Seed of the annual species can be sown in late winter for an early crop. Protect from snails.

Borago officinalis
(below)

BORAGE

This annual herb is grown for its cucumber-flavored leaves and pretty, purplish blue star-shaped flowers. The plant grows to around 30 in (75 cm) high with clusters of flowers in spring and summer. The fresh young leaves are used raw in salads and cool drinks or cooked with vegetables. The edible flowers have long been used to decorate salads. ZONES 5–10.

BOYKINIA
syn. *Telesonix*

A North American and Japanese genus of 9 species of woodland and alpine perennials, these plants spread by shortly creeping rhizomes. They resemble the closely related genera *Heuchera* and *Tiarella*, and have lobed and toothed, roughly heart- or kidney-shaped hairy leaves, varying in size depending on the species. Stalked panicles of small, 5-petalled, white, cream or reddish flowers open through spring or summer. While not spectacular, they are graceful plants that help to lighten shady corners. Botanists differ on the question of whether *Telesonix* should be united with *Boykinia*.

CULTIVATION
Plant in moist, humus-rich, well-drained soil in dappled shade. Hardiness varies, though all species will tolerate at least moderate frosts. Propagate by division in late winter.

Boykinia jamesii (above)
syns *Boykinia heucheriformis, Telesonix jamesii*

A native of Colorado, this is one of the more cold-hardy species and also among the smallest. Its kidney-shaped leaves are usually less than 2 in (5 cm) wide and the plant forms a compact mound of fresh green foliage around 4 in (10 cm) high and up to 6 in (15 cm) in diameter. Its narrow 6 in (15 cm) stems bear purplered flowers, larger than those of other boykinias, and it needs to be treated as an alpine. ZONES 5–8.

Brachycome 'Sunburst'
(left)

Brachycome 'Outback
Sunburst' *(below left)*

Brachycome 'Amethyst' *(below)*

A long-flowering perennial with purple-blue
flowers, this recent hybrid grows to about 12 in
(30 cm) tall and wide. ZONES 9–11.

BRACHYCOME
syn. *Brachyscome*

Native to Australia, the low-growing annuals
and evergreen perennials of this genus are
attractive ground cover or rockery plants.
Many of the perennials are mound-forming,
spreading by underground runners and having finely divided, soft, fern-like foliage. They
bear a profusion of daisy-like flowerheads in
shades of blue, mauve, pink and yellow, with
orange or brownish centers or yellow as in the
hybrids 'Sunburst' and 'Outback Sunburst',
both with white ray florets. Australian botanists have disputed over the spelling of this
genus, the debate hingeing on whether the
nineteenth-century botanist who spelt it
Brachyscome had the right to subsequently
correct his bad Greek, as he did (it combines
brachys, short, with *kome*, hair, referring to a
seed feature, but the 's' is dropped when they
are joined).

CULTIVATION
They require a sunny situation and a light,
well-drained garden soil. Many are moderately frost hardy and some will tolerate
coastal salt spray. Do not over-water as they
prefer dry conditions. Pinch out early shoots
to encourage branching and propagate from
ripe seed or stem cuttings or by division in
spring or autumn.

Brachycome multifida *(right)*

This perennial species is a charming ground cover in warm-temperate climates, though it is not long lived and should be renewed every few years. It grows 4–6 in (10–15 cm) high and spreads to about 18 in (45 cm). The mauve-pink flower-heads bloom for weeks in late spring and summer. It likes sunshine and perfect drainage and is propagated by layers or from cuttings. **'Break O' Day'** is a selected form with finer leaves, profuse mauve-blue flowers and a very compact habit. **ZONES 9–11.**

Brachycome iberidifolia 'Blue Star'

(below)

Brachycome iberidifolia

SWAN RIVER DAISY

This daisy is a weak-stemmed annual, long grown as a bedding or border plant, that grows to a height and spread of around 12 in (30 cm), sometimes taller. It has deeply dissected leaves with very narrow segments. Small, fragrant, daisy-like flowerheads, normally mauve-blue but sometimes white, pink or purple, appear in great profusion in summer and early autumn. **'Blue Star'** is a cultivar with massed flowers that are small and mauve to purple-blue. **ZONES 9–11.**

B

BRACTEANTHA
syn. Helichrysum
STRAWFLOWER, EVERLASTING DAISY

This Australian genus of 7 species of annuals and perennials, until recently classified in *Helichrysum*, differs from true helichrysums in their large, decorative flowerheads carried singly or a few together at the end of the flowering branches, each consisting of golden yellow to white bracts of straw-like texture surrounding a disc of tiny yellow or brownish florets. The leaves, mostly broad and thin, are often downy on their undersides, or can be very sticky in some species. Most of the cultivated forms and seedling strains are treated as forms of *Bracteantha bracteata*, but further botanical study is likely to result in new species being recognized.

CULTIVATION
Plant in moist, well-drained soil in full sun. The summer-flowering annuals may be planted from late winter for an early display. Provided they are not waterlogged, most species will tolerate light to moderate frosts. Propagate annuals from seed and perennials from seed or tip cuttings.

Bracteantha bracteata 'Dargon Hill Monarch' *(center right)*

Bracteantha bracteata cultivar *(top right)*

Bracteantha bracteata 'Diamond Head' *(right)*

Bracteantha bracteata *(left)*
syn. *Helichrysum bracteatum*

This annual or short-lived perennial has an erect habit and grows to a height of around 3 ft (1 m). It has weak, hollow stems, thin green leaves and from summer to early autumn bears golden yellow blooms up to 2 in (5 cm) in diameter at the branch tips. In the mid-nineteenth century annual strains with larger flowerheads in shades of pink, bronze red, cream, purple and yellow were developed; these plants were generally more vigorous; **Bright Bikinis Series** is a modern descendant of these. Some more spreading, shrubby perennial plants from eastern Australia, which may be recognized as distinct species, have been named as cultivars. These include the popular '**Dargan Hill Monarch**', with rich yellow blooms up to 3 in (8 cm) across that emerge over several months; and '**Diamond Head**', which is similar but lower and more compact. ZONES 8–11.

B

BROMELIA

This genus gives its name to the large family Bromeliaceae (the bromeliads). The 50 or so species of *Bromelia* are scattered widely through South America and parts of Central America and the West Indies. They are mostly ground-dwelling perennials resembling pineapple plants, with strong, hooked spines along the margins of their long, stiff leaves which generally turn a bronzy color in strong sun. The leaves form large rosettes, which in some species can multiply by sending out long rhizomes to make extensive clumps. A stout flower spike arises from the center of the rosette surrounded by leaf-like bracts that may be brilliantly colored; the flowers are tubular and densely packed and give way to large fleshy yellow fruits, which in some species are used medicinally.

CULTIVATION
Bromelia species are mostly grown outdoors in frost-free climates, thriving in full sun and well-drained soil. They are relatively free from diseases and pests. Propagate from offsets or seeds, keeping seedlings well ventilated to discourage damping off fungus.

Bromelia balansae
(above)
HEART OF FLAME

This vigorous species reaches a height of 5 ft (1.5 m) and can spread extensively. Its flower spike is up to 3 ft (1 m) tall and is surrounded by glossy, brilliant scarlet, spiny-edged bracts, the longer, lower ones only colored at the base. The purple flowers, borne in late summer, are in a series of dense heads among shorter whitish bracts. The dull orange-yellow berries can form very large clusters, taking almost a year to ripen. This plant has been used in South America as an impenetrable living fence. ZONES 10–12.

BRUNNERA

This is a genus of 3 species of perennials
closely related to the forget-me-not
(Myosotis) and *Anchusa.* They range in
the wild from eastern Europe to western
Siberia and form clumps of heart-shaped
to rather narrow basal leaves on long
stalks. Leafy, branched flowering stems
bear panicles of tiny 5-petalled purple or
blue flowers in spring and early summer.
There are cultivated forms with white
flowers and variegated foliage.

CULTIVATION

Essentially woodland plants, they prefer
humus-rich, moist soil with a leafy mulch
and a position in dappled shade. They are
very cold hardy and in suitable conditions
will self-sow and naturalize. Propagate
from seed, by removing small rooted
pieces or by taking cuttings of the soft
spring shoots.

Brunnera
macrophylla (above)
SIBERIAN BUGLOSS

The small violet flowers
of this species show their
relationship to the for-
get-me-nots; they are
held on slender stems
18–24 in (45–60 cm)
tall above the bold
mounds of heart-
shaped leaves. When
the flowers appear the
new leaves grow to their
full length of 4–6 in
(10–15 cm). Clumps
spread slowly under-
ground but self-seed
readily, making excellent
ground cover under
trees and large shrubs.
'Hadspen Cream' has
paler green leaves pret-
tily edged with cream,
and paler blue flowers.
ZONES 3–9.

B

BULBINELLA

This southern hemisphere genus has an unusual distribution, with 6 species endemic to New Zealand and the remainder of its 20 or so species native to southern Africa. They are fleshy-rooted perennial lilies similar to the related *Bulbine* but with mostly broader, thinner leaves and crowded spikes of golden yellow flowers terminating the long, hollow stems. They form clumps of somewhat untidy foliage. Some of the larger South African species, such as *Bulbinella floribunda*, make excellent cut flowers. The alpine species are much smaller but not so easily grown.

CULTIVATION

In the wild, many species grow in very damp areas and in cultivation they demand moist, humus-rich soil that never dries out entirely in summer. A position in sun or semi-shade is best. Most species are at least slightly frost hardy and are propagated from seed or by dividing established clumps. The fleshy roots should be planted with the root-crown at soil level.

Bulbinella floribunda (above)
CAT'S-TAIL

This native of South Africa produces 24–36 in (60–90 cm) tall flower stalks from late winter to mid-spring. Each stalk is topped with a broad, 4 in (10 cm) spike crammed with tiny orange-yellow flowers and terminating in tight green buds. Long, narrow basal leaves appear in winter, forming a large tangled clump. The plant dies back in summer and autumn. It is excellent as a long-lasting cut flower. **ZONES 8–10.**

Bulbinella hookeri (left)

Found in the subalpine grasslands of both the main islands of New Zealand, this species has very narrow, grassy leaves and develops into a thick clump of foliage. The flower stems are around 24 in (60 cm) tall, half of which is the densely packed spike of ¼ in (6 mm) wide flowers. **ZONES 8–10.**

CALAMINTHA
CALAMINT

Seven species make up this genus of aromatic perennial herbs, occurring as natives mainly in Europe and temperate Asia but with 2 species confined to the USA. In growth habit they are quite like the true mints *(Mentha)*, with creeping rhizomes and leaves in opposite pairs on square stems, but the white, pink or purplish flowers are mostly larger and are borne in looser terminal sprays. The leaves of several species are used in herbal medicine, as well as being infused to make herbal teas. The name *Calamintha* (beautiful mint) goes back to ancient Greek, referring originally to an aromatic herb of this general kind but now not identifiable.

CULTIVATION
Mostly fairly frost hardy, calaminthas are easily grown in moist but well-drained soil in a sheltered position; some species prefer woodland conditions in part-shade, others thrive best in full sun. Propagate by division of rhizomes or from seed sown in spring.

Calamintha nepeta
LESSER CALAMINT

Native to much of Europe, also North Africa and western Asia, this unassuming plant to 12–24 in (30–60 cm) tall favors dry, well-drained conditions in full sun. Its small leaves are hardly toothed and the small summer flowers, held in long, erect, rather open sprays, are pale mauve or almost white. The epithet *nepeta* was presumably given to indicate its resemblance to the catmint genus *Nepeta*. **Calamintha nepeta subsp. *glandulosa* 'White Cloud' and 'Blue Cloud'** are popular cultivars. ZONES 4–10.

Calamintha nepeta subsp. *glandulosa* 'White Cloud' *(left)*

Calathea makoyana (below)
PEACOCK PLANT, CATHEDRAL-WINDOWS

From eastern Brazil, this dwarf species grows to
no more than 18 in (45 cm) but has the most
gorgeously patterned leaves, well justifying its
common name; they are broadly oval, with a
feathery design of dark green markings on a pale
creamy background grading to mid-green at the
margins. The undersides have the same markings
in purple. Makoy, after whom the species is
named, was a renowned nineteenth-century
Belgian grower of hothouse plants. ZONES 11–12.

CALATHEA

Consisting of 300 or so species of evergreen perennials of the
arrowroot family, native to Central and South America and the
West Indies, this genus is prized for its decorative foliage. At
least one species is grown as a food crop, yielding small starchy
tubers. The long-stalked, mostly upright leaves are usually
large and often beautifully variegated in shades of green, white,
pink, purple and maroon, and usually purplish on the undersides. The flowers are interesting but rarely showy, in short
dense spikes with overlapping bracts that may be white or variously colored and often partly hidden beneath the foliage.

CULTIVATION
In the wet tropics and subtropics calatheas make attractive foliage plants for outdoor landscaping in shaded areas beneath
trees or in courtyards. In colder parts of the world they are
grown indoors. Many will thrive in low light levels. Plant in
humus-rich, moist but well-drained soil. Water freely in
warmer weather and fertilize regularly. Propagate by division
of rhizomes. The sheathing leaf bases often harbor mealybugs,
and the foliage is affected by aphids, spider mites and thrips.

Calathea burle-marxii
(above)

Named in honor of the re-
nowned Brazilian landscape
designer, Roberto Burle
Marx, whose gardens fea-
tured dramatic swathes of
plants such as calatheas, this
east Brazilian species grows
rapidly up to 5 ft (1.5 m)
high, with short bamboo-
like stems growing erect
from the rhizomes. The
leaves may be over 24 in
(60 cm) long and half as
wide, bright green with a
yellowish central stripe on
the upper surface, duller
gray-green beneath. The
¾ in (20 mm) long pale
violet flowers emerge from
waxy white bracts grouped
in a large spike. ZONES 11–12.

C

Calathea veitchiana (left)

One of the taller growing calatheas, to 3 ft (1 m) or more in height, this species from Peru has leaves blotched light green along the center, the blotches bordered by scalloped bands of dull green, these in turn are bordered greenish yellow, while on the underside the dark green areas become purple. The small white flowers are borne in a club-shaped spike with green bracts.

This species is named after a horticulturalist, James Veitch, whose famous English nursery continued throughout the nineteenth century. ZONES 11–12.

Calathea zebrina (right)
ZEBRA PLANT

This vigorous species from Brazil is usually 24–36 in (60–90 cm) tall, and can develop into a broad clump of crowded stems, its habit reminiscent of a dwarf canna except that the large, velvety, deep green leaves are marked by parallel stripes or bars of pale chartreuse; the undersides are purplish red. It will thrive in somewhat cooler climates than most calatheas, making a fine ground cover plant, though the leaves turn yellowish in winter; they can be trimmed away to reveal clusters of chocolate brown bracts which protect the spring flowers. ZONES 10–12.

CALCEOLARIA
LADIES' PURSE, SLIPPER FLOWER, POCKETBOOK FLOWER

Gardeners who know this genus only in the form of the gaudy 'slipper flowers' sold by florists may be surprised to learn that it contains upward of 300 species, ranging from tiny annuals to herbaceous perennials and even scrambling climbers and quite woody shrubs. All are native to the Americas, from Mexico southward to Tierra del Fuego, and all share the same curious flower structure, with a lower lip inflated like a rather bulbous slipper. Flower colors are mainly yellows and oranges, often with red or purple spots.

CULTIVATION

Calceolarias come from a wide range of natural habitats and vary greatly in cold hardiness. When grown outdoors they prefer a shady, cool site in moist, well-drained soil with added compost. Provide shelter from heavy winds as the flowers are easily damaged. Shrubby species may benefit from being pruned back by half in winter. Propagate from seed or softwood cuttings in summer or late spring. The Herbeohybrida Group, grown mainly in cool greenhouses, are fed and watered liberally in the summer growing season; they are subject to a number of diseases and pest infestations.

Calceolaria,
Herbeohybrida Group
cultivar *(below)*

Calceolaria, Herbeohybrida Group

These are the popular florists' calceolarias, a group of hybrids derived from 3 Chilean species. They are soft-stemmed, compact, bushy biennials often treated as annuals, producing in spring and summer blooms in a range of bright colors from yellow to deep red and so densely massed they almost hide the soft green foliage. Innumerable named varieties have appeared over the years, and they are now mostly sold as mixed-color seedling strains and series. Marginally frost hardy, they can be used for summer bedding but do not tolerate very hot, dry weather. Normally 12–18 in (30–45 cm) tall, dwarf strains can be as small as 6 in (15 cm). **'Sunset Mixed'** are bushy F1 hybrids 12 in (30 cm) tall with flowers in vibrant shades of red, orange and mixes of these two; they are useful in massed bedding. **'Sunshine'** is also an F1 hybrid of compact form around 10 in (25 cm) high, with bright golden yellow blooms, bred for planting in massed displays or for use in borders. ZONES 9–11.

C

Calceolaria,
Herbeohybrida Group
cultivar *(left)*

Calceolaria tomentosa
(left)

A native of Peru, this soft-
stemmed perennial species
grows to about 3 ft (1 m) with
broad, soft, heart-shaped
leaves with toothed margins.
The golden-yellow flowers
have an almost globular
'slipper' about $1\frac{1}{2}$ in (35 mm)
wide. **ZONES 9–10.**

Calceolaria,
Herbeohybrida Group,
'Sunset Mixed' *(left)*

CALENDULA
MARIGOLD

It is thought that St Hildegard of Bingen (1098–1179) dedicated *Calendula officinalis* to the Virgin Mary and gave the flowers the name Mary's gold, or marigold. To gardeners of today 'marigold' generally signifies the unrelated *Tagetes* from Mexico (the so-called 'African' and 'French' marigolds). In the Middle Ages marigolds were considered a certain remedy for all sorts of ills ranging from smallpox to indigestion and 'evil humors of the head', and even today the marigold is a favorite of herbalists. The genus *Calendula* consists of 20-odd species of bushy annuals and evergreen perennials, occurring wild from the Canary Islands through the Mediterranean region to Iran in the east. They have simple, somewhat aromatic leaves and daisy-like, orange or yellow flowers.

CULTIVATION
Calendulas are mostly fairly frost-hardy plants and are readily grown in well-drained soil of any quality in sun or part-shade. Flowering will be prolonged with regular deadheading. Propagate from seed, and watch for aphids and powdery mildew.

Calendula arvensis
(below)
FIELD MARIGOLD

This sprawling annual is a common wildflower in Mediterranean countries, where it grows among the long grass of fields and displays its golden flowers from spring to autumn and on into winter if the weather is mild. The name *Calendula* comes from the same root as calendar and refers to the almost all-year blooming. It is rarely cultivated but, transplanted to gardens, it can make a bright show. **ZONES 6–10.**

C

Calendula officinalis (left)

POT MARIGOLD, ENGLISH MARIGOLD

Originally native to southern Europe and long valued for its medicinal qualities, this species is known in gardens only by its many cultivars and seedling strains, popular winter- and spring-flowering annuals that remain in bloom for a long time. There are tall and dwarf forms, all of bushy habit, the tall growing to a height and spread of 24 in (60 cm) and the dwarf to 12 in (30 cm). All forms have lance-shaped, strongly scented, pale green leaves and single or double flowerheads. Tall cultivars include **'Geisha Girl'** with double orange flowers; the **Pacific Beauty Series** with double flowers in a number of different colors including bicolors; **'Princess'** with crested orange, gold or yellow flowers; and the **Touch of Red Series** with double flowers in tones of deep orange-red. Dwarf cultivars include **'Fiesta Gitana'** with double flowers in colors ranging from cream to orange, and **'Honey Babe'** with apricot, yellow and orange flowers. ZONES 6–10.

Calendula officinalis 'Fiesta Gitana' *(below)*

Calendula officinalis, Pacific Beauty Series *(right)*

Callistephus chinensis (right)
syn. *Aster chinensis*

This erect, bushy, fast-growing annual has oval, toothed, mid-green leaves and long-stalked flowerheads. There are many seedling strains available, ranging from tall, up to 3 ft (1 m), to dwarf, about 8 in (20 cm). Stake tall cultivars and remove spent flowers regularly. The **Milady Series** are vigorous cultivars to 12 in (30 cm) in height with double flowerheads in pinks, reds, white, purplish blue and mixed colors.
ZONES 6–10.

CALLISTEPHUS
CHINA ASTER

This genus contains one annual species, native to China and once included in the genus *Aster*. It is a colorful garden flower, with summer blooms in a wonderful array of shades from white to pink, blue, red and purple, popular both for bedding and as a cut flower. Long cultivation has given rise to many variants, and plant breeders add new strains almost every year. The 3–4 in (8–10 cm) flowerheads can be either yellow-centered single daisies or fully double. The doubles can have petals that are plume-like and shaggy, more formal and straight or very short, making the blooms like perfect pompons.

CULTIVATION
China aster is usually sown in spring to flower during summer, but the season of bloom is not long and it is usual to make successive sowings to prolong it. It is superlative for cutting and will grow in any climate, from the coolest temperate to subtropical. Give it sunshine and fertile, well-drained soil, and do not plant it in the same bed 2 years in a row—a rest of 2 or 3 years between plantings is desirable to guard against aster wilt, a soil-borne fungus.

CALTHA

There are about 10 species of moisture-loving perennials in this genus of the ranunculus family, all occurring in cold marshlands and alpine bogs of the cool-temperate zones in both northern and southern hemispheres. With their cup-shaped, white or yellow flowers and kidney- or heart-shaped leaves, they bring bright color to the edges of garden ponds or to mixed borders in moist soil. They spread by thick rhizomes and often come into leaf and flower very early, appearing from beneath melting snow.

CULTIVATION
These frost-hardy plants prefer full sun and rich, damp soil at the water's edge or in any damp spot. Propagate by division in autumn or early spring, or from seed in autumn. Watch for rust fungus, which should be treated with a fungicide.

Caltha palustris
MARSH MARIGOLD, KINGCUP

Occurring widely in temperate regions of the northern hemisphere, this semi-aquatic or bog plant is sometimes grown for its attractive flowers. It is deciduous or semi-evergreen with dark green, rounded leaves and glistening buttercup-like, golden yellow flowers borne from early spring to mid-summer. It grows to a height and spread of 18 in (45 cm). The cultivars **'Monstrosa'** and **'Flore Pleno'** both have double flowers, while *Caltha palustris* var. *alba* has single white flowers with yellow stamens.
ZONES 3–8.

Caltha palustris
'Flore Pleno' *(left)*

Caltha palustris
'Monstrosa' *(below)*

C

Campanula carpatica *(below)*

CARPATHIAN BELLFLOWER, TUSSOCK BELLFLOWER

The slowly spreading clumps of basal leaves of this species make it well suited for use as an edging or rock garden plant. From late spring through summer, 8–12 in (20–30 cm) stems rise above the foliage, carrying upward-facing, 1–2 in (2.5 –5 cm) wide, bowl-shaped flowers in blue, lavender or white. The most common cultivars available are the compact-growing **'Blue Clips'** and **'White Clips'**, and the bright violet blue **'Wedgwood Blue'**. ZONES 3–9.

Campanula 'Burghaltii' *(above)*

This cross between *Campanula latifolia* and *C. punctata* has interesting flowers, up to 3 in (8 cm) long and amethyst purple in the bud stage opening to pale gray-mauve. Rhizomes do not creep to any great degree. It grows to about 24 in (60 cm) in height. ZONES 4–9.

Campanula 'Birch Hybrid' *(above right)*

A hybrid between *Campanula portenschlagiana* and *C. poscharskyana*, this delightful miniature campanula grows up to 6 in (15 cm) high with blooms of a light blue color. ZONES 4–9.

CAMPANULA
BELLFLOWER, BLUEBELL

Native to temperate parts of the northern hemisphere, this large genus includes about 250 species of showy herbaceous plants, mostly perennials but a few annual or biennial. The leaves vary in shape and size, mainly arising from upright stems or sometimes only in basal clusters. The flowers are mostly bell-shaped but in some species are more tubular, urn-shaped or star- shaped, and come mainly in shades of blue and purple with some pinks and whites.

CULTIVATION

Campanulas are useful for rockeries, borders, wild gardens and hanging baskets. All do best in a moderately rich, moist, well-drained soil. They grow in sun or shade, but flower color remains brightest in shady situations. Protect from drying winds and stake taller varieties, which make good cut flowers. Remove spent flower stems. Propagate from seed in spring (sow alpines in autumn), by division in spring or autumn, or from basal cuttings in spring. They are very frost hardy to frost tender. Transplant during winter and watch for slugs.

Campanula glomerata
'Superba' *(above)*

Campanula isophylla

ITALIAN BELLFLOWER

This dwarf evergreen
trailing perennial
grows to 4 in (10 cm)
high with a spread of
12 in (30 cm) or more.
It is only moderately
frost hardy and is com-
monly grown indoors.
It bears large star-
shaped blue or white
flowers in summer.
The leaves are small
and heart-shaped.
'**Alba**' has white
flowers. The so-called
Campanula isophylla
Kristal hybrids, '**Kristal
Blau**' and '**Krystal
Weiss**', are not really
hybrids but selected
forms with particularly
showy blue and white
flowers respectively.
ZONES 8–10.

Campanula isophylla
'Krystal Weiss' *(right)*

Campanula isophylla
'Kristal Blau' *(below)*

Campanula glomerata

CLUSTERED BELLFLOWER

This variable species is found throughout Europe
and temperate Asia. The violet-blue flowers are
grouped in almost globular clusters on 10–15 in
(25–38 cm) tall stems in early summer and again
later if the old flower stems are removed.
'**Superba**' grows to 24 in (60 cm); *Campanula
glomerata* var. *dahurica* is a deeper violet than
the species. There are also double-flowered and
white versions. ZONES 3–9.

C

Campanula lactiflora
MILKY BELLFLOWER

Native to the Caucasus region and eastern Turkey, this popular strong-growing perennial reaches a height of 5 ft (1.5 m) and spreads into a broad clump. The strong stems bear many narrow oval leaves. In summer it produces very large and dense panicles of bell-shaped lilac-blue flowers (occasionally pink or white). If the flowering stem is cut back after flowering, side shoots may bear blooms in late autumn. **'Loddon Anna'** has lilac-pink flowers; **'Pritchard's Variety'** has deep violet-blue flowers. ZONES 5–9.

Campanula lactiflora cultivar *(above right)*
Campanula lactiflora 'Pritchard's Variety' *(right)*

Campanula latifolia *(above)*
GREAT BELLFLOWER

Widely distributed in Europe and temperate Asia, this attractive species grows to 3 ft (1 m) tall with long-stalked basal leaves and strong leafy stems ascending from a compact rootstock. The upper leaves grade into bracts with lilac to white flowers arising from the axils; the flowers are up to 2 in (5 cm) across, bell-shaped and with elegantly recurved petals. ZONES 5–9.

Campanula medium *(below)*
CANTERBURY BELL

A biennial species from southern Europe, this is a slow-growing, erect plant with narrow basal leaves. In spring and early summer it has stout spires up to 4 ft (1.2 m) tall of crowded, white, pink or blue, bell-shaped flowers with recurved rims and prominent large green calyces. Dwarf cultivars grow to 24 in (60 cm), and double forms have a colored calyx like a second petal tube. Grow as border plants in part-shade. ZONES 6–10.

C

Campanula rotundifolia *(below)*
HAREBELL, SCOTTISH BLUEBELL

This variable species, widely distributed around the temperate northern hemisphere, has a hardy nature. Loose rosettes of rounded, long-stalked leaves arise from creeping rhizomes, followed by slender, wiry stems holding nodding lilac-blue to white bells during the summer months. ZONES 3–9.

Campanula persicifolia *(left)*
PEACH-LEAFED BELLFLOWER

Native to southern and eastern Europe and temperate Asia, this well-known species has large, nodding, bowl-shaped purplish blue or white flowers borne above narrow, lance-shaped, bright green leaves in summer. It is a rosette-forming perennial spreading by rhizomes and reaching a height of 3 ft (1 m). Pinch individual blooms off upright stems as soon as they fade. **'Alba'** has white flowers; **'Boule de Neige'** and **'Fleur de Neige'** have double white flowers. ZONES 3–9.

Campanula portenschlagiana *(below)*
syn. *Campanula muralis*
DALMATIAN BELLFLOWER

Native to a small area of the Dalmatian limestone mountains of Croatia, this is a dwarf, evergreen perennial growing to a maximum height of 6 in (15 cm) with an indefinite spread. It has crowded small violet-like leaves and a profusion of small, star-shaped, violet flowers in late spring and early summer. Best suited to rockeries and wall crevices, it likes a cool, partially shaded site with good drainage. ZONES 5–10.

Campanula rapunculoides *(left)*
CREEPING BELLFLOWER, ROVER BELLFLOWER

Considered by some a weed on account of the difficulty of eradicating its long rhizomes, this common European native may conversely be useful for the wild woodland garden as it spreads and self-seeds easily. It sends up widely spaced stems to about 3 ft (1 m) tall with serrated nettle-like leaves and nodding violet-blue bell-shaped flowers during the summer months. ZONES 4–10.

C

Campanula vidalii
(above)

syn. *Azorina vidalii*

AZORES BELLFLOWER

Campanula vidalii is so different from other campanulas that some botanists place it in a genus of its own *(Azorina)*. A shrubby evergreen perennial, it has crowded, narrow, fleshy leaves and bears nodding flesh pink or white bells of a remarkable waxy texture in early summer on 18 in (45 cm) tall stems. It is a garden plant for warm-temperate climates only—in cool climates it is best grown in a mildly warmed greenhouse. ZONES 9–11.

Campanula takesimana *(top right)*

A native of Korea, this striking perennial has unusually long bell-shaped flowers, satiny creamy white to lilac-pink outside but spotted with darker purple-brown inside. The large leaves form loose basal rosettes, and the roots tend to spread so the plant forms a large clump. The flowering stems are up to 3 ft (1 m) long but are usually weak and reclining. The cultivar **'Alba'** has white flowers. ZONES 5–9.

Campanula takesimana
'Alba' *(above)*

C

CANISTRUM

This bromeliad genus has 7 species, all native to eastern Brazil where they grow as epiphytes or rock dwellers. They are rosette plants rather like neoregelias, the rosette funnel-shaped and holding water in the base. In the center of the rosette appears a short flowerhead, consisting of a tight clump of small flowers enclosed by a neat ring of short but colorful bracts.

CULTIVATION

Usually grown as indoor plants in cooler climates, in the wet tropics and subtropics canistrums do well outdoors in a partially shaded position planted in low forks of trees or on rock piles, or in raised beds in a very open, humus-rich soil mixture. In dry summer weather, mist-spray frequently. Propagate from offsets or seed; protect seedlings from fungus and scale insects.

Canistrum lindenii
(below)
syns *Aechmea rosea*, *Canistrum roseum*

The stemless rosettes of this species consist of broad, spiny edged leaves up to 18 in (45 cm) long, green with silvery scales on the undersides. The crowded small flowers are white and the surrounding bracts are pale green to white (pink or reddish in '**Roseum**'); it blooms in summer. **ZONES 11–12.**

CANNA

This genus of robust rhizomatous perennials consists of about 25 species, all native to tropical and South America. Belonging to the same broad grouping as gingers and bananas, they resemble these in that their apparent aboveground stems are not true stems but collections of tightly furled leaf bases, rising from the thick knotty rhizomes. Slender flowering stems grow up through the centers of these false stems, emerging at the top with showy flowers of asymmetrical structure. Most of the wild species have rather narrow-petalled flowers in shades of yellow, red or purple. All garden cannas are hybrids with much broader petals, originating as crosses between several species in the mid-nineteenth century. Early hybrids had fairly smooth petals in single colors but the addition of *Canna flaccida* genes resulted in larger, crumpled flowers with striking variegations ('orchid-flowered cannas'). The colors of cannas range from the common reds, oranges and yellows through to apricots, creams and pinks. The leaves can be green, bronze or purple, or sometimes white or yellow striped. Plants range in height from 18 in (45 cm) to 8 ft (2.4 m).

CULTIVATION

Cannas thrive outdoors in frost-free, warm climates but if grown outside in colder areas the roots need to be protected with thick mulch in winter, or else the rhizomes may be lifted in autumn and stored until spring—alternatively they can be grown in containers in a conservatory or greenhouse. They are sun-loving plants and thrive in hot dry weather as long as water can be kept up to the roots, and they respond well to heavy feeding. Cut back to the ground after flowers finish. Propagate in spring by division.

Canna × generalis cultivars
(top, center & right)

C

Canna × generalis

Canna × generalis is a large, highly variable group of canna hybrids of unknown or complex parentage. Plants are extremely variable, ranging from dwarfs less than 3 ft (1 m) to large growers that reach 6 ft (1.8 m). Foliage is also variable and may be plain green, reddish, purple or variegated. Flowers come in all the warm shades, either in plain single colors like the orange-red **'Brandywine'** or spotted or streaked as in the yellow and red **'King Numbert'**. **'Königin Charlotte'** has dazzling red flowers. **'Lenape'** is a dwarf hybrid with bright yellow flowers with a red throat and brownish red spots; it grows to a height of only 30 in (75 cm). **'Lucifer'** is a most attractive hybrid with yellow-edged red petals and purple-toned leaves. It is one of the newer dwarf types, growing to 3 ft (1 m). **ZONES 9–12.**

Canna × generalis
'Lucifer' *(left)*

Canna × generalis
'Königin Charlotte'
(below left)

Canna × generalis
'Brandywine' *(below)*

Canna × generalis
'Lenape' *(right)*

Canna indica
(below right)
syn. *Canna edulis*
INDIAN SHOT

Despite the common name, this species is native to northern South America, although it is commonly naturalized in warm regions elsewhere. Growing to about 8 ft (2.4 m) tall, it has dark green leaves with purple tones and in summer bears dark red to yellow flowers with very narrow petals, followed shortly by fleshy spined capsules containing black seeds—their hardness and smooth spherical shape allowed them to be substituted for shotgun pellets, hence the common name. Some strains, once distinguished as *Canna edulis*, have been cultivated for the edible starch in their rhizomes, known as 'Queensland arrowroot'. ZONES 9–12.

CARDAMINE
BITTERCRESS

This genus of the mustard family includes 150 or more species of annuals and perennials from most parts of the world, usually with dissected or compound leaves forming basal tufts and on lower parts of the flowering stems. Small, 4-petalled, white, pink or purple flowers like small stocks open progressively up the stem and are followed by slender pods that split apart suddenly, flinging the minute seeds a short distance. They are found in shady, moist habitats, some forming large mats, but the genus also includes several common small weeds, for example *Cardamine hirsuta* which can be eaten like watercress.

CULTIVATION
Given moist soil and full or part shade, these soft-leafed plants can be planted in a woodland garden or in an informal border, where their foliage makes an attractive ground cover.

Cardamine raphanifolia
(above)
syn. *Cardamine latifolia*

The botanical name of this species, native to southern Europe and western Asia, means 'radish-leafed' and its leaves do resemble those of a small radish plant. It is a perennial of up to about 24 in (60 cm) in height, the stems springing from a creeping rhizome. The flowers are pinkish purple and are borne from late spring to mid-summer. Coming from stream banks and damp woodland, the plant will take sun as long as its roots are kept moist.
ZONES 7–9.

CARTHAMUS

This genus of prickly composites of the thistle tribe consists of
14 species of annuals and perennials from the Mediterranean
region and western Asia. Some are nuisance weeds but one species, safflower, is of commercial importance as an oil seed, and
was also the source of red and yellow dyes used for rouge and
food coloring. They are plants of upright growth with very sharp
spines bordering the parchment-textured leaves; the thistle-like
flowerheads are smallish, mostly with yellow florets surrounded
by a ring of fiercely spiny bracts.

CULTIVATION

Not fussy as to soil but enjoying a full sun position, these plants
need little care and their flowers make good, though not long
lasting, cut flowers that can be easily dried. Propagate from seed
in spring.

**Carthamus
tinctorius** (left)

SAFFLOWER, FALSE SAFFRON

A fast-growing annual
24–36 in (60–90 cm)
tall, this thistle is
valued for its orange-
yellow flowers in
summer and for the oil
contained in its seeds.
Its leaves are spiny and
oblong, running down
the stems. Safflower is
frost hardy and grows
best in fertile, well-
drained soil. **ZONES 7–11.**

CATHARANTHUS
MADAGASCAR PERIWINKLE

Although still referred to as *Vinca* by many gardeners, this genus is in fact quite distinct. It consists of 8 species of annuals and evergreen perennials or subshrubs, all originally from Madagascar though one widespread and often weedy species, *Catharanthus roseus,* has spread throughout warmer regions of the world. It has given rise to many horticultural selections, grown as bedding and border plants or sold in pots by florists. They are plants with repeatedly branched, rather fleshy stems and plain, smooth-edged leaves. The flowers are clustered in the upper leaf axils and are somewhat oleander-like, with a short tube opening by a very narrow mouth into 5 flat, radiating petals, the whole effect being very neat and star-like.

CULTIVATION

In cooler areas *Catharanthus* can be can be grown in a sunny conservatory or as summer bedding plants. In warm climates they are moderately tolerant of deep shade, the fiercest sun, and a dry atmosphere. Grow in free-draining soil, which should be kept moist in the growing period. Tip prune to keep bushy, but not so heavily as to inhibit flowering. They can be propagated from seed or from cuttings in summer.

Catharanthus roseus
syns *Lochnera rosea,* *Vinca rosea*
PINK PERIWINKLE

In its original form this shrubby perennial is a rather slender plant about 24 in (60 cm) high, with white to rose pink flowers shading to a darker red eye in the center. Garden forms are generally lower and more compact with larger flowers in a wider range of colors, blooming almost throughout the year in warm climates but mainly in spring and summer in cooler climates. Some mixed color series have flowers ranging from purple through pink to white, while others have pale colors (or are white) with prominent red eyes. All plant parts contain poisonous alkaloids from which drugs of value in the treatment of leukaemia have been refined. ZONES 9–12.

Catharanthus roseus cultivar *(left)*

Celmisia
asteliifolia (right)
SILVER SNOW DAISY

This species is native to
Tasmania and south-
eastern mainland Aus-
tralia, forming large
swathes of silvery gray
foliage over grassy
mountain slopes above
the treeline. A dense
network of woody
rhizomes connects
tangled rosettes of
narrow, curving leaves
that are white-felty on
the undersides and
dark gray-green on the
upper. In mid-summer
appear profuse 2–3 in
(5–8 cm) wide flower-
heads with white ray
florets that are purplish
on the reverse, on stalks
8–12 in (20–30 cm)
tall. ZONES 6–9.

CELMISIA
SNOW DAISY, MOUNTAIN DAISY, NEW ZEALAND DAISY

Sixty or so species of rhizomatous perennials and subshrubs with
white daisy-like flowerheads make up this genus, the majority native
to New Zealand but with a smaller number native to Tasmania
and southeastern mainland Australia. Mostly occurring in higher
mountain grasslands, meadows and rocky places, they are attractive evergreen plants with tufts of narrow silvery gray leaves
and a profuse display of yellow-centered white flowers, mostly
solitary on scaly stalks. The leaf undersides of most species are
covered with a thick silvery white fur.

CULTIVATION

Most celmisias are true alpine plants that resent lowland conditions,
but a few will grow successfully in rockeries, peat beds or scree
gardens in temperate climates. Plant in full sun or part-shade
and in moist, well-drained, gritty, acid soil. Protect from hot sun
in drier areas and from excessive moisture in cool climates.
Propagate from seed in autumn or by division in late spring.

Celmisia hookeri *(below)*

From the South Island of New Zealand, where it occurs in dry grasslands from the coast to lower mountain slopes, this larger-leaved species bears leaves to 12 in (30 cm) long and 3 in (8 cm) wide, glossy deep green above, thick white felty beneath. Flowerheads are up to 4 in (10 cm) across on short, thick stems, with a wide disc and a narrow rim of ray florets. **ZONES 7–9.**

Celmisia semicordata *(above)* syn. *Celmisia coriacea*

This is one of the largest-growing species, also from low to medium altitudes on the South Island of New Zealand. Forming with age large mounds of rosettes, the striking silvery leaves are stiff and straight, up to 18 in (45 cm) long and 1–3 in (2.5–8 cm) wide. The white flowerheads are up to 4 in (10 cm) across, on slender stems to 15 in (38 cm) long. Generally regarded as the easiest celmisia to grow, *Celmisia semicordata* is more tolerant than most of heat and dry conditions but likes ample summer moisture. **ZONES 7–9.**

CELOSIA
COCKSCOMB, CHINESE WOOLFLOWER

This genus of erect annuals, perennials and shrubs in the amaranthus family contains 50 or more species from warmer parts of the Americas, Asia and Africa, but only *Celosia argentea* is widely cultivated as a bedding annual and for cut flowers. It has evolved in cultivation into numerous forms, hardly recognizable as belonging to the one species. It has simple, soft, strongly veined leaves; the variation is almost wholly in the structure of the heads of the small flowers, which have undergone proliferation and deformation in the two major cultivated races.

Celosia argentea, Plumosa Group cultivar *(above)*

CULTIVATION
In cool climates celosias are treated as conservatory plants, or planted out for summer bedding after raising seedlings under glass in spring. Better adapted to hot climates, they can withstand the fiercest summer heat. They require full sun, rich, well-drained soil and constant moisture. Propagate from seed in spring.

Celosia argentea, Cristata Group cultivars *(above & below)*

Celosia argentea
syns *Celosia cristata*, *C. pyramidalis*

Probably native to tropical Asia, this erect, summer-flowering annual reaches 3 ft (1 m) high or more. The leaves are mid-green; the silvery white flowers appear in summer in dense, erect, pointed spikes with a silvery sheen. The species is best known in the guise of two strikingly different cultivar groups, which are hardly recognizable as belonging to the species. These are the **Plumosa Group**, with erect, plume-like heads of tiny deformed flowers in a range of hot colors, and the **Cristata Group** (cockscombs), with bizarre wavy crests of fused flower stalks also in many colors. Both have been developed in cultivation with a range of seedling strains, differing in height as well as size and the color of the flowerheads. The Plumosa Group in particular are favored for cut flowers and sale in pots for indoor decoration. Some dwarf strains are no more than 6 in (15 cm) tall, while the old-fashioned bedding strains are about 24 in (60 cm). Most strains are sold as mixed colors. **ZONES 10–12.**

C

Celosia spicata *(left)*

Of uncertain origin, this annual species has appeared in recent years as a cut flower. Growing to 24 in (60 cm) or more, it has an erect, slender habit and much narrower leaves than *Celosia argentea*. The summer flowers are neatly crowded onto terminal spikes, opening progressively from the base with the buds purplish pink and the flowers ageing to pale silvery pink as the spikes elongate. The flowers last well when dried. There are many cultivars available. **'Caracas'** is an example. ZONES 10–12.

Celosia spicata 'Caracas' *(above)*

CENIA

These low-growing annuals and perennials in the daisy family are closely related to *Cotula*, in which they were formerly included. The plants have rather the aspect of *Anthemis* but the yellow flowerheads lack ray florets, appearing like large buttons, borne singly on slender stalks. The finely divided leaves are softly hairy and slightly aromatic.

CULTIVATION

Easily grown as rock garden or edging plants, they produce a succession of cheerful blooms, though the plants can become straggly as they age. Sow seed in autumn, and plant out in a sunny spot when seedlings are about 1 in (25 mm) high.

Cenia turbinata (below)
syn. *Cotula turbinata*
BACHELOR'S BUTTONS

Native to coastal areas of South Africa's Cape Province, this species is a short-lived perennial but in the garden is most often treated as an annual. The sprawling stems radiate from a central rootstock, concealed beneath the pale green, dissected, hairy foliage. In spring it produces a succession of bright yellow 'buttons' about 1¼ in (30 mm) in diameter on short, weak stalks. The plant grows 4–6 in (10–15 cm) high and spreads to about 24 in (60 cm). **ZONES 8–10.**

C

Centaurea cineraria (above)
syns *Centaurea candidissima* of gardens,
C. gymnocarpa
DUSTY MILLER

A shrubby perennial from the Mediterranean region, *Centaurea cineraria* is grown mainly for its beautiful, much divided silvery white foliage. When not in flower the plant is easily mistaken for the unrelated *Senecio cineraria*, also known as dusty miller. Small thistle-like, lilac-pink flowerheads held on much-branched flower stems reveal delicate symmetry and color. The silveriness of the foliage can vary from plant to plant, the best being selected for propagation. ZONES 7–10.

CENTAUREA
CORNFLOWER, KNAPWEED

This genus, belonging to the thistle tribe of composites, is a huge one with around 450 species scattered all over the temperate, grassy regions of Eurasia and north Africa, with one or two in America. It includes annuals, biennials and perennials. Some spiny-leafed species are troublesome weeds in some parts of the world. Apart from the common annual cornflower, some of the perennial species are desirable garden plants; they come in various colors, from white through shades of blue, red, pink, purple and yellow. The flowerheads typically have an urn-shaped receptacle of fringed or spiny bracts, from the mouth of which radiate the quite large florets, each deeply divided into 5 colored petals; smaller florets occupy the center of the head, but do not form a distinct disc as in other members of the daisy or Compositae family.

CULTIVATION

Cornflowers do well in well-drained soil in a sunny position. Propagate from seed in spring or autumn; perennials can also be divided in spring or autumn.

Centaurea cyanus (left)
BLUE-BOTTLE, BACHELOR'S BUTTON, CORNFLOWER

One of the best known wildflowers of Europe and northern Asia, this species is also a common weed of cereal crops. It is a weak-stemmed erect annual 24–36 in (60–90 cm) tall with very narrow leaves and small, rather untidy flowerheads that are typically a slightly purplish shade of blue. Garden varieties have been developed with larger flowers in shades of pale and deep pink, cerise, crimson, white, purple and blue, some of them dwarf and more compact. Best displayed in large clumps, it will flower for months if deadheads are removed regularly. ZONES 5–10.

Centaurea montana
(above left)

PERENNIAL CORNFLOWER,
MOUNTAIN BLUET

From the mountains of
Europe, this long-
cultivated perennial
species is up to 30 in
(75 cm) high and has
creeping rhizomes; it
may form large clumps
when conditions are to
its liking. The leaves
are usually smooth
edged and green, and
the 2 in (5 cm) wide
violet flowerheads,
borne in early summer,
are distinctive for their
widely spaced florets,
giving them a delicate
lacy effect. **ZONES 3–9.**

Centaurea hypoleuca
'John Coutts' (above)

Centaurea hypoleuca

Also from the Caucasus
and Iran as well as east-
ern Turkey, this spread-
ing perennial has
fragrant pale to deep
pink flowerheads, pro-
duced singly on stalks
up to 24 in (60 cm) high
in early summer often
with a second flush in
autumn. It has long,
lobed leaves, green on
top and gray under-
neath, and forms a
clump 18 in (45 cm)
across. **'John Coutts'**
bears deep rose pink
flowers. **ZONES 5–9.**

Centaurea dealbata (above)

PERSIAN CORNFLOWER

Native to the Caucasus
region and northern
Iran, this very leafy
perennial has deeply
cut foliage that is grayish
green underneath. Lilac-
purple to lilac-pink
flowerheads appear
from late spring on-
wards. An erect plant,
Centaurea dealbeata
grows to 3 ft (1 m)
high. **'Steenbergii'** has
larger, deep pink
blooms. **ZONES 4–9.**

Centaurea macrocephala (right)

GLOBE CORNFLOWER

With foliage a bit like a
large dandelion, this
perennial comes from
the subalpine fields of
Armenia and nearby
parts of Turkey. In
summer, stout leafy
stems, up to 3 ft (1 m)
tall, carry yellow
flowerheads 2 in (5 cm)
across with a club-like
base of shiny brown
bracts. **ZONES 4–9.**

CENTRANTHUS
VALERIAN

Around 10 species belong to this genus of annual and perennial
herbs closely related to *Valeriana,* native to the Mediterranean
region and western Asia, but only one, *Centranthus ruber,* is
widely planted for ornament. They make tufts of soft leaves that
may be simple and smooth edged or less commonly dissected,
and the leafy, branched flowering stems bear many irregular
heads of tiny tubular flowers.

CULTIVATION

Grow in full sun in moderately fertile, chalk or lime soil that is
well drained. Deadhead regularly. These plants are not long lived
and are best divided every 3 years to ensure a good display.
Propagate from seed or by division.

Centranthus ruber
(left)

RED VALERIAN, JUPITER'S BEARD,
KISS-ME-QUICK

This perennial is often
seen as a naturalized
plant on dry banks and
is ideal for dry rock
gardens as well as
borders. It forms loose
clumps of somewhat
fleshy leaves and grows
to a height of 24–36 in
(60–90 cm). From late
spring to autumn it
produces dense clusters
of small, star-shaped,
deep reddish pink to
pale pink flowers that
last for a long time.
The cultivar **'Albus'**
has white flowers. One
of the easiest plants to
grow, it requires sun
and good drainage and
will tolerate exposed
positions and poor al-
kaline soil. ZONES 5–10.

C

Cerastium alpinum
(right)

ALPINE MOUSE-EAR

This cold-loving perennial species is widely distributed across subarctic regions of the northern hemisphere, coming south in Europe in the mountains. Forming a mat or small hummock, *Cerastium alpinum* has hairy rounded leaves and in summer bears conspicuous white flowers with broad petals purple-lined in the throat, singly or in 2s or 3s on short, erect stalks. It does not adapt well to cultivation in warmer climates, requiring cool, humid summers. ZONES 2–8.

CERASTIUM

Sixty or so species of low-growing annuals and perennials belong to this genus. They occur in most temperate regions of the world though mainly in the northern hemisphere, where some extend into arctic regions. The annuals include some common weeds of lawns (mouse-eared chickweeds), proliferating in winter and spring, but some of the perennials are useful garden plants grown as ground covers or rock garden subjects, for example, *Cerastium boissieri.* They have very weak stems from a network of thin rhizomes, and small leaves, usually clothed in whitish hairs, tapering to narrow bases. The flowers are white with 5 petals, each notched at the apex, held in stalked clusters above the leaves.

Cerastium boissieri
(below)

CULTIVATION

Easily cultivated, some cerastiums can be invasive if planted in confined spaces in a rock garden. All are frost hardy and like full sun and well-drained soil. Their foliage should, if possible, be kept dry both in winter and during humid summer weather, as the fine hairs on the leaves tend to retain moisture and become mildewed. They are easily propagated by division of rhizomes.

C

Ceratostigma plumbaginoides (left)
syn. *Plumbago larpentae*

CHINESE PLUMBAGO, PERENNIAL
LEADWORT, DWARF PLUMBAGO

Native to western China,
this bushy perennial
grows to 18 in (45 cm)
high with rather erect,
crowded stems arising
from much-branched rhi-
zomes. It has oval, mid-
green leaves that turn a
rich orange and red in
autumn. The flowers are
plumbago-like, with small
clusters of single corn-
flower blue blooms ap-
pearing on reddish,
branched stems in late
summer and autumn.
ZONES 6–9.

CERATOSTIGMA

This genus of 8 species of herbaceous perennials and small shrubs
is primarily of Himalayan and East Asian origin, with one species endemic to the Horn of Africa. Most of the species grown in
gardens are small deciduous shrubs and from spring to autumn
they produce loose heads of blue flowers that indicate the genus's relationship with *Plumbago*. The small leaves are deep
green, turning to bronze or crimson in autumn before dropping.

CULTIVATION

Ceratostigma species will grow in any moist, well-drained soil
in sun or part-shade. Propagate from seed or semi-ripe cuttings,
or by division. In cold climates they will reshoot from the roots
even though the top growth may die back to ground level.

CHELIDONIUM
GREATER CELANDINE, SWALLOWWORT

A single species of short-lived perennial belongs to this genus of the poppy family, native to Europe and western Asia. It forms a clump of leafy stems, the slightly brittle leaves divided into several irregular leaflets with scalloped edges. Short sprays of small 4-petalled bright yellow flowers are produced over a long season, each flower soon succeeded by a slender pod that splits to release tiny black seeds. Broken leaves and stems bleed an orange latex which is irritating to the skin and has been used to cure warts; the plant has many other traditional medicinal uses but is quite poisonous.

Chelidonium majus
'Flore Pleno' *(above)*

C

CULTIVATION

The plant is very frost hardy and is easily grown in sun or light shade, adapting to all except very wet soils. Its duration may be only biennial, but it self-seeds readily and can become invasive. Propagate from seed or by division in autumn and cut back after flowering to keep under control.

Chelidonium majus *(right)*

This quick-growing perennial can form an effective ground cover if a number of seedlings are planted closely together. It is an erect to rather sprawling plant about 2–4 ft (0.6–1.2 m) high and wide, with attractive pale green foliage. From mid-spring to mid-autumn it produces a continuous scatter of bright golden yellow flowers about 1 in (25 mm) across; the slender seed capsules are 2 in (5 cm) long. **'Flore Pleno'** has double flowers.
ZONES 6–9.

CHELONE
TURTLEHEAD

This genus of 6 species of rather coarse but showy perennials from North America is related to *Penstemon*, which they resemble in growth habit and foliage. The name comes from the Greek *kelone* meaning a tortoise or turtle, and refers to the hooded, gaping flowers, borne in short terminal spikes. Leaves are toothed and shiny in most species.

CULTIVATION
They are best along streams or pond edges, but also adapt to a moist border planting with rich soil in full sun or part-shade. Propagate by dividing clumps in early spring, from cuttings in summer or from seed in spring or autumn.

Chelone lyonii (left)
PINK TURTLEHEAD

This species from the mountains of southeastern USA grows to a height of at least 3 ft (1 m), with erect, angled stems and dark green leaves up to 6 in (15 cm) long. The summer flowers are rosy purple and are produced in axillary and terminal spikes terminating the stems, and in upper leaf axils. ZONES 6–9.

Chelone obliqua
(above)

ROSE TURTLEHEAD

Also from southeastern USA, this is the showiest of the turtleheads and the best as a garden plant. Pairs of rich green leaves line 3 ft (1 m) tall vertical stems topped with short spikes of rosy-purple flowers in late summer and autumn. ZONES 6–9.

C

CHIASTOPHYLLUM

This genus in the crassula family consists of a single species of somewhat succulent evergreen perennial native to the Caucasus Mountains. It has leafy stems arising from a rootstock, the rounded, blunt-toothed leaves arranged in opposite pairs. The stems terminate in branched, drooping spikes of small yellow, bell-shaped flowers.

CULTIVATION

Its natural habitat is cool, moist crevices among rocks, and this should be simulated in the garden, for example on the shady side of a stone wall or bank, or a cool position in the rock garden. Watch for snails and slugs. Propagate from seed in autumn or by division in summer.

Chiastophyllum oppositifolium
(above)
syn. *Cotyledon simplicifolia*

This plant grows to no more than 8 in (20 cm) high but can spread by rhizomes to make a mat of indefinite width. The leaves are rather like some of the herbaceous sedums, pale green and thinly succulent with scalloped margins, the rusty red lower ones about 1½ in (38 mm) long. The golden yellow flowers are ¼ in (6 mm) long, appearing in late spring and early summer. ZONES 7–9.

CHRYSANTHEMUM
CHRYSANTHEMUM

C

Although the garden (or florists') chrysanthemums are so well known, the history of *Chrysanthemum* as a botanical name is very confusing. At one time this was used by botanists in a very broad sense to include not only the florists' chrysanthemums but several other related groups such as the Shasta daisies, marguerites, tansies and pyrethrums. After World War II the scientific evidence against this broad view began to mount, and a number of genera were split off *Chrysanthemum* to contain these rather distinct groups. For a while the florists' chrysanthemums themselves were given another genus name *(Dendranthema)* but a recent decision by an international committee on botanical nomenclature has brought their scientific name back into line with popular usage and they are now treated as the rightful claimants to the name *Chrysanthemum.*

The genus in this present, redefined sense consists of 37 species of perennials occurring wild mostly in eastern Asia, though two extend into northern Europe. They have lobed, somewhat aromatic leaves and panicles of daisy-like flowerheads in shades of red, purple, pink, yellow or white. Some of the species were taken into cultivation in China, possibly over 1000 years ago, and by the seventeenth century hundreds of named cultivars were recorded. News of these gorgeous flowers reached the West and by the early nineteenth century a number of cultivars had been introduced to Europe. Breeding continued in both China and western countries to produce the extraordinary array of forms and colors available today. The largest and most striking cultivars are grown only for exhibition by chrysanthemum enthusiasts, but commercial growers raise other varieties by the millions for sale either as cut flowers or as flowering pot plants; their normal late summer-autumn flowering season is frequently extended by manipulation of day length and temperature in greenhouses.

Genera listed elsewhere in this book whose species were once classified under *Chrysanthemum* are: *Argyranthemum,* the marguerites, evergreen subshrubs from the Canary Islands and Madeira; *Leucanthemum,* white-flowered perennials from the Mediterranean and Europe, including the ox-eye and Shasta daisies; *Tanacetum,* perennials and subshrubs from temperate Eurasia and North Africa, with very aromatic foliage and yellow, red or white flowers—they include the insecticidal pyrethrum, tansy and feverfew; *Ajania,* perennials from eastern and northern Asia rather like the florists' chrysanthemums but with flowers in numerous yellow button-like heads. And finally, 'Chrysanthemum' in the sense recognized before the recent decision, is the group of 5 annuals from Europe and North Africa including the crown daisy, corn marigold and painted daisy. The correct genus name for this group is still uncertain, so they are listed hereunder but with the genus in quotes, indicating they are no longer true *Chrysanthemums.*

CULTIVATION

Chrysanthemums are generally frost-hardy, though some forms are a little more tender than others. They can be grown outdoors in most temperate climates but, for indoor use, exhibition purposes or choice cut flowers, are usually raised under glass. Plant outdoors in full sun in a well-drained, slightly acid soil improved with compost and well-rotted manure. For pot culture, use a rich, organic growing medium. Avoid excessive watering and in early summer feed with low-nitrogen, high-potassium fertilizer. Pinching out stem tips when they are 6–12 in (15–30 cm) high promotes flowering lateral stems with many flowers (known as 'sprays'), but for the largest exhibition blooms all lateral buds are removed at an early stage, leaving a single terminal bud—a 'disbudded chrysanthemum'. Stake tall plants with canes. Propagate bedding types from seed, named varieties from root divisions or basal cuttings of late autumn shoots. The annual species of 'Chrysanthemum' are easily grown in any good garden soil in a sunny position, by sowing seed in spring in cool climates or in autumn in warmer climates.

Chrysanthemum × grandiflorum
syns *Chrysanthemum morifolium,*
Dendranthema × grandiflorum
FLORISTS' CHRYSANTHEMUM

Thought to be derived mainly from the Chinese species *Chrysanthemum indicum*, this hybrid group includes most of the cultivated chrysanthemums, and all of those with large double blooms. A more recent development is the breeding of the 'Korean chrysanthemums', introducing genes from *C. zawadskii* for more compact plants with smaller single heads, good for bedding. The chrysanthemum plant can be up to 5 ft (1.5 m) tall though mostly smaller; it has rather woody stems rising from a mass of creeping rhizomes, bluntly lobed leaves up to 3 in (8 cm) long with gray felted undersides; flowerheads may be anywhere from 1 to 6 in (2.5–15 cm) across, borne on a broad panicle and ranging from white, pink or yellow through various bronze colors to deep red or purple. Most of the larger types are 'double' lacking disc florets.

Chrysanthemum × grandiflorum, Single Form cultivar *(right)*

C

Chrysanthemum enthusiasts and societies have classified the thousands of cultivars into 10 groups, based on the overall form of the blooms and the shape and orientation of the florets. The full range of colors is represented in each group. The groups are:

Anemone-centered: daisy-like but with a pincushion center and a single or double row of radiating flat florets; normally grown as sprays rather than single blooms.

Incurved: fully double globular blooms with firm-textured florets curving inward and packed closely together, used for cut flowers as well as exhibition, long-lasting when cut. Cream **'Gillette'** and yellow **'Max Riley'** are examples.

Intermediate: falling somewhat between incurved and reflexed, these have ball-like blooms, sometimes with recurving florets at the base. Pale bronze **'Crimson Tide'** and deep pink **'Elizabeth Shoesmith'** are examples. Another Intermediate is **'Jane Sharpe'**, which has salmon florets and a deep pink reverse.

Pompon: globular double blooms formed of numerous, tightly packed florets; normally grown as sprays rather than single blooms, they make excellent cut flowers.

Quill-shaped: double blooms with narrow tubular florets that open out at the tips. **'Yellow Nightingale'** is an example.

*Chrysanthemum ×
grandiflorum*
'Elizabeth Shoesmith'
(above left)

*Chrysanthemum ×
grandiflorum* 'Jane
Sharpe' *(above)*

*Chrysanthemum ×
grandiflorum* 'Yellow
Nightingale' *(below)*

Chrysanthemum × *grandiflorum* 'Flame Symbol' *(right)*

Reflexed: rounded or dome-shaped, fully double blooms, the florets curved out and down, often with a curl or twist. Burnt-orange **'Flame Symbol'**, deep pink **'Matthew Scaelle'**, mid-pink **'Debonair'** and **'Yellow Symbol'** are examples.

Fully reflexed: perfectly rounded double blooms with florets that curve out and down, lowermost florets touching the stem.

Single: daisy-like blooms with up to 5 rows of radiating florets around a flattened yellow disc; excellent for massed planting.

Spider: double blooms with long narrow tubular florets that spread out in all directions, usually curled or twisted at the end. Golden-orange **'Dusky Queen'** and white **'Sterling Silver'** are examples.

Spoon-shaped: double blooms with radiating narrow, tubular florets with the tips expanded to form spoon shapes. **'Spears'** is an example. **ZONES 4–10.**

Chrysanthemum × *grandiflorum* 'Matthew Scaelle' *(above)*
Chrysanthemum × *grandiflorum* 'Dusky Queen' *(below)*

Chrysanthemum × *grandiflorum* 'Yellow Symbol' *(above)*
Chrysanthemum × *grandiflorum* 'Sterling Silver' *(below)*

C

'Chrysanthemum' carinatum (left)
syn. Chrysanthemum tricolor

PAINTED DAISY, SUMMER CHRYSANTHEMUM, TRICOLOR CHRYSANTHEMUM

This and some of the following species are considered to belong to a separate genus from the florists' chrysanthemums but its name is yet to be determined, hence the quotes. It is a colorful garden flower from Morocco that grows to 24 in (60 cm), spreading to about 12 in (30 cm) with much-divided, fleshy leaves and banded, multi-colored flowers in spring and early summer. **'Monarch Court Jesters'** comes in red with yellow centers or white with red centers, and the **Tricolor Series** has many color combinations. They are excellent as bedding plants and cut flowers. ZONES 8–10.

'Chrysanthemum' coronarium (left)
CROWN DAISY

Chrysanthemum × grandiflorum
'Spears' (above)

This is a fast-growing annual from the Mediterranean that will grow to a height of about 3 ft (1 m). The light green leaves are deeply divided and feathery. Daisy-like flowerheads are single or semi-double, very pale to deep yellow and up to 2 in (5 cm) across. The tender young shoots of selected strains are used in oriental cooking, where they are known as *shungiku* or chop suey greens; they can also be used raw in salads but have a strong aromatic taste. ZONES 7–11.

C

'Chrysanthemum'
segetum *(below)*
CORN MARIGOLD

Originating from the eastern Mediterranean area and North Africa, this fast-growing annual is now widely naturalized in temperate regions. Up to about 24 in (60 cm) tall, it has gray-green leaves that are toothed or, on the lower stem, deeply cut. The daisy-like flowerheads, 1½–2½ in (4–6 cm) across, appear in summer and early autumn in various shades of yellow. They make good cut flowers. **'Zebra'** has brick red outer florets. **ZONES 7–10.**

'Chrysanthemum'
segetum 'Zebra' *(right)*

Chrysocephalum apiculatum
(above)
syn. *Helichrysum apiculatum*
YELLOW BUTTONS, COMMON EVERLASTING

Occurring over a large part of the Australian continent and also Tasmania, this species is highly variable in growth habit and foliage characters. Some forms are up to 24 in (60 cm) high, others much lower, some make compact clumps of basal rosettes, others spread extensively. The simple, flat leaves vary from gray-felted to green and only slightly hairy. Flowerheads are golden yellow, in small to large clusters, appearing mainly in spring or summer but can appear at any time of year. Some very attractive forms have been introduced to cultivation. ZONES 8–11.

CHRYSOCEPHALUM

All 8 species of this Australian genus of perennials were formerly included in *Helichrysum,* a genus of the daisy family that botanists are still in the process of redefining and narrowing in scope. *Chrysocephalum* species are mostly evergreens, with slender leafy stems arising from wiry rhizomes by which the plants may spread extensively, though some species have more compact rootstocks. The small 'everlasting' type flowerheads are mostly clustered at the stem apex, and have many rows of tiny yellow or white chaffy bracts surrounding a small group of orange disc-florets. Some species are vigorous growers and make useful ground covers, as well as providing a fine display of spring and summer blooms.

CULTIVATION
These plants prefer a climate with warm, dry summers but are nonetheless fairly adaptable if grown in well-drained, open soil of moderate fertility and in a sunny spot. Propagate from seed, rhizome division, or cuttings from lower stems.

Chrysocephalum baxteri (left)
syn. *Helichrysum baxteri*
FRINGED EVERLASTING, WHITE EVERLASTING

Native mainly to Victoria, Australia, this compact perennial has narrow, almost grass-like dark green leaves, woolly white underneath, forming a mound to about 6 in (15 cm) high. The 4–8 in (10–20 cm) flowering stems each carry a single daisy-like flowerhead, with showy white or cream (sometimes buff or pinkish) papery bracts surrounding yellow disc-florets. It can flower at any time but peaks in spring. This species makes an attractive rock garden plant. ZONES 8–10.

C

**Chrysogonum
virginianum** (above)

This low growing, mat-
forming perennial suit-
able for a rock garden
spreads by under-
ground runners, but is
not normally invasive.
It bears yellow daisy-
like flowerheads
through summer into
autumn. ZONES 6–9.

CHRYSOGONUM
GOLDEN KNEE, GOLDEN STAR

This genus of only a single species of herbaceous perennial from
eastern USA belongs to the sunflower tribe of the very large
daisy or composite family. The botanical name is Latinized
Greek for 'golden knee', alluding to the joint-like stem nodes
from which the flower stalks arise. Plants spread by long-
running rhizomes, sending up short erect stems with heart-
shaped leaves arranged in opposite pairs. The bright yellow
flowerheads have only 5 broad ray-florets and are produced
over a very long flowering season in spring and summer.

CULTIVATION
Easy to grow, *Chrysogonum* can spread over a large area of
ground but prefers light shade and a rather peaty, moist soil.
Propagate from seed or by division.

CHRYSOSPLENIUM

GOLDEN SAXIFRAGE

A genus of 50 or more species of low-growing perennials of the saxifrage family, native in temperate regions of the northern hemisphere except for a handful in temperate South America. They are interesting little plants with creeping fleshy stems and round or kidney-shaped leaves, and little flat heads of golden yellow flowers sitting in a circle of leaf-like bracts which may be yellow at the base but are usually green tipped.

CULTIVATION

They prefer moist, sheltered spots in semi-shade and grow well in boggy edges of streams or ponds. Propagate from seed or by division.

Chrysosplenium davidianum (below)

Native to western China, this species forms low carpets of hairy stems and rounded leaves that are hairy on the undersides and have strongly scalloped edges. The flattened heads of tiny yellow flowers with yellow-tinted bracts are borne from late spring to early summer. ZONES 5–9.

CIMICIFUGA
BUGBANE

This genus of about 15 species of perennials in the ranunculus family, native to cooler regions of the northern hemisphere. The name literally means 'bug repellent', from the Latin *cimex*, the bedbug, and *fugare*, to repel, reflecting an early use of one species. The foliage is reminiscent of astilbes, having large compound leaves with toothed leaflets, but the branched flowering stems terminate in long, erect spikes of small white, cream or pinkish flowers, the many stamens being the conspicuous part of each flower. Some North American species are important in herbal medicine.

CULTIVATION
These plants are bold additions to the summer garden, at the back of borders or in open woodland situations. They prefer part-shade and a deep, rich soil and need regular watering but otherwise need little attention. Plant rhizome divisions in spring or autumn, but do not disturb the root; they flower best when established, and seldom need staking.

Cimicifuga japonica var. *acerina* (below)

Cimicifuga simplex 'Hanse Herms' (above)

Cimicifuga simplex (below)
KAMCHATKA BUGBANE

From Japan and far eastern Siberia, this species is the latest to flower of the whole genus, the flowers coming in late autumn. It is also smaller, reaching a height of about 4 ft (1.2 m). The flowers are white, carried on long arching wands, and the foliage is much divided. **'Elstead'** has purplish buds opening to pure white and is a very graceful plant. **'Hanse Herms'** is another popular cultivar. ZONES 3–9.

Cimicifuga japonica
JAPANESE BUGBANE

From woodlands of Japan, this species is distinguished by its very long-stalked leaves with shallowly lobed leaflets up to 4 in (10 cm) wide. The flowering stems are slender and leafless, up to 4 ft (1.2 m) high, bearing rather undistinguished small white flowers from mid-summer to early autumn. ***Cimicifuga japonica*** var. *acerina* (syn. *C. acerina*) has long drawn-out points on the leaf lobes. ZONES 5–9.

C

CINERARIA

This name has been the source of much confusion. The true
Cineraria, as botanists understand it, is a genus of about
50 species from southern Africa and Madagascar, little known in
gardens. The florists' 'cinerarias' are a colorful group of hybrids
of Canary Island origin now referred to as *Pericallis × hybrida*
though once placed in the genus *Senecio;* and the gray-leafed
Cineraria maritima of gardens is correctly *Senecio cineraria,* a
Mediterranean plant. The true (African) cinerarias are perennials
and subshrubs with broad, rather fleshy leaves that are often
heart-shaped or kidney-shaped and may be hairy or woolly. They
produce numerous stalked flowerheads with yellow ray-florets,
like small daisies.

CULTIVATION

Only a few South African species have ever been cultivated, making attractive low plants for rockeries or banks, or used as
ground covers. They are not very frost hardy and like well-
drained, humus-rich soil and plenty of sun. Propagate from seed,
cuttings, or by root divisions.

Cineraria
saxifraga *(above)*

This South African
perennial is broadly
spreading and usually
about 8 in (20 cm)
high, with prostrate
branches that root into
the soil. The pale green
somewhat succulent
leaves, to about 1½ in
(38 mm) long, are
almost kidney-shaped
and coarsely toothed.
Numerous small,
yellow, daisy-like
flowerheads appear
through spring,
summer and autumn,
on weak slender stalks.
ZONES 9–11.

CIRSIUM

This name of this genus of 200 species of thistles from the cooler parts of the northern hemisphere comes from the Greek *kirsos* (swollen vein). Several species are cursed by farmers as noxious weeds, but others make attractive ornamentals. There are both annual and perennial species. They are mostly very spiny plants, with a basal leaf rosette and branched flowering stems bearing spiny flowerheads of typical thistle form.

CULTIVATION

They can be grown in average garden soil but like good drainage. They are easily raised from seed, but care must be taken when planting them in situations where seed may escape into surrounding areas.

Cirsium occidentale (below)
COBWEB THISTLE

Native to central western and southwestern California, this biennial grows to 3 ft (1 m) tall with leaves that are deeply divided, rather hairy and armed with numerous needle-like spines. The clustered flowerheads, borne in spring and summer, are enclosed in striking white woolly bracts and the florets are scarlet in color. ZONES 9–11.

C

CLARKIA
syn. *Godetia*

This genus, allied to the evening primroses *(Oenothera)* and consisting of about 36 species, was named in honor of Captain William Clark, of the famous Lewis and Clark expedition that crossed the American continent in 1806. They are bushy annuals, undistinguished in foliage but spectacular in their all too short flowering season when they are covered in showy funnel-shaped flowers in various shades of pink, white and carmine. The flowers can be 4 in (10 cm) across, and they look a little like azaleas—in Germany they are called *Sommerazalee*, the summer azalea. They are very good as cut flowers, borne on long stems and lasting a week in water.

CULTIVATION
They are easily grown in full sun in any temperate climate. They prefer moist but well-drained, slightly acid soil; soil that is too fertile will see good foliage but poor flower production. Propagate from seed in autumn or spring.

Clarkia unguiculata (above)
syn. *Clarkia elegans*
MOUNTAIN GARLAND

This species is usually taller than its fellow-Californian *Clarkia amoena* but with smaller flowers, only 1 in (25 mm) across, often frilled and doubled. The flowers, produced at the tops of slender, reddish stems 3 ft (1 m) or more in height, have a broader color range, including orange and purple. ZONES 7–11.

Clarkia amoena
(left)
syn. *Clarkia grandiflora*
FAREWELL-TO-SPRING

A free-flowering annual, this Californian native is fast growing to a height of 24 in (60 cm) and spread of 12 in (30 cm). It has lance-shaped, mid-green leaves, thin upright stems, and in summer bears spikes of open, cup-like, single or double flowers in shades of pink; a number of cultivars have been produced from this species. Allow it to dry out between waterings and watch for signs of botrytis. ZONES 7–11.

Clematis integrifolia (right)

From southern Europe, this herbaceous clematis is hardly recognizable as belonging to this genus, at least until it flowers. It forms a gradually expanding clump with masses of stems arising from the base each spring, each one ending in a single, nodding flower of four 1 in (25 mm) long petals. It is normally purpleblue, deeper in the center. The stamens are creamy white and tightly packed. The flower stalks tend to flop and may need support. Improved forms like 'Hendersonii', 'Rosea' and 'Tapestry' are rather more reliable in this regard than the species. ZONES 3–9.

CLEMATIS
VIRGIN'S BOWER, TRAVELLER'S JOY

The 200 or more species of deciduous or evergreen woody climbers or woody-based perennials in this genus are scattered throughout the world's temperate regions, but most of the popular, larger-flowered garden plants have come from Japan and China. They climb by twisting their leaf-stalk tendrils about a support and are ideal for training on verandah posts, arbors, bowers and trellises. Showy bell-shaped or flattish flowers with 4 to 8 petals (*sepals* really) are followed by masses of fluffy seed heads, often lasting well into winter.

CULTIVATION
The most important requirement for successful cultivation is a well-drained, humus-rich, permanently cool soil with good moisture retention. The plants like to climb up to the sun with their roots in the shade. Prune old twiggy growth in spring and propagate from cuttings or by layering in summer. In some areas where growing clematis is a problem, plants are often grafted. Clematis wilt can be a problem.

Clematis mandshurica (above)
syn. *Clematis recta* var. *mandshurica*

A native of China and Japan, this herbaceous perennial species has a sprawling habit or may climb to about 3–6 ft (1–1.8 m) in height. The small white flowers, about 1¼ in (3 cm) across, are borne in erect terminal umbels, while the smooth dark brown seeds have long yellowish tails. Plant in a protected, part-shaded position. ZONES 7–9.

C

Cleome hassleriana
(left)
syn. *Cleome spinosa* of gardens

Native to subtropical South America, this fast-growing, bushy annual is valued for its unusual spidery flowers. An erect plant, it grows to 4 ft (1.2 m) tall with a spread of 18 in (45 cm). It has large palmate leaves and the hairy, slightly prickly stems are topped in summer with heads of airy, pink and white flowers with long, protruding stamens. Several cultivars are available as seed, and these range in color from pure white to purple. ZONES 9–11.

CLEOME
SPIDER FLOWER, SPIDER PLANT

This genus of 150 species of bushy annuals and short-lived ever-green shrubs, from subtropical and tropical zones all over the world, is characterized by its spidery flowers with 4 petals that narrow into basal stalks and mostly long, spidery stamens and styles. The leaves are composed of from 5 to 7 palmate leaflets. One species is widely grown as a background bedding plant, use-ful for its rapid growth and delicate floral effect.

CULTIVATION
Marginally frost hardy, they require full sun and fertile, well-drained soil, regular water and shelter from strong winds. Taller growth can be encouraged by removing side branches, and dead flowers should also be removed. Propagate from seed in spring or early summer. Check for aphids.

CLINTONIA

Five species of woodland lilies from North America and eastern Asia make up this genus, all rhizomatous perennials with rich green smooth foliage rather like that of *Convallaria*, and erect spikes or umbels (solitary in one species) of small, starry 6-petalled flowers.

CULTIVATION

All species need a cool, peaty, lime-free soil and a shaded, humid position, and so are best suited to a woodland garden. Winter mulching will protect from frost. Propagate from seed or division of rhizomes.

Clintonia borealis
(below)

CORN LILY, BLUEBEARD

From eastern and central North America, this species has loose clusters of yellowish white flowers with recurving petals and protruding stamens, followed by blue berries. It reaches a height of 6–12 in (15–30 cm) and blooms in late spring and early summer. **ZONES 3–9.**

Clintonia umbellulata *(above)*

SPECKLED WOOD-LILY

From eastern USA, this is one of the prettiest species with dense umbels of fragrant white flowers, often speckled green or purplish, rising on stems up to 15 in (40 cm) tall above dense patches of luxuriant foliage. The flowers appear in late spring and early summer and are followed by black berries. **ZONES 4–9.**

Clintonia andrewsiana *(right)*

A native of northern California and Oregon, this species has small bell-like flowers that are poised in a cluster at the top of the stems; they are colored a rich carmine red, the three inner petals with a central creamy vein. The flowers are followed by violet-blue berries. This plant increases slowly, reaching a height of about 24 in (60 cm). **ZONES 7–9.**

CLIVIA
KAFFIR LILY

This genus of southern African lilies was named after Lady Clive, Duchess of Northumberland, whose grandfather was the famous Clive of India. She was a patron of gardening and *Clivia nobilis* first flowered in the UK in her greenhouses. The genus consists of 4 species of evergreen perennials with thick, strap-like, deep green leaves springing from short rhizomes with thick roots. Flowers are borne in dense umbels terminating somewhat flattened stems and are funnel-shaped to trumpet-shaped, with 6 red to orange, sometimes green-tipped petals that are partially fused into a tube. They are sometimes followed by quite conspicuous, deep red, berry-like fruits.

CULTIVATION

They will grow well outdoors in a mild, frost-free climate, or in a conservatory or greenhouse in regions with colder climates. Plant in a shaded or part-shaded, position in friable, well-drained soil. They are surface-rooting, however, and dislike soil disturbance. Keep fairly dry in winter and increase watering in spring and summer. Propagate by division after flowering. Clivias may also be grown from seed, but can be slow to flower.

Clivia miniata
(below left)
BUSH LILY, FIRE LILY

This most commonly cultivated and showiest species is distributed widely in eastern South Africa. About 18 in (45 cm) in height, it has broad leaves, sometimes up to 3 in (8 cm) wide and bears clusters of broadly funnel-shaped flowers up to 3 in (8 cm) long, mostly orange to scarlet with a yellow throat, usually in spring but with the occasional bloom at other times. Many cultivars have been selected over the years, including yellow and cream forms. There is a group of especially prized forms commonly called 'hybrids' with tulip-shaped, deep, rich scarlet blooms. **ZONES 10–11.**

C

*Codonopsis
convolvulacea* 'Alba'
(left)

CODONOPSIS

Native to eastern Asia and higher mountains of the Malay region, this genus allied to *Campanula* consists of about 30 species of perennials with swollen roots, some with scrambling or climbing stems, and simple, broad to narrow leaves that smell slightly unpleasant when bruised. The flowers are pendent or nodding, basically bell-shaped but with many variations, and in many cases prettily veined.

CULTIVATION

They require a moist, cool-temperate climate and most species grow best in a light, well-drained soil in part or complete shade. For best effect, plant in a raised bed or on a bank where the insides of the nodding flowers can be seen. Propagate from seed or by division with care.

Codonopsis convolvulacea

This species from the Himalayas and Western China sends up twining stems to as much as 8 ft (2.4 m) high if a suitable support is available or it may hang down a bank or wall. The broadly bell-shaped flowers are up to 2 in (5 cm) across, range in color from violet to almost white and are carried singly on long stalks at ends of lateral branches. **'Alba'** has white flowers. *Codonopsis clematidea* from central Asia is very similar to *C. convolvulacea*, but has nodding flowers with purple veining. ZONES 5–9.

Codonopsis clematidea
(right)

C

Columnea arguta
(left)

A native of Panama, this is one of the most beautiful species which is at its best grown in a large hanging basket in a humid conservatory. The pendulous stems grow up to 6 ft (1.8 m) long, forming a dense curtain of foliage; the small, crowded leaves are dark green on their convex uppersides with velvety purplish hairs, and the strongly hooded flowers, about 3 in (8 cm) long, make a display of brilliant color. ZONES 11–12.

COLUMNEA

With over 150 species of shrubs, subshrubs and climbers from tropical America, this is one of the largest genera of the African violet and gloxinia family, as well as being one of the most important in terms of ornamental indoor plants. Coming from regions of high rainfall and humidity, many grow as epiphytes, with long trailing stems and rather fleshy leaves. The beautiful and unusual flowers, mostly in colors of red, orange and yellow, have a long tube and often a hooded or helmet-shaped upper lip; they are adapted to pollination by hummingbirds, which hover under the flower and brush pollen from anthers beneath the hood onto their heads while sipping nectar from the tube.

CULTIVATION

Some species demand constant high humidity, but many can grow outdoors in warm climates in a suitably sheltered spot in filtered light; in cooler climates they need the protection of a greenhouse or conservatory. Hanging baskets are ideal for most columneas, whether they are of the type with quite pendulous stems or more erect, scrambling plants. Grow in an open, fibrous compost, including, for example, sphagnum moss, peat and charcoal. Water freely in summer, reducing water as the weather cools. Propagate from cuttings.

CONSOLIDA

LARKSPUR

Botanists in the past often treated these annuals as species of *Delphinium*, but the consensus now is that the 40 or so species constitute a distinct genus, occurring in the Mediterranean region and west and central Asia. The name *Consolida* was bestowed in the Middle Ages in recognition of the plants' use in the healing of wounds; they were believed to help the clotting (consolidating) of the blood. The larkspurs grown in gardens are mostly derived from the one species, *Consolida ajacis,* and include many strains, mostly grown as mixed colors. The flowers of the taller kinds will last a long time when cut. They have finely divided, feather-like leaves and poisonous seeds.

CULTIVATION

They are not difficult to grow, succeeding in any temperate or even mildly subtropical climate and liking full sun and rich, well-drained soil. Tall cultivars need to be staked. Propagate from seed and watch for snails and slugs and for powdery mildew.

Consolida ajacis (below)
syns *Consolida ambigua, Delphinium consolida*

The name larkspur comes from the nectar spur at the back of the flowers, hidden in the open blooms but clearly visible on the unopened buds. This Mediterranean species originally had blue flowers. Present-day garden larkspurs are the result of hybridizing this species with *Consolida orientalis* to give the 'rocket larkspurs', or may be derived mainly from *C. regalis* in the case of the 'forking larkspurs'. Their blooms may be pink, white or purple and are usually double, borne mainly in summer. Some can reach a height of 4 ft (1.2 m). ZONES 7–11.

CONVALLARIA
LILY-OF-THE-VALLEY

Some botanists have recognized several species of *Convallaria*, but most believe there is only one, occurring wild in forests from France to Siberia, also cooler parts of North America. The plant spreads over the forest floor by slender underground rhizomes which at intervals send up pointed oval leaves and slender flowering stems adorned with little white bells, shining like pearls against the dull green of the foliage. The red berries that follow have their uses in medicine, but they are poisonous—dangerously so, as they are sweet enough to tempt children to eat them.

CULTIVATION

The rhizomes, or 'pips' as they are commonly known from their growing tips, should be planted in autumn in a part-shaded position. Given the right conditions, lily-of-the-valley spreads freely and in a confined space sometimes becomes overcrowded, when it will benefit from lifting and thinning. Grow in fertile, humus-rich, moist soil. They can be potted for display indoors, then replanted outdoors after flowering. Propagate from seed or by division.

Convallaria majalis (below)

Renowned for its glorious perfume, this beautiful plant does best in cool climates. It is low growing, 8–12 in (20–30 cm) high but of indefinite spread, with mid-green leaves. The dainty white bell-shaped flowers, ¼–½ in (6–12 mm) across, appear in spring. Pink-flowered variants are known, collectively referred to as *Convallaria majalis* var. *rosea*, and there are several cultivars with variegated or gold foliage. ZONES 3–9.

CONVOLVULUS

Found in many temperate regions of the world, this genus consists mainly of slender, twining creepers (the bindweeds) and
small herbaceous plants. Only a few species are shrubby, and
even these are soft stemmed and renewed by shooting from the
base. They have simple, thin-textured, usually narrow leaves, and
flowers like morning glories, with a strongly flared tube that
opens by unfurling 'pleats'. However, *Convolvulus* species differ
from morning glories *(Ipomoea)* in having flowers that stay open
all day, rather than shrivelling by mid-morning or early afternoon; they usually open in succession over a long season.

CULTIVATION

These easily grown plants adapt to most soils and exposed as well
as sheltered positions, but prefer full sun. Cut back hard after
flowering to promote thicker growth. Propagation is from cuttings.

**Convolvulus
althaeoides** *(above)*

Native to the Mediter-
ranean region, this is a
perennial which can
spread by underground
rhizomes. It has trail-
ing or twining stems
and oval to heart-
shaped leaves that may
be strongly lobed and
slightly overlaid with
silver. The profuse
bright pink flowers are
1–1½ in (25–38 mm)
across, and they are
borne in late spring
and summer. In a mild
climate the plants may
become invasive. If not
supported, they will
mound untidily to
about 6 in (15 cm)
high. **ZONES 8–10.**

C

Convolvulus tricolor
syn. *Convolvulus minor*

This bedding annual
from the Mediterranean
bears profuse deep purple-
blue or white flowers
with banded yellow and
white throats. The small
leaves are lance-shaped
and mid-green. A slen-
der, few-branched plant,
it grows to a height of
8–12 in (20–30 cm) and
blooms from late spring
to early autumn, but
each flowers lasts only
one day. **'Blue Ensign'**
has very deep blue
flowers with pale yellow
centers. ZONES 8–11.

Convolvulus tricolor
'Blue Ensign' *(above left)*

Convolvulus tricolor,
mixed *(left)*

Convolvulus
cneorum *(below left)*
BUSH MORNING GLORY

This attractive plant from
Mediterranean Europe
has crowded, weak,
upcurving stems sprout-
ing from the base to
1–2 ft (0.3–0.6 m). The
leaves, in tufts along
the stems, are soft and
narrow with a coating of
silky hairs, giving them a
silvery sheen. The stems
terminate in dense clus-
ters of silky buds, each
producing a long succes-
sion of flowers through
spring and summer,
flesh pink in bud open-
ing pure dazzling white
with a small yellow 'eye'.
ZONES 8–10.

C

COREOPSIS

These 80 species of annuals and perennials from cooler or drier regions of the Americas make up this genus of the daisy family. The flowerheads, borne on slender stems mainly in summer, are mostly shades of gold or yellow, some bicolored. Leaves vary from simple, narrow and toothed, to deeply divided. They may be basal or scattered up the stems. *Coreopsis rosea* 'American Queen' is a popular cultivar.

Coreopsis rosea
'American Queen' *(above)*

Coreopsis auriculata
'Nana' *(below)*

CULTIVATION

The annuals are grown as bedding plants, while the perennials are excellent for herbaceous borders. Perennials prefer full sun and a fertile, well-drained soil but also grow well in coastal regions and in poor, stony soil. Propagate by dividing old clumps in winter or spring, or by spring cuttings. Annuals also prefer full sun and a fertile, well-drained soil; they will not tolerate heavy clay soil. Stake tall varieties. Propagate from seed in spring or autumn.

Coreopsis auriculata

This is a frost-hardy but short-lived perennial from southeastern USA that will grow to a height of 18 in (45 cm). The flowerheads are a rich yellow, produced through summer. The leaves are oval or lance-shaped. There are several improved forms, such as **'Perry's Variety'**, which has semi-double flowers. **'Nana'** is a compact form growing to 6 in (15 cm) tall. **ZONES 4–9**.

Coreopsis grandiflora

(below right)

TICKSEED

Among the easiest of perennials, this golden yellow daisy from southeastern and central USA provides color from late spring to mid-summer. Somewhat hairy leaves and stems form a loose mound to 12–24 in (30–60 cm) tall and wide, the flower stems rising to nearly 24 in (60 cm) or usually flopping on their neighbors. Best suited to a meadow garden, it can be treated as an annual and self-seeds freely. More compact cultivars such as **'Badengold'**, **'Sunray'** or **'Early Sunrise'** are the best choices for the well-maintained border. **ZONES 6–10**.

C

Coreopsis verticillata

This perennial produces crowded erect stems to 30 in (75 cm) tall from a tangled mass of thin rhizomes. The leaves, in whorls of 3, are divided into very narrow segments. The abundant bright yellow flowerheads appear from late spring until autumn. It does best in light soil of low fertility. **'Moonbeam'** is slightly lower and more compact with lemon yellow blooms. ZONES 6–10.

Coreopsis verticillata 'Moonbeam' *(above left)*

Coreopsis lanceolata 'Baby Sun' *(left)*

Coreopsis lanceolata *(below)*

This is a tufted perennial with long-stalked, lance-shaped basal leaves and bright golden yellow flowerheads on leafy stems up to about 24 in (60 cm) high. It is extremely floriferous and when mass planted can make sheets of gold in spring and early summer. Short lived, it is very free-seeding, and is a weed in parts of Australia. Double forms are sometimes grown. **'Baby Sun'** is a compact long blooming cultivar about 12 in (30 cm) high; suitable for bedding. ZONES 3–11.

Coreopsis tinctoria *(left)*
TICKSEED, PLAINS COREOPSIS, CALLIOPSIS

This fast-growing, showy annual produces clusters of bright yellow flowerheads with red centers during summer and autumn. Of slender, weak habit, and 24–36 in (60–90 cm) tall, the plants tend to incline over and may need staking. It provides good cut flowers. ZONES 4–10.

CORONILLA
CROWN VETCH

A legume genus of 20 or so species of annuals, perennials and low, wiry shrubs, native to Europe, western Asia and northern Africa. They have pinnate leaves with small, thin or somewhat fleshy leaflets, and stalked umbels of small pea-flowers a little like some clover or medic flowers. Certain perennial and shrub species are grown as ornamentals, valued for their profuse flowers blooming over a long season, though not especially showy. *Coronilla* is Latin for 'little crown', referring to the neat circular umbels of some species.

CULTIVATION
They need full sun, moderately fertile, well-drained soil and protection from cold winds. Cut leggy plants back to the base in spring. Propagate from seed, cuttings, or division of rootstock.

Coronilla varia (below)
syn. *Securigera varia*
CROWN VETCH

A sprawling perennial from Europe, crown vetch has run wild in some parts of the USA. It can spread quite rapidly by a deep network of thin rhizomes, the weak leafy stems rising to about 24 in (60 cm) tall. The soft pinnate leaves resemble those of the true vetches (*Vicia*) and the clover-like heads of pink to lilac-pink flowers appear throughout summer. Not suited to a formal garden, it can be rather invasive, but makes a good soil-binding plant for a sunny bank, stopping erosion while slower plants take hold. Some botanists now place it in the genus *Securigera*. ZONES 6–10.

CORYDALIS

The 300 or so species in this genus, allied to the fumitories *(Fumaria)*, occur in temperate regions of the northern hemisphere. Mostly perennials, but with some annuals, their basal tufts of ferny, deeply dissected leaves spring from fleshy rhizomes or tubers. The smallish tubular flowers, with a short backward-pointing spur that may be curved, are usually in short spikes. They are mostly creams, yellows, pinks and purples, and a few have clear blue flowers.

CULTIVATION

The sun-loving species do well in rock gardens, while the shade lovers are best beneath border shrubs or in a woodland garden. Soil should be moist but well drained, and rich in humus for woodland species. Several, such as *Corydalis lutea,* self-seed freely in cracks between paving or on walls. Propagate from seed or by division.

Corydalis lutea *(left)*
YELLOW CORYDALIS

The most easily grown species, this native of Europe's southern Alps is widely naturalized in temperate climates around the world. A rhizomatous perennial, it makes broad clumps or mounds of fresh green foliage to 12 in (30 cm) high, and is dotted from spring to autumn with short sprays of soft yellow flowers. It will grow in many situations but often self-seeds in wall crevices or moist chinks in rockeries. In a woodland garden it makes an attractive ground cover. ZONES 6–10.

Corydalis flexuosa
(above)

This species forms a small clump of green foliage around 12 in (30 cm) tall. During late spring and early summer, short spikes of long-spurred, tubular, clear blue flowers, each about 1 in (25 mm) long, appear above the foliage. It requires a cool spot in part-shade and moist soil.
ZONES 5–9.

C

Corydalis solida (right)

FUMEWORT

This species from northern Europe and Asia is similar to *Corydalis cava* differing, as its name suggests, in having a solid, not hollow, tuber and stem base. Each 6–10 in (15–25 cm) erect stem has only 2 or 3 dissected leaves, one at the base, and terminates in a dense spike of pink to purplish red flowers in spring. It dies back in summer. The cultivar **'George Baker'** has rich salmon-red flowers. **ZONES 6–9.**

Corydalis wilsonii
(below)

This species from China forms low mounds of blue-green foliage to 8 in (20 cm) high and wide. Loose spikes of bright yellow flowers are borne in spring. **ZONES 7–9.**

C

Cosmos bipinnatus
cultivar *(left)*

Cosmos bipinnatus
(below far left)
COMMON COSMOS, MEXICAN ASTER

This feathery-leafed annual from Mexico and far southern USA reaches 5–6 ft (1.5–1.8 m) in height with showy daisy-like flowerheads in summer and autumn, in shades of pink, red, purple or white. Taller plants may need staking. Newer strains are usually more compact and can have double flowers and striped petals. 'Sea Shells' has usually pink, sometimes crimson or white flowerheads with edges of ray-florets curled into a tube. ZONES 8–11.

Cosmos atrosanguineus *(left)*
BLACK COSMOS, CHOCOLATE COSMOS

A tuberous-rooted, clump-forming perennial growing to 24 in (60 cm) in height and spread, the unusual black cosmos from Mexico has long-stalked, very dark maroon flowerheads that have a chocolate scent, most noticeable on warm days. It flowers from summer to autumn. The leaves are rather few-lobed and tinged dull purplish. It normally dies back in autumn and requires fairly dry soil if the rootstock is not to rot; alternatively the roots can be lifted and stored for the winter like dahlias. ZONES 8–10.

COSMOS
MEXICAN ASTER

This genus of 25 annuals and perennials allied to *Dahlia*, contains a couple of well-known garden flowers. They have erect but weak, leafy stems and the leaves are variously lobed or deeply and finely dissected. Flowerheads, on slender stalks that terminate branches, are daisy-like with showy, broad ray-florets surrounding a small disc; they range in color from white through pinks, yellows, oranges, reds and purples to deep maroon.

CULTIVATION

They are only moderately frost hardy and in cold climates need protection in winter. Seedlings should be planted out only after all danger of frost has passed. They require a sunny situation with protection from strong winds and will grow in any well-drained soil as long as it is not over-rich. Mulch with compost and water well in hot, dry weather. Propagate annuals from seed in spring or autumn, the perennials from basal cuttings in spring. Deadhead regularly, and in humid weather check for insect pests and mildew.

COSTUS
SPIRAL FLAG, SPIRAL GINGER

Belonging to the ginger family, this genus of clump-forming ever-green perennials consists of some 150 species scattered throughout the wet tropics, though concentrated mainly in tropical America and West Africa. The ginger-like leaves are arranged in an ascending spiral around the stem, and attractive terminal flowerheads with overlapping bracts, rather like a pine cone. The flowers which emerge between the bracts are orange, yellow, pink, red or white.

CULTIVATION
They are suitable for planting outdoors only in tropical or sub-tropical regions. In cooler climates they make showy indoor plants but require high humidity and a heated greenhouse or conservatory in winter. Grow in humus-rich soil in a well-lit position, but not direct sunlight. Propagate by division or from seed in spring. Plants grown indoors may be affected by red spider mite.

Costus speciosus
CREPE GINGER, SPIRAL GINGER

Of wide distribution in tropical Asia, this tall-growing species has short elliptic leaves running in a conspicuous spiral up the slender cane-like stems that are themselves gently twisted into a spiral, and up to 8 ft (2.4 m) tall. The large flowerheads consist of tightly overlapping green bracts tinged reddish, and white, sometimes pinkish flowers with yellow centers and petals like silky crêpe, emerging one or two at a time over much of the year. ZONES 11–12.

Costus speciosus
cultivar *(right)*

C

CRAMBE

This genus, related to *Brassica*, consists of 20 species of annuals and perennials, ranging in the wild from central Europe to central Asia, also in parts of Africa. They have large, cabbage-like basal leaves that are shallowly to very deeply lobed, and large panicles of small, 4-petalled white flowers with a somewhat cabbage-like smell. They are attractive to bees.

CULTIVATION

Mostly very frost hardy, they will grow in any well-drained soil and prefer an open, sunny position, although they will tolerate some shade. Propagation is by division in early spring or from seed sown in spring or autumn.

Crambe cordifolia
(below left & far left)
COLEWORT

From the Caucasus region, this very spectacular perennial has lobed leaves up to about 18 in (45 cm) long and almost as wide, forming a broad but untidy rosette. The stout, much-branched flowering stem bursts into a cloud of small, white, starry flowers, the whole measuring 4 ft (1.2 m) across with a total height of 6 ft (1.8 m). It is very deep rooted and will produce numerous offsets. **ZONES 6–9.**

Crambe maritima
(below left)
SEA KALE

Occurring wild along cooler European coast-lines, this robust small perennial forms a mound of broad bluish green or even purplish, cabbage-like leaves with curled and crisped margins. In late spring and summer it produces dense, erect panicles of honey-scented white flowers, as much as 2½ ft (75 cm) tall. The young leafy shoots are used as a green vegetable, often blanched to lessen the bitterness. **ZONES 5–9.**

Cryptanthus
zonatus *(right)*
ZEBRA PLANT

This species is pre-
sumed to be native to
Brazil but has not been
found in the wild. It
forms flattish rosettes of
rather irregular shape
and up to about 12 in
(30 cm) in diameter.
The attractive wavy-
edged leaves are dark
green to somewhat pur-
plish and banded cross-
wise with silvery gray or
pale brownish mark-
ings. In summer a clus-
ter of tubular white
flowers appears in the
center of each rosette.
'Zebrinus' has more
highly colored leaves
with a chocolate-brown
background color.
ZONES 10–12.

CRYPTANTHUS
EARTH STAR

One of the most distinctive and easily recognized genera of
bromeliads, *Cryptanthus* consists of 20 or more species of rosette-
forming perennials, all native to eastern Brazil where they reportedly
grow on the ground, though in cultivation they are quite happy
when treated as epiphytes. They have shortly creeping rhizomes
that branch into small, flat rosettes of star-like form, usually with a
small central funnel. The leaves have finely toothed, wavy edges
and in many species and cultivars are striped or barred with white
or red. Small white flowers emerge from the center of the rosettes.

CULTIVATION
They require similar growing conditions to most of the epiphytic
bromeliads, but their compact size makes them especially suitable as indoor plants. Ensure a position in weak sun or partial
shade, planting in a standard potting mix with some sphagnum
moss or peat added. All need protection from frost and like a
high level of humidity. They are susceptible to scale insect and
mealybug. Propagate from seed or offsets.

Cryptanthus bivittatus
'Pink Starlight' *(above)*

Cryptanthus
bivittatus *(top right)*

This species has not
been found in the wild
since its introduction to
cultivation. The rosette
is 12 in (30 cm) or more
across, the dark green
leaves each with longi-
tudinal yellow stripes
and very rippled edges.
Cryptanthus bivittatus
var. *atropurpureus* has
leaves suffused with red
and the stripes pale red,
turning purple in full
sun. **'Pink Starlight'**
has pinkish white leaves
with an olive green cen-
tral stripe. ZONES 10–12.

C

CTENANTHE

The ancient Greeks, it seems, could pronounce the 2 consonants that begin words such as this (*kteis*, comb; *anthos*, flower), but present-day English speakers normally pretend that the 'c' is not there. Around 15 species belong to this genus of tropical plants closely related to *Maranta* and *Calathea*, all but one of them native to Brazil (the exception is a native of Costa Rica). They are evergreen perennials or subshrubs with short rhizomes; the taller species produce forking, somewhat bamboo-like aerial stems with a single leaf at each node. The rather leathery, lance-shaped or almost oblong leaves are borne on slender stalks which broaden into sheathing bases. The flowers are borne in spikes with tightly overlapping bracts and are not showy.

CULTIVATION

Several species are widely grown as indoor foliage plants, or in frost-free climates they are easily grown outdoors in the shade of trees, protected from drying winds. Indoors they require bright to moderate light but direct sunlight may cause the leaves to curl. They need ample water during the growing season and dislike low humidity. Propagation is usually from basal offshoots.

Ctenanthe lubbersiana (left)
BAMBURANTA

Endemic to Brazil, this most commonly grown ctenanthe is a splendidly marked foliage plant, growing to 30 in (75 cm) with branching stems that spread laterally. The oblong green leaves are patterned in irregularly shaded bands of pale yellow-green, with pale green undersides. Small, white flowers on one-sided spikes are produced intermittently. ZONES 10–12.

Ctenanthe oppenheimiana (below left)

From Brazil, this widely grown species is normally about 18 in (45 cm) high but can grow taller under good conditions. Its 10–12 in (25–30 cm) long leaves are oblong and have a herringbone pattern of broad grayish bars on a dull green background, with dull red undersides. Most commonly grown is the cultivar **'Tricolor'** with irregular blotches of creamy yellow on its leaves; the red undersides give it a reddish glow from above. ZONES 10–12.

CYNOGLOSSUM

A genus of 55 species of annuals, biennials and perennials from most temperate regions of the world. All species are frost hardy and valued for their long flowering period. They are related to the common forget-me-not, which many resemble.

CULTIVATION

All species need a fertile but not over-rich soil; if over-nourished the plants tend to flop over. Propagation is from seed sown in autumn or spring or, in the case of perennial species, by division.

Cynoglossum amabile *(right)*
CHINESE FORGET-ME-NOT

This upright annual or biennial, growing to a height of about 20 in (50 cm) has dull green hairy lanceolate leaves and flowers in racemes, generally blue although white and pink forms can occur. Flowers are produced in spring and early summer. It self-seeds very readily. **'Firmament'** has pendulous sky blue flowers. ZONES 5–9.

Cynoglossum amabile
'Firmament' *(below)*

D

D

The following are the 10 main classification groups of Dahlia hybrids.

Single-flowered (Group 1): As the name of this group suggests, these hybrids have a single ring of ray petals (sometimes 2) with an open center. Most singles are small plants usually growing no more than 18 in (45 cm) high, so they are ideal for bedding and are often sold as seed strains. **'Yellow Hammer'** is a popular bedding variety with bronze foliage and rich yellow flowers. **'Schneekönigin'** has pure white flowers.

Dahlia, Group 1, 'Schneekönigin'
(left)

DAHLIA

This comparatively small genus of about 30 species from Mexico and Central America has had as much impact on gardens as almost any other group of herbaceous perennials. Of this number only 2 or 3 species were used to create the thousands of named varieties of the past and present. Progeny of *Dahlia coccinea* and *D. pinnata* originally formed the nucleus of the modern hybrid dahlias. Others are derived from forms of *D. hortensis* such as the popular cultivar 'Ellen Huston'. So many different flower forms have been developed that the hybrids are classified into about 10 different groups, determined by the size and type of their flowerheads. Some authorities suggest that there should be more, as group 10 consists of disparate classes as yet too small to give groupings of their own, known as the miscellaneous group. Most groups have small-, medium- and large-flowered subdivisions.

CULTIVATION

Dahlias are not particularly frost resistant so in cold climates the tubers are usually lifted each year and stored in a frost-free place to be split and replanted in spring. Most prefer a sunny, sheltered position in well-fertilized, well-drained soil. Feed monthly and water well when in flower. Increase flower size by pinching out the 2 buds alongside each center bud. All, apart from bedding forms, need staking. Propagate bedding forms from seed, others from seed, cuttings from tubers or by division.

Anemone-flowered (Group 2): This group includes fewer cultivars than most of the others. They have one or more rows of outer ray florets; instead of the yellow center, these tiny flowers have mutated into outward-pointing tubular florets.

Collarette (Group 3): This group, once again becoming popular, has a single row of 8 outer large florets which are usually flat and rounded at the tips. Then comes a row of shorter tubular, wavy florets often in a contrasting color and finally the normally yellow center.

Waterlily or nymphaea-flowered (Group 4): These fully double-flowered dahlias have slightly cupped petals that have a more than passing resemblance to their namesakes, the waterlilies. The overall effect is of a flattish flower. **'Cameo'** has white flowers with a cream base; **'Gerrie Hoek'** has pink waterlily flowers on strong stems and is popular as a cut flower. **'Emanuel Friediirkeit'** has bright red flowers.

Decorative (Group 5): This group are fully double-flowered dahlias with no central disc showing. The petals are more numerous and slightly twisted making the flower look fuller than the waterlily types. This group, which can produce some truly giant forms, may be subdivided into formal decoratives and informal ones. Informal decoratives have petals that are twisted or pointed and of an irregular arrangement. **'Hamari Gold'** is a giant decorative with golden-bronze flowers. **'Evening Mail'** is also a giant decorative. **'Majuba'** is a very free-flowering compact, medium-sized decorative dahlia bearing deep red blooms on strong stems. Large informal decorative types include **'Almand's Climax'** which has lavender blooms with paler tips; **'Alva's Supreme'** with yellow flowers; **'Golden Ballade'** with deep golden flowers and **'Suffolk Punch'** with rich purple flowers.

D

Dahlia, Group 4, 'Emanuel Friediirkeit' *(below)*   *Dahlia,* Group 4, 'Gerrie Hoek' *(above)*

Dahlia, Group 5, 'Golden Ballade' *(below left)*   *Dahlia,* Group 5, 'Majuba' *(below)*

Dahlia, Group 5, 'Suffolk Punch' *(above)*

Dahlia, Group 6, 'Rose Cupid' *(below)*

Ball (Group 6): As the name suggests these dahlias are full doubles and almost ball-shaped. Miniature, small, medium and large forms are available. **'Rose Cupid'** is a medium-sized ball dahlia with salmon pink blooms; **'Wotton Cupid'** is a dark pink miniature.

Pompon (Group 7): These are similar to ball dahlias but even more globose and usually not much more than 2 in (5 cm) across. They are sometimes called 'Drum Stick' dahlias. **'Buttercup'** is a yellow pompon form.

Cactus-flowered (Group 8): This group of fully double-flowered dahlias have long, narrow rolled petals giving the flowers a spidery look. This group can be divided further by size as well as into classes with straight petals, incurved petals or recurved petals. **'Hamari Bride'** is a medium-sized white form.

Semi-cactus (Group 9): As the name suggests this group is close to Group 8 but the petals are broader at the base and less rolled back at the edges. **'So Dainty'** is a miniature with golden bronze and apricot flowers; **'Brandaris'** is a medium form with soft orange and golden yellow flowers; **'Hayley Jane'** is a small form with purplish pink flowers and white bases; and **'Salmon Keene'** has large salmon pink to golden flowers. **'Danbarkeit'** has pale salmon pink flowers and **'Vulkan'** has orange-red.

Dahlia, Group 9, 'Brandaris' *(below left)*

Dahlia, Group 9, 'Dankbarkeit' *(below)*

Miscellaneous (Group 10): This category consists of small groups and unique forms of dahlias that do not fit into any of the above groups. If breeders increase the numbers in any of the forms in this category, they will probably be split off to form new groups. Under this heading can be found such forms as orchid types which are single with revolute petals: **'Giraffe'** with its banded yellow and bronze flowers is an example. The star dahlias are also single in appearance and produce very pointed, widely spaced petals. Peony-flowered dahlias, which are still kept as a separate group in some countries, usually have one or two rows of flat petals with a center which can be open or partly covered by small twisted petals; examples of this form include **'Bishop of Llandaff'** with its brilliant scarlet blooms above its beautiful deep burgundy leaves, **'Fascination'** with light pinkish purple flowers and dark bronze foliage, and **'Tally Ho'** with deep orange flowers and gray-green leaves, tinged with purple.

Dahlia, Group 9, **'Vulkan'** *(above)*

Dahlia, Group 10, **'Bishop of Llandaff'** *(right)*

Dahlia, Group 10, **'Tally Ho'** *(right)*

D

DARMERA
syn. Peltiphyllum

UMBRELLA PLANT, INDIAN RHUBARB

A genus of only one species, this is a herbaceous perennial with very large handsome leaves that follow the flowers in spring. The flowers, usually white or pink and in clusters on unbranched stems, are followed by attractive inedible fruit. It is native to northwestern California and southwestern Oregon.

CULTIVATION

As this plant comes from cool areas and damp to wet situations, it makes a good specimen in muddy banks and by streams. It is frost tolerant but not drought resistant. Propagation is by division or from seed.

Darmera peltata *(above & below)*
syn. ***Peltiphyllum peltatum***

This dramatic foliage plant can have leaves up to 24 in (60 cm) across on 6 ft (1.8 m) stalks. It bears attractive pink to white flowers in early spring. The dwarf form called **'Nana'** only grows to 12 in (30 cm). **ZONES 5–9.**

Datura innoxia
(right)
syn. *Datura meteloides*

Though sometimes classed with *Brugmansia*, this bushy perennial from Central America is in fact a true *Datura*. It has pink or white flowers, the latter resembling those of *Datura stramonium,* but it is less poisonous, as its specific name suggests. If grown as an annual it makes a bush just under 3 ft (1 m) tall. ZONES 9–11.

D

DATURA
ANGEL'S TRUMPET

The tropical and subtropical genera *Brugmansia* and *Datura* are closely related; the taller, woody species with pendulous flowers are now included in *Brugmansia*. The genus contains 8 species of annuals or short-lived perennials, grown for their large, handsome and usually fragrant flowers. They bloom throughout summer and are white, sometimes blotched with purple, yellow or violet-purple. The foliage has an unpleasant odor, and all parts of the plants are narcotic and poisonous.

CULTIVATION
They need full sun and fertile, moist but well-drained soil. Propagate from seed.

Datura stramonium *(right)*

JIMSON WEED, JAMESTOWN WEED, COMMON THORN APPLE

This American annual is a common weed in many countries. It grows to 6 ft (1.8 m) and its 3 in (8 cm) long trumpets, which are produced throughout summer and autumn, can be white or purple. ZONES 7–11.

D

DELPHINIUM

This genus contains 250 or so species native to mainly northern hemisphere temperate zones, with a few found in scattered, high-altitude areas of Africa. They range from attractive self-seeding annuals or dwarf alpine plants up to statuesque perennials that can exceed 8 ft (2.4 m) in height. Nearly all start growth as a tuft of long-stalked basal leaves, their blades divided into 3 to 7 radiating lobes or segments. The tufts elongate into erect, sometimes branched flowering stems that bear stalked, 5-petalled flowers each with a backward-pointing nectar spur. Garden delphiniums are mainly derived from *Delphinium elatum* and its hybrids. Recognized groups include the Belladonna, Elatum and Pacific hybrids. Many other hybrids are available. An example is *Delphinium* 'Polamacht'. The annual larkspurs have now been placed in the genus *Consolida*.

Delphinium elatum
(above)

Delphinium,
Belladonna Group
(below right)

These perennials
(*Delphinium elatum* ×
D. grandiflorum) have
an upright, loosely
branching form and
are frost-hardy. Their
widely-spaced blue or
white flowers, 1 in
(25 mm) or more wide,
are single or sometimes
semi-double and borne
on loose spikes up to
4 ft (1.2 m) tall. They
bloom in summer.
Propagate by division
or from basal cuttings
in spring. ZONES 3–9.

CULTIVATION

Very frost hardy, most like a cool to cold winter. They prefer full sun with shelter from strong winds, and well-drained, fertile soil with plenty of organic matter. Stake tall cultivars. Apply a liquid fertilizer at 2–3 weekly intervals. To maintain type, propagate from cuttings or by division though some species have been bred to come true from seed.

D

Delphinium, Pacific Hybrids

These short-lived perennials, usually grown as biennials, were bred in California with the main parent being the perennial *Delphinium elatum.* They are stately plants to 5 ft (1.5 m) or more in height with star-like single, semi-double or double flowers of mostly blue, purple or white, clustered on erect rigid spikes. Some of the named cultivars are: **'Astolat'**, a perennial with lavender-mauve flowers with dark eyes; **'Black Knight'**, with deep rich purple flowers with black eyes; **'Galahad'** has pure white flowers. **'Guinevere'** bears pale purple flowers with a pinkish tinge and white eyes; **'King Arthur'** has purple flowers with white eyes; and **'Summer Skies'** has pale sky blue flowers. ZONES 7–9.

Delphinium grandiflorum

syn. *Delphinium chinense*

BUTTERFLY DELPHINIUM, CHINESE DELPHINIUM

Native to China, Siberia, Japan and Mongolia, this tufted perennial grows to a height of 18 in (45 cm) and a spread of 12 in (30 cm), the leaf segments further divided into narrow lobes. Its large bright blue flowers, with the long spurs finely warted, bloom over a long period in summer. It is fully frost hardy. **'Azure Fairy'** has pale blue flowers; **'Blue Butterfly'** has bright blue flowers. ZONES 3–9.

Delphinium grandiflorum 'Blue Butterfly' *(above)*

Delphinium cardinale *(below)*

SCARLET LARKSPUR

This short-lived upright perennial to 6 ft (2 m) tall is native to California and Mexico. It has finely divided leaves and bears slender loose spikes of small, single red blooms with yellow centers in summer. Provide a rich, moist soil and a little shade. ZONES 8–9.

Delphinium, Pacific Hybrid 'Black Knight' *(below)*

D

Delphinium semibarbatum *(below)*
syn. *Delphinium zalil*

This short-lived, tuberous delphinium is indigenous to Iran and central Asia, where its flowers are used to dye silk. It is a rare plant of great beauty, producing spikes of sulfur yellow flowers with orange tips from spring to mid-summer. It grows to a height of 3 ft (1 m) with a 10 in (25 cm) spread. **ZONES 6–9.**

Delphinium
'Polamacht' *(above)*

Delphinium, Pacific Hybrid
'Galahad' *(below)*

Delphinium 'Tempelgong' *(right)*
syn. *Delphinium* 'Temple Gong'

This *Delphinium elatum* hybrid was raised by Foerster of Germany in 1936. It has deep-centered violet-blue flowers and grows 5–6 ft (1.5–1.8 m) tall. **ZONES 3–10.**

DIANELLA
FLAX LILY

This genus of small-flowered lilies is named after Diana, the ancient Roman goddess of hunting. It consists of 25 to 30 species of evergreen, clump-forming perennials from Australia, New Zealand and the Pacific Islands; they grow in woodlands and are delightful plants for a shaded place in a warm-temperate garden. They are mostly under 3 ft (1 m) tall and are alike in their long leaves and sprays of small, deep or bright blue flowers in spring and early summer. Long-lasting, bright blue berries follow the flowers.

CULTIVATION
They prefer sun or part-shade and a moderately fertile, humus-rich, well-drained, neutral to acidic soil. Propagate by division, or rooted offsets, or from seed in spring and autumn. They naturalize in mild climates.

Dianella caerulea
(right)
BLUE FLAX-LILY

The evergreen foliage of this species from eastern Australia arises in clumps from a creeping rhizome often with elongated, cane-like aerial stems. The grass-like leaves, up to 3 ft (1 m) long, have rough margins and the open panicles, up to 24 in (60 cm) tall, support small starry blue or, rarely, white flowers in spring and summer. These are followed in autumn by deep purple-blue berries which are sometimes more ornamental than the flowers. ZONES 9–11.

DIANTHUS
CARNATION, PINK

This large genus of some 300 species occurs mostly in Europe and Asia with one species in Arctic North America and a few in southern Africa. Most are rock garden or edging plants. Much hybridizing has bred pinks and carnations for specific purposes. Border Carnations, annuals or perennials up to 24 in (60 cm), are used in borders and for cut flowers. Perpetual-flowering Carnations are mainly grown in the open but may be grown under cover to produce unblemished blooms; these are often disbudded leaving only the top bud to develop. American Spray Carnations are treated like perpetuals except that no disbudding is carried out. Malmaison Carnations, now undergoing a revival in popularity, are so-called because of their supposed resemblance to the Bourbon rose 'Souvenir de la Malmaison'; highly perfumed, they are grown in the same way as the perpetuals but need more care. Other groups of hybrids for the garden and cutting are the Modern Pinks and the Old-fashioned Pinks. Finally comes the Alpine or Rock Pinks bred from alpine species and used mostly in rock gardens. In all groups, some cultivars are all the same color (self-colored), and others are flecked, picotee or laced; the latter two types have petals narrowly edged with a different color.

CULTIVATION
Ranging from fully to marginally frost hardy, *Dianthus* species like a sunny position, protection from strong winds, and well-drained, slightly alkaline soil. Stake taller varieties. Prune stems after flowering. Propagate perennials by layering or from cuttings in summer; annuals and biennials from seed in autumn or early spring. Watch for aphids, thrips and caterpillars, rust and virus infections.

Dianthus barbatus
(below)
SWEET WILLIAM

A slow-growing, frost-hardy perennial often treated as a biennial, sweet William self-sows readily and grows 18 in (45 cm) high and 6 in (15 cm) wide. The crowded, flattened heads of fragrant flowers range from white through pinks to carmine and crimson-purple and are often zoned in two tones. They flower in late spring and early summer and are ideal for massed planting. The dwarf cultivars, about 4 in (10 cm) tall, are usually treated as annuals. It has been crossed with Modern Pinks to produce a strain of hybrids, known as 'Sweet Wivelsfield'. ZONES 4–10.

Dianthus caryophyllus *(right)*

WILD CARNATION, CLOVE PINK

The wild carnation is a loosely tufted woody-based perennial species from the Mediterranean area with a history of cultivation dating back to classical times. It has pink-purple, pink or white flowers in summer, their perfume is sweet with a spicy overtone somewhat like cloves, and grows to about 30 in (75 cm) tall by 9 in (23 cm) wide or more. From this species have been raised over the years many varieties of Annual or Marguerite Carnations and the hardy Border Carnations, in addition to the modern Perpetual-flowering Carnations commonly grown for the cut-flower trade. ZONES 8–10.

Dianthus erinaceus

(right)

This attractive cushion-forming species from Turkey forms a lovely rock garden plant that will trail over the top of rocks. It rarely grows more than 2 in (5 cm) tall but can exceed 24 in (60 cm) in spread and its gray-green foliage is surprisingly prickly. The small single pink flowers are produced on short stems not much above the mat in summer. ZONES 7–9.

Dianthus chinensis

CHINESE PINK, INDIAN PINK

This popular annual, originally from China, has a short, tufted growth habit, and gray-green, lance-shaped leaves. In late spring and summer it bears masses of single or double, sweetly scented flowers in shades of pink, red, lavender and white. It is slow growing to a height and spread of 6–12 in (15–30 cm), and is frost hardy. **'Strawberry Parfait'** has single pink flowers, lightly fringed with deep red centers. ZONES 7–10.

Dianthus chinensis
'Strawberry Parfait' *(left)*

D

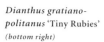

Dianthus gratiano-politanus 'Tiny Rubies'
(bottom right)

Dianthus giganteus
(below)

As its name implies this is a comparatively tall species reaching up to 3 ft (1 m) tall. It comes from the Balkan Peninsula. In summer it produces dense heads of purple-pink flowers. ZONES 5–9.

Dianthus gratianopolitanus *(above)*
syn. *Dianthus caesius*

CHEDDAR PINK

The English common name comes about because in the UK this species is only known from the limestone of Cheddar Gorge, but in fact it is widely distributed in continental Europe. It makes tidy mounds of blue-gray, linear leaves developing into broad mats 12 in (30 cm) or more wide. Delightfully fragrant, purplish pink blossoms with toothed ('pinked') petals are borne on 6–8 in (15–20 cm) wiry stems in spring; the flowers will often continue until frost. It requires a very well-drained, alkaline soil and full sun. **'Tiny Rubies'** is ideal as a neat compact ground cover. **'Tiny Tim'** has ½ in (12 mm), double, deep pink flowers on 4 in (10 cm) stems. ZONES 5–9.

Dianthus 'First Love' *(right)*

There are many annual strains of Pinks, some descended from the Chinese Pink, *Dianthus chinensis*, others from sweet William *(D. barbatus)*. **'First Love'**, a low grower at 6 in (15 cm), may be a cross between these groups. The fringed magenta and white flowers, often bicolored, are scented. ZONES 6–10.

Dianthus plumarius
(right)

GARDEN OR COTTAGE PINK

A loosely tufted, evergreen perennial with pale pink or white flowers with strongly fringed petals, this species grows 12–18 in (30–45 cm) high and spreads to 10 in (25 cm) across. A native of Europe, this is one of the main parents of the Old-fashioned Pinks and Modern Pinks. There are many named cultivars, bearing sprays of single or fully double, sweetly scented flowers in red, pink, purple-red, mauve and white. Many have fringed petals and a contrasting eye. ZONES 3–10.

Dianthus pavonius
(above)

syn. *Dianthus neglectus*

This is usually a tufted or mat-forming perennial to 6 in (15 cm) tall and up to 10 in (25 cm) across. It comes from the Alps of France and Italy. The flowers are usually solitary occasionally up to 3, pale pink with toothed petals. ZONES 4–9.

Dianthus superbus
(left)

Native to mountains in Europe and temperate Asia, this species is a loosely tufted perennial sometimes as much as 3 ft (1 m) high. Its leaves are mid-green and about 3 in (8 cm) long. The rich purple-pink fragrant flowers, produced singly or in pairs through summer, have petals deeply divided giving flowers a loosely fringed appearance. Seldom grown, it has been used in producing garden hybrids. It is better known as a parent of the Loveliness Strain which includes **'Rainbow Loveliness'**, with deeply fringed single flowers of mauve and pink shades carried on slender stems in spring. ZONES 4–10.

Dianthus superbus 'Rainbow Loveliness' *(above)*

D

Dianthus, Alpine Pinks

Also known as Rock Pinks, the cultivars of this hybrid group are compact plants forming mounds or mats of crowded fine leaves. The flowers come in many colors and shapes and are usually held 6–12 in (15–30 cm) above the foliage. **'La Bourboule'** (syn. 'La Bourbille') bears a profusion of single clove-scented pink flowers with fringed petals; **'Pike's Pink'** has gray-green foliage and rounded double pink flowers with a darker zone at the base; **'Nancy Colman'** is very similar but without the darker zone. ZONES 4–9.

Dianthus, Alpine Pink, *Dianthus,* Alpine Pink,
'Pike's Pink' *(left)* 'Nancy Colman' *(below)*

Dianthus, Ideal Series

These short-lived perennial hybrids between *Dianthus barbatus* and *D. chinensis,* are usually grown as annuals or biennials, flowering in the first season. They grow to 14 in (35 cm) and have bright green leaves. They bear clusters of fringed, 5-petalled flowers in shades of deep violet, purple, deep pink and red in summer. **'Ideal Violet'** has deep purple-pink flowers with paler margins. ZONES 5–10.

Dianthus, Ideal Series, *Dianthus,* Modern Pink,
'Ideal Violet' *(left)* 'Allwoodii' *(above)*

Dianthus, Modern Pink
cultivar *(right)*

Dianthus, Modern Pinks

These densely leaved, mound-forming perennials are derived from crosses between cultivars of *Dianthus plumarius* and *D. caryophyllus.* Early hybrids were called *D.* × *allwoodii,* but these hardly stand apart from the rest of the Modern Pinks now. Modern Pinks have gray-green foliage and many erect flowering stems, each carrying 4 to 6 fragrant, single to fully double flowers in shades of white, pink or crimson, often with dark centers and with plain or fringed petals. Most are 12–18 in (30–45 cm) tall, spreading 18 in (45 cm) and flowering from late spring until early autumn; some are clove-scented. **'Allwoodii'** bears fringed, pale purple-pink flowers with deep red central zones; **'Becky Robinson'** bears laced pink, clove-scented double blooms with ruby centers and margins; **'Dick Portman'** bears double crimson flowers with pink-ish cream centers and margins; **'Doris'** is a scented pale pink double with deep pink centers; **'Gran's Favourite'** is a sweetly scented, short-stemmed double, white with maroon centers and margins; **'Joy'** has semi-double carmine-pink flowers on strong upright stems; **'Laced Monarch'** bears deep pink to cerise double flowers with pale pink markings; **'Monica Wyatt'** has full double clove-scented pale pink flowers with dark centers; **'Valda Wyatt'** has clove-scented, rich pink double flowers with darker centers; and **'Warrior'** has double pink flowers with deep red centers and margins. ZONES 5–10.

Dianthus, Modern Pink, 'Dick Portman' *(above)*

Dianthus, Modern Pink, 'Doris' *(below)*

D

D

Dianthus, Modern
Pink, 'Laced Monarch'
(top)

Dianthus, Modern
Pink, 'Gran's Favourite'
(above left)

Dianthus, Modern
Pink, 'Joy' *(above)*

Dianthus, Modern
Pink, 'Warrior' *(left)*

Dianthus, Old-Fashioned Pink, 'Clare'
(above)

Dianthus, Old-Fashioned Pinks

These are tuft-forming perennials that grow to 18 in (45 cm) high. In late spring and early summer they bear single to fully double, clove-scented flowers to 2½ in (6 cm) across in colors varying from white, through pale pink and magenta to red, often fringed and with contrasting centers. **'Mrs Sinkins'** is a famous Old-fashioned Pink with pure white shaggy flowers prone to split at the calyx; it is highly perfumed. **'Pink Mrs Sinkins'** is a pale pink form of **'Mrs Sinkins'**. Other Old-fashioned Pinks include **'Clare'**, which produces bicolored clove-scented double pink fringed flowers with maroon centers, and **'Rose de Mai'**, which bears clove-scented single pink flowers with deep pink eyes. **ZONES 5–9.**

Dianthus, Old-Fashioned Pink, 'Mrs Sinkins' and 'Pink Mrs Sinkins' *(center)*

Dianthus, Old-Fashioned Pink, 'Rose de Mai' *(right)*

D

Dianthus, Perpetual-flowering Carnations

These popular flowers are marginally frost hardy perennials that reach at least 3 ft (1 m) high with a spread of 12 in (30 cm). Their stems will need support. Fully double flowers, usually fringed, are produced all year. Disbud large-flowered varieties; spray types produce about 5 flowers per stem and do not need disbudding. Cultivars include 'Charlotte' which bears cream flowers striped salmon pink; 'Malaga' has salmon pink flowers; 'Olivia' has salmon pink flowers with fringed petals; 'Raggio di Sole' has bright orange flowers with red specks; 'Sofia' bears white flowers with clear red stripes. ZONES 8–11.

Dianthus, Perpetual-flowering Carnation, 'Charlotte' *(above)*

Dianthus, P-fC, 'Malaga' *(above)*

Dianthus, P-fC , 'Olivia' *(above left)*

Dianthus, P-fC, 'Raggio di Sole' *(below)*

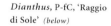

Dianthus, P-fC 'Sofia' *(above)*

DIASCIA
TWINSPUR

This genus of about 50 species of delicate but long-blooming perennials from South Africa is popular in rockeries, borders and as potted specimens. They bear terminal racemes of flat, generally pink flowers with double nectar spurs on the back, and have erect or prostrate stems with toothed, mid-green leaves. A number of attractive cultivars are available including 'Kelly's Eye', and 'Rose Queen', which is an excellent bedding plant.

CULTIVATION
Full sun is best, with afternoon shade in hot areas; most are frost hardy, but they dislike humidity. A fertile, moist but well-drained soil and regular summer watering are vital. Pinch out tips to increase bushiness and cut back old stems after flowering. Propagate from seed in autumn, or cuttings in autumn, to overwinter in a cool greenhouse.

Diascia barberae
(below)

This low-growing, rather fragile perennial has small, heart-shaped, pale green leaves; it bears clusters of twin-spurred, salmon pink flowers from spring to early autumn. It grows 6–12 in (15–30 cm) tall with a spread of 8 in (20 cm). **'Ruby Field'** bears salmon pink, wide-lipped flowers that are produced over a long period from summer to autumn. **ZONES 8–10.**

Diascia 'Rose Queen'
(above)

Diascia barberae
'Ruby Field' *(right)*

D

Diascia 'Rupert Lambert' *(left)*

This cultivar grows to about 10 in (25 cm) tall by 20 in (50 cm) wide and has narrow, shallowly toothed pointed leaves. The deep pink flowers with parallel spurs are produced during summer and autumn. **ZONES 8–10.**

Diascia 'Blackthorn Apricot' *(above)*

This is probably another selection from *Diascia barberae*. It grows to 16 in (25 cm) tall by at least 20 in (50 cm) wide and its apricot pink flowers, with downward-pointing spurs, are produced on loose spikes from summer well into autumn. **ZONES 8–10.**

Diascia fetcaniensis *(left)*
syn. *Diascia felthamii*

Indigenous to the Drakensburg Mountains, this fairly compact plant with ovate hairy leaves to 1 in (25 mm) long grows to a height of 12 in (30 cm) and spreads about 3–4 ft (1–1.2 m). It produces loose racemes of rose pink flowers with downward-curved spurs from summer well into autumn. **ZONES 8–10.**

Diascia stachyoides
(above)

Growing to 16 in (40 cm) tall, this perennial has slightly serrated leaves decreasing in size up the flower stems, which are sparsely clad in deep rose pink flowers in summer, their spurs pointing down and outwards. **ZONES 8–10.**

Diascia vigilis (right)
syn. *Diascia elegans*

A vigorous plant with a strongly stoloniferous habit, it grows to 20 in (50 cm) tall. The foliage is light green and glossy. It produces loose racemes of clear pink flowers from summer into early winter with incurved spurs. This is one of the most frost hardy and floriferous species.
ZONES 8–10.

D

Dicentra spectabilis *(left)*
BLEEDING HEART

This popular garden perennial grows 24–36 in (60–90 cm) tall with a spread of 18–24 in (45–60 cm). Pink and white heart-shaped flowers on long arching stems appear in late spring and summer. After flowering, the foliage usually dies down to the ground. **'Alba'** is a pure white form with green-yellow markings and pale green leaves that will grow true from seed. ZONES 2–9.

Dicentra formosa
WESTERN BLEEDING HEART

This spreading plant grows to about 18 in (45 cm) high with a spread of 12 in (30 cm). Dainty pink and red flowers appear on slender arching stems during spring and summer. **'Alba'** is a white-flowered form. ZONES 3–9.

Dicentra formosa
'Alba' *(below)*

DICENTRA
BLEEDING HEART

This genus consists of about 20 species of annuals and perennials much admired for their feathery leaves and the graceful carriage of their flowers, although they do not grow or flower well without a period of winter chill. The flowers, pendent and heart-shaped, come in red, pink, white, purple and yellow. They flower from mid-spring into early summer, though potted plants can be gently forced into early spring bloom if taken into a mildly warmed greenhouse at mid-winter. From Asia and North America, they are usually found in woodland and mountainous areas.

CULTIVATION
Mostly quite frost hardy, dicentras love humus-rich, moist but well-drained soil and some light shade. Propagate from seed in autumn or by division in late winter.

Dicentra spectabilis
'Alba' *(below left)*

Dicentra formosa
(below)

DICHORISANDRA

This genus of about 25 species from Central and South America is related to the common wandering Jew *(Tradescantia)*. The foliage of these soft-stemmed perennials may be glossy green or banded or striped with cream. The small cup-shaped flowers are purple or blue and are followed by fleshy orange fruits.

CULTIVATION

In warm-temperate climates they can be grown in well-drained, shady spots; however, they cannot survive frost and must be overwintered in a greenhouse in colder climates. They require adequate moisture at all times and high humidity in summer. Propagate by division in early spring or from cuttings in summer.

Dichorisandra reginae (below)

This soft-stemmed clump-forming perennial to 12 in (30 cm) high has erect stems and dark green leaves to 7 in (18 cm) long that are purplish beneath and are often flecked with silver. Small dense spikes of purple-blue flowers are produced from summer to autumn. ZONES 11–12.

D

Dichorisandra thyrsiflora (right)
BLUE GINGER, BRAZILIAN GINGER

The common name for this species is a misnomer, arising from its ginger-like stems covered in tightly sheathing leaf bases. This perennial has glossy, dark green leaves 12 in (30 cm) long that are spirally arranged along the upright stems. It produces dense terminal clusters of deep purple-blue flowers in autumn, and grows to a height of 8 ft (2.4 m) and spread of 3 ft (1 m). ZONES 10–12.

DICLIPTERA

This genus of the acanthus family consists of some 150 species of annuals, perennials, subshrubs or scrambling climbers. The simple, smooth-edged leaves are arranged in opposite pairs. The tubular flowers are in terminal or sometimes axillary clusters. They range in the wild through most tropical and subtropical regions of the world.

CULTIVATION
In frosty areas lift and store in greenhouses for the winter or take cuttings which can then be held over indoors until after spring frosts. Propagate from cuttings.

***Dicliptera
suberecta*** (left)
syns *Jacobinia
suberecta, Justicia
suberecta*

This is the only species commonly found in cultivation. It comes from Uruguay and makes a soft-wooded, sprawling perennial up to about 24 in (60 cm) and sometimes wider. Its stems and leaves are covered with velvety gray felt which makes a dramatic setting for the tubular orange-red flowers, which are pro-duced through late summer and autumn. It is a good pot plant and somewhat shade tolerant. **ZONES 8–11.**

D

Dictamnus albus
(right)
syn. *Dictamnus*
fraxinella

BURNING BUSH, DITTANY,
GAS PLANT

This herbaceous, woody-stemmed perennial bears early summer spikes of fragrant, star-shaped, white, pink or lilac flowers with long stamens. It grows to 3 ft (1.2 m) tall with a spread of 36 in (90 cm) and has glossy light green leaves. It is quite frost hardy. **Dictamnus albus var. purpureus** (syn. *D. a.* var. *rubra*) bears purple-pink flowers with purple veins. ZONES 3–9.

DICTAMNUS
BURNING BUSH

The Book of Exodus tells how God spoke to Moses on Mount Sinai from a bush that burned yet was not consumed by the fire. Theologians point out that since this was a miracle the species is irrelevant. Gardeners insist that it must have been *Dictamnus albus*, the only species in its genus and indeed indigenous to the Mediterranean and temperate Asia. In still, warm conditions so much aromatic oil evaporates from the leaves that if you strike a match near it the vapor ignites and the bush is engulfed in flame, but so briefly that it is not damaged.

CULTIVATION
This perennial needs full sun and fertile, well-drained soil. It resents disturbance. Propagate from fresh seed in summer.

D

Dierama pendulum
syn. *Dierama ensifolium*

This perennial from South Africa has flower stems up to 4 ft (1.2 m) high and grass-like leaves to 20 in (50 cm) or more long. The open bell-shaped flowers in shades of pink or magenta are produced on wiry pendulous stems in summer. **'Album'** produces white flowers. **ZONES 8–10.**

Dierama pendulum 'Album' *(left)*

DIERAMA

This genus of about 40 species of evergreen perennials of the iris family is indigenous to tropical Africa and South Africa. Growing from corms, the plants produce tufts of upright, grass-like leaves up to 3 ft (1 m) long, and fine wiry flower stems which bend like fishing rods under the weight of the flower clusters. These charming plants thrive and also look good near a pool or water feature. Several fine hybrid cultivars have been raised.

CULTIVATION
These warm-temperate plants demand a sheltered, sunny spot in cool areas, and rich, moist, well-drained soil. They are marginally frost hardy and dislike being disturbed. Propagate by corm division in spring, or from seed in spring and autumn.

DIETES
FORTNIGHT LILY

Native to southern Africa and to Lord Howe Island off eastern Australia, this genus contains 6 species of evergreen rhizomatous perennials that are grown for their attractive, iris-like flowers. The flowers usually last only for a day but new buds open over a long period in spring and summer. They have leathery, erect, sword-like leaves which form large clumps. In the past the species were included in the genus *Moraea*, from which they differ in being rhizomatous.

CULTIVATION

All species thrive in part-shade or full sun, and prefer humus-rich, well-drained soil that does not dry out too quickly. Marginally frost hardy, they are tough enough to serve as low hedges and, once established, self-seed readily. Propagate from seed in spring or autumn or by division in spring.

Dietes iridioides (above)
syns *Dietes vegeta, Moraea iridioides*

This species has branching, wiry stems that carry 2½–3 in (6–8 cm) wide, iris-like flowers that are white with central yellow marks. It grows to a height of 24 in (60 cm) and a spread of 12–24 in (30–60 cm), forming dense clumps of basal leaves in a spreading fan. Its preferred habitat is in semi-shade under tall, open trees. **ZONES 8–11.**

Dietes bicolor (left)
syn. *Moraea bicolor*

Sometimes called the Spanish iris, though it is neither an iris nor Spanish (it comes from South Africa), *Dietes bicolor* has pale green sword-shaped basal leaves and pale yellow flowers that appear from spring to summer. Each of the 3 larger petals has a central brown mark. It grows to around 3 ft (1 m) in height. **ZONES 9–11.**

D

Digitalis lanata (above)
GRECIAN FOXGLOVE

A clump-forming biennial or short-lived perennial, this subtle species produces flowers in mid- to late summer on stems up to 36 in (90 cm) tall. The flowers are strange but appealing: they are pale cream to fawn, finely veined with brown inside and a lighter cream lower lip. ZONES 4–9.

Digitalis grandiflora
syns *Digitalis ambigua*,
D. orientalis
YELLOW FOXGLOVE

A charming pale lemon-flowered foxglove, this species grows to 3 ft (1 m) when in flower from early to mid-summer and has rich green, prominently veined leaves. It can be a biennial or a short-lived perennial. **'Dwarf Temple Bells'** (syn. 'Temple Bells') is a smaller form but with larger pale yellow flowers. ZONES 4–9.

Digitalis grandiflora
'Dwarf Temple Bells' (right)

DIGITALIS
FOXGLOVE

Natives of Europe, northern Africa and western Asia, these 22 species of biennials and perennials, some of them evergreen, are grown for their tall spikes of tubular, 2-lipped flowers which come in many colors including magenta, purple, white, cream, yellow, pink and lavender. The leaves are simple, mid-green and entire or toothed. The medicinal properties of digitalis have been known since ancient times, and these plants are still used in the treatment of heart ailments.

CULTIVATION
Marginally frost hardy to fully frost hardy, they grow in most sheltered conditions, doing best in cool climates in part-shade and humus-rich, well-drained soil. Cut flowering stems down to the ground after spring flowering to encourage secondary spikes. Propagate from seed in autumn or by division; they self-seed readily.

Digitalis ferruginea (above)
RUSTY FOXGLOVE

A biennial or short-lived perennial, this robust plant can reach 4 ft (1.2 m) or so tall. The leaves are comparatively narrow and rich green. The trumpet-shaped flowers are golden brown with darker red-brown veins and are produced in summer. ZONES 7–10.

Digitalis lutea *(right)*

This foxglove is a 24 in (60 cm) tall, clump-forming, summer-flowering perennial from Europe. It is admired for its elegance and unusual color, which varies from almost white to canary yellow, and there are usually purple spots in the flowers' throats. It has hairless, glossy, dark green leaves and is sometimes cultivated for medicinal use. **ZONES 4–9.**

Digitalis purpurea f. *albiflora* *(above)*

Digitalis × mertonensis
(above center)

A hybrid of *Digitalis grandiflora* and *D. purpurea*, this frost-hardy perennial forms a clump about 3 ft (1 m) tall and 12 in (30 cm) wide. Summer flowering, it bears spikes of tubular, pink to salmon flowers above a rosette of soft, hairy, oval leaves. Divide after flowering. **ZONES 4–9.**

Digitalis purpurea *(right)*

This is the common foxglove, a short-lived, frost-hardy perennial with an upright habit, a height of 3–5 ft (1–1.5 m) and a spread of 24 in (60 cm). The flowers come in purple, pink, rosy magenta, white or pale yellow, above a rosette of rough, oval, deep green leaves. All parts of the plant, especially the leaves, are poisonous. Many seedling strains are available, grown as bedding annuals, the **Excelsior Hybrids** in mixed colors being very popular. *Digitalis purpurea* f. *albiflora* has pure white flowers sometimes lightly spotted brown inside; it will usually come true from seed especially if it is isolated from other colored forms. **ZONES 5–10.**

DIMORPHOTHECA

AFRICAN DAISY, CAPE MARIGOLD

These 7 species of annuals, perennials and evergreen subshrubs from South Africa have colorful, daisy-like flowers from late winter. Related to *Osteospermum*, they are useful for rock gardens and borders.

CULTIVATION

They need an open sunny situation and fertile, well-drained soil; they are salt tolerant. The flowers only open in sunshine. Prune lightly after flowering; deadheading prolongs flowering. Propagate annuals from seed in spring and perennials from cuttings in summer. Watch for fungal diseases in summer rainfall areas.

Dimorphotheca pluvialis (below) syn. *Dimorphotheca annua*

RAIN DAISY

This bedding annual produces small flowerheads in late winter and spring that are snow white above and purple beneath, with brownish purple centers. Low growing, it reaches 8–12 in (20–30 cm) in height with a similar spread. ZONES 8–10.

DIONAEA
VENUS FLYTRAP

This genus contains only one species, the best known of all carnivorous plants, though it is quite small. The rosettes of leaves
rarely exceed 8 in (20 cm) across, while the flower stems reach
about 12 in (30 cm) high; and the white, 5-petalled flowers are
about ½ in (12 mm) wide. Each leaf has 2 flattened lobes with
stiff spines along the margins. Minute glands secrete insect-
attracting nectar; when the insect alights, it stimulates 3 hairs on
each lobe, and the trap closes shut. The nectar digests the insect
by liquefying it. When only the hard bits are left, the leaf opens
and the remains are blown away.

CULTIVATION
Marginally frost hardy, grow in peat kept saturated by standing
the pot in a saucer of rainwater in full sun. Pinching out emerging flower stems and removing dead traps will encourage new
traps to grow. Feed plants tiny pieces of meat or cheese and
watch the flytrap in action. Without some animal protein,
it will not flower. Propagate from seed or leaf cuttings or by
division in spring.

Dionaea muscipula
(above)

This rosette-forming
perennial comes from
southeastern USA,
where it grows in mossy
bogs. The rounded
leaves are yellow-green
or red and have winged
stalks. Like so many
carnivorous plants, it is
very sensitive to pollu-
tion and is becoming
rare in the wild.
ZONES 8–10.

D

DIONYSIA

A genus of 42 species in the primula family from the arid mountains of southwestern and central Asia, these tufted or cushion-forming alpine plants, much admired by alpine plant enthusiasts, usually grow in moist shaded crevices. The flowers are tubular and flared out nearly flat at the end.

CULTIVATION

Only grown in climates with cool to cold winters and needing protection from excessive damp on the foliage, these plants are normally grown under cover in pots or in the hollows of tufa rocks. Make sure that the cushions are sitting up on a bed of coarse gravel to stop crown rot. Propagate from seed or by division.

Dionysia involucrata (above)

Considered to be relatively easy to grow, this species forms a dense cushion of rich green foliage from which are borne in early summer masses of violet to violet-purple flowers with white eyes that darken with age. ZONES 4–9.

DIPSACUS
TEASEL

Related to *Scabiosa*, this genus consists of 15 species of biennials and short-lived perennials from Europe, North Africa and temperate Asia. They have harsh bristly or prickly leaves arranged in opposite pairs on the strong stems, which branch into long-stalked, erect, barrel-shaped flowerheads. At the base of each flowerhead is a circle of long, springy, spine-like bracts. The small white, pink or purple flowers open progressively from the base of the head; an additional short springy bract accompanies each small flower. Apart from fuller's teasel, they are known as wildflowers or weeds. They are popular with landscape designers because of their statuesque habit.

CULTIVATION
Teasels are happy in well-drained garden soil of moderate fertility, in sun or light shade. They are frost hardy and will generally self-seed freely in the garden. Propagate from seed.

D

Dipsacus fullonum
(below)
syn. *Dipsacus sylvestris*
WILD TEASEL

Native to Europe and western Asia, this common wildflower is a prickly biennial up to 6 ft (1.8 m) tall, initially with a basal rosette of long, pointed leaves though these shrivel by the time the plant flowers; the stem leaves are shorter. The long-stalked flowerheads, borne mid- to late summer, are about 3 in (8 cm) long, with mauve-pink flowers emerging between small, curved, springy bracts which persist long after the flowers are gone. In more recent times *Dipsacus sativus* has been the species principally used for fulling—the dressing of cloth after it is woven. ZONES 4–10.

Dipsacus sativus *(above)*
syn. *Dipsacus fullonum* subsp. *sativus*
FULLER'S TEASEL

This biennial species is known only as a cultivated plant, though botanists now believe it may be derived from the wild Mediterranean species *Dipsacus ferox*. It is similar in most respects to *D. fullonum* but the small bracts that cover the flowerheads are shorter and broader and slightly hooked at the apex—it is the dried heads of this teasel, gathered after flowering, that are used to 'card' woollen cloth, the springy hooks raising the nap as the cloth is dragged past. It is also grown as a curiosity and for dried flowers. ZONES 5–10.

D

DISPORUM
FAIRY BELLS

Disporum is a genus of between 10 and 20 species of elegant and attractive woodland plants related to and similar to Solomon's seal *(Polygonatum)*. Species are native to the USA, eastern Asia and the Himalayas. They have creeping rhizomes that can travel some distance but they are not invasive. The arching stems are often slightly branched and clothed with attractive alternating leaves. The flowers are bell-shaped and hang under the stems. They can be white to green-yellow.

CULTIVATION
As these are woodland plants give them a cool part-shaded position with ample organic material like leafmold. They are definitely not for tropical or arid zones. Propagate from seed or by division.

Disporum flavens (above)

This Korean woodland perennial grows in neat clumps to 30 in (75 cm) high by 12 in (30 cm) across. It has attractive lance-shaped leaves and in early spring will produce up to 3 drooping soft yellow flowers per stem. These are followed in autumn by small black berries. ZONES 5–9.

Disporum smilacinum (left)

Also from Korea as well as Japan, this species grows to about 16 in (40 cm) tall and will spread to at least 12 in (30 cm) wide. It is sparsely branched with oval and oblong-shaped leaves to 3 in (7 cm) long. It produces one or two drooping cup-shaped white flowers per stem in mid- to late spring. ZONES 5–9.

DODECATHEON
SHOOTING STAR

The shooting stars (about 14 species) are western North America's equivalent to Europe's cyclamens and, like them, they are perennials and cousins of the primrose. Most are rosette-forming and grow to about 15 in (38 cm) high, with pink or white flower clusters. They have swept-back petals and protruding stamens.

CULTIVATION
Fully frost hardy, they prefer part-shade in moist, well-drained acidic soil. Most require a dry dormant summer period after flowering. They resent disturbance. Propagate from seed in autumn or by division in winter.

Dodecatheon pulchellum
'Red Wings' *(right)*

Dodecatheon pulchellum
syns *Dodecatheon amethystinum,*
D. pauciflorum, D. radicatum

Native to the mountains of western North America, this clump-forming perennial has mid-green 8 in (20 cm) long leaves in rosettes and produces up to 30 deep cerise to lilac flowers per stem. White forms are known as well as a form named **'Red Wings'** which has magenta-pink flowers on strong stems in late spring and early summer. ZONES 4–9.

Dodecatheon jeffreyi *(below right)*
SIERRA SHOOTING STAR

Occurring from California to Alaska, this plant grows to about 18 in (45 cm) tall. Its flower spike is topped with many red-purple flowers with deep purple stamens. Its leaves are slightly sticky and about 12 in (30 cm) long. ZONES 5–9.

Dodecatheon meadia *(right)*

From eastern North America, this is the best-known species, bearing white, rose pink or cyclamen pink, nodding flowers. It has primula-like, clumped rosettes of pale green leaves, and ranges from 6–18 in (15–45 cm) high with a spread of 18 in (45 cm). It was named for the English scientist Richard Mead (1673–1754), a patron of Ameri-can botanical studies. ZONES 3–9.

D

Doronicum orientale 'Magnificum' (left)

This clump-forming perennial grows to about 20 in (50 cm) tall and has bright green ovate leaves. The flowers, up to 2 in (5 cm) across, are produced in mid- to late spring. This cultivar apparently comes true from seed. ZONES 4–9.

Doronicum columnae 'Miss Mason' (below left)

This is a large-flowered selection with blooms about 3 in (8 cm) across in mid- to late spring. Its bright yellow daisies are held well above its heart-shaped leaves on stems up to 24 in (60 cm) tall. ZONES 5–9.

DORONICUM
LEOPARD'S BANE

The 35 species of herbaceous perennials that make up this genus extend from Europe through western Asia to Siberia. Species are grown for their attractive, bright yellow daisy-like flowers which are produced in spring and summer above fresh bright green foliage. Most species make attractive border plants of restrained habit and are also good as cut flowers.

CULTIVATION

Doronicums will cope with a range of habitats, but for best results give them a moisture-retentive but not wet soil, high in humus; part-shade or morning sun is preferred but never heavy dark shade. Propagate from seed or by division.

Doronicum pardalianches (above)
syn. Doronicum cordatum
LEOPARD'S BANE

Doronicum pardalianches is a spreading, clump-forming perennial to 3 ft (1 m) tall and wide. The oval basal leaves, to 5 in (12 cm) long, have heart-shaped bases. Bright yellow daisy-like flowers are borne on slender, branching stems from late spring to mid-summer. ZONES 5–9.

Dorotheanthus
bellidiformis (below)

ICE PLANT, LIVINGSTONE DAISY,
BOKBAAI VYGIE

This small succulent
annual has daisy-like
flowerheads in dazzling
shades of yellow, white,
red or pink in summer
sun, although the
flowers close in dull
weather. It grows to 6 in
(15 cm) tall and spreads
to 12 in (30 cm), and
has fleshy light green
leaves to 3 in (7 cm)
long with glistening sur-
face cells. **ZONES 9–11.**

DOROTHEANTHUS

ICE PLANT, LIVINGSTONE DAISY

A genus of about 10 species of succulent
annuals from South Africa, these mat-
forming plants bear masses of daisy-like
flowers in bright shades of red, pink, white
or bicolored with dark centers in summer.
Ideal for borders and massed displays.

CULTIVATION

Marginally frost hardy, grow in well-
drained soil in a sunny position.
Deadhead to improve appearance and prolong flowering. In frost-prone areas plant
out once the danger of frost has passed.
Propagate from seed.

D

D

DORYANTHES

The 2 species of *Doryanthes* are large evergreen perennials indigenous to the east coast of Australia. Somewhat resembling agaves in growth habit, they have loose rosettes of sword-shaped leaves and bear large red flowers with spreading petals, at the end of very tall stalks. The nectar attracts birds. Although requiring up to 10 years to bloom, they are popular in warm climates.

CULTIVATION
Frost tender, they do best in full sun or part-shade in warm, frost-free conditions in light, humus-rich, well-drained soil. Water well during the growing season. Propagate from seed or by division.

Doryanthes excelsa
(left)

GYMEA LILY

The larger and more common of the 2 species, *Doryanthes excelsa* is one of the largest lilies in the world. The large rounded head of deep red, torch-like flowers is borne terminally on a stem that can reach 20 ft (6 m) tall, arising from a rosette of sword-shaped leaves that can spread to about 8 ft (2.4 m) wide. It makes a spectacular feature plant for a large garden. **ZONES 9–11.**

Doryanthes palmeri *(above)*

This species forms a dense rosette of lance-shaped, bright green leaves up to 10 ft (3 m) long. The flower stalk, up to 18 ft (5 m) tall, carries numerous scarlet, funnel-shaped flowers with white throats. They are arranged along the upper part of the stalk and appear in spring. **ZONES 9–11.**

Draba
sachalinensis (right)

From the far northeast of Asia, this is a tufted perennial with velvety mid-green obovate to spoon-shaped leaves. Its small white flowers are borne in dense racemes up to 8 in (20 cm) tall. **ZONES 5–9.**

D

DRABA

Draba is a mainly Arctic and alpine genus of perennial or occasionally annual tufted or cushion plants. There are about 300 species and they range through the northern temperate regions as well as some of the mountains of South America. Some of the very tight cushion-forming species are much prized by alpine plant enthusiasts.

CULTIVATION
Most are frost hardy but they do require ample light, good drainage and protection from winter wet. They are handsome plants in rock gardens, troughs or individually in shallow terracotta pots. Propagate from seed, cuttings or by careful division.

Draba aizoides (center)
YELLOW WHITLOW GRASS

A variable species native to the UK and the mountains of central and southern Europe, this tufted plant usually grows 4 in (10 cm) tall by 10 in (25 cm) wide. Its bright yellow flowers are borne in late spring. This is one of the most easily grown species. **ZONES 5–9.**

Draba rigida var. bryoides (right)
syn. *Draba bryoides*

From Turkey and Armenia this species makes tufts about 3 in (8 cm) each way. Its bright yellow flowers are produced on stems up to 4 in (10 cm) long. It forms tight rosettes of minute dark green leaves with inrolled margins. **ZONES 6–9.**

D

Dracocephalum forrestii *(left)*

This clump-forming perennial from western China grows 18 in (45 cm) tall by 12 in (30 cm) wide. Its stems are erect and densely leafy. It produces deep purple-blue flowers with a white hairy exterior from late summer until mid-autumn. **ZONES 4–9.**

DRACOCEPHALUM
DRAGON'S HEAD

Related to mints, this genus consists of 50 or more species mainly from temperate Asia but with a few native to Europe and North Africa and one to North America. *Nepeta* is its closest ally, but in general appearance *Dracocephalum* shows parallels with salvias. The common name is merely a translation of the botanical name (of Greek origin) and refers to a fancied resemblance of the flower to a miniature dragon's head. The plants include annuals and perennials and, like most other members of the mint family, have stems that are squarish in cross-section and leaves that are aromatic when crushed and are arranged in strictly opposite pairs. The stems terminate in whorls of 2-lipped flowers, mostly blues and purples, the upper lip hooded and the lower 3-lobed.

CULTIVATION
They are frost-hardy and easily cultivated in a temperate climate in reasonably fertile soil with ample moisture in spring and summer. A sunny but sheltered position suits them best. Propagate by division of established clumps.

DROSERA
SUNDEW, DAILY DEW

This genus of carnivorous perennials consists of around 100 species; more than half of these are indigenous to Australia, and the rest are widely distributed throughout the world. They usually grow in highly acidic, damp to wet soils. Sticky glandular hairs on the leaf surfaces attract and catch insects, closing over the prey and slowly absorbing its nutrients. The fork-leafed sundews are among the easiest to cultivate and include the very attractive 'Marston Dragon' with narrow green leaves glistening with red glandular hairs.

CULTIVATION

Due to their wide distribution, great differences in hardiness exist. Some species require heated greenhouse conditions if taken from their tropical home; others are very cold tolerant. Grow in damp to wet conditions in a nutrient-deficient mix of peat moss and sand. Most like plenty of light. Propagate from seed, by division or root cuttings.

D

Drosera aliciae
(below)

This is a South African species with a rosetting habit to 2 in (5 cm) across and dark green leaves with bright red glandular hairs. Flowers are pink and produced on fine stems up to 18 in (45 cm) tall. ZONES 9–11.

D

Drosera capensis
(left)

CAPE SUNDEW

This species grows to
6 in (15 cm) tall, with
small rosettes of narrow
linear leaves covered in
sensitive, red, glandular
hairs which secrete
fluid. In summer many
small, purple flowers
are produced on leafless
stems. Water only with
rainwater as it is very
sensitive to the impuri-
ties found in tapwater.
ZONES 9–11.

Drosera binata
(right)

FORKED SUNDEW

A native of southeastern
Australia, this erect
growing sundew has
once- or twice-forked
leaves to 24 in (60 cm)
long. They are pale
green to reddish and are
covered in glandular
hairs. Numerous white
or pink flowers are
borne on erect stems to
30 in (75 cm) tall from
spring to mid-autumn.
ZONES 9–11.

Drosera regia *(right)*

GIANT SUNDEW

As its common name and the specific epithet *regia* imply, this South African species is among the largest in the genus. It produces rosettes of strappy leaves up to 28 in (70 cm) long, wider in the center than the ends. Its flower stems are up to 28 in (70 cm) high and bear 1½ in (35 mm) wide, pale pink to purple flowers in summer. The species produces rhizomes, around 2 in (5 cm) long, that are usually at soil level and covered in dead foliage. **ZONES 9–11.**

Drosera 'Marston Dragon' *(below)*

Possibly a hybrid of *Drosera binata*, this cultivar is notable for its large size, up to 24 in (60 cm) wide, and the large number of traps it carries. Its stems bend down under the weight of the traps and sprawl over the ground. The young growth and the traps are tinted pinkish red. **ZONES 9–10.**

D

Drosera cuneifolia

(right)

This South African species has 1 in (25 mm) wide basal rosettes of foliage and small purple flowers on stems 2–10 in (5–25 cm) tall. The leaves are a rounded wedge shape with short stems and are edged with fine hairs. *Drosera cuneifolia* flowers in summer. **ZONES 9–11.**

DROSOPHYLLUM
PORTUGUESE SUNDEW

The sole species in this genus is a carnivorous perennial native to Portugal, southern Spain and Morocco. It traps its prey using sticky hairs that cover the foliage. These hairs then secrete a digestive solution. Its flowers appear in spring and summer and are quite showy, being held clear of the foliage.

CULTIVATION

Usually found in dry areas in the wild, in cultivation Portuguese sundew does best in well drained gritty soil with added leaf mold for humus. It can be grown in sun or partial shade and is among the simpler carnivorous plants to grow.

Drosophyllum lusitanicum
(below)

This native of Portugal, southern Spain and Morocco is a woody stemmed carnivorous perennial up to 12 in (30 cm) high. Its stems, which are sometimes branched are covered with old dry leaves that hang on long after they have died. When alive, the leaves are around 10 in (20 cm) long by just over 1 in (25 mm) wide. They are covered in sticky hairs that entrap insects that are then digested by a fluid excreted from the hairs. In spring and summer, branched stems carry sprays of bright yellow 5-petalled flowers up to 1 in (25 mm) wide. **ZONES 9–11.**

Dryas octopetala var.
argentea (above)

DRYAS
MOUNTAIN AVENS

A small genus of 3 species from alpine and
Arctic regions of the northern hemisphere,
Dryas species make dense mats of ever-
green foliage somewhat like tiny oak leaves; these often turn dark
bronze in winter. Although the foliage and stems hug the ground,
the showy flowers and seed heads sit up well above them.

CULTIVATION
Completely cold tolerant they may be less than satisfactory in
warm climates. They make attractive rock garden or ground
cover plants and are also useful between paving slabs. Grow in
full sun or part-shade in a well-drained, humus-rich soil.
Propagate from seed or cuttings.

Dryas octopetala
'Minor' *(right)*

Dryas octopetala
(above)

MOUNTAIN AVENS

This lovely European
alpine plant can make
evergreen mats up to
4 in (10 cm) tall in
flower with a spread
exceeding 3 ft (1 m).
It has dark green scal-
loped leaves to 1½ in
(4 cm) long. The pure
white flowers, 1½ in
(4 cm) across and with
a boss of golden sta-
mens in the center, are
produced in late spring
and early summer and
followed by equally
ornamental fluffy silver
seed heads. *Dryas
octopetala* var.
argentea (syn. *lanata*)
has felted leaves on
both sides; '**Minor**' has
smaller flowers and
leaves. ZONES 2–9.

D

DUCHESNEA
INDIAN STRAWBERRY, MOCK STRAWBERRY

There are 6 species of these perennial plants, closely related to and very similar in appearance to the true strawberries. The leaves are divided into 3 to 5 leaflets and the plant spreads vegetatively with long fine stolons that produce more rosettes. Native to eastern and southern Asia, they differ from strawberries in having yellow flowers instead of white flowers and the red fruits are dry and unpalatable.

CULTIVATION
These frost-hardy plants can be quite aggressive so they should be placed with care; they are probably best as ground covers in less cultivated parts of the garden. They prefer part-shade and are not really fussy about the soil. Propagate by division.

Duchesnea indica (above)
syns *Fragaria indica,*
Potentilla indica

A semi-evergreen trailing perennial, this species grows to a height of 4 in (10 cm) and multiplies rapidly by runners to an indefinite spread. It is useful as a ground cover and for bed edges, hanging baskets and pots. It has dark green leaves and bright, 1 in (25 mm) wide, yellow flowers from spring to early summer. Ornamental, strawberry-like small red fruits appear in late summer. ZONES 5–11.

DYMONDIA

A South African genus of one species, rather like a gazania in miniature, this mat-forming perennial is ideal for rock gardens, borders, edging and as a ground cover in warm gardens.

CULTIVATION

In frost-prone climates grow in hanging baskets and containers. In warmer areas plant in the rock garden or in paving crevices in well-drained, moderately fertile soil in full sun. Propagate from seed or by division.

D

Dymondia margaretae (below)

This prostrate ground-covering perennial will spread to 20 in (50 cm) in diameter. The linear dark green leaves to 2 in (5 cm) or less long have 2 or 3 teeth and silvery undersides. Very small bright yellow daisy-like flowerheads on very short stalks are produced in spring. ZONES 8–11.

E

E

Echinacea purpurea *(left)*
syn. *Rudbeckia purpurea*
PURPLE CONEFLOWER

This showy, summer-flowering perennial has dark green, lance-shaped leaves and large, daisy-like, rosy purple flowers with high, orange-brown central cones. The flowerheads, about 4 in (10 cm) wide, are borne singly on strong stems and are useful for cutting. Of upright habit, it grows to 4 ft (1.2 m) tall and spreads about 18 in (45 cm). **'Robert Bloom'** has dark pink flowers with orange-brown centers, while **'White Swan'** has large, pure white flowers with orange-brown centers. ZONES 3–10.

Echinacea pallida *(below left)*
PINK CONEFLOWER

This species is an upright perennial to 4 ft (1.2 m) differing from *Echinacea purpurea* in that its petals are longer and tend to hang down. The petal (ray floret) color is usually a pink-mauve, although purple and white forms are known. ZONES 5–9.

ECHINACEA
CONEFLOWER

The 9 coneflower species, all native to the USA, share their common name with their close cousins the rudbeckias. They are clump-forming plants with thick edible roots. The daisy-like flowerheads are usually mauve-pink or purple, with darker and paler garden forms available. The dried root and rhizome of *Echinacea angustifolia* and *E. purpurea* are used in herbal medicine and allegedly increase the body's resistance to infection.

CULTIVATION
Very frost hardy, these plants like full sun and fertile soil, and resent disturbance—divide them only to increase stock, otherwise leave them alone and mulch each spring. Deadhead regularly to prolong flowering. Propagate by division or from root cuttings from winter to early spring.

Echinops ritro (right)

This perennial is a useful plant for the herbaceous border, and its globe-like, spiky flowers can be cut and dried for winter decoration. It has large, deeply cut, prickly leaves with downy undersides, silvery white stems and round, thistle-like, purplish blue flowerheads in summer. Of upright habit, it grows 30 in (75 cm) tall and wide. ZONES 3–10.

E

ECHINOPS
GLOBE THISTLE

This genus, related to thistles, contains about 120 species of erect perennials, biennials and annuals. The perennials are most commonly grown in gardens. They are native to southern Europe, central Asia as well as some of the mountainous areas of tropical Africa. The cultivated species are considered bold, attractive additions to mixed or herbaceous borders and many are used in dried flower arrangements. The foliage is usually gray-green and thistle-like though usually not as spiny. The ball-shaped flowerheads can be blue, blue-gray or white, the rich blues being the most favored, and up to 2 in (5 cm) in diameter. Most cultivated species grow to 4 ft (1.2 m) or more.

Echinops bannaticus

Native to southeastern Europe, this perennial grows to 4 ft (1.2 m) tall and bears spherical, blue-toned flowers during mid- to late summer. It has downy stems and gray-green leaves up to 10 in (25 cm) long. **'Taplow Blue'** is taller and produces vivid blue flowers. ZONES 3–10.

CULTIVATION

These plants are usually fully frost hardy and heat tolerant, requiring nothing more than a sunny aspect with a well-drained soil of any quality. Like most herbaceous perennials, cut them to the ground in autumn or early winter. Propagate by division or from seed.

Echinops bannaticus 'Taplow Blue' (right)

ECHIUM

Indigenous to the Mediterranean, Canary Islands and Madeira in western Europe, the 40 or so species of annuals, perennials and shrubs in this genus are grown for their spectacular bright blue, purple or pink flowers that appear in late spring and summer. The hairy leaves form rosettes at the bases of the flowering stems. They look best in mixed borders. Ingestion of the plants can cause stomach upsets.

CULTIVATION

Very frost hardy to frost tender, *Echium* species require a dry climate, full sun and a light to medium, well-drained soil. They become unwieldy in soil that is too rich or damp. Prune gently after flowering to keep them compact. Coastal planting is ideal. Propagate from seed or cuttings in spring or summer. In mild climates they self-seed readily.

Echium plantagineum (top)
syn. *Echium lycopsis*

This annual or biennial to 24 in (60 cm) and native to warm, dry areas of Europe produces a basal rosette of bristly leaves up to 6 in (15 cm) long. The flower stems produced in late spring and summer form a panicle of rich blue-purple, occasionally red flowers. This is an attractive bedding plant but it tends to self-seed in dry climates; in southern Australia it has become a notorious weed known as Paterson's curse. **ZONES 9–10.**

Echium pininana (left)

Indigenous to La Palma in the Canary Islands, this biennial species bears striking tapered spires of funnel-shaped, lavender-blue flowers, soaring to 10 ft (3 m) or more in height. The leaves appear in the first year, the flowers the next, and after flowering the plant dies. **ZONES 9–10.**

Echium wildpretii
(right & below left)
syn. *Echium bourgaeanum*
TOWER OF JEWELS

A striking biennial from the
Canary Islands, this evergreen
plant makes a rosette of narrow, silvery leaves and, in its
second season, bears a single,
bold spike of small, funnel-
shaped, rich coral flowers. It
has an erect habit, growing to
6 ft (1.8 m) or more high and
about 24 in (60 cm) wide.
ZONES 9–10.

Echium vulgare *(right)*
VIPER'S BUGLOSS

This spectacular European
biennial to 3 ft (1 m) tall has
erect leafy stems. The funnel-
shaped flowers, borne in
spikes or panicles, are usually
a rich violet, although white
and pink forms exist. A dwarf
form is available with white,
blue, pink or purple flowers.
ZONES 7–10.

EICHHORNIA
WATER HYACINTH

This is a genus of 7 species of aquatic perennials native to tropical America. They form rosettes of stalked, broadly oval or heart-shaped leaves and terminal spikes of showy, funnel-shaped flowers. They grow floating in water, with no need to anchor their roots; a raft of connected plants can rapidly cover a large area of water, choking rivers and blocking sunlight to other marine life. Grow only where they can be controlled and never in open watercourses.

CULTIVATION
Reasonably frost hardy, they thrive in warm, slowly moving water in full sun. Propagate by division.

Eichhornia crassipes (above)

This species from South America spreads to around 18 in (45 cm). The pale violet flowers are marked with bright blue and gold, and occur in upright terminal spikes. The rounded, glossy green leaves are arranged in rosettes. Its cultivation is prohibited in most warmer countries. ZONES 9–12.

ELEGIA
CAPE REED

This genus consists of 32 species restricted to the Fynbos (a type of heath-like vegetation) region of southern Africa. Fynbos is typified by poor soils, wet periods and hot, dry, fire-prone seasons. In their native home, many species have been used as thatching and for making brooms. They are also becoming very popular in the florist trade as foliage; the strong, fine stems of *Elegia grandispicata* makes excellent accent foliage as does *E. persistens* with its terminal ochre-colored bracts. Some species can exceed 10 ft (3 m), although most are smaller. Most are soft rush-like plants that look good by ponds or among rocks. Some species may have weed potential in Mediterranean climates.

CULTIVATION
Most are sun-loving plants requiring nothing more than some moisture and good drainage in a frost-free climate. Cut back any old stems that are dying off. Propagate from seed or by division of young plants.

Elegia capensis
(above)
BESEMRIET, BERGBAMBOES

This is possibly the most attractive and one of the easiest species to grow. It has fluffy, branching, green stems that perform the function of leaves (the leaves are attractive bronze bracts that run up the stems at the nodes). These stems are usually about 5 ft (1.5 m) tall, although they can reach nearly 10 ft (3 m) under ideal conditions. Tiny brown flowers are produced at the ends of the stems. ZONES 9–10.

Elegia cuspidata
(left)
BLOMBIESIES

This species rarely exceeds 3 ft (1 m) tall. The sturdy upright stems support dense bronze flowerheads surrounded by papery brown bracts. ZONES 9–10.

E

ENSETE

At one time the 7 species of this remarkable genus of gigantic tropical herbs were included in the banana genus *Musa*, of which they are undoubtedly the closest relatives. They are native to tropical Africa and Asia and have a non-branching underground stem, which results in only a single, trunk-like false stem being produced. The flowering stem grows through the middle of the crown of large spreading leaves, to produce a pendulous spike of flowers half-hidden among large bracts. After the small banana-like fruits mature the whole plant dies. They make dramatic, yet short-lived ornamentals.

CULTIVATION

Frost-tender, they should be grown in full sun or part-shade in a rich, moist but well-drained soil and given shelter from winds. Propagate from seed in spring; germination can be erratic without the provision of a warm seed-bed.

Ensete ventricosum
(above)

ABYSSINIAN BANANA,
WILD BANANA

Native to tropical Africa, this large leafy perennial to 30 ft (9 m) tall has huge leaves up to 12 ft (3.5 m) long with a bright red midrib. In late spring, flowers surrounded by deep red bracts droop in spikes to 10 ft (3 m) long. The fruit are not edible. ZONES 10–12.

EPILOBIUM
syn. *Chamaenerion*

WILLOW HERB

This is a large genus of about 200 species of annuals, biennials, perennials and subshrubs in the evening primrose family, widely distributed throughout the temperate and cold zones of both hemispheres. Most species are invasive, but some are valued in cultivation for their pretty deep pink or white flowers produced over a long period from summer to autumn.

CULTIVATION
Plant in sun or shade in moist, well-drained soil. They are mostly quite frost hardy. Remove spent flowers to prevent seeding. Propagate from seed in spring or autumn, or from cuttings.

Epilobium angustifolium (below)
syn. *Chamaenerion angustifolium*

FIREWEED, ROSE BAY WILLOW HERB

This is a tall, vigorous perennial to 5 ft (1.5 m) found throughout the northern and mountainous parts of Eurasia and North America, most widespread in areas that have been recently burned or logged. Drifts of rose-pink flowering spikes are produced in late summer. It will spread indefinitely unless confined by pruning or containing the root system, and self-seeds freely. **ZONES 2–9.**

E

EPIMEDIUM
BARRENWORT

This genus of about 40 species comes mainly from temperate Asia with a few species extending to the Mediterranean. Among the most useful low-growing perennials for shady situations, the barrenworts produce elegant foliage. Sometimes evergreen, the compound leaves are composed of heart-shaped leaflets. Delightful sprays of delicate, often spurred flowers appear in late spring or early summer just above the foliage. Slowly spreading to form a broad mound or mat, they serve well as ground covers in open woodland or in the foreground of borders and rockeries. A number of cultivars are available. 'Enchantress' has large pale pink flowers and foliage that is copper-tinted when young.

CULTIVATION

Frost hardy, most are tolerant of dry conditions, especially in the shade. All prefer a woodland environment and well-drained soil. Old leaves are best cut back in early spring to display the new foliage and flowers. Propagate from ripe seed or by division in autumn.

Epimedium 'Enchantress' *(above)*

Epimedium alpinum *(below)*

An evergreen, low-growing perennial from southern Europe, this plant makes a good ground cover under azaleas and rhododendrons. The finely toothed, glossy leaves are bronze-red when young, turning to mid-green with age. In spring it bears racemes of pendent yellow and crimson flowers. It grows to a height of 10 in (25 cm) and spread of 12 in (30 cm). It prefers cooler climates. ZONES 5–9.

Epimedium grandiflorum
syn. *Epimedium macranthum*

BISHOP'S HAT, LONGSPUR EPIMEDIUM

This species from northern China, Korea and Japan is deciduous, except in mild climates. It has toothed leaflets often edged with red. Spidery pink or purple flowers with white spurs are held above the foliage on 12 in (30 cm) slender stems in spring. It is best displayed as a clump rather than as a ground cover. **'Rose Queen'** bears clusters of cup-shaped rose-pink flowers with long, white-tipped spurs. **'White Queen'** has large pure white flowers. ZONES 4–9.

Epimedium grandiflorum 'Rose Queen' *(above)*

Epimedium grandiflorum 'White Queen' *(right)*

Epimedium diphyllum *(right)*

From Japan, this dainty semi-evergreen plant to 12 in (30 cm) tall and wide has leaves divided into 2 leaflets. The small, bell-shaped, pure white, spurless flowers are borne in spring. Purple flowering forms are also known. ZONES 5–9.

E

Epimedium pinnatum
subsp. *colchicum* (below)

Epimedium pinnatum (left)

Native to northeastern Turkey, this carpeting perennial grows to about 12 in (30 cm) high and wide. The leaflets are 3 in (8 cm) long and are somewhat leathery, evergreen and with spiny edges. The bright yellow flowers with purplish brown spurs are produced in late spring and early summer. **Epimedium pinnatum** subsp. *colchicum,* the Persian epimedium, has showy panicles of larger, yellow flowers with short brown spurs. **ZONES 6–9.**

Epimedium × versicolor

This hybrid of *Epimedium grandiflorum* and *E. pinnatum* is the best known of the epimediums. It is a carpeting perennial to 12 in (30 cm) high and wide. The green, heart-shaped leaves are tinted reddish when young. Clusters of pendent, pink and yellow flowers with red spurs are produced in spring. **'Sulphureum'** has sulfur yellow flowers and reddish, bronze-tinted young foliage. As summer advances it turns green, then russet again in autumn. **ZONES 5–9.**

Epimedium × versicolor
'Sulphureum' (left)

Epimedium × *youngianum* (right)

This hybrid between *Epimedium diphyllum* and *E. grandiflorum* is possibly of wild origin. It forms attractive, neat clumps 18 in (45 cm) high and 30 in (75 cm) wide. The leaves can have up to 9 leaflets and are tinted red in spring and autumn. The flowers come in colors varying from white through to pink-mauve and may have spurs or may not. **'Niveum'** is a lovely, white-flowered form with bronze-tinged foliage in spring. **'Roseum'** (syn. 'Lilacinum') has soft pink-mauve flowers. ZONES 5–9.

Epimedium × *youngianum* 'Niveum' (right)

Epimedium × *youngianum* 'Roseum' (below)

EPISCIA

From the jungles of tropical America and the West Indies, the 6 species of this genus are related to the African violet and make ideal plants for hanging baskets. Long runners bear tufts of ornamental leaves, which are hairy and produced in whorls or rosettes; they cascade down the sides of the pot or basket, and given the right conditions produce long-lasting, colorful flowers. The flowers, either solitary or in small racemes, have 5 lobes and appear from spring to autumn.

CULTIVATION

Plant in African violet mix or porous, peaty, indoor plant mix, in bright indirect light. Poor light may result in few flowers. They require constant warmth and humidity, so are well suited to a sunny bathroom or conservatory. Keep moist at all times, but take care not to over-water as it leads to rotting. Pinch back stems after flowering to encourage branching, and repot every year in spring. Propagate in summer by laying runners in compost, from cuttings or by division.

Episcia dianthiflora
(left)
LACE FLOWER VINE

A native of Central America and Mexico, this evergreen, low-creeping perennial has rooting stems that provide an easy means of propagation. Its small leaves, to 2 in (5 cm) long, are dark green often with red veins. Its pure white flowers have purple spotting at the base and inside the spur. The edges of the petals are deeply and attractively fringed. ZONES 10–12.

Episcia cupreata
'Mosaica' *(above)*

Episcia cupreata
(top)
FLAME VIOLET

This evergreen creeping perennial, native to northern South America, grows to a height of about 6 in (15 cm). The attractive, felted, bronze leaves have silver veins. It intermittently produces tubular, scarlet flowers with yellow centers. 'Mosaica' has dark, almost black leaves with an embossed appearance. ZONES 10–12.

E

E

EQUISETUM
HORSETAIL, SCOUR RUSH

Some 25 species of rush-like perennials belong to this ancient group of plants, distantly related to the ferns. They occur mainly in the northern hemisphere although a few cross the Equator to Africa and South America. The cylindrical stems are usually erect and may be unbranched or have whorled branches at the nodes. They rarely exceed 10 ft (3 m) tall and grow from vigorous creeping rhizomes. Although quite ornamental, their use in gardens is limited because they can become invasive and are difficult to

eradicate. Horsetails have been used since Roman times to scour pots and medically as a general tonic and an astringent.

CULTIVATION
Most species are very frost hardy. Grow plants in containers and make sure the rhizomes don't escape out the drainage holes. Give them a sunny aspect and plenty of water. Propagation is usually by division.

Equisetum trachyodon (above)

This horsetail is unbranched. It makes an attractive potted specimen and needs shade during the hottest hours. ZONES 5–9.

Equisetum scirpoides (left)
DWARF SCOURING RUSH

This is a fairly small species to 6 in (15 cm) or so tall from Eurasia, Greenland and North America. Its stems are very fine and not usually branched, with 3, or rarely, 4 ridges. This is not a very ornamental species. ZONES 2–9.

Eremurus × isabellinus,
'Shelford Desert Candle' *(above)*

EREMURUS
FOXTAIL LILY, DESERT CANDLE

This is a genus of 50 or so species, all native to the cold, high plains of central and western Asia. Among the most dramatic of early summer perennials, they are mainly clump forming with a rosette of strap-shaped leaves. Their flower spikes, each of which can contain hundreds of flowers in pale shades of white, yellow or pink, rise to well over head height. The foliage is luxuriant but low, so the flower stems rise almost naked, which makes them all the more imposing.

CULTIVATION

In the wild these cool- to cold-climate plants are protected from the winter cold by a thick blanket of snow; in milder climates they must be given a winter mulch to ensure the soil does not freeze. The other requirements are sun, a well-drained soil and shelter from strong winds. Propagate from fresh seed in autumn or by careful division after flowering.

Eremurus × isabellinus, Shelford Hybrids

These frost-hardy perennials are grown for their lofty spikes of close-packed flowers, magnificent for floral displays. They produce rosettes of strap-like leaves and in mid-summer each crown yields spikes of blooms with strong stems and hundreds of shallow cup-shaped flowers in a wide range of colors including white, pink, salmon, yellow, apricot and coppery tones. **'Shelford Desert Candle'** is a particularly lovely pure white form. The plants grow to about 4 ft (1.2 m) in height with a spread of 24 in (60 cm). **ZONES 5–9.**

Eremurus × isabellinus,
Shelford Hybrid cultivar
(left)

Eremurus stenophyllus (right)

This species from southwestern or central Asia
has tufted basal leaves that are gray-green in
color. The flowers are bright yellow and produced
on spikes up to 3 ft (1 m) tall. **ZONES 5–9.**

Eremurus robustus (above)

The tallest of the foxtail
lilies, this upright per-
ennial from central
Asia flowers profusely
in early summer. The
individual flowers are
smallish stars in palest
peach-pink and are
produced by the hun-
dreds in spires that can
reach nearly 10 ft (3 m)
in height. They need to
be staked. **ZONES 6–9.**

Eremurus spectabilis (right)

This is a tufted perennial
with strap-like, rough-
margined, gray-green
leaves. In mid-summer
it sends up rigid spikes
of sulfur-yellow flowers
to 4–6 ft (1.2–1.8 m).
The individual blooms
are star-shaped and
½ in (12 mm) across.
This species ranges
from Turkey to
Pakistan. **ZONES 6–9.**

ERIGERON

FLEABANE

This large genus of about 200 species of annuals, biennials and perennials, some evergreen, occurs throughout temperate regions of the world but predominantly in North America. Some species were believed to repel fleas. The mainly erect stems are capped by masses of pink, white or blue, daisy-like flowers and are well suited to the front of a mixed herbaceous border or rock garden. They flower between late spring and mid-summer. There are many garden forms; **Wayne Roderick** is but one example.

Erigeron 'Wayne Roderick' *(above)*

CULTIVATION

Frost hardy, they prefer a sunny position sheltered from strong winds and moderately fertile, well-drained soil. Do not allow to dry out during the growing season. Cut back immediately after flowering to encourage compact growth and prevent unwanted self-seeding. Some erigerons can become invasive. Propagate from seed or by division in spring.

Erigeron aureus 'Canary Bird' *(below)*

Erigeron aureus

The wild forms of *Erigeron aureus* are short-lived perennials from the mountains of western North America. The selected form **'Canary Bird'** is a much longer lived plant that grows to 4 in (10 cm) tall in flower. Its flowers are soft to bright yellow and are held singly on stems above its spoon-shaped, hairy, gray-green leaves. ZONES 5–9.

Erigeron 'Charity' *(above)*

This perennial cultivar produces a profusion of
pale lilac-pink flowers with yellowy green centers
over a long period in summer. Clump forming,
it grows to a height and spread of about 24 in
(60 cm) and may require support. **ZONES 5–9.**

Erigeron compositus *(right)*

This tufted perennial
to 6 in (15 cm) tall is
native to Greenland
and western North
America. It has rosettes
of hairy leaves that may
be lobed or dissected.
Its summer flowers can
be white, pink, lilac or
blue with a yellow
center. **ZONES 5–9.**

E

Erigeron foliosus
(left)

This clump-forming species grows to about 8 in (20 cm) in flower and comes from western North America. Its leaves are narrow-oblong and reduce in size up the stem. The flowers are usually blue with a yellow center. ZONES 5–9.

Erigeron formosissimus *(left)*

This clumping perennial from the southern Rocky Mountains has usually basal leaves that vary somewhat in shape. Its daisy flowers can be blue or pink or, rarely, white. ZONES 6–9.

Erigeron 'Dunkelste Aller' *(left)*

'Dunkelste Aller' ('Darkest of All') is a clump-forming perennial reaching a height of 24 in (60 cm) and spread of 18 in (45 cm). It produces semi-double, deep purple flowers with yellow centers in summer and has lance-shaped, grayish green leaves. ZONES 5–9.

Erigeron glaucus 'Cape Sebastian' *(right)*

Erigeron glaucus *(below)*
SEASIDE DAISY, BEACH ASTER

This clump-forming perennial grows to about 10 in (25 cm) in height with a spread of about 8 in (20 cm). The spoon-shaped leaves are glaucous. Lilac-pink flowers are borne in summer. **'Cape Sebastian'** has compact growth and flowers profusely. ZONES 3–10.

Erigeron 'Strahlenmeer' *(below)*
syn. *Erigeron* 'Shining Sea'

Usually regarded as a cultivar of *Erigeron speciosus*, though possibly a hybrid, this German-raised perennial grows to around 28 in (70 cm) high and has soft violet flowers. Its foliage is the same as that of *E. speciosus*: clumped spatula-shaped basal leaves up to 6 in (15 cm) long with smaller leaves on the lower parts of the flower stems. ZONES 3–9.

ERINUS
ALPINE BALSAM, FAIRY FOXGLOVE

This genus contains 2 species of semi-evergreen, small-growing perennials from northern Africa and southern and central Europe. Only one species, *Erinus alpinus*, is usually found in cultivation. They rarely exceed 3 in (8 cm) tall and 4 in (10 cm) wide so make attractive little tufting plants for a sunny rock garden or between paving slabs.

CULTIVATION
Very frost hardy, grow in a sunny or part-shaded, well-drained site and provide adequate water during summer. Although short lived, they will often self-seed into cracks and gaps helping to soften edges. Propagate from seed in autumn.

Erinus alpinus
(above)

This species is native to the European Alps and is ideal for planting in wall crevices and rock gardens. It forms rosettes of soft, medium green leaves and bears a profusion of starry, rosy purple or white flowers in late spring and summer. It grows to 2–3 in (5–8 cm) in height and spread.
ZONES 6–9.

ERIOGONUM
WILD BUCKWHEAT, UMBRELLA PLANT

This is a large genus of the polygonum family, of some 150 species native to North America, mainly the western side. They may be annuals, perennials or small shrubs often with silvery or white leaves. Some of the smaller ones are ideal rock garden plants and many of the taller species make good cut flowers, both fresh and dried. The long-lasting flowers are small but are produced in clusters surrounded by attractive toothed or lobed bracts. Most come from mountain habitats or alkaline desert areas.

CULTIVATION
Due to the wide distribution of the genus their frost tolerance varies, but all like a sunny, well-drained site. If kept dry in winter they will stand more cold than if damp. Cut back immediately after flowering unless seed is required. Propagate from seed in spring or autumn or by careful division in spring or early summer.

Eriogonum nervulosum *(above)*
SNOW MOUNTAIN BUCKWHEAT

This spreading, mat-forming species to about 4–6 in (10–15 cm) tall has small, obovate, fleshy leaves. Tight, hemispherical heads of pale yellow to reddish flowers are produced atop short, leafless stems. This is an unusual ground cover for gravelly soil. **ZONES 8–10.**

Eriogonum umbellatum *(below)*
SULFUR BUCKWHEAT

This woody-based perennial from the Rocky Mountains in British Columbia is grown for its attractive heads of tiny, bright yellow flowers borne in summer and turning copper with age. It is a useful rock garden plant, growing to a height of 12 in (30 cm) and a spread of 24 in (60 cm). It has a prostrate to upright form and the dense green leaves have white, downy undersides. In cooler, wetter areas some shelter is required. *Erigonum umbellatum* var. *subalpinum* has creamy yellow flowers that turn dull mauve with age. **ZONES 6–9.**

E

Eriophyllum lanatum (left)
WOOLLY SUNFLOWER

This charming, brilliant yellow daisy from northwestern North America grows up to 24 in (60 cm) tall. It has erect to spreading stems clothed in white-felted, silvery leaves. The basal leaves are usually entire with the leaves decreasing in size and often becoming dissected as they go up the stems. The flowerheads can be up to 1½ in (35 mm) across and are produced in late spring and summer. **ZONES 5–9.**

ERIOPHYLLUM

This genus of 11 species of yellow-flowered, herbaceous perennials from western North America belongs to the sunflower tribe of the daisy (or Compositae) family. The genus name, latinized Greek for 'woolly leaf', refers to the whitish coating of felty hairs that is a conspicuous feature of the foliage of most species. Stems branch from the base and can form a dense clump, and the narrow leaves, often with toothed margins, are arranged on them in opposite pairs. The long-stalked flowerheads grow terminally on the branches, and both ray florets and disc florets are bright golden yellow.

CULTIVATION
Frost hardy, they like moderately fertile, very well-drained soil and a sunny position and may be short lived in climates with warm, wet summers. Propagate from seed or by division.

Erodium chrysanthum *(left)*

This Greek tufted perennial grows to about 6 in (15 cm) tall and up to 15 in (38 cm) wide. It has soft, silvery green, dissected foliage and produces its soft creamy yellow to sulfur-yellow flowers throughout summer. It is a lovely plant for a sunny rock garden. ZONES 6–9.

ERODIUM
HERONSBILL

This is a cosmopolitan genus of about 60 species of annuals and perennials in the geranium family. The evergreen leaves are often finely divided and quite attractive, and the 5-petalled flowers are quite like those of the true geranium though generally smaller. They are mostly low-growing, clumping plants and are best suited for ground cover, rock gardens or for cracks in a stone wall.

CULTIVATION
Frost hardy, all species prefer full sun, doing well in warm, dry regions. Soil must be well drained and not too fertile. Propagate from cuttings in summer or from seed when ripe.

Erodium cheilanthifolium *(above)*
syn. *Erodium petraeum* subsp. *crispum*

This tufted perennial to 8 in (20 cm) tall and 12 in (30 cm) across from southern Spain and the mountains of Morocco has crinkled, dissected, gray-green foliage. In summer it produces pale pink to white flowers veined with deep pink and with purple blotches on the base of the 2 upper petals. ZONES 6–9.

E

Erodium × kolbianum 'Natasha'
(below)

This 6 in (15 cm) tall plant has a spread of around 10 in (25 cm). The dainty flowers of **'Natasha'** have more prominent veins and central blotches than the usual type. The leaves are gray-green and somewhat fern-like. **ZONES 6–9.**

Erodium glandulosum *(above)*
syns *Erodium macradenum, E. petraeum* subsp. *glandulosum*

This clumping perennial from northern Spain has silvery, dissected foliage. In summer it produces its flowers in clusters of up to 5; they are pink with purple markings on the upper 2 petals. It grows to 8 in (20 cm) tall and wide. **ZONES 7–9.**

Erodium manescaui *(right)*
syn. *Erodium manescavii*

This perennial to 18 in (45 cm) tall produces very few leaves, all basal and up to 12 in (30 cm) long and 4 in (10 cm) wide. They are hairy and lanceolate with toothed edges. Its flowers are 1½ in (35 mm) across, saucer-shaped and in clusters of up to 20. They are bright magenta with darker markings on the 2 upper petals. This native of the Pyrenees Mountains can self-seed. **ZONES 6–9.**

Erodium
pelargoniiflorum
(below center)

Native to Turkey, this mound-forming, tufted perennial is ideal for rock gardens or alpine houses, reaching a height of about 12 in (30 cm). It has prostrate, woody stems and heart-shaped, lightly lobed, green leaves. Umbels of white, purple-veined flowers are produced from late spring to autumn. It is prone to aphid infestation. **ZONES 6–9.**

Erodium trifolium
var. *montanum*
(below)

A low-growing, compact perennial from higher elevations in the Atlas Mountains of North Africa, this species is suitable for the alpine house, rock or scree garden. The lobed, toothed leaves are dull green and the simple flowers, in 2 shades of pink, appear in clusters atop slender stems. **ZONES 7–9.**

Erodium × variabile
'Bishop's Form'
(left & bottom right)

As the name would suggest, this is a variable hybrid, its parents being *Erodium corsicum* and *E. reichardii*. This selected form grows up to 24 in (60 cm) tall. Its branched flower stems produce bright pink flowers throughout summer. **ZONES 7–9.**

E

E

ERYNGIUM
SEA HOLLY

Mostly native to South America and
Europe, these 230 species of biennials
and perennials are members of the same
family as the carrot, and are grown for
their interesting foliage and spiny collared
flowerheads that usually have a bluish
metallic sheen. They flower over a long
period in summer and may be cut before
they fully open, and dried for winter decoration. The spiny margins of the strongly
colored, thistle-like bracts, which surround the central flower,
give rise to the common name 'holly'. A number of named hybrids are available including the rather striking 'Jos Eijking'.

Eryngium 'Jos Eijking'
(above)

CULTIVATION
Mostly frost hardy, they need sun, good drainage and sandy soil.
Plants tend to collapse in wet, heavy ground in winter. Propagate
species from fresh seed and selected forms by root cuttings in
winter or by division in spring.

Eryngium alpinum
(right)

Considered one of the
most beautiful of the
genus, this perennial
species from south-
eastern Europe has
green, heart-shaped,
spiny basal leaves but
with upper stems and
leaves suffused with a
soft blue. The 1½ in
(35 mm) conical
flowerheads and
showy, intricately cut,
feathery bracts are
purplish blue. It
reaches 30 in (75 cm)
in height with a spread
of 18 in (45 cm) and is
superb in the border,
where it will tolerate
very light shade.
ZONES 3–9.

Eryngium amethystinum
(left)

This perennial to 30 in (75 cm) tall comes from Italy and the Balkans. Its leaves are basal to 6 in (15 cm) long, spiny and mid-green. The ovoid flowerheads are amethyst surrounded by silvery blue bracts about 2 in (5 cm) long and are produced on silvery blue stems. **ZONES 7–10.**

E

Eryngium bourgatii *(below)*

This striking herbaceous perennial from the eastern Mediterranean has basal leaves that are leathery, gray-green and silver veined. Its flower spikes rise up to 30 in (75 cm) tall and support numerous blue or gray-green flowers surrounded by silvery spiny bracts. **'Othello'** is a compact form that produces shorter flowers on strong, thick stems. **ZONES 5–9.**

Eryngium bourgatii 'Othello'
(below left)

Eryngium proteiflorum
(right)

syn. *Eryngium delaroux*

This very handsome, ever-green perennial to 3 ft (1 m) high has tapered leaves to 12 in (30 cm) or more long and 1 in (25 mm) wide. These have white spines along their edges and form a cluster like the top of a pineapple. The heads of small flowers are whitish and surrounded by masses of long, narrow, silvery white bracts to 4 in (10 cm) in length. This species is less frost hardy than others. **ZONES 8–11.**

Eryngium giganteum (below)
MISS WILLMOTT'S GHOST

This short-lived, clump-forming perennial grows 3–4 ft (1–1.2 m) tall and spreads about 30 in (75 cm). The leaves are heart-shaped and mid-green, and it bears large, rounded, blue or pale green thistle heads surrounded by silvery bracts. It dies after flowering, but its seeds will thrive in good conditions. **ZONES 6–9.**

Eryngium × tripartitum (right)

Of Mediterranean origin, this perennial hybrid is not as spiny as some of the other species. It has coarsely toothed, smooth, dark green, wedge-shaped leaves and bears globular, magenta flowerheads on blue stems from summer through to autumn. Frost hardy, it reaches a height of about 3 ft (1 m) and a spread of about 18 in (45 cm). It requires some support in exposed conditions. ZONES 5–9.

Eryngium variifolium (above)

Distinctive for its variegated white and green foliage which forms an attractive evergreen clump, this species has silvery blue stems to 18 in (45 cm) that are topped by 1 in (25 mm) flowerheads surrounded by similar silvery blue bracts. It is good for the front of the border, where the foliage will provide interest all year round. ZONES 7–10.

ERYSIMUM
syn. *Cheiranthus*
WALLFLOWER

These 80 species of annuals and perennials range in the wild from Europe to central Asia, with a smaller number in North America. Some are suitable for rock gardens, such as the hybrid 'Orange Flame', others fit nicely into the border, such as 'Winter Cheer'. Short-lived species are best grown as biennials. Some form woody bases and become leggy after a few years, at which time they are best replaced with younger specimens. A number are fine winter to spring-flowering plants, while some flower all winter or all year in very mild regions. The older types are sweetly scented, while the newer cultivars have no fragrance but bloom well over a long season. Botanists have now placed all species of *Cheiranthus* into this genus.

Erysimum 'Orange Flame' *(below)*

CULTIVATION
Mostly frost hardy, they do best in well-drained, fertile soil in an open, sunny position. Cut back perennials after flowering so only a few leaves remain on each stem. Propagate from seed in spring or cuttings in summer.

Erysimum 'Winter Cheer' *(below)*

E

Erysimum × allionii
(left)

syn. *Cheiranthus × allionii*

SIBERIAN WALLFLOWER

This slow-growing but short-lived hybrid is a bushy evergreen suitable for rock gardens, banks and borders. It has toothed, mid-green leaves and bears bright yellow or orange flowers in spring, putting on a dazzling display for a long period. It reaches a height and spread of 12–18 in (30–45 cm). ZONES 3–10.

Erysimum 'Bowles' Mauve' *(right)*
syn. *Erysimum* 'E. A. Bowles'

This shrubby evergreen flowers almost continuously in mild climates. The deep rosy purple flowers on elongating stems are nicely set off against the glaucous foliage. Plants develop into mounds 3 ft (1 m) tall and 4 ft (1.2 m) wide. Prune back lightly when flowering slows to encourage another flush of blooms. Flowering ceases in very hot weather, but will continue through winter in spite of occasional light frosts. ZONES 6–11.

Erysimum cheiri *(left)*
syn. *Cheiranthus cheiri*

ENGLISH WALLFLOWER

This bushy species from southern Europe is grown as an annual or biennial and has been part of the cottage garden for centuries. Cultivars vary in height from 8–24 in (20–60 cm) and spread to 15 in (38 cm). Fragrant, 4-petalled flowers appear in spring, or during winter in mild-winter regions. Colors range from pastel pink and yellow to deep brown, bronze, orange, bright yellow, dark red and scarlet. All have lance-shaped leaves. They do best where summers are cool. **'Monarch Fair Lady'**, to 18 in (45 cm) high, has single, deep orange to bright yellow flowers; **'Orange Bedder'**, to 12 in (30 cm) high, is grown as a biennial and has abundant, scented, brilliant orange flowers. ZONES 7–10.

E

Erysimum 'Jubilee Gold' *(below)*

This is a bushy plant to 15 in (38 cm) high with lance-shaped leaves and golden yellow flowers in short clusters in spring. ZONES 7–10.

Erysimum 'Golden Bedder' *(above)*
syn. *Cheiranthus* 'Golden Bedder'

This is one of the color forms of the Bedder Series, bred for compact shape and available in shades from cream through yellow to orange and red. They can flower for months, often starting in winter in mild climates. 'Golden Bedder' is a rich golden yellow. ZONES 8–10.

Erysimum cheiri 'Monarch Fair Lady' *(below)*

Erysimum linifolium (above)

Native to Spain and Portugal, this narrow-leafed, mat-forming perennial grows to about 30 in (75 cm) tall and has long spikes of comparatively small, deep mauve flowers almost all year round in mild climates. Several forms exist including **'Bicolor'**, with pink-mauve as well as white flowers, and **'Variegatum'**, with mauve flowers and white-edged leaves. **ZONES 6–10.**

Erysimum 'Moonlight' (above)

This is a mat-forming evergreen perennial to 10 in (25 cm) tall and about 18 in (45 cm) wide. It flowers from early spring well into summer and produces short racemes of cheerful sulfur-yellow flowers. *Erysimum* 'Moonlight' would make a most attractive rock garden plant or subject for the front of a border. **ZONES 6–9.**

Erysimum mutabile (right)
syn. *Cheiranthus mutabilis*

This much-branched shrub from the Canary Islands and Madeira grows to 3 ft (1 m) high and has narrow, lance-shaped leaves. In spring the flowers open pale yellow and age to a purplish color. It is marginally frost hardy. **ZONES 9–11.**

E

Erysimum ochroleucum *(below)* syn. *Erysimum decumbens*

This short-lived perennial should be grown as a biennial. It has spreading stems to 12 in (30 cm) or more tall, lance-shaped leaves and bright yellow flowers in spring and summer. **ZONES 6–9.**

Erysimum perofskianum *(above)*

This biennial or short-lived perennial is usually treated as an annual in gardens. It grows to 15 in (38 cm) tall and about 10 in (25 cm) wide and has dark green, slightly toothed leaves to 4 in (10 cm) long. It produces its orange to orange-red flowers in spikes of up to 40 blooms in summer. This rosette-forming plant is native to Afghanistan and Pakistan. **ZONES 7–9.**

Eschscholzia californica
(bottom far right)

This short-lived perennial, the official floral emblem of California, has cup-shaped flowers that open out from gray-green feathery foliage into vivid shades of orange. Cultivated strains have extended the color range to bronze, yellow, cream, scarlet, mauve and rose. It flowers in spring with intermittent blooms in summer and autumn, although the flowers close on cloudy days. Of rounded habit, it grows to 12 in (30 cm) high with a similar or wider spread. **'Mission Bells Mixed'** is a seedling strain with double and semi-double blooms in both pastel and strong colors; **'Thai Silk Series'** consists of compact plants with large single or semi-double flowers with fluted and striped petals in orange, pink and bronze-red. ZONES 6–11.

Eschscholzia californica (orange) and *E. caespitosa* (yellow) *(above right)*

Eschscholzia caespitosa *(right)*

This fast-growing, slender, erect annual bears cup-shaped, solitary yellow flowers 1 in (25 mm) wide in summer and early autumn. It has bluish green leaves and reaches a height of 6 in (15 cm). ZONES 7–10.

ESCHSCHOLZIA
CALIFORNIA POPPY

This genus from western North America was named by botanist and poet Adalbert von Chamisso (1781–1838) in honor of his friend, Johan Friedrich Eschscholz. It is a genus of 8 to 10 annuals and perennials with deeply dissected leaves. They bear capsular fruits and yellow to orange poppy-like flowers that close up in dull weather.

CULTIVATION

Species of *Eschscholzia* thrive in warm, dry climates but will tolerate quite severe frosts. They do not like transplanting, so should be sown directly where they are to grow. Grow in poor, well-drained soil and deadhead regularly to prolong flowering. The best method of propagation is from seed which should be sown in spring.

E

E

ESPELETIA

This genus contains up to 80 species of perennials, shrubs and trees from South America. The leaves are often crowded in a terminal cluster. Daisy-like flowerheads are generally borne in terminal panicles or racemes.

CULTIVATION
Frost tender, these plants require a well-drained soil in an open, sunny position. Indoors, provide them with adequate air movement, good light and a fertile, free-draining potting mixture. Propagate by division in spring.

Espeletia schultzii
(below)

From Venezuela, this perennial to 3 ft (1 m) tall has stems and oblong leaves covered in long, felt-like hair. The yellow daisy-like flowerheads are also felty. ZONES 10–12.

E

Eupatorium fistulosum
JOE PYE WEED

Native to the southeastern
states of the USA, this variable perennial grows 3–10 ft
(1–3 m) tall and about as wide.
It enjoys constantly moist,
humus-rich soil and will
tolerate periods of wetness.
It produces heads of rosy-
mauve flowers from mid-
summer to early autumn. It
can be invasive in rich, moist
soil but is easily controlled by
division every second year.
'Filigrankuppel' is an improved flowering form.
ZONES 7–10.

Eupatorium fistulosum
'Filigrankuppel' *(right)*

Eupatorium maculatum *(above)*

This perennial has stems marked with purple
blotches and serrated, lance-shaped leaves in whorls
of three or four. In late summer and autumn rose-
purple flowers are produced in rather flattened
terminal clusters. ZONES 5–10.

EUPATORIUM

This genus contains about 40 species of
perennials and subshrubs, mainly from
the Americas but a few from Asia and
Europe. Only a few are cultivated for
their large terminal panicles of small
flowerheads, which come in white or
shades of purple, mauve or pink.

CULTIVATION
Mostly quite frost hardy, they need full
sun or part-shade and moist but well-
drained soil. The shrubs should be
pruned lightly in spring or after flowering. Propagate from seed in spring,
from cuttings in summer or by division
in early spring or autumn.

EUPHORBIA
MILKWEED, SPURGE

The genus is very large, with close to 2000 species, among numerous succulent species that at first sight look remarkably like cacti. There is a great variety of forms, which suggests that the genus should be divided, but the flowers of all species are almost identical. They are very much reduced, consisting of only a stigma and a stamen, always green, and usually carried in small clusters. Many species have showy bracts, these are the most widely cultivated; examples include *Euphorbia cognata* and *E.* 'Excalibur'. Mainly tropical and subtropical, the genus also includes many temperate species.

CULTIVATION

Plant species of *Euphorbia* in sun or part-shade in moist, well-drained soil. Cold tolerance varies greatly depending on the species; the more highly succulent species are generally frost tender. Propagate from cuttings in spring or summer, allowing succulent species to dry and callus before placing in barely damp sand, by division in early spring or autumn or from seed in autumn or spring.

Euphorbia amygdaloides 'Rubra'
(below)

Euphorbia characias subsp. *wulfenii*
(above right)

Euphorbia characias

This is a sun-loving, frost-hardy shrubby perennial usually up to 3 ft (1 m) tall. It is native to the Mediterranean region from Portugal and Morocco to Turkey. It likes a sunny, well-drained site and where happy, it will self-seed. It has deep brown nectaries giving a brown spot in the center of each yellow-green bract. *Euphorbia characias* subsp. *wulfenii* (syn. *Euphorbia wulfenii*) has blue-green leaves densely clothing the erect stems, which in spring are topped by dome-like chartreuse flowerheads. ZONES 8–10.

Euphorbia amygdaloides
WOOD SPURGE

Native to much of Europe and also Asia Minor, this erect perennial to 3 ft (1 m) high has dark green leaves to 3 in (8 cm) long and flowerheads with yellowish green bracts from mid-spring to early summer. It is generally represented in cultivation by its frost-hardy, selected, colorful varieties and forms. *Euphorbia amygdaloides* var. *robbiae* (syn. *E. robbiae*), Mrs Robb's bonnet, forms spreading rosettes of dark green leaves to 24 in (60 cm) high and wide and bears rounded heads of lime-green floral bracts; **'Rubra'** has light green leaves heavily suffused with burgundy and acid green floral bracts. ZONES 7–9.

E

Euphorbia griffithii *(right)*

This perennial from the eastern Himalayas, which grows to a height of 3 ft (1 m), produces small, yellow flowers surrounded by brilliant orange-red bracts in summer. The lanceolate, green leaves have prominent pinkish midribs and turn red and yellow in autumn. **'Fireglow'** produces orange-red floral bracts in early summer. **ZONES 6–9.**

E

Euphorbia griffithii 'Fireglow' *(right)*

Euphorbia glauca
(below right)

MAORI SPURGE, WAINATUA, SHORE SPURGE

This shrubby perennial species is native to New Zealand and is that country's only member of the genus; its Maori name means 'milk of the demons'. It is an erect plant to about 24 in (60 cm) tall with blue-green foliage. Its flowerheads are only fractionally paler in color than the leaves, but it has tiny red nectaries. **ZONES 9–11.**

E

Euphorbia marginata *(left)*
SNOW ON THE MOUNTAIN, GHOSTWEED

Native to central areas of North America, this bushy annual makes an excellent foil for brighter flowers. It has pointed, oval, bright green leaves sharply margined with white, and broad, petal-like white bracts surrounding small flowers in summer. *Euphorbia marginata* is fairly fast growing to about 24 in (60 cm) tall with a spread of about 12 in (30 cm). It will endure cold conditions. **ZONES 4–10.**

Euphorbia palustris *(center left)*

This bushy, evergreen perennial occurs through most of Europe and western Asia. It grows to about 3 ft (1 m) tall and has mid-green, lance-shaped foliage and flattish heads of deep yellow flowers and bracts in late spring. Frost hardy, this is one of the few euphorbias that will grow well in damp soil. Prune out flowered stems to ground level. **ZONES 5–9.**

Euphorbia polychroma *(below left)*
syn. *Euphorbia epithymoides*
CUSHION SPURGE

Native to central and southern Europe, this frost-hardy, clump-forming perennial is grown for its heads of bright chrome-yellow flowers produced from spring to summer. It has softly hairy, deep green leaves and a rounded, bushy habit, reaching a height and spread of about 18 in (45 cm). **'Major'** has yellowish green flowers in loose clusters. **ZONES 6–9.**

Euphorbia polychroma 'Major' *(below)*

Euphorbia
sikkimensis (top)

This herbaceous perennial from the eastern Himalayas has a somewhat suckering, spreading root system that produces upright stems to 3 ft (1 m) tall. In late winter its foliage is rich burgundy, fading to green as the season progresses although it keeps a lovely pinkish midrib. By mid-summer it produces flat heads of lime-yellow bracts.
ZONES 6–9.

Euphorbia
schillingii (center)
SCHILLING'S SPURGE

This is a frost-hardy, clump-forming, perennial species to 3 ft (1 m) tall. It is a comparative newcomer to horticulture, discovered in Nepal by Tony Schilling in 1975. It has unbranched, well-clothed stems with foliage of a soft green with a white midrib. The flat flowerheads are produced from mid-summer to mid-autumn. In some climates—usually with dry autumn weather—its foliage will color well before dying.
ZONES 5–9.

Euphorbia
seguieriana subsp. *niciciana* (right)
syn. *Euphorbia reflexa*

This perennial plant has several slender stems arising from a central woody crown. Its foliage is fine and blue-green and in late summer it bears terminal heads of small yellow-green bracts, sometimes ageing reddish. This frost-hardy plant is a good rock garden subject or suits the edge of a border where it can trail out over gravel or paving. It is native to southeastern Europe and southwestern Asia.
ZONES 5–9.

E

E

Eustoma grandiflorum
cultivar *(above)*

EUSTOMA
syn. *Lisianthius*

Belonging to the gentian family, this genus consists of 3 species of annuals, biennials and perennials, ranging in the wild from southern USA to northern South America. One species, *Eustoma grandiflorum*, has very showy, tulip-like flowers that have become popular as cut flowers in recent years, and has been the subject of considerable breeding work. Japanese plant breeders extended the pastel color range to white, pale blue and pink as well as the original violet, and also developed double-flowered strains. Any unopened buds on the spray develop beautifully in water, so these continue the display for an extended period.

CULTIVATION
Usually regarded as frost tender, the plants are easy to cultivate in any warm-temperate climate. Give them sun, perfect drainage and fertile soil, but they rarely perform well after their first year. Propagate from seed in spring or from cuttings in late spring or summer.

Eustoma grandiflorum
syn. *Lisianthus russellianus*

PRAIRIE GENTIAN, TEXAS BLUEBELL, LISIANTHUS

Native to America's Midwest from Nebraska to Texas, this biennial's flowers last up to 3 weeks in water after cutting. It can also be grown as a container plant. It has gray-green leaves and 2 in (5 cm) wide, flared, tulip-like flowers in colors of rich purple, pink, blue or white. Of an upright habit, the plant is slow growing to a height of 24 in (60 cm) and spread of 12 in (30 cm). ZONES 9–11.

E

Exacum affine
(below)

PERSIAN VIOLET, GERMAN VIOLET

This showy miniature has shiny, oval leaves and bears a profusion of small, 5-petalled, saucer-shaped, usually purple-blue flowers with yellow stamens during summer. A biennial usually treated as an annual, *Exacum affine* grows to a height and spread of 8–12 in (20–30 cm). **'Blue Midget'** grows to only half as big and has lavender-blue flowers, while **'White Midget'** has white flowers. ZONES 10–12.

EXACUM

Like *Eustoma*, this genus belongs to the gentian family. It consists of about 25 species of annuals, biennials or perennials, widely distributed through tropical Africa and Asia. They have mostly yellow, white, blue or purple flowers that are often broadly cup-shaped or flat, unlike the tubular flowers of gentians. Only one species, *Exacum affine*, has become widely cultivated. It is a miniature plant from the hot, dry island of Socotra, just off the horn of Africa at the mouth of the Red Sea, and is grown as an indoor plant, popular for its neat, shrub-like habit and long succession of flowers.

CULTIVATION

These plants can only be grown outdoors in warm, frost-free climates, where they do best in a sunny position in rich, moist but well-drained soil. Indoors they like diffused sun and a night temperature not below 50°F (10°C). Propagate from seed in early spring.

FAGOPYRUM
BUCKWHEAT

This small genus of annuals and perennials are grown for their richly flavored, highly nutritious seeds which are processed into grits or flour. It is unsatisfactory for bread, but is used to make pancakes and ordinary cakes particularly in Europe and eastern Asia; it is also used to make buckwheat pasta. In the USA and Canada the flour is used in griddle cakes and in Japan it is made into thin green-brown noodles called soba. The leaves are alternate, and the small white flowers appear in racemes or corymbs.

CULTIVATION
Buckwheat are frost-hardy plants that will grow in poor soil. They mature within 2 months, which makes it possible to harvest 2 crops per season. Propagate from seed in spring and summer.

Fagopyrum esculentum (below)
syn. *Polygonum fagopyrum*
BUCKWHEAT

A native of northern Asia, this annual species grows to 3 ft (1 m) tall. It has reddish stems and short dense racemes of white fragrant flowers followed by triangular fruit that are enclosed in a tough, dark-brown rind.
ZONES 3–9.

Farfugium
japonicum (right)
syns *Farfugium*
tussilagineum,
Ligularia tussilaginea

Native to Japan, this
clump-forming peren-
nial to 24 in (60 cm)
high has glossy, kidney-
shaped leaves on long
stalks, above which
arise downy branched
stems bearing clusters
of flowers from autumn
to winter. **'Aureo-**
maculatum', the leop-
ard plant, has variegated
leaves with circular
yellow blotches.
ZONES 7–10.

F

FARFUGIUM

From temperate Asia, and closely allied to *Ligularia*, the 2 species
of evergreen perennials in this genus are grown for their large,
leathery foliage and daisy-like, yellow flowerheads. They are suitable for containers.

CULTIVATION
These frost-hardy plants do best in part-shade in fertile, moist
but well-drained soil. Propagate from seed in spring, or divide
variegated cultivars in spring.

Farfugium japonicum
'Aureomaculatum'
(right)

F

FASCICULARIA

This genus is made up of 5 species of ever-green, rosette-forming, perennial plants of the bromeliad family. They all originate from Chile and are valued for their spreading leaves which form large rosettes and for their exotic, long-lasting blue flowers, which are followed by scaly fruits.

CULTIVATION

These frost-tender plants are best grown in a greenhouse in cool climates. In warmer areas grow outside in poor, very well-drained soil in full sun. Water moder-ately during the growing season and spar-ingly in winter. Propagate from seed or by division in spring or summer.

Fascicularia bicolor (above) syn. *Fascicularia andina*

So named because of its green and red inner leaves, this vigorous bromeliad is one of the most attractive of Chile's native plants when in full flower. It has compact clusters of narrow, gray-green leaves with serrated edges which form a large rosette. Its inner leaves turn a vivid fiery red in autumn. The flowers are borne in dense corymbs in summer. ZONES 8–11.

Felicia amelloides (below)

BLUE MARGUERITE

This bushy, evergreen perennial has a spreading habit, and grows to 24 in (60 cm) in height and twice as wide. It has roundish, bright green leaves and pale to deep blue flowerheads with bright yellow centers that are borne on long stalks from late spring to autumn. Frost tender, it is fast growing in temperate climates and is suitable for seaside gardens. It is often grown as an annual in cool areas. **'Santa Anita'** has extra large blue flowers and **'Alba'** is a white form. *Felicia pappei* is like a miniature version of *F. amelloides* in growth, foliage and are an even richer, purer blue. It reaches 20 in (50 cm) in height. **ZONES 9–11.**

FELICIA

BLUE DAISY

This genus, which ranges from southern Africa to Arabia, consists of 80 species of annuals, perennials and evergreen subshrubs. Named after Herr Felix, mayor of Regensburg on the Danube in the 1800s, they are sprawling plants with aromatic foliage. In mild climates, they flower on and off almost all year. The daisy-like, usually blue flowerheads with yellow disc florets are borne in masses.

F

CULTIVATION

They are fully frost hardy to frost tender and require full sun and well-drained, humus-rich, gravelly soil. They do not tolerate wet conditions. In all but the mildest areas, the frost-tender perennial species need protection in winter with open-ended cloches. Deadheading prolongs the flowering season. Prune straggly shoots regularly. Propagate from cuttings taken in late summer or autumn or from seed in spring.

Felicia heterophylla *(left)*

This dome-shaped, mat-forming annual from South Africa grows to 20 in (50 cm) high and wide. It has lance-shaped, gray-green leaves and solitary blue flowerheads in summer. **ZONES 9–11.**

Felicia petiolata *(below)*

This mat-forming prostrate perennial with a spread of up to 3 ft (1 m) has small, sparsely lobed leaves and bears solitary white to violet flowerheads in summer. **ZONES 9–11.**

Ferula communis
(right)

GIANT FENNEL

Found in most parts of the Mediterranean region, this tall robust perennial to 15 ft (4.5 m) high has narrowly lobed leaves and leaf stalks that sheath the stems. The 5-petalled yellow flowers appear in early summer. Plants may take several years to flower. **ZONES 8–10.**

F

FERULA
GIANT FENNEL

This genus consists of about 170 species of aromatic herbaceous perennials from central Asia to the Mediterranean, with finely cut pinnate leaves and large rounded umbels of greenish white or yellow flowers borne on tall branching stems. These plants are grown for their strong architectural form and are ideal for the back of a border. They should not be confused with culinary fennel *(Foeniculum)*.

CULTIVATION
Grow these frost-hardy plants in full sun in fertile, well-drained soil. Plants often die after seeding. Propagate from seed in late summer. They are prone to attack from aphids and slugs.

FILIPENDULA

This is a genus of 10 species of herbaceous
perennials from northern temperate regions.
All except *Filipendula vulgaris* occur
naturally in moist waterside habitats. They
have alternate pinnate leaves and erect
stems bearing large panicle-like clusters of
tiny, 5-petalled flowers with fluffy stamens.
They do well at the back of large perennial
borders and in waterside positions.

CULTIVATION
Grow these fully frost-hardy plants in full
sun or part-shade in any moisture-retentive
but well-drained soil. *Filipendula rubra*
and *F. ulmaria* will thrive in swampy,
boggy sites. Propagate from seed or by
division in spring or autumn. Check for
powdery mildew.

Filipendula purpurea
'Elegans' *(below)*

Filipendula purpurea
JAPANESE MEADOWSWEET

From Japan, this up-
right clump-forming
perennial reaches
4 ft (1.2 m) high with
deeply divided toothed
leaves. In summer it
bears large terminal
heads composed of
masses of tiny crimson-
purple flowers. This is
a beautiful plant for
growing near a water
feature. **'Elegans'** has
light, greenish yellow
foliage, and
Filipendula purpurea
f. *albiflora* has white
flowers. ZONES 6–9.

F

Filipendula vulgaris
(right)
syn. *Filipendula hexapetala*

DROPWORT

From Europe and Asia, this species reaches 24–36 in (60–90 cm) high and has fleshy swollen roots. It is grown for its attractive, deeply cut, fern-like foliage, and showy, crowded heads of tiny white flowers; some garden varieties are pink. This species will tolerate fairly dry conditions and must have good drainage. **ZONES 3–9.**

F

Filipendula ulmaria
syn. *Spiraea ulmaria*

MEADOWSWEET, QUEEN-OF-THE-MEADOW

Native to Europe and western Asia, this clump-forming perennial grows to 6 ft (1.8 m) high. It has pinnate leaves to 12 in (30 cm) long with sharply toothed ovate leaflets. The creamy white flowers are borne in dense heads to 10 in (25 cm) across in summer. **'Aurea'** has golden-green leaves that are yellow when young; the leaves of **'Variegata'** are striped and mostly blotched yellow. **ZONES 2–9.**

Filipendula ulmaria
'Variegata' *(above)*

Filipendula ulmaria
'Aurea' *(right)*

FITTONIA
NERVE PLANT, PAINTED NET LEAF

This genus consists of 2 species of ever-green, creeping perennials from tropical rainforests in South America. They are grown mainly for their leaves, which are opposite, short-stemmed and have brightly colored veins. They are popular conservatory and house plants. Occasionally, white to reddish white, insignificant flowers are borne on short spikes. In warm, frost-free climates they make excellent ground covers or trailing plants.

CULTIVATION
Grow in part-shade and provide a humus-rich, well-drained soil and plenty of water. Where temperatures drop below 50°F (15°C), grow indoors in a good potting mix and keep evenly moist. They make excellent hanging basket subjects. Cut back straggly stems in spring. Propagate from cuttings or by layering stems in summer.

Fittonia verschaffeltii (above)

This species reaches about 6 in (15 cm) high with an indefinite spread and has dark green oval leaves with conspicuous red veins. The insignificant flowers are irregular and best removed. *Fittonia verschaffeltii* var. *argyroneura* (syn. *F. argyroneura*), the silver net leaf, has rooting stems and mid- to dark green leaves with conspicuous white veins. ZONES 11–12.

FRAGARIA
STRAWBERRY

The dozen or so species in this genus are mostly native to temperate areas of the northern hemisphere. They are low-growing, creeping or tufted perennials popular as ornamental ground covers and for their fleshy red fruit. The palmate leaves are composed of 3 toothed leaflets, and the white or pink, 5-petalled flowers appear in cymes. The strawberry itself is a false fruit; a a large fleshy receptacle covered with tiny pips. Modern, more robust cultivars can fruit 6 months, or all year round in a warm climate. There are many named varieties with varying flavors. 'Red Ruby' is an interesting cultivar with bright pink-red flowers.

CULTIVATION

Grow these frost-hardy plants in containers or beds lined with straw in free-draining, acidic soil. The plants need full sun or light shade and protection from wind; in cold climates grow them in slits in sheets of plastic. Propagate from seed in spring or autumn or by runners and replant with fresh stock every few years. Protect them from snails, strawberry aphids and birds. Botrytis can be a problem in high rainfall areas.

F

Fragaria 'Red Ruby'
(below)

F

Fragaria 'Pink Panda' (above)

This spreading, ground cover perennial to 6 in (15 cm) high with an indefinite spread is grown for its pretty bright pink flowers to 1 in (2.5 cm) across, which appear from late spring to autumn. It rarely bears fruit. ZONES 4–10.

Fragaria chiloensis (left)
SAND STRAWBERRY

This species grows wild in coastal North and South America and is one of the parents of modern strawberries. It spreads by runners in dense tufts, the lower leaves forming rosettes. It reaches a height of 12 in (30 cm) and spreads to 18 in (45 cm). The 2 in (5 cm) long, obovate, trifoliate leaves are a lustrous deep green, and hairy underneath. ZONES 4–10.

FRANCOA

MAIDEN'S WREATH, BRIDAL WREATH

The 5 species of evergreen perennials that make up this genus from Chile are grown for their flowers, which are used in floral arrangements. The plants form a basal rosette of wavy, lobed leaves, each with a large terminal lobe. The 5-petalled bell-shaped flowers in white, pink or red with darker markings at the base are borne in terminal, spike-like racemes in summer and early autumn.

CULTIVATION

Mostly frost hardy, but in very cold climates plants make good potted specimens for a cool greenhouse. Outdoors grow in humus-rich, moist but well-drained soil in a sheltered sunny or part-shaded position. Water sparingly in winter. Propagate from seed or by division in spring.

Francoa sonchifolia (below)

This species to 3 ft (1 m) tall has oblong to oval, crinkled dark green basal leaves. The pale pink flowers, spotted deep pink within, appear on erect, sparsely branched stems from summer to early autumn. ZONES 7–10.

GAILLARDIA
BLANKET FLOWER

This genus of around 30 species of annuals, perennials and biennials are all native to the USA, with the exception of 2 South American species. The perennials are better suited to cool-temperate climates. All plants bloom for a very long season from summer until the first frosts. The daisy-like flowers are either single, like small sunflowers, or double and as much as 6 in (15 cm) wide. The common name arose because the colors of the flowers resemble the bright yellows, oranges and reds of the blankets traditionally worn by Native Americans. Gaillardias are a colorful addition to the flower border and meadow garden. They are also very good for cutting.

CULTIVATION
Among the hardiest of garden flowers, they tolerate extreme heat, cold, dryness, strong winds and poor soils. Plant in full sun in well-drained soil and stake if necessary. In cool climates, the stems of perennials should be cut back in late summer in order to recover before frosts. Propagate from seed in spring or early summer. Perennials may be divided in spring.

Gaillardia ×
grandiflora (left)

These hybrids of
Gaillardia aristata and
G. pulchella are the
most commonly grown
of the blanket flowers.
The plants form mounds
up to 3 ft (1 m) high
and wide and have narrow, slightly lobed,
hairy leaves. The flowerheads, 3–4 in (8–10 cm)
in diameter, come in
hot colors: red, yellow,
orange and burgundy.
They are propagated
by division or from
cuttings. There are
several named
cultivars: **'Burgunder'**
('Burgundy') has deep
maroon-colored
blooms; **'Dazzler'** has
bright orange-yellow
flowers with maroon
centers; **'Kobold'**
('Goblin') has compact
growth to 12 in (30 cm)
high and rich red
flowers with yellow
tips. ZONES 5–10.

Gaillardia × grandiflora
'Kobold' *(above)*

Gaillardia × grandiflora
'Dazzler' *(below)*

G

Galium verum (left)
LADY'S BEDSTRAW

This sprawling perennial from temperate Eurasia and North America grows to about 12 in (30 cm) high forming a dense mass of fine foliage up to 4 ft (1.2 m) across. It has linear leaves arranged in whorls and tiny, bright yellow flowers borne in dense terminal heads in summer and early autumn. ZONES 3–10.

GALIUM
BEDSTRAW

This genus contains about 400 species of annuals and perennials of cosmopolitan distribution. Some have become naturalized beyond their native regions and are weeds. They have weak sprawling stems and whorls of narrow green leaves. Many species spread by slender, much-branched rhizomes. The small star-shaped flowers are white, pink or yellow.

CULTIVATION
Grow these frost-hardy plants in part-shade in well-drained but moist soil. Propagate from fresh ripe seed or by division in early spring or autumn.

Galium odoratum
(above left & above)
syn. *Asperula odorata*
SWEET WOODRUFF

This delicate European perennial produces a beautiful pattern of whorled leaves, making a dense mass of foliage about 12 in (30 cm) high and greater spread. The tiny white flowers appear in few-flowered clusters in late spring. The fragrant foliage was traditionally added to white wine to produce May wine in Europe. ZONES 5–10.

GAURA

Related to the evening primrose *(Oenothera)*, this genus of about 20 species of annuals, biennials, perennials and subshrubs are from North America. They are apt to be weedy, despite their showy flowers and the genus name that translates as 'gorgeous'. They have simple, narrow leaves and clusters of flat, star-shaped, pink or white flowers.

CULTIVATION
They prefer full sun and light, well-drained soil. Cut ruthlessly to the ground when flowering has finished. Propagate from seed in autumn or spring, or from cuttings in summer.

G

Gaura lindheimeri
(right)

Native to the USA–Mexico border region, this clump-forming, long-flowering perennial is useful for backgrounds and mixed flower borders. It has loosely branched stems covered with tiny hairs, and from spring to autumn produces long sprays of beautiful flowers that open white from pink buds. It grows to 4 ft (1.2 m) in height with a spread of 3 ft (1 m). **ZONES 5–10.**

GAZANIA

From tropical and southern Africa, this
genus consists of about 16 species of low-
growing annuals and perennials grown for
their bright, colorful flowers. The genus
name honors the medieval scholar
Theodore of Gaza (1398–1478). The leaves
are entire or deeply lobed, long and narrow,
often dark green on top and white- or silver-
gray-felted beneath, or in some species

silvery haired on both sides. The flowerheads borne singly on short
stalks range from cream to yellow, gold, pink, red, buff, brown and
intermediate shades, usually with contrasting bands or spots at the
petal bases. They appear from early spring until summer. Most
modern varieties are hybrids from several South African species;
they are marginally frost hardy and useful for coastal areas for
bedding, rock gardens, pots and tubs and for binding soil on
slopes. Cultivars include **'Double Orange'**, bearing large orange
flowers with double centers on short stems just above the leaves;
'Flore Pleno', with bright yellow double flowers; and **'Gwen's
Pink'**, with salmon-pink single flowers with yellow centers and
dark brown rings. Plants in the **Chansonette Series** are strong but
low growers, reaching just 8 in (20 cm) in height. There are many
color varieties, mostly with contrasting dark centers.

Gazania 'Flore Pleno'
(above)

CULTIVATION

Grow in full sun in sandy, fairly dry, well-drained soil. Mulch with
compost and water during dry periods. Propagate by division or
from cuttings in autumn, or from seed in late winter to early spring.

Gazania 'Gwen's Pink'
(left)

Gazania Sunshine
Hybrid cultivar
(opposite page right)

Gazania rigens var.
leucolaena
(opposite page far right)

G

Gazania krebsiana (above)

From South Africa, this stemless perennial has slender lance-shaped leaves with a smooth upper surface and white downy underside. The flowers range from yellow to orange-red with a contrasting darker color around their centers. **ZONES 9–11.**

Gazania, Sunshine Hybrids

These mat-forming perennials may be grown as annuals. The height and spread is around 8 in (20 cm). Its solitary flowers, which are borne in summer, range in color with the disc-florets usually ringed in a darker color. **ZONES 9–11.**

Gazania rigens

This perennial species grows to a height of 12 in (30 cm) with a similar spread. It is a mat-forming plant with crowded rosettes of mostly unlobed leaves that are green above and whitish beneath. The orange flowerheads have a black eye spot at the petal bases. The leaves of **Gazania rigens var. leucolaena** are silvery green on both sides and the flowers are yellow; **G. r. var. uniflora** has flowers that are smaller and short stalked. **ZONES 9–11.**

G

Gentiana asclepiadea *(above)*
WILLOW GENTIAN

The arching stems of this perennial bear slender, willow-like leaves. In early autumn many rich violet-blue flowers appear in the leaf axils on the upper stems. It forms a loose clump 3 ft (1 m) high and 24 in (60 cm) wide. ZONES 6–9.

GENTIANA
GENTIAN

Occurring worldwide, mostly in alpine meadows and occasionally in woodlands, this is a genus of around 400 species of annuals, biennials and perennials, some of them evergreen. Intense deep blues and sky blues are the usual flower colors, but whites, creams, yellows and even red are also found. The mostly trumpet-shaped flowers are borne from spring to autumn. They are useful in rock gardens and sloping hillside gardens.

CULTIVATION
They prefer cooler regions and well-drained, but moisture-retentive soil rich in humus. Some species grow naturally in limestone soil. Plant in either sun or semi-shade. Propagate by division in spring or from fresh seed in autumn. Divide autumn-flowering species every 3 years in early spring, planting out in fresh soil.

Gentiana acaulis *(below)*
syns *Gentiana excisa, G. kochiana*
STEMLESS GENTIAN, TRUMPET GENTIAN

The stemless gentian is an evergreen, rhizomatous perennial from southern Europe. It makes a striking carpet of small, crowded leaves and disproportionately large, vivid blue trumpet flowers with green-spotted throats in spring and early summer. The foliage is only about 1 in (25 mm) high. It needs a deep root run and benefits from a light application of lime. ZONES 3–9.

Gentiana dinarica
(below)

From Italy and the Balkans, this small, tufted perennial grows to about 6 in (15 cm) high with a basal rosette of broadly elliptic leaves to 1½ in (35 mm) long. In summer it bears solitary, deep blue, narrowly bell-shaped flowers on stems to 3 in (8 cm) long. **ZONES 6–9.**

Gentiana bellidifolia *(right)*

The 'daisy-leafed' gentian is typical of the New Zealand species in having white flowers in clusters. It is variable, reaching 6 in (15 cm) at the most. The flowers appear in summer, and the leaves are usually brown tinted. **ZONES 7–9.**

G

Gentiana farreri *(below)*

This 4 in (10 cm) tall semi-evergreen perennial from the borders of China and Tibet is one of the most beautiful of the Asiatic gentians. It has trailing stems with rosettes of small lance-shaped leaves. The turquoise blue, trumpet-shaped flowers with a white stripe appear in autumn. **ZONES 5–9.**

G

Gentiana paradoxa
(left)

This beautiful perennial species has prostrate stems with linear, lance-shaped, finely pointed leaves up to 2 in (5 cm) long. The trumpet-shaped, bright blue flowers have deep purple and white stripes at the throat. ZONES 6–9.

Gentiana 'Inverleith' *(below)*

This robust hybrid of *Gentiana farreri* and *G. veitchiorum* has trailing stems with basal rosettes of linear, lance-shaped leaves. The pale blue trumpet-shaped flowers have deep blue stripes and appear in autumn. ZONES 5–9.

Gentiana lutea
(right)

GREAT YELLOW GENTIAN

This robust, erect, clump-forming perennial from the mountains of Europe produces tubular yellow flowers in clusters in the upper axils of tall stems in summer. It grows to 3–6 ft (1–1.8 m) high and 24 in (60 cm) wide and has oval, stem-clasping leaves to 12 in (30 cm) long. This is the main commercial source of gentian root, used medicinally and to flavor vermouth. ZONES 5–9.

G

Gentiana sino-ornata
'Alba' *(above)*

Gentiana septemfida *(below)*

CRESTED GENTIAN

Native to mountains of
western and central
Asia, this sun-loving
perennial grows about
8 in (20 cm) tall and has
paired oval leaves. The
rich blue flowers with
white throats are borne
in terminal clusters of
up to 8 in summer.
ZONES 3–9.

Gentiana sino-ornata *(right)*

This evergreen perennial
from western China
flowers in autumn and
bears deep blue trumpet
flowers that are paler
at the base and banded
purplish blue. It has a
prostrate, spreading
habit, reaching 2 in
(5 cm) tall and 12 in
(30 cm) wide. **'Alba'**
has white flowers.
ZONES 6–9.

Gentiana verna

SPRING GENTIAN

This spring-flowering perennial to 2 in (5 cm) high
has a scattered distribution
in mountainous regions in
Europe from Ireland to
Russia. Often short-lived, it
forms compact clumps of
basal rosettes of broadly
ovate leaves. Short, erect
stems bear solitary brilliant
blue flowers with a white
throat and spreading petals
in early spring. **'Angulosa'**
has larger, more robust
flowers. **ZONES 5–9.**

Gentiana verna
'Angulosa' *(below)*

GERANIUM
CRANESBILL

Over 300 species of annual, biennial and perennial geraniums, some evergreen, grow all over the world mainly in cool-temperate regions. The leaves are on long stalks, broadly circular in outline but usually palmately lobed. They make small, showy clumps with pink to blue or purple and white, 5-petalled flowers. The true geraniums or cranesbills, so-called for the shape of their small, dry fruitlets, are often confused with species of the genus *Pelargonium,* also commonly known as 'geraniums'. Symmetrical flowers are their chief point of distinction from pelargoniums, which produce irregularly shaped or marked flowers. With their attractive flowers they are useful for rock gardens, ground covers and borders. Compact species and hybrids such as **'Brookside'** and *Geranium goldmanii* are also good for containers.

CULTIVATION
Mostly quite frost hardy, they prefer a sunny situation and damp, well-drained soil. Transplant during winter. Propagate from cuttings in summer or seed in spring, or by division in autumn.

Geranium 'Brookside' *(below)*

**Geranium ×
cantabrigiense**
(above)

This hybrid between *Geranium dalmaticum* and *G. macrorrhizum* to 12 in (30 cm) high spreads by runners to 24 in (60 cm) wide. It has aromatic, light green basal leaves and bright purplish pink flowers in summer. **'Biokovo'** has pink-tinged, white flowers. ZONES 5–9.

Geranium endressii *(right)*

From the Pyrenees, this rhizomatous perennial forms clumps to 18 in (45 cm) high and 24 in (60 cm) across. The leaves are deeply lobed and toothed and pale pink flowers, becoming darker with age, are produced from early summer to early autumn. **ZONES 5–9.**

Geranium cinereum

This small, tufted perennial to 6 in (15 cm) forms a basal rosette of soft, deeply divided leaves. The cup-shaped flowers, white or pale pink often with purple veins, are produced in late spring or early summer. **'Ballerina'** bears purplish pink flowers with distinct purple veins; *Geranium cinereum* subsp. *subcaulescens* has darker green leaves and magenta flowers with a black center. **ZONES 5–9.**

Geranium clarkei

From the western Himalayas, this perennial is up to 18 in (45 cm) high and has spreading stems and deeply divided leaves. Its saucer-shaped flowers, borne in summer, are white or violet with pink veins. **'Kashmir Purple'** bears lilac-blue flowers with red veins. **ZONES 7–9.**

Geranium cinereum subsp. *subcaulescens* *(below)*

Geranium cinereum 'Ballerina' *(above)*

Geranium clarkei 'Kashmir Purple' *(below)*

G

Geranium himalayense *(below)*
syn. *Geranium grandiflorum*

This clump-forming perennial has cushions of neatly cut leaves and grows to 18 in (45 cm) high and 24 in (60 cm) wide. In summer large cup-shaped violet-blue flowers with white centers appear on long stalks. **'Gravetye'** (syn. *Geranium grandiflorum* var. *alpinum*) has lilac-blue flowers with reddish centers and leaves that turn russet before dying down in autumn. **'Plenum'** (syn. 'Birch Double') has double, purplish pink flowers with darker veins. **ZONES 4–9.**

Geranium erianthum *(above)*

This is a clump-forming perennial from north-eastern Asia and north-western North America. It has erect stems to 24 in (60 cm) tall and light green, deeply lobed and toothed leaves, which have a rich autumn coloring. Clusters of saucer-shaped, violet flowers are borne in early summer. **ZONES 3–9.**

Geranium himalayense 'Plenum' *(left)*

Geranium himalayense 'Gravetye' *(left)*

Geranium ibericum (below)

Although 'ibericum' is normally taken to mean 'Spanish' in Latin, it can also refer to the Caucasus region, where in fact this species comes from. This clump-forming perennial grows to a height and spread of 18 in (45 cm). It has heart-shaped, hairy leaves and produces large sprays of saucer-shaped violet flowers with faint darker veins in early summer. ZONES 6–9.

Geranium 'Johnson's Blue' (above)

This rhizomatous perennial may be merely a form of *Geranium himalayense*. It has deeply divided leaves and bears cup-shaped lavender-blue flowers with pale centers throughout summer. It has a spreading habit, reaching 18 in (45 cm) tall and 30 in (75 cm) wide. ZONES 5–9.

Geranium incanum (right)

This South African evergreen perennial grows up to 15 in (38 cm) high and 3 ft (1 m) wide. Its green leaves are deeply cut and feathery with a spicy aroma. The cup-shaped blooms are deep pink with deeper colored veins. It is marginally frost hardy. ZONES 8–10.

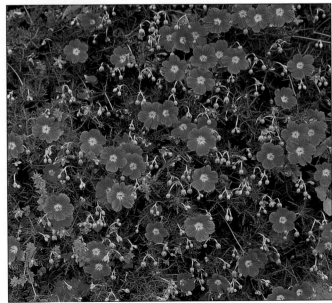

G

Geranium
macrorrhizum (right)

This clump-forming
perennial often forms
large colonies in its
shady mountain habi-
tats of southern Europe.
The sticky, deeply lobed
leaves are aromatic,
often turning red or
bronze in autumn. The
flowers appear on 12 in
(30 cm) stems above
the foliage in spring and
early summer. Flower
color varies from pink
or purplish to pure
white. It makes an ex-
cellent ground cover
for a dry, shady site.
'Album' has white petals with reddish calyces;
'Ingwersen's Variety'
has pale pink flowers
and smoother glossy
leaves. **'Spessart'** is an
attractive German
cultivar. ZONES 4–9.

Geranium
maculatum (above)

Native to eastern
American woodlands,
this species is best used
in woodland gardens
as it is less showy and
more open in habit
than others. It is an
erect, clump-forming
perennial to 30 in
(75 cm) tall with deeply
lobed, glossy leaves and
bears saucer-shaped,
lilac-pink flowers with
white centers in late
spring to mid-summer.
ZONES 6–9.

Geranium
macrorrhizum
'Ingwersen's Variety'
(left)

Geranium × magnificum (right)

This vigorous garden hybrid of *Geranium ibericum* and *G. platypetalum* forms clumps to 24 in (60 cm) high. It has hairy deeply cut leaves that color in autumn. Abundant, violet-blue, reddish veined, saucer-shaped flowers appear in mid-summer. Propagate by division or from cuttings. **ZONES 5–9.**

Geranium malviflorum (below)
syn. *Geranium atlanticum* of gardens

From southern Spain and northern Africa, this tuberous perennial to 12 in (30 cm) tall has deeply cut dark green leaves and violet-blue, red-veined, saucer-shaped flowers in spring. It flowers best in a poor soil, although better soil promotes a fine display of foliage. **ZONES 9–10.**

Geranium maderense (above)

Native to Madeira, this short-lived, evergreen, bushy perennial to 5 ft (1.5 m) tall has huge leaves for a geranium, often 12 in (30 cm) or more across. They are divided in a striking snowflake pattern and turn reddish in autumn. Shallowly cup-shaped, pinkish magenta flowers with darker centers are borne in tall panicles from late winter to late summer. Old leaves should not be removed too soon, as the plant props itself on them to resist wind-loosening. **ZONES 9–10.**

G

Geranium × oxonianum (right)

This vigorous upright hybrid of *Geranium endressi* and *G. versicolor* forms clumps to 30 in (75 cm) high; it has light green wrinkled leaves with conspicuous veining. Trumpet-shaped flushed pink flowers with darker veins are produced over a long period from late spring to mid-autumn. **'Claridge Druce'** has mauve-pink darker veined flowers in summer; **'Wargrave Pink'** has bright pink flowers. **ZONES 5–9.**

Geranium × oxonianum 'Claridge Druce' (above)

Geranium × oxonianum 'Wargrave Pink' (right)

Geranium phaeum
'Variegatum' *(left)*

Geranium phaeum
'Samobor' *(above)*

Geranium phaeum *(below)*
MOURNING WIDOW, DUSKY CRANESBILL

From Europe and western Russia, this clump-forming perennial to 30 in (75 cm) high and 18 in (45 cm) wide has soft green, densely lobed leaves. Its flowers are a deep, brownish purple with a paler center ring, borne in late spring or early summer. **'Lily Lovell'** has large white flowers; ***Geranium phaeum* var.** *lividum* has pale pink or lilac flowers; **'Variegatum'** has leaves with yellow margins and pink splotches. Another cultivar is **'Samobor'**. ZONES 5–10.

Geranium phaeum
'Lily Lovell' *(below)*

Geranium phaeum
var. *lividum* *(above)*

G

Geranium pratense
MEADOW CRANESBILL

From Europe, Siberia and China, this clump-forming perennial species reaches 3 ft (1 m) in height. It has hairy stems and the leaves are deeply lobed almost to the base. They become bronze in autumn. Saucer-shaped, violet-blue flowers are carried on erect branching stems in summer. **'Plenum Violaceum'** (syn. 'Flore Pleno') has double, deep violet-blue flowers. ZONES 5–9.

Geranium pratense **'Plenum Violaceum'** *(left)*

Geranium psilostemon *(right)*
syn. *Geranium armenum*
ARMENIAN CRANESBILL

This robust, clump-forming perennial grows 2–4 ft (0.6–1.2 m) high and 24 in (60 cm) wide. It has lobed, deeply toothed leaves, often reddish in autumn. Striking, large, cup-shaped, magenta flowers with a black eye appear in summer. ZONES 6–9.

Geranium renardii *(left)*

This clump-forming perennial develops into a neat mound to 12 in (30 cm) high and wide. It has lobed, circular, finely wrinkled leaves with a velvety underside. The saucer-shaped white flowers with bold purple veins are borne in early summer. ZONES 6–9.

Geranium sanguineum

BLOODY CRANESBILL

In flower color this European species is often less 'bloody' than many other geraniums, but then coiners of English plant names had a weakness for translating the Latin name wherever possible. It is a low-growing perennial of around 8 in (20 cm) tall spreading by rhizomes. The dark green leaves are deeply cut into toothed lobes. Abundant cup-shaped bright magenta flowers with notched petals are produced during summer. **Geranium sanguineum var. striatum** is a pink version; **'Vision'** is a compact form with deep pink flowers. **ZONES 5–9.**

Geranium sanguineum var. striatum (left)

Geranium sanguineum 'Vision' (below)

Geranium robertianum *(top)*

HERB ROBERT, RED ROBIN

Late in the season, this scrambling annual or biennial, found widespread in regions of the northern hemisphere, takes on an overall red color. The 'Robert' in the name is in fact a corruption of *ruberta*, from the Latin adjective ruber meaning 'red'. Herb Robert derived its traditional uses from the medieval Doctrine of Signatures which stated that a plant's medicinal qualities were revealed in its external features—in this case for diseases of the blood. The plant has deeply cut ferny leaves with a rather strong, not altogether pleasant, scent. Small star-shaped pink or rose flowers are produced from summer to autumn. It is self-seeding, often to the point of being a nuisance. **ZONES 6–10.**

G

Geranium sylvaticum *(below)*
WOOD CRANESBILL

Another well-known European species, this upright, clump-forming perennial to 30 in (75 cm) tall has deeply divided basal leaves from which arise branching stems carrying bluish purple, cup-shaped flowers with white centers from late spring to summer. **'Album'** has white flowers; **'Mayflower'** has rich violet-blue flowers with white centers. ZONES 4–9.

Geranium sylvaticum
'Album' *(below)*

Geranium sylvaticum
'Mayflower' *(above)*

Geranium traversii

From coastal cliffs on the Chatham Islands off southern New Zealand, this perennial of up to 6 in (15 cm) high forms mounds of silvery, gray-green, lobed leaves. The pink or sometimes white saucer-shaped flowers are carried on slender stems above the foliage in summer to autumn. It is ***Geranium traversii* var. *elegans*** rather than the type that is found in cultivation; **'Seaspray'** has small, pale pink flowers on short stems. ZONES 8–9.

Geranium
traversii
'Seaspray'
(right)

GERBERA

This genus of around 40 perennial species is from Africa, Madagascar and Asia. The showy flowerheads, in almost every color except blue and purple, are carried on bare stems 18 in (45 cm) long. Linnaeus named the genus to honor a German colleague, Traugott Gerber. They are ideal rockery plants in frost-free climates. Only one species, *Gerbera jamesonii,* is commonly cultivated, along with its numerous hybrids.

CULTIVATION

They need full sun to part-shade in hot areas, and fertile, well-drained soil. Water well during summer. Gerberas make good greenhouse plants, where they require good light and regular feeding during the growing season. Propagate from seed in autumn or early spring, from cuttings in summer or by division from late winter to early spring.

G

Gerbera jamesonii 'Brigadoon Red' *(below)*

Gerbera jamesonii

BARBERTON DAISY, TRANSVAAL DAISY

Native to South Africa, this is one of the most decorative daisies and is an excellent cut flower. From a basal rosette of deeply lobed, lance-shaped leaves, white, pink, yellow, orange or red flowerheads, up to 3 in (8 cm) wide, are borne singly on long stems in spring and summer. Modern florists' gerberas derive from crosses between *Gerbera jamesonii* and the tropical *G. viridifolia*. Some have flowerheads as much as 12 in (30 cm) across, others in a wide range of colors, as well as double, for example **'Brigadoon Red',** and quilled forms. ZONES 8–11.

Gerbera jamesonii cultivars *(left & below)*

GEUM
AVENS

This genus of 50 or so herbaceous perennials is from the temperate and colder zones of both northern and southern hemispheres. Species form basal rosettes of hairy, lobed leaves. Masses of red, orange and yellow flowers with prominent stamens are borne from late spring until early autumn, and almost all year in frost-free areas. They suit mixed herbaceous borders and rock gardens, but may require a lot of room. *Geum capense* is suitable for a rock garden.

CULTIVATION
Frost hardy, they prefer a sunny, open position and moist, well-drained soil. Propagate from seed or by division in autumn or spring.

Geum chiloense
'Mrs Bradshaw' *(below)*

Geum chiloense
'Lady Stratheden' *(above)*

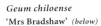

Geum chiloense
syns *Geum coccineum* of gardens, *G. quellyon*
SCARLET AVENS

This Chilean native grows to 24 in (60 cm) in height with a spread of 12 in (30 cm). It forms a basal rosette of deep green, pinnate leaves to 12 in (30 cm) long. The vivid scarlet, cup-shaped flowers appear in terminal panicles in summer. **'Lady Stratheden'** (syn. 'Goldball') has semi-double, golden yellow flowers. **'Mrs Bradshaw'** bears rounded, semi-double, scarlet flowers. ZONES 5–9.

Geum capense (below)

G

Geum montanum
(left)

ALPINE AVENS

From mountainous regions of southern and central Europe, this clump-forming perennial forms mats of up to 6 in (10 cm) high and 12 in (30 cm) wide. The basal leaves are pinnately divided, each with a large, rounded, terminal lobe. Solitary golden-yellow flowers are carried on short stems from spring to early summer. **ZONES 6–9.**

Geum triflorum
(left)

PRAIRIE SMOKE, PURPLE AVENS

Geum triflorum, native to northern USA and Canada, is a plant of 12–18 in (30–45 cm) with crowded leaves that have regularly incised margins. In summer it bears sprays of nodding, pinkish white flowers with long protruding styles. The flowers are followed by feathery, smoky gray seed heads that make a striking display in autumn. **ZONES 3–9.**

GILIA

From temperate western regions of both North and South America, this is a genus of about 30 species of annuals, biennials and perennials in the phlox family. The basal leaves are feathery and finely divided, and erect panicles of small, funnel- to trumpet-shaped flowers, often densely clustered, appear in spring and summer.

CULTIVATION

Moderately to very frost hardy, gilias prefer a climate with cool wet winters and hot summers, and well-drained soils in full sun. Water lightly and regularly. They are particularly sensitive to drought and heat and wilt rapidly. Light stakes may be needed for support on windy sites. Propagate from seed in spring directly where they are to grow when the soil has warmed up.

G

Gilia capitata (right)

QUEEN ANNE'S THIMBLES, BLUE THIMBLE FLOWER

Native to the west-coastal ranges of Canada, the USA and Mexico, this erect, branching annual to 24 in (60 cm) high has mid-green, fern-like leaves and tiny, soft lavender blue flowers that appear in a pincushion-like mass in summer and early autumn. It is a good cut flower and useful border plant. ZONES 7–9.

GILLENIA

This genus of the rose family consists of
2 species of rhizomatous perennials from
temperate North America. They are clump
forming with stalkless leaves consisting of
3 leaflets and starry, 5-petalled flowers.
After flowering the sepals enlarge and turn
red. They are easy to grow in a shady
position and make good cut flowers.

CULTIVATION

Very frost hardy, they prefer humus-rich,
moist but well-drained soil, preferably in
part-shade. Propagate from seed in spring
or by division in spring or autumn.

Gillenia trifoliata
(below)

INDIAN PHYSIC, BOWMAN'S
ROOT

This species is up to 4 ft
(1.2 m) tall and has red-
dish stems and bronze
green leaves composed
of 3 oval toothed leaf-
lets, each 3 in (8 cm)
long. Open panicles of
white or pale pink
starry flowers are pro-
duced throughout
summer. ZONES 3–9.

G

Glaucidium palmatum var. *leucanthum* (above)

Glaucidium palmatum

This clump-forming perennial has a height and spread of 15 in (40 cm). It has light green, palmately lobed leaves with crinkly surfaces and irregularly toothed edges. The large, cup-shaped, 4-petalled lilac or mauve flowers are borne in late spring and early summer. *Glaucidium palmatum* var. *leucanthum* (syn. 'Album') has white flowers. ZONES 6–9.

GLAUCIDIUM

This genus of a single species is indigenous to northern Japan. A rhizomatous perennial, its large pink to lilac flowers are somewhat poppy-like but in fact the genus is a relative of *Paeonia*.

CULTIVATION

Plant in rich, peaty soil with plenty of moisture. It prefers part- to deep shade and shelter from drying winds. Propagate from seed in spring or by careful division in early spring.

Glechoma hederacea
'Variegata' *(above)*

GLECHOMA

This genus consists of 12 species of low-growing, perennial plants. The stems root at the nodes, often forming extensive mats of coarsely toothed, rounded or broadly oval, soft hairy leaves. Ascending shoots bear pairs of small, tubular, 2-lipped flowers in the leaf axils in summer. They make good carpeting ground covers, but can be very invasive and should be kept away from heavily planted beds. They are good for containers and hanging baskets.

CULTIVATION

They prefer full sun or part-shade and moderately fertile, moist but well-drained soil. Propagate from cuttings in late spring or by division in spring or autumn.

Glechoma hederacea

GROUND IVY, RUNAWAY ROBIN

This prostrate species often forms mats to 6 ft (1.8 m) or more across, producing an unpleasant smell when bruised. The opposite, almost kidney-shaped leaves have scalloped margins. Small violet flowers are borne in late spring and early summer. **'Variegata'** has pretty, soft pale green leaves with white marbling. ZONES 6–10.

GLOBULARIA

GLOBE DAISY

The 20 or so species of this genus of mainly evergreen, tufted or sometimes mat-forming perennials or subshrubs are grown for their neat rounded habit and compact heads of many tiny tubular flowers in shades of blue. Many are suitable for a rock garden or container, such as the tight, cushion-forming 'Hort's Variety'. The bushy subshrubs such as *Globularia* × *indubia* and *G. sarcophylla* are attractive planted among other small shrubs or against low walls.

Globularia sarcophylla *(below)*

CULTIVATION

Most cultivated species are only moderately frost hardy. Grow in full sun in well-drained soil. Water sparingly and keep dry in winter. Propagate from seed in autumn or by division in spring and early summer.

Globularia × *indubia* *(below)*

G

Globularia gracilis
(left)

This tufted, upright perennial has dark green, spoon-shaped leaves on long stalks. The lavender-blue flowerheads are borne in summer. **ZONES 7–9.**

Globularia punctata *(left)*
syns *Globularia aphyllanthes, G. wilkommii*

Native to Europe, this is a tufted perennial to 12 in (30 cm) high with a basal rosette of long-stalked, somewhat spoon-shaped leaves. Indigo flowerheads are produced in summer. **ZONES 5–9.**

Globularia cordifolia *(below left)*

This evergreen mini-ature subshrubby per-ennial, found in central and southern Europe, has creeping woody stems with unusual tiny, spoon-shaped leaves, and produces solitary, stemless, fluffy blue to pale mauve flowerheads from late spring to early summer. It forms a dense mat or hummock, growing to a height of only 1–5 in (2.5–12 cm) and gradu-ally spreading to 8 in (20 cm) or more. **ZONES 6–9.**

GUNNERA

This is a genus of around 45 species of rhizomatous perennials from temperate regions of Africa, Australasia and South America. Occurring in moist habitats, they range in size from small, mat-forming plants to very large clumps with some of the largest leaves of any broad-leaved specimens. They are grown mainly for their striking foliage, although some species have attractive flower spikes and fruits.

CULTIVATION

Most species enjoy moist but well-aerated soil at the edge of a pond or stream. Plant in rich soil in full sun, although they may need shelter from very hot sun (which can scorch the leaves) and wind (which can reduce the leaves to tatters). Propagate from seed in autumn or spring, or by division in early spring. Protect from slugs and snails.

Gunnera tinctoria (above)
syn. *Gunnera chilensis*

Next in size to *Gunnera manicata*, this is a slow-growing species from Chile with large, heart-shaped, sharply toothed, deep green leaves up to 5 ft (1.5 m) wide and borne on prickly stalks to 5 ft (1.5 m) in length. Numerous tiny, rusty flowers are borne on erect cylindrical panicles up to 24 in (60 cm) high; they are followed in summer by rounded green fruit suffused with red. ZONES 6–7.

Gunnera manicata
(left)
syn. *Gunnera brasiliensis*

GIANT ORNAMENTAL RHUBARB

Native to the high mountain swamps of Brazil and Colombia, this huge plant thrives in boggy soil and is usually grown on the margins of a pond. The massive leaves quickly unfurl in spring to as wide as 8 ft (2.4 m) on prickly stalks about 6 ft (1.8 m) high. Long spikes of greenish red flowers are borne in summer. Give the dormant crown a protective mulch of straw in winter. ZONES 7–9.

GUZMANIA

The 120 species in this genus of evergreen, mostly epiphytic bromeliads have lance-shaped leaves that form funnel-shaped rosettes. The flowerheads of tubular white or yellow flowers are usually surrounded by colorful bracts on yellow, orange or bright red stems. Guzmanias are mostly rain-forest plants from the American tropics, and are therefore frost tender.

CULTIVATION

They require a position in part-shade in a well-drained compost. Water moderately during the growing season, less at other times, but always keep the leaf vases filled with water. If potting, leave enough room for just one year's growth and then repot. They make good indoor or greenhouse plants where they need plenty of indirect light. Fertilize only when in full growth, during the warmer months. Propagate from seed or offsets in spring or summer.

Guzmania lingulata

Ranging in the wild from Honduras to Bolivia, this is the most commonly grown species. It has basal rosettes of strap-like, apple-green leaves and grows to 12–18 in (30–45 cm) tall. Striking colored bracts surround clusters of tubular, white to yellow flowers in summer. *Guzmania lingulata* **var.** *minor* grows to 12 in (30 cm) high and across and has creamy yellow flowers and orange-red bracts. It is easily grown in a greenhouse. **'Indiana'** has erect golden yellow bracts tipped with orange-red. ZONES 10–12.

Guzmania 'Squarrosa' *(above)*

This cultivar is a clump-forming epiphyte with rosettes of colorful bronzy leaves that grow up to 3 ft (1 m) in length. The center of the foliage flares a brilliant red for a short period during bloom time. The bright red inflorescence is borne on a short erect stem, and the flowers are white. ZONES 11–12.

Guzmania lingulata 'Indiana' *(left)*

Gypsophila paniculata *(right)*

BABY'S BREATH

This short-lived perennial, mostly treated as an annual, has small, dark green leaves and sprays of tiny, white spring flowers. It reaches a height and spread of 3 ft (1 m) or more. **'Bristol Fairy'** has double white flowers. **'Compact Plena'** has double white or soft pink flowers. ZONES 4–10.

G

Gypsophila paniculata 'Compacta Plena' *(above)*

Gypsophila repens 'Rosea' *(below)*

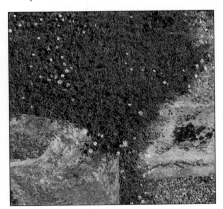

GYPSOPHILA

Native to Europe, Asia and North Africa, there are over 100 species of these annuals and perennials, some of which are semi-evergreen. They are grown for their masses of small, dainty, white or pink flowers, often used by florists as a foil for bolder flowers or foliage. The narrow leaves are borne in opposite pairs.

CULTIVATION

Plant in full sun with shelter from strong winds. Fully frost hardy, they will tolerate most soils, but do best in deep, well-drained soil lightened with compost or peat, and grow well in limy soil. Cut back after flowering to encourage a second flush. Transplant when dormant during winter. Propagate from cuttings in summer or from seed in spring or autumn.

Gypsophila repens

This prostrate perennial has stems forming low mounds up to 8 in (20 cm) high and 18 in (45 cm) wide. It has narrow, bluish green leaves and bears panicles of star-shaped, white, lilac or pale purple flowers in summer. It is an ideal plant for trailing over rocks. **'Dorothy Teacher'** has abundant pale pink flowers that age to deep pink. **'Rosea'** has deep pink flowers. ZONES 4–9.

H

HABERLEA

Of the more than 2000 species of the large African violet and gloxinia family (Gesneriaceae) only a small proportion extend beyond the tropics, and of these a mere half-dozen are native to Europe. The European species are shared among 3 genera, *Ramonda, Jankaea* and *Haberlea,* all perennials and restricted to small regions in the Pyrenees or the Balkans. *Haberlea* consists of 2 species only, occurring in Bulgaria and northern Greece. They are rosette plants that grow on rock ledges and in crevices, resembling some of the smaller *Streptocarpus* species in leaf and flower.

CULTIVATION

They require a climate with warm dry summers and cool wet winters but dislike excessive wetness around the roots at any time. Plant in freely draining crevices in a rock garden or a stone wall, or grow in pots with coarse gravel in an alpine house. Choose an aspect where the roots remain shaded but foliage gets some sun. Propagate from seed, by division of rhizomes, or from leaf cuttings.

Haberlea rhodopensis (left)

This pretty plant grows only to about 4–6 in (10–15 cm) in height, with spatulate, scalloped leaves arising from a short rhizome. In spring and early summer it produces stalked umbels of lilac flowers about 1 in (25 mm) across, the 3 lower petals much longer than the 2 upper. There is also a pure white-flowered form, 'Virginalis'. ZONES 6–9.

HACQUETIA
syn. *Dondia*

There is one species only in this genus: a tiny perennial from the woodlands of eastern Europe. At most it grows to 4 in (10 cm) tall, spreading very slowly into a small mat. The flowers appear in spring before the leaves and the plant is usually grown in rock gardens or in small pots in collections of alpine plants. It requires a cold winter for success.

CULTIVATION
Grow in porous, gritty soil that contains leafmold or other rotted organic matter in part- or dappled shade. Keep moist always but give more water from the time the flower buds appear until the leaves begin to yellow in autumn. Propagate from seed sown as soon as it is ripe or by division of clumps in late winter, before flower buds appear. Divide infrequently as it resents root disturbance.

Hacquetia epipactis
(right)
syn. *Dondia epipactis*

The pinhead-sized, bright yellow flowers of this species are surrounded by glossy green bracts, giving the effect of a most unusual bright green flower. Appearing straight from the ground in earliest spring, they are followed by 3-lobed leaves. This is a most unusual and desirable plant for cooler areas.
ZONES 6–9.

H

HEDYCHIUM
GINGER LILY

Ginger lilies, like frangipanis and hibiscus, are associated with
the tropics because of their lush foliage, glamorous flowers and
heady scent. Yet, of the 40 species of *Hedychium*, many grow
quite high on the mountains, indicating their tolerance for cooler
weather. Some recently introduced species are hardy enough to
be grown even in temperate gardens. They are perennials that
grow from rhizomes to form clumps up to 6 ft (1.8 m) high and
4 ft (1.2 m) wide. For most of the year in warm climates
(summer elsewhere) they bear spikes or heads of fragrant flowers
that last well and are good for cutting.

CULTIVATION

They prefer humus-rich, moist but well-drained soil in part-
shade. They flower in summer, and spent stems should be cut
out each season to ensure
vigorous growth—or cut
blooms for indoors.
Propagate from fresh seed
or by division.

Hedychium coccineum
(right)
RED GINGER LILY

This species from the Himalayas forms a low clump with
spreading stems and narrow
leaves. Its spectacular erect
flower spikes, which carry only
a few flowers, can reach 10 in
(25 cm) high. The blooms vary
from pale coral to a bright red,
always with the exaggerated
stamen in pink. The cultivar
'Tara' has brilliant orange
flowers and is more frost
hardy than the species.
ZONES 9–11.

Hedychium gardnerianum (below)

KAHILI GINGER

This species from the Himalayas grows to 8 ft (2.4 m) tall with long, bright green leaves clasping the tall stems. This is the most widely cultivated species; it prefers a warm climate although it will grow outside in temperate areas that have light, infrequent frosts. The fragrant, red and pale yellow flowers held in dense spikes, appear towards the end of summer. This species is considered a weed in some regions, such as in the north of New Zealand. **ZONES 9–11.**

Helenium 'Moerheim Beauty' *(left)*

This upright perennial has sprays of daisy-like, rich orange-red flower-heads with prominent, chocolate-brown central discs. They are borne in summer and early autumn above mid-green foliage. Easily grown, it gives color to borders and is useful for cut flowers. Slow growing to 3 ft (1 m) high and 24 in (60 cm) wide, it enjoys hot summers. **ZONES 5–9.**

HELENIUM
SNEEZEWEED, HELEN'S FLOWER

This genus, native to the Americas, consists of about 40 species of annual, biennial or perennial herbs. The mid-green leaves, which are alternate on erect stems, are oval to lance-shaped. The daisy-like flowerheads appear in summer and have yellow, red-brown or orange ray florets and yellow, yellow-green, red or brown disc florets. The flowers make a good border and are ideal for cutting.

CULTIVATION

Frost hardy, heleniums are easy to grow in any temperate climate as long as they get sun. The soil should be moist and well drained. Remove spent flowers regularly to prolong the flowering period. Propagate by division of old clumps in winter or from seed in spring or autumn.

Helenium autumnale *(above)*

COMMON SNEEZEWEED

This perennial from North America grows about
5 ft (1.5 m) tall. The flowers occur from late summer to mid-autumn. This species has given rise to
a number of named garden forms, whose flowers
range from yellow to maroon, with many being a
blend of yellow and russet tones. **ZONES 3–9.**

Heliamphora heterodoxa (left)

This sun pitcher is from the swampy mountains of Venezuela and grows to about 15 in (38 cm) in height. It has funnels up to 2 in (5 cm) in diameter and white to pink flowers in early winter. There are a number of forms. **ZONES 11–12.**

HELIAMPHORA

SUN PITCHERS

This genus contains 6 species of rhizomatous, carnivorous plants, allied to sarracenias, and is found on very wet mountains in Venezuela and Guyana. They have funnel-shaped, green to reddish leaves with, in most cases, a small overhanging cap. Each leaf has a nectar-secreting gland designed to attract small insects to their last meal. The flower stems may be up to 24 in (60 cm) tall, each with several delicate white flowers changing to pink with age.

CULTIVATION

These plants grow naturally in wet, peaty soil and prefer warm, humid conditions, though preferably less than 86°F (30°C); they tolerate a minimum temperature of 40°F (5°C). They are best grown in a pot with a mixture of peat, sand and sphagnum moss placed in a saucer of water. Propagate by division of rhizomes in spring or from seed.

Heliamphora nutans (below)

This is an intriguing sun pitcher with green, basal, pitcher-shaped leaves with red margins and a constriction in the middle. It grows 4–8 in (10–20 cm) high and has large, nodding white to pink flowers on 6–12 in (15–30 cm) stalks. **ZONES 11–12.**

HELIANTHEMUM
ROCK ROSE, SUN ROSE

Helianthemum means flower of sunshine, an appropriate name for flowers that only open in bright sunlight. Allied to *Cistus*, the genus contains over 100 species found on rocky and scrubby ground in temperate zones around the world. Sun roses are sturdy, short-lived, evergreen or semi-evergreen shrubs or subshrubs. Their bushy foliage ranges in color from silver to mid-green. There are many garden forms, mostly of low, spreading habit. Wild plants have flowers resembling 1 in (25 mm) wide wild roses, but garden forms can be anything from white through yellow and salmon-pink to red and orange, and some varieties have double flowers.

CULTIVATION
Plant in full sun in freely draining, coarse soil with a little peat or compost added during dry periods. As the flowers fade, they should be cut back lightly to encourage a second flush of bloom in autumn. Propagate from seed or cuttings.

Helianthemum nummularium
(below)

A variable species from Europe and Turkey, *Helianthemum nummularium* has a neat, prostrate habit. Its small but profuse flowers vary in color from yellow or cream to pink and orange. Most of the cultivars that are traditionally listed under this name are in fact of hybrid origin. ZONES 5–10.

HELIANTHUS

This genus of the daisy family includes plants used for livestock fodder, the Jerusalem artichoke with edible tubers, many ornamentals, and one of the world's most important oilseed plants. Consisting of around 70 species of annuals and perennials, all native to the Americas, they have large, daisy-like, usually golden yellow flowerheads, which are on prolonged display from summer to autumn. The plants have hairy, often sticky leaves and tall, rough stems.

CULTIVATION

Frost hardy, they prefer full sun and protection from wind. The soil should be well drained. Fertilize in spring to promote large blooms and water generously in dry conditions. Perennials should be cut down to the base after flowering. Propagate from seed or by division in autumn or early spring.

Helianthus annuus (below)
COMMON SUNFLOWER

This fast-growing, upright annual can reach a height of 10 ft (3 m) or more. Large, daisy-like, 12 in (30 cm) wide, yellow flowerheads with brown centers are borne in summer. They are tall, leggy plants with broad, mid-green leaves. This species produces one of the world's most important oilseeds. It can be a little large for small gardens, but newer varieties have been developed that grow to a more manageable size, about 6 ft (1.8 m). They include **'Autumn Beauty'**, with medium-sized flowers usually brownish red, deep red, light yellow or golden yellow; and **'Teddy Bear'**, a compact grower with double, dark yellow flowers. ZONES 4–11.

H

Helianthus
maximilianii *(above)*

Growing to at least
10 ft (3 m) tall, this
perennial has rough
stems densely covered
with spearhead-shaped
leaves about 8 in
(20 cm) long. Golden
yellow flowers 4–6 in
(10–15 cm) across
appear in summer and
autumn. ZONES 4–9.

Helianthus ×
multiflorus *(right)*

This hybrid is a clump-
forming perennial to
6 ft (1.8 m) in height
and 3 ft (1 m) in spread.
The domed flowers can
be up to 6 in (15 cm)
across and appear in
late summer and mid-
autumn. The most
popular cultivars in-
clude **'Capenoch Star'**,
'Loddon Gold', **'Soleil
d'Or'** and **'Triomphe
de Gand'**. ZONES 5–9.

H

Helianthus ×
multiflorus 'Loddon
Gold' *(above)*

Helianthus ×
multiflorus
'Triomphe de Gand'
(left)

HELICHRYSUM
EVERLASTING, PAPER DAISY, STRAWFLOWER

As understood until recently, this is a genus of around 500 species of annuals, perennials and shrubs, their highest concentration being in southern Africa followed by Australia, with smaller numbers in the Mediterranean, west and central Asia, and New Zealand. Belonging to the daisy family, they all have flowerheads with no ray florets or 'petals' but instead papery, mostly whitish bracts that are long-lasting when dried, hence the common names. But study by botanists has shown this to be an unnatural group, and they have been busy carving off both large and small groups of species and renaming them as distinct genera. This study is ongoing, and many species still in *Helichrysum* will eventually be reclassified, particularly among the South African species. The 'true' helichrysums include the Mediterranean and Asian species and an uncertain number from southern Africa; some well-known Australasian species have been reclassified under genera such as *Bracteantha*, *Ozothamnus* and *Chrysocephalum*.

CULTIVATION
Most species will tolerate only light frosts and are best suited to mild climates with low summer humidity, but a few are more frost hardy. They are mostly rock garden plants, requiring gritty, well-drained soil that is not too fertile and a warm, sunny position. Propagate from seed, cuttings, or rhizome divisions.

Helichrysum argyrophyllum
(below)

This shrubby perennial from eastern South Africa grows to 4 in (10 cm) and is used as a ground cover. It has silvery leaves and clusters of yellow flowers from summer to early winter. The 'petals' are in fact brightly colored bracts surrounding the central florets. ZONES 9–11.

H

H

Helichrysum petiolare (right)
syn. *Helichrysum petiolatum* of gardens
LICORICE PLANT

This South African evergreen is an excellent foliage plant; its gray, heart-shaped leaves and its stems are covered with cobweb-like white hairs. It is a sprawling subshrub forming dense mounds 24 in (60 cm) or more high and 6 ft (1.8 m) or more wide, with new stems springing from a network of rhizomes. It is well adapted to sun or shade and to dry conditions. The flowers, only occasionally produced, are not showy. **'Limelight'** has pale chartreuse foliage, and **'Variegatum'** has a creamy variegation. Both of these cultivars do better in shade and are superb summer container plants in cold climates. ZONES 9–10.

Helichrysum retortum (below)

This prostrate perennial from the Cape region of South Africa can grow to 8 in (20 cm) with a spread of 18 in (45 cm). It has contorted stems with bright, silvery-gray oval leaves and pretty, white papery flowers in spring. It is marginally frost hardy. ZONES 9–11.

HELICONIA
LOBSTER CLAW, FALSE BIRD-OF-PARADISE

From tropical America, Southeast Asia and some Pacific Islands, these beautiful, exotic plants have large leaves and spikes of colorful bracts enclosing relatively insignificant flowers. There are around 100 evergreen perennial species and hybrids in this genus, which is related to bananas and strelitzias. Planted *en masse*, heliconias create an eye-catching show of color all year round. The bracts may be red, yellow or orange, or scarlet tipped with yellow and green, or lipstick red and luminous yellow. The leaves are spoon-shaped and grow to 6 ft (1.8 m) long. Heliconias make excellent cut flowers.

H

CULTIVATION
Grow only in warm, tropical gardens with a winter minimum of 64°F (18°C). Plant in humus-rich, well-drained soil in filtered sun and with summer humidity. Water well during the growing season. To encourage new growth, remove all dead leaves and flowers. Propagate by division of the rootstock in spring, ensuring there are 2 shoots on each division. Check for spider mites, snails and mealybugs.

Heliconia bihai (right)
syns *Heliconia humilis*, *H. jacquinii*
FIREBIRD, MACAW FLOWER

The large, paddle-shaped, green leaves of this species surround a flower stem of pointed, scarlet bracts tipped with green and inconspicuous white flowers. This is the most familiar species and is popular for flower arrangements.
ZONES 11–12.

H

Heliconia collinsiana *(left)*

COLLINS' HELICONIA,
HANGING HELICONIA

Growing to around 12 ft (3.5 m) tall, this heliconia grows into a dense clump of thin stems from which the pendulous flowers hang in long strings. Bracts are 8–10 in (20–25 cm) long, bright red and sheath the golden yellow true flowers. The whole plant is dusted with a staining, powdery bloom. **ZONES 11–12.**

Heliconia latispatha *(below)*

This big, vigorous plant of wide occurrence in tropical America needs plenty of room to spread. It has showy bracts that may be yellow, red or a combination of both. Bracts appear atop tall, erect stems, each pointing in a different direction. In the wild, they are pollinated by hummingbirds. **ZONES 11–12.**

Heliconia rostrata (above)

FISHTAIL HELICONIA

Possibly the most striking of the heliconias, this species from Peru and Argentina has a large, pendulous cascade of alternating bracts of scarlet tipped with yellow and green. It grows 3–20 ft (1–6 m) in height. **ZONES 11–12.**

Heliconia wagneriana (right)

RAINBOW HELICONIA, EASTER HELICONIA

From steamy Central America, this magnificent heliconia with its cream, red and green bracts cannot fail to impress. They grow at least 12 ft (3.5 m) tall, but the spring flowering season is relatively short for heliconias. **ZONES 11–12.**

Heliconia psittacorum (below)

PARROT FLOWER

Ranging from eastern Brazil to the West Indies, this smaller species is good for mass planting. It has long-stalked, lance-like, rich green leaves. Narrow, pinkish, orange or pale red bracts surrounding yellow or red flowers with green tips are produced in summer. It is usually 3–5 ft (1–1.5 m) tall. **ZONES 11–12.**

H

HELIOPSIS
ORANGE SUNFLOWER, OX EYE

The name *Heliopsis* means resembling a sunflower, and these perennials from the North American prairies do look like sunflowers, though on a rather reduced and more manageable scale. There are about 12 species, with stiff, branching stems and toothed, mid- to dark green leaves. The solitary, usually yellow flowers are up to 3 in (8 cm) wide and make good cut flowers.

CULTIVATION
These plants are easily grown, and will even tolerate poor conditions. However, they thrive in fertile, moist but well-drained soil and a sunny position. They are all very frost hardy. Deadhead regularly to prolong the flower display and cut back to ground level after flowering finishes. Propagate from seed or cuttings in spring, or by division in spring or autumn.

Heliopsis helianthoides

This species grows to 5 ft (1.5 m) tall and 3 ft (1 m) in spread. It has coarse, hairy leaves and golden yellow flowers in summer. The cultivar **'Patula'** has semi-double orange flowers. **'Light of Loddon'** has rough, hairy leaves and strong stems that carry dahlia-like, bright yellow, double flowers in late summer. It grows to a height of 3 ft (1 m) and a spread of 24 in (60 cm). ZONES 4–9.

Heliopsis helianthoides
'Light of Loddon' *(right)*

HELIOTROPIUM
HELIOTROPE

This genus consists of over 250 species of annuals, perennials, shrubs and subshrubs from most warmer parts of the world. The leaves are simple and usually alternate. The clusters of flowers can be purple, blue, white or yellow and are deliciously scented. They appear in summer and are attractive to butterflies. The smaller varieties make excellent pot plants.

CULTIVATION
Heliotropes grow wild in both subtropical and cooler temperate climates and hence vary in frost hardiness. They prefer moist, well-drained, moderately fertile soil. Cut plants back by about half in early spring to promote bushiness. Propagate from seed in spring or cuttings in early autumn.

Heliotropium arborescens
(above)

syn. *Heliotropium peruvianum*
CHERRY PIE, COMMON HELIOTROPE

Traditionally treated as a perennial, this attractive, soft-wooded evergreen shrub bears clusters of fragrant, purple to lavender flowers, with a delicate scent similar to stewed cherries, from late spring to autumn. From the Peruvian Andes, it grows fast to 30 in (75 cm) tall and 3 ft (1 m) wide. It has dark green, wrinkled leaves, golden to lime-green in the cultivar '**Aurea**', and dark purplish green in '**Lord Robert**'. In cold climates it is grown as a conservatory or summer bedding plant. ZONES 9–11.

HELLEBORUS
HELLEBORE

Native to areas of Europe and western Asia, these 15 perennial or evergreen species are useful winter- and spring-flowering plants for cooler climates. They bear beautiful, open flowers in white or shades of green, red and purple and are effective planted in drifts or massed in the shade of deciduous trees. All hellebores are poisonous.

CULTIVATION

Grow in part-shade and moist, well-drained, humus-rich soil, which is not allowed to dry out in summer. Cut off old leaves from deciduous species just as the buds start to appear. Remove flowerheads after seeds drop. A top-dressing of compost or manure after flowering is beneficial. Propagate from seed or by division in autumn or early spring. Check for aphids.

Helleborus foetidus (above)
STINKING HELLEBORE

This clump-forming perennial has attractive, dark green, divided leaves that remain all year. In winter or early spring the clusters of pale green, bell-shaped flowers, delicately edged with red, are borne on short stems. Established plants will often self-seed readily. ZONES 6–10.

Helleborus argutifolius
(right)
syns *Helleborus corsicus*,
H. lividus subsp. *corsicus*
CORSICAN HELLEBORE

This is one of the earliest flower-ing hellebores, with blooms appearing in late winter and early spring. It is a robust evergreen that bears large clusters of cup-shaped, nodding, 2 in (5 cm) wide, green flowers on an upright spike above divided, spiny-margined, deep green foliage. It has a clump-forming habit, growing to a height of 24 in (60 cm) and a spread of 24–36 in (60–90 cm). This is the most sun- and drought-tolerant species of the genus. ZONES 6–9.

H

Helleborus lividus
(below)

This species from the islands of the western Mediterranean has deep green or bluish green leaves and bowl-shaped, creamy green flowers from winter to spring. It is slow to establish after being transplanted. **ZONES 7–9.**

Helleborus orientalis *(above)*
LENTEN ROSE

The most widely grown of the genus, this evergreen, clump-forming species from Greece, Turkey and the Caucasus grows to 24 in (60 cm) high and wide. The large nodding flowers come in a great variety of colors from white, green, pink and rose to purple, sometimes with dark spots. Very frost hardy, it flowers in winter or early spring. The dense foliage fades and can be trimmed back before flowering. **ZONES 6–10.**

Helleborus niger *(right)*
CHRISTMAS ROSE

Popular for its white, mid-winter flowers, often appearing in the snow, this is one of the more temperamental species. It is often worth covering the plant with a cloche before the flowers open, to protect them from the winter weather. The mid-green, deeply lobed leaves are evergreen; mounds are 12 in (30 cm) high with a spread of 12–18 in (30–45 cm). They need steady moisture. **ZONES 3–9.**

H

Helleborus 'Queen of the Night'
(left)

Possibly a hybrid between *Helleborus orientalis* and *H. purpurascens*, this plant produces simple, open-faced flowers that are a brownish purple color. ZONES 6–10.

Helleborus purpurascens (below)

Flowering from about mid-winter, even in cool climates, this frost-hardy, deciduous perennial from eastern Europe blooms before the new season's leaves appear. Plants grow anywhere up to 12 in (30 cm) tall but often less and the clumps spread at least 12 in (30 cm) across. The compound leaves are big and lobed and the flowers are an odd gray-green-pink combination. ZONES 6–9.

HEMEROCALLIS
DAYLILY

Native to temperate east Asia, these perennials, some of which are semi-evergreen or evergreen, are grown for their showy, often fragrant flowers that come in a vibrant range of colors. Individual blooms last only for a day, but are borne in great numbers on strong stems above tall, grassy foliage and continue to flower from early summer to autumn. The flower size varies from 3 in (8 cm) miniatures to giants of 6 in (15 cm) or more, single or double. Plant heights range from about 24 in (60 cm) to 3 ft (1 m). Grow in a herbaceous border among shrubs or naturalize in grassy woodland areas.

CULTIVATION
Position carefully when planting because the flowers turn their heads towards the sun. Most daylilies are fully hardy. They prefer sun but will grow well and give brighter colors in part-shade. Plant in a reasonably good soil that does not dry out. Propagate by division in autumn or spring, and divide clumps every 3 or 4 years. Cultivars raised from seed do not come true to type. Check for slugs and snails in early spring. Plants may also suffer from aphid or spider mite attack.

Hemerocallis forrestii (below)

Collected from the Yunnan Province of China by the plant hunter George Forrest in 1906, this species grows to 18 in (45 cm) with evergreen leaves to 12 in (30 cm). The flower stem rises from the outer foliage and bears 5 to 10 yellow, funnel-shaped flowers. It is less frost hardy than most other species. **ZONES 5–10.**

Hemerocallis fulva
TAWNY DAYLILY

This clump-forming species to 3 ft (1 m) high and 30 in (75 cm) wide, bears rich orange-red, trumpet-shaped, 3–6 in (8–15 cm) wide flowers from mid- to late summer. It has been in cultivation for centuries, and in China and Japan the flower buds are sold as food. **'Flore Pleno'** (syn. 'Kwanzo') has 6 in (15 cm), double, orange flowers with sepals curved back and a red eye. **'Kwanzo Variegata'** bears similar flowers to 'Flore Pleno' and has leaves with a white margin. **ZONES 4–11.**

Hemerocallis fulva
'Flore Pleno' *(below)*

Hemerocallis Hybrids

Almost all the cultivated species of *Hemerocallis* have played their part in producing the vast range of modern daylily hybrids. Most have been bred for size and texture of blooms, together with rich or delicate coloring, often with an 'eye' of contrasting color in the center; but some others are grown more for the massed effect of smaller or more spidery flowers which can be of great elegance. A recent development is a range of miniatures, in many colors and with either broad or narrow petals: one of the most popular is **'Stella d'Oro'** with clear golden yellow flowers of almost circular outline. **ZONES 5–11.**

Hemerocallis Hybrid, 'Berlin Lemon' *(below)*

Hemerocallis Hybrid, 'Apricot Queen' *(below)*

Hemerocallis Hybrid,
'Baldone' *(right)*

H

Hemerocallis Hybrid,
'Bonus' *(left)*

H

Hemerocallis Hybrid,
'Brownie the Gold'
(above)

Hemerocallis Hybrid,
'Gone Native' *(right)*

Hemerocallis Hybrid,
'Grand Prize' *(right)*

H

Hemerocallis Hybrid,
'Egyptian Ruffles' *(left)*

Hemerocallis Hybrid,
'Grown Fire' *(below)*

H

Hemerocallis Hybrid,
'Chemistry' *(left)*

Hemerocallis Hybrid,
'Christmas Day' *(below)*

Hemerocallis Hybrid,
'Constant Eye' *(below)*

Hemerocallis Hybrid,
'Custom Design' *(above)*

Hemerocallis Hybrid,
'Coquetry' *(right)*

H

H

Hemerocallis Hybrid,
'High Priestess' *(above)*

Hemerocallis Hybrid,
'Esau' *(left)*

Hemerocallis Hybrid,
'Florisant Snow' *(right)*

Hemerocallis Hybrid,
'Golden Wonder' *(left)*

Hemerocallis Hybrid,
'Holy Mackerel' *(right)*

H

Hemerocallis Hybrid, 'Irish Ranger' *(above)*   *Hemerocallis* Hybrid, 'Jadis' *(above)*

Hemerocallis Hybrid,
'Silver Threads' *(left)*

Hemerocallis Hybrid,
'Ming Porcelain' *(above)*

Hemerocallis Hybrid,
'Mama Joe' *(left)*

H

Hemerocallis Hybrid,
'Memories' *(left)*

Hemerocallis Hybrid,
'Red Waves' *(below)*

Hemerocallis Hybrid,
'Rocket City' *(above)*

Hemerocallis Hybrid,
'Russian Rhapsody'
(left)

Hemerocallis Hybrid,
'Scarlet Pansy' *(left)*

Hemerocallis Hybrid,
'Rose Tapestry' *(right)*

Hemerocallis Hybrid,
'Velvet Shadow' *(left)*

H

Hemerocallis Hybrid,
'So Excited' *(right)*

H

Hemerocallis Hybrid,
'Stella d'Oro' *(left)*

Hemerocallis Hybrid,
'Wynnson' *(right)*

Hemerocallis lilioasphodelus *(left)*
syn. *Hemerocallis flava*

PALE DAYLILY, LEMON DAYLILY

This was one of the first daylilies to be used for
breeding. It is found across China, where it forms
large, spreading clumps with leaves up to 30 in
(75 cm) long. The lemon yellow flowers are
sweetly scented and borne in a cluster of 3 to 9
blooms. It has a range of uses in Chinese herbal
medicine: some parts may be eaten, while others
may be hallucinogenic. ZONES 4–9.

HEPATICA
LIVERLEAF

Hepatica is closely related to *Anemone,* as the flower shape suggests. There are 10 species from North America, Europe and temperate Asia. They are all small, hairy, spring-flowering perennial herbs. The supposed resemblance of their leaves to a liver gave them their common and botanical names: *hepar* is Latin for liver. They have medicinal uses in liver and respiratory complaints, as well as for indigestion. There are a number of garden varieties with white, blue or purple flowers, sometimes double.

CULTIVATION
They occur naturally in woodlands so prefer part-shade and rich, moist but well-drained soil. Propagate from seed or by division, especially for the double varieties.

Hepatica nobilis
(right)
syns *Anemone hepatica, Hepatica triloba*

An inhabitant of mountain woods across much of Europe, this small perennial has solitary blue, pink or white ½–1¼ in (12–30 mm) flowers on long stalks. It has evergreen leaves with 3 broad, rounded lobes, usually purplish beneath. Although the plant is poisonous, it has been used as a herbal remedy for coughs and chest complaints. ZONES 5–9.

H

Hesperis matronalis *(left)*
DAME'S ROCKET, SWEET ROCKET

Ranging from Europe to central
Asia, *Hesperis matronalis* is
grown for its flowers which become very fragrant on humid
evenings. It has smooth, narrowly oval leaves and branching
flowerheads with white to lilac
flowers borne in summer. Upright in habit, this species grows
12–36 in (30–90 cm) in height
with a spread of about 24 in
(60 cm). Plants lose their vigor
after a time and are best renewed
every 2 to 3 years. **ZONES 3–9.**

HESPERIS

From the Mediterranean and temperate Asia, this genus
consists of 60 species of biennials and herbaceous perennials allied to stocks *(Matthiola)*. They have narrow,
usually undivided leaves that may be toothed or tooth-
less, and showy pink, purple or white flowers in long
racemes. The flowers of some species are fragrant.

CULTIVATION

The species are readily grown in temperate areas and
will naturalize, but cultivars sometimes prove more difficult. Frost hardy, they prefer full sun and moist but
well-drained, neutral to alkaline, not too fertile soil.
Propagate from seed or cuttings and check regularly for
mildew and also for attack from slugs and snails.

HETEROCENTRON
syn. *Schizocentron*

About 27 species of shrubby or creeping plants make up this genus which is allied to *Tibouchina*. Originating in Mexico and Central and South America, *Heterocentron* are grown for their showy, 4-petalled, white, pink, mauve or purple flowers which appear from summer to winter.

CULTIVATION
These plants grow well in sun or part-shade in well-drained soil. They are frost tender, and need a minimum temperature of 40°F (5°C). Propagate from cuttings in late winter or early spring.

Heterocentron elegans (above)
syn. *Schizocentron elegans*
SPANISH SHAWL

Native to Central America, *Heterocentron elegans* is a prostrate, evergreen perennial. It is a popular ground cover in areas of warm climate. The foliage is dense, trailing and mid-green, and masses of bright carmine-purple flowers cover the plant in summer. This plant grows to a height of 2 in (5 cm) with an indefinite spread. ZONES 10–11.

HETEROTHECA

From the southern parts of the USA and Mexico
comes this genus of around 20 species of annuals and
perennials in the daisy family. The leaves, which may
be silvery or green, smooth edged or toothed, form
a basal clump from which (usually) branched flower
stems arise. Species vary in height from about
8 in (20 cm) to 5 ft (1.5 m).

CULTIVATION

They are best grown in dry, sandy or gravelly soil in
full sun. Where winters are always frosty, plants may
rot if that season is also rainy and will need some shelter. In areas with milder winters, rain has no ill-effect
so long as soil drains fast. Propagate annuals from
seed sown in spring; perennial species by division
in spring.

H

Heterotheca villosa
'San Bruno Mountain'
(left)

Heterotheca villosa
syn. *Chrysopsis villosa*
HAIRY GOLDEN ASTER

A variable perennial from Texas and New Mexico, this species is
sometimes erect, sometimes sprawling, and has hairy, gray-
green leaves and 1 in (25 mm) wide golden yellow flowerheads
in summer and autumn. In hot, dry locations, this species may
only reach a height of 8 in (20 cm) but in better soil with regular
water it may grow over 30 in (75 cm) tall. It is frost hardy. **'San
Bruno Mountain'** is a form selected for attractive foliage and
profusion of flowers. ZONES 5–9.

HEUCHERA
ALUM ROOT, CORAL BELLS

There are about 55 species of these evergreen and semi-evergreen perennials, which are native to North America and Mexico. They form neat clumps of scalloped leaves, often tinted bronze or purple, from which arise stems bearing masses of dainty, nodding, white, crimson or pink bell-shaped flowers often over a long flowering season. They make useful woodland, rock garden, edging plants or can be used as ground covers.

CULTIVATION
Mostly very frost hardy, they grow well in either full sun or semi-shade and like well-drained, coarse, moisture-retentive soil. Propagate species from seed in autumn or by division in spring or autumn. Cultivars can be divided in autumn or early spring. Remove spent flower stems and divide established clumps every 3 or 4 years.

Heuchera × *brizoides* 'June Bride' *(above)*

Heuchera × brizoides *(left)*
This group are all complex hybrids involving *Heuchera sanguinea* and several other species. Highly attractive, they produce mounds of rounded, lobed leaves that are prettily marbled. Above these rise tall, slender, arching stems bearing dainty bell-like flowers in white, as in **'June Bride'**, or shades of pink or red. Foliage mounds are about 12 in (30 cm) tall with flower stems rising at least another 12 in (30 cm). **ZONES 3–10.**

H

Heuchera maxima
(left)

ISLAND ALUMROOT

Found only on the islands off the southern Californian coast, this species has big, coarse, deeply lobed and cut leaves and bears its small, pinkish white flowers on thick, sturdy stems. It grows well in dry, dappled shade and is marginally frost hardy. ZONES 9–10.

Heuchera micrantha var. diversifolia
'Palace Purple' *(right)*

This cultivar is grown for its striking, purple, palmate leaves and panicles of tiny white flowers in summer. It is clump forming, with a height and spread of about 18 in (45 cm). The leaves last well as indoor decoration. ZONES 5–10.

Heuchera 'Pewter Veil' *(left)*

This beautiful hybrid has silvery green leaves with a contrasting network of deep green veins. Pinkish red flowers appear on stout, red stems. ZONES 5–10.

Heuchera pilosissima (right)
SHAGGY ALUMROOT

Compact and free flowering, this Californian species has maple-like lobed and toothed leaves that are rather hairy to the touch. In late spring, pink or white flowers are generously borne on the tall stems typical of the genus. ZONES 6–10.

H

Heuchera sanguinea
(left)
CORAL BELLS

This is the most commonly grown species, and occurs naturally from Arizona to New Mexico. It grows to 18 in (45 cm) tall and has sprays of scarlet or coral red flowers above toothed, deeply lobed leaves. British and American gardeners have developed cultivars with a wider color range, from pale pink to deep red, and slightly larger flowers. **Bressingham hybrids** are a typical example. ZONES 6–10.

Heuchera villosa (right)

From the mountains of eastern USA, this species has glossy, bronze-green leaves with pointed, triangular lobes. The flowers are usually white but may be pink. ZONES 5–10.

× HEUCHERELLA

This hybrid genus is the result of a cross between *Heuchera* and *Tiarella*, both members of the saxifrage family. Plants are evergreen, clumping or ground-covering perennials with tall, airy stems of dainty pink or white flowers. These are produced over a long season beginning in late spring. The leaves are rounded, lobed and have distinct veins. When young they are bronze-red, turning green during summer then reddish in autumn.

CULTIVATION

Heucherellas are easy to grow and enjoy leafy, rich, moist but well-drained soil. Where summers are mild, full sun is best, but in hotter areas dappled or part-shade suits them and they will do reasonably well in full shade that is not too dark. Propagation by division is easy and this should be done in autumn or winter in mild areas, spring in cooler places.

H

× *Heucherella tiarelloides*

Growing about 12 in (30 cm) tall with flower stems rising a further 12–15 in (30–38 cm), this fully hardy perennial spreads by creeping stolons. The leaves are lobed and toothed and form a dense, rounded mound. Small pink flowers appear on red stems. In the cultivar **'Bridget Bloom'** the flowers are a soft, pastel pink and very freely produced. ZONES 5–9.

× *Heucherella tiarelloides* 'Bridget Bloom' *(above)*

Hibiscus
moscheutos (left)

COMMON ROSE MALLOW,
SWAMP ROSE MALLOW

This herbaceous peren-
nial grows to 8 ft
(2.4 m) high and 3–5 ft
(1–1.5 m) wide. Single,
hollyhock-like flowers,
4–8 in (10–20 cm)
wide, are carried on
robust, unbranched
stems in late summer
and autumn. Colors
vary from white to
pink, some with deeper
throat markings.
The leaves are large,
toothed and softly
hairy beneath. A range
of lower-growing
cultivars with dramatic
large flowers have been
bred, including '**South-
ern Belle**', with rose
pink blooms up to
10 in (25 cm) across.
ZONES 5–9.

H

HIBISCUS

While the genus name conjures up the innumerable cultivars of
Hibiscus rosa-sinensis, the genus of around 220 species is quite
diverse, including hot-climate evergreen shrubs and small trees
and also a few deciduous, temperate-zone shrubs and some
annuals and perennials. The leaves are mostly toothed or lobed
and the flowers, borne singly or in terminal spikes, are of characteristic shape with a funnel of 5 overlapping petals and a central
column of fused stamens.

CULTIVATION
Easy to grow, the shrubby species thrive in sun and slightly acid,
well-drained soil. Water regularly and feed during the flowering
period. Trim after flowering to maintain shape. Propagate from
seed or cuttings or by division, depending on the species. Check
for aphids, mealybugs and white fly. The *H. rosa-sinensis* cultivars make greenhouse subjects in frosty climates, and compact-
growing cultivars are gaining popularity as house plants.

HOSTA
PLANTAIN LILY

Natives of Japan and China, the 40 species in this genus of easily grown, frost-hardy perennials are valued for their decorative foliage. They all produce wide, handsome leaves, some being marbled or marked with white and others a bluish green. All-yellow foliage forms are also available. They do well in large pots or planters, are excellent for ground cover, and add an exotic touch planted on the margins of lily ponds or in bog gardens. Tall stems to about 18 in (45 cm) tall, bear nodding, white, pink or shades of purple and blue, bell- or trumpet-shaped flowers during warmer weather. Both the leaves and the flowers are popular for floral arrangements.

CULTIVATION
They grow well in shade and rich, moist, neutral, well-drained soil. Feed regularly during the growing season. Propagate by division in early spring, and guard against snails and slugs.

Hosta crispula (left)

This handsome species has elongated, lanceolate, distinctly pleated leaves. They are gray-green with creamy white margins. Pale lavender flowers are produced in early summer but it is the foliage that is the chief attraction. ZONES 6–10.

Hosta 'Birchwood Parky's Gold' *(right)*
syn. *Hosta* 'Golden Nakaiana'

The big leaves of this hybrid open yellowish green but turn golden with age and as summer progresses. It is a strong-growing plant up to 18 in (45 cm) tall that slowly spreads to form large colonies. Mauve flowers are produced in late spring or summer. ZONES 6–10.

Hosta 'Eric Smith' *(left)*

This hybrid has big, rounded leaves with a blue-green bloom and is best grown where summers are mild with cool nights. **ZONES 6–10.**

Hosta fluctuans 'Sagae' *(below)*

H

Hosta fluctuans
KURONAMI-GIBOSHI

This Japanese species has very unusual foliage. The leaves, up to 10 in (25 cm) long, taper markedly from a broad base and are wavy and twisted. They are a deep olive shade on their upper surface with noticeably gray undersides. The flower scape is blue-green, around 3 ft (1 m) tall and carries pale violet flowers. **'Sagae'** or **'Sagae-giboshi'** is a Japanese form that has leaves with creamy white edges. **ZONES 7–10.**

Hosta fortunei 'Aureomarginata' *(below)*

Hosta fortunei

This strong-growing perennial has given rise to many hybrids. It has ovate or broad lanceolate, pleated and pointed leaves that are a dull mid-green. In summer, tall flower stems are produced from which hang lavender flowers. Plants grow at least 18 in (45 cm) tall but spread nearly twice as wide. **'Albomarginata'** has gray-green leaves with creamy yellow to white margins; **'Albopicta'** has leaves marbled or irregularly marked in 2 shades of green; **'Aurea'** is a luminous golden green; and **'Aureomarginata'** has leaves edged with yellow. **ZONES 6–10.**

H

Hosta fortunei 'Aurea'
(right)

Hosta fortunei
'Albomarginata' *(above)*

Hosta fortunei
'Albopicta' *(right)*

Hosta 'Frances Williams' *(right)*

This large-growing vigorous variegated hybrid was raised by F. & C. Williams in 1986. Although it is slow to propagate, it has quickly become one of most popular hostas. It has large gray-green, heart-shaped, puckered leaves heavily edged with pale greenish yellow. The flowers are lavender. **ZONES 6–10.**

Hosta 'Gold Edger' *(left)*

'Gold Edger' forms a 12 in (30 cm) tall mound of broad, yellowish green leaves and produces tall spikes of almost white flowers in summer. **ZONES 6–10.**

Hosta 'Golden Sculpture' *(left)*

This big-leafed plant with quilted foliage is a combination of yellow and green overlaid with a powdery bloom. It is a vigorous grower. **ZONES 6–10.**

H

Hosta 'Halcyon' *(right)*

Striking gray-blue leaves
make 'Halcyon' an arrest-
ing sight, especially when
contrasted against green
or yellow foliage. Its summer flowers are a dusty
mauve color. **ZONES 6–10.**

Hosta 'Golden Tiara' *(below)*

'Golden Tiara' forms a dense mound of dull green
leaves edged in golden green. As a bonus,
it produces unusual striped purple flowers in
summer. A compact plant, it rarely exceeds 12 in
(30 cm) in height. **ZONES 6–10.**

Hosta 'Honeybells' *(left)*

'Honeybells' has oval to heart-shaped leaves, about 10 in (25 cm) long, with strong veins. The short-lived white flowers, opening from mauvish buds, are borne in late summer. Some are pleasantly scented in the evening. ZONES 6–10.

Hosta 'Hydon Sunset' *(above)*

The leaves of this hybrid open lime green but age to yellow, creating a dense clump of various shades of yellow-green. The flowers are a deep lavender purple. ZONES 6–10.

Hosta 'June' *(below)*

'June' has similar gray-blue leaves to its parent *Hosta* 'Halcyon', overlaid with splashes of yellow and green. ZONES 6–10.

H

Hosta lancifolia *(above)*
NARROW LEAFED PLANTAIN LILY

This smaller-leafed species forms a clump to 18 in (45 cm) high and 30 in (75 cm) wide. It has narrow, lance-shaped, glossy mid-green leaves. It bears racemes of trumpet-shaped, pale lilac flowers in late summer and early autumn. **ZONES 6–10.**

Hosta 'Krossa Regal' *(below)*

This hybrid has beautiful powdery gray-green leaves that are upward folded, wavy edged and distinctly pleated. **ZONES 6–10.**

Hosta 'Pearl Lake' *(above)*

The 4 in (10 cm) long leaves of this hybrid are plain gray-green with a slight powdery bloom. The lavender-blue flowers are are quite showy. **ZONES 6–10.**

Hosta 'Royal Standard'
(left)

This *Hosta plantaginea* hybrid was registered in 1986 by Wayside Gardens. It forms clumps of deep green glossy foliage with fragrant, white, lily-like flowers on 24 in (60cm) stems from late summer. One of the few hostas grown as much for its flowers as its foliage. The only drawback is that it needs reasonably mild late summer and early autumn weather to perform well. ZONES 8–10.

H

Hosta plantaginea
(right)

AUGUST LILY, FRAGRANT PLANTAIN LILY

Popular for its pure white, fragrant flowers on 30 in (75 cm) stems, this species has mid-green leaves forming a mound 3 ft (1 m) across. It flowers in late summer. ZONES 3–10.

H

Hosta sieboldiana *(left)*

This robust, clump-forming plant grows to 3 ft
(1 m) high and 5 ft (1.5 m) wide. It has puckered,
heart-shaped, bluish gray leaves and bears racemes
of mauve buds, opening to trumpet-shaped white
flowers in early summer. **'Frances Williams'** has
heart-shaped, puckered blue-green leaves with
yellowish green margins. ***Hosta sieboldiana* var.
*elegans*** also has heart-shaped, puckered leaves.
ZONES 6–10.

Hosta tokudama *(right)*

This very slow-growing perennial, native to
Japan, has racemes of trumpet-shaped, pale
mauve flowers that are borne above cup-shaped
blue leaves in mid-summer. Clump forming, it
reaches a height of 18 in (45 cm) and a spread of
30 in (75 cm). There are several cultivars available: **'Aureonebulosa'** has leaves splashed with
green and yellow; **'Flavocircinalis'** has heart-
shaped leaves with creamy margins. ZONES 6–10.

Hosta tokudama
'Aureonebulosa' *(left)*

H

Hosta undulata

(above)

WAVY LEAFED PLANTAIN LILY

Hosta undulata has creamy white, wavy or twisted leaves that are splashed and streaked green along their edges. Mauve flowers on tall stems in summer complete this attractive and desirable specimen. **ZONES 6–10.**

Hosta 'Wide Brim'

(right)

This hybrid has dark green heavily puckered leaves with a broad white margin. Its flowers are pale lavender. It was registered in 1979 by the well-known hosta authority Paul Aden. **ZONES 6–10.**

HOUTTUYNIA

There is only one species in this genus, a wide-spreading, creeping herbaceous perennial native to eastern Asia. It grows in moist or wet, part- or fully shaded areas. It is a good ground cover in moist, woodland gardens or beside ponds and can also grow in shallow water or boggy ground. The wild form has dark green, heart-shaped, red-margined, plain green leaves, and in summer bears spikes of tiny yellowish flowers with 4 pure white bracts at the base of each spike.

CULTIVATION

Grow this frost-hardy plant in moist, leafy rich soil. In cooler climates the plant will tolerate sun so long as the ground is moist, but in hotter places some shade is desirable. Where winters are always cold, reduce water in winter or cover the roots with a thick layer of straw. Propagate from ripe seed or from cuttings in late spring and early summer, or by division in spring.

Houttuynia cordata (below)

Ranging from the Himalayas to Japan, this water-loving deciduous perennial makes a good ground cover but may become invasive. It is a vigorous plant, growing to 12 in (30 cm) in height with an indefinite spread. It grows from underground runners that send up bright red branched stems bearing aromatic green leaves. However, the most popular form, **'Chameleon'** (syns 'Tricolor', 'Variegata') is strikingly variegated in red, cream, pink and green. ZONES 5–11.

H

HUNNEMANNIA
MEXICAN TULIP POPPY, GOLDEN CUP

This genus consists of one species of poppy found in dry, elevated parts of Mexico. It has an upright habit and is fast growing to a height of 24 in (60 cm) with a spread of 8 in (20 cm). It has decorative, oblong, finely dissected, bluish green leaves and bears rich, glowing yellow, single or semi-double, 3 in (8 cm) wide, poppy-like flowers in summer and early autumn.

CULTIVATION
Grow in full sun in free-draining, sandy or gravelly soil. Plants do not enjoy cold, wet winters although they can withstand considerable frost in their native range where winter days are sunny. In the UK and similar cool, rainy climates they are often grown as annuals, the seed sown under glass in late winter or early spring. Deadhead plants regularly to prolong flowering and provide support in exposed areas. Water liberally during hot weather.

Hunnemannia fumariifolia (above)

One of the best yellow-flowered perennials, this relative of the California poppy (*Eschscholzia californica*) is grown as an annual in frost-prone areas. ZONES 8–10.

H

HYPERICUM
ST JOHN'S WORT

This is a large and varied genus of 400 species
of annuals, perennials, shrubs and a few small
trees, some evergreen but mostly deciduous,
grown for their showy flowers in shades of
yellow with a central mass of prominent golden
stamens. They are found throughout the world
in a broad range of habitats. Species range in
size from tiny perennials for rockeries to over
10 ft (3 m) tall.

CULTIVATION
Mostly cool-climate plants, they prefer full sun
but will tolerate some shade. They do best in
fertile, well-drained soil, with plentiful water in
late spring and summer. Remove seed capsules
after flowering and prune in winter to maintain
a rounded shape. Cultivars are propagated
from cuttings in summer, and species from
seed in autumn or from cuttings in summer.
Some species are susceptible to rust.

*Hypericum
cerastoides* (above)
syn. *Hypericum
rhodoppeum*

This densely mounding
perennial has oval, gray-
green leaves and terminal
clusters of bright yellow,
cup-shaped flowers in late
spring and early summer.
It has an upright, slightly
spreading habit and grows
to 12 in (30 cm) tall with
a 18 in (45 cm) spread.
Frost hardy, it is useful in
rock gardens. ZONES 6–9.

HYSSOPUS
HYSSOP

This genus of aromatic culinary and medicinal herbs belongs to the mint family and includes about 5 species of herbaceous perennials and shrubs. All are found in poor soils around the northern Mediterranean coasts and also in Asia Minor. The leaves vary with species from linear to ovate and may be green or blue-green in color. The flowers are small, tubular with protruding stamens, and usually a shade of blue although they may also be white or pink.

CULTIVATION
All species do best in full sun and although they will grow in dry sandy soil, in gardens they look much better when grown in friable, fertile loam though good drainage is essential. Ensure adequate water particularly in autumn and winter. Propagate from cuttings taken in early summer or from seed sown in autumn. Prune by shearing plants all over.

H

Hyssopus
officinalis (left)
HYSSOP

This bushy perennial herb grows to 24 in (60 cm) and has narrow, pointed, dark green leaves. Spikes of small violet-blue flowers, which are attractive to bees and butterflies, are borne in late summer. White and pink flowering forms are also available. Fully frost hardy, hyssop is evergreen in mild climates; in cool areas it dies down for the winter. The slightly bitter leaves are used in small quantities with fatty meats and fish. The essential oil made from the leaves has antiseptic properties and is used in the manufacture of perfumes. ZONES 3–11.

IBERIS

This genus consists of around 50 species of annuals, perennials and evergreen subshrubs, which are mainly from southern Europe, northern Africa and western Asia. Highly regarded as decorative plants they are excellent for rock gardens, bedding and borders.

Iberis spathulata
(below)

The showy flowers are borne in either flattish heads in colors of white, red and purple, or in erect racemes of pure white. *Iberis spathulata* is an alpine perennial endemic to the Pyrenees.

CULTIVATION

Fully to marginally frost hardy, they require a warm, sunny position and a well-drained, light soil, preferably with added lime or dolomite. Propagate from seed in spring or autumn—they may self-sow, but are unlikely to become invasive—or cuttings in summer.

Iberis amara cultivar
(left)

Iberis amara

CANDYTUFT, HYACINTH-
FLOWERED CANDYTUFT

This frost-hardy, fast-growing and erect bushy annual has lance-shaped, mid-green leaves and reaches a height of 12 in (30 cm), with a spread of 6 in (15 cm). It produces large racemes of small, fragrant, pure white flowers in early spring and summer. Various strains are available. The **Hyacinth-flowered Series** has large fragrant flowers in varying shades of pink; these are sometimes used as cut flowers. ZONES 7–11.

Iberis umbellata
(right)

GLOBE CANDYTUFT

Native to the Mediter-
ranean region, this up-
right bushy annual has
lance-shaped, mid-
green leaves. Flattish
heads of small, mauve,
lilac, pink, purple, car-
mine or white flowers
are produced in late
spring and summer.
Iberis umbellata grows
to a height of 6–12 in
(15–30 cm) and a
spread of 8 in (20 cm).
It is frost hardy and is a
useful cut flower. The
Fairy Series has flowers
in shades of pink, red,
purple or white which
appear in spring.
Bushes in this series
grow to a height and
spread of 8 in (20 cm).
Lightly trim after flow-
ering. **ZONES 7–11.**

Iberis pruitii
(below right)
syn. *Iberis jordanii*

A short-lived perennial
or occasionally an
annual, this species is
native to the Mediter-
ranean. It grows to
about 6 in (15 cm) tall
with a spread of 8 in
(20 cm). *Iberis pruitti*
has slightly fleshy, dark
green rosette-forming
leaves and produces
tight clusters of lilac to
white flowers in sum-
mer. It is frost hardy,
but is susceptible in
wet winter conditions.
ZONES 7–11.

Iberis sempervirens
(right)

**CANDYTUFT,
EVERGREEN CANDYTUFT**

A low, spreading, ever-
green perennial, this
species from southern
Europe is ideal for rock
gardens. It has narrow,
dark green leaves and
dense, rounded heads
of unscented white
flowers in spring and
early summer. It is
frost hardy, and grows
6–12 in (15–30 cm)
high with a spread of
18–24 in (45–60 cm).
The cultivar '**Snow-
flake**' is most attrac-
tive, with glossy, dark
green leaves and semi-
spherical heads of
white flowers. Lightly
trim after flowering.
ZONES 4–11.

Impatiens glandulifera (left)
syn. *Impatiens roylei*

POLICEMAN'S HELMET, HIMALAYAN BALSAM

A native of the Himalayas, this plant has naturalized in both the UK and northern North America. A frost-hardy annual with a strong self-seeding tendency, it grows to about 6 ft (1.8 m) tall. It has thick fleshy stems, particularly at the bottom, and produces masses of flowers during summer. Its flowers are rose-purple to lilac or even white with a yellow-spotted interior. **ZONES 6–10.**

IMPATIENS

This large genus of around 850 species of succulent-stemmed annuals, evergreen perennials and subshrubs is widely distributed, especially in the subtropics and tropics of Asia and Africa. They are useful for colorful summer bedding displays and for indoor and patio plants. The flowers come in an ever-increasing range of colors. Many hybrid strains are perennial in mild climates, but in colder climates are usually grown as annuals. Their botanical name, *Impatiens,* refers to the impatience with which they grow and multiply.

CULTIVATION

Frost hardy to frost tender, they will grow in sun or part-shade: many species do well under overhanging trees. They prefer a moist but freely drained soil, and need protection from strong winds. Tip prune the fast-growing shoots to encourage shrubby growth and more abundant flowers. Propagate from seed or stem cuttings in spring and summer.

Impatiens, New Guinea Hybrids

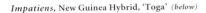

Hybrids from a New Guinean species, members of this group of fast-growing perennials are also grown as annuals in cool climates. They are frost tender and grow to a height and spread of 12–18 in (30–45 cm). The leaves are oval, pointed and bronze green, or may be variegated with cream, white or yellow. The flat, spurred flowers are pink, orange, red or cerise, sometimes with white markings. Cultivars include **'Cheers'**, with its coral flowers and yellow leaves; **'Concerto'**, with crimson-centered deep pink flowers; **'Tango'**, with deep orange flowers; and **'Red Magic'**, which has scarlet flowers and bronze-red leaves. They do well in brightly lit positions indoors in cooler climates, or on enclosed verandahs or patios in warmer areas. **'Toga'** has blueish pink flowers. **ZONES 10–12.**

Impatiens, New Guinea Hybrid, 'Toga' *(below)*   *Impatiens,* New Guinea Hybrid, 'Concerto' *(above)*

I

Impatiens pseudoviola *(left)*

This semi-trailing East African species is a perennial. It produces white flowers suffused with rose pink, with violet-rose central stripes on the wing petals. **'Woodcote'** is a shrubby, pale pink-lilac form. **ZONES 10–12.**

Impatiens pseudoviola 'Woodcote' *(below)*

*Impatiens usambarensis ×
walleriana* (above)

Impatiens
usambarensis

This tropical African species gets its name from the
Usambara Mountains on
the borders of Kenya and
Tanzania, where it was
first discovered. It is related to the better known
Impatiens walleriana, and
has been used in the
breeding of the many
colorful 'busy lizzie' hybrids in this group. *I. u. ×
walleriana*, seen here,
displays just one of the
many possible color out-
comes in such crosses.
ZONES 10–12.

Impatiens repens *(below)*

GOLDEN DRAGON

This evergreen, creeping perennial is native to Sri Lanka.
It bears golden, hooded flowers with a large hairy spur in
summer; these stand out against the small, kidney-
shaped leaves with red stems. *Impatiens repens* is frost
tender, and grows to a height of 2 in (5 cm). This species
is especially suited to hanging baskets. **ZONES 10–12.**

INCARVILLEA

This genus of the bignonia family (Bignoniaceae) consists of 14 species native to central and East Asia, including the Himalayas. They are suitable for rock gardens and the taller species are more at home in herbaceous borders. Some species are annuals, although those in cultivation are usually perennial. From mountain habitats, some of the shorter growing types from higher altitudes have, strangely enough, the largest and most exotic flowers. Most species have flowers in shades of magenta and deep rose pink, although 1 or 2 have flowers in shades of yellow or white.

CULTIVATION

Most species of *Incarvillea* are frost hardy, but do not tolerate overly wet or water-logged soil in winter. They usually require an aspect that has rich, moisture-retentive, well-drained soil, in a position that receives ample sun except in the very hottest part of the day. These plants prefer cold to temperate climates. Propagation is usually by seed in autumn or spring; division in spring or autumn is possible, but difficult, as mature plants resent disturbance.

Incarvillea delavayi (above)
PRIDE OF CHINA, HARDY GLOXINIA

This fleshy-rooted, clump-forming perennial is useful for rock gardens and borders. It has handsome, fern-like foliage and erect stems bearing large, trumpet-shaped, rosy purple flowers in summer. It grows to a height of 24 in (60 cm) with a spread of 12 in (30 cm), but dies down early in autumn. It is very frost hardy, but should be protected with a compost mulch during cold winters. ZONES 6–10.

Incarvillea arguta (left)

This hardy species from the Himalayas and western and southwestern China grows to about 3 ft (1 m) tall with a spread of 12 in (30 cm). It is more suitable for a border than a rock garden, although it will grow in a crevice in a wall. It will flower in the first year from seed and although perennial is sometimes treated as an annual. Its 1½ in (35 mm) long trumpet-shaped flowers are usually deep pink or sometimes white, and are produced through summer. ZONES 8–10.

Inula helenium
(left)

ELECAMPANE, SCABWORT

Believed to have originated in central Asia, this plant has become widely naturalized. It is one of the largest *Inula* species at 8 ft (2.4 m) tall with a spread of 3 ft (1 m). As it is rhizomatous, it is also one of the most invasive. It produces its large, yellow daisy-like flowers in summer and should be planted with due deference to its invasive potential. *Inula helenium* was used in medicine as a tonic, astringent, demulcent and diuretic. Because of this, it is often planted in herb gardens. **ZONES 5–10.**

INULA

Native to Asia, Africa and Europe, this genus of about 90 species in the daisy family are mostly herbaceous perennials, although some are subshrubs, biennials or annuals. The different species vary in size from quite tiny plants suited to the rock garden up to towering perennials that can exceed 10 ft (3 m) tall. Often in the case of the larger species, the leaves can also be impressive if somewhat rank. Inulas are well known for their fine-petalled, invariably yellow daisies, some species of which are quite large and showy. Several species have been cultivated since ancient times and the name *Inula* was used by the Romans.

CULTIVATION

Inulas are frost hardy plants. They will grow in any deep, fertile, well-drained or moist soil, but not one that is wet. They prefer a sunny to part-shaded aspect. Propagation is usually from seed or by division in either spring or autumn.

IPOMOEA
syns *Calonyction, Mina, Pharbitis, Quamoclit*
MORNING GLORY

This large genus of some 300 mostly climbing, evergreen shrubs, perennials and annuals is widespread throughout the tropics and warm-temperate regions of the world. It includes sweet potato and some of the loveliest of the tropical flowering vines. Most species have a twining habit and masses of funnel-shaped flowers, which in many species wither by midday. The flowers are usually short-lived, lasting only one day (or night), but bloom prolifically and in succession. They are useful for covering sheds, fences, trellises and banks, and may also be grown in containers.

CULTIVATION
Marginally frost hardy to frost tender, they are best suited to warm coastal districts or tropical areas. They prefer moderately fertile, well-drained soil and a sunny position. Care should be taken when choosing species, as some can become extremely invasive in warm districts. Propagate in spring from seed that has been gently filed and pre-soaked to aid germination, or from cuttings in summer (for perennial species).

Ipomoea nil (above)
syns *Ipomoea imperialis, Pharbitis nil*

This soft-stemmed, short-lived, twining perennial is best treated as an annual. Marginally frost hardy, it grows to 12 ft (3.5 m) in height. Its stems are covered with hairs, and the leaves are heart-shaped. Large, trumpet-shaped flowers appear from summer through to early autumn in a variety of shades. **'Scarlett O'Hara'** is a cultivar with dark crimson blooms. ZONES 9–12.

Ipomoea × multifida (right)
syn. *Ipomoea × sloteri*
CARDINAL CLIMBER

This is a hybrid of *Ipomoea coccinea* and *I. quamoclit* of garden origin. A frost-tender annual climber with slender twining stems, it reaches 10 ft (3 m) in height. The foliage is mid-green and divided into several lobes. Its tubular flowers, produced during summer, are crimson-red with white throats. **ZONES 9–12.**

Ipomoea tricolor 'Heavenly Blue' *(below)*

Ipomoea tricolor
syns *Ipomoea rubrocaerulea, I. violacea, Pharbitis tricolor*

This Mexican perennial vine is more often grown as an annual. It can reach a height of 10 ft (3 m) with a spread of 5 ft (1.5 m), and has cord-like, twining stems and heart-shaped, light green leaves. From summer to early autumn, *Ipomoea tricolor* bears large, blue to mauve, funnel-shaped flowers that open in the morning and gradually fade during the day. Widening to a trumpet as they open, the flowers can reach 6 in (15 cm) across. The cultivar **'Heavenly Blue'** is particularly admired for its color, as is the very similar **'Clarke's Himmelblau'**. **ZONES 8–12.**

IRESINE

Belonging to the amaranthus family, these tropical perennials from the Americas and Australia—some 80 species in all—are sometimes treated as annuals. They vary in habit from upright to ground-hugging. The flowers are insignificant and not the reason for which these plants are grown. It is for their often brilliantly colored leaves that they merit attention.

CULTIVATION

These frost-tender plants only make permanent garden plants in tropical to warm-temperate climates, where there is no incidence of frost. In cooler areas they can be grown in greenhouses and planted out once all chance of frost has passed. They prefer good loamy, well-drained soil and must be kept moist during the growth period. They also need bright light, with some direct sun, to retain the brilliant color in their leaves. Tips should be pinched out in the growing season to encourage bushy plants. Propagate from cuttings in spring.

Iresine herbstii 'Brilliantissima' *(below)*

Iresine herbstii *(above left)*
syn. *Iresine reticulata*
BEEFSTEAK PLANT, BLOODLEAF

Native to Brazil, this species makes an attractive tropical bedding or pot plant. Although perennial, it is often treated as an annual that is overwintered as struck cuttings in a greenhouse in cold areas. It grows to 24 in (60 cm) tall with a spread of 18 in (45 cm), but usually much less if grown as an annual. It has red stems and rounded, purple-red leaves up to 4 in (10 cm) long, with notches at the tips and yellowish red veins. Garden forms have a range of color, from bright green leaves with bright yellow veins, through to cultivars such as 'Brilliantissima', with its rich purple-green leaves and beetroot-pink veins. ZONES 10–12.

IRIS

This wide-ranging genus of more than 200 species, native to the temperate regions of the northern hemisphere, is named for the Greek goddess of the rainbow, and is valued for its beautiful and distinctive flowers. Each flower has 6 petals: 3 outer petals, called 'falls', which droop away from the center and alternate with the inner petals, called 'standards'. There are many hybrids. Irises are divided into 2 main groups: **rhizomatous** and **bulbous**.

Rhizomatous irises have sword-shaped leaves, are sometimes evergreen, and are subdivided into 3 groups: **bearded** (or flag) irises, with a tuft of hairs (the 'beard') on the 3 lower petals; **beardless** irises, without the tuft; **crested** or Evansia irises, with a raised crest instead of a beard.

The bearded types include the rare and beautiful **Oncocyclus** and **Regelia** irises, native to the eastern Mediterranean and Central Asia. Therefore they need cold winters and hot, dry summers to flourish. Hybrids between these 2 groups are called **Regeliocyclus** irises, while hybrids between either of them and other bearded irises are called **Arilbred** irises. But the main group of bearded irises consists of numerous species with thick, creeping rhizomes, mainly from temperate Eurasia, and countless hybrids bred from these: both species and hybrids can be subdivided into the 3 classes **Tall Bearded**, **Intermediate Bearded** and **Dwarf Bearded** irises, depending mainly on the plant's height but some other characteristics as well. Tall bearded irises are the most popular class of irises, with by far the largest number of hybrid cultivars.

The beardless irises mostly have long, narrow leaves and include several identifiable groups of species and hybrids. Most notable are the East Asian **Laevigatae** or **Water** irises, including the large-flowered 'Kaempferi' irises derived from *I. ensata*, the **Louisiana** irises from southeastern USA and their hybrids, the **Pacific Coast** irises from the west side of North America, also with many hybrids, and the Eurasian **Spuria** and **Siberian** irises, consisting of numerous species and a scattering of hybrids.

The bulbous irises are also divided into 3 groups, the **Juno**, **Reticulata** and **Xiphium** irises. The first 2 consist of beautiful, but mostly difficult bulbs, from west and central Asia. The Xiphium irises, though, are centered on the Mediterranean and are more easy to grow; they have given rise to a group of bulbous hybrids including the so-called **English**, **Spanish** and **Dutch** irises. It is the latter that are commonly seen in florist shops.

CULTIVATION

Growing conditions vary greatly. As a rule, rhizomatous irises, with the exception of the crested or Evansia irises, are also very frost hardy and prefer a sunny position; some of the beardless types like very moist soil. Bulbous irises are also very frost hardy, and prefer a sunny position with ample moisture during growth, but very little during their summer dormancy. Bulbous irises should be planted in autumn and are prone to virus infection and so need to be kept free of aphids, which will spread the infection. Propagate irises by division in late summer after flowering or from seed in autumn. Named cultivars should only be divided.

Iris bracteata (above)

SISKIYOU IRIS

So called because its leaves on the flowering stems are short and bract-like, this native of Oregon inhabits dry conifer forests. Its flowers are usually predominantly cream or yellow, but some plants with reddish toned flowers exist. The falls are flared with reddish veins, and its standards are erect. The flowers are held on stems 12 in (30 cm) tall. Although frost hardy, this species is not easy to grow; it resents being lifted and divided, so is best raised from seed. ZONES 7–9.

Iris cristata (below)

CRESTED IRIS

A woodland crested or Evansia iris native to southeastern USA, this rhizomatous species grows 4–9 in (10–22.5 cm) in height. In spring, it bears faintly fragrant, pale blue to lavender or purple flowers held just above the foliage; each fall has a white patch with an orange crest. It prefers a moist soil in part-shade, making it suitable as a ground cover in shaded gardens; it spreads slowly by rhizomes. 'Alba' is a vigorous cultivar with white flowers. ZONES 6–9.

Iris cristata 'Alba' *(left)*

Iris ensata *(right)*
syn. *Iris kaempferi*
JAPANESE FLAG, HIGO IRIS

Native to Japan and cultivated there for centuries, this beardless iris grows to 3 ft (1 m) tall. It has purple flowers that appear from late spring to early summer, with yellow blotches on each fall. The leaves have a prominent midrib. The many cultivars bear huge flowers, up to 10 in (25 cm) wide, in shades of white, lavender, blue and purple, often blending 2 shades, and some with double flowers. These plants prefer part-shade in hot areas, rich, acid soil and plenty of moisture. They can even grow in shallow water provided they are not submerged during the winter months. The foliage dies down in winter. **'Exception'** has particularly large falls and deep purple flowers; **'Mystic Buddha'** has purple-blue flowers with red edging. **ZONES 4–10.**

Iris ensata 'Exception' *(right)*

Iris douglasiana *(below)*
DOUGLAS IRIS

One of the chief parents of the Pacific Coast irises, this evergreen, rhizomatous beardless species comes from the coastal mountain ranges of California. It reaches 10–30 in (25–75 cm) in height and its branched stems produce 1 to 3 flowers in early spring. The flowers are variable in color, from rich blue-purple to almost white, while the leathery, dark green leaves are stained with maroon at the base. It readily hybridizes with other species from its region. **ZONES 8–10.**

I

Iris germanica var.
biliottii (left)

Iris germanica
'Florentina' (below)

Iris germanica (above)
COMMON FLAG, GERMAN IRIS

The putative ancestor of the
modern bearded irises, this
rhizomatous, bearded species is
easy to grow in just about any
temperate climate. Its creeping
rhizomes multiply rapidly into
large clumps. The sparsely
branched stem produces up to
6 yellow-bearded, blue-purple
to blue-violet flowers in spring.
Iris germanica var. biliottii
(syn. Iris biliottii) occurs naturally in the Black Sea region of
Turkey. It grows to about 3 ft
(1 m) tall and, like I. germanica,
has scented flowers. This variety
has reddish purple falls with
standards of a more blue-purple
shade, and the beard is white
with yellow tips. Another form
of I. germanica is 'Florentina',
which has scented white flowers
with a bluish flush and yellow
beards. Its bracts are brown and
papery during flowering.
'Florentina' is cultivated in
Italy, for its perfume (orris
root), which is released when
the roots are dried. It is an
early-flowering variety that prefers a position in full sun.
ZONES 4–10.

Iris innominata *(below)*
DEL NORTE COUNTY IRIS

Native to the northwest coast of the
USA, this rhizomatous, beardless iris
is one of the parent species of the
Pacific Coast Hybrids. It reaches
6–10 in (15–25 cm) in height. Its
evergreen, narrow, deep green leaves
are up to 12 in (30 cm) long and are
purple at their bases. The unbranched stems bear 1 or 2 flowers
in early summer. They range in
color from bright yellow to cream,
and from pale lavender-blue to
purple. The falls may be veined with
brown or maroon. **ZONES 8–10.**

Iris japonica *(top right & right)*
syn. *Iris fimbriata*
CRESTED IRIS

This is the best known of the
crested or Evansia species. It grows
to 18–32 in (45–80 cm) in height,
forming large clumps of almost
evergreen, glossy mid-green leaves.
In late winter and spring, it bears
sprays of 2½ in (6 cm) wide, ruffled, pale blue or white flowers;
each fall has a violet patch around
an orange crest. It prefers an acidic
soil, a lightly shaded position, and a
mild climate. It must be kept shaded
from afternoon sun. **ZONES 8–11.**

Iris lutescens
syn. *Iris chamaeiris*

Iris lutescens is a variable rhizomatous, dwarf bearded iris from southwestern Europe similar to *I. pumila*. It is fast growing and can have foliage that is less than ½ in (12 mm) to more than 1 in (2.5 cm) wide and up to 12 in (30 cm) long. The flowers, borne in early spring, can be yellow, violet blue, white or bicolored; the beard is yellow. This is an easy-to-grow and showy species, but it does need winter cold to flower well. **'Caerulea'** is a bluish version of *I. lutescens*. ZONES 5–9.

Iris lutescens 'Caerulea'
(above)

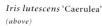

Iris lactea *(below)*

This widespread beardless species allied to *Iris ensata* is found from central Russia to Korea and the Himalayas. It has stiff, upright, gray-green leaves up to about 2 in (5 cm) wide which can overtop the 12 in (30 cm) tall flower spikes. These are produced in early summer and have 1 or 2 fragrant pale lavender-blue or rarely white flowers. This strong plant will cope with both frost and heat, but is one of the less spectacular irises. ZONES 4–9.

Iris maackii *(left)*

This little known and comparatively newly described species from China is related to *Iris laevigata*. The flowers are more than 2 in (5 cm) wide and completely yellow. It should prove to be a hardy and dainty iris, growing up to about 12 in (30 cm) tall. ZONES 4–9.

Iris orientalis *(right)*
syn. *Iris ochroleuca*
SWAMP IRIS

This 4 ft (1.2 m) tall, almost evergreen, rhizomatous beardless iris from western Asia has mid-green leaves and white and yellow flowers in early summer. **Iris orientalis var. monnieri** is an all-yellow form. Although these plants will grow in damp ground, they are perfectly happy in any rich, well-watered garden soil in a sunny position. ZONES 6–9.

Iris missouriensis
(center)
syn. *Iris tolmeiana*
MISSOURI FLAG,
ROCKY MOUNTAIN IRIS

A widespread rhizomatous, beardless iris extending through western and central North America from Mexico to British Columbia, this is a very frost-hardy and easy-to-grow plant, although quite variable in appearance. It reaches 30 in (75 cm) in height. It likes moist soil up until it flowers in early spring and drier conditions during summer. This species can make substantial clumps with slender leaves. Its flowers vary in color from very pale blue through to deep blue or lavender, with some white forms. The falls, veined with deep purple, usually have a yellow blaze. ZONES 3–9.

Iris munzii *(right)*
MUNZ'S IRIS

One of the largest flowering of the Pacific Coast irises, this species grows up to 30 in (75 cm) tall. Blooms up to 3 in (8 cm) wide are borne in summer. The flowers vary in color from pale blue through lavender to dark red-purple, with the veins often darker. This species is not very frost hardy. ZONES 8–10.

Iris pallida (left)
DALMATIAN IRIS

This bearded iris from the Dalmatian region of Croatia has fragrant, pale blue flowers with yellow beards, which are borne on 4 ft (1.2 m) high stems in late spring. It is often grown as a source of orris (also obtained from *I. germanica* 'Florentina'), a volatile substance that develops in the dried and aged rhizomes and is used in perfumes, dental preparations and breath fresheners. **'Variegata'** (syn. 'Aurea Variegata') has handsome leaves striped in gray-green and cream. **ZONES 5–10.**

Iris pallida 'Variegata' *(above)*

Iris pseudacorus
'Variegata' *(right)*

Iris pseudacorus (left)
WATER FLAG, YELLOW FLAG

A robust beardless iris from Europe, the water flag has handsome, mid-green leaves and profuse bright yellow flowers on 3 ft (1 m) stems which are borne in early spring. The flowers usually have brown or violet veining, with a darker yellow patch on the falls. It prefers to grow in shallow water and rich soil; plant in autumn in a box of rich earth and place in a sunny position in the garden pond. The cultivar **'Variegata'** has yellow- and green-striped foliage during the spring months, often turning green in summer; it is less vigorous than the species. **ZONES 5–9.**

Iris setosa subsp. *canadensis* *(right)*

This subspecies of a more widely spread species is found from Newfoundland to Ontario and south to Maine in North America. It grows to 24 in (60 cm) tall, although it is often shorter. A beardless iris, it flowers from late spring to early summer. Its flowers are usually solitary and are lavender-blue in color. This is a tough, easy-to-grow plant ideal for rock gardens. **ZONES 3–9.**

Iris 'Roy Davidson' *(center)*

This beardless iris is a hybrid of *Iris pseudacorus* and as such is a suitable plant for a boggy site, although it is equally happy in moist garden conditions. It grows to slightly more than 3 ft (1 m) tall and has yellow flowers very like its parent, except that they last longer and are about 4 in (10 cm) across. **ZONES 5–9.**

Iris pumila

This dainty little bearded iris is distributed throughout central and eastern Europe and Turkey, varying considerably over its range. It has thick fleshy rhizomes and, in flower, rarely exceeds 6 in (15 cm) in height. The color also varies greatly and may be white, yellow, violet, purple or blue, with yellow or blue beards on the falls. It prefers a sunny position and well-drained, slightly alkaline soil. **'Purpurea'** is a deep purple form. **ZONES 4–9.**

Iris pumila 'Purpurea' *(below)*

Iris sibirica 'Perry's Blue' *(left)*

Iris sibirica 'Vi Luihn' *(left)*

Iris sibirica *(above)*
SIBERIAN FLAG

Despite the name, this well-known species has a natural distribution across temperate Eurasia from France to Lake Baikal. It is one of the most popular beardless irises, usually found in gardens in one of its cultivars rather than its wild form. The plants make strongly vertical clumps of slender bright green leaves 2–4 ft (0.6–1.2 m) high. In late spring or early summer, flowering stems rise above the foliage with narrow-petalled, blue, purple or white flowers, often veined in a deeper color. It prefers full sun to very light shade (particularly in hot areas), a moderately moist, rich soil that may be slightly acid and water during the hottest periods. It will grow in a wet soil and does best in cold winter climates. Some of the available cultivars include **'Cleave Dodge'**, with mid-blue flowers; **'Perry's Blue'**, which has rich lilac-blue flowers with yellow markings and netted brown towards the base of the falls; **'Ruby'**, which has purplish blue flowers; **'White Swirl'**, which has pure white flowers with yellow at the base and flared, rounded petals; and **'Vi Luihn'**, with flowers in a rich violet shade. ZONES 4–9.

Iris sibirica 'Cleave Dodge' *(left)*

Iris tenax (right)
syn. *Iris gormanii*
OREGON IRIS

This is a deciduous beardless Pacific
Coast iris from Oregon and Washington which grows to about 15 in (30 cm)
tall. Its dark green foliage is stained
pink at the base. It flowers from mid-spring into summer; the blooms are
about 3½ in (9 cm) across and can be
blue, lavender, yellow or white, and often have yellow and white markings on
the falls. This species is relatively easy
to grow and prefers sun or part-shade.
ZONES 8–10.

Iris tectorum (left)
JAPANESE ROOF IRIS, WALL FLAG

So-called because in Japan this species was said to have been
grown on thatched roofs in times of hardship when all available ground was needed for food crops. Originally native to
China, it is a hardy crested or Evansia iris with thick rhizomes and broad, bright green leaves in fans to 12 in
(30 cm) long. The flowers, produced in spring and early
summer, are about 4 in (10 cm) across and are lilac-blue
with darker veins and blotches, and a white crest on each
fall. It prefers part-shade in a sheltered position with protection from afternoon sun. It also has a white form called
'Alba'. ZONES 5–10.

Iris unguicularis (right)
syn. *Iris stylosa*
WINTER IRIS, ALGERIAN IRIS

This evergreen, beardless species from
northern Africa is notable for bearing its
flowers deep down among the clumps of
grassy, dark green leaves, on stems no
more than 8 in (20 cm) long. The flowers
are typically pale blue, but white and
darker blue to purple varieties are also
available; the falls have yellow centers. It
blooms from autumn to spring and the
flowers are primrose-scented. Although
moderately frost hardy, it does best in a
warm, sheltered, sunny position, in
slightly alkaline soil. To make the flowers
more conspicuous cut the tough foliage
back early each winter. **ZONES 7–10.**

Iris, Bearded Hybrid, 'Orange Celebrity' *(left)*

Iris, Bearded Hybrids

Often classed under *Iris germanica* or
I. pallida, which are only 2 of their ancestral
species, the bearded irises are among the
most widely grown of late-spring flowers,
with fat creeping rhizomes, sword-shaped,
grayish foliage and stems bearing several
large flowers. They are available in an enormous range of colors—everything but true
red—with many varieties featuring blended
colors, contrasting standards and falls, or a
broad band of color around basically white
flowers (this pattern is called 'plicata'). Some
of the newer varieties, described as 'remon-
tant', flower a second time in late summer
or autumn, though rather erratically. All
prefer a temperate climate, sun and mildly
alkaline, well-drained soil, and flower most
freely if not over-watered in summer.
Bearded irises are subdivided into 3 groups:

Dwarf Bearded, which grow 6–15 in
(15–40 cm) tall and flower earlier than
the others.

Intermediate Bearded, about 24 in (60 cm)
tall, which flower a fortnight or so later
than the dwarf varieties. **'Sunny Dawn'** is
typical, with yellow flowers with red beards.

Tall Bearded irises are the last to bloom
and grow to 3 ft (1 m) tall or slightly higher.
Representative Tall Bearded cultivars include
'Blue Shimmer' which has white flowers
with lilac-blue stitching; **'Dancer's Veil'**, to
3 ft (1 m) tall, has white flowers with plicata
edges in blue-violet; **'Light Beam'** has
yellow standards and white falls edged with
yellow; and **'Orange Celebrity'** is renowned
for its ideal form and brilliant yet delicate
colors, including apricot and pink shades
with a flaming orange beard. **'Cannington
Skies'** has mid-blue standards and falls.
'Supreme Sultan' has butterscotch-yellow
standards and crimson-brown falls. **'Sun
and Sand'** has apricot-yellow standards
and yellow falls. **'White City'** has pure
white flowers. ZONES 5–10.

Iris, Bearded Hybrid, 'Dancer's Veil' *(left)*

Iris, Bearded Hybrid,
'Light Beam' *(right)*

Iris, Bearded Hybrid,
'Sunny Dawn' *(below)*

Iris, Bearded Hybrid,
'White City' *(below)*

Iris, Bearded Hybrid,
'Blue Shimmer' *(below)*

I

Iris, Bearded Hybrid,
'Supreme Sultan' *(left)*

Iris, Bearded Hybrid,
'Sun and Sand'
(below left)

Iris, Bearded Hybrid,
'Cannington Skies'
(below)

Iris, Louisiana Hybrids

This extremely colorful group of rhizomatous, beardless hybrid irises include *Iris fulva* and *I. brevicaulis* among their ancestral species. They are evergreen with fine strap-like foliage and can build into substantial clumps; divide after 2 to 3 years. The Louisiana hybrids are not fully frost hardy in very cold climates, but are becoming increasingly popular in Australia and southern parts of the USA. Although basically swamp or water irises, they will happily grow in the garden if kept very well watered. They do best in a sunny position with average to damp, humus-rich garden soil. This group rarely exceeds 3 ft (1 m) in height and is usually much shorter. Some of the available hybrids include **'Art World'**, with mauve-pink duo-toned flowers; **'Bluebonnet Sue'**, with rich violet-blue blooms; **'Guessing Game'**, with a pale mauve flower with darker violet veins and irregular markings; **'Insider'**, a new Australian hybrid which has yellow-edged reddish brown standards and falls of reddish brown with yellow spray patterning; and **'Vermilion Treasure'**, with a red-violet flower with lighter spray patterning. ZONES 7–10.

Iris, Louisiana Hybrid, 'Guessing Game' *(below)*

Iris, Louisiana Hybrid, 'Bluebonnet Sue' *(above)*

Iris, Louisiana Hybrid, 'Insider' *(below)*

Iris, Louisiana Hybrid, 'Vermilion Treasure' *(left)*

Iris, Louisiana Hybrid, 'Art World' *(above)*

Iris, Spuria Hybrids

While *Iris spuria* (from northern Africa and southern France), *I. sibirica* (from eastern Europe) and their allied species are beautiful plants in their own right, they have been much hybridized. The more common hybrids bear numerous 4 in (10 cm) wide flowers on 4 ft (1.2 m) long stems in early summer. Colors are mainly in the white to blue range, with some yellow and white forms. All prefer sun, rich soil and lavish watering while they are growing and flowering. **'Clarke Cosgrove'** is mauve-blue with a yellow splash. ZONES 4–9.

Iris, Louisiana Hybrid, 'Impressioned' *(above)*

Iris, Spuria Hybrid, 'Clarke Cosgrove' *(left)*

Jeffersonia diphylla (right)

RHEUMATISM ROOT, TWIN LEAF

This North American species grows in rich woodland from Ontario to Tennessee. Slow-growing, its attractive kidney-shaped, deeply incised leaves are about 6 in (15 cm) across and gray tinted. The dainty, white, cup-shaped flowers are 1 in (25 mm) wide and produced in late spring or early summer; they have prominent yellow stamens. The plant increases in height after flowering and can reach 18 in (45 cm) with a similar spread by the time it sets seed. Do not disturb its roots. ZONES 5–9.

JEFFERSONIA
TWIN LEAF

This genus of just 2 species of herbaceous perennials is named after Thomas Jefferson, the third president of the USA. The species are dainty woodland plants—one from North America, the other from northeast Asia. Although they are part of the *Berberis* family, this fact is not at all obvious to most gardeners. The rounded, mid-green leaves consist of 2 even lobes, hence the common name.

CULTIVATION
As much as possible, try to simulate their natural woodland homes. They are fully hardy plants and prefer a cool, part-shaded position and humus-rich soil; top-dress with leafmold regularly. Propagation is usually from fresh seed in autumn or by careful division in late winter or early spring.

JOVIBARBA

This small genus of 5 species of evergreen, succulent perennials has a rosette-forming habit much like the closely related *Sempervivum* genus. Some species have attractive colored leaves, which are the reason why these plants are grown; all have pale yellow flowers, but these are insignificant. The rosettes die after flowering, but the gaps are soon filled with new growth.

CULTIVATION

Unlike many succulents, these plants are fully frost hardy and only require a well-drained, sunny aspect in temperate to cold climates to succeed. Some shade is necessary in warmer areas. They are ideal in rock gardens, troughs or in dry stone walls packed with a little soil. Propagate from offsets in summer. Simply remove a rosette with a piece of stem; once planted, it will quickly take root.

Jovibarba hirta
(left)
syn. *Jovibarba globifera*

The rosettes of this mat-forming species are usually about 2 in (5 cm) across. If the plants become dry, their leaves will curl up; otherwise, they radiate outwards. The thick, fleshy leaves are mid-green and often tipped red or reddish brown; star-shaped flowers are borne in summer. **Jovibarba hirta subsp. *arenaria*** has smaller rosettes— usually only about 1 in (25 mm) across, with occasional red tips on the leaves. These plants dislike winter-wet conditions. ZONES 7–10.

*Keckiella
antirrhinoides* var.
antirrhinoides (left)
syn. *Penstemon
antirrhinoides*

BUSH SNAPDRAGON, SNAP-
DRAGON KECKIELLA, YELLOW
PENSTEMON

This species is a large,
well-branched, spread-
ing to erect shrub reach-
ing 5–8 ft (1.5–2.4 m)
tall and wider. Leafy
clusters of bright,
yellow, snapdragon-like
flowers appear from
scarlet buds in spring.
The bush snapdragon
prefers hot locations; it
sheds many leaves dur-
ing the hot dry months.
ZONES 9–11.

K

KECKIELLA

This is a small group of 7 species of shrubs
formerly in the genus *Penstemon.*
Keckiellas are grown for their brightly
colored, tubular flowers which attract
birds. Found mostly in the California
chaparral community, they also are native
to Arizona and Baja, Mexico.

CULTIVATION

All keckiellas need well-drained soils and
part-shade to full sun. Only occasional
watering is required in summer. Shrubby
keckiellas tend to become scraggly and
require pruning to promote compact
growth. Propagation is from seed or
cuttings.

Keckiella corymbosa (below)
syn. *Penstemon corymbosa*
RED-FLOWERED ROCK PENSTEMON

Summertime clusters of tubular, wide-mouthed,
scarlet flowers grace this sprawling, much-branched
shrub, which grows up to 18 in (45 cm) tall and
wider. Native to rocky slopes in northwest and central western California, it tolerates abundant winter
rains when planted in well-drained soils; it is an excellent rock garden plant. ZONES 8–11.

K

KIRENGESHOMA

This aristocrat from the cool forests of Japan and Korea is represented by only one species, although the Korean form which
differs little from the Japanese one is sometimes accorded species
status. An upright perennial, it has arching, usually black stems
with large, lobed, soft green leaves and flowers in summer.

CULTIVATION

This fully frost-hardy perennial suits cool to cold areas in part-
shade. It also requires a moist, humus-rich, lime-free soil and
complements plants such as hostas and rodgersias. Propagation
is from seed or by careful division in autumn or spring.

Kirengeshoma
palmata (above)
YELLOW WAXBELLS

This unusual perennial
thrives in cool, moist
conditions. In late sum-
mer to autumn, it bears
sprays of pale yellow,
narrow, shuttlecock-
shaped flowers on arch-
ing stems 3 ft (1 m)
high, forming a clump
about the same distance
across. ZONES 5–10.

KNAUTIA

Consisting of 60 species of annuals and perennials, this genus is found extensively throughout temperate Eurasia, from the Mediterranean to Siberia. Their flowers are very like the related *Scabiosa*, but few are ornamental enough to be grown in gardens except for the 2 described here. These have a rosette of basal leaves through which the flower stems grow; these are branched and support some leaves.

CULTIVATION

Occurring in meadows, hedgerows and open woodland, these frost-hardy plants prefer sun or part-shade. Although often found growing in limy soil in their natural habitat, they will grow happily in any well-drained loam, but require staking. Propagate from seed in autumn or by basal cuttings in spring.

Knautia macedonica (right)

A showy species from the central Balkans to Romania, this makes an attractive subject for herbaceous borders. Erect branched stems to 30 in (75 cm) come from basal rosettes of lyre-shaped foliage. The flowers are usually deep purple-red, and occasionally pale pink or white. The darker shades are the best. ZONES 6–10.

KNIPHOFIA
RED-HOT POKER, TORCH LILY, TRITOMA

This genus of 68 species of stately perennials, some of which are
evergreen, are native to southern and eastern Africa. They are
upright, tufted plants with long leaves. In summer, they carry
showy, brightly colored, tubular flowers in dense spikes on tall
bare stems; some cultivars flower in winter and early spring.
Originally the flowers were mostly flame colored (the common
name, red-hot poker, dates from the days of coal fires), but due
to the work of German plant breeder Max Leichtlin (1831–1910)
and others, the flowers can also be pink, orange or yellow. They
range from head-high to miniature types, which grow to 24 in
(60 cm) or less, and are attractive to nectar-feeding birds.

CULTIVATION
Frost hardy to somewhat frost tender, they require an open position
in full sun, well-drained soil and plenty of water in summer. In areas
with winter temperatures below 5°F (–15°C), they can be carefully
lifted and stored indoors to be planted again in spring, although
heavy mulching is preferable. They will tolerate wind and coastal
conditions. From spring onwards, fertilize monthly. Remove dead
flower stems and leaves in late autumn. Propagate species from
seed or by division in spring; cultivars by division in spring.

Kniphofia 'Atlanta'
(below)

One of many fine hy-
brids and selected
forms, 'Atlanta' grows
to 4 ft (1.2 m) tall. It
has gray-green leaves
and orange-red flowers
fading to lemon yellow.
ZONES 7–10.

Kniphofia caulescens (right)

This majestic, frost-hardy evergreen grows on mountainsides up to altitudes of 10,000 ft (3,000 m). The 12 in (30 cm) rust-colored stems are topped with cream to coral pink flowers that fade to yellow; these appear from late summer to mid-autumn. The narrow leaves are blue green. It reaches 4 ft (1.2 m) in height. **ZONES 7–10.**

Kniphofia ensifolia (below right)

WINTER POKER

This moderately frost-hardy evergreen perennial forms a dense clump, growing to 5 ft (1.5 m) tall with a spread of 24 in (60 cm). It has slender, sword-shaped, mid-green leaves and bears torches of prolific, lemon-yellow flowers in late autumn and winter. **ZONES 8–10.**

Kniphofia 'Cobra' (far right)

'Cobra' is a compact form with relatively short-stemmed, pale orange flowers that age to cream. **ZONES 7–10.**

K

K

Kniphofia 'Erecta'
(below)

'Erecta' is an unusual deciduous form with orange-red flowers that point upwards when open. It grows to 3 ft (1 m) and flowers from late summer to mid-autumn. **ZONES 7–10.**

Kniphofia 'John Benary' *(above)*

'John Benary' grows to 5 ft (1.5 m) tall and has loose spikes of deep scarlet flowers. **ZONES 7–10.**

Kniphofia 'Gold Crest' *(right)*

This cultivar forms a clump of bright green, grassy foliage with fine-stemmed, somewhat loose flowerheads that open orange and age to bright yellow. **ZONES 8–10.**

Kniphofia 'Little Maid' *(right)*

'Little Maid' is a dwarf form that reaches a height of 24 in (60 cm). It has buff-tinted, soft yellow flowers opening from pale green buds. **ZONES 7–10.**

Kniphofia × praecox *(below)*

RED-HOT POKER

This South African perennial is the most common species in the wild and reaches up to 5 ft (1.5 m) tall when in bloom. Its slender leaves, up to 24 in (60 cm) long, are heavily keeled and serrated. Vivid red or yellow flowers appear in early summer. It is able to survive long dry periods and enjoys full sun. **ZONES 7–10.**

Kniphofia 'Lemon Green' *(left)*

Yellow green in bud, the flowers of this form open soft yellow and become brighter with age. **ZONES 8–10.**

K

Kniphofia 'Royal Standard' *(below)*

This upright perennial reaches 4 ft (1.2 m) in height with a spread of 24 in (60 cm). Moderately frost hardy, it has grass-like leaves and bears terminal spikes of scarlet buds, which open to lemon-yellow flowers in late summer. In cold areas, use a winter mulch to protect the crowns. ZONES 7–10.

Kniphofia 'Star of Baden-Baden' *(above)*

Forming large clumps with age, this cultivar has 5 ft (1.5 m) flower stems with flowerheads that are mainly bright orange-red except for the oldest flowers, which fade to yellow. ZONES 7–10.

K

Kniphofia tuckii (right)

This species closely resembles *Kniphofia ensifolia*, the winter poker, with its heads of greenish white flowers from reddish buds. However, it is not as tall, reaching only 4 ft (1.2 m) in height. ZONES 7–10.

Kniphofia 'Underway'
(above)

'Underway' has slightly blue-green foliage with small flowerheads that open rusty orange and fade to buff yellow. ZONES 8–10.

Kniphofia triangularis
(right)
syns *Kniphofia galpinii* of gardens, *K. macowanii*, *K. nelsonii*

This poker from South Africa grows to about 3 ft (1 m) tall and is usually deciduous. Its flowers are a rich orange, yellowing slightly with age. This species has probably contributed the coral shade to the gene pool of hybrids. ZONES 7–10.

K

Kniphofia uvaria var.
maxima *(left)*

K

Kniphofia 'Yellow Hammer' *(below)*

This pale yellow
Kniphofia hybrid, one
of the best of the
shorter-growing plants,
raises its 3 ft (1 m)
flower stems in sum-
mer. The flowers are
excellent for cutting.
ZONES 7–10.

Kniphofia uvaria

This tall perennial, the
source of many hybrids,
grows to 4 ft (1.2 m) high
and 18 in (45 cm) wide. It
has thick, strongly channeled
leaves. In late summer and
autumn, it bears dense racemes of tubular scarlet
flowers becoming orange-
yellow with age. It is fully
frost hardy. **Kniphofia
uvaria var. maxima** is
slightly larger, reaching
6 ft (1.8 m) in height. It also
has larger, rich orange-red
flowers which fade slightly
with age. **ZONES 5–10.**

KOHLERIA

This attractive genus of the African violet family consists of about 50 species of rhizome-forming perennials or subshrubs from tropical regions of the Americas. Their tubular flowers are usually felty, pendulous, single or in clusters, in an outrageous array of gaudy colors. The entire plant, including the flowers, is covered in bristles.

CULTIVATION

These plants are tropical and frost tender; in all but tropical climates they are treated as plants for heated greenhouses or as indoor plants. In the tropics, give them a moist shaded site in which to grow. Water sparingly in winter. Propagation is by division of clumping species in spring or soft cuttings from shrubby types.

Kohleria eriantha
(below)

This robust, shrubby perennial, to 4 ft (1.2 m) or more tall, has a rhizomatous root system. Its foliage is avate to lance shaped and up to 5 in (12 cm) long. In summer, it produces brilliant orange to orange-red pendulous trumpets, either singly or in clusters of 3 to 4. **ZONES 10–11.**

K

L

LAMIUM
syns *Galeobdolon, Lamiastrum*
DEADNETTLE

This genus of over 50 species of annuals and rhizomatous perennials, native to Europe, Asia and North Africa, belongs to the
mint family, not the nettle family as the common name would
seem to indicate. They include some common weeds and hedge-
row plants and a few that are cultivated for ornament. Some have
astringent properties and have been used in folk medicine, or
have been grown as pot herbs in parts of Europe. Some are an
important source of nectar for bees. They have leaves with
toothed margins, arranged in opposite pairs and sometimes
splashed with paler gray-green or white. Short spikes or axillary
whorls of white, yellow, pink or purple, 2-lipped flowers are produced. The upper lip curves over in a helmet-like shape.

CULTIVATION
Lamiums are frost hardy and grow well in most soils. Flower
color determines planting season and light requirement. White-
and purple-flowered species are planted in spring and prefer full
sun; the yellow-flowered ones are planted in autumn and prefer
shade. They often have invasive habits and need plenty of room.
Propagate from seed or by division in early spring.

Lamium album
(below left)
WHITE DEADNETTLE, ARCHANGEL

Ranging right across
Europe and northern
Asia, this species has
foliage that superfi-
cially resembles that of
the common nettle
(*Urtica urens*). An erect
perennial of 12–24 in
(30–60 cm) high, it
produces whorls of
pure white flowers
from late spring to
early autumn. It
became known as arch-
angel because it flowers
around the 8th of May,
the feast day of the
Archangel Michael in
the old calendar. It is
sometimes known to
flower in mid-winter.
ZONES 4–10.

Lamium galeobdolon
syns *Galeobdolon luteum,*
G. argentatum, Lamiastrum galeobdolon
YELLOW ARCHANGEL

This perennial species from Europe and western
Asia spreads both by rhizomes and surface runners
to form extensive, loose mats of foliage usually about
12 in (30 cm) deep, spreading over moist, shady
areas beneath trees. Its leaves are variably splashed
with silvery gray and in summer it bears leafy spikes
of bright yellow flowers each about ¾ in (18 mm)
long. **'Florentinum'** has leaves splashed with silver that become purple-tinged in winter. **'Hermann's
Pride'** is densely mat forming and has narrow
leaves streaked and spotted with silver. ZONES 6–10.

Lamium galeobdolon
'Hermann's Pride'
(above)

Lamium garganicum *(below)*

The specific name refers to the Garganian Prom-
ontory which extends into the Adriatic from Italy,
whence this species extends eastward to Turkey
and Iraq. It is a mound-forming perennial up to
18 in (45 cm) tall with toothed, heart-shaped
leaves and produces pink, red, purple or, rarely,
white flowers in early summer. ZONES 6–10.

L

L

Lamium maculatum
'Roseum' *(above)*

Lamium maculatum
'Golden Anniversary'
(left)

Lamium maculatum
'White Nancy'
(below left)

Lamium maculatum
'Beacon's Silver' *(below)*

Lamium maculatum

SPOTTED DEADNETTLE

Its wild forms often regarded almost as weeds, this semi-evergreen perennial is native to Europe and western Asia. It is also naturalized in North America. A variable species, it may have erect stems to 24 in (60 cm) tall, or have a lower, more spreading habit. The strongly toothed leaves have a central blotch or stripe of pale silvery green, and leafy whorled spikes of very pale pink to deep rose flowers appear in spring and summer. The cultivars are more desirable garden plants, mostly with a compact, mat-forming habit and not more than 6 in (15 cm) high. **'Beacon's Silver'** has purplish flowers with silvery green leaves edged dark green; **'Golden Anniversary'** has leaves with bright golden-yellow edges and a splash of silver in the center; **'Pink Pewter'** has silvery leaves that highlight the beautiful pink flowers; **'Roseum'** has silver-striped foliage and pinkish lilac flowers; and **'White Nancy'** has silvery green leaves and white flowers. **ZONES 4–10.**

LATHRAEA

The name of this genus comes from the Greek *lathraios*, meaning hidden, because most of the plant is underground. In fact the 7 species of this Eurasian genus are parasites, lacking chlorophyll of their own and attaching to the roots of trees and shrubs. The fleshy, ivory to mauve leaves are borne in 4 rows on subterranean rhizomes; the interesting fleshy flowers are borne on stems arising from the rhizome and, together with the capsular fruits that succeed them, are the only parts of the plant normally visible.

CULTIVATION

These frost-hardy plants can sometimes be induced to grow in a woodland setting if the right host genera are present. Scatter seed among the tree roots in shade, in moist but well-drained soil with a mulch of leaves in autumn.

Lathraea clandestina (below)
PURPLE TOOTHWORT

This parasitic plant from southwestern Europe bears dense clusters of showy purplish flowers with hooded apices just 2 in (5 cm) above the soil. The scale-like leaves are kidney-shaped and white. The host trees for this species are poplars, willows and alders. **ZONES 6–10.**

L

Lathyrus nervosus
(below right)
syn. *Lathyrus magellanicus* of gardens

This perennial climber from temperate South America can grow to a height of 10 ft (3 m) and has conspicuously veined, leathery leaves. The racemes of fragrant, purplish blue flowers are borne in summer. ZONES 8–10.

Lathyrus vernus 'Cyaneus' *(below)*

LATHYRUS

Closely allied to the garden peas *(Pisum)* and vetches *(Vicia)*, this genus of 150 or so species of annuals and perennials are mainly tendril climbers, and some of them are edible. They are native mainly to temperate northern hemisphere regions, but with a significant number also in Andean South America. The leaves are pinnate with the uppermost pair of leaflets usually modified into tendrils. The pea-shaped flowers come in a wide range of colors, from red, mauve and white to blue and even pale yellow. Flat seed pods follow the flowers. *Lathyrus odoratus*, the sweet pea, has a proud place in the history of science: it was one of the chief plants used by Gregor Mendel (1822–84) in his hybridizing experiments that laid the foundations for the science of genetics.

CULTIVATION
These frost-hardy plants need fertile, well-drained soil and full sun. Stake or train on wires and deadhead regularly. Propagate annuals from seed in early summer or early autumn, and perennials from seed in autumn or by division in spring. They may be affected by mildew and botrytis.

Lathyrus vernus
SPRING VETCH

This 24 in (60 cm) high European and west Asian perennial pea is an excellent rockery or bright woodland plant. It doesn't really climb, but instead scrambles over the ground and any low vegetation. The flowers, which open from late winter and continue well into spring, are purple-red when first open, passing through mauve to blue-green as they age. '**Cyaneus**' is a cultivar with purplish blue flowers. ZONES 4–10.

Lathyrus odoratus
(right)

SWEET PEA

Native to Italy, the wild form has been much improved by gardeners. It is a vigorous, climbing annual, grown for its abundant, sweetly scented flowers. The $1^1/_2$ in (35 mm) wide flowers, in colors of white, cream, pink, blue, mauve, lavender, maroon and scarlet, bloom several to the stem from late winter to early summer and make excellent cut flowers. The plant grows to 6 ft (1.8 m) or more in height, although there are dwarf, non-climbing cultivars available. The climbers will need a good support, such as wire netting or lattice, and are ideal for covering sunny walls or fences. Over many years of development, sweet peas have become less scented and mixed color seedling strains, for example 'Carnival', tended to predominate. With the resurgence of interest in cottage gardens, breeders mainly in the UK and New Zealand, have developed a range of very fragrant cultivars in single colors. These include 'Apricot Sprite', deep apricot fading with age; 'Bandaid', with pale pink flowers; 'Elegance', with pure white flowers; 'Esther Ranson', with mauve flowers; 'Felicity Kendall', with deep purplish pink flowers; 'Hampton Court', with purple to mauve flowers; 'Katherine', with bright red-pink flowers; 'Kiri Te Kanawa', with pinkish purple flowers; and 'Lucy', with apricot-pink flowers. The Knee-hi Group, although a little taller than the name suggests, to around 24–30 in (60–75 cm) high, is a bushy strain that flowers heavily in colors from white through red to blue. Cultivars in the Supersnoop Group have no tendrils and may be grown as bushes rather than as climbers. ZONES 4–10.

Lathyrus odoratus
cultivar *(right)*

Lathyrus odoratus
'Hampton Court'
(below)

L

LAVATERA

Closely related to the mallows and holly-hocks, this genus of 25 species of annuals, biennials, perennials and softwooded shrubs has a scattered, patchy distribution around temperate regions of the world, mostly in Mediterranean or similar climates. Some of them favor seashores. A few species are cultivated for their colorful mallow flowers, generally produced over a long season. These plants are upright in habit with simple to palmately lobed leaves, often downy to the touch. The shrubs and perennials in this genus are not very long-lived.

CULTIVATION

Moderately to very frost-hardy, these plants prefer a sunny site in any well-drained soil. Prune after a flush of blooms to encourage branching and more flowers. Propagate annuals, biennials and peren-nials in spring or early autumn from seed sown *in situ* (cuttings do not strike well), and shrubs from cuttings in early spring or summer.

Lavatera trimestris
ANNUAL MALLOW

This shrubby annual, native to the Mediterranean, is grown mainly for its silken, trumpet-shaped, brilliant white or pink flowers. The flowers are 3 in (8 cm) wide and appear from summer to early autumn. They are short lived but are borne in profusion, benefiting from regular dead-heading. The annual mallow has an erect, branch-ing habit and is moderately fast growing to a height of 24 in (60 cm) and a spread of 18 in (45 cm). **'Mont Blanc'** (syn. *Lavatera* 'Mont Blanc') has pure white flowers; **'Silver Cup'** has lovely dark pink flowers. ZONES 8–11.

Lavatera trimestris
'Mont Blanc' *(above)*

Lavatera trimestris
'Silver Cup' *(left)*

Leontopodium ochroleucum var. campestre *(left)* syn. *Leontopodium palibinianum*

This species from Asia is a loosely tufted perennial growing 6–15 in (15–38 cm) tall. It has attractive yellowish, nearly white bracts that almost enclose the inconspicuous disc florets. ZONES 4–9.

LEONTOPODIUM
EDELWEISS

Occurring wild in the mountains of Europe and temperate Asia, this genus consists of about 35 species of short-lived, downy perennials in the daisy family. Their distinctive feature is the flowerheads, with a central disc of rather inconspicuous cream florets surrounded by a ring of overlapping, pointed bracts of unequal length and coated with sparse to dense white wool. The simple, lance-shaped leaves are also covered with white hairs, which protect the plant from cold and from intense ultraviolet sunlight. They are suitable for rock gardens in cool to cold climates.

CULTIVATION
Plant in full sun or part-shade (in hot climates) in gritty, well-drained soil. They are very frost hardy but need shelter from winter rain. Propagate from fresh seed or by division in spring.

Leontopodium alpinum *(below)*

Much loved by the Swiss, the European edelweiss is often regarded as a symbol of the Alps. It reaches a height and spread of around 8 in (20 cm). Each silvery white flowerhead is 2–3 in (5–8 cm) across, the bracts so thickly felted they look like strips of flannel. It blooms in spring or early summer. ZONES 5–9.

L

Leucanthemum vulgare (above)
syn. *Chrysanthemum leucanthemum*
OX-EYE DAISY, MOON DAISY

This native of Europe and temperate Asia is like
a small version of the Shasta daisy, though the
pretty white flowerheads, borne in early summer,
are no more than 2 in (5 cm) in diameter.
A clump-forming perennial up to 30 in (75 cm)
tall, it is freely self-seeding and has become abundantly naturalized in parts of North America,
Australia and New Zealand. ZONES 3–10.

LEUCANTHEMUM

There are about 25 species of annuals or
perennials in this genus from Europe and
temperate Asia. They were previously
included in *Chrysanthemum* by many
botanists, though some botanists always
treated them as a distinct genus. They are
clump-forming plants with variably
toothed or lobed leaves that are neither
grayish hairy nor aromatic, unlike those
of other chrysanthemum relatives. Long-
stalked, daisy-like flowerheads arise from
leafy stems, with white or yellow ray florets and yellow disc florets. While mostly
vigorous, adaptable plants, some do not
do well in warmer climates.

CULTIVATION

Largely undemanding, these plants grow
well in a perennial border or garden bed
in full sun or morning shade in moderately
fertile, moist but well-drained soil. Propagate from seed, cuttings or by division.

Leucanthemum
paludosum
syn. *Chrysanthemum*
paludosum

This southern Euro-
pean annual grows to
6 in (15 cm) in height.
It has pale yellow or
white-tinged yellow
flowers. **'Show Star'**
has bright yellow
flowers and wavy edged
leaves. ZONES 7–11.

Leucanthemum
paludosum 'Show Star'
(left)

**Leucanthemum ×
superbum** *(below)*
syns *Chrysanthemum
maximum* of gardens,
C. × superbum

SHASTA DAISY

Growing to a height
and spread of 2–3 ft
(60–90 cm), this robust
perennial has large,
daisy-like, white
flowerheads with pale
golden centers. These
may be 3 in (8 cm)
across and are carried
high above the dark,
shiny, toothed leaves in
summer and early
autumn. The Shasta
daisies were once
thought to be
**Leucanthemum
maximum**, a native of
the Pyrenees, but are
now believed to be
hybrids between that
species and the Portu-
guese *L. lacustre*. They
were first noticed natu-
ralized on the slopes of
Mount Shasta in Wash-
ington State, USA and
attracted the attention
of the famous plant
breeder Luther Burbank.
There are now many
cultivars, always white-
flowered, but including

doubles as well as sin-
gles, some with fringed
petals. '**Aglaia**' grows
to 12 in (30 cm) tall
and is noted for its semi-
double flowers that last
through summer;
'**Esther Read**' grows to
3 ft (1 m) tall with a
profusion of semi-
double flowers; '**Wirral
Pride**' reaches 30 in
(75 cm) in height with
double white flower-
heads; and '**Wirral
Supreme**' is noted for
its anemone-centered
double flowers.
'**Tinkerbell**' and '**Snow
Lady**' are low-growing
forms with single
flowers. ZONES 5–10.

*Leucanthemum ×
superbum* cultivar
(above right)

*Leucanthemum ×
superbum* 'Wirral
Pride' *(right)*

*Leucanthemum ×
superbum* 'Tinkerbell'
(right)

Lewisia columbiana *(left)*

Named after the Columbia River region from whence it originates, this evergreen species forms a clump of narrow, fleshy basal leaves. The foliage clump is around 6 in (15 cm) high with an 8 in (20 cm) spread and in summer it produces heads of pink-veined white to pale pink flowers on 12 in (30 cm) stems. ZONES 5–9.

Lewisia 'Ben Chase' *(left)*

LEWISIA
BITTER ROOT

This genus, which honors the explorer Meriwether Lewis (1774–1838), contains about 20 species of small perennials with deep tap roots, leathery leaves and starry flowers, all native to the Rocky Mountains of the USA. The roots are endowed with wonderful powers of survival: Lewis returned to civilization in 1806 and it is said that a botanist in London, studying his dried plant specimens nearly 5 years later, found that one was trying to grow. He planted it and it duly revived, and the following summer bore its beautiful pink flowers. Hybrid lewisias such as 'Ben Chase', flower over a long period in summer in a range of colors—pink, white, apricot, red or flame.

CULTIVATION

Give them a cool climate, full sun or part-shade in warm climates and excellent drainage, so there will be no chance of winter-wet rotting the roots. Propagate herbaceous species from seed in spring or autumn, and evergreen species from seed in spring or offsets in summer.

Lewisia tweedyi
(right)

Growing to 8 in
(20 cm) tall and 12 in
(30 cm) wide, this ever-
green species has suc-
culent stems, small
fleshy leaves and pale
to peach-pink open-
faced flowers from
spring to summer.
ZONES 5–9.

Lewisia cotyledon
'Pinkie' *(below)*
Lewisia cotyledon var.
howellii *(bottom right)*

Lewisia cotyledon
(below)

This evergreen, which
hybridizes readily, has
rosettes of fleshy,
toothed leaves and
bears clusters of white
to yellow, apricot and
pink to purple flowers
on upright stems. It
grows to a height of
12 in (30 cm). *Lewisia
cotyledon* var. *howellii*
spreads to 6 in (15 cm).
'**Pinkie**', with pink
flowers grows 1 in
(25 mm) tall and 2 in
(5 cm) wide. **ZONES 6–10.**

L

LIATRIS

BLAZING STAR

These 40 species of perennials come from the central and eastern regions of North America. In summer they sprout tall, cylindrical spikes of fluffy flowers from a knobby rootstock that remains visible during the rest of the year. They belong to the daisy or composite family, but their spike-like inflorescences, crowded with small flowerheads opening from the top downward, are so unlike those of other daisies that it is hard to recognize their affinity.

CULTIVATION

These plants will grow in most soils and conditions including damp places such as stream banks and ditches. However, they do best in climates with low humidity. They thrive with minimum care and attention, making excellent border plants. Propagation is from seed or by division of old clumps in winter.

Liatris punctata
(below)
SNAKEROOT

Ranging from eastern Canada to New Mexico, this species reaches nearly 3 ft (1 m) in height and has purple, occasionally white, flowers in autumn. Flowering is prolonged by cutting and the stems make an attractive indoor display. They perform best in fertile, well-drained soil. ZONES 3–10.

Liatris spicata (right)
syn. *Liatris callilepis* of gardens
GAY FEATHER, SPIKE GAY FEATHER

This low-growing species is a desirable cut flower and good for attracting bees or butterflies. The flowers are lilac-purple, although they can occur in pink and white. They are produced in crowded, fluffy spikes—like a feather duster—in late summer, and open from the top downwards, which is the opposite of most flower spikes. It grows to a height of 24 in (60 cm), with thickened, corm-like rootstocks and basal tufts of grassy, mid-green foliage. **'Floristan'** is a seedling strain growing to 5 ft (1.5 m) tall, and is available in 2 colors: deep violet (**'Floristan Violett'**) and white (**'Floristan Weiss'**). **'Kobold'** is a dwarf cultivar reaching 15 in (38 cm) and producing bright purple flowers. ZONES 3–10.

Liatris spicata
'Floristan Violett' *(left)*

Liatris spicata 'Kobold'
(below)

L

Libertia
peregrinans *(left)*

This New Zealand
species is remarkable
for its long, branching
rhizomes that send up
sparse tufts of narrow,
strongly veined leaves
at intervals. These
turn a striking orange-
brown shade in
autumn and winter.
It reaches 30 in (75 cm)
in height and has a
yellowish bronze-green
flowering stem with
white flowers with
orange-brown anthers.
ZONES 8–10.

LIBERTIA

These 20 species of perennials in the iris family have tufts of
grass-like leaves springing from rhizomes that may be very short
or long creeping. They are found on both sides of the Pacific
Ocean in New Zealand, Australia, New Guinea and the Andes of
South and Central America. They grow easily in a temperate
climate, producing erect, wiry stems bearing clusters of small,
white, iris-like flowers in spring and summer.

CULTIVATION

Moderately frost hardy, they require a sheltered, sunny or part-
shaded position and well-drained, peaty soil with plenty of moisture in spring and summer. Propagate by division in spring, or
from seed in spring or autumn. Some species naturalize freely.

LIGULARIA

There are at least 150 species of perennials in this genus, which is closely related to *Senecio*, found mainly in temperate eastern Asia, though a smaller number occur in northern Asia and Europe. Many species are large-leaved, clump-forming plants that produce tall spires of daisy-like flowerheads, mostly in shades of yellow or orange. The cultivated ligularias are stately plants and vigorous growers, adapted to moist, sheltered sites such as stream banks and woodland glades. They flower mainly in summer and early autumn. The spring foliage is almost as ornamental as the summer blooms.

CULTIVATION

Quite frost hardy, they prefer moist, well-drained soil in either sun or part-shade. Propagate by division in spring or from seed in spring or autumn. They are prone to attack by slugs and snails.

Ligularia dentata *(above)*
syns *Ligularia clivorum, Senecio clivorum*

This compact species from China and Japan is grown for its striking foliage and showy flowerheads. It grows to a height of 4 ft (1.2 m) and a spread of 3 ft (1 m). It has kidney-shaped, long-stalked, leathery, brownish green leaves and bears clusters of large, 3 in (8 cm) wide, orange-yellow flowerheads on long branching stems in summer. It will grow happily at the edge of ponds. Cultivars worth growing are **'Othello'** and **'Desdemona'**, which has green leaves heavily overlaid with bronze and maroon. **'Gregynog Gold'** has round green leaves and orange flowers. ZONES 4–9.

Ligularia stenocephala *(right)*

This species from Japan, China and Taiwan grows to 5 ft (1.5 m). It has dark purple stems and slender racemes of yellow flowers in summer. The leaves are triangular and toothed. ZONES 5–10.

LIMONIUM
STATICE, SEA LAVENDER

This genus of around 150 species scattered around the world's temperate regions mostly in saline coastal and desert environments, with major concentrations in the Mediterranean, central Asia and the Canary Islands. They include evergreen and deciduous subshrubs, perennials, biennials and annuals. Some of the latter are grown as border plants and are popular for their many-colored heads of small papery flowers, which can be cut and dried for decoration. The flowers should be cut just as they open and hung upside down to dry in a cool, airy place. The tapered, almost stalkless leaves appear in basal rosettes.

CULTIVATION
Statices are easily grown in full sun and well-drained, sandy soil. Their tolerance to sea spray and low rainfall make them a good choice for seaside and low-maintenance holiday-house gardens. Plants will benefit from light fertilizing in spring, while the flowerheads are developing. Propagate by division in spring, from seed in early spring or autumn or from root cuttings in late winter. Transplant during winter or early spring.

Limonium perezii
(below)

Limonium perezii comes from the Canary Islands and is a species of more or less shrubby habit with glossy leaves. The leafless flower stems bear many small flowers, whose insignificant white petals make less impact in the garden than the long-lasting, deep mauve-blue calyces. It grows about 24 in (60 cm) tall and flowers in summer. ZONES 9–11.

Limonium sinuatum,
Petite Bouquet Series
cultivar *(below)*

Limonium latifolium *(above)*
syn. *Limonium platyphyllum*

From eastern Europe, this tall-stemmed perennial bears clusters of lavender-blue or white flowers over summer. Clump forming and large leafed, it grows 24 in (60 cm) tall and spreads 18 in (45 cm). The dried flower stems have a delicate appearance. **ZONES 5–10.**

Limonium gmelinii *(above)*

This robust perennial from eastern Europe and Siberia grows to 24 in (60 cm) tall in any deep, well-drained soil in full sun. It has leaves in spikelets and lilac tubular flowers. **ZONES 4–10.**

Limonium sinuatum
syn. *Statice sinuata*

This Mediterranean species is a bushy, upright perennial almost always grown as an annual. It produces dense rosettes of oblong, deeply waved leaves and bears masses of tiny papery flowers on winged stems. It flowers in summer and early autumn and is fairly slow growing, reaching a height of 18 in (45 cm) with a spread of 12 in (30 cm). One of the most popular cut flowers, seedling strains are available in a rainbow of colors. The **Petite Bouquet Series** are dwarf plants to 12 in (30 cm) in height and with golden or lemon yellow, white, cream, salmon-pink, purple or blue spikelets. **ZONES 9–10.**

Limonium minutum *(above)*

This spreading perennial from southern Europe reaches 4 in (10 cm) tall and is suited to rockeries. It has tiny rosettes of leaves and lilac flowers. **ZONES 8–10.**

Linaria alpina *(left)*

This trailing perennial from Europe grows to about 3 in (8 cm) in height with a 6 in (15 cm) spread. It has violet, yellow, white or pink flowers and narrow blue-gray leaves. **ZONES 4–10.**

L

LINARIA
EGGS AND BACON, TOADFLAX

Native mainly to the Mediterranean region and western Europe, these 100 species of adaptable annuals, biennials and perennials are related to snapdragons and have naturalized in many places. They grow to 18 in (45 cm) with masses of tiny snapdragon-like blooms in many colors. The erect stems have stalkless, usually gray-green leaves. They are ideally suited to rock gardens, borders and cottage gardens.

CULTIVATION
They require rich, well-drained, preferably sandy soil, moderate water and full sun. Seed sown directly in autumn or very early spring will germinate in 2 weeks. Seedlings need to be thinned to a 6 in (15 cm) spacing and weeded to ensure there is no over-shadowing. Cutting back after the first flush will produce more flowers.

Linaria vulgaris
(above)

A 3 ft (1 m) tall perennial that occurs wild in the Mediterranean and much of Europe, this species has reddish brown stems, numerous pale blue-green leaves and yellow flowers appearing in summer and autumn. It can be grown from seed and will self-seed. It has traditional uses as a medicinal herb. **ZONES 4–10.**

Linaria purpurea
'Canon J. Went' *(right)*

Linaria purpurea
(below)

PURPLE TOADFLAX

This perennial from
Europe is naturalized
in some areas and
grows to 3 ft (1 m).
It bears violet-tinged
purple flowers in
summer. **'Canon J.
Went'** is a tall cultivar
of the species with tiny
pale pink flowers.
ZONES 6–10.

L

LINDERNIA

A genus of annuals and perennials from most warmer parts of the world, *Lindernia* consists of about 50 species. Related to the snapdragons and toadflaxes, they have colorful flowers on erect racemes or arising singly from leaf axils, and fruits that are narrow capsules.

CULTIVATION

They grow well in moist soil, some liking almost boggy situations, in full sun. Propagate from fresh seed.

L

Lindernia americana (below)

This species from North America has bright green, rounded, fleshy leaves. Long-tubed, violet-like flowers are borne in the leaf axils and open from spring. **ZONES 9–11.**

LINDHEIMERA
STAR DAISY

This genus consists of a single species of annual from the limestone soils of Texas, USA. It grows to just over 24 in (60 cm) tall, and has yellow flowers suitable for cutting and bright green, bract-like leaves that obscure the seed heads.

CULTIVATION
Grow this plant in moderately fertile, well-drained soil in full sun. Propagate from seed sown direct.

Lindheimera texana (above)

This frost-hardy annual is grown for its dainty, daisy-like yellow flowers, borne in late summer and early autumn. It is moderately fast growing, with hairy stems and pointed to oval, serrated, hairy fresh green leaves. Of an erect, branching habit, it grows from 12–24 in (30–60 cm) in height with a spread of 12 in (30 cm). **ZONES 6–10.**

L

Linum doerfleri (above)

LINUM
FLAX

This genus contains 200 species of annuals, biennials, perennials, subshrubs and shrubs, some of which are evergreen, and are distributed widely in temperate regions. It includes the commercial flax, *Linum usitatissimum,* grown for fiber and oilseed. Several ornamental species are valued for their profusely blooming, 5-petalled flowers, which can be yellow, white, blue, red or pink. They are useful plants in a rock garden or border. *Linum doerfleri* is a yellow-flowered species.

CULTIVATION
They are mostly quite frost hardy, although some need shelter in cool climates. Grow in a sunny spot in humus-rich, well-drained, peaty soil. After perennial species flower, prune them back hard. Propagate the annuals, biennials and perennials from seed in autumn and perennials by division in spring or autumn. Most self-sow readily. Transplant from late autumn until early spring.

Linum capitatum
(above)

This European rhizomatous perennial grows to about 18 in (45 cm) high. When in flower, it forms a basal clump of foliage from which emerge leafy flower stems bearing heads of 5 or more flowers. ZONES 7–10.

Linum campanulatum
(left)

This small southern European perennial is reminiscent of some of the oxalises or of California poppy (*Eschscholzia californica*). It has small, slightly glaucous leaves and during summer produces small, 3- to 5-flowered heads of yellow to orange flowers. ZONES 7–10.

L

Linum flavum

GOLDEN FLAX, YELLOW FLAX

A 12–24 in (30–60 cm) tall, somewhat woody perennial with a strongly erect habit, this southern European species has dark green, pointed or blunt-ended leaves about 1 in (25 mm) long. The golden yellow, trumpet-shaped flowers, many to each stem, appear in summer. **'Compactum'** is a dwarf variety growing just 6–8 in (15–20 cm) tall. **ZONES 5–10.**

Linum flavum **'Compactum'** *(above)*

Linum narbonense

(right)

A perennial native of the Mediterranean region, this is the most handsome of all the blue flaxes. It has violet, funnel-shaped flowers borne on slender stems, which last for many weeks in summer. It has soft, green leaves and forms clumps 18 in (45 cm) high and wide. **ZONES 5–10.**

Linum perenne subsp. *lewisii* (left)

L

Linum perenne
(above & left)
syn. *Linum sibiricum*

Of wide occurrence in Europe and temperate Asia, this is a vigorous, upright perennial that forms a shapely, bushy plant 24 in (60 cm) high with a spread of 12 in (30 cm). It has slender stems with grass-like leaves and clusters of open, funnel-shaped, light blue flowers are borne throughout summer. **'Alba'** is a pure white form. Prairie flax **(*Linum perenne* subsp. *lewisii*)** is a more compact plant than the species but has slightly longer leaves. **ZONES 7–10.**

LIRIOPE

This genus contains 5 species of clump-forming, rhizomatous, evergreen perennials native to Vietnam, China, Taiwan and Japan. Some cultivars are so dark in leaf they are practically black, a most unusual color for the designer to play with. They do not creep, and for ground cover have to be planted 6 in (15 cm) apart. *Liriope* flowers range from white through to pale purple.

CULTIVATION

Grow in full sun or part-shade in well-drained soil. In early spring, cut back shabby leaves just before the new ones appear. Propagate from seed in autumn or by division in early spring.

Liriope muscari
(right)
syns *Liriope platyphylla, L. graminifolia*

This clumping, ever-green perennial is a useful ground cover or path edging. It has grass-like, shining, dark green leaves and bears erect spikes of rounded, bell-shaped, violet flowers in late summer. It grows to a height of 12–24 in (30–60 cm) with a spread of 18 in (45 cm). The flower spikes are held just above the foliage. **'Lilac Beauty'** comes from China and Japan and is a larger example of the species. Its leaves are 1 in (25 mm) wide and 12–18 in (30–45 cm) long with stiff lilac flowers rising above the foliage. **'Majestic'** has large violet-blue

flowers. **'Variegata'** is the most common of the variegated forms. Its leaf margins are lined with cream, and it has lovely lilac flowers. ZONES 6–10.

Linum muscari
'Variegata' *(below)*

Linum muscari
'Lilac Beauty' *(below)*

L

LITHODORA

This genus of 7 species of dwarf evergreen subshrubby perennials and shrubs from Europe, Turkey and North Africa is well suited to rockeries. Most are known for their 5-lobed, funnel-shaped intense blue flowers, borne over a long season in small sprays at the growth tips. The deep green leaves are hairy.

CULTIVATION

Most species prefer well-drained, alkaline soil; water lightly even in summer. They do well in full sun if grown in not too hot an area. Shearing after flowering will promote a compact habit and encourage dense flowering the following year. Propagate from cuttings of last year's growth and strike in a mix of peat and sand.

Lithodora 'Star'
(below)
syn. *Lithospermum* 'Star'

This shrub grows to 12 in (30 cm) in height and has star-shaped, lilac flowers with a purple stripe down the center of each lobe.
ZONES 7–10.

LOBELIA

This genus of 370 species of annuals, perennials and shrubs is widely distributed in temperate regions, particularly the Americas and Africa. Growth habits vary from low bedding plants to tall herbaceous perennials or shrubs. They are all grown for their ornamental flowers and neat foliage and make excellent edging, flower box, hanging basket and rock garden specimens. Some are suitable in wild gardens or by the side of water.

CULTIVATION

These frost-hardy to somewhat frost-tender plants are best grown in well-drained, moist, light loam enriched with animal manure or compost. Most grow in sun or part-shade but resent wet conditions in winter. Prune after the first flush of flowers to encourage repeat flowering, and fertilize weekly with a liquid manure in this season. Propagate annuals from seed in spring, perennial species from seed or by division in spring or autumn, and perennial cultivars by division only. Transplant from late autumn until early spring.

Lobelia cardinalis (below)
CARDINAL FLOWER

This clump-forming perennial from eastern North America is useful for growing in wet places and beside streams and ponds. From late summer to mid-autumn it produces spikes of brilliant, scarlet-red flowers on branching stems above green or deep bronze-purple foliage. It grows to a height of 3 ft (1 m) and a spread of 12 in (30 cm).
ZONES 3–10.

Lobelia × speciosa
(right)

This is one of a group of hybrid lobelias derived from the American species *Lobelia cardinalis*, *L. splendens* and *L. siphilitica*, noted for their tall spikes of flowers that range in color from pink to mauve, red or purple.
ZONES 4–10.

Lobelia erinus *(left)*

EDGING LOBELIA

This slow-growing, compact annual is native to South Africa and grows to a height of 4–8 in (10–20 cm) and spread of 4–6 in (10–15 cm). It has a tufted, often semi-trailing habit, with dense, oval to lance-shaped leaves tapering at the base. It bears small, 2-lipped pinkish purple flowers continuously from spring to early autumn. **'Cambridge Blue'** is a popular hybrid along with **'Colour Cascade'**, with a mass of blue to violet to pink and white flowers. **'Crystal Palace'** is a very small variety with dense foliage, and is smothered in deep violet-blue flowers. **'Tim Riece'** is pale violet-blue. ZONES 7–11.

Lobelia erinus 'Tim Riece' *(left)*

Lobelia erinus 'Crystal Palace' *(below)*

Lobelia × gerardii (right)

This hybrid between the North American species *Lobelia cardinalis* and *L. siphilitica* is a robust perennial that can grow as tall as 5 ft (1.5 m). It has pink, violet or purple flowers and makes a beautiful garden specimen. **'Vedrariensis'**, its best-known cultivar, produces racemes of violet-blue flowers in late summer. Its leaves are dark green and lance-shaped. These hybrids prefer to grow in moist but well-drained soil in full sun. ZONES 7–10.

Lobelia tupa (below)

This vigorous, upright perennial from Chile is a rather coarse plant with large, light gray-green leaves and grows to about 6 ft (1.8 m) in height. In late summer and autumn the stems terminate in striking many-flowered erect racemes of tubular, 2-lipped flowers in shades from scarlet to deep, dull scarlet. ZONES 8–10.

Lobelia splendens (above)
syn. *Lobelia fulgens*
SCARLET LOBELIA

Native to southern USA and Mexico, *Lobelia splendens* bears tubular, 2-lipped, scarlet flowers in one-sided racemes in late summer. It has lance-shaped, mid-green leaves that are sometimes flushed red, and grows 3 ft (1 m) tall. ZONES 8–10.

L

Lobularia maritima
syn. *Alyssum maritimum*
SWEET ALYSSUM, SWEET ALICE

This fast-growing, spreading annual is a popular edging, rock garden or window box plant. It produces masses of tiny, honey-scented, 4-petalled white flowers over a long season, from spring to early autumn. Lilac, pink and violet shades are also available. It has a low, rounded, compact habit with lance-shaped, grayish green leaves, and grows to a height of 3–12 in (8–30 cm) and a spread of 8–12 in (20–30 cm). **'Violet Queen'** is the darkest of the garden varieties. ZONES 7–10.

Lobularia maritima
cultivars
(left & below left)

Lobularia maritima
'Violet Queen' *(below)*

L

LOBULARIA

This genus consists of 5 species of frost-hardy, dwarf plants from the Mediterranean and the Canary Islands. They are useful for rockeries, window boxes and borders. Although there are both annual and perennial forms, the annuals are most commonly grown. They bear tiny, 4-petalled, fragrant flowers in compact, terminal racemes in summer and early autumn.

CULTIVATION
Grow in full sun in fertile, well-drained soil. Continuous flowering can be encouraged by regular deadheading. Propagate from seed in spring or, if outdoors, from late spring to autumn.

Lotus berthelotii (right)

CORAL GEM, PARROT'S BEAK, PELICAN'S BEAK

Native to the Cape Verde and Canary Islands, this semi-evergreen, trailing perennial is suitable for hanging baskets, ground cover or for spilling over rockeries, banks or the tops of walls. It has hairy, silvery branches of fine needle leaves, and clusters of 1 in (25 mm), pea-like, orange to scarlet flowers that cover the plant in spring and early summer. It grows to 8 in (20 cm) tall with an indefinite spread. Frost tender, it suits warm coastal gardens. Tip prune young shoots to encourage dense foliage. ZONES 10–11.

Lotus maculatus
(left)

This trailing perennial from the Canary Islands grows to 8 in (20 cm) high and has silver needle-like leaves and claw-like tawny yellow flowers. It also has trailing, cascading fruit. **'Gold Flame'** has golden yellow to orange flowers. ZONES 10–11.

L

LOTUS

This legume genus of 150 species from temperate regions worldwide includes summer-flowering annuals, short-lived perennials and deciduous, semi-evergreen and evergreen subshrubs. They are grown for their foliage and pea-like flowers, which come in a range of colors. They should not be confused with the aquatic plants *(Nelumbo* and *Nymphaea)* commonly known as lotus.

CULTIVATION

Fully frost hardy to frost tender, they prefer moderately fertile, well-drained soil in full sun. Propagate from cuttings in early summer or from seed in autumn or spring.

Lotus maculatus
'Gold Flame' *(above)*

LUNARIA
HONESTY

Allied to stocks *(Matthiola)*, the origin of the common name for this genus of 3 species of annuals, biennials and perennials is uncertain. It could be from the way the silver lining of the seed pods is concealed in the brown husk like a silver coin, the reward of virtue that does not flaunt itself. Sprays of honesty have been popular as dried flower arrangements since the eighteenth century.

CULTIVATION

Plant in full sun or part-shade in fertile, moist but well-drained soil. Propagate perennials from seed or by division in autumn or spring, biennials from seed. They self-seed quite readily.

L

Lunaria rediviva (below)
PERENNIAL HONESTY

This perennial grows to 3 ft (1 m) high with a spread of 12 in (30 cm). It has hairy stems, heart-shaped leaves and pale violet flowers; the fruit are silver pods. **ZONES 8–10.**

Lunaria annua
(left & below left)
syn. *Lunaria biennis*

This fast-growing biennial, native to southern Europe and the Mediterranean coast, is grown for its attractive flowers and curious fruit. It has pointed, oval, serrated, bright green leaves and bears heads of scented, 4-petalled, rosy magenta, white or violet-purple flowers throughout spring and early summer. These are followed by circular seed pods with a silvery, translucent membrane. Erect in habit, it grows to a height of 30 in (75 cm) and a spread of 12 in (30 cm). **ZONES 8–10.**

LUPINUS
LUPIN, LUPINE

This legume genus of 200 species of annuals, perennials and semi-evergreen and evergreen shrubs and subshrubs, is mainly native to North America, southern Europe and North Africa. They are popular for their ease of culture, rapid growth and long, erect spikes of showy pea-flowers in a range of colors including blue, purple, pink, white, yellow, orange and red. Apart from being ornamentals, they are used for animal fodder, as a 'green manure' crop because of their nitrogen-fixing capacity. A few species are grown for grain, used as food by both humans and livestock. The compound leaves are distinct among legumes in being palmate, with 5 or more leaflets radiating from a common stalk, rather than the usual pinnate arrangement. *Lupinus purpurescens* is a seldom cultivated species, at one time grown for medicinal purposes.

CULTIVATION
Most lupins prefer climates with cool wet winters and long dry summers. They should be planted in full sun and in well-drained, moderately fertile, slightly acidic, sandy soil. They like plenty of water in the growing season and should be mulched in dry areas. Spent flowers should be cut away to prolong plant life and to prevent self-seeding. The foliage adds nitrogen to the soil when dug in. Propagate species from seed in autumn and Russell hybrids from cuttings or by division in early spring. Watch for slugs and snails.

Lupinus hartwegii (above)
HAIRY LUPIN

Native to Mexico, this fast-growing annual has a compact, erect growth habit and reaches 30 in (75 cm) in height with a spread of 15 in (38 cm). It has hairy, dark green leaves, and slender spikes of flowers in shades of blue, white or pink are borne abundantly in late winter, spring and early summer. ZONES 7–11.

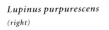

Lupinus purpurescens
(right)

Lupinus, Russell Hybrids

George Russell was a gardener fond of growing lupins, and over the years selected the best seedlings from open-pollinated plants of *Lupinus polyphyllus*. Around 1937, a colorful selection of his perennial lupins was released and rapidly became popular, known as 'Russell lupins'. It is thought that they are hybrids, the other major parent being the annual *L. hartwegii*. This fine strain of strong-growing lupins bears long spikes of large, strongly colored flowers in cream, pink, orange, blue or violet, some varieties bicolored, in late spring and summer. They produce a magnificent clump of deeply divided, mid-green leaves, growing to a height of 3 ft (1 m). **'Blue Jacket'** has dark blue-purple flowers; **'Noble Maiden'**, one of the Band of Nobles series, has cream flowers; **'Polar Princess'** has white flowers; and the blooms of **'Troop the Colour'** are bright red. There are also dwarf strains, such as the 24 in (60 cm) high **'Lulu'**. ZONES 3–9.

Lupinus 'Troop the Colour' *(above)*

Lupinus 'Noble Maiden' *(below)*

Lupinus 'Polar Princess' *(right)*

Lupinus 'Blue Jacket'
(above)

Lupinus texensis
(right)

TEXAS BLUE BONNET

A bushy annual reaching a height of 12 in (30 cm), this species has bright green leaves divided into 5 small leaflets that are hairy on the undersides, and bears dark blue and white flowers in late spring. Easily grown, it thrives in poor soil and is quick to flower from seed. This is the state flower of Texas, beyond which it does not occur wild. **ZONES 8–10.**

L

LYCHNIS
CAMPION, CATCHFLY

Native to temperate regions of the northern hemisphere, these 15 to 20 species of biennials and perennials include some that have been cultivated for many centuries. They are grown for their summer flowers that range in color from white through pinks and oranges to deep red. All have flat 5-petalled flowers, but in many species the petals are notched or deeply forked or sometimes divided into narrow teeth. The genus is related to *Silene,* and the boundary between the 2 genera has shifted with varying botanical opinion.

CULTIVATION

They are frost hardy and easily grown in cool climates, preferably in sunny sites and in any well-drained soil. The higher mountain species do best in soil that is protected from being excessively warmed by the sun. Remove spent stems after flowering and deadhead frequently to prolong the flowering period. Propagate by division or from seed in autumn or early spring. Some species self-seed readily.

Lychnis chalcedonica *(below)*
MALTESE CROSS

This perennial species from far eastern Europe has been a favorite with gardeners since the seventeenth century. Its color is such a dazzling orange-red that its garden companions should be chosen with care. It flowers for a rather short season in early summer, grows about 4 ft (1.2 m) tall, and takes its common name from the shape of the flower. White and pink varieties and one with double flowers exist, but these are fairly rare. ZONES 4–10.

Lychnis × arkwrightii 'Vesuvius' *(left)*
syn. *Lychnis × haageana* 'Vesuvius'

This hybrid is probably a cross between *Lychnis fulgens* and *L. sieboldii* and is a singularly striking perennial in all respects. Often short-lived, it is nonetheless worth growing for its deep bronze green foliage and its large, vivid orange flowers. It reaches around 24 in (60 cm) high and blooms from mid-summer. It is a spectacular plant to contrast against light green foliage and pale flowers. ZONES 6–10.

Lychnis coronaria *(below)*

ROSE CAMPION, DUSTY MILLER, MULLEIN PINK

This clump-forming perennial, sometimes grown as a biennial, is a striking plant that grows to a height of 30 in (75 cm) and a spread of 18 in (45 cm). It forms a dense clump of silvery white, downy leaves and many-branched gray stems that carry large, deep rose-pink to scarlet flowers throughout summer. **'Alba'** is a white-flowered cultivar. In ancient times the flowers were used for garlands and crowns. It is drought tolerant, requires little or no cultivation or watering, and often self-seeds. ZONES 4–10.

Lychnis viscaria

GERMAN CATCHFLY

This perennial is widely distributed through Europe and western Asia. Growing to 18 in (45 cm) tall and with a similar spread, it is a densely clumping plant with bronze stems and narrow dark green leaves with sticky hairs. It produces spike-like panicles of mauve to magenta flowers in early summer. **'Splendens Plena'** (syn. 'Flore Pleno') has larger, bright magenta double flowers. ZONES 4–9.

Lychnis flos-jovis *(below)*

FLOWER OF JOVE, FLOWER OF JUPITER

This perennial species from the Alps grows to a height of 18 in (45 cm). It has tufts of ground-hugging leaves, from the midst of which the flower stems arise to carry the blooms in clusters in summer. The leaves are gray and downy and the flowers are bright pink. ZONES 5–9.

L

Lychnis coronaria
'Alba' *(above)*

Lychnis viscaria
'Splendens Plena' *(right)*

Lycopodium phletmaria *(left)*
LAYERED TASSEL FERN

This elegant species is widely distributed in rainforests of tropical Asia and the South Pacific. It features small, shiny, lacquered leaves that line the long, pendent stems in 4 rows. In this and many related species the ends of the stems branch into groups of fine, elongated strobili-like green tassels, earning this group the name tassel ferns. They form large clumps of hanging stems that look good in baskets. ZONES 11–12.

LYCOPODIUM
CLUBMOSS

Widespread throughout most moister regions of the world, the 100 or more species in this genus are an ancient group of plants whose larger ancestors, along with those of the horsetails *(Equisetum)*, dominated the world's vegetation around 250 million years ago. Considered more primitive than the ferns but more advanced than the mosses, they range from tiny thread-stemmed plants that grow in boggy ground below heath, to large epiphytes that form curtains of ferny foliage on the limbs of tropical rainforest trees. All share similar cord-like stems clothed with overlapping, bright green or golden-green scale-like leaves. Club mosses do not flower but instead bear tiny spore capsules between the scales of delicate small cones (strobili).

CULTIVATION
Only the epiphytic species are cultivated to any extent, mainly by fern enthusiasts. Outdoors in the tropics they prefer part-shade and a permanently moist niche in the fork of a tree. Elsewhere they require a greenhouse or conservatory maintained at high humidity, and can make dramatic specimens in hanging baskets. Hang in positions with some air movement; they are sensitive to excess water around the roots. Propagate from cuttings or by layering fertile stem tips.

L

LYSICHITON
syn. *Lysichitum*

SKUNK CABBAGE

This unusual genus of the arum family is composed of 2 species of rhizomatous perennials, one from northeastern Asia, the other from western North America. They flower in spring as or before the new foliage develops. The stout-stemmed, pointed, heart-shaped leaves are quite large, sometimes as much as 4 ft (1.2 m) long when fully expanded. The spathes, white or yellow depending on the species, are around 15 in (38 cm) long and partially enclose the flower spike (spadix). The flowers have a musky smell that is nowhere near as bad as the common name suggests.

CULTIVATION
Skunk cabbages are frost-hardy plants suited only to cool climates. They normally grow in damp or boggy ground and are best positioned at the edges of ponds or streams. Propagate from seed or by division.

Lysichiton camtschatcensis (right)

WHITE SKUNK CABBAGE

As the name suggests, this species occurs on the Kamchatka Peninsula of far eastern Siberia, but its range includes other nearby parts of Siberia and northern Japan. The name skunk cabbage is not at all apt for this species, as its pure white spathes are odorless or even slightly sweet-scented. They appear before the leaves in early spring and stand about 24 in (60 cm) high. The conspicuously veined leaves are up to 3 ft (1 m) long. ZONES 5–9.

Lysichiton americanus (left)

YELLOW SKUNK CABBAGE

This species ranges in the wild from coastal Alaska to northern California and east to Montana. It has large butter-yellow spathes that appear in mid-spring before the leaves, though still present when the leaves have expanded, making a dramatic contrast. It grows to a height of around 3 ft (1 m). ZONES 5–9.

LYSIMACHIA
LOOSESTRIFE

Ranging through temperate and subtropical regions of the northern hemisphere, this genus of mainly evergreen perennials and shrubs of the primula family consists of around 150 species, of which about 130 are found in China. There are also a few species in Africa, Australia and South America. They vary greatly in growth habit from low, creeping plants to stately clumps with tall, spike-like racemes of crowded flowers. The 5-petalled flowers are mostly yellow or white, less commonly pink or purple. The botanical name is Latinized Greek for 'ending strife' and the English common name is a version of the same, though why these plants deserve such a name is now unclear.

CULTIVATION
They prefer slightly acidic soil with a good mix of organic matter and medium to moist conditions in sun or part-shade. Some species are marsh plants that grow best at the edge of a pond or stream. Propagate from seed or cuttings, or by division.

Lysimachia
clethroides (below)
JAPANESE LOOSESTRIFE

This somewhat hairy perennial from China, Korea and Japan grows to 3 ft (1 m) high making a broad, leafy clump of erect stems. In summer it produces tapering terminal spikes, gracefully nodding in bud but becoming erect with maturity, of crowded starry white flowers. ZONES 4–10.

Lysimachia
congestiflora (left)

A spreading perennial ground cover sometimes treated as an annual, this species roots at the nodes as it spreads and eventually covers an area over 3 ft (1 m) wide. A native of the damp meadows and streamsides of China and nearby parts of the Himalayan region, Thailand and Vietnam, it is prized for its bright golden yellow flowers, which are produced in globular terminal clusters in late summer. Where it occurs naturally it is used in herbal medicines to treat fractures, bruises and strains. ZONES 7–10.

Lysimachia ephemerum (right)

A native of south-western Europe, this handsome summer-flowering perennial has stems up to 3 ft (1 m) tall, rather narrow gray-green leaves and erect, tapering spikes of $^1/_2$ in (12 mm) wide, starry white flowers at the stem tips.
ZONES 6–10.

Lysimachia vulgaris (right)

YELLOW LOOSESTRIFE

·This perennial is a common wildflower in Europe and western Asia, growing in wet meadows and along streams. It has creeping rhizomes with erect stems that can be 4 ft (1.2 m) or more in height, with broad green leaves in whorls of three or four. The starry golden yellow flowers, about $^3/_4$ in (18 mm) wide, are borne in loose terminal spikes in summer.
ZONES 5–10.

L

Lysimachia nummularia

CREEPING JENNY, MONEYWORT

Native to much of Europe and also Turkey and the Caucasus, this vigorous creeping perennial has become widely naturalized in North America. Various medicinal properties were attributed to it by herbalists. The prostrate stems take root wherever they touch damp ground, forming a dense, rapidly spreading mat usually no more than 3 in (8 cm) deep. The deep yellow bowl-shaped flowers are up to 1 in (25 mm) wide, borne singly on short stalks from the leaf axils over a long summer period. **'Aurea'**, golden creeping Jenny, is a popular cultivar with pale yellow-green leaves and stems; when grown in shade it turns an interesting lime green. Both green and gold forms are useful ground cover plants for moist or even boggy soil and can tolerate occasional light foot traffic. **ZONES 4–10.**

Lysimachia nummularia 'Aurea'
(left)

Lysimachia punctata

(above & below left)

GOLDEN LOOSESTRIFE, GARDEN LOOSESTRIFE

A vigorous clump-forming perennial, this species is native to central and southern Europe and Turkey. It grows erect to a height of 3 ft (1 m) with broad mid-green leaves in whorls of 4, grading into floral bracts on the upper stems which carry in summer a massed display of brilliant yellow starry flowers, each about 1 in (25 mm) across. Golden loosestrife looks best planted in large groups. It is suitable for bedding, large rock gardens, or pool and streamside plantings. **ZONES 5–10.**

LYTHRUM

LOOSESTRIFE

This genus of annuals, perennials and subshrubs shares the common name 'loosestrife' with *Lysimachia*, though the 2 genera are quite unrelated; however, the long, erect flower spikes of some *Lythrum* species and their boggy habitats are like those of some lysimachias. There are around 35 species, scattered through all continents except South America. They vary from small creeping plants with stems rooting in the mud of ditches, to plants 6 ft (1.8 m) or more tall with showy spikes of pink to purple flowers.

CULTIVATION

These plants will grow in most soil conditions as long as moisture is adequate, and in bogs and other wetlands some species can be quite invasive. Propagation is very easy from seed or by division.

Lythrum virgatum
(below left)

This species extends in the wild from central Europe through central Asia as far as northern China. It is a handsome, vigorous perennial growing to as much as 6 ft (1.8 m) tall, with pretty pinkish red flowers arranged rather loosely in erect spikes. Like the similar *Lythrum salicaria*, it has become a weed in North America. **ZONES 4–10.**

Lythrum salicaria *(right)*

PURPLE LOOSESTRIFE

This perennial always grows in wet ground, often spreading into the shallow water at the edges of ponds. Erect stems arise from a knotty rhizome 3–6 ft (1–1.8 m) tall depending on soil moisture and fertility. It produces showy long spikes of pink to magenta flowers from mid-summer to autumn. In some areas it is detested as a weed, displacing native wildflowers. Purple loosestrife was used in folk medicine for centuries: its tannins have coagulent properties, hence staunching the flow of blood, and it was also used to treat cholera. There are a number of garden forms, with flowers in the deep rose red to deep pink range, some double-flowered. **'Feuerkerze'** ('Firecandle') is a cultivar with more reddish flowers. **ZONES 3–10.**

MALVA
MALLOW

This genus is made up of 30 species of annuals, biennials and perennials that originate in Europe, North Africa and Asia, but have in some cases naturalized elsewhere. The flowers are similar to but smaller than the popular *Lavatera* to which the malvas are related; they are single, 5-petalled flowers in shades of white, pink, blue or purple. Although they may not be quite as showy as those of *Lavatera,* they do make attractive subjects for the border or wild garden.

CULTIVATION
These plants flourish in sunny, well-drained aspects and tend to be more robust and longer lived in not too rich soil. They are fully frost hardy. Cut plants back after the first flowers have faded. Propagate from cuttings or seed in spring; the perennials often self-seed. Watch for rust disease in spring.

M

Malva moschata
MUSK MALLOW

Useful for naturalizing in a wild garden or odd corner, this perennial has narrow, lobed, divided leaves with a sticky, hairy texture which emit a musky, cheesy odor when crushed. A native of Europe, *Malva moschata* bears profuse spikes of saucer-shaped pink flowers in summer. **'Alba'**, a white cultivar, is also very popular. It has a bushy, branching habit and can grow to a height of 3 ft (1 m). **ZONES 3–10.**

Malva moschata 'Alba'
(left)

MARANTA

This is a genus of 32 species of evergreen rhizomatous perennials from the tropical forests of Central and South America. Apart from the beautifully marked and textured leaves, they are known for their habit of 'going to sleep' at night. The leaves spread by day and stand erect at night. One species, *Maranta arundinacea*, is an important crop plant: it is better known to cooks as arrowroot.

CULTIVATION

Marantas are usually grown in greenhouses or as indoor plants. They like humidity and bright light without direct sunlight. In tropical areas, they make a good ground cover under large trees. Propagation is usually done by dividing established clumps or from basal cuttings struck on bottom heat.

Maranta leuconeura
PRAYER PLANT, TEN COMMANDMENTS

This variable species contains most of the best foliage forms of this genus. It usually grows to about 12 in (30 cm) in height and spread, and produces its inconspicuous white flowers with foliate spots in slender spikes during summer. The dark green leaves are usually about 6 in (15 cm) long. They have silver to pink veins and the reverse side can be purple or gray-green. In the cultivar '**Erythroneura**', the herringbone plant, the leaves are velvety and very dark black-green with a brilliant green irregular zone along the midrib. It also has bright pink veins and a deep red reverse. '**Kerchoviana**', known as rabbit tracks, has oval, light green leaves with green to brown blotches on either side of the central vein. Its insignificant white to mauve flowers appear intermittently. ZONES 11–12.

Maranta leuconeura 'Kerchoviana' *(below)*

M

MARRUBIUM
HOREHOUND

This genus of around 40 species of aromatic perennial herbs is found in temperate regions of Europe and Asia, often by the roadside and in wastelands. *Marrubium* is a member of the mint family and characteristically has square branching stems and opposite pairs of toothed, ovate leaves with soft hairs and conspicuous veining. The whorls of small flowers are borne in the leaf axils. The botanical name is believed to have evolved from *marob*, a Hebrew word meaning a bitter juice, as this was one of the bitter herbs eaten by Jews to commemorate the feast of Passover.

Marrubium kotschyi (below) syn. *Marrubium astracanicum*

This native of Iraq and Kurdistan grows up to 15 in (38 cm) in height. It has elliptic-toothed leaves and whorls of reddish purple flowers are produced in summer. ZONES 7–10.

CULTIVATION
These fully frost-hardy plants prefer full sun in poor, well-drained soil. Although trouble free, avoid planting them in an over-rich soil and protect from drying winds. Propagate by root division in mid-spring or from seed in late spring.

Marrubium supinum (left)

A native of mountainous regions in central and southern Spain, this species grows to 18 in (45 cm) in height and has kidney-shaped, toothed leaves and pink or lilac flowers in summer. ZONES 7–10.

MATRICARIA

This extensively revised genus of aromatic annual herbs consists of 5 species, native to the temperate regions of the northern hemisphere. They have finely dissected leaves with numerous linear segments and produce terminal, white daisy-like flowerheads from spring to late summer. They can be grown in a rockery, herb garden or as a border edging. Some species produce good cut flowers and *Matricaria recutita* is valued for its herbal use.

CULTIVATION

These fully frost-hardy plants prefer well-drained, light sandy soil in full sun. Propagate from seed in summer.

Matricaria recutita

(below)

syn. *Matricaria chamomilla*

GERMAN CHAMOMILE

This is an aromatic annual with stems to 24 in (60 cm) and finely divided, light green leaves. It has white daisy-like flowers with golden centers. The flowers appear in summer and autumn. The fully opened flowers can be harvested and dried. This species is used in a similar fashion to *Chamaeleum nobile,* chamomile. Use discarded tea flowers on the compost pile to activate decomposition. ZONES 6–10.

M

Matthiola incana
(left)

Best grown as an annual, this upright, bushy plant grows up to 24 in (60 cm) with a spread of 12 in (30 cm). Fully frost hardy, it has lance-shaped, gray-green leaves and fragrant, 3–6 in (8–15 cm) long spikes of flowers in shades of pink, purple, red or white, borne in spring. Many cultivars are available. **'Mammoth Column'** reaches 30 in (75 cm) in height, and produces a single, 12–15 in (30–38 cm) tall spike of scented flowers in spring in mixed or separate colors. ZONES 6–10.

MATTHIOLA
STOCK, GILLYFLOWER

This genus contains some 55 species of annuals, biennials and subshrubby perennials, very few of which are grown in gardens with the exceptions of the night-scented stock *Matthiola longipetala* subsp. *bicornis* and the cultivars of *M. incana*. The species are native to Europe, central and southwestern Asia and North Africa. The leaves are usually gray-green and the perfumed flowers can be produced from spring to autumn. They are attractive both for bedding out and as cut flowers. Unfortunately, stocks are prone to quite a few pests and diseases, including downy mildew, club-root, gray mold and cabbage root fly.

CULTIVATION
Matthiola prefer a sunny aspect in moist but well-drained, neutral or alkaline soil. Shelter from strong winds and stake some of the larger forms. Propagate from seed sown *in situ* for night-scented stock, which should be staggered to prolong flowering season, or in spring sow seed of *M. incana* types into seed trays and move to beds later.

Meconopsis betonicifolia (right)
syn. *Meconopsis baileyi*

BLUE POPPY, TIBETAN POPPY, HIMALAYAN POPPY

This clump-forming woodland species bears sky blue, saucer-shaped, 2–3 in (5–8 cm) wide satiny flowers with yellow stamens in late spring and early summer. The oblong, mid-green leaves are in basal rosettes. It grows 3–5 ft (1–1.5 m) tall and 18 in (45 cm) wide. It does not bloom in the first season, and dies down completely over winter. ZONES 7–9.

MECONOPSIS

This genus consists of about 45 species of annuals, biennials and short-lived perennials. They bear large, exotic flowers with papery petals and a bold, central boss of stamens on tall stems. The flower stalks lengthen after flowering as the fruits develop. The hairy leaves are either simple or pinnate.

M

CULTIVATION
Mostly frost hardy, they need a moist but not over-wet, lime-free, humus-rich soil and a cool site in part- or full shade with shelter from strong winds. Propagate from seed in late summer.

Meconopsis cambrica (right)
WELSH POPPY

Native to western Europe and the UK, this species is more easily grown than *Meconopsis betonicifolia*. The slightly hairy, deeply divided, mid-green leaves form basal rosettes. Lemon yellow or rich orange blooms are freely borne from mid-spring to autumn. It has a spreading habit, reaching 12–18 in (30–45 cm) tall and 12 in (30 cm) wide. Though short lived, it self-seeds read-ily, given the right conditions. ZONES 6–10.

M

Meconopsis grandis (left)
HIMALAYAN BLUE POPPY

This stunning rich blue poppy is more solidly
perennial than the better known *Meconopsis
betonicifolia*. It has rosettes of irregularly toothed,
deciduous green leaves with red-brown or rust
colored hairs. The brilliant, early summer flowers
can be up to 6 in (15 cm) across on stems up to
4 ft (1.2 m) tall. ZONES 5–9.

Meconopsis × *sheldonii*
'Slieve Donard' (below)

Meconopsis × sheldonii (above)

These hybrids between
Meconopsis betonicifolia
and *M. grandis* are
rosette-forming,
hairy perennials with
12 in (30 cm) leaves.
They can grow up to
5 ft (1.5 m) tall in good
conditions. The blue
flowers are borne
from late spring to
early summer. **'Slieve
Donard'** is vigorous
brilliant blue form with
long pointed petals,
growing to 3 ft (1 m)
tall. ZONES 6–9.

Meconopsis pseudointegrifolia (right)

As the name suggests,
this species is similar to
Meconopsis integrifolia.
However, it differs in
bearing heads of
downward-facing
blooms at the top of
strong stems. The
flowers are soft yellow
with conspicuous
golden stamens and are
borne in late spring
and early summer. The
plant is covered in fine
golden brown hairs.
ZONES 7–9.

MELISSA
BALM

This genus of 3 species of perennial herbs has representatives from Europe to central Asia. The name *Melissa* is derived from a Greek word meaning bee, owing to the abundance of nectar in the flowers which attracts bees. Borne in opposite pairs on square stems, the crinkled ovate or heart-shaped leaves emit a lemony odor when bruised. Axillary spikes of white or yellowish flowers appear in summer. These quick-growing, decorative foliage plants look good along paths, in herb gardens, among ferns and when grown in pots.

CULTIVATION
Very frost hardy, they prefer full sun or light shade if summers are hot. Slightly moist, well-drained soil is best. Propagate from seed sown in spring. Variegated forms are propagated by root division or from young spring cuttings.

Melissa officinalis
(below)
LEMON BALM, BEE BALM

This perennial to 24 in (60 cm) high is grown for its fresh, lemon-scented and lemon-flavored leaves. Small white flowers appear in late summer and attract pollinating bees into the garden. Lemon balm spreads rapidly, dies down in winter but shoots again in spring. The leaves are valued as a calming herbal tea. They also give a light, lemon flavor to fruit salads, jellies, iced tea and summer drinks, and can be used as a substitute for lemon peel in cooking. ZONES 4–10.

M

MENTHA
MINT

This genus contains 25 species of aromatic, perennial herbs, some evergreen and some semi-evergreen, from Europe, Asia and Africa. Most are cultivated for their fragrance, some for their flavor or ornamental appeal. Several species make attractive ground covers. They vary in size from tiny creeping forms to bushy plants, and vary in flavor from refreshing to very strong.

CULTIVATION
Most are very frost hardy, like sunshine and rich soil and need lots of moisture. They are invasive, spreading rapidly by runners; to keep them under control, try growing them in large pots, watering regularly and repotting annually. Propagate from seed or by root division in spring or autumn.

M

Mentha arvensis
(below)
CORN MINT, FIELD MINT

This erect hairy perennial reaches up to 24 in (60 cm) in height. It occurs throughout most of Europe on disturbed, often damp ground. The lance-shaped leaves are shallowly toothed. The lilac flowers appear in dense axillary whorls from mid-summer until autumn. This species has the property of being able to prevent milk from curdling and was once cultivated solely for this purpose.
ZONES 4–10.

Mentha pulegium
(right)

PENNYROYAL, EUROPEAN
PENNYROYAL MINT

A native of Asia and
Europe with small,
elliptical, gray-green,
hairy leaves, this species
has spreading stems
that form a foliage clump
around 4 in (10 cm)
high and 18 in (45 cm)
wide. In summer and
early autumn, the plant
produces upright spikes
with whorls of white to
pale lilac to soft purple-
pink flowers. Plant
in shade if the soil is
inclined to dry out.
Prostrate dwarf forms
grow well in hanging
baskets. It is renowned
for its curative value in
treating colds, nausea,
headaches, nervous
disorders and various
skin conditions.
ZONES 7–10.

M

Mentha × piperita (above)
PEPPERMINT

This spreading perennial, grown for its aromatic
foliage and culinary uses, grows to 24 in (60 cm)
high and wide. Using underground stems, it
forms a carpet of oval, toothed, mid-green and
reddish green leaves. Purple flowers appear in
spring. **Mentha × piperita f. citrata,** eau de
cologne mint, is too strong and bitter for culinary
use but is grown for its distinctive perfume.
ZONES 3–10.

M

MENYANTHES

There is only one species in this genus, with a very wide distribution through Europe, northern Asia, northwestern India and North America. It is an aquatic or marginal water plant with creeping rhizomes to 4 ft (1.2 m) long. This plant has long been used in herbal medicine to relieve gout and fever. The Inuit ground it into a flour and the leaves have been used in Scandinavia to make beer.

CULTIVATION

This plant is fully frost hardy and is happy grown in wet mud in, or on the edge of, water. Propagate from seed sown in wet soil or cuttings of pre-rooted rhizomes in spring.

Menyanthes trifoliata (above)
BOG BEAN

This plant has attractive foliage divided into 3 leaflets of rich green supported by dark-colored stems. The tiny fringed flowers are produced in erect spikes and are white, but pink in bud. This species grows to about 12 in (30 cm) tall and spreads out over a considerable area of water. ZONES 3–10.

Mertensia ciliata
CHIMING BELLS

This species from western USA grows to about 24 in (60 cm) tall. Its leaves are lanceolate and bluish green. The flower stems support nodding, blue, trumpet-shaped flowers, $1/_3$ in (8 mm) long during summer. 'Blue Drops' is a selection by the famous British perennial specialist Alan Bloom of Bressingham Gardens. It gives a particularly fine display of bright blue flowers. ZONES 4–10.

Mertensia ciliata 'Blue Drops' *(above)*

MERTENSIA

This genus from northern temperate areas consists of about 50 species of herbaceous perennials. The foliage is usually lanceolate and hairy. They produce terminal panicles of tubular flowers, usually blue, in spring.

CULTIVATION

Some species are small alpines ideal for cool rock gardens; others are taller, making them suitable for most borders and woodland gardens. All species prefer full sun and moisture-retentive soil but in most cases, especially the alpines, sharp drainage is important. All are fully frost hardy. Propagate from seed, although some species can be carefully divided. Check for slugs and snails.

Mertensia pulmonarioides *(above)*
syn. *Mertensia virginica*
VIRGINIA BLUEBELLS

Native to the cooler parts of North America, this perennial is one of the loveliest of all blue spring flowers. It has smooth, oblong, soft blue-green foliage, and bears clusters of rich blue, tubular 1 in (25 mm) long flowers, 20 or more on each stem. It is effective planted with daffodils and polyanthus, and is seen at its best naturalized in woodlands or alongside streams. It grows to a height and spread of around 18 in (45 cm). ZONES 3–9.

MEUM

BALDMONEY, SPIGNEL

There is only one species in this genus of the carrot family. It is a clump-forming herbaceous perennial to 24 in (60 cm) tall with attractive foliage and umbels of small white flowers in summer. This plant occurs naturally in western and central Europe.

CULTIVATION

An attractive addition to the perennial border or wild garden, it is simple to grow in any well-drained but moist soil in full sun and does best in temperate to cold climates. It is very frost hardy. Propagate from fresh seed. It will often self-seed if happy.

M

Meum athamanticum (below)

The pretty soft mid-green basal foliage is the major asset of this plant. In early summer it will start to produce its tiny white or purple-tinged white flowers in small umbels. It spreads to 12 in (30 cm). The foliage is aromatic. ZONES 4–9.

MIMULUS
syn. *Diplacus*
MONKEY FLOWER, MUSK

The 180 or so species of annuals, perennials and shrubs of this genus are characterized by tubular flowers with flared mouths, often curiously spotted and mottled. They have been likened to grinning monkey faces, and come in a large range of colors, including brown, orange, yellow, red, pink and crimson. Mainly native to the cool Pacific coastal areas of Chile and the USA, most species are suited to bog gardens or other moist situations, although some are excellent rock garden plants.

CULTIVATION
Grow these plants in full sun or part-shade in wet or moist soil. Propagate perennials by division in spring and annuals from seed in autumn or early spring.

Mimulus cardinalis
(right)

CARDINAL MONKEY FLOWER,
SCARLET MONKEY FLOWER

From southwestern USA and Mexico, this herbaceous perennial grows at least 3 ft (1 m) tall and 12 in (30 cm) wide. It has sharply toothed, hairy, mid-green leaves and produces racemes of scarlet flowers from summer through to autumn. Found on banks of streams and ponds, it needs a sheltered position as it tends to sprawl if battered by rain and wind. ZONES 7–11.

Mimulus × hybridus Hybrids

These popular hybrids between *Mimulus guttatus* and *M. luteus* blend parental characters in various ways. The funnel-shaped, open-mouthed flowers can be up to 2 in (5 cm) wide and come in red, yellow, cream and white, or mixed variations of these colors, plus red mottling, spotting or freckling. Although reasonably hardy and perennial, they rapidly deteriorate in hot sunlight and become straggly after a few months, and so are treated as annuals. **'Ruiter's Hybrid'** bears orange trumpet-shaped flowers with wavy petal margins. ZONES 6–10.

M

Mimulus × hybridus
'Ruiter's Hybrid'
(below)

Mimulus luteus
(left)

**YELLOW MUSK, GOLDEN
MONKEY FLOWER**

A spreading perennial
often grown as an an-
nual, this plant bears a
profusion of yellow
flowers above mid-
green foliage through-
out summer. It grows
to a height and spread
of 12 in (30 cm). It is
very frost hardy, and
needs part-shade and
moist soil. **ZONES 7–10.**

M

Mimulus moschatus *(above)*
MONKEY MUSK

This small, creeping, water-loving perennial
grows to a height and spread of 6–12 in
(15–30 cm). It bears pale yellow flowers, lightly
dotted with brown, in summer to autumn. It is
very frost hardy. This plant was once grown for its
musk scent, but it has been mysteriously odorless
for many years. **ZONES 7–10.**

M

MIRABILIS
UMBRELLA WORT

This Central and South American genus consists of about 50 species of annuals or herbaceous perennials that make showy garden plants in virtually frost-free climates. Some can become invasive and difficult to eradicate as they can be quite deep rooted. The flowers are often brightly colored and in one case at least are variegated in bold colors like magenta and orange. Most have a pleasant fragrance.

CULTIVATION

In frost-free and dry tropical climates, they are quite easy plants to grow. All that is required is a sunny, well-drained aspect. In colder climates, the tubers of perennial species can be lifted and stored over winter like dahlias. Propagate from seed or by division of the tubers.

Mirabilis jalapa
(above)

MARVEL OF PERU, FOUR-O'CLOCK FLOWER

This bushy tuberous perennial, native to tropical America, is grown for its fragrant, trumpet-shaped, crimson, pink, white or yellow flowers that open in late afternoon and remain open all night, closing again at dawn. It is good as a pot or bedding plant or as a dwarf hedge. It is summer flowering and grows to around 3 ft (1 m) high with a spread of 24–30 in (60–75 cm). ZONES 8–11.

MOLTKIA

This genus of 6 species comes from northern Italy to northern Greece and southwestern Asia. All are perennials or small shrubs found on rocky, sunny hillsides. They have lance-shaped, hairy, mid- to dark green leaves. The flowers are usually tubular and pendulous in shades of blue, purple and occasionally yellow. These attractive plants can be useful in rock gardens as ground covers or in the front of perennial borders.

CULTIVATION

They all like full sun and alkaline, well-drained soil, especially in winter. Some species can be invasive and are best in wilder parts of the garden. Propagate from seed or cuttings or by layering the woody species.

Moltkia doerfleri
(left)
syn. *Lithospermum doerfleri*

This is a suckering herbaceous species to 18 in (45 cm) in height and spread with unbranched, erect stems topped with drooping clusters of deep purple flowers from late spring to mid-summer. From Albania, it can be invasive in gardens and swamp smaller plants. ZONES 6–10.

M

MOLUCCELLA

The origin of this genus name is a puzzle, since none of its 4 species get any closer to the Moluccas than northwestern India, from where they extend to the eastern Mediterranean. They are annuals or short-lived perennials, although it is only the annual species that are usually grown. They are tall, upright, branched plants to 3 ft (1 m) or more with toothed leaves and small white fragrant flowers. It is, however, for the large green calyces that *Moluccella* species are grown; these are attractive in the garden or as cut flowers, fresh or dried.

CULTIVATION

Marginally frost hardy, these plants prefer full sun and moderately fertile, moist but well-drained soil. Propagate from seed.

Moluccella laevis
(right)

BELLS OF IRELAND, SHELL FLOWER

This summer-flowering annual, native to Turkey, Syria and the Caucasus, is grown for its flower spikes, surrounded by shell-like, apple green calyces, which are very popular for fresh or dried floral work; the tiny white flowers are insignificant. Its rounded leaves are pale green. This plant is fairly fast growing to a height of 3 ft (1 m) and spread of 12 in (30 cm), and has an erect, branching habit. **ZONES 7–10.**

M

MONARDA
BERGAMOT, HORSEMINT

This is a genus of 15 species of perennials or annuals from North America with green, sometimes purple-tinged, veined, aromatic leaves. They are much loved by bees and are used for flavoring teas and in potpourris, as well as for their colorful, scented flowers. Plants can be single stemmed or sparsely branching, and bear 2-lipped, tubular flowers from mid-summer to early autumn.

CULTIVATION
They are very frost hardy and are best planted in full sun although some shade is acceptable. They must be well drained, and the annual species do best on sandy soil. The perennials are happy in moist soil and in some climates like a good feed of manure or compost. Annuals are sown directly into their permanent spot, and perennials are usually grown by division of established clumps.

Monarda didyma
(left)
BEE BALM, OSWEGO TEA

This plant was used by the Native Americans and early colonists as a herbal tea. With its spidery white, pink or red flowers borne in late summer, it is one of the showiest of the culinary herbs. The young leaves may be used in salads or as a stuffing for roast meat. The species grows 3 ft (1 m) or more tall. **'Aquarius'** has deep, purple-lilac flowers with purplish green bracts. **'Cambridge Scarlet'** is a vigorous perennial to 3 ft (1 m) with dark green, slightly toothed leaves that when crushed or brushed against emit an exotic, citrus-like scent. **'Croftway Pink'** grows to 30 in (75 cm) tall and has rose-pink flowers from mid-summer to early autumn. ZONES 4–10.

M

Monarda didyma
'Aquarius' *(right)*

Monarda
citriodora *(right)*
LEMON MINT

This annual species
from central and
southern USA and
northern Mexico grows
to 24 in (60 cm) tall. Its
curved tubular flowers
are scented and usually
white, pink or purplish,
and have a hairy
mouth. **ZONES 5–11.**

M

Monarda
'Mahogany' *(right)*

This is a hybrid
between *Monarda
didyma* and *M. fistulosa*.
It is a tall variety that
grows to 3 ft (1 m) with
handsome wine-red
or lilac flowers from
mid-summer well into
autumn. **ZONES 4–10.**

MONARDELLA

This is a small genus of annuals and perennials from western
North America, some 20 species in all. They are grown for their
highly aromatic foliage, which in some species is used for herbal
teas. The 2-lipped, tubular flowers are formed in terminal clusters and are most usually red, pink or purple in color.

CULTIVATION
Most like a sunny, sharply drained site and can be attractive
in a rock garden or pot in the alpine house if smaller species are
selected. The taller ones can be used at the front of a dry sunny
border. They have reasonable frost resistance, but do resent
dampness in winter. Propagate from seed or summer cuttings of
perennial species or by division.

Monardella villosa (above)
COYOTE MINT

This species is a trailing, woody stemmed,
suckering perennial from California. The flowers
are usually pale pink to rose purple. It can vary in
height from 4 in (10 cm) up to 24 in (60 cm).
ZONES 8–11.

MONOPSIS

This is a genus of 18 species of annuals from tropical and southern Africa that are quite similar to the annual lobelias. They can be used in much the same way in borders of flower beds. The tubular flowers flare at the tips into spreading lobes and are usually in shades of blue or yellow. The tube is split all the way to the base on the top side.

CULTIVATION
They do best in climates with cool summers and prefer full sun or part-shade and well-drained soil of moderate richness. Propagate from seed either planted *in situ* or raised under glass and planted out after frosts are over.

M

Monopsis lutea (above)

This spreading, trailing plant has thin wiry stems to 12 in (30 cm) or more long, sometimes taking root from the lower nodes. It has alternate, linear to lance-shaped leaves with toothed margins. In spring and summer, bright yellow flowers are produced towards the ends of the stems. This is a pretty cascading plant for a rock garden or wall. **ZONES 10–11.**

M

MORINA

This is a small genus of 4 species of prickly, rosette-form perennials that until they flower look for all the world like some species of thistle. The tall flower spikes produce whorls of long tubular curved flowers supported by collars of prickly bracts. These cold-hardy perennials come from mountainous regions of eastern Europe and the Himalayas and make statuesque foliage and flowering plants for the flower border.

CULTIVATION

They prefer full sun and very well-drained soil enriched with compost. Propagate from ripe seed or from root cuttings.

Morina longifolia
(above)
WHORL FLOWER

This is probably the best known species in the genus and grows to 4 ft (1.2 m) or more tall. Its foliage is basal and spiny. The flowers open white and turn deep cerise; after pollination both colors will be seen together. The flowers are supported by bronze-tinged spiny bracts and the calyxes stay ornamental after flowering. ZONES 6–10.

MUSA
BANANA, PLANTAIN

Bananas, native to Southeast Asia, are now cultivated throughout the tropics. Since they can ripen in transit, they have become a very familiar fruit in most temperate countries. Nearly all the edible varieties, including red and green fruit, lack seeds entirely. The genus includes several important species, such as *Musa textilis*, which yields strong fiber known as Manila hemp; others are grown for their enormous leaves or colored flowers. The flowers are borne in large spikes, erect or pendulous depending on species, the buds enclosed in large purplish bracts. Female flowers are borne at the base of the spikes, male ones further up. Although they often grow to tree size, they are really giant herbaceous perennials: each 'trunk' is composed of leaf bases and, when the flowering shoot has risen and borne fruit, it dies.

CULTIVATION
Some of the smaller species can be grown as house plants or in greenhouses in temperate climates. Banana crops require fertile, moist soil and full sun. Protect from winds, which will cause new growth to shred. Propagate from ripe seed or by division of clumps.

Musa velutina
(below left & right)

Banana flowers are admired more for their curiosity value than their beauty. This dwarf species grows no higher than 6 ft (1.8 m) with yellow flowers highlighted by red bracts and small, velvety, red, inedible bananas. The fruit unpeel themselves when ripe, hence one common name of self-peeling banana. ZONES 9–12.

M

MYOSOTIDIUM
CHATHAM ISLAND FORGET-ME-NOT

Though the Chatham Islands lie east of New Zealand, this forget-me-not gives a glimpse of what Antarctic flora might have been like before the continent settled at the South Pole. The scientific name of the only species, *Myosotidium hortensia,* emphasizes the plant's close relationship to the true forget-me-not, *Myosotis.*

CULTIVATION
The instructions that accompanied the plant's introduction to England in 1858 were to give it a cool, rather damp position and mulch it twice a year with rotting fish, a practice that has happily proved unnecessary. Salt tolerant and marginally frost hardy, it requires semi-shade and a humus-rich, moist soil. Propagate by division in spring or from seed in summer or autumn. Once growing well, it should not be disturbed and will naturalize freely.

Myosotidium hortensia (below)

This evergreen, clump-forming perennial is the giant of the forget-me-not family, growing to a height and spread of 24 in (60 cm). It has a basal mound of large, glossy, rich green, pleated leaves, and in spring and summer bears large clusters of bright purple-blue flowers, slightly paler at the edges, on tall flower stems. A white-flowered cultivar is also available. ZONES 9–11.

M

MYOSOTIS

FORGET-ME-NOT

This genus of annuals and perennials includes 34 New Zealand natives among its 50 or so species, but the most commonly cultivated are from the temperate regions of Europe, Asia and the Americas. Their dainty blue (sometimes pink or white) flowers bloom in spring, and most species are useful in rock gardens and borders, or as ground cover under trees and shrubs. The plants fade after flowering. *Myosotis*, from the Greek for 'mouse ear', refers to the pointed leaves. The flowers have long been associated with love and remembrance.

CULTIVATION

Mostly frost hardy, they prefer a semi-shaded setting or a sunny spot protected by larger plants, and fertile, well-drained soil. They are rarely affected by pests or diseases and like fertilizing before the flowering period. Propagate from seed in autumn. Once established, they self-seed freely.

Myosotis sylvatica

(center)

GARDEN FORGET-ME-NOT

This European biennial or short-lived perennial is usually grown as an annual for its bright lavender-blue, yellow-eyed flowers in spring and early summer. It forms mounds of fuzzy foliage 18 in (45 cm) tall and 12 in (30 cm) wide, with taller stems uncurling as the flower buds open. There are many named selections, some more compact, some pink or white. **'Blue Ball'** has tiny, deep blue flowers and is good for edging. ZONES 5–10.

Myosotis sylvatica 'Blue Ball' (below)

M

Myosotis alpestris (below)

ALPINE FORGET-ME-NOT

This short-lived perennial from Europe (usually grown as an annual or biennial) forms clumps to a height and spread of 4–6 in (10–15 cm). In late spring and early summer, it bears clusters of dainty, bright blue, pink or white flowers with creamy yellow eyes. ZONES 4–10.

MYRIOPHYLLUM
MILFOIL

This genus consists of 45 species, mainly aquatic annuals and perennials with representatives worldwide. They are usually submerged plants rooted in the bottom silt of ponds or slow-moving streams. As their wiry stems elongate they reach the surface, where they float and produce emergent leaves. The submerged leaves are very finely cut, feathery and whorled around the stems, while the emergent leaves are often simple and narrow. Spikes of minute flowers develop in summer, usually at the tips of the emergent stems.

CULTIVATION

Little effort is required in cultivation provided a species appropriate to the climate is chosen. As long as the stems have soil to root in, they should thrive. They prefer sun, but will tolerate part-shade. Hardiness varies with the species. Propagate by breaking off rooted pieces of stem.

Myriophyllum aquaticum (below) syns *Myriophyllum brasiliense*, *M. proserpinacoides*

PARROT FEATHER, DIAMOND MILFOIL

This perennial species found wild in Australia, New Zealand and South America produces stems up to 6 ft (1.8 m) long often with their tips well up out of the water. The finely dissected foliage appears yellow-green if submerged, blue-green out of the water. Tiny, bright yellow-green flowers appear among the submerged leaves in summer. ZONES 10–12.

M

Myrrhis odorata
(above)

This graceful perennial to 6 ft (1.8 m) high is excellent as a background plant in the herb garden or mixed flower border. It will tolerate shade and can be sited beneath garden trees. It self-seeds readily and the strongest seedlings may be transplanted. ZONES 5–10.

MYRRHIS
SWEET CICELY, MYRRH

This is a genus of only one species, an attractive long-lived perennial in the carrot family, native to southern Europe. It has aromatic, fern-like leaves and fragrant creamy white flowers in flattened heads in early summer, followed by ribbed, shiny brown seeds that have a very brief viability. The leaves and seeds have a sweet aniseed flavor and are cooked with fruit as a sugar substitute. They are also good in raw vegetable juices.

CULTIVATION
Fully frost hardy, they should be grown in part-shade in moist but well-drained, fertile soil. Propagate from fresh seed in autumn or spring or by division in autumn or early spring.

NELUMBO
LOTUS

This is a genus of 2 species of deciduous, perennial water plants found in North America, Asia and northern Australia. Lotuses resemble waterlilies, but raise both their leaves and flowers well clear of the muddy water of the ponds and ditches in which they grow, blossoming unsullied. The leaves are waxy and almost circular, while the solitary, fragrant flowers are borne on long stalks. Flowers left on the stem develop into decorative seed pods. When these are dried, they can be used in flower arrangements. Lotus seeds found in Japan, shown by carbon dating to be 2000 years old, have germinated and borne flowers.

CULTIVATION
Frost hardiness varies, some tropical forms of *Nelumbo nucifera* being quite frost tender. They prefer an open, sunny position in 24 in (60 cm) of water. Plant in large pots in heavy loam and submerge. Propagate from seed or by division in spring.

Nelumbo lutea (left)
WATER CHINQUAPIN, AMERICAN LOTUS

This American species, suitable for larger waterscapes, has leaves almost 24 in (60 cm) across emerging 6 ft (1.8 m) or more above the water surface. Pale yellow, 10 in (25 cm) wide summer flowers, held on solitary stalks, are followed by attractive seed heads. ZONES 6–11.

Nelumbo nucifera (left)
SACRED LOTUS, INDIAN LOTUS

The sacred lotus has leaves that emerge 6 ft (1.8 m) or more above the water. The plant spreads to 4 ft (1.2 m) wide. Large, fragrant, pink or white, 10 in (25 cm) wide flowers are borne above large, shield-shaped, pale green leaves. This vigorous plant from Asia and northern Australia grows well in large ponds. Buddha is often depicted in the center of such a lotus. ZONES 8–12.

NEMESIA

This genus of 50-odd species of annuals, perennials and subshrubs comes from South Africa. Their flowering period is short, although if they are cut back hard when flowering slows down they will flower again. The flowers are showy, being trumpet-shaped and 2-lipped, and are borne singly in the upper leaf axils or in terminal racemes. The leaves are opposite and simple.

CULTIVATION

These plants need a protected, sunny position and fertile, well-drained soil. They cannot tolerate very hot, humid climates. Pinch out growing shoots on young plants to ensure a bushy habit. Propagate from seed in early autumn or early spring in cool areas.

Nemesia caerulea *(below)*
syn. *Nemesia fruticans*

This perennial can grow up to 24 in (60 cm) in height if conditions are to its liking. Becoming slightly woody at the base, it tends to sprawl, branching into erect stems holding small mid-green leaves and terminal heads of soft pink, lavender or blue flowers. **'Elliott's Variety'** is very free-flowering, with bright mauve-blue flowers with a white eye. ZONES 8–10.

Nemesia caerulea
'Elliot's Variety' *(left)*

Nemesia strumosa *(right)*

This plant is a colorful, fast-growing, bushy annual, popular as a bedding plant. It has lance-shaped, pale green, prominently toothed leaves, and grows to a height of 8–12 in (20–30 cm) and a spread of 10 in (25 cm). Large flowers in yellow, white, red or orange are borne in spring on short terminal racemes. **'Blue Gem'** is a compact cultivar to 8 in (20 cm), with small, clear blue flowers. **'Prince of Orange'** also grows to about 8 in (20 cm), and bears orange flowers with a purple blotch. **'Red and White'** has flowers strikingly bicolored, the upper lip bright red and the lower lip white. ZONES 9–11.

N

Nemsia strumosa 'Blue Gem' *(above)*

Nemsia strumosa 'Prince of Orange' *(below)*

Nemsia strumosa 'Red and White' *(below)*

N

Nemophila maculata *(right)*
FIVE SPOT

Commonly referred to as five spot because each veined, white petal has a prominent deep purple blotch at its tip, this plant grows to 12 in (30 cm) tall. It is used extensively in massed displays as plants hold their profusion of blooms above the ferny foliage over a long period during summer. ZONES 7–11.

Nemophila menziesii *(below)*
syn. *Nemophila insignis*
BABY BLUE-EYES

A charming little Californian wildflower, this spreading annual is a useful ground cover under shrubs such as roses, as well as in rock gardens and around edges. It is particularly effective overplanted in a bed with spring bulbs. It bears small, bowl-shaped, sapphire-blue flowers with a well-defined concentric ring of white in the center. It has dainty, serrated foliage, and grows to a height and width of 6–10 in (15–25 cm). These plants dislike heat and transplanting. ZONES 7–11.

NEMOPHILA

This is a group of 11 species of annuals grown for their bright, open, 5-petalled flowers. Originating from western USA, these annuals make good borders and are attractive in window boxes. They produce colorful spring–summer blooms mainly in a range of blues.

CULTIVATION

These quick-growing annuals grow best in full sun or part-shade in friable, moisture-retentive soil. As the foliage is rather soft, provide protection from wind and position plants away from high-traffic pathways. Regular watering will help prolong blooming. Check for aphids. Propagate from seed, which can be sown *in situ* during the autumn months.

N

NEOMARICA

Related to irises, the 15 species in this genus are herbaceous perennials from tropical America and western Africa. The strappy leaves rise from a basal rhizome in fan formation to a height of around 3 ft (1 m). The flowering stems bear masses of short-lived blooms, which have 3 distinct, somewhat flattened outer petals in intense colors. The central segments have interesting markings.

CULTIVATION

They are easily grown plants, but frost tender. Grow in part-shade or full sun in well-drained, humus-rich soil. Water well in summer and ensure the soil does not dry out during the winter months. Propagate by division of the rhizomes, or from seed in spring. Transplant from late autumn until early spring.

Neomarica
northiana (below)
WALKING IRIS, APOSTLE PLANT

With long, heavily ribbed leaves up to 24 in (60 cm), this plant from Brazil provides textural interest to warm-climate gardens. Plants flower for a long period during spring and summer, with each stem carrying scented, multi-colored blooms in white, mottled crimson with a violet-blue banding. ZONES 10–11.

N

NEOREGELIA

The 70 or so members of this stemless bromeliad genus vary greatly in size, texture and color. Native to South America, the genus was named after Edward von Regel, Superintendent of the Imperial Botanic Gardens in St Petersburg, Russia. Many species turn a brilliant rose, violet or red color in the center of the rosette when flowering approaches. The flowers may be blue or white and the spined foliage ranges from green to maroon, striped, spotted or marbled. The leaves form a wide funnel-shaped or tube-like rosette, which ranges from 6 in (15 cm) to 5 ft (1.5 m) across.

CULTIVATION

Neoregelias prefer well-drained soil and dislike strong light, but they require some direct light to maintain their color. These plants thrive in a humid atmosphere and are best grown in pots or hanging baskets where they will enjoy good air circulation. Do not allow the center cup to dry out and ensure it stays warm in winter. Propagate from offsets in spring or summer.

Neoregelia carolinae 'Fendleri' *(below)*

Neoregelia carolinae *(below right)*
HEART OF FLAME, BLUSHING BROMELIAD

This is the most widely cultivated species of the genus and forms a spreading rosette 15–24 in (38–60 cm) across, composed of light olive green, strap-shaped, saw-toothed leaves. Immediately before flowering, which can be at any time of the year, the youngest inner leaves turn deep red. The cluster of inconspicuous, blue-purple flowers is surrounded by crimson-red bracts. **'Fendleri'** is bright green and has leaves neatly edged with bands of cream. *Neoregelia carolinae* × *concentrica*, an unnamed cross between 2 of the most colorful species, displays the variegation found in some forms of *N. carolinae*, combined with the purple leaf tips of *N. concentrica*. **'Tricolor'** has cream-striped foliage. Its inner leaves turn a rich crimson before producing purple flowers and then the entire plant turns pink. **'Tricolor Perfecta'** is a variety susceptible to cold. ZONES 10–12.

N

Neoregelia carolinae
× *concentrica*
(above)

Neoregelia carolinae
'Tricolor Perfecta'
(above left)

N

Neoregelia concentrica
'Aztec' *(left)*

Neoregelia concentrica

This Brazilian species has a flat, outstretched funnel-shaped rosette 30–36 in (75–90 cm) across. It has broad, leathery leaves with a center becoming deep purple as the flower buds form. The flowers are blue. **'Aztec'** is possibly of hybrid origin, but shows a strong influence of this species; its leaves are heavily blotched with deep purple. ZONES 10–12.

Neoregelia chlorosticta *(left)*
syn. *Neoregelia sarmentosa* var. *chlorosticta*

This species from Brazil is distinguished by its green-lilac-brown leaf blotching. The flowers are white, opening on short stalks 1 in (25 mm) long. ZONES 10–12.

NEPENTHES

PITCHER PLANT

This genus of nearly 70 species, mainly from Indonesia and tropical Asia, includes some tall climbing perennials, capable of ascending nearly 70 ft (21 m) into any handy tree, but their preference for swampy land means they often have to make do without support. They bear inconspicuous purple or brownish flowers in spikes among the upper leaves; the leaves often terminate in pendulous, colored 'pitchers' with lids strikingly tinted in shades of russet, green or even red and pink. Insects are attracted to them and drown in the liquid held in the pitcher before being absorbed into the plant as food.

CULTIVATION

They require a humid atmosphere, part-shade and moist, fertile soil. Species from tropical lowlands require higher temperatures (minimum winter temperature of 65°F/18°C) than those from the tropical highlands (minimum winter temperature of 50°F/10°C). Propagate from seed in spring or from stem cuttings in spring and summer, although air layering may prove more successful.

Nepenthes
bicalcarata (below)

This native of Borneo has dimorphic pitchers, which means that they occur in two forms. Those found among the climbing stems are predominantly green, bell-shaped or funnel-shaped and around 5 in (12 cm), while those found near the base of the plant are rounded, about 4 in (10 cm) in diameter and may be green, green mottled with red, or red. The lower pitchers also have winged kidney-shaped lids. ZONES 11–12.

N

N

Nepenthes × coccinea (left)

A garden crossing of 2 tall perennial climbers, *Nepenthes × coccinea* produces pitchers measuring up to 6 in (15 cm) in length. These are yellow-green in color, mottled with purple-red streaks and blotches. **ZONES 11–12.**

Nepenthes maxima (right)

As its name implies, the pitchers on this species are extremely large, often measuring up to 8 in (20 cm) in length. Because this species comes from the high-altitude areas of Indonesia and New Guinea, its temperature requirements are lower than the lowland species. **ZONES 11–12.**

NEPETA

This large genus of more than 200 species of perennial, rarely annual, plants is used extensively in herbaceous borders and for edgings or as ground cover plants. Some species have highly aromatic silver-gray foliage and are naturally compact, while others tend to be taller growing plants and may benefit from staking. Originating from a wide area of Eurasia, North Africa and the mountains of tropical Africa, many species have been extensively hybridized to produce exceptional garden plants.

CULTIVATION

Provide a well-drained soil in a sunny position. Some of the vigorous herbaceous species make good single species ground covers as they have a tendency to over-power less robust plants. However, they can be kept in check by light trimming during the growing season and can be cut back each year to prevent the plants from becoming too straggly. Propagation is by division, from cuttings taken during late spring or from seed.

Nepeta clarkei (below)

This species from Pakistan and Kashmir forms large clumps up to 30 in (75 cm) high. The leaves are green and the upright flowering stems hold masses of lilac-blue blooms, each with a white patch on the lower lip. This is an very cold-hardy species. **ZONES 3–9.**

N

Nepeta cataria
(*right*)
CATNIP, CATMINT

Catnip is a frost-hardy perennial with branching, upright stems growing up to 3 ft (1 m). It has aromatic, green leaves and whorls of white flowers from late spring through to autumn. Cats are attracted to this plant and will lie in it or play in it and sometimes dig it up. A tea made from the leaves is said to be relaxing. **ZONES 3–10.**

Nepeta racemosa
(below)

syn. *Nepeta mussinii*

Native to the Caucasus region and northern Iran, this species is generally known as *Nepeta mussinii* in gardens, though many plants sold under that name are in fact the hybrid *N. × faassenii*. It is a vigorous perennial up to about 12 in (30 cm) high with gray-green, densely hairy leaves and lavender-blue summer flowers in long racemes. **'Blue Wonder'** is a very free-flowering form of spreading habit with violet-blue flowers; **'Snowflake'** has pure white flowers. ZONES 3–10.

Nepeta racemosa 'Blue Wonder' *(right)*

Nepeta racemosa 'Snowflake' *(left)*

Nepeta nervosa
(right)

This showy species forms a bushy habit to 24 in (60 cm) tall. It has long, narrow, deeply veined leaves and dense spikes of purplish blue flowers, although they can occasionally be yellow in the wilds of its native Kashmir. ZONES 5–9.

Nepeta × *faassenii*
(right)

CATMINT

This is a bushy, clump-forming perennial, useful for separating strong colors in the shrub or flower border. It is very effective when used with stone, either in walls, paving or rock gardens or as an edging plant. It forms spreading mounds of grayish green leaves that are aromatic when crushed, and the numerous flower stems carry hundreds of small, violet-blue flowers throughout summer. It grows to a height and spread of 18 in (45 cm). Many cultivars are available, including **'Dropmore Blue'**, with upright, tall flower spikes of lavender blue; and **'Six Hills Giant'**, a robust plant growing to around 18 in (45 cm) with gray foliage complemented by tall spikes of lavender-blue blooms that will appear continuously throughout the summer if spent flowers are kept clipped. **'Walker's Blue'** has finer foliage and flowers than the other 2 hybrids. **ZONES 3–10.**

Nepeta × *faassenii*
'Dropmore Blue'
(above)

Nepeta × *faassenii*
'Six Hills Giant'
(right)

N

NERTERA

These neat perennial plants, with their prostrate or creeping habit, are native to cool, moist habitats. There are 15 species, all of which form small mats or hummocks of moss-like foliage. It is their bead-like fruits that attract the gardener's interest. Some species make excellent alpine-house plants or they can be used in rock gardens where frosts are only light and infrequent.

CULTIVATION

Nerteras thrive in a cool, sheltered, part-shaded site with gritty, moist but well-drained sandy soil, which can be provided in a sink garden, for example. Water well in summer but keep dryish in winter. Propagate by division or from seed or tip cuttings in spring.

Nertera granadensis (below)
syn. *Nertera depressa*
BEAD PLANT, CORAL MOSS

This carpeting species is grown for the masses of spherical, orange or red, bead-like berries it bears in autumn. It has a prostrate habit, growing to ½ in (12 mm) in height with a spread of 4 in (10 cm), and forms compact cushions of tiny, bright green leaves with extremely small, greenish white flowers in early summer. A variety with purple-tinged foliage is also available. ZONES 8–11.

N

NICOTIANA
FLOWERING TOBACCO

The 67 species of annuals, biennials, perennials and shrubs in this genus from America and Australia include the commercial tobacco plant. Other species are grown for the fragrance of their warm-weather flowers, which usually open at night. The flowers of modern strains remain open all day, but have limited perfume. They are good for cutting, although the plants are sticky to handle.

CULTIVATION
Marginally frost hardy to frost tender, they need full sun or light shade and fertile, moist but well-drained soil. Propagate from seed in early spring. Check carefully for snails and caterpillars.

Nicotiana alata
(right)
syn. *Nicotiana affinis*

A short-lived perennial often grown as an annual, this marginally frost-hardy plant bears clusters of attractive, tubular flowers in white, red or various shades of pink. The flowers open towards evening and fill the garden with scent on warm, still nights. Rosette forming, it has oval leaves and grows to a height of about 3 ft (1 m) with a spread of 12 in (30 cm). It flowers throughout summer and early autumn. **ZONES 7–11.**

N

Nicotiana langsdorfii *(right)*

This annual species grows to 5 ft (1.5 m) tall and has erect and branching stems that produce masses of fine, tubular lime-green flowers during the summer months. Do not be in a hurry to deadhead the last of the blooms as they may self-seed if conditions are favorable, even though the seeds themselves are extremely small. **ZONES 9–11.**

Nicotiana × sanderae

This hybrid is a slow-growing, bushy annual reaching a height of 15 in (38 cm) and spread of 8 in (20 cm). In summer and early autumn, it bears long, trumpet-shaped flowers in shades of white, pink, red, cerise, bright crimson and purple. The flowers stay open during the day and are fragrant in the evening. Many cultivars have been developed from this garden hybrid, including **'Lime Green'**, which has abundant, vivid lime green blooms held over a long summer season. The flowers of **'Falling Star'** range from white to pale pink to deep pink. ZONES 8–11.

Nicotiana × *sanderae* 'Falling Star'
(above)

Nicotiana sylvestris *(left)*

This is one of the few summer-flowering annuals that thrive in shade. It is also one of the taller-growing species, with flowers that remain open even in deep shade or on overcast days. It is robust, though tender, and grows to 5 ft (1.5 m) or more, and bears tall, stately flowering stems that arise from a mass of large, bright green lush foliage. The long, tubular, white flowers are particularly fragrant on warm summer evenings, so plant it where the scent can be appreciated. ZONES 8–11.

Nicotiana tabacum *(right)*

TOBACCO

The flowers of this plant are pretty and offer a pleasant, if faint, perfume. They are rather small, about 1 in (25 mm) wide, and they are borne atop a head-high plant with coarse leaves. The plant is scarcely decorative enough for a flower garden, but the leaves make tobacco. Although different cultivars have been developed for processing into cigarettes, pipe tobacco or cigars, it is the way the leaves are processed that determines their ultimate use. ZONES 8–11.

NIDULARIUM

From the Latin *nidulus*, which means little nest, this genus of bromeliads is characterized by an inflorescence that, in most species, nestles in the rosette. There are 46 species. The flowers vary in color from red to white.

CULTIVATION

These frost-tender plants grow best in moist, rich soil. They prefer warm temperatures in semi-shady to shady positions. Position in an area of bright light for good foliage and color. Water regularly, keeping the rosettes full from spring to the end of summer. Propagate from offsets or seeds.

Nidularium innocentii (below) syns *Ikaratas innocentii*, *Regelia innocentii*

The rosette of this stemless bromeliad has a spread up to 24 in (60 cm) across. Its leaves are dark green to reddish brown on the upperside and brown-violet on the underside. White flowers appear on red-brown primary bracts. ZONES 10–12.

N

NIGELLA

Nigellas are a genus of about 15 species of annuals from the Mediterranean region and western Asia. The flowers and ornamental seed pods are attractive and are popular for flower arrangements.

CULTIVATION

Nigella seedlings hate being transplanted, but if seeds are sown where the plants are to grow, and some of the flowers are allowed to go to seed, new plants will come up of their own accord for years. Plant in full sun in fertile, well-drained soil and deadhead to prolong flowering if the seed pods are not needed. Propagate from seed in autumn or spring.

N

Nigella damascena
(left)

LOVE-IN-A-MIST,
DEVIL-IN-A-BUSH

This fully frost-hardy annual bears spurred, many-petalled, pale to lilac-blue or white flowers in spring and early summer. They are almost hidden by the bright green, feathery foliage, and are followed by rounded, green seed pods that mature to brown. Upright and fast growing, it reaches 24 in (60 cm) in height with a spread of 8 in (20 cm). 'Miss Jekyll' is a double blue form. ZONES 6–10.

Nigella damascena
'Miss Jekyll' *(left)*

NOLANA

Found in Chile, Peru and the Galapagos Islands, this genus consists of 18 species of annuals, perennials and subshrubs. Most are clump forming to semi-trailing and rarely exceed 8 in (20 cm) in height, although they may spread to 18 in (45 cm) or more. The bright green foliage can be slightly succulent, is elliptical and 1–2½ in (2.5–6 cm) long. Long-tubed, bell-shaped flowers, carried singly or in small clusters, develop in the leaf axils near the stem tips. They are up to 1½ in (35 mm) in diameter and appear throughout the growing season. They are generally white to purple with yellow throats.

CULTIVATION

Plant in humus-rich, well-drained soil in sun or part-shade. The semi-trailing types grow well in hanging baskets. Pinch the stem tips back occasionally to keep them bushy. They are only hardy to the lightest frosts. Propagate from seed, layers or tip cuttings.

Nolana paradoxa
(above)

N

This annual has a dwarf, creeping habit, and is ideal as a colorful ground cover in an open sunny position or for pots and hanging baskets. Low growing, up to 10 in (25 cm) high and 15 in (38 cm) wide, it produces masses of trumpet-shaped, purple-blue flowers, each with a pronounced white throat, over the summer. Many hybrids have evolved: **'Blue Bird'** has flowers in a rich, deep blue shade, again with the white throat. ZONES 8–11.

NUPHAR
SPATTERDOCK, POND LILY, YELLOW POND LILY

Made up of 25 species of perennial aquatic herbs with creeping rhizomes, these pond lilies from the temperate northern hemisphere have large, floating and submerged leaves. The flowers, usually in yellow or green tones, are held on stalks above the water surface.

CULTIVATION

Requirements are very similar to the hardy species of *Nymphaea* with the additional benefit that they will flower in shade and some are suited to being planted in slow-moving water. They prefer to be planted in pots of rich soil and carefully submerged to around 24 in (60 cm) deep, depending on the species. Propagation is by division and best carried out in spring.

Nuphar lutea (above)
YELLOW POND LILY

This species is native to eastern USA, the West Indies, northern Africa and large tracts of Eurasia. It thrives in deep water and has large orbicular leaves that emerge when the water is shallow or float when planted in deeper ponds. Summer-flowering, deep yellow-orange blooms held just above the surface emit a distinct odor. This is a vigorous species. ZONES 4–11.

Nuphar polysepala (below)

In this species from the USA, the large, round, floating leaves, with their distinct V-shaped lobe, offset the greenish blooms which are tinged with purple-brown. ZONES 4–9.

NYMPHAEA

WATERLILY

This genus of 50 species of deciduous and evergreen perennial aquatic plants with fleshy roots is named after the Greek goddess Nymphe. They are grown for their rounded, floating leaves that are cleft at the base and for their attractive large flowers which come in shades of white and cream, brilliant yellows and oranges, pinks and deep reds, blues and purple. They may be night blooming, depending on species, and sometimes fragrant. The berry-like fruits mature underwater. There are both frost-hardy and tropical varieties.

CULTIVATION

Frost-hardy waterlilies grow in most climates and flower freely throughout summer. Faded foliage should be removed. Divide the tuber-like rhizomes and replant in spring or summer every 3 or 4 years. Tropical waterlilies are all frost tender, and require a very warm, sunny situation. They flower from mid-summer into autumn. In cooler areas, the tubers of tropical waterlilies should be lifted and stored in moist sand over winter. All species need still water and annual fertilizing as they are gross feeders. Propagate from seed or by separating plantlets in spring or early autumn. Check for insects, particularly aphids; goldfish kept in the pool will eat most pests.

Nymphaea capensis

CAPE BLUE WATERLILY

This bright blue, fragrant day-opening waterlily from southern and eastern Africa has floating leaves up to 15 in (38 cm) in diameter with acute, over-lapping petals. When young, its foliage is spotted with purple below. Some plants cultivated as *Nymphaea capensis* may in fact be *N. caerulea*. **ZONES 9–11.**

Nymphaea gigantea *(left)*
AUSTRALIAN WATERLILY

This tuberous-rooted plant from the tropical areas of Australia and New Guinea has large leaves, often up to 24 in (60 cm) in diameter. Day-blooming, 12 in (30 cm) flowers range from sky to deeper purple-blue. ZONES 10–12.

Nymphaea, Hardy Hybrid, 'Atropurpurea' *(below)*

Nymphaea, Hardy Hybrid, 'Attraction' *(bottom)*

Nymphaea, Hardy Hybrids

These cold-hardy and colorful hybrids have been bred from several European and North American species, principally *Nymphaea alba*, *N. odorata* and *N. mexicana*. The day-blooming flowers are 3–6 in (8–15 cm) across, mostly in shades of white, yellow, pink or red, set on or just above the surface of the water. **'Atropurpurea'** has reddish purple foliage complementing its dark red, wide-open flowers with golden stamens. **'Attraction'** will grow in quite deep water; its crimson-red flowers with contrasting white sepals deepen to a rich garnet red as they age. **'Aurora'** is smaller, spreading to 30 in (75 cm), and has olive-green leaves blotched with purple; its semi-double flowers are star-shaped, 2 in (5 cm) wide and they turn from cream to yellow, to orange, to blood red as they age. **'Escarboucle'**, with masses of blooms and a long flowering season, has wine-crimson flowers with contrasting golden stamens. **'Formosa'** is a profuse bloomer, producing many large flowers in a soft rosy pink shade on opening, becoming deeper in coloring as the flower ages. **'Gladstoniana'** is generally a very hardy and vigorous plant, its deep red foliage contrasting with very large, pure white flowers that have thick and incurving petals. **'Gonnère'**, once known as **'Snowball'**, is a multi-petalled or double hybrid in pure white with a moderately contained leaf spread. **'James Brydon'** flowers in part-shade, its scented blooms opening pink and ageing to rosy red. **'Lucida'** has large green leaves and attractive deep red flowers with

N

paler outer petals, 5–6 in (12–15 cm) across;
'Mme Wilfon Gonnère' produces 6 in (15 cm)
wide flowers in 2 shades of pink; reddish leaves
age to bright green. **'Rose Arey'** has dark pink,
sweetly fragrant flowers; leaves are reddish purple
ageing to reddish green. The compact-growing
'Paul Hariot', suited to small and medium ponds,
has foliage streaked maroon and flowers that
open pale peach and darken to rich coppery red
with maturity. Other hybrids include **'Caroliniana
Perfecta'**, **'Colonel Welch'**, **'Colossea'** and
'Helvola'. The compact **Laydeckeri hybrids** are
very free flowering yet produce comparatively
little foliage. Colors range from soft rose pink to
deep pink and rosy
crimson, and they have
a spread of around
24 in (60 cm). **'Fulgens'**
has star-shaped, semi-
double, crimson to
magenta flowers. The
Marliacea hybrids are
among the most elegant
of all the hardy water-
lilies, raised by M.
Latour-Marliac in the
1880s. They have dark
green leaves and star-
shaped, semi-double,
soft pink flowers with
golden centers, which
appear in summer.
The large flowers stand
slightly above the
water. **'Albida'** is a
strong-growing plant
bearing free-blooming
white flowers.
'Chromatella' is a very
free-flowering and
reliable hybrid, even
flowering in part-
shade; it has creamy
yellow blooms and
foliage marked with
bronze. **'Rosea'** has
pale salmon flowers,
flushed with pink at the
base of the petals.
ZONES 5–10.

Nymphaea, Hardy
Hybrid, 'Formosa'
(above right)

Nymphaea, Hardy
Hybrid, 'Gladstoniana'
(right)

Nymphaea, Hardy
Hybrid, 'Caroliniana
Perfecta' *(below)*

N

Nymphaea, Hardy Hybrid, 'Rosea' *(above)*

Nymphaea, Hardy Hybrid, 'Colossea' *(above left)*

Nymphaea, Hardy Hybrid, 'Albida' *(top)*

Nymphaea, Hardy Hybrid, 'Colonel Welch' *(left)*

Nymphaea nouchali *(right)*

SHAPLA

This tropical species has a wide distribution from southern Asia to northern Australia. Its flower is the national emblem of Bangladesh and it is used there and in India in perfumery and cosmetics. It is a rather small waterlily with floating leaves normally only 3–6 in (8–15 cm) across, and 3 in (8 cm) wide flowers held at or just above the water surface; they open during the day and have 10 or fewer pointed petals that may be blue, pink or white, with a distinct gap between the petals and the bunch of yellow stamens. **ZONES 11–12.**

Nymphaea 'Maurice Laydecker' (pink) and
Nymphaea odorata (white) *(above)*

Nymphaea odorata

POND LILY, WHITE WATERLILY

This native of North and tropical America has white fragrant, many-petalled flowers 3–5 in (8–12 cm) across, appearing by day in summer. The leaves are thick, glossy and mid-green. It spreads to 4 ft (1.2 m). **ZONES 3–11.**

N

Nymphaea tetragona 'Helvola' *(right)*

This true miniature waterlily bears soft yellow, star-shaped, semi-double flowers 2–3 in (5–8 cm) across. The leaves are handsome, too, being dark olive green splashed with maroon. The species is widely distributed around the temperate northern hemisphere. Plant with around 10 in (25 cm) of water over the crown of the plant. It is the smallest of the miniature waterlilies. **ZONES 7–10.**

Nymphaea, Tropical
Day-blooming Hybrid,
'St Louis Gold' *(right)*

Nymphaea, TD-bH,
'Pink Platter' *(below left)*

Nymphaea, TD-bH,
'Margaret Randig'
(below right)

Nymphaea, TD-bH,
'Blue Beauty'
(bottom left)

Nymphaea, TD-bH,
'William B. Shaw'
(bottom right)

Nymphaea, Tropical Day-blooming Hybrids

Tropical hybrids can bear day- or night-time flowers. **'Blue Beauty'** is a deciduous or ever-green, day-blooming waterlily with large, brown-speckled, dark green leaves with purplish undersides. Its flowers are rounded, semi-double, 12 in (30 cm) across, and deep purple-blue with yellow centers, and it spreads to 8 ft (2.4 m). **'Margaret Randig'** has mottled purple foliage

with fragrant, large, open, sky blue petals with yellow centers and blue-tipped stamens. Bright green leaves mottled with rich brown offset the open, soft pink blooms of **'Pink Platter'**; those of **'St Louis'** are scented and pale yellow. **'St Louis Gold'**, with abundant blooms of deep gold, is a good variety for smaller pools or tubs. Others include **'Bob Trickett'**, **'Lucida'** and **'William B. Shaw'**. ZONES 10–12.

Nymphaea, Tropical Night-blooming Hybrids

Of the night-bloomers, **'H. T. Haarstick'** is notable. Both have tall stems, the former carrying deep red flowers over deep coppery red leaves with very serrated edges, and the latter bearing creamy white flowers over mid-green leaves that also have serrated margins. **'Emily Grant Hutchings'** has enormous deep pink flowers that can reach 12 in (30 cm) across. ZONES 10–12.

Nymphaea, TD-bH, 'St Louis' *(above)*

Nymphaea, TD-bH, 'Bob Trickett' *(left)*

Nymphaea, Tropical Night-blooming Hybrid, 'E. T. Haarstick' *(below left)*

Nymphaea, TN-bH, 'Emily Grant Hutchings' *(below right)*

N

NYMPHOIDES
FAIRY WATERLILY, WATER SNOWFLAKE

Resembling miniature waterlilies, the 20 species of rhizomatous, aquatic perennials in this genus are distributed throughout the world. Their rootstocks embed in the pond bottom while the long-stalked, oval, round or kidney-shaped, wavy-edged leaves float on the surface. The foliage ranges in diameter from 1–6 in (2.5–15 cm), and is usually slightly glossy and olive green, occasionally purple mottled. The $^{1}/_{2}$–1 in (12–25 mm) diameter flowers, with 5 often fimbriated (fringed) petals, may be white or yellow; they appear in summer and are held just above the foliage.

CULTIVATION
Plant in soil with a water depth of 4–18 in (10–45 cm) in full or half-day sun. The runners can spread to 6 ft (1.8 m), so allow room for development. Propagate by dividing the rootstock in late winter or early spring.

Nymphoides peltata (below)
WATER FRINGE, YELLOW FLOATING HEART

This is a very hardy species from a vast area of Eurasia and Japan. The small, heart-shaped submerged leaves grow near the very long rhizomes, while surface leaves are bright green with blackish markings on their upper sides and reddish tinges below. The flowers are bright golden yellow. ZONES 6–10.

Nymphoides indica (left)
WATER SNOWFLAKE, FALSE INDIAN WATERLILY

These plants are found throughout the tropics with separate subspecies found in different continents. This hardy perennial has rounded surface leaves ranging from 2–8 in (5–20 cm) across with a heart-shaped base. The flowers are white with a deep yellow center and the petals have characteristic fringed margins. ZONES 10–12.

N

OCIMUM
BASIL

This genus of approximately 35 species of rather frost-tender annuals, perennials and shrubs is native to tropical Asia and Africa. They are now widely cultivated in many other countries for their highly aromatic leaves, which are used for medicinal purposes or to flavor salads, soups, sauces, stews and curries. They have mostly oval leaves in opposite pairs and small tubular flowers borne in whorls towards the ends of the stems in late summer.

CULTIVATION
Grow in a protected, warm, sunny position in a moist but well-drained soil. Regularly pinch back plants to encourage bushy growth and to prevent them going to seed quickly. Propagate from seed in mid-spring. Protect from late frosts and check for chewing insects and snails.

Ocimum tenuiflorum (below)
syn. *Ocimum sanctum*
HOLY BASIL

This flavorsome aromatic herb from India is an important sacred plant in the Hindu religion. It is a short-lived perennial that dies back to a few woody stems near ground level. It grows to about 3 ft (1 m) tall with many upright stems clothed in oval, toothed leaves. Small, not very showy flowers appear on a spike from the tips of the branches. It is not particularly frost hardy and in cooler areas is usually raised as a summer annual. ZONES 10–12.

O

OENANTHE
WATER DROPWORT

Native to very damp areas of the northern hemisphere and tropical Africa, this genus of the carrot family consists of about 30 species of perennials, found mainly in damp habitats such as marshland and water meadows. Tiny white flowers appear in umbels, while the leaves are divided into many small leaflets. Care must be taken with these plants, as some species are quite toxic.

CULTIVATION
These plants can be naturalized in informal situations, requiring moist, fertile soil and doing well in either shade or sun. Propagate from seed or stem tip cuttings or by division or layering.

Oenanthe crocata
(above)
HEMLOCK, WATER DROPWORT

This European species is extremely poisonous and dangerous to livestock, so care should be taken when planting. It grows to a height of 5 ft (1.5 m) with a robust branching habit and has a very strong smell. Terminal heads of white flowers are borne in winter. ZONES 5–10.

OENOTHERA
EVENING PRIMROSE

Native to temperate regions of both North and South America but widely naturalized elsewhere, this genus consists of more than 120 species of annuals, biennials and perennials. Their short-lived flowers, borne during summer, have 4 delicate petals, yellow, red white or (less commonly) pink, and a long basal tube. Most species are pollinated by nocturnal insects and only release their fragrance at night. Some do not even open their petals during the day. Evening primrose oil is extracted from the tiny seeds. It contains certain fatty acids believed to be beneficial to health if consumed regularly in modest quantities.

CULTIVATION
They are mostly frost hardy and grow best in a well-drained, sandy soil in an open, sunny situation. They will tolerate dry conditions. Propagate from seed or by division in spring or autumn, or from softwood cuttings in late spring.

Oenothera elata subsp. *hookeri* (above)
HOOKER'S EVENING PRIMROSE

This species from western North America grows to a height of 6 ft (1.8 m). An erect perennial or biennial, it bears its lemon-gold turning to red-orange flowers in summer; the flowers open just as the sun sets. ZONES 7–9.

O

Oenothera biennis
(right)
COMMON EVENING PRIMROSE

A showy plant, this upright, hairy biennial has large, scented yellow flowers in tall spikes, opening in the evening and shrivelling before noon. It is erect and fast growing to a height of 5 ft (1.5 m). ZONES 4–10.

Oenothera fruticosa
SUNDROPS

This biennial or perennial species from eastern North America sometimes grows to a height of 3 ft (1 m), but is usually smaller. It has a reddish, erect, branching stem and narrow leaves. Deep yellow 1–2 in (2.5–5 cm) wide flowers open by day. ***Oenothera fruticosa* subsp. *glauca*** has broader, less hairy leaves with red tints when young. **'Fyrverker'** (syn. 'Fireworks') has yellow flowers that open from red buds. **'Sonnenwende'** grows to 2 ft (60 cm) tall. It has red-tinted autumn foliage and orange-red flower buds. ZONES 4–10.

Oenothera fruticosa subsp. *glauca* (yellow) with *Erigeron* 'Quakeress' *(above)*

Oenothera fruticosa 'Sonnenwende' *(left)*

O

Oenothera macrocarpa *(left)*
syn. *Oenothera missouriensis*
OZARK SUNDROPS, MISSOURI PRIMROSE, FLUTTERMILLS

This perennial is usually almost stemless with large rosettes of narrow tapering leaves. The flowers are large, reaching 4 in (10 cm) in diameter, lemon yellow in color and open in the evening in summer. This plant reaches a height of no more than 6 in (15 cm), but spreads to 24 in (60 cm) or more across, the flowers appearing singly from between the leaves. ZONES 5–9.

Oenothera speciosa

**WHITE EVENING PRIMROSE,
SHOWY EVENING PRIMROSE**

This short-lived, rhizomatous perennial native to southern USA and Mexico bears spikes of profuse, fragrant, saucer-shaped, pink-tinted white blooms. Fresh flowerheads open daily during summer. The small leaves often turn red in hot or cold weather. Clump forming, it grows to 18–24 in (45–60 cm) in height with a spread of 18 in (45 cm) or more. **'Rosea'** (syns 'Childsii', *Oenothera berlandieri*) is lower growing, with flowers edged and heavily veined rose pink, yellow in the center. **'Siskiyou'** is similar but with larger flowers. These pink forms have often been confused with *O. rosea*, which has much smaller flowers. **ZONES 5–10.**

Oenothera speciosa
'Rosea' *(above right)*

Oenothera speciosa
'Siskiyou' *(right)*

Oenothera odorata *(left)*

This perennial, native to South America, was introduced into England by Sir Joseph Banks in 1790. It has erect red-tinted stems with a rosette of narrow leaves at the base. The fragrant yellow flowers appear in summer, turning red with age and opening at dusk. It reaches a height of 24–36 in (60–90 cm) and a spread of 12 in (30 cm). **ZONES 7–10.**

OMPHALODES
NAVELWORT

From Europe, Asia and Mexico, this genus consists of 28 species of forget-me-not–like annuals and perennials that are either evergreen or semi-evergreen. These plants make excellent ground covers, and they are most suited to rock gardens.

CULTIVATION

These plants prefer shade or part-shade with moist but well-drained soil (except for *Omphalodes linifolia*, which prefers a sunny position). They are mostly frost hardy. Propagate from seed in spring or by division in autumn.

Omphalodes cappadocica 'Cherry Ingram' *(below)*

Omphalodes cappadocica 'Starry Eyes' *(bottom)*

O

Omphalodes cappadocica
(below left)

This spreading perennial from Turkey has creeping underground stems. It produces numerous sprays of flat, bright purple-blue flowers in spring that arise from clumps of densely hairy, oval to heart-shaped leaves that are found at the base of the plant. This plant reaches a height of 6–8 in (15–20 cm) and a spread of 10 in (25 cm) and is fully frost hardy. '**Cherry Ingram**' is a vigorous grower to 10 in (25 cm) in height with purplish blue flowers. '**Starry Eyes**' has relatively big flowers, with each blue petal edged in white giving a starry effect. ZONES 6–9.

Omphalodes verna *(below)*
BLUE-EYED MARY, CREEPING FORGET-ME-NOT

This semi-evergreen thrives in shady conditions. During spring, it produces long, loose sprays of flat, bright blue flowers with white eyes. This plant has heart-shaped, mid-green leaves that form clumps. It reaches a height and spread of 8 in (20 cm). ZONES 6–9.

ONOPORDUM
syn. *Onopordon*

Found naturally in Europe, North Africa and western Asia, this is a genus of about 40 species of large biennial thistles. They have a basal rosette of large, gray-green, lightly felted leaves, deeply toothed, with a spine at the tip of each tooth. The flowerheads are of typical thistle form: globose with a dense tuft of purple florets at the top and covered in spiny bracts. They are borne at the top of branched stems up to 10 ft (3 m) tall, and mature in mid-summer. On drying, they release downy seeds. In the first year the plants form an attractive foliage clump with a few flowerheads. In the second year they grow rapidly to full height, flower heavily then die.

CULTIVATION
Onopordums are easily cultivated in any well-drained soil in full sun with shelter from strong winds. Offsets and seedlings often naturally replace spent plants. They are frost hardy and are propagated from seed.

Onopordum acanthium (right)

SCOTCH THISTLE, COTTON THISTLE

Despite its common name, it is doubtful that this European and west Asian species is a true native of Scotland or indeed of the British Isles, but it is the thistle usually regarded as the one shown on the Scottish royal emblem. It has a thick, downy stem with many wing-like ridges on its numerous branches. Its leaves are large and also downy, with wavy, sharply prickly edges. The flowers appear in late summer and autumn and are light purple in color. It reaches a height of up to 10 ft (3 m) and a spread of 6 ft (1.8 m) or more. ZONES 6–10.

ONOSMA

This genus comprises 150 species of semi-evergreen biennials, perennials and subshrubs, allied to the comfreys (*Symphytum*), cultivated particularly for their gracefully pendent, tubular flowers. The densely tufted leaves are tongue-like with rather stiff, prickly hairs. Native to the Mediterranean region, they are most useful in rock gardens and along banks.

CULTIVATION

They are moderately frost hardy. Full sun is essential, although in warmer climates some shade must be provided for them to flourish. They prefer well-drained soil and dislike wet summers. They can be propagated from cuttings in summer or from seed in autumn.

Onosma tauricum (below)
GOLDEN DROP

Nodding spikes of pale yellow flowers are borne on this 12 in (30 cm) tall perennial. The erect stems are sparsely branched and the lower surfaces of the leaves have minute tufts of short, spreading hairs. ZONES 6–9.

Onosma alborosea (left)

This semi-evergreen perennial is covered with fine hairs that may be an irritant to some people. The drooping tubular flowers open as white and then turn pink and appear for a long period during summer. Clump forming, it reaches a height of 6–12 in (15–30 cm) and spread of 8 in (20 cm). ZONES 7–9.

O

OPHIOPOGON

MONDO GRASS, SNAKEBEARD, LILYTURF

This genus contains 50 or so species of evergreen perennials. They are valued for their attractive, long-lived clumps of grass-like foliage springing from underground rhizomes. The summer flowers are small and can be white or blue through to purple. The berry-like fruits each contain one seed. They are trouble-free plants that will last indefinitely, providing an attractive ground cover that effectively suppresses leaves.

CULTIVATION

Most are fairly frost hardy and will tolerate sun or part-shade in moist, well-drained soil. Propagate by division of clumps in spring, or from seed in autumn. For a quick ground cover, plant divisions at 8 in (20 cm) intervals.

Ophiopogon japonicus (below) syn. *Liriope japonica*
MONDO GRASS

This fine-leaved species has dark green recurving foliage that arises from deep rhizomes, spreading to form dense, soft mats up to about 8 in (20 cm) deep. Pale purple flowers are hidden among the leaves in mid-summer, followed by bright blue, pea-sized fruit. **'Kyoto Dwarf'** is only 2–4 in (5–10 cm) high, with very short leaves.
ZONES 8–11.

Origanum 'Barbara Tingey' *(left)*

This cultivar of possible hybrid origin has rounded, felty, blue-tinged leaves that are reddish purple beneath. In summer, pink flowers appear nestled in bracts which are green at first, but age to a purplish pink color. It grows 4–6 in (10–15 cm) tall, but spreads to at least 10–12 in (25–30 cm) across. ZONES 7–9.

ORIGANUM
syn. *Majorana*
MARJORAM, OREGANO

Native to the Mediterranean region and temperate Asia, these perennials and subshrubs in the mint family have aromatic leaves and stalked spikes or heads of small tubular flowers with crowded, overlapping bracts. Some species are grown as culinary herbs, while others are grown for their decorative pink flowerheads. With arching or prostrate stems arising from vigorously spreading rhizomes, they make useful plants for trailing over rocks, banks and walls.

CULTIVATION

These plants like full sun and a moderately fertile, well-drained soil. Trim excess growth regularly and propagate from seed in spring or by root division in autumn or spring.

Origanum laevigatum *(above)*

This vigorous and ornamental species has spreading woody rhizomes and densely massed evergreen leaves, from which arise numerous flowering stems 18–24 in (45–60 cm) high. Tiny flowers with purple bracts create a cloud of lavender at the top of the stems all summer long, and provide nectar for bees and butterflies. An excellent filler for the perennial border as well as the herb garden, it also makes a delightful addition to dried flower arrangements. **'Hopleys'** and **'Herrenhausen'** are recent cultivars with richer flower color. ZONES 7–11.

Origanum vulgare

COMMON OREGANO, WILD MARJORAM

The common oregano has a sharper, more pungent flavor than marjoram. It has a sprawling habit and grows to 24 in (60 cm) high with dark green, oval leaves and small, white or pink flowers in summer. The leaves are used, fresh or dried, in many Mediterranean-inspired dishes. In Italy, oregano is used in pizza toppings and pasta dishes. **'Aureum'** has a less sprawling habit and bright greenish gold leaves. **'Thumble's Variety'** is a low, mound-forming selection with yellow-green leaves. **ZONES 5–9.**

Origanum libanoticum *(right)*

From Lebanon, this 24 in (60 cm) tall species produces nodding spikes of quite large pink flowers with dull pink bracts in summer. **ZONES 8–10.**

Origanum vulgare 'Aureum' *(above right)*

Origanum vulgare 'Thumble's Variety' *(right)*

O

ORONTIUM
GOLDEN CLUB

The single species in this genus is an unusual member of the arum family from eastern USA. An aquatic perennial, it has thick rhizomes and broad spatulate leaves on long-stalked spadices of minute flowers surrounded by a membranous spathe that shrivels at an early stage.

CULTIVATION
This very frost-hardy plant will overwinter in any pond or slow-moving stream with water over 6 in (15 cm) deep that does not freeze solid. The roots need to be in soil, either in silt at the pond bottom or in tubs. The foliage is best in sun or morning shade. Propagate by breaking up the rhizome in late winter as dormancy finishes.

Orontium aquaticum *(below & bottom)*

This species has simple, leathery leaves up to 10 in (25 cm) long that may be submerged, floating or held erect above the water surface. The leaves have metallic blue-green upper surfaces, purple undersides and stalks up to 15 in (38 cm) long. Flower spikes appear in summer and are short lived; the papery spathe is insignificant and quickly withers, but the bright yellow spadix, around 6 in (15 cm) long, is held above the surface on a long stem. ZONES 7–9.

Orthophytum gurkenii *(below)*

This curious bromeliad has purple-bronze leaves strikingly barred with rows of silvery scales. The erect flowering stem bears bracts like the leaves but broader, and the upper bracts have brilliant green bases the same color as the small tubular flowers. ZONES 9–12.

ORTHOPHYTUM

This bromeliad genus is endemic to eastern Brazil and consists of about 17 species, all terrestrial and forming rosettes of stiff, prickly edged leaves, spreading by stolons and sometimes forming extensive mats. The flowering stems may rise well above the leaf rosettes with interesting broad bracts, or the flowers may be in stemless clusters in the center of the rosette.

CULTIVATION

These plants are frost tender and should be grown in fertile, well-drained soil in full sun. Water moderately in the growing season and keep dry in winter. Propagate from seed in early spring. They are susceptible to aphids while flowering.

Orthophytum navioides *(right)*

Found in the wild in rocky crevices, this species has long narrow leaves edged with very short, delicate spines. The white flowers are borne in a dense hemispherical cluster in the center of the rosette, the inner leaves turning deep reddish purple at flowering time. It is easy to grow but needs strong light. ZONES 9–12.

Orthrosanthus multiflorus *(left)*

This native of south-western Australia makes an erect tufted plant with narrow, grass-like leaves and spikes of starry blue to purple flowers which appear in spring. It reaches a height of 24 in (60 cm) and a spread of 12 in (30 cm). **ZONES 9–10.**

ORTHROSANTHUS

Found in the mountains of Central and South America and the sandy plains of southern Australia, the 7 species of this genus of the iris family are grass-like perennials with short, woody rhizomes and flattened fans of sword-shaped leaves up to 18 in (45 cm) long. Blue or yellow 6-petalled flowers up to 2 in (5 cm) in diameter open in spring and summer. In some species, the flowers have dark veining. They are carried in clusters of 2 to 8 blooms on wiry stems.

CULTIVATION
Plant in moist, well-drained soil in sun or part-shade. Light frosts are tolerated, but *Orthrosanthus* species are best grown in a mild, frost-free climate. They are often short lived. Propagate from seed or by division of the rhizomes in late winter.

OSTEOSPERMUM

This genus of 70 or so species of evergreen shrubs, semi-woody perennials and annuals is mostly indigenous to South Africa. Allied to *Dimorphotheca*, they have irregularly toothed leaves and produce a profusion of large, daisy-like flowerheads in the white, pink, violet and purple range. Most of the commonly grown osteospermums are cultivars of uncertain origin, suspected to be hybrids. Tough plants, they are useful for rock gardens, dry embankments or the front rows of shrub borders, particularly as temporary filler plants.

CULTIVATION

Osteospermums are marginally to moderately frost hardy and do best in open, well-drained soil of medium fertility. An open, sunny position is essential. Light pruning after flowering helps maintain shape and extends the ultimate lifespan. Propagate from cuttings of non-flowering shoots or from seed in summer.

Osteospermum fruticosum
syn. *Dimorphotheca fruticosa*

FREEWAY DAISY, TRAILING AFRICAN DAISY

This perennial has prostrate or trailing stems that spread to cover large areas when planted along freeways in coastal California. Masses of palest lilac daisies are borne on stalks up to 12 in (30 cm) above the ground; the heaviest bloom is in winter, with some blossoms year-round. Named selections are available with pure white, burgundy or purple flowers. ZONES 9–11.

Osteospermum fruticosum cultivar *(below)*

Osteospermum 'Pink Whirls' *(left)*

This new, pink-flowering cultivar has a slight constriction in each petal on some flowerheads, although others may have more normal petals. It reaches a height of about 18 in (45 cm) and spread of 3 ft (1 m). **ZONES 8–10.**

Osteospermum 'Whirligig' *(below)*
syn. *Osteospermum* 'Starry Eyes'

This somewhat bizarre cultivar has white petals above and gray-blue beneath, each with their edges pinched together in the outer part, but remaining flat right at the tip; the effect is curious but quite decorative. It reaches a height of about 24 in (60 cm) with a spreading habit. **ZONES 8–10.**

O

Oxalis articulata
(right)

This Paraguayan species has numerous fleshy, caterpillar-like rhizomes which readily disperse when soil is disturbed. In some mild, moist climates it has become a minor nuisance. The 3-lobed, hairy edged leaves are long stalked and the rose-pink flowers are borne above the foliage in dense, showy sprays in summer and autumn. ZONES 8–11.

Oxalis massoniana
(below)

Its orange-toned flowers make *Oxalis massoniana* something of a novelty. From southern Africa, it was named after Francis Masson, a Scot who made notable collections in South Africa in the late eighteenth century. ZONES 9–10.

OXALIS
WOOD-SORREL

This is a genus of 500 or so species of bulbous, rhizomatous and fibrous-rooted perennials and a few small, weak shrubs. Most are native to South Africa and South America. Some have become garden and greenhouse weeds which, though pretty in flower, have given a bad name to the genus; the species listed here are more restrained in growth and make choice additions to the garden. The leaves are always compound, divided into 3 or more heart-shaped or more deeply 2-lobed leaflets in a palmate arrangement (like clover). The funnel-shaped flowers are usually pink, white or yellow, and are carried in an umbel-like cluster on slender stalks.

CULTIVATION
Most species grow from bulbs or corms, which multiply readily. A position in sun or part-shade suits most, along with a mulched, well-drained soil and moderate water. Propagate by division of the bulbs or from seed in autumn.

Oxalis oregana *(below)*
REDWOOD SORREL

This species from western USA and Canada spreads by creeping rhizomes and forms large, dense mats in moist, shady woodlands and forests. It grows 10 in (25 cm) high and has 1 in (25 mm) or more long, broadly heart-shaped dark green leaflets. Rosy pink to white flowers are borne on solitary stems from spring to autumn. ZONES 7–10.

O

Paeonia bakeri
(below)

This species grows to 24 in (60 cm) tall with leaves composed of two sets of three, 3–4 in (8–10 cm) long leaflets. The leaves are dark green above, blue-green below. The flowers, over 4 in (10 cm) in diameter, open from late spring and have rounded purple-red petals and bright golden anthers. **ZONES 5–9.**

Paeonia 'Skylark Saunders' *(right)*

This hybrid has beautiful single pale pink flowers with prominent golden stameNs. **ZONES 7–9.**

Paeonia 'Ludovica'
(bottom)

This semi-double hybrid has reddish pink to salmon pink flowers with conspicuous golden stamens. It flowers very early. **ZONES 7–9.**

PAEONIA
PEONY

There are 33 species in this genus of beautiful perennials and shrubs. The genus name goes back to classical Greek and arose from the supposed medicinal properties of some species. Peonies are all deciduous and have long-lived, rather woody rootstocks with swollen roots, and large compound leaves with the leaflets usually toothed or lobed. Each new stem in spring terminates in one to several large, rose-like flowers. Their centers are a mass of short stamens that almost conceal the 2 to 5 large ovaries, which develop into short pods containing large seeds. The flowers are mostly in shades of pink or red, but there are also white and yellow-flowered species. The great majority of peonies are herbaceous, dying back to the ground in autumn, but there is a small group of Chinese species, known as the 'tree peonies' that have woody stems, although no more than about 8 ft (2.4 m) in height, so strictly they are shrubs. Cultivars of this tree peony group produce the largest and most magnificent of all peony flowers, some approaching a diameter of 12 in (30 cm), mostly double and often beautifully frilled or ruffled.

Paeonia 'Sophie' *(above)*

This hybrid peony, popular in Germany, has
single soft crimson red flowers and a few similarly
colored central petaloids with golden stamens.
ZONES 7–9.

Paeonia lactiflora
'Yangfeichuyu' *(above)*

Paeonia lactiflora
'Sarah Bernhardt'
(below)

Paeonia lactiflora Hybrids

CULTIVATION

Most peonies will only succeed in climates
with a cold winter, allowing dormancy and
initiation of flower buds, but new foliage
and flower buds can be damaged by late
frosts. They appreciate a sheltered position
in full or slightly filtered sunlight, but
with soil kept cool and moist. Mulch and
feed with well-rotted manure when leaf
growth starts, but avoid disturbing roots.
Pruning of the tree peonies should be
minimal, consisting of trimming out
weaker side shoots. Propagate from seed
in autumn, or by division in the case of
named cultivars. Tree peony cultivars are
best propagated from basal suckers, but
few are produced. Hence, plants on their
own roots are very expensive. A faster and
cheaper method is to graft them onto herbaceous rootstocks, but the resulting
plants are often short lived.

These herbaceous Chinese peonies are derived
mainly from *Paeonia lactiflora*. They have handsome foliage, which is maroon tinted when it first
appears in spring, and usually scented flowers in a
huge range of colors and forms. **'Beacon Flame'**
has deep red, semi-double flowers. **'Bowl of
Beauty'** grows to 3 ft (1 m) tall and between late
spring and mid-summer bears dense clusters of
slender, creamy white petaloids nesting in the
center of broad, pink outer petals. **'Coral Charm'**
has deep apricot buds fading to soft orange-pink
as they mature. **'Cora Stubbs'** has broad outer
petals and smaller central ones in contrasting

tones. **'Duchesse de Nemours'** is a fairly tall grower with fragrant, white to soft yellow flowers with frilled incurving petals. **'Félix Crousse'** is a deep pink double with a red center. **'Festiva Maxima'** has large, fully double, scented flowers with frilled petals that are white with red flecks. **'Inspecteur Lavergne'** is late-flowering and fully double red. **'Kelway's Glorious'** has highly scented, creamy white, double flowers. **'Miss America'** has large, highly scented white flowers with gold stamens. **'Monsieur Jules Elie'** has very deep cerise-pink single flowers. **'President Roosevelt'** is a luxuriant 'rose' or 'bomb' double peony. **'Sarah Bernhardt'** has scented, double, rose pink flowers with silvery margins. **'Whitleyi Major'** has single, ivory-white flowers with yellow stamens. Others include **'Moonstone'**, **'Scarlett O'Hara'** and **'Yangfeichuyu'**. ZONES 6–9.

Paeonia lactiflora 'Moonstone' *(above)*

Paeonia lactiflora 'Cora Stubbs' *(above left)*

Paeonia lactiflora 'Bowl of Beauty' *(left)*

Paeonia lactiflora
'President Roosevelt'
(*right*)

Paeonia lactiflora
'Kelway's Glorious'
(*below*)

Paeonia lactiflora
'Scarlett O'Hara' (*above right*)

Paeonia lactiflora
cultivar (*right*)

P

Paeonia mascula
subsp. *russii* (left)

Paeonia mascula

Found from the north-west Balkans to the Himalayas, this herbaceous perennial is a very variable species. It usually has very stout stems 10–24 in (25–60 cm) tall. The leaves vary considerably, some forms having broad leaflets, others narrow and some with serrated edges. The flowers are deep pink, red or white, more than 4 in (10 cm) wide and open early. *Paeonia mascula* subsp. *russii* from Greece and the islands of the Mediterranean differs from the species in having broader, more rounded leaves with hairy undersides. ZONES 8–10.

Paeonia mollis
(above)

Of unknown origin and considered to be a garden variety rather than a true species, this 18 in (45 cm) tall herbaceous peony has biternate (made up of two, 3-leaflet sections) leaves with lobed leaflets up to 4 in (10 cm) long. Its 3 in (8 cm) wide, deep pink or white flowers open from early summer. ZONES 6–9.

Paeonia mlokosewitschii
(below)

CAUCASIAN PEONY

From late spring to mid-summer, this European peony bears big, open, pale to bright yellow flowers atop soft green leaves that have hairy undersides and are sometimes tinged purple at the edges. An erect, herbaceous perennial, it grows to 30 in (75 cm) high and wide, enjoys semi-shade and is resistant to frost. The seed pods split open to reveal black seeds on a red background. ZONES 6–9.

P

Paeonia officinalis
'Rosea' *(below)*

Paeonia officinalis
(above)

Of European origin,
this herbaceous peren-
nial reaches a height
and spread of 24 in
(60 cm) and from
spring to mid-summer
bears single, purple or
red, rose-like flowers.
Although poisonous, it
has been used medici-
nally. Of similar size,
'Rubra Plena' bears
flowers that consist of
clusters of many small,
mid-magenta petals.
The more compact
'China Rose' bears
darker green foliage
and salmon-pink
flowers with yellow-
orange anthers. **'Rosea'**
has deep pink flowers.
ZONES 8–10.

P

Paeonia officinalis
cultivar *(left)*

Paeonia officinalis
'Rubra Plena' *(left)*

P

Paeonia peregrina
(left)

Native to southern
Europe, this 18 in
(45 cm) herbaceous
species has sticky stems
and leaves made up of
15 to 17 leaflets. The
leaves have a blue-green
tinge. Cup-shaped, 4 in
(10 cm) wide, deep red
flowers with golden
anthers open from late
spring. **'Sunshine'**
(syn. 'Otto Froebel')
is an early-flowering
cultivar with vivid deep
orange-red flowers.
ZONES 8–10.

Papaver alpinum *(right)*

A short-lived perennial, this tuft-forming semi-
evergreen alpine poppy (a miniature Iceland
poppy) grows to 8 in (20 cm) high with a spread
of 4 in (10 cm) and has fine, grayish leaves. It
bears white or yellow flowers in summer. This
species prefers a little lime in the soil. Use on
banks or in rock gardens. ZONES 5–10.

PAPAVER
POPPY

The 50 or so annual, biennial or perennial
species of the genus *Papaver* are mainly
from the temperate parts of Eurasia and
Africa, with a couple from eastern USA.
Their characteristic cupped petals and
nodding buds that turn skywards upon
opening make them popular bedding
flowers. Several of their close relatives take
their name in common usage, such as the
tree poppy *(Romneya)*, the Californian
poppy *(Eschscholzia)* or the blue poppy
(Meconopsis).

CULTIVATION
Poppies are fully frost hardy and prefer
little or no shade and deep, moist,
well-drained soil. Sow seed in spring or
autumn; many species self-seed readily.

P

Papaver atlanticum *(center)*

This perennial from Morocco has a woody rhizome and 6 in (15 cm) long, toothed-edged,
downy leaves. The flowers are borne on 18 in
(45 cm) stems and are pale orange to red, around
4 in (10 cm) wide, and open in summer. **'Flore
Semi-Pleno'** has semi-double flowers on slightly
shorter stems than the species. ZONES 6–10.

Papaver atlanticum
'Flore Semi-Pleno'
(right)

Papaver
bracteatum (right)

Occurring naturally
from the Caucasus to
the Himalayas, this
summer-flowering
species is very similar
to *Papaver orientale*. It
is a perennial with 3 ft
(1 m) tall flower stems
and 18 in (45 cm) long
pinnate leaves. The
foliage and stems are
covered with white
hairs. The flowers,
usually red with purple
centers, are 4 in (10 cm)
wide. **ZONES 5–10.**

Papaver
commutatum
(below)

A close relative of the
blood-red *Papaver
rhoeas*, this annual
species can be massed
in a garden to create an
effect resembling an
Impressionist painting.
The flowers, bright red
on hairy stems, appear
in summer but only
last for about 3 weeks.
ZONES 8–10.

Papaver nudicaule
(left)

ICELAND POPPY

This tuft-forming per-
ennial from North
America and Asia
Minor is almost always
grown as an annual. It
is good for rock gar-
dens and for cutting.
Large scented flowers,
borne in winter and
spring, are white,
yellow, orange or pink,
and have a crinkled
texture. The leaves are
pale green, and the
stems are long and
hairy. It grows 12–24 in
(30–60 cm) tall with a
6–8 in (15–20 cm)
spread. ZONES 2–10.

Papaver orientale
(center)

ORIENTAL POPPY

This herbaceous peren-
nial is native to south-
west Asia. In summer,
it bears spectacular
flowers as big as peo-
nies in shades of pink
through to red with
dark centers to 4 in
(10 cm) in diameter.
The cultivated varieties,
sometimes double,
come in a wide range of
colors and many feature
a dark basal blotch on
each petal. It has hairy,
lance-like, bluish green
leaves and can become
straggly. According to
the variety, it grows
from 18 in (45 cm) to
more than 3 ft (1 m)
tall. **'Cedric Morris'** is
a big-flowered form
with individual blooms
up to 6 in (15 cm)
across. Its shell-pink
flowers have frilly
petals, each with an
almost black blotch at
the base. **'Mrs Perry'**
has large, coral pink
flowers. **'Feuerriese'**
(syn. 'Fire Giant') is a
30 in (80 cm) tall Ger-
man Foerster cultivar
with brick red flowers
on stiffly erect stems.
Other cultivars include
'China Boy' and **'Rosenwelle'**. ZONES 3–9.

Papaver orientale
'Feuerriese' and
Delphinium elatum
hybrid *(below)*

Papaver orientale
'Rosenwelle' *(left)*

Papaver orientale
'China Boy' *(above)*

Papaver rhoeas *(below)*

CORN POPPY, FIELD POPPY, FLANDERS POPPY

The cupped flowers on this fast-growing annual
are small, delicate, scarlet and single. The cultivated varieties (**Shirley Series**) come in reds,
pinks, whites and bicolors. They have a pale heart
instead of the black cross that marks the center of
the wild poppy. The leaves are light green and
lobed. This species grows to 24 in (60 cm) high
with a 12 in (30 cm) spread. Double-flowered
strains are also available. '**Mother of Pearl**' has
gray, pink or blue-purple flowers. ZONES 5–9.

Papaver somniferum *(above)*
OPIUM POPPY

The grayish green leaves on this fast-growing annual from the Middle East are lobed and elliptical with serrated edges. It blooms in summer, to display big flowers in white, pink, red or purple, usually as doubles. Opium poppies are cultivated for the milky sap produced in their seed capsules, which is the source of the narcotic drug opium and its derivatives. The flowers of '**Hungarian Blue**' are more intense in color than those of the wild plants. **ZONES 7–10.**

P

Papaver rhoeas
'Mother of Pearl'
(below)

Papaver somniferum
'Hungarian Blue'
(below right)

PARIS
syn. *Daiswa*

This genus consists of 20 species of herbaceous, rhizomatous perennials and is closely related to the trilliums. It is found from Europe to eastern Asia. They form clumps and their leaves are carried in whorls at the top of stems up to 3 ft (1 m) long. Unlike trilliums, the 1–4 in (2.5–10 cm) long, oval to lance-shaped leaves are not always in 3s, but in groups of 4 to 12 depending on the species. The flowers, borne singly at the stem tips in spring and summer, have 4 to 6 petals and sepals that are usually green or yellow-green.

CULTIVATION
Plant in cool, moist, woodland conditions in dappled shade. Most species are vigorous and are not difficult to cultivate. They are very frost hardy. Propagate from seed or by dividing established clumps. Divide only every 3 to 4 years or the plants may be weakened.

Paris lanceolata
(below)

This species has long, narrow leaves that form a very distinct collar around a central stem. At its tip, the stem carries a flower with golden anthers and petals reduced to filaments. ZONES 7–10.

Paris japonica (left)
syn. *Kinugasa japonica*

This Japanese species has stems up to 30 in (75 cm) tall and whorls of 8–12 in (20–30 cm) long elliptical leaves. The flowers are borne singly on 1–3 in (2.5–8 cm) pedicels at the stem tips and have white sepals up to 2 in (5 cm) long. The petals are much reduced or absent. The flowers are followed by small, fleshy red fruit. ZONES 8–10.

Paris polyphylla
(right)
syn. *Daiswa polyphylla*

This Chinese species grows to 3 ft (1 m) tall with 6 in (15 cm) leaves. The flowers have very narrow, almost filamentous petals up to 4 in (10 cm) long. Although scarcely a feature, they are yellow-green while the center of the flower is purple with brown stigmas. The flowers are followed by red fruit. **Paris polyphylla var. *yunnanensis*,** from Yunnan Province has slightly broader petals. **ZONES 7–10.**

Paris tetraphylla
(below)
syn. *Paris quadrifolia*

This very frost-hardy species from Eurasia, which grows to 15 in (38 cm) in height, bears its star-shaped, green and white flowers in late spring. The mid-green leaves are from 2–6 in (5–15 cm) long. **ZONES 8–10.**

Paris polyphylla var. *yunnanensis* *(right)*

Parnassia grandifolia (above)

This species from central and southeastern USA grows to 24 in (60 cm) tall. It has rounded $1^1/_2$–4 in (3.5–10 cm) long leaves on $1^1/_2$–6 in (3.5–15 cm) stems. Its flowers are white with very narrow petals. ZONES 6–10.

PARNASSIA
BOG STAR, PARNASSUS GRASS

This is a genus of around 15 species of perennials found over much of the northern temperate zone. They have long-stemmed, kidney-shaped to near round, 1–4 in (2.5–10 cm) long leaves in basal rosettes. The wiry flowers stem, which grow up to 24 in (60 cm) tall, bear a single, 5-petalled, 1–$1^1/_2$ in (25–35 mm) wide flower backed by a single bract. The flowers open in summer.

CULTIVATION
Plant in moist, well-drained soil in sun or part-shade and do not allow to become dry in summer. Some species are very difficult to cultivate and will only grow well in naturally damp, grassy meadows or damp, peaty soil. All species are very hardy. Propagate from seed in autumn or by very careful division of established clumps.

PAROCHETUS
SHAMROCK PEA, CLOVER PEA, BLUE PEA

This genus contains a single species of prostrate perennial with clover-like, trifoliate leaves. The leaflets are about $^1/_2$ in (12 mm) long. For most of the year it looks exactly like a small patch of clover. However, from late summer to winter, depending on the climate, it is studded with $^1/_2$–1 in (12–25 mm) wide bright blue, pea-like flowers borne singly or in pairs.

CULTIVATION
It is an excellent plant for rockeries, in an alpine house or in a hanging basket. It prefers to grow in moist, humus-rich soil in sun or part-shade. Although it tolerates only light frosts, in the right conditions it can spread quickly. Propagate from seed or by division.

Parochetus communis (above)

From the mountains of southwest China, Southeast Asia and the Himalayas to Sri Lanka and tropical Africa, this deciduous species grows to a height of 4 in (10 cm) with a 12 in (30 cm) spread. The flowers are borne late in the growing season. ZONES 9–11.

P

PARONYCHIA
WHITLOW WORT

This widespread genus consists of around 50 species of usually mat- or clump-forming, dianthus- or thyme-like annuals or perennials. Most occur naturally in the Mediterranean region and have wiry stems and tiny linear to rounded leaves, often in pairs. The minute flower inflorescences, in themselves quite inconspicuous, smother the plants in early summer and are highlighted by the surrounding silvery bracts.

CULTIVATION

These are very much plants for well-drained, sunny positions and are at home in rockeries or alpine houses. Most are quite frost hardy, but suffer if kept wet and cold in winter. Propagate from seed or by layering (they are often self-layering) or by division.

Paronychia argentea (above)

This species from southern Europe, North Africa and southwest Asia forms a mat of wiry stems with rounded leaves. In summer, it is smothered in small, dull yellow inflorescences partially covered by silvery bracts. ZONES 7–11.

Paronychia capitata (below)

This Mediterranean species is very similar to *Paronychia argentea*. However, its leaves are linear to lance-shaped rather than rounded and its bracts are an even brighter silver. ZONES 5–10.

P

PELARGONIUM

The widely grown hybrid pelargoniums are popularly known as 'geraniums', but should not be confused with members of the genus *Geranium* of the same plant family. The genus *Pelargonium* consists of perhaps 280 species, the vast majority endemic to South Africa and adjacent Namibia, but a sprinkling of species are found elsewhere in the world including other parts of Africa, southwest Asia, Arabia, Australia, New Zealand and some Atlantic Ocean islands. Although pelargoniums are mostly soft-wooded shrubs and subshrubs, some are herbaceous perennials or even annuals; there is also a large but little known group of species that have succulent stems, leaves or roots and are grown by succulent collectors. The leaves of pelargoniums are often as broad as they are long and are variously toothed, scalloped, lobed or dissected, depending on species; they are usually aromatic, containing a wide range of essential oils, and may secrete resin droplets which give the leaves a sticky feel. Flowers of the wild

Pelargonium zonale (above)

This South African species is rarely seen in gardens, being best known for its genetic contribution to the Zonal pelargonium hybrids. ZONES 9–11.

species have the 2 upper petals differently colored or marked from the 3 lower ones, a feature that distinguishes pelargoniums from true geraniums. Their seeds are plumed like thistledown, another distinguishing feature.

Only a few groups of hybrid pelargoniums are widely grown in gardens and as indoor plants, originating in the early nineteenth century from a small number of South African shrub species. The common garden and pot 'geraniums' are the **Zonal pelargoniums**, once known botanically as *Pelargonium* × *hortorum.* They have almost circular leaves with scalloped margins, often with horseshoe-shaped zones of brown, red or purple, and flower almost continuously. Somewhat similar are the **Ivy-leafed pelargoniums**, with their semi-scrambling habit and leaves that are fleshier with more pointed lobes;

P

these are also the subject of intensive breeding, and are tending to merge with zonals in some of their characteristics. Another major group is the **Regal pelargoniums**, sometimes known as the **Martha Washington geraniums** or *Pelargonium* × *domesticum*; these have woody stems and sharply toothed and creased leaves, and the large flowers come in a range of gaudy colors and patterns. There are some smaller groups of hybrids bred for their flowers, most significant being the **Unique** and **Angel pelargoniums**. And then there is a large and varied group, grown primarily for their foliage, known as the **Scented-leafed pelargoniums**: these are mostly shrubby and usually have deeply lobed or dissected leaves that give off a quite remarkable range of odors when bruised or crushed, depending on the variety. They include both species and hybrids, and some also have quite pretty flowers. Some of these are grown commercially for 'geranium oil', used in perfumery.

CULTIVATION

These frost-tender plants are often treated like annuals for summer bedding in colder climates. In warmer climates with long hours of daylight they flower almost all the time, although they do not do well in extreme heat and humidity. Plant in pots or beds. The site should be sunny with light, well-drained, neutral soil. If grown in pots, fertilize regularly and cull dead heads. Avoid over-watering; Zonals in particular rot at the base if soil remains wet, although stems re-root higher up (but weaker plants result). Propagate from softwood cuttings from spring to autumn.

Pelargonium crispum (below)
LEMON GERANIUM, FINGER-BOWL GERANIUM

A distinctive species from South Africa's southwest Cape Province, *Pelargonium crispum* is an erect, few-branched shrubby perennial to 3 ft (1 m) high, its straight stems regularly lined with small lobed leaves with crinkled margins, lemon-scented when bruised. The scattered pink flowers appear large in proportion, up to 1 in (25 mm) across with darker markings. **'Variegatum'** (syn. 'Prince Rupert Variegated') is a widely grown form with cream-edged leaves. **'Prince Rupert'** is a vigorous, larger-leafed form. ZONES 9–11.

Pelargonium tricolor (above)

This species is a sprawling, wiry-stemmed shrubby perennial about 12 in (30 cm) tall. It has narrow, hairy, gray-green leaves with a few deeply cut teeth, and are seldom more than 1¹/₂ in (35 mm) long. The distinctive flowers are pansy-like, 1¹/₂ in (35 mm) wide; the upper petals are red with a black base and the lower petals are white. ZONES 9–11.

Pelargonium, Ivy-leafed Hybrids

These are derived mainly from the South African *Pelargonium peltatum*, which has a scrambling or trailing habit with fleshy, pointed-lobed, hairless leaves and small pink flowers. The many cultivars retain the leaf characteristics, but have larger flowers in conspicuous long-stalked heads, often double and in a wide range of colors. Easily grown, they tolerate wetter conditions than the Zonals, and are especially suited to hanging baskets and the tops of retaining walls. Recent developments include variegated leaves and compact or miniature plants. Hybridization of Ivy-leafed and Zonal pelargoniums has resulted in plants with leaves like the former, and flowers more like the latter. The popular **'Blooming Gem'** has bright pink flowers. The **Cascade Series** of miniature Ivy-leafed pelargoniums have small leaves and masses of small flowers. It includes **'Laced Red Cascade'**, with red flowers flecked with white, and **'Chic'**, with deep pink, double flowers. **'Galilee'**, one of the best known Ivy-leafed cultivars, is compact and has leaves that may be variegated with cream or cream and pink; its densely massed double flowers are flesh pink. ZONES 9–11.

Pelargonium,
Ivy-leafed Hybrid,
'Blooming Gem' *(above)*

Pelargonium cucullatum *(above)*
WILDEMALVA

This South African species is one of the original parents of the Regal pelargonium hybrids; like many other significant species it is restricted in the wild to the southwest Cape Province. It makes a very attractive shrubby perennial of sprawling habit to around 3 ft (1 m) in height; the downy gray-green leaves are sharply toothed and lobed and somewhat cupped. In spring and summer, it bears clusters of bright reddish mauve flowers with darker veins, up to 2 in (5 cm) in diameter. ZONES 9–11.

Pelargonium 'Splendide' *(below)*

Believed to be a hybrid between the South African species *Pelargonium tricolor* and *P. ovale*, this subshrubby 6–12 in (15–30 cm) tall plant, often sold as *P. tricolor* **'Arborea'**, has knotted woody stems with toothed, long-stalked, oval, hairy, gray-green leaves. It produces branched flowering stems ending in 2- to 3-flowered clusters of striking bicolored flowers. They have red upper petals, dark purple at the base, and pure white lower petals, about 1 1/2 in (35 mm) wide. **'Pretty Lady'** is similar. ZONES 9–11.

P

Pelargonium odoratissimum *(left)*
APPLE GERANIUM

A strong, sweet smell of apples comes off the
small, roughly heart-shaped, lobed, gray-green
leaves of this very bushy, many-branched geranium. It reaches a height and spread of 12 in
(30 cm). The flowers are small and white, sometimes with red veins in the upper petals. In warm-
temperate climates, flowers may be borne almost
continuously, although it dislikes hot, humid
conditions. **ZONES 10–11.**

Pelargonium, Scented-leafed Hybrids

This varied group of hybrids derives from quite a
few wild South African species. Most have dense
branches and shallowly to deeply lobed or dissected leaves that in some are quite hairy. The
range of essential oils in the leaves is very large,
their scents ranging through peppermint, euca-
lyptus, lemon, cloves, aniseed, apple, rose and
even coconut. Often a hot day will bring out the
aroma, but it is released most strongly when the
foliage is bruised or crushed. Some have quite
showy flowers, in others they are small but still
pretty. **'Fragrans'** (apple geranium) is a bushy,
many-branched shrub reaching 12 in (30 cm)
high and wide. A strong spicy smell like green
apples comes off the small, roughly heart-shaped,
lobed, gray-green leaves. Its flowers are small and
white, sometimes with red veining on the upper
petals. **ZONES 8–11.**

Pelargonium,
Scented-leafed Hybrid,
'Fragrans' *(left)*

Pelargonium peltatum *(left)*
IVY-LEAFED GERANIUM

From coastal areas of South Africa's Cape Province, this species has trailing or scrambling stems
up to 3 ft (1 m) long. Its bright green leaves have
5 sharp lobes, the shape reminiscent of ivy leaves,
and are up to 3 in (8 cm) across. The flowers of
the original wild form are pale pink and have
quite narrow petals, appearing mainly in spring
and summer. This species is the chief ancestor of
the Ivy-leafed hybrids. **ZONES 9–11.**

PENSTEMON

This large genus consists of 250 species of deciduous, evergreen or semi-evergreen subshrubs and perennials, mostly native to Central and North America. The leaves appear in opposite pairs or whorls, while the flowers have 2 lobes on the upper lip and 3 on the lower. Hybrids are valued for their showy flower spikes in blues, reds, whites, and bicolors. Tall varieties suit sheltered borders, and dwarf strains brighten up bedding schemes. 'Bev Jensen' is red and 'Holly's White' is a favorite in the USA.

CULTIVATION

These marginally to very frost-hardy plants do best in fertile, well-drained soil and full sun. Cut plants back hard after flowering. They can be propagated from seed in spring or autumn, by division in spring, or from cuttings of non-flowering shoots in late summer (the only method for cultivars).

Penstemon 'Alice Hindley' *(below)*
syn. *Penstemon* 'Gentianoides'

This cultivar was raised in 1931. It is tall, around 4 ft (1.2 m) and has pale mauve flowers with a white mouth. Each bloom is a little under 2 in (5 cm) long. The only drawbacks with this impressive plant are that it is inclined to be rather sparsely foliaged and that it often needs staking. ZONES 8–10.

Penstemon 'Andenken an Friedrich Hahn' *(above)*
syn. *Penstemon* 'Garnet'

This very frost-hardy perennial, which grows to 30 in (75 cm) with a 24 in (60 cm) spread, bears its dark pink flowers from mid-summer to autumn. ZONES 7–10.

Penstemon barbatus *(right)*
syn. *Chelone barbata*
CORAL PENSTEMON, BEARD-LIP PENSTEMON

The scarlet flowers on this semi-evergreen, very frost-hardy perennial are tubular with 2 lips. They bloom on racemes from mid-summer to early autumn above narrow, lance-shaped, green leaves. The plant grows to 3 ft (1 m) high, with a spread of 12 in (30 cm). ZONES 3–10.

Penstemon campanulatus *(below)*

This frost-hardy, semi-evergreen perennial from Mexico and Guatemala is 12–24 in (30–60 cm) tall with narrow, serrated, 3 in (8 cm) long leaves. Its flowers are funnel- to bell-shaped, reddish purple to violet and are carried on a lax inflorescence. They open from early summer. ZONES 9–11.

Penstemon 'Bev Jensen' *(right)*

This cultivar grows to about 28 in (70 cm) high in flower and has mauve to pale purple flowers with light throats. ZONES 8–10.

Penstemon cardwellii *(above)*

From northwestern USA, this very frost-hardy evergreen perennial forms broad 4–8 in (10–20 cm) high clumps with $^1/_2$–2 in (1.2–5 cm) long, elliptical, serrated-edged leaves. Its flowers are 1–1$^1/_2$ in (25–35 mm) long, bright purple and open in summer. ZONES 8–10.

Penstemon 'Blue of Zurich' *(left)*
syn. *Penstemon* 'Zuriblau'

This 18 in (45 cm) tall cultivar has particularly bright blue flowers. ZONES 8–10.

P

Penstemon digitalis
(below)

Native to eastern North America, this very frost-hardy perennial species is usually seen with white or pale lavender flowers, neither particularly exciting. **'Husker's Red'**, however, is notable for its deep reddish purple foliage. A robust plant, it reaches a height of 30 in (75 cm) and spread of 24 in (60 cm), and is attractive to hummingbirds. **ZONES 3–9.**

Penstemon 'Firebird' *(left)*
syn. *Penstemon* 'Schoenholzen'

This cultivar grows to around 30 in (75 cm) and has vivid orange-red flowers. **ZONES 7–10.**

Penstemon digitalis 'Husker's Red' *(right)*

Penstemon 'Cherry Ripe' *(above)*

This is a 4 ft (1.2 m) tall hybrid with narrow, warm red blooms on wiry stems. **ZONES 7–10.**

P

Penstemon 'Evelyn'
(above left)

This is a 30 in (75 cm) tall perennial hybrid with very narrow leaves and masses of slightly curved pale pink flowers. It was raised by the famous Slieve Donard nursery of Northern Ireland and is very frost hardy. ZONES 7–10.

Penstemon 'Connie's Pink'
(above)

This 4 ft (1.2 m) tall hybrid has fine wiry stems with a coating of hairs. Its flowers are rose pink and rather narrow. ZONES 7–10.

P

Penstemon 'White Bedder' (above)
syns Penstemon 'Burford White', P. 'Royal White', P. 'Snow Storm'

This frost-hardy, 30 in (75 cm) tall perennial has white flowers with a pale yellow-cream tinge and an occasional hint of pale pink. The buds are often pink tinted. ZONES 7–10.

Penstemon glaber
(left)

This perennial grows to about 24 in (60 cm) tall. Its leaves are 1¹/₂–4 in (3.5–10 cm) long and lance-shaped. The inflorescence is up to 10 in (25 cm) long and is composed of 1–1¹/₂ in (25–35 mm) flowers that are purple-red at the base and white near the tips. It blooms from late summer. ZONES 3–10.

Penstemon × gloxinioides *(right)*

BORDER PENSTEMON

This name applies to a group of hybrids raised in the middle of the nineteenth century from *Penstemon cobaea* and *P. hartwegii*. They have some of the largest and showiest flowers of any penstemons, mainly in rich reds and pinks and usually with a white throat. However, they are often short lived and not so cold hardy as other penstemons, and have declined in popularity. **ZONES 7–9.**

Penstemon heterophyllus *(below)*

FOOTHILL PENSTEMON, BLUE BEDDER PENSTEMON

From California, this very frost-hardy, summer-flowering species grows to about 18 in (45 cm) tall. Its leaves are 1–2 in (2.5–5 cm) long, lance-shaped and slightly blue-green. The $1–1^1/_2$ in (25–35 mm) long flowers vary from deep violet-pink to near blue. **ZONES 8–10.**

Penstemon 'Hidcote Pink' *(right)*

Up to 4 ft (1.2 m) tall, this narrow-leafed perennial has gray-green foliage and rose-pink flowers with deep pink streaks. It is very frost hardy. **ZONES 7–10.**

P

Penstemon hirsutus *(below)*

A penstemon from the northeastern and central states of the USA, this species reaches about 24 in (60 cm) in height and has hairy stems and rather narrow, dark green leaves. The flowers, crowded at the ends of the stems in summer, are pale purple outside with a coating of fine fuzzy hairs, and white in the throat. **Penstemon hirsutus var. pygmaeus** is a loosely mat-forming plant no more than 4 in (10 cm) high with short, spreading flowering stems and purple-flushed foliage; it is popular as a rock garden plant. ZONES 3–9.

Penstemon 'Pennington Gem' *(below)*

This 30 in (75 cm) tall, frost-hardy perennial has deep pink, white-throated flowers with a few purple-red stripes. ZONES 7–10.

Penstemon hirsutus
var. *pygmaeus* *(above)*

P

Penstemon pinifolius (opposite page, left)

This sprightly evergreen species is best suited to a
well-drained rock garden. A moderately frost-
hardy native of southwest USA and Mexico, it
thrives in heat and needs little water beyond the
normal rainfall. The flowers are typically 2 lipped
and bright orange-red, and are produced for
much of the summer. The leaves are needle-like.
ZONES 8–11.

Penstemon serrulatus (below)

CASCADE PENSTEMON

Found from Oregon to southern Alaska, this
12–30 in (30–75 cm) tall, very frost-hardy species
has broad, lance-shaped, 1–4 in (2.5–10 cm) long
leaves with serrated edges. The flowers, in dense
clusters, are less than 1 in (25 mm) long, tubular-
to bell-shaped, deep blue to purple and open
from late summer. ZONES 5–10.

Penstemon 'Stapleford Gem'
(above)

P

A very frost-hardy
strong grower to 4 ft
(1.2 m) tall, this peren-
nial has flowers in
a glowing shade of
purple-pink. The color
varies somewhat with
the climate and soil
pH. ZONES 7–10.

Penstemon 'Thorn'
(left)

This hybrid grows to
3 ft (1 m) in height and
has narrow pink and
white flowers.
ZONES 7–10.

PENTAPHRAGMA

This genus of about 25 species from the rainforests of Southeast Asia is related to the bellflowers (*Campanula*) but the relationship would only be evident to a botanist. They evergreen perennials have fleshy, creeping stems, broad, simple leaves that are often one-sided at the base, and dense clusters of rather insignificant circular flowers in the leaf axils. Foliage of some species is gathered by local people for use as a green vegetable.

CULTIVATION

These plants are seldom cultivated except in botanical gardens, and outside the wet tropics would need a heated greenhouse.

Pentaphragma horsfieldii (below)

Native to Java, Sumatra and the Malay Peninsula, this low-growing plant has creeping stems and broad, heavily veined green leaves. The tightly clustered small flowers are fleshy, disc-shaped and cream in color, changing to green as they age. ZONES 11–12.

PENTAS

This genus of around 40 species of biennials, perennials and subshrubs is found in tropical parts of Arabia and Africa. They have bright green, lance-shaped, 3–8 in (8–20 cm) long leaves, sometimes coated with a fine down or tiny hairs. The small, starry, long-tubed flowers are massed in flat-topped heads and appear throughout the warmer months. They are usually bright pink, but also occur in red and purple shades and white.

Pentas lanceolata
(below)
syn. *Pentas carnea*
EGYPTIAN STAR, STAR CLUSTER

This erect, straggling shrubby perennial grows to a height of 2–3 ft (0.6–1 m) with a slightly wider spread. It is grown for its clusters of tubular, red, pink, lilac or white flowers, among bright green, hairy leaves during spring and summer. ZONES 10–12.

CULTIVATION

Although very frost tender and only suitable for outdoor cultivation in very mild climates, they are easily grown as house plants. The new dwarf strains can be treated as bedding or pot annuals. Plant in moist, well-drained soil in full sun or part-shade and pinch back regularly to maintain a compact habit and to encourage bloom. Deadhead as required and trim lightly in early spring. Water well when in full growth. Propagate from seed in spring or from softwood cuttings in summer. Watch for aphids and red spider mites.

P

Peperomia argyreia (left)
WATERMELON PEPEROMIA

Found in northern South America, this is a compact, nearly stemless perennial with rosettes of glossy, rounded, 3–4 in (8–10 cm) long, gray-striped leaves on long red stems. The flower spikes are small, but extend beyond the foliage. ZONES 11–12.

PEPEROMIA
RADIATOR PLANT

This genus from tropical and subtropical regions worldwide contains 1000 species of evergreen or succulent perennials. Ideal in terrariums or dish gardens, they have diverse and beautifully marked and shaped, fleshy, usually long-stalked leaves. Long-stemmed spikes of minute, greenish white to cream flowers appear erratically in late summer.

CULTIVATION

Frost tender, these make good house plants. Peperomias like bright light, but not direct sun, especially near a window, with high humidity in summer. Keep moist in warm weather, and be sure to water them from below as the leaves mark easily. In winter, allow the plants to dry out between waterings. Use a half-strength, soluble fertilizer once a month in spring and summer. Peperomias are easily propagated from leaf or stem cuttings in spring or summer, and should be repotted annually. Watch for mealybugs, spider mites and white fly.

Peperomia caperata
EMERALD RIPPLE

This perennial species has oval, deeply corrugated and veined, heart-shaped, dark green, sometimes purplish leaves. They are pale green underneath and about 1¹/₂ in (35 mm) across, carried on pinkish stems. Tight clusters of white flower spikes appear irregularly. 'Silver Ripples' has silver-gray markings on the ridges of the corrugations. ZONES 11–12.

Peperomia caperata 'Silver Ripples' *(left)*

P

PERICALLIS

CINERARIA

This genus has about 15 species of perennials and subshrubs closely allied to *Senecio*, where they were once included. They are distributed throughout the mid-latitude islands of the Atlantic Ocean. Best known in cultivation for the florist's cineraria *(Pericallis × hybrida)*, the wild species are nowhere near as fancy. The leaves, which form basal rosettes in the perennials, are usually oval to lance-shaped, 2–6 in (5–15 cm) long, with finely toothed edges and covered in small hairs. The flowers are usually pink, mauve or purple, $1/_2$–2 in (1.2–5 cm) wide and carried in open heads.

CULTIVATION

Although easily cultivated in any moist, well-drained soil in part- to full shade, few species will tolerate anything other than very light frosts. The florist's strains are often used as winter-flowering house plants. Propagate from seed or cuttings or by division, depending on the growth form.

Pericallis × hybrida

(below)
syns *Senecio cruentus,*
S. × hybrida

This hybrid reaches 12 in (30 cm) tall and wide. It is a multi-purpose bloomer for grouping or for formal bedding in part-shaded spots. It is ideal for window boxes, for contain-ers on balconies or in court-yards. The color of the daisy-like flowers ranges from pink, red, purple and crimson through to white, as well as the traditional blue. They are very tolerant of heat, salt air and poor soil, but suffer in high humidity or excessive rain.
ZONES 9–11.

P

Pericallis × *hybrida*
(above, above left & left)

Pericallis lanata *(left)*
syn. *Senecio heritieri*

This 3 ft (1 m) tall species from Tenerife in the
Canary Islands has flexible stems that may be upright or spreading. It leaves, which are hairy and
up to 6 in (15 cm) long, are usually oval and
finely toothed, but sometimes have 5 to 7 deep
lobes. The flowers may be borne singly or in loose
heads and are white and purple, up to $1^1/_2$ in
(35 mm) wide and sweetly scented. **ZONES 9–11.**

P

PEROVSKIA

Found in western Asia and the Himalayan region, the 7 species of deciduous shrubby perennials in this genus have gray-white stems and aromatic leaves that are covered with gray felt when young. As they mature, the deeply lobed, 2–3 in (5–8 cm) long leaves lose their felting and become gray-green. They form large clumps to 3–5 ft (1–1.5 m) tall and are topped in late summer with 12–18 in (30–45 cm) panicles of tiny purple-blue flowers.

CULTIVATION

They are very easily grown in any well-drained, rather dry soil in a sunny position. It is often best to contain their growth by planting them beside a path, wall or border edge. If allowed free rein, smaller, less vigorous plants may be smothered. They are very frost hardy and may be propagated from seed, or by cuttings of non-flowering stems.

Perovskia atriplicifolia *(above)*
RUSSIAN SAGE

This tall, tough species produces soft, gray-green foliage that beautifully complements the haze of pale lavender-blue flowers, which appear on panicles in late summer and autumn. The plants are upright to 5 ft (1.5 m), with a spread of 3 ft (1 m) or more. They are long lived.
ZONES 6–9.

PERSICARIA
syns *Aconogonon, Bistorta, Tovara*

KNOTWEED

This genus of 50 to 80 species of annuals, perennials or subshrubs have strong wiry stems with variously shaped leaves $1^1/_2$–10 in (3.5–25 cm) long. The foliage often has purple-gray markings and may develop red and gold tints in autumn. The flowers, usually pink or cream, are small and are sometimes borne in showy panicles or spikes.

CULTIVATION

Most are vigorous and very frost hardy, easily cultivated in any well-drained soil in sun or part-shade. Some may become invasive: the stronger growers are best contained. Propagate from seed in spring or by division in spring or autumn.

Persicaria
amplexicaulis

syns *Bistorta*
amplexicaulis,
Polygonum
amplexicaule

BISTORT, MOUNTAIN FLEECE

Persicaria amplexicaulis is a clump-forming, leafy, semi-evergreen perennial from the Himalayas. It has oval to heart-shaped mid-green leaves and grows to a height and spread of 4 ft (1.2 m). Its profuse spikes of small, rich red flowers are borne from summer to autumn. *P. amplexicaulis* **'Firetail'** is a low grower with vivid crimson flowers. **'Inverleith'** is a dwarf cultivar with short spikes of deep crimson flowers. ZONES 5–9.

Persicaria
amplexicaulis 'Firetail'
(left)

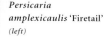

Persicaria
amplexicaulis
'Inverleith' *(left)*

P

Persicaria bistorta
syn. *Polygonum bistorta*

BISTORT, SNAKEWEED

A vigorous perennial
with heavy rootstock,
Persicaria bistorta is
found from Europe to
western Asia. This spe-
cies grows to around
24 in (60 cm) tall. Its
leaves are oblong with
wavy margins and grow
4–8 in (10–20 cm)
long. The flowers
open in summer and
are white or pink.
'Superba' is a tall form
which has densely
packed spikes of pink
flowers. ZONES 4–9.

Persicaria campanulata *(right)*
syn. *Polygonum campanulatum*

LESSER KNOTWEED

This Himalayan species
is a spreading perennial
that forms a clump of
unbranched wiry stems.
Its leaves are 1½–4 in
(3.5–10 cm) long and
are lance-shaped, bright
green on top with pale
gray to pink under-
sides. The flowering
stems are erect, 2–4 ft
(0.6–1.2 m) tall with
pink or white flowers
from late summer.
'Rosenrot' is an upright
grower with deep pink
flowers. ZONES 8–10.

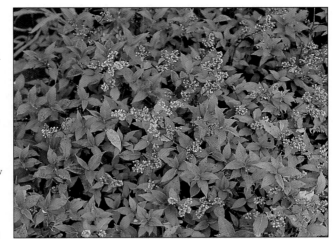

Persicaria campanulata 'Rosenrot' *(above)*

Persicaria bistorta 'Superba' *(below)*

Persicaria filiformis (left)
syn. *Polygonum filiforme*

Up to 4 ft (1.2 m) tall, *Persicaria filiformis* comes from Japan, the Himalayas and northeastern USA. It has 3–6 in (8–15 cm) long elliptical leaves with a covering of short, rough hairs and often marked with rows of chocolate-brown flecks. The flower spikes are slender and the green-white or pale pink flowers are not particularly showy. ZONES 5–10.

Persicaria macrophylla (left)
syn. *Polygonum macrophyllum*

This spreading Himalayan and western Chinese semi-evergreen perennial rarely exceeds 6 in (15 cm) in height, but has leaves up to 4 in (10 cm) long. The foliage forms a basal clump that slowly enlarges and spreads. The pink or red flowers open in summer. ZONES 5–9.

Persicaria orientale (left)
syn. *Polygonum orientale*
PRINCE'S FEATHER, PRINCESS FEATHER

From eastern and Southeast Asia and Australia, this species is an annual that reaches 5 ft (1.5 m) tall. Its leaves are large, up to 8 in (20 cm) long, and are roughly an elongated heart shape. The flowers open from late summer and are bright pink to purple-pink or white and are borne in large, slightly pendulous, branched spikes. ZONES 8–11.

P

PETUNIA

'Petun' means 'tobacco' in a South American Indian dialect, and petunias are indeed relatives of the tobaccos *(Nicotiana)*. Their leaves have a similar narcotic effect on humans, and both genera belong to the same family as potatoes (Solanaceae). There are around 35 species in the genus, occurring in warmer parts of South America. They include annuals, biennials and shrubby perennials. The leaves are dark green, rather hairy and smooth-edged and the trumpet-shaped flowers are white, purple, red, blue, pink or mixed hues. It is doubtful whether any other group of garden annuals has been the subject of such intense selection by plant breeders over such a long period as the petunias. Interestingly, from what has been revealed of their work, it seems to have been concentrated almost entirely on the one hybrid combination, *Petunia* × *hybrida.*

Petunia × *hybrida,* Surfinia Series, 'Pink Vein' *(above)*

CULTIVATION

The garden petunias are frost-tender plants always grown as annuals. They are popular worldwide as bedding plants and for window boxes, hanging baskets and planters. Fairly fast growing, they like well-drained, fertile soil and a sunny location and thrive where summers are hot, although they do need shelter from wind. Flowers of some of the larger **Grandiflora hybrids** are damaged by rain, but others, mainly the **Multiflora hybrids**, are more resistant. Sow seed under glass in early spring, or plant purchased seedlings at beginning of summer. Fertilize every month until flowering is well advanced. Pinch back hard to encourage branching and deadhead regularly. Watch for cucumber mosaic and tomato spotted wilt.

P

P

Petunia × *hybrida*
'Shihi Purple' *(left)*

Petunia × *hybrida*

Believed to have originated as a cross between the
white-flowered *Petunia axillaris* and the pink to
purple-flowered *P. integrifolia*, the garden petunia
was a well-known summer bedding plant in Europe
by the middle of the nineteenth century. From an
early stage, the garden petunias were divided into
4 groups of cultivars and seedling strains, desig-
nated by Latin names, and this classification still
survives. The 2 most important groups are the
Grandiflora and **Multiflora** petunias, both with
plants around 12 in (30 cm) tall at maturity.
Flowers of the former are very wide and shallow,
scattered over the somewhat sprawling plants,
while Multifloras are more compact in growth with
densely massed and somewhat narrower blooms.
The **Nana Compacta** petunias are generally less
than 6 in (15 cm) high, of compact habit, and
with profuse small flowers. The **Pendula** petunias
have prostrate, trailing stems and are grown
mainly in hanging baskets. It is the Grandiflora
petunias that are now the most popular, with a
dazzling range of newer F1 hybrids, although they
are more easily rain damaged and susceptible to
disfiguring botrytis rot. They include the **Cascade**

Petunia × *hybrida,*
Celebrity Series,
'Pink Morn' *(left)*

Petunia × *hybrida*
cultivars
(below left & below right)

Petunia × *hybrida*
'Flamingo' *(right)*

and **Supercascade Series** (or Magic Series), available in a wide range of colors, with single flowers and somewhat trailing stems suitable for hanging baskets. **'Giants of California'** is not so profusely blooming, but individual blossoms are very large with ruffled edges and are white, pink or mauve. The Multifloras have smaller blooms but are more prolific flowerers. They include the **Plum Series**, with delightfully veined flowers and **Bonanza Series** with frilly, trumpet-shaped double flowers in a multitude of colors. The **Celebrity Series**, including cultivars such as **'Pink Morn'**, also covers a wide color range, and are mainly in pastel shades. They can be distinguished by their light-throated flowers. The **Madness Series** have small single-color flowers. **'Purple Wave'** is a seedling strain with prolific flowers of a single, magenta-purple color. It has a cascading growth habit and is similar to the vegetatively propagated **'Colorwave'** petunias. **Surfinia Series** petunias are extremely vigorous disease-resistant trailing plants that are smothered throughout the warmer months with rain-tolerant blooms. Other petunia cultivars include **'Flamingo'**, **'Frenzy Rose'**, **'Pink Flamingo'**, and **'Shihi Purple'**. ZONES 9–11.

Petunia × *hybrida*
'Frenzy Rose' *(below)*
Petunia × *hybrida*
cultivar *(below right)*

Petunia × *hybrida*,
Madness Series, 'Purple
Wave' *(right)*

Petunia integrifolia,
Million Bells Series,
'Terracotta' *(left)*

Petunia integrifolia (below)
syn. *Petunia violacea*

Sometimes sold as
'Burgundy Pet', this
Argentinian species is a
short-lived shrubby
perennial that pro-
duces masses of small,
dark-throated, rose
purple flowers on
sprawling plants. It is a
weather- and disease-
tolerant species that is
being increasingly used
in hybridizing. Some
very free-flowering
cultivars recently re-
leased under the trade
name **Million Bells**
may belong to this
species. ZONES 9–11.

Petunia × *hybrida,* Surfinia Series,
'Blue Vein' and *Petunia integrifolia,*
Million Bells Series, 'Blue' *(below)*

Petunia × *hybrida*
'Pink Flamingo' *(below)*

Petunia × *hybrida,*
Surfinia Series, 'White'
(below right)

Petunia × *hybrida,* Surfinia Series,
'Hot Pink' and *Petunia integrifolia,*
Million Bells Series, 'Trailing Pink' *(above)*

PHACELIA
SCORPION WEED

This is a genus of around 150 species of annuals, biennials and perennials native to the Americas. They are generally shrubby, but vary considerably in size, ranging from as little as 6 in (15 cm) to over 5 ft (1.5 m) tall. The young shoots and leaves are sometimes downy and the leaves are often toothed or lobed, sometimes to the point of being pinnate. They all have clusters of small 5-petalled flowers at the stem tips. The flowers are usually in blue or purple shades, often with white centers, and can be quite striking. *Phacelia bolanderi* is a delicate shade of lilac.

Phacelia grandiflora (below)

This species from southern California is a 3 ft (1 m) tall annual with serrated-edged, elliptical leaves up to 8 in (20 cm) long. Its flowers are 1^1/$_2$ in (35 mm) wide and are mauve to white. ZONES 8–11.

CULTIVATION
Most species are very easily grown in any light but moist, well-drained soil in full sun. They are fully frost hardy. Propagate the annuals and biennials from seed, the perennials from seed or cuttings.

Phacelia bolanderi
(below)

PHLOMIS

This is a genus of around 150 species of often downy-leaved perennials, subshrubs and shrubs found from the Mediterranean region to China. Although variable, in most cases their leaves are large, over 4 in (10 cm) long, and densely covered with hair-like felting. Typical of members of the nettle family, the leaves occur in whorls on upright stems. The tubular flowers, borne on upright verticillasters, curl downwards and have 2 lips at the tip, the upper lip hooded over the lower. They occur in clusters of 2 to 40 blooms, depending on the species, and are usually in shades of cream, yellow, pink, mauve or purple.

CULTIVATION

Hardiness varies, though most will tolerate moderate frosts. Species with heavily felted foliage suffer in prolonged wet weather and are best grown in exposed positions where the foliage dries quickly after rain. Plant in moist, well-drained soil in full sun or part-shade. Propagate from seed or from small cuttings of non-flowering shoots, or by division where possible.

Phlomis tuberosa
(right)

This 5 ft (1.5 m) tall species develops small tubers on its roots. Its leaves are an elongated heart shape, up to 10 in (25 cm) long with toothed edges. They have a covering of fine hairs, but are not felted. The flowers open in summer, are pink to purple and quite small, but there are up to 40 in each whorl. ZONES 7–10.

Phlomis russeliana *(below)*

This easily grown perennial thrives in any ordinary soil given a reasonable amount of sun. The large, heart-shaped, fresh green leaves make excellent ground cover if planted in quantity, forming clumps around 12 in (30 cm) high and up to 24 in (60 cm) across. In summer, it bears stout stems 3 ft (1 m) high topped with several whorls of hooded, butter yellow flowers. ZONES 7–10.

Phlox adsurgens 'Wagon Wheel' *(below)*

Phlox adsurgens
WOODLAND PHLOX

This prostrate to slightly mounding perennial is native to Oregon and northern California. Its leaves are rounded, shiny, usually less than 1 in (25 mm) long and slightly hairy. Sprays of bright pink flowers up to 1 in (25 mm) wide open from late spring. It prefers a cool, lightly shaded position. **'Wagon Wheel'** is a popular cultivar with drooping stems of large flowers with strappy petals. ZONES 6–10.

PHLOX

This genus contains more than 60 species of evergreen and semi-evergreen annuals and perennials, mostly native to North America. They are grown for their profuse, fragrant flowers and the symmetry of the flower clusters. The name *phlox* means 'flame', appropriate for these brightly colored, showy flowers popular in bedding and border displays. *Phlox purpurea* × *lutea* has deep pink flowers with pale yellow centers.

CULTIVATION
Perennials are easily grown in any temperate climate, and need a lot of water while they grow. Annuals grow in almost any climate. Plant in fertile, moist but well-drained soil in a sunny or part-shaded position. Propagate from seed or cuttings or by division. Watch out for red spider mite, eelworm and powdery mildew.

Phlox douglasii 'Waterloo' *(below)*

Phlox douglasii

This evergreen perennial, occurring naturally from Washington to California in the USA, bears white, lavender-blue or pink flowers and grows to 8 in (20 cm) in height. **'Boothman's Variety'** is a dwarf form with blue-centered lavender flowers. **'Crackerjack'** is a compact cultivar with crimson to magenta flowers. **'Red Admiral'** is a strong-growing yet compact form with vivid crimson flowers. **'Rosea'** forms a neat mat with silver-pink flowers. **'Waterloo'** has deep crimson flowers. **'Rose Cushion'** is a very compact plant that covers itself with dusky pink flowers. ZONES 5–10.

Phlox purpurea × *lutea* *(above)*

Phlox douglasii 'Rose Cushion' *(right)*

Phlox douglasii 'Rosea' *(below)*

Phlox maculata
MEADOW PHLOX

Phlox maculata is a perennial that grows to 3 ft (1 m) tall and bears scented, white, pink or purple flowers in mid-summer. **'Alpha'** is around 30 in (75 cm) tall with deep pink flowers. **'Miss Lingard'** is up to 3 ft (1 m) tall with fragrant white flowers that sometimes have a central pink ring. **'Omega'** is around 30 in (75 cm) tall with fragrant white, lilac-centered flowers. ZONES 5–10.

Phlox maculata 'Omega' *(above)*

Phlox maculata 'Alpha' *(left)*

Phlox drummondii 'Sternenzauber' *(left)*

Phlox drummondii
ANNUAL PHLOX

This bushy annual grows quickly to 15 in (38 cm) tall and half that in spread. In summer and autumn, it bears closely clustered, small, flattish flowers with 5 petals in reds, pinks, purples and creams. It has lanceolate, light green leaves and is frost resistant. **'Sternenzauber'** (syn. 'Twinkle') bears star-like flowers that have pointed petals. There are dwarf strains that grow to 4 in (10 cm). ZONES 6–10.

Phlox paniculata
(right)

SUMMER PHLOX, PERENNIAL
PHLOX

This tall perennial to 3 ft (1 m) bears long-lasting flowerheads of many small flowers in summer. **'Amethyst'** has violet flowers. **'Brigadier'** has very deep green leaves and pink flowers suffused with orange. **'Bright Eyes'** has pink flowers with red eyes. **'Eventide'** has light mauve or lavender blue flowers. **'Fujiyama'** has pure white flowers on stems up to 30 in (75 cm) tall. **'Graf Zeppelin'** has white flowers with pinkish red centers. **'Mother of Pearl'** has white to pale pink flowers suffused pink on stems up to 30 in (75 cm) tall. **'Prince of Orange'** has deep pink flowers flushed with orange on stems up to 3 ft (1 m) tall. **'Prospero'** is an award-winning cultivar with white-edged, mauve flowers. **'Sir John Falstaff'** has salmon-pink flowers. **'Snow Hare'** has snow white flowers. **'White Admiral'** bears pure white flowers. **'Windsor'** has deep pink flowers. ZONES 4–10.

Phlox paniculata
'Prince of Orange'
(right)

Phlox paniculata
'Graf Zeppelin' *(below)*

Phlox paniculata
'Snow Hare' *(above)*

Phlox paniculata
'Mother of Pearl' *(left)*

Phlox paniculata
'Amethyst' and
P. p. 'Europa' *(below)*

Phlox subulata
MOSS PHLOX

Throughout spring, this prostrate alpine perennial produces masses of 1 in (25 mm) wide, star-shaped flowers in blue, mauve, carmine, pink and white, the petals being notched and open. Its fine-leaved foliage grows carpet-like to 4 in (10 cm) high with a spread twice that. Fully frost hardy and ever-green, it is suitable for sunny rock gardens. **'Greencourt Purple'** has a rich color and likes a little shade. **'McDaniel's Cushion'** (syn. 'Daniel's Cush-ion') is best in small groups among shrubs or taller perennials. **'Maischnee'** (syn. 'May Snow') is a beautiful snow white form. **'Marjorie'** has glowing deep pink flowers. **'Oakington Blue Eyes'** forms large mats and is smothered with light blue flowers. **ZONES 3–10.**

Phlox pilosa subsp. ozarkana *(right)*
PRAIRIE PHLOX

This form of a peren-nial widespread in the USA grows to 24 in (60 cm) tall with lance-shaped leaves up to 6 in (15 cm) long. The spring flowers, in large panicles, are up to 1 in (25 mm) wide, white, purple or pink. **ZONES 5–10.**

Phlox subulata 'McDaniel's Cushion' *(above)*

Phlox subulata 'Greencourt Purple' *(right)*

P

PHORMIUM
NEW ZEALAND FLAX

Valued for the dramatic effect of their stiff, vertical leaves, these 2 species of large, clumping plants from New Zealand grow well in most conditions. In summer, they produce panicles of flowers that attract nectar-feeding birds. The large, arching, striped leaves appear in clumps and can be anything from dark green to green-yellow. There are many cultivars with variegated or brightly colored foliage. They range in height from 3 ft (1 m) to 6 ft (1.8 m). The fiber of these flaxes has been used commercially, but is now largely confined to traditional Maori crafts.

CULTIVATION
They make splendid container plants as well as useful garden specimens in almost any climate. They are fairly frost hardy, and respond well to generous watering and permanently moist conditions. Propagate from seed or by division in spring.

Phormium 'Apricot Queen' *(below)*

This form has dark green, arching leaves to 4 ft (1.2 m) long with apricot striping and bronze edges. The young foliage is creamy yellow. ZONES 8–11.

Phormium cookianum *(right)*
syn. *Phormium colensoi*

Found throughout New Zealand in a wide range of conditions, this species has leaves 2–5 ft (0.6–1.5 m) long and up to $2^{1}/_{2}$ in (6 cm) wide. Its flowers are yellow to red-brown with yellow interiors, and are carried on stiffly erect stems that extend well above the foliage clump. **'Dark Delight'** has deep wine-red leaves up to 4 ft (1.2 m) long. **'Duet'** is a 12 in (30 cm) tall dwarf cultivar with cream and green foliage. **'Maori Maiden'** (syn. 'Rainbow Maiden') is an upright grower with 3 ft (1 m) long bronze leaves striped red. **'Sundowner'** has extremely long leaves, almost 6 ft (1.8 m), that are bronze-green with cream or pinkish edges. **'Tricolor'** is an evergreen, upright perennial with bold spiky leaves prettily striped with red, yellow and green, and panicles of tubular, pale yellowish green flowers. ZONES 8–11.

Phormium cookianum
'Duet' *(left)*

Phormium cookianum
'Maori Maiden' *(right)*

P

Phormium cookianum
'Sundowner' *(left)*

Phormium tenax *(left)*

The larger of the flax species, this has olive green, strap-like leaves 6–10 ft (1.8–3 m) tall in clumps about 6 ft (1.8 m) across. It grows well by the sea. Hybrids of *Phormium tenax* and *P. cookianum* are often more compact than their parents, and their foliage varies from bronze or purplish chartreuse to pink and salmon. The leaves may be variegated with vertical stripes of 2 or more colors. **'Bronze Baby'** has wide, fibrous, copper-toned leaves with sharply pointed tips. In summer, it bears tubular, bronze-red flowers on a strong stem from the base of the clump. **'Dazzler'** has red leaves edged with plum-purple. **'Purpureum'** has stiff, pointed, plum-purple to dark copper leaves and in summer bears reddish flowers on purplish blue stems. **'Variegatum'** has foliage marked with a lighter colored stripe. **'Tom Thumb'** has green leaves with bronze margins growing to 24 in (60 cm). **'Coffee'** is another popular cultivar. ZONES 8–11.

Phormium tenax
'Bronze Baby' *(left)*

Phormium tenax
'Purpureum' *(above)*

Phormium tenax
'Variegatum' *(below)*

Phormium tenax
'Coffee' *(above)*

Phormium
'Rainbow Warrior'
(right)

This is a recently
released cultivar that
makes a luxuriant
clump of foliage. It has
long arching and
drooping leaves that
are predominantly
pinkish red and irregu-
larly striped with
bronze green.
ZONES 8–11.

PHUOPSIS

This is a genus of just one species, a small clump- or mat-forming perennial native to the Caucasus and northern Iran. Its whorled foliage is reminiscent of the closely related woodruff *(Galium odoratum)* with tiny, narrow leaves in starry clusters at intervals along the 6–8 in (15–20 cm) stems. Its flowers are bright pink, $^1/_2$ in (12 mm) long, 5-petalled tubes with a protruding style. They are massed in rounded heads of 30 to 50 blooms and open in summer.

CULTIVATION

This plant is very frost hardy and is best grown in gritty, humus-rich, moist soil in sun or part-shade. Propagate from seed or cuttings of non-flowering shoots or by division.

Phuopsis stylosa
(below)

This charming little plant is most at home in a corner of a rockery that doesn't get too hot and dry in summer. Remove the heads of small pink flowers as they deteriorate and the display should last well into autumn. ZONES 7–9.

PHYSALIS
GROUND CHERRY

This is a genus of about 80 species of annuals and perennials with a widespread distribution, especially in the Americas. Most form a clump of upright leafy stems 2–4 ft (0.6–1.2 m) tall. The leaves are variable in shape, usually lance-shaped, oval or deltoid (like a poplar leaf), often with lobes or shallow-toothed edges. The flowers are small, usually white or yellow blotched purple, and are backed by calyces that enlarge to enclose the fruit as they develop. The fruit are yellow, orange or red berries, and are often edible. They are ripe when the calyces start to dry out.

CULTIVATION
Hardiness varies, but most species tolerate moderate frosts. They prefer moist, well-drained soil and a position in sun or part-shade. Propagate from seed or by division.

Physalis alkekengi
(right)

CHINESE LANTERN, WINTER CHERRY

This 24 in (60 cm) tall perennial found from southern Europe to Japan is most notable for the vivid orange calyx that surrounds the ripening fruit, giving rise to one of its common names. The narrow leaves, about 3 in (8 cm) long, are midgreen. The flowers are small and white with yellow centers. The fruiting stems are often used fresh in floral arrangements or dried for winter decoration. **Physalis alkekengi var. franchetii** has minute, creamy white flowers. ZONES 6–10.

P

Physalis alkekengi var.
franchetii (left)

Physalis peruviana
(above right & right)

CAPE GOOSEBERRY, GROUND
CHERRY

This perennial South
American species grows
to around 3 ft (1 m)
tall. It is often treated
as an annual and is
grown for its crop of
bright yellow to purple,
edible berries. Its
leaves are oval to heart-
shaped and up to 4 in
(10 cm) long. The
yellow-blotched purple
flowers are $^1/_2$ in
(12 mm) wide and are
quickly enveloped by
the calyces. **ZONES 8–11.**

P

Physostegia virginiana
'Summer Spire'
(above left)

Physostegia
virginiana *(above)*

P

PHYSOSTEGIA
OBEDIENT PLANT, FALSE DRAGON HEAD

This is a North American genus of some 12 species of rhizomatous perennials. They are vigorous growers and quickly develop in spring to form clumps of unbranched, upright stems clothed in narrow, lance-shaped, long leaves with toothed edges. Plant size varies from 2–6 ft (0.6–1.8 m) tall and the leaves are 2–6 in (5–15 cm) long. From mid-summer, spikes of flowers develop at the stem tips. The flowers are tubular to bell-shaped with 2 upper lobes and 3 lower lobes. They are usually less than $^1/_2$ in (12 mm) long and in shades of lavender, pink or purple and white. If a flower is moved, it will not spring back into position but will stay put, owing to a stalk with a hinge-like structure.

CULTIVATION
Obedient plants prefer moist, well-drained soil in sun or very light shade. They are very easy to grow and can be slightly invasive. Hardiness varies, though all species tolerate at least moderate frosts. Propagate from seed, from small basal cuttings or by division.

The showy flowers of this herbaceous perennial, which bloom in erect terminal spikes late in summer, are tubular, have 2 lips and are available in pale pink, magenta (**'Vivid'**) or white. It grows to 3 ft (1 m) and gives a striking display suitable for a mixed border. **'Summer Snow'** has white flowers. **'Summer Spire'** is around 24 in (60 cm) tall with deep pink flowers.
ZONES 3–10.

PHYTEUMA
HORNED RAMPION

This Eurasian genus of around 40 species of small perennials is instantly recognizable for the unusually structured flowerheads. The plants vary in size from 4–30 in (10–75 cm) tall. Their basal leaves are usually heart-shaped, while the upper leaves are oval to lance-shaped. The leaves are sometimes sharply toothed. The flowers are borne on rounded heads and are tubular, often swelling at the base, with scarcely open tips from which the stigma protrudes; they are usually in lavender, blue or purple shades tinged with white.

CULTIVATION

The small alpine species should be grown in light, gritty soil with added humus in a rockery or alpine house; the large species will grow in a normal perennial border, but take care that they do not become overgrown by more vigorous plants. Plant in sun or part-shade. Propagate from seed or by division where possible.

Phyteuma comosum (below) syn. *Physoplexis comosa*

Native to the European Alps, this tufted perennial rarely exceeds 4 in (10 cm) in height. It has toothed, heart-shaped leaves and heads of violet-blue flowers. A favorite of alpine enthusiasts, it requires a gritty soil with added humus for moisture retention. ZONES 6–9.

Phyteuma comosum
(right)

*Phyteuma
spicatum* *(right)*

SPIKED RAMPION

Up to 30 in (75 cm)
tall, this European
species is suitable for
general garden use. Its
lower leaves are heart-
shaped, toothed and
around 4 in (10 cm)
long. The upper leaves
are more oval in shape
and are less sharply
toothed. The densely
packed flowerheads are
backed by narrow leafy
bracts and the flowers
are white, cream or
blue. **ZONES 6–10**.

P

PHYTOLACCA
POKEWEED, POKEBERRY

The 35 species in this genus are native to warm-temperate and tropical areas of the Americas, Africa and Asia. Taller plants can grow to 50 ft (15 m). These perennials, evergreen trees and shrubs are valued for their general appearance and decorative, though often poisonous, rounded berries. The leaves can be quite large and have colored stems and attractive hues in autumn; the white flowers are small and are arranged in clusters.

CULTIVATION
They prefer rich soil in a sheltered position in full sun to part-shade and need adequate moisture to thrive. Propagate from seed in spring or autumn.

Phytolacca americana (above)

This soft-wooded shrub from North America is often treated as an herbaceous perennial. The white flowers in summer are followed by purple-blue berries in autumn. All parts of the plant are poisonous. ZONES 2–11.

PILEA

This is a genus of around 600 species of annuals and perennials that are widely distributed in the tropics with the exception of Australia. They may be creeping or erect and are usually small, though the larger species can reach 6 ft (1.8 m) tall. The foliage is variable: many have simple lance-shaped leaves, others have heart-shaped peperomia-like foliage and a few have tiny, clustered, moss-like leaves. The flowers are tiny, cream to pink structures that are easily over-looked. They are sometimes followed by seed pods that for-cibly eject their seed when ripe.

CULTIVATION

All frost tender, pileas are widely grown as house plants. The smaller species prefer warm, humid conditions and are ideal for terrariums and heated greenhouses. In subtropical or tropical gardens grow in moist, well-drained, humus-rich soil in part-shade. Propagate from seed or cuttings or by division.

Pilea involucrata (below)
FRIENDSHIP PLANT

From Central and South America, this trailing species that sometimes mounds to 12 in (30 cm) tall has hairy, toothed-edged, $2^1/_2$ in (6 cm) long, oval leaves. The foliage has a puckered surface and is usually bronze-green above and reddish beneath. There are several cultivated forms with varying leaf colors, shapes and sizes. **ZONES 10–12.**

P

Pilea nummulariifolia (right)

Usually seen spilling from a hanging basket, this trailing perennial from tropical South America and the West Indies has 1 in (25 mm) long, rounded leaves with toothed edges. In summer it produces small cream flowers in the leaf axils and at the stem tips. **ZONES 10–12.**

PILOSELLA

This is a genus of some 20 species of small, rosette-forming, dandelion-like perennials from Eurasia and North Africa. At least one species, *Pilosella aurantiaca,* is a serious weed in the western USA and New Zealand. The clump of basal leaves is composed of simple, hairy, oblong, lance- or spatula-shaped leaves, 1–8 in (2.5–20 cm) long depending on the species. Loose, open heads of small yellow or orange daisy-like flowerheads are carried on wiry stems up to 24 in (60 cm) tall. Most species flower continuously through summer.

CULTIVATION

They are not difficult to cultivate in any light, well-drained soil in full sun and are really plants that are more likely to pop up by chance than to be actively cultivated. Most species are very frost hardy. Propagate from seed or by division.

Pilosella laticeps
(below)

The species name means 'wide head' and aptly describes the showy golden flowerheads of this uncommon species, larger than those of most other pilosellas. It shows promise as a rock garden and ground cover plant; the spatula-shaped leaves are glossy deep green above and whitish beneath. The plant spreads to form a mat of foliage 24 in (60 cm) or more across. **ZONES 8–10.**

PINGUICULA
BUTTERWORT

This widely distributed genus consists of about 45 species of carnivorous perennials. Their 1–2^1/$_2$ in (2.5–6 cm), pointed oval leaves in basal rosettes develop from overwintering buds. The leaves are succulent and their sticky surface traps small insects. The leaf coating also contains an anesthetic that immobilizes the insects, and the leaf edges curl in to trap them. After closing, the leaf secretes a substance to digest the prey and extract its nutrients. In summer the long-spurred, 1–2^1/$_2$ in (2.5–6 cm) long flowers, usually purple, are borne singly on 2–12 in (5–30 cm) stems.

Pinguicula gypsicola (below)

This Mexican species has lance-shaped, 2–3 in (5–8 cm) long leaves and dark-veined lavender to purple flowers on stems up to 5 in (12 cm) high. ZONES 10–12.

CULTIVATION
Growing naturally in wet, mossy bogs, these plants are not easy to cultivate outside their natural environment. Bell jars and terrariums can provide the necessary humidity, but keeping the soil damp but not putrid is difficult. Frost hardiness varies considerably with the species. Propagate from seed or by division.

Pinguicula moranensis (right)

This Mexican species has 2–4 in (5–10 cm) long, rounded leaves. Its flowers are on 4–8 in (10–20 cm) stems and are 1^1/$_2$–2 in (3.5–5 cm) wide, crimson or pink with a red throat. ZONES 10–11.

PISTIA
WATER LETTUCE, SHELL FLOWER

The sole species in this genus is an aquatic perennial, widespread in the tropics and a noxious weed in some areas. The name water lettuce is an apt description: the 6 in (15 cm) wide, floating rosettes of ribbed, wedge-shaped leaves resemble blue-green lettuce heads. The base of the leaves is spongy, which keeps them buoyant, and the fine roots that emerge from the base of the rosette extract nutrients directly from the water. Although connected by stolons, the rosettes can survive independently. The arum-like inflorescence is enclosed in a leaf-like spathe that makes it inconspicuous.

CULTIVATION
Apart from needing warm subtropical to tropical conditions, water lettuce is easily grown in any pond or slow-moving water. It multiplies rapidly and can quickly clog streams. It is usually self-propagating.

Pistia stratiotes
(above)

Forming large clumps of felted rosettes, this species is an aggressive colonizer that can easily smother a small pond. Although it does not oxygenate the water, fish will feed on its roots. It also helps to shade the surface and keep the water cool. **ZONES 10–12.**

P

Pitcairnia ringens
(right)

This is one of the *Pitcairnia* species adapted to drier environments. It has underground growing points which produce sparse tufts of short, narrowly lance-shaped leaves and spreading spikes about 18 in (45 cm) tall of progressively opening scarlet flowers about 2 in (5 cm) long. **ZONES 10–12.**

PITCAIRNIA

This genus of bromeliads is native to Central and South America, Mexico and the West Indies. Mostly rock dwellers or ground dwellers, they are occasionally epiphytic. They produce clumps of somewhat grass-like foliage and spikes of variously colored tubular flowers with recurved petals. The 260 species vary widely in their styles of growth but all of them require a rest period with minimum water in cold months.

CULTIVATION
Some species like full sun while the evergreen species prefer a part-shaded position. The leaf-dropping species need plenty of water and fertilizer as soon as the first regrowth appears. Generally it is a frost-tender genus. All prefer well-drained soil. Propagate from seed or by division of the rhizomes.

PLATYCODON

BALLOON FLOWER, CHINESE BELLFLOWER

The sole species in this genus is a semi-tuberous perennial with flower stems up to 30 in (75 cm) tall. It is native to China, Japan, Korea and eastern Siberia. In spring it forms a clump of 2–3 in (5–8 cm) long, toothed-edged, elliptical to lance-shaped light blue-green foliage. The leafy flower stems develop quickly from mid-summer, and are topped with heads of inflated buds that open into broad, bell-shaped, white, pink, blue or purple flowers up to 2 in (5 cm) wide.

CULTIVATION

Very frost hardy and easily grown in any well-drained soil in full sun, this plant may take a few years to become established. Propagate from seed or by division. Because it resents disturbance, divide it as little as possible.

Platycodon grandiflorus var. *mariesii* (below)

Platycodon grandiflorus

On this species, balloon-like buds open out into 5-petalled summer flowers like bells, colored blue, purple, pink or white. The serrated, elliptical leaves with a silvery blue cast form in a neat clump up to 24 in (60 cm) high and half that in spread. **'Fuji Blue'** is very erect to 30 in (75 cm) tall with large blue flowers. *Platycodon grandiflorus* var. *mariesii* is more compact than the species, and grows to 18 in (45 cm) tall and with glossy, lance-shaped leaves. **ZONES 4–10.**

Platycodon grandiflorus 'Fuji Blue'
(above)

Platycodon grandiflorus cultivar
(right)

P

P

*Plectranthus
neochilus* (above)

This is one of a group
of species allied to
Plectranthus caninus
that range from south-
eastern Africa to south-
ern Arabia. Its flowers
are pale lavender on
short dense spikes that
terminate in a group of
purplish bud bracts, cast
off as flowers open. The
fleshy leaves have a
strong musky smell.
They have a mat-form-
ing habit of growth and
are fairly drought toler-
ant. ZONES 10–12.

PLECTRANTHUS

This genus contains more than 350 species of annuals, perennials
and shrubs. Most are rather frost tender and several species are
grown as house plants, others as garden ornamentals or herbs.
They generally have succulent or semi-succulent stems. The
leaves, too, are often fleshy and frequently oval to heart-shaped.
The flowers are small and tubular, sometimes borne in showy
spikes that extend above the foliage.

CULTIVATION

Plant in moist, well-drained soil in part-shade. Protect from frost
and prolonged dry conditions. Propagate from seed or cuttings
or by layering. Many species are spreading and will self-layer.

PODOPHYLLUM

Although the 9 perennials in this genus have a superficial resemblance to trilliums, they are actually in the berberis family. Native to eastern North America, East Asia and the Himalayas, they have stout rhizomes that in early spring sprout large, peltate leaves up to 12 in (30 cm) across. The leaflets are broad with toothed edges and often lobed. Cup-shaped, upward-facing, 6- to 9-petalled flowers soon follow. They are around 2 in (5 cm) wide, white or soft pink and are often followed by red berries up to 2 in (5 cm) across.

CULTIVATION

These essentially woodland plants prefer moist, humus-rich, well-drained soil and dappled shade. Most tolerate hard frosts provided the rootstock is insulated. Propagate from seed or by division.

Podophyllum peltatum (below)
MAY APPLE

This is a popular eastern American wildflower, appearing before the leaves on deciduous forest trees. Deeply lobed, peltate leaves around 12 in (30 cm) long shelter creamy white blossoms resembling single roses, almost hidden under the leaves. Edible yellow fruit follow. It spreads rampantly to form a bold ground cover, so it is not for the small garden. Propagate by dividing the rhizomes in early spring. **ZONES 3–9.**

P

POGOSTEMON
PATCHOULI

Famed for their aromatic oils, which are used in perfumes and aromatherapy, the patchouli plants are native to tropical East Asia. They are shrubby with upright stems and have large, nettle-like leaves that are roughly heart-shaped with shallowly lobed edges. Their flowers are white, mauve or pink, and are carried on a typical mint-family verticillaster (whorled flower stem).

CULTIVATION

All species have tropical origins and demand warm, frost-free conditions. They prefer moist, humus-rich, well-drained soil in sun or part-shade. Propagate from seed or cuttings.

Pogostemon cablin

Native to Indonesia, the Philippines and Malaysia, this is the species most often cultivated. It has narrow leaves and hairy stems. Because it seldom flowers, seeds are rarely available so it is usually grown from cuttings. **Pogostemon heyneanus,** often grown as a substitute for *P. cablin*, has smooth stems and slightly bronze new growth, and flowers reliably. ZONES 11–12.

Pogostemon heyneanus (left)

POLEMONIUM

JACOB'S LADDER

This genus of around 25 species of annuals and perennials is distributed over the Arctic and temperate regions of the northern hemisphere. They form clumps of soft, bright green, ferny, pinnate leaves from which emerge upright stems topped with heads of short, tubular, bell-or funnel-shaped flowers usually in white or shades of blue or pink. Completely dormant in winter, they develop quickly in spring and are in flower by early summer.

CULTIVATION

Most species are very frost hardy and easily cultivated in moist, well-drained soil in sun or part-shade. Propagate annuals from seed and perennials from seed or cuttings of young shoots or by division. Some species self-sow freely.

Polemonium 'Brise d'Anjou' *(left)*

This cultivar of uncertain origin but clearly part of the *Polemonium caeruleum* complex, is distinguished by its neatly variegated foliage—the upper and lower edge of each leaflet has a narrow pale yellow stripe. ZONES 3–9.

Polemonium boreale *(right)*

NORTHERN JACOB'S LADDER

Found north of the Arctic tree line, this perennial species has basal leaves made up of 13 to 23, $^1/_2$ in (12 mm) leaflets. Its flower stems are 3–12 in (8–30 cm) tall, and the blue to purple flowers are about $^1/_2$ in (12 mm) long. It is a dwarf species for rock gardens or alpine troughs. ZONES 3–9.

Polemonium caeruleum (right)

Yellowy orange stamens provide a colorful contrast against the light purplish blue of this perennial's bell-shaped flowers when they open in summer. The flowers cluster among lance-shaped leaflets arranged in many pairs like the rungs of a ladder. The plant grows in a clump to a height and spread of up to 24 in (60 cm) or more. The stem is hollow and upright. A native of temperate Europe, it suits cooler climates. **ZONES 2–9.**

Polemonium delicatum (below)

SKUNKLEAF JACOB'S LADDER

This native of the Midwest and western USA has leaves less than 4 in (10 cm) long made up of 5 to 11, $^1\!/_2$–1 in (12–25 mm) long leaflets. The flowers are also small, blue to violet and open in summer. It is an excellent rockery species. **ZONES 6–9.**

Polemonium reptans
'Blue Pearl' *(right)*

Polemonium reptans

GREEK VALERIAN, CREEPING
POLEMONIUM

This large perennial
species from eastern
USA forms a 12–24 in
(30–60 cm) high foli-
age clump with leaves
composed of 7 to 19
leaflets. The inflores-
cence is inclined to be
lax and the flowers,
which are bright blue,
are large: $^1/_2$–1 in
(12–25 mm) in diam-
eter. Low-growing and
spreading forms have
given rise to several
cultivars. **'Blue Pearl'**
grows to 10 in (25 cm)
tall and has bright blue
flowers. ZONES 4–9.

Polemonium 'Sapphire' *(right)*

A cultivar probably de-
rived from *Polemonium
reptans*, P. 'Sapphire'
forms a compact clump
of foliage with flower
stems 12–15 in
(30–38 cm) tall. The
flowers are light blue
and about $^1/_2$ in (12 mm)
wide. ZONES 4–9.

POLYGONATUM
SOLOMON'S SEAL

The 30 or so species in this genus of forest-floor perennials are distributed all over the temperate zones of the northern hemisphere. The most likely explanation of the common name is that the scars left on the creeping rhizomes, after the flowering stems die off in autumn, are thought to resemble the 6-pointed star associated with kings Solomon and David. King Solomon is thought to have first discovered the medicinal qualities of the plants, which are credited with healing wounds. The distilled sap of the rhizomes is still used in the cosmetics industry. The plants' fresh greenery and delicate white flowers make them favorites for planting in woodland gardens.

CULTIVATION
They need rich, moist soil and a shady spot. Cut back to the rhizome in autumn as they are completely dormant in winter. Propagate from seed or by division of the rhizomes in spring or autumn.

*Polygonatum
falcatum* (below)

With stems to 3 ft (1 m) long and long, rather narrow leaves, this Japanese and Korean species is not as attractive as some of the others. Its flowers tend to be small and are carried singly rather than in small clusters. The stems are red tinted. ZONES 6–9.

Polygonatum × hybridum (right)

This hybrid species does best in cool to cold areas. In spring, the white, green-tipped, tubular flowers hang down from the drooping 3 ft (1 m) stems at the leaf axils. It is difficult to grow from seed. **ZONES 6–9.**

Polygonatum multiflorum (below)

This Eurasian species has arching 3 ft (1 m) stems with large, broad leaves that point upwards very distinctly. Its flowers are cream with green tips in 2- to 5-flowered clusters. It has vigorous rhizomes and can be invasive. Although often found on limestone soil in the wild, it does not seem fussy about soil type. **ZONES 4–9.**

P

Polygonatum odoratum (right)

From Europe, Russia, Japan and the Caucasus, this perennial to 3 ft (1 m) tall has long, hairless leaves in 2 rows. The fragrant, tubular, white flowers have green tips and appear in late spring and early summer. They are followed by rounded black fruit. **ZONES 4–9.**

PONTEDERIA
PICKEREL WEED

The 5 or so aquatic perennials in this genus are all native to river shallows in North and South America. They have distinctive, lance-shaped leaves and bell-shaped, usually blue flowers in terminal spikes. The Latin name has nothing to do with ponds; it honors Guilio Pontedera (1688–1757), who was a professor of botany at the University of Padua in Italy.

CULTIVATION
Easily grown, pickerel weed flourishes in almost any climate, from cold to subtropical. Plant it in full sun in up to 10 in (25 cm) of water. Only the spent flower stems need pruning, to encourage successive batches of flowers from spring to autumn. Propagate from seed or by division in spring.

Pontederia cordata
(left)
PICKEREL RUSH

This species grows on the east coast of North America. A very frost-hardy, marginal water plant, it grows to 30 in (75 cm) with a 18 in (45 cm) spread. Its tapered, heart-shaped leaves are dark green and shiny. In summer, it produces intense blue flowers in dense, terminal spikes. ZONES 3–10.

P

PORTEA

This bromeliad genus has 7 species of rock or ground dwellers native to Brazil. Generally they are large rosette-forming perennials with stiff-spined green leaves that vary in height from 30 in (75 cm) to over 6 ft (1.8 m) when in flower.

CULTIVATION

Plants enjoy bright light and warm conditions. Plant in humus-rich, loamy soil. Some species are cold sensitive. Propagate from offsets or seed.

Portea petropolitana
(right & above right)
syns *Aechmea petropolitana, Portea gardneri, Streptocalyx podantha*

This is a large species with varying lengths of branches and flower stalks. The plant is stemless, with thick, heavily spined leaves, and reaches over 3 ft (1 m) in height when in bloom. Narrow, blue-violet flowers are 1½ in (35 mm) long and the inflorescences upright in length to 15 in (38 cm) long. ZONES 9–12.

PORTULACA

There are about 100 species of semi-succulent annuals or perennials in this genus, indigenous to the warm, dry regions of the world. The fleshy leaves vary in color from white to green or red, but it is for their cup-shaped flowers that they are grown, which are white, yellow, apricot, pink, purple or scarlet and resembling roses in form.

CULTIVATION

They are easily grown in all climates. In cooler areas they should not be planted out until the danger of frost has passed. Because they are plants of the deserts they need sun, well-drained soil and only occasional watering. Propagate from seed in spring or cuttings in summer. Check for aphids.

Portulaca grandiflora (above)
ROSE MOSS, SUN PLANT

Native to South America and one of the few annual succulents, this low-growing plant reaches 8 in (20 cm) high and spreads to 6 in (15 cm). It has small, lance-shaped, fleshy, bright green leaves like beads on their reddish stems. Its large, open flowers, usually double and borne in summer, are 3 in (8 cm) wide and come in bright colors including yellow, pink, red or orange. The flowers close at night and on cloudy days. It is suitable as a ground cover or in a rockery or border. ZONES 10–11.

P

POTENTILLA
CINQUEFOIL

This genus of approximately 500 perennials, annuals, biennials and deciduous shrubs is indigenous mainly to the northern hemisphere, from temperate to arctic regions. Most species have 5-parted leaves (hence the common name cinquefoil), and range from only 1 in (25 mm) or so tall to about 18 in (45 cm). They bear clusters of 1 in (25 mm), rounded, bright flowers in profusion through spring and summer. Some *Potentilla* species are used medicinally: the root bark of one species is said to stop nose bleeds and even internal bleeding.

CULTIVATION
Plant all species in well-drained, fertile soil. Lime does not upset them. Although the species all thrive in full sun in temperate climates, the colors of pink, red and orange cultivars will be brighter if protected from very strong sun. Perennials are generally frost hardy. Propagate by division in spring, or from seed or by division in autumn. Shrubs can be propagated from seed in autumn or from cuttings in summer.

Potentilla cuneata
(above)

This Himalayan perennial develops a woody base and can form a rather upright mound or be a low, spreading plant. Its leaves are trifoliate, up to 6 in (15 cm) long, leathery, deep green above and blue-green below. The flowers are bright yellow, 1 in (25 mm) wide and carried singly. ZONES 5–9.

P

Potentilla alba *(left)*

This low, spreading perennial from Europe rarely exceeds 4 in (10 cm) high. It has hand-shaped basal leaves with 5 leaflets, each up to $2^1/_2$ in (6 cm) long. The young growth has a dense covering of fine hairs that gives it a silver sheen. The white flowers are 1 in (25 mm) wide, in clusters of up to 5 blooms. ZONES 5–9.

Potentilla megalantha *(left)*

This perennial from Japan forms a mound of foliage about 12 in (30 cm) wide. Its leaves are trifoliate with hairy undersides. Its $1^1/_2$ in (35 mm) wide, bright yellow flowers are carried singly and are produced in summer. ZONES 5–9.

Potentilla nepalensis *(left)*

A profusion of flowers in shades of pink or apricot with cherry red centers appears throughout summer on the slim branching stems of this Himalayan perennial. With bright green, strawberry-like leaves, this species grows to 12 in (30 cm) or more high and twice that in width. **'Miss Willmott'** is a 18 in (45 cm) high cultivar with deep pink flowers. ZONES 5–9.

P

Potentilla nepalensis
'Miss Willmott' *(right)*

Potentilla neumanniana
(right)

syn. *Potentilla verna*

This herbaceous, mat-forming perennial grows to 4 in (10 cm) in height. Golden yellow flowers to 1 in (25 mm) are borne from spring onwards. ZONES 5–9.

Potentilla × tonguei *(right)*

This hybrid derives from the Himalayan *Potentilla nepalensis* crossed with **P. anglica**, a European species. It is a sprawling perennial with attractive leaves and abundant 1 in (25 mm) wide, tangerine-colored flowers in summer. If spent flower stalks are trimmed, the plant usually responds with more flowers. ZONES 5–9.

PRATIA

This genus includes 20 species of evergreen perennials. They have multiple branching stems and little toothed leaves. A profusion of starry flowers is followed by globular berries. Most are carpet forming and make excellent rockery specimens, but tend to over-run the garden.

CULTIVATION

Ranging from very frost hardy to frost hardy, these plants generally enjoy damp but porous soil, total sun or part-shade and protection from the elements. Water liberally during the growth period and sparingly in winter. Some species are susceptible to slugs if over-moist. Propagate by division or from seed in autumn.

Pratia perpusilla
(below)

The specific name of this coastal New Zealand species is Latin for 'extremely small'. Its prostrate stems which root at the nodes are very thin and weak, and the narrow, toothed, slightly hairy leaves are little more than $^1/_8$ in (3 mm) long. The $^1/_4$ in (6 mm) long white flowers are held just above the foliage on very slender stems. **ZONES 8–10.**

PRIMULA
PRIMROSE

This well-known and much-loved genus of perennials has about 400 species, found throughout the temperate regions of the northern hemisphere, although most densely concentrated in China and the Himalayas. They also occur on high mountains in the tropics, extending as far south as Papua New Guinea. They are mainly rhizomatous, though some have poorly developed rhizomes and are short lived (*Primula malacoides,* for example). The foliage is usually crowded into a basal tuft or rosette, and the leaves are mostly broadest toward their tips, with toothed or scalloped margins. The flowering stems vary in form, but most often carry successive whorls or a single umbel of flowers. In a few species, the flowers are tightly crowded into a terminal head or a short spike, or they emerge singly or in small groups from among the leaves on short stalks. Flower shape, size and color vary so much that it is hard to generalize, though basically all have tubular flowers that open into a funnel or flat disc with five or more petals that are often notched at their tips.

CULTIVATION
Primulas like fertile, well-drained soil, part-shade and ample water. Propagate from seed in spring, early summer or autumn, by division or from root cuttings. Remove dead heads and old foliage after blooming. There is a primula for virtually every position and purpose.

Primula beesiana (above)

This candelabra-style primrose from western China has tapering, toothed-edged leaves, which together with their stems are up to 6 in (15 cm) long. The 24 in (60 cm) flower stems hold 5 to 7 whorls of yellow-eyed red-purple flowers. This deep-rooted species is not a bog plant but does require deep watering. ZONES 5–9.

Primula species (right)

Primula allionii
(left)

From the coastal ranges of France and Italy comes this low, evergreen perennial. The leaves, produced in basal rosettes, are sticky, hairy, gray-green and have toothed edges. In winter or early spring stems of up to 5 white, pink or rose flowers, each about 1 in (25 mm) across, rise above the foliage. Plants grow 4–6 in (10–15 cm) tall with a spread of about 8 in (20 cm). **ZONES 7–9.**

P

Primula auricula *(left)*

This small, central European perennial has yellow flowers in spring and furry leaves (hence the old common name, bear's ear—*auricula* means a 'little ear'). Garden varieties come in a wide range of colors. In the mid-eighteenth century a mutation resulted in flowers in shades of gray, pale green and almost black with centers covered with a white powder called 'paste'. Such flowers, called show auriculas, were once great favorites, but now have few devotees. **ZONES 3–9.**

Primula capitata
subsp. *mooreana*
(right)

This northern Indian subspecies differs from the species in having white powdering on the underside of the foliage and a slightly different leaf shape. Its leaves are up to 6 in (15 cm) long and it has drumstick heads of violet flowers on 12 in (30 cm) stems. **ZONES 5–9.**

Primula bulleyana

This western Chinese candelabra primrose is very similar to *Primula beesiana* except that its leaves have reddish midribs and its flowers are bright yellow. It dies down completely over winter. **'Ceperley Hybrid'** has yellow, orange and pink flowers. **ZONES 6–9.**

Primula bulleyana
'Ceperley Hybrid'
(right)

Primula cockburniana *(right)*

Native to China, this candelabra primrose has relatively few 6 in (15 cm) toothed-edged leaves and 12–15 in (30–38 cm) stems with 3 to 5 whorls of orange-red flowers. It is less robust than other candelabra primroses but makes up for that with its vivid color. **ZONES 5–9.**

P

Primula denticulata (left)

DRUMSTICK PRIMROSE

The botanical name of this very frost-hardy Himalayan perennial refers to the toothed profile of the mid-green, broadly lanceolate leaves. A neat and vigorous grower, it reaches a height and spread of 12 in (30 cm). In early to mid-spring its open, yellow-centered flowers of pink, purple or lilac crowd in rounded terminal clusters atop thick hairy stems. **Primula denticulata subsp. alba** has white flowers usually on slightly shorter stems than the species. ZONES 6–9.

Primula denticulata
subsp. *alba (below)*

Primula forrestii (right)

This Chinese species is often found growing in
soil pockets among limestone rocks. It has woody
rhizomes and $1^1/_2$–3 in (3.5–8 cm) leaves with
toothed edges and powdering on the undersides.
The flowers are bright yellow and are carried in
polyanthus-like heads on 6–8 in (15–20 cm)
stems. **ZONES 6–9.**

Primula elatior (below)
OXLIP

This European species has 2–8 in (5–20 cm) long
leaves with finely hairy undersides. Its 4–12 in
(10–30 cm) flower stems carry a heavy crop of
long-tubed, 1 in (25 mm) wide yellow to orange-
yellow flowers. **ZONES 5–9.**

P

Primula sinopurpurea (below)

This late-flowering Chinese species has very distinctive, nearly smooth-edged, narrow, bright green leaves that are 2–12 in (5–30 cm) long. It produces its purple-pink flowers when the stems are around 12 in (30 cm) tall, but the stem continues to grow as the seed matures and eventually reaches 30 in (75 cm). **ZONES 5–9.**

Primula florindae (below)

TIBETAN PRIMROSE

In spring this perennial carries up to 60 bright yellow flowers to an umbel, hanging like little bells against a backdrop of broad, mid-green leaves with serrated edges. It grows 24–36 in (60–90 cm) high and likes wet conditions, thriving by the edge of a pond or stream. **ZONES 6–9.**

Primula malacoides (left)

FAIRY PRIMROSE

This is a native of China. Small, open flowers bloom in spiral masses on this frost-tender perennial, sometimes grown as an annual. The single or double flowers range from white to pink to magenta. Its oval, light green leaves and erect stem have a hairy texture. It reaches a height and spread of 12 in (30 cm) or more. **ZONES 8–11.**

P

Primula frondosa
(right)

This species has 4 in (10 cm) long, toothed-edged leaves with powdering on the undersides. Its flower stems are 2–6 in (5–15 cm) tall and carry as few as 1 or as many as 30, $^1/_2$ in (12 mm) wide yellow-eyed lilac to purple flowers. **ZONES 5–9.**

Primula juliae
(below)

This low-growing, rosette-forming miniature primrose has 4 in (10 cm) long, dark green leaves. It bears bright purple, yellow-centered flowers and has given rise to a series of garden varieties. **ZONES 5–9.**

Primula poissonii (left)

This is a Chinese species with rather open rosettes of 6–8 in (15–20 cm) long, blue-green leaves. Its flower stems are up to 18 in (45 cm) tall with 2 to 6 whorls of yellow-eyed deep pink to crimson flowers. It blooms late, prefers wet soil and can be somewhat sparse. **ZONES 6–9.**

Primula japonica (below)
JAPANESE PRIMROSE

Forming a clump up to 24 in (60 cm) high and 18 in (45 cm) across, this fully frost-hardy perennial flowers in tiers on tall, sturdy stems like a candelabra. Its shiny flowers are borne in spring and early summer, and range through pink, crimson and purple to nearly pure white, usually with a distinct eye of another color. The leaves are elliptical, serrated and pale green. This species does best in a moist situation. **'Postford White'** offers a white, flattish round flower. **ZONES 5–10.**

Primula pulverulenta *(right)*

This is a Chinese candelabra primrose with deep green, wrinkled leaves 12 in (30 cm) or more long. Its flower stems are 3 ft (1 m) tall, white powdered with whorls of 1 in (25 mm) wide flowers. The flowers are white, pink or red with a contrasting eye. **ZONES 6–9.**

Primula obconica *(below)*

POISON PRIMROSE

Dense flower clusters grow in an umbellate arrangement on hairy, erect stems of this perennial. Native to China, it grows to 12 in (30 cm) high and wide and flowers from winter through spring. The yellow-eyed, flattish flowers, 1 in (25 mm) across, range from white to pink to purple. The light green leaves are elliptical and serrated. **ZONES 8–11.**

P

Primula, Polyanthus Group *(left)*
syn. *Primula* × *polyantha*

These fully frost-hardy perennials, sometimes grown as annuals, reach 12 in (30 cm) in spread and height. Large, flat, scented flowers in every color but green bloom on dense umbels from winter to spring. Polyanthus are cultivars derived from *Primula vulgaris* crossed with *P. veris*, and have been grown since the seventeenth century. **'Garryarde Guinevere'** has pink flowers and bronze foliage. ZONES 6–10.

Primula, Polyanthus Group cultivar *(left)*

Primula 'Wanda'
(left)

This little plant disappears entirely over winter and begins to burst into flower as the new foliage develops. The leaves are deep green, heavily crinkled and about 3 in (8 cm) long. The short-stemmed flowers are deep magenta to purple with a yellow eye. It is an easily grown plant that quickly forms a small clump. ZONES 6–9.

Primula polyneura
(right)

This Chinese species
has rounded, light
green, softly hairy
leaves 2–10 in
(5–25 cm) wide on
wiry stems. Its flower
stems are 8–18 in
(20–45 cm) tall with
1, 2 or several whorls
of deep pink to purple-
red flowers. It spreads
freely. **ZONES 5–9.**

Primula sieboldii *(left)*

This species from Japan and northeast Asia has
large, scalloped-edged leaves 4–15 in (10–38 cm)
long. Its flowers, which may be white, pink or
purple, are carried in 6- to 20-flowered heads on
6–15 in (10–38 cm) stems. There are several cultivated forms, grown mainly in Japan. **ZONES 5–9.**

Primula veris *(right)*
COWSLIP

A European wildflower
of open woods and
meadows, this species
blooms a little later than
the common primrose
does. It is easily distinguished by the clusters
of flowers carried on
6 in (15 cm) tall stalks
and its sweeter scent.
This plant is easy to
grow. **ZONES 5–9.**

P

Primula vialii *(left)*

This 24 in (60 cm) tall perennial species from Yunnan Province in China is remarkable for carrying its purple flowers in short spikes, quite unlike any other primula. The buds are bright crimson, giving the inflorescence a two-toned effect. The foliage is lush and bright green. It needs a cool, moist climate. **ZONES 7–9.**

Primula vulgaris *(below left)*
ENGLISH PRIMROSE, COMMON PRIMROSE

This common European wildflower likes its cultivated conditions to resemble the cool woodland of its native environment. Low growing to 8 in (20 cm) and usually frost hardy, it produces a carpet of bright flowers in spring. The flattish flowers are pale yellow with dark eyes (but the garden forms come in every color), and bloom singly on hairy stems above rosettes of crinkled, lance-shaped, serrated leaves. Both the leaves and the flowers are edible. **'Gigha White'** has white flowers with yellow centers. **ZONES 6–9.**

Primula vulgaris
'Gigha White' *(below)*

*Protasparagus
densiflorus* 'Myersii'
(right)

**Protasparagus
densiflorus**
syn. *Asparagus
densiflorus*
EMERALD ASPARAGUS FERN

Although frequently
used as an indoor plant,
this South African
species is hardy to
about 25°F (−4°C) and
can be grown outdoors
in many areas. It pro-
duces sprays of 24–36 in
(60–90 cm) long, wiry,
rather spiny stems cov-
ered with very fine, al-
most needle-like bright
green leaves. Small but
fragrant white flowers
are followed by bright
red berries. **'Myersii'**,
the foxtail fern, has
mainly upright stems
with dense foliage
cover, which gives
them a tapering,
cylindrical shape.
'Sprengeri' is a sprawling perennial with
bright green leaves and
bears abundant tiny,
white, heavily scented
flowers, usually fol-
lowed by red berries.
ZONES 9–11.

PROTASPARAGUS
syn. *Asparagus*
ASPARAGUS FERN

Primarily native to southern Africa, these tuberous perennials
have now been separated from the true rhizomatous asparagus,
although some botanists disagree with this reclassification. Widely
grown as garden plants in warm-temperate to tropical areas,
they are popular house plants everywhere. Grown primarily for
their sprays of fern-like foliage, they may be shrubby or semi-
climbing. Their stems are often protected by small but vicious
thorns. The tiny white, cream or green flowers are inconspicuous
but the red or black berries can be a feature.

CULTIVATION

They are undemanding plants that are tolerant of neglect, hence
their popularity as house plants. Grow in moist, well-drained,
humus-rich soil in sun or part-shade. Propagate from seed or by
division, but do not divide into very small pieces as plants so
treated seldom recover quickly.

P

PRUNELLA
SELF-HEAL

This is a genus of 7 species of semi-evergreen perennials from Europe, Asia, North Africa and North America. They form low, spreading clumps and bear opposite pairs of ovate to oblong, sometimes deeply lobed leaves. Erect flowering stems bear whorled spikes of 2-lipped tubular flowers in shades of white, pink or purple.

CULTIVATION

Most species spread from creeping stems that readily take root at the nodes, making them excellent ground covering plants for creating large drifts. They are fully frost hardy and will grow in sun or part-shade in moist, well-drained soil. Propagate from seed or by division in spring or autumn.

Prunella grandiflora
LARGE SELF-HEAL

Purple, 2-lipped flowers grow in erect spikes above leafy stubs in spring and summer. A native of Europe, it is good for ground cover or rock gardens, having a spread and height of 18 in (45 cm). **'Loveliness'** has soft mauve flowers. ZONES 5–9.

Prunella grandiflora 'Loveliness' *(below)*

PSYLLIOSTACHYS

STATICE

Psylliostachys
suworowii (below)
syn. *Limonium*
suworowii

RUSSIAN STATICE, RAT'S TAIL
STATICE

Native to Iran, Afghanistan and central Asia, this species has sticky 2–6 in (5–15 cm) leaves and relatively large pink flowers on wavy, 6 in (15 cm) spikes. ZONES 6–10.

This genus of 6 to 8 species of annuals was once included with *Statice* (*Limonium*), but is now classified separately. Rarely over 15 in (38 cm) tall in flower, the plants form a clump of basal leaves, sometimes hairy, that are often deeply cut so they are almost pinnate. The tiny, papery flowers are white, pink or mauve, and borne on upright spikes that only rarely branch. They are dried or used fresh in floral arrangements.

CULTIVATION

Plant in moist, well-drained soil in full sun and allow to dry off after flowering. Propagate from seed.

P

P

PTILOTUS

This is a genus of around 100 species of annuals, perennials and subshrubs from Australasia. Their leaves are often rather thick and heavy and are stemless. The foliage tends to be red tinted and frequently has wavy edges. The flowers are tiny, usually a shade of green, pink or purple, and are carried on shaggy spikes up to 6 in (15 cm) long.

CULTIVATION

Apart from being frost tender, they are easily cultivated in any well-drained soil in full sun. Propagate the annuals from seed, the perennials and shrubs from seed or cuttings.

Ptilotus manglesii (above)

This is an Australian species that flowers from late winter to early summer when it is covered in rounded, 4 in (10 cm) spikes of pink to purple flowers. Sometimes grown as an annual, it is a short-lived spreading perennial that grows to around 12 in (30 cm) high. The leaves vary in shape: the basal leaves are oval and up to 3 in (8 cm) long, while the upper leaves are narrow. ZONES 9–11.

Pulmonaria longifolia
'Lewis Palmer' *(above)*

Pulmonaria longifolia

This European species has particularly large leaves. They are up to 20 in (50 cm) long, but only 3 in (8 cm) wide, and usually white-spotted. There is a sparse covering of fine hairs on both the upper and lower surfaces of the leaves. The flowers are blue to violet and start to open early in spring, well before the foliage is fully grown. '**Lewis Palmer**' has wider, faintly spotted leaves and pink-tinted pale blue flowers. ZONES 6–9.

PULMONARIA
LUNGWORT

This is a Eurasian genus that consists of 14 species of perennial, rhizomatous, forget-me-not-like plants. The common name refers to their former medicinal use, not their appearance. The most common species are low, spreading plants 6–10 in (15–25 cm) high with a spread of 24 in (60 cm) or more. The simple, oval to lance-shaped leaves are sometimes slightly downy and often spotted silver-white. From very early spring, small deep blue, pink or white flowers open from pink or white buds.

CULTIVATION
These woodland plants are easily grown in cool, moist, humus-rich soil in light shade. All are very frost hardy. Propagate from seed or cuttings or by division.

P

Pulmonaria 'Mawson's Blue'

(left)

syn. *Pulmonaria* 'Mawson's Variety'

'Mawson's Blue' is a deep blue-flowered deciduous perennial with narrow 12 in (30 cm) unspotted leaves and very bristly flower stems. It grows to a height of 15 in (38 cm) with an 18 in (45 cm) spread. ZONES 5–9.

Pulmonaria officinalis

JERUSALEM COWSLIP, COMMON LUNGWORT

Often recommended by herbalists as a treatment for coughs, bronchitis and other breathing disorders, this evergreen perennial is widely grown as an ornamental. It has heavily white-spotted 4–6 in (10–15 cm) long leaves and deep blue flowers on stems up to 12 in (30 cm) tall. **'Sissinghurst White'** is an early-blooming, white-flowered cultivar that does not develop pink tints as the flowers age; it grows up to 12 in (30 cm) tall with large leaves. ZONES 6–9.

Pulmonaria officinalis 'Sissinghurst White'

(left)

Pulmonaria saccharata

JERUSALEM SAGE, BETHLEHEM SAGE

This evergreen perennial has heavily spotted, hairy, 10 in (25 cm) leaves and has given rise to numerous cultivars with flowers in white and all shades of pink and blue. **'Highdown'** is 12 in (30 cm) tall with silver-frosted leaves and pendulous clusters of blue flowers. The cultivars of the **Argentea Group** have silver leaves and red flowers that age to dark purple. **ZONES 3–9.**

Pulmonaria saccharata 'Highdown' *(right)*

Pulmonaria rubra

RED LUNGWORT

This evergreen perennial has leaves up to 18 in (45 cm) long, only rarely spotted and relatively hairless. The flower stems are covered with fine bristles and bear purple to blue flowers. Near red-flowered forms occur and there are several cultivars in shades of pink and white. **'Redstart'** is up to 15 in (40 cm) high with bright green foliage and large pinkish red flowers. **ZONES 6–9.**

Pulmonaria rubra 'Redstart' *(right)*

P

PULSATILLA
PASQUE FLOWER

This genus contains 30 species of spring-flowering, deciduous perennials from Eurasia and North America. They form mounds of very finely divided, almost ferny foliaged rosettes. The leaves and flower stems are covered with downy silver-gray hairs. The general effect is that of a hairy anemone with large flowers. The flower color range includes white, pink, purple and red.

CULTIVATION
Most often grown in rockeries, these very frost-hardy plants are also suitable for borders and troughs and prefer a moist, gritty, scree soil in sun or part-shade. They do best with cool to cold winters and cool summers and tend to be short lived in mild areas. Propagate from seed or by division.

Pulsatilla halleri
subsp. *slavica (below)*

Pulsatilla halleri

This species has white, lavender or purple flowers that open from purple-pink to purple buds. Its new growth is a light green and very hairy. The first flowers are usually open before the early leaves are fully unfurled. The whole plant is covered in fine hairs and has a very silky feel. **Pulsatilla halleri subsp. *slavica*** has deep violet flowers and woolly foliage that is less finely divided than that of the species. ZONES 5–9.

Pulsatilla alpina subsp. *apiifolia*
(right)

This is a yellow-flowered form of a normally white-flowered species found through much of southern Europe and the Caucasus. It usually occurs on slightly acid soil and has flower stems to 18 in (45 cm) tall with 2 in (5 cm) wide flowers. **ZONES 5–9.**

Pulsatilla *bungeana* (right)

This Siberian species is very small with flower stems scarcely 2 in (5 cm) high. Its flowers are upward facing, bell-shaped and violet-blue when young. They are a little over $1/2$ in (12 mm) wide. **ZONES 4–9.**

P

Pulsatilla montana (above)

This species from Switzerland, Romania and Bulgaria has very finely divided leaves, each of the 3 main leaflets having up to 150 lobes. The flowers are $1^1/_2$ in (35 mm) wide, deep blue to purple, and bell-shaped. They are carried on 6 in (15 cm) stems that continue to grow after flowering and reach 18 in (45 cm) tall when the seed ripens. **ZONES 6–9.**

Pulsatilla vulgaris (left)
syns *Anemone pulsatilla, A. vulgaris*

Nodding, 6-petalled flowers bloom in spring on this species from Europe. The yellow centers of the flowers are a stark color contrast to the petals, which can range through white, pink and red to purple. The finely divided leaves are pale green and very hairy. Reaching 10 in (25 cm) in height and spread, the species is good in a sunny rock garden. Avoid disturbing the roots. **'Alba'** has pure white flowers and needs protection from sun and frost for the flowers to last. **'Rode Klokke'** (syn. 'Rote Glocke') is a free-flowering form with dark red blooms. **'Rubra'** has purplish red or rusty flowers. **ZONES 5–9.**

P

Pulsatilla vulgaris
'Alba' *(right)*

Pulsatilla vulgaris
'Rubra' *(right)*

P

PUYA

This large genus of terrestrial bromeliads from South America consists of 170 species. They include the largest of all bromeliads, some species growing to about 20 ft (6 m). They are cultivated in gardens as shrubs. The leaves stand out boldly from a basal rosette and they often have hollow stems. Large blue, purple or yellow flowers are held on unbranched spikes or in dense panicles. The fruit are capsules that enclose winged seeds.

CULTIVATION

These plants can grow in a wide range of soils provided they are well drained, and prefer a sunny position. As with all members of the bromeliad family, keep them away from footpaths because the leaves bear sharp spines along their margins. Prune to remove damaged foliage and propagate by division of offsets or from seed. In cool climates they can be grown in a greenhouse.

Puya alpestris
(above)

Although plants are often sold under this name, those in cultivation are usually *Puya berteroniana*. The true species is a native of southern and central Chile. It grows 4–5 ft (1.2–1.5 m) tall with spine-edged leaves up to 24 in (60 cm) long. The leaves form dense rosettes from which emerge strong flower stems topped with pyramidal heads of tubular blue green flowers. ZONES 8–9.

Puya berteroniana
(right)

This species from Chile has blue-green foliage. The stems are prostrate, and the 3 ft (1 m) long narrow leaves are strap-like and arching. During summer, metallic blue flowers with vivid orange stamens form dense panicles up to 6–10 ft (1.8–3 m) tall at the ends of long stems. The rosette of leaves dies after flowering, leaving offsets to carry on. This plant benefits from mulch to prevent water evaporation from its roots. **ZONES 9–10.**

Puya mirabilis
(right)

Native to Argentina and Bolivia, this species has 24–30 in (60–75 cm) long leaves that are silvery brown with fine spines along the edges. Its flower stems are around 5 ft (1.5 m) tall and the flowers are green to white. **ZONES 9–10.**

QUESNELIA

This bromeliad genus consists of 15 species of stemless, evergreen perennials found originally in rocky outcrops in eastern Brazil. Some species are also epiphytic. They have a medium-sized rosette of lance-shaped, stiff, spiny leaves. The inflorescences, which are either upright or hanging, are composed of tubular or ovoid flowers that appear among showy bracts.

CULTIVATION
These frost-tender plants prefer part-shade and coarse, humus-rich, moist but well-drained soil. They need the protection of a greenhouse where temperatures drop below 55°F (13°C). Water moderately, but reduce watering levels over the winter period. Propagate from seed or offsets.

Quesnelia liboniana
(above)

This species features navy blue flowers and orange-red bracts. It is a stemless plant that grows to 30 in (75 cm) high. The foliage forms a tube-shaped rosette composed of light green leaves with gray scales on the undersides and spines on the leaf edges. ZONES 11–12.

Q

RAMONDA

This genus from Spain, the Pyrenees and the Balkans contains 3 species of evergreen perennials that have rosettes of hairy, usually wrinkled leaves with toothed, wavy edges. Doing well in rock gardens or in cracks in stone walls, they are also grown for their brightly colored, 4- to 5-petalled flowers, which appear in late spring and early summer.

CULTIVATION

Excessive water in the leaf rosettes may cause rotting, so these plants are best grown on an angle in part-shade and very well-drained, humus-rich soil. Propagate from seed or cuttings.

Ramonda nathaliae (right)

This species, which reaches a height and spread of 4 in (10 cm), bears panicles of flat, 4-petalled, deep purple flowers with orange-yellow centers. The mid- to dark green leaves, hairier on the undersides than on top, grow to 2 in (5 cm) in length. ZONES 6–9.

R

Ranunculus acris
MEADOW BUTTERCUP

This clump-forming perennial from Europe and western Asia has wiry stems with lobed and cut leaves. Panicles of saucer-shaped, bright yellow flowers appear in mid-summer. It grows from 8–36 in (20–90 cm) in height. **'Flore Pleno'** has double, rosetted, golden yellow flowers. ZONES 5–9.

Ranunculus cortusifolius (below)

Found on the Atlantic islands of the Azores, Canaries and Madeira, this species has thick, rounded, leathery basal leaves with toothed edges and shallow lobes. The flower stems, up to 4 ft (1.2 m) tall, bear reduced leaves and many-flowered corymbs of 2 in (5 cm) wide bright yellow flowers. ZONES 9–10.

RANUNCULUS
BUTTERCUP

Ranunculus acris 'Flore Pleno' *(above)*

This genus of some 400 annuals and perennials is distributed throughout temperate regions worldwide. They are grown for their colorful flowers, which are bowl- or cup-shaped, 5-petalled and yellow, white, red, orange or pink. The name derives from the Latin for 'frog', due to the tendency of some species to grow in bogs or shallow water. Two species of buttercups are popular folk cures for arthritis, sciatica, rheumatism and skin conditions, including the removal of warts.

CULTIVATION
Most species of *Ranunculus* are easy to grow and thrive in well-drained soil, cool, moist conditions and sunny or shady locations. They are mostly fully frost hardy. Propagate from fresh seed or by division in spring or autumn. Water well through the growing season and allow to dry out after flowering. Keep an eye out for powdery mildew and for attacks by slugs, snails and aphids.

Ranunculus ficaria (below)

LESSER CELANDINE, PILEWORT

From southwestern Asia, Europe and northwestern Africa, this perennial has single, almost cup-shaped, bright yellow flowers that appear in spring. It reaches only 2 in (5 cm) in height, and has glossy green leaves with silver or gold markings; the leaves die down after the flowers appear. 'Albus' has single, creamy white flowers with glossy petals. 'Brazen Hussy' has deep bronze-green leaves and shiny, deep golden yellow flowers with bronze under-sides. ZONES 5–10.

Ranunculus gramineus (above)

With hairy, bluish green leaves shaped like grass, this clump-forming perennial from south-western Europe has a compact spread and grows 18 in (45 cm) tall. In late spring and early summer it produces yellow, cup-shaped flowers. Plant it in rich soil. ZONES 7–10.

Ranunculus lyallii (below)

MT COOK LILY, GIANT MOUNTAIN BUTTERCUP, MOUNTAIN LILY

Native to New Zealand's South Island, this thicket-forming perennial grows to 3 ft (1 m) tall. Its broad, leathery leaves can reach 8 in (20 cm) wide and are lustrous deep green. Glossy, white, cup-shaped flowers appear in clusters in summer. Moderately frost hardy, it can be difficult to grow. ZONES 7–9.

R

RAOULIA

VEGETABLE SHEEP

This is a genus of about 20 species of evergreen perennials or subshrubs confined to New Zealand. They mostly form slow-growing, ground-hugging carpets of downy leaves and in summer bear small white or pale yellow, papery textured daisies. They are excellent foliage plants for rock gardens or raised beds.

CULTIVATION

Most require a cool-temperate climate, moist, acidic, sharply drained soil and protection from heavy winter rain (other-wise they will rot). They prefer an open, sunny position or part-shade in warmer areas. Propagate from fresh seed or by division in spring.

Raoulia haastii

(right)

This frost-hardy peren-nial grows to only ½ in (12 mm) in height with a 12 in (30 cm) spread. The pale green, silky leaves overlap slightly in dense cushions. Yel-low flowerheads appear in spring. ZONES 7–9.

Raoulia australis

(above)

syn. Raoulia lutescens

GOLDEN SCABWEED

Suitable for rock gar-dens, this prostrate, mat-forming perennial native to New Zealand lays down a solid carpet of silvery leaves ½ in (12 mm) deep over a 10 in (25 cm) spread. In summer it produces minuscule flowerheads of fluffy yellow blooms. ZONES 7–9.

Raoulia eximia (left)

This perennial makes tight hummocks of growth 3 ft (1 m) across and completely covered with gray hairs. In late spring or summer it bears yellowish white flowerheads. It grows to only 2 in (5 cm) in height. ZONES 7–9.

R

Rehmannia elata *(above & below)*
syn. *Rehmannia angulata* of gardens
CHINESE FOXGLOVE

This is the best known *Rehmannia*. It bears semi-
pendent, tubular, bright pink flowers from summer
to autumn and grows to 3 ft (1 m) high. Though
perennial, it is only short lived. ZONES 9–10.

REHMANNIA

From China, these perennials are sometimes classed with the foxgloves and the
snapdragons, or grouped as cousins of the
the African violet. The uncertainty is due
to the 2-lipped flowers, which look a bit
like foxgloves, snapdragons and African
violets. They all have an attractive shape
and delicate color, usually some shade of
cool pink with pink and gold at their
throats. The leaves are large, oblong,
veined and hairy, and form basal rosettes.

CULTIVATION

Plant in a warm-temperate climate (or a
mildly warmed greenhouse in cool climates) in a sheltered spot in full sun and
in rich, leafy soil. Propagate from seed in
winter or cuttings in late autumn. Watch
for attack by slugs and snails.

R

REINECKEA

From Japan and China and allied to *Ophiopogon,* this genus contains a single species, an evergreen, rhizomatous perennial that has arching, glossy green leaves and small, scented flowers.

CULTIVATION

This frost-hardy plant prefers part-shade and moist but well-drained, humus-rich soil. Propagate from seed or by separation of the rhizomes. It may be prone to attack by snails and slugs.

R

Reineckea carnea
(above)

This species, which reaches 8 in (20 cm) in height with a 15 in (38 cm) spread, produces its almost cup-shaped, white or pink flowers to ½ in (12 mm) wide in late spring. If the summer months are warm, round berries will appear in autumn. ZONES 7–10.

Reseda odorata

(center right)

COMMON MIGNONETTE

From northern Africa, this moderately fast-growing annual is renowned for the strong fragrance of its flowers. The conical heads of tiny greenish flowers with touches of red, have dark orange stamens, but are otherwise unspectacular. They appear from summer to early autumn. The plants grow to 24 in (60 cm) high and about half that in spread. ZONES 6–10.

RESEDA
MIGNONETTE

This genus from Asia, Africa and Europe contains about 60 species of erect or spreading, branching annuals and perennials. They bear star-shaped, greenish white or greenish yellow flowers in spike-like racemes from spring to autumn. These are attractive to bees. Mignonette used to be a favorite with perfumers and the plant is still cultivated in France for its essential oils.

CULTIVATION
Plant in full sun or part-shade in well-drained, fertile, preferably alkaline soil. Deadheading will prolong flowering. Propagate from seed in late winter.

Reseda luteola

(below right)

WELD, WILD MIGNONETTE, DYER'S ROCKET

This biennial or short-lived perennial from Europe and central Asia yields a yellow dye that has been used as a paint pigment and in textile making. Weld grows to 4 ft (1.2 m) tall with narrow bright green leaves; almost half its height is made up of narrow, sometimes branched flower spikes, composed of whorls of small pale yellow to yellow-green flowers. The flowers appear in the second summer of growth, the first season being spent developing the large tap root. ZONES 6–10.

R

RHEUM

This genus contains 50 species of rhizomatous perennials, including the edible rhubarb and several ornamental plants. From eastern Europe and central Asia to the Himalayas and China, they are grown for their striking appearance and for their large basal leaves, which are coarsely toothed and have prominent midribs and veins. The minute, star-shaped flowers appear in summer and are followed by winged fruits.

Rheum palmatum
'Atrosanguineum'
(below)

CULTIVATION

These very frost-hardy plants prefer full sun or part-shade and deep, moist, humus-rich soil. Propagate from seed or by division, and watch out for slugs and crown rot.

Rheum officinale *(below)*

Sometimes used in weight control drugs and herbal medicine, this species from western China and Tibet can grow to 10 ft (3 m) tall. Its leaves are kidney-shaped to round, 5-lobed and up to 30 in (75 cm) wide. In summer it produces large branched heads of white to greenish white flowers. ZONES 7–10.

Rheum palmatum
CHINESE RHUBARB

This species bears panicles of small, dark red to creamy green flowers that open early in summer. It has deep green leaves with decoratively cut edges, and reaches up to 8 ft (2.4 m) in height and 6 ft (1.8 m) in spread. **'Atrosanguineum'** has dark pink flowers and crimson leaves that fade to dark green. ZONES 6–10.

Rhodanthe
chlorocephala
subsp. *rosea* (right)
syns *Helipterum*
roseum, Acroclinium
roseum

This annual grows to a
height of 24 in (60 cm)
and a spread of 6 in
(15 cm). The flower-
heads are composed
of white to pale pink
bracts surrounding a
yellow center, and close
in cloudy weather. It is
widely grown for cut
flowers. ZONES 9–11.

Rhodanthe 'Paper
Star' (below)

This cultivar has pro-
fuse white flowerheads.
While not very long
lasting as a cut flower,
it is an impressive,
long-flowering garden
specimen of semi-pros-
trate habit. ZONES 7–11.

RHODANTHE
STRAWFLOWER

The 40 species of erect annuals, perennials and subshrubs in
this genus all come from arid areas of Australia. Their daisy-like,
everlasting, pink, yellow or white summer flowers are keenly
sought for cut flowers and in dried arrangements. They have
alternate, mid-green to gray-green leaves.

CULTIVATION
These marginally frost-hardy plants prefer full sun and well-drained soil of poor
quality. The flowerheads can be cut for
drying and hung upside down in a dark,
cool place. Propagate from seed.

R

Rhodiola
heterodonta (left)
syn. *Sedum*
heterodontum

This rhizomatous, clump-forming species from Afghanistan, the Himalayas and Tibet grows to a height and spread of 15 in (38 cm). It bears flattish heads of yellow to orange-red or greenish flowers in spring to early summer and has thick, unbranched stems with oval, toothed, blue-green leaves. ZONES 5–10.

RHODIOLA

Similar to *Hylotelephium* and the larger *Sedum* species, this genus includes around 50 species of fleshy leafed, rhizomatous perennials widely distributed in the northern hemisphere. The plants are composed of a mass of thickened stems clothed with simple, often toothed, gray-green leaves. The individual, star-shaped flowers, in shades of yellow, orange, red, occasionally green or white, appear in dense, rounded heads.

CULTIVATION
Most are very frost-hardy and undemanding. Plant in an area that remains moist in summer but which is not boggy in winter. A sunny rockery is ideal. Propagate by division in spring or take cuttings of the young growth. They may be attacked by aphids.

R

Rhodiola kirilowii
(left)
syn. *Sedum kirilowii*

Found from central Asia to Mongolia, this species has heavy, branched rhizomes from which develop stout, upright stems that grow to 3 ft (1 m) tall. The narrow to lance-shaped leaves are unusually large, sometimes over 10 ft (3 m) long. The flowers are yellow-green to rusty red, and open from early summer.
ZONES 5–10.

Rhodiola rosea *(below)*
syn. *Sedum rosea*

ROSEROOT

The tightly massed heads of pink buds produced by
this perennial in late spring or early summer open to
small, star-shaped flowers in pale purple, green or
yellow. The saw-edged, elliptical leaves are fleshy.
This species grows into a clump 12 in (30 cm) in
height and spread. The name comes from the scent
of the fleshy roots, used in making perfume. It is a
highly sociable species that occurs right around the
temperate northern hemisphere. **ZONES 2–9.**

Rhodiola purpureoviridis *(above)*
syn. *Sedum purpureoviride*

This dense species has rounded, ovate leaves with
densely hairy, toothed margins. The flowering
stems grow to 18 in (45 cm) and bear pale green-
yellow flowers in early summer. It comes from
western China and Tibet. **ZONES 6–10.**

Rhodiola stephanii *(right)*
syn. *Sedum stephanii*

This rhizomatous,
branching species
from eastern Siberia
has bright yellow-
green, deeply
toothed leaves. The
flowering stems, to
10 in (25 cm) in
length, bear their
creamy white
flowers in summer.
ZONES 5–10.

R

RODGERSIA

Native to Burma, China, Korea and Japan, this genus consists of 6 species of moisture-loving perennials. They have handsome foliage and flowers, but tend to be grown more for their bold leaves than for their plumes of fluffy flowers, borne in mid- to late summer. The stems unfurl in mid-spring and spread out to form a fan of leaves on top of stout stems.

CULTIVATION

Their liking for moist soil makes them excellent plants for marshy ground at the edge of a pond or in a bog garden in sun or part-shade. They do best in a site sheltered from strong winds, which can damage the foliage. Propagate by division in spring or from seed in autumn.

Rodgersia aesculifolia (below)

This Chinese species has lobed, 10 in (25 cm) wide leaves that are borne on hairy stalks, forming a clump 24 in (60 cm) high and wide. The large, cone-shaped clusters of small, starry flowers are cream or pale pink, and are borne on stout stems up to 4 ft (1.2 m) tall. **ZONES 5–9.**

R

Rodgersia pinnata
(above)

This rhizomatous, clump-forming plant produces bold, dark green leaves arranged in pairs. Star-shaped, yellowish white, pink or red flowers are borne in panicles on reddish green stems in mid- to late summer. It reaches a height of 4 ft (1.2 m) and a spread of 30 in (75 cm). **'Superba'** has bright pink flowers and purplish bronze leaves. **'Serenade'** has pale pink flowers. **ZONES 6–9.**

R

Rodgersia pinnata
'Serenade' *(above)*

Rodgersia sambucifolia (above)

This clump-forming, rhizomatous species from western China has emerald-green, occasionally bronze-tinted leaves with large leaflets. It reaches 3 ft (1 m) high and wide and bears sprays of creamy white flowers above the foliage in summer. ZONES 6–10.

Rodgersia podophylla (left)

Suited to pond surrounds, this rhizomatous species has green, copper-tinted leaves comprising 5 to 9 large leaflets. It bears multi-branched panicles of cream, star-shaped flowers. It tolerates full shade but does better in part-shade, and grows 3–4 ft (1–1.2 m) tall by 30 in (75 cm) wide. ZONES 5–9.

R

ROMNEYA
TREE POPPY

The 2 species in this genus from North America are summer-flowering, woody based perennials and deciduous subshrubs. They have blue-green foliage composed of alternate leaves and poppy-like, 6-petalled flowers with glossy yellow stamens.

CULTIVATION
They prefer a warm, sunny position and fertile, well-drained soil. They are difficult to establish (although once established they may become invasive), and they resent transplanting. Protect the roots in very cold areas in winter. Propagate from seed or cuttings.

Romneya coulteri (below)
CALIFORNIA TREE POPPY, MATILIJA POPPY

This shrubby Californian perennial produces large, sweetly scented, poppy-like white flowers highlighted with fluffy gold stamens. The silvery green leaves are deeply divided, their edges sparsely fringed with hairs. Fully frost hardy, it forms a bush up to 8 ft (2.4 m) high with a spread of 3 ft (1 m). **Romneya coulteri** var. **trichocalyx** has pointed, rather bristly sepals. ZONES 7–10.

ROSCOEA

These 18 species of tuberous perennials from China and the Himalayas are related to ginger *(Zingiber)*, but in appearance are more reminiscent of irises. They are grown for their orchid-like flowers, which have hooded upper petals, wide-lobed lower lips and 2 narrower petals. The leaves are lance-shaped and erect. They are most suitable for open borders and rock and woodland gardens.

CULTIVATION

They prefer part-shade and cool, fertile, humus-rich soil that should be kept moist but well drained in summer. Provide a top-dressing of leafmold or well-rotted compost in winter, when the plants die down. Propagate from seed or by division.

Roscoea cautleoides (left)

Bearing its yellow or orange flowers in summer, this frost-hardy species from China grows to 10 in (25 cm) tall with a 6 in (15 cm) spread. The glossy leaves are lance-shaped and erect and wrap into a hollow stem-like structure at their base. ZONES 6–9.

Rosmarinus officinalis
'Prostratus' *(right)*

Rosmarinus officinalis

Widely grown as a culinary herb, this species is also ornamental. It is upright with strong woody branches densely clothed with narrow, 1 in (25 mm), deep green leaves. Simple, lavender-blue to deep blue flowers smother the bush in autumn, winter and spring. **'Benenden Blue'** has vivid blue flowers; **'Huntingdon Carpet'** is a low spreader with bluish flowers; **'Lockwood de Forest'** has deep blue flowers and a spreading habit; **'Majorca Pink'** is an upright grower with soft pink flowers; **'Miss Jessop's Upright'** grows vigorously to 6 ft (1.8 m); **'Prostratus'** (syn. *Rosmarinus lavandulaceus* of gardens), a ground cover form, is ideal for spilling over walls or covering banks; and **'Tuscan Blue'** bears dark blue flowers. ZONES 6–11.

ROSMARINUS
ROSEMARY

Some botanists recognize up to 12 species in this genus, but most suggest there is only one, an evergreen native to the Mediterranean. It has been valued for centuries for its perfume and for medicinal and culinary uses. A small shrub rarely growing more than 4 ft (1.2 m) tall, it has narrow, needle-like leaves that are dark green and aromatic. The blue flowers are held in short clusters.

CULTIVATION

Rosmarinus prefers a sunny site and thrives in poor soil if it is well drained; it is salt tolerant. Prune regularly to keep it compact and promote new growth. It can be grown as a specimen shrub or as a low hedge. Propagate from seed or cuttings in summer.

R

Rudbeckia fulgida

BLACK-EYED SUSAN, ORANGE CONEFLOWER

This rhizomatous perennial, to 3 ft (1 m) tall, has branched stems, mid-green, slightly hairy leaves with prominent veins, and daisy-like, orange-yellow flowers with dark brown centers. ***Rudbeckia fulgida* var. *deamii*** has very hairy stems and is free flowering; ***R. f.* var. *speciosa*** has elliptic to lance-shaped basal leaves and toothed stem leaves; ***R. f.* var. *sullivantii* 'Goldsturm'** (syn. *R.* 'Goldsturm') grows to 24 in (60 cm) tall and has crowded stems that bear lanceolate leaves. **ZONES 3–10.**

Rudbeckia fulgida var.
deamii (above)
Rudbeckia fulgida var.
speciosa (below)

RUDBECKIA
CONEFLOWER

This popular genus from North America has about 15 species of annuals, biennials and perennials. The plants in this genus have bright, daisy-like, composite flowers with prominent central cones (hence the common name). The single, double or semi-double flowers are usually in tones of yellow. The cones, however, vary from green through rust, purple and black. Species range in height from 24 in (60 cm) to 10 ft (3 m). A number of rudbeckias make excellent cut flowers.

CULTIVATION
Coneflowers prefer loamy, moisture-retentive soil in full sun or part-shade. Propagate from seed or by division in spring or autumn. They are moderately to fully frost hardy. Aphids may be a problem.

Rudbeckia fulgida
var. *sullivantii*
'Goldsturm' (left)

Rudbeckia hirta 'Toto'

Rudbeckia hirta

(below right)

BLACK-EYED SUSAN

The flowerheads on this biennial or short-lived perennial are bright yellow, with central cones of purplish brown, and its lanceolate leaves are mid-green and hairy. It reaches 12–36 in (30–90 cm) tall, with a spread of 12 in (30 cm). **'Irish Eyes'** is noteworthy for its olive green center. **'Marmalade'** has large flowerheads with golden orange ray florets. Many dwarf cultivars such as **'Becky Mixed'** are available in a range of colors from pale lemon to orange and red. They are usually treated as annuals. **'Toto'** is a compact strain that flowers heavily and is very even in size and flower distribution. It is ideal for massed plantings. **ZONES 3–10.**

R

Rudbeckia laciniata *(left)*
CUTLEAF CONEFLOWER

This species is a splendid summer-flowering perennial that can reach 10 ft (3 m) tall, though 6 ft (1.8 m) is more usual. The drooping ray florets give the flowerhead an informal elegance. **'Golden Glow'** is a striking, if somewhat floppy, double cultivar. **'Goldquelle'** grows to around 30 in (75 cm) tall and has large, yellow, double flowers. ZONES 3–10.

Rudbeckia laciniata
'Goldquelle' *(right)*

Rudbeckia subtomentosa *(left)*
SWEET CONEFLOWER

Found naturally in the central United States, sweet coneflower has branched stems up to 28 in (70 cm) tall with mid-green leaves up to 6 in (15 cm) long. The leaves are covered in fine gray hairs. The flower heads, composed of yellow ray florets around a purple-brown disc, are carried individually and are up to 3 in (8 cm) wide. Sweet coneflower is so called because of the honeyed scent of its blooms, which open in autumn. ZONES 5–10.

RUMEX
DOCK, SORREL

Chiefly found in northern hemisphere temperate regions, this genus comprises around 200 species of annual, biennial and perennial herbs, usually with a deep tap root. Many species have been introduced to other parts of the world and have become invasive weeds. Docks are erect plants, usually with a basal rosette of simple leaves and with or without stem leaves. Flowers are borne in whorls in spikes or panicles, followed by small, oval, pointed fruits. A few species are cultivated for their ornamental foliage or as herbs mainly used as a vegetable.

CULTIVATION
Most docks thrive in full sun in moderately fertile, well-drained soil. They are marginally to fully frost hardy. Propagation is from seed sown in spring or by division in autumn; broken pieces of root will also sprout. Protect young plants from slugs and snails.

Rumex patienta
(right)

PATIENCE DOCK, PATIENCE HERB,
SPINACH DOCK

This vigorous Eurasian perennial is up to 7 ft (2 m) high when in flower. Its basal leaves are 6–18 (15–45 cm) long, oval to lance-shaped and wavy. Their size is enhanced by the 12 in (30 cm) stems on which they are carried. The flower stem develops rapidly and starts to bloom around midsummer. ZONES 6–9.

R

SAGITTARIA
ARROWHEAD, WAPATO, DUCK POTATO

About 20 species of submerged or partially emergent temperate and tropical aquatic perennials, some tuberous, make up this genus. The emersed leaves are often linear to oval, but a few species have sagittate (arrowhead-shaped) leaves, hence the common name. They are usually about 10–12 in (25–30 cm) long. The submerged leaves are ribbon like, up to 4 ft (1.2 m) long including the petioles, and may form dense underwater meadows. In summer showy, purple-spotted white flowers open. They are 3-petalled, borne on branched stems that extend above the foliage and are ½–2 in (1.2–5 cm) wide.

CULTIVATION
Emergent species generally grow in ponds and fully submerged species prefer streams. All are bottom rooting and require a soil base and a position in full sun. Frost hardiness varies considerably according to the species. Propagate from seed or by division of the roots or tubers.

Sagittaria lancifolia 'Rubra' *(left)*

Sagittaria lancifolia

With this species from North Carolina down to northern South America and the West Indies, most leaves are above the water, the whole plant growing to 6 ft (1.8 m). The leaves may be linear, oval or elliptical and up to 15 in (38 cm) long, leathery and pale green. The white flowers may be 2 in (5 cm) wide in several whorls. 'Gigantea' is larger in all aspects, while 'Rubra' has a reddish tint to its leaves and flowers. ZONES 9–12.

S

SAINTPAULIA
AFRICAN VIOLET

Natives of eastern Africa, saintpaulias were originally collected in the late nineteenth century by Baron von Saint-Paul. There are 20 species of these low-growing, evergreen perennials and several thousand varieties. Some of these are the most popular flowering indoor plants because of their attractive foliage, compact nature, long flowering periods and wide range of flower colors. Cultivars include **'Chimera Monique'**, with purple and white flowers; **'Chimera Myrthe'**, with crimson and white flowers; **'Nada'**, with white flowers; and **'Ramona'**, with flowers a rich crimson. The flowers are 5-petalled and the succulent leaves are usually hairy.

CULTIVATION
Although African violets have a reputation for being difficult to grow, in the right conditions this is generally not so. They do demand certain soil, so plant them in commercial African violet mix. Constant temperature, moderate humidity and bright, indirect light ensure prolonged flowering; in winter they may also need artificial light. Use room temperature water, allow the surface soil to dry out a little between waterings, and avoid splashing the leaves. They bloom best when slightly potbound, so repot when very leafy and no longer flowering well. Propagate from leaf cuttings rooted in water or stuck in a layer of pebbles on top of a moist sand and peat mixture. African violets are vulnerable to cyclamen mite, mealybug and powdery mildew.

S

Saintpaulia 'Chimera Myrthe' *(above)*

Saintpaulia 'Nada' *(left)*

Saintpaulia 'Ramona' *(below)*

Saintpaulia ionantha *(below)*

COMMON AFRICAN VIOLET

This species has clusters of tubular, semi-succulent violet-blue flowers, growing on stems above the leaves. The green leaves, with reddish green undersides, are scalloped, fleshy and hairy. Thousands of cultivars are available, now far removed from the species. The flowers can be single or double, usually $1\frac{1}{2}$ in (35 mm) across, and come in shades from white through mauve and blue to purple, and pale and deep pink to crimson. **ZONES 11–12.**

Saintpaulia ionantha hybrids *(top & bottom)*

Saintpaulia magungensis *(above)*

This plant from Tanzania has purple flowers $\frac{3}{4}$ in (18 mm) across in groups of 2 or 4, held just above the leaves. Branched stems up to 6 in (15 cm) long bear leaves with petioles (leaf stems) up to 2 in (5 cm) long. The leaves are oval or round, about $2\frac{1}{2}$ in (6 cm) across, with a wavy edge and both long and short hairs on the upper surface. **ZONES 10–12.**

S

Salpiglossis sinuata
(left & below)

PAINTED TONGUE

Offering a variety of flower colors including red, orange, yellow, blue and purple, this annual from Peru and Argentina blooms in summer and early autumn. The 2 in (5 cm) wide, heavily veined flowers are like small flaring trumpets, while the lanceolate leaves are light green. A fast grower, it reaches a height of 18–24 in (45–60 cm) and a spread of at least 15 in (38 cm). It is frost tender and dislikes dry conditions. ZONES 8–11.

SALPIGLOSSIS

These species from the southern Andes are not seen very often in gardens as they can be tricky to grow, but patient gardeners who live in mild climates with fairly cool summers will be rewarded by a short but beautiful display of flowers like petunias (they are re-

lated). They come in rich shades of crimson, scarlet, orange, blue, purple and white, all veined and laced with gold. There are 2 species of annuals and perennials providing color in borders or as greenhouse plants in cold climates.

CULTIVATION
Plant in full sun in rich, well-drained soil. Deadhead regularly. *Salpiglossis* species are best sown in early spring directly in the place they are to grow, as seedlings do not always survive transplanting. They are prone to attack by aphids.

SALVIA
SAGE

The largest genus of the mint family, *Salvia* consists of as many as 900 species of annuals, perennials and soft-wooded shrubs, distributed through most parts of the world except very cold regions and tropical rainforests. Their tubular, 2-lipped flowers are very distinctive. The lower lip is flat but the upper lip helmet- or boat-shaped; the calyx is also 2-lipped and may be colored. The flowers come in a wide range of colors, including some of the brightest blues and scarlets of any plants, though yellows are rare. Many beautiful sage species are grown as garden plants, including some with aromatic leaves grown primarily as culinary herbs, but even these can be grown for their ornamental value alone. The genus name goes back to Roman times and derives from the Latin *salvus*, 'safe' or 'well', referring to the supposed healing properties of *Salvia officinalis*.

CULTIVATION
Most of the shrubby Mexican and South American species will tolerate only light frosts, but some of the perennials are more frost-hardy. Sages generally do best planted in full sun in well drained, light-textured soil with adequate watering in summer. Propagate from seed in spring, cuttings in early summer, or division of rhizomatous species at almost any time. Foliage of many species is attacked by snails, slugs and caterpillars.

Salvia argentea (right)
SILVER SAGE

Silver sage is a biennial or short-lived perennial native to southern Europe and North Africa. It has large, silver-felted leaves forming a flat basal rosette that builds up in autumn and winter to as much as 3 ft (1 m) wide before sending up 3 ft (1 m) panicles of small white flowers in spring and summer. Its main attraction is its foliage, which can be maintained for longer if inflorescence buds are removed. Allow to seed in the second or third year to maintain a supply of replacement seedlings. ZONES 6–9.

S

Salvia blepharophylla
(left)
EYELASH LEAFED SAGE

This Mexican species is a subshrubby perennial of similar style to the better-known *Salvia greggii* and *S. microphylla*. It is almost evergreen and spreads by creeping rhizomes, reaching about 15 in (38 cm) in height and somewhat greater spread, with rich green foliage. Through summer and autumn it produces a succession of bright red flowers suffused with paler orange or pink. It likes part-shade and moist soil. ZONES 8–11.

Salvia cacaliifolia *(left)*
GUATEMALAN BLUE SAGE

From the highlands of Mexico, Guatemala and Honduras, this is one of the most distinctive sages: its name signifies a resemblance between its leaves and those of *Cacalia*, a genus allied to *Senecio*. It is a perennial to about 3 ft (1 m) high with stems springing from a creeping rootstock, bearing pairs of glossy bright green triangular leaves that are about as broad as long, with 3 sharp points. In summer and autumn it produces a profusion of small deep blue flowers on branched spikes. ZONES 8–10.

Salvia austriaca *(left)*
AUSTRIAN SAGE

From eastern Europe, this is one of a large group of cold-hardy perennial sages with basal rosettes of closely veined, jaggedly toothed or lobed leaves, and long, erect spikes of smallish flowers in regular whorls. In *Salvia austriaca* the stalked leaves may be over 12 in (30 cm) long and the pale yellow flowers with protruding stamens are borne in summer on spikes to 3 ft (1 m) tall. ZONES 6–10.

Salvia confertiflora *(right)*

SABRA SPIKE SAGE

From Brazil, this perennial plant can reach a height of 6 ft (1.8 m). It has large, 8 in (20 cm) wide, mid-green oval leaves with downy undersides. The flower spikes are in 12 in (30 cm) unbranched heads with red flowers and deep red calyces during late summer and autumn. ZONES 9–11.

Salvia coccinea
'Coral Nymph'
(below)

Salvia chamaedryoides *(above)*

GERMANDER SAGE

From Texas and Mexico, this tiny leafed perennial is suitable for the rock garden, being multi-branched and very compact. The foliage is gray-blue and masses of small deep violet-blue flowers appear in summer. It grows to 12 in (30 cm) high and 24 in (60 cm) wide. ZONES 8–11.

Salvia coccinea

RED TEXAS SAGE

This compact, bushy, short-lived perennial from South America is treated as an annual in colder climates. It has small mid-green leaves and an abundance of scarlet flowers from early summer to late autumn. It is normally grown in full sun, but when placed in light shade and protected from frost it can survive another season or two. Many forms are known, including a pure white and a lovely salmon pink and white bicolor. **'Coral Nymph'** is a compact form with coral pink flowers; **'Lady in Red'** is also compact, growing just 15 in (38 cm) tall with bright red flowers. ZONES 8–11.

S

Salvia dolomitica (left)

This native of South Africa is still rare in cultivation. It has gray-green foliage, grows to around 4 ft (1.2 m) tall and spreads slowly by rhizomes to eventually form a dense thicket of stems. Its flowers are dusky lavender-pink and appear in spring. The calyces are purple-red and last well after the flowers have fallen. **ZONES 9–11.**

Salvia elegans 'Scarlet Pineapple' *(above)*

Salvia darcyi (left)

DARCY SAGE

This rare perennial from high in the mountains of northeastern Mexico is a recent discovery only named in 1994, although introduced to cultivation in the USA about 5 years earlier. Growing to about 3 ft (1 m) high, it is a little like *Salvia coccinea* but its rich scarlet flowers are larger, about 1½ in (35 mm) long, and borne in greater profusion in erect panicles. It flowers in summer and early autumn and dies back in winter. Easily grown in fertile soil with ample water in summer, *S. darcyi* is proving an outstanding ornamental. **ZONES 8–10.**

Salvia elegans

PINEAPPLE-SCENTED SAGE

This open-branched perennial or subshrub from Mexico and Guatemala can reach 6 ft (1.8 m) in milder areas and is grown for its light green foliage. It has a distinctive pineapple scent and flavor. Its whorls of small bright red flowers are borne in late summer and autumn. The leaves are used fresh but sparingly in fruit salads, summer drinks and teas. The flowers are delicious, and may be added to desserts and salads for color and flavor. **'Scarlet Pineapple'** (syn. *Salvia rutilans)* is more floriferous with larger scarlet flowers which, in milder areas, will persist to midwinter and are most attractive to honey-eating birds. **ZONES 8–11.**

S

Salvia farinacea

MEALY-CUP SAGE

This species is grown as an annual in regions that have cold winters and is at its best when mass planted. It is a short-lived perennial in warmer climates, although if planted in a little shade to protect it from hot afternoon sun and pruned hard in mid-autumn it can live up to 5 years. Growing to 24–36 in (60–90 cm), it bears lavender-like, deep violet-blue flowers on slender stems. It is a good cut flower and comes from Texas and Mexico. **'Blue Bedder'** is an improved cultivar; **'Strata'** has blue and white flowers; and **'Victoria'** has deep blue flowers. **'Argent'** (syn. 'Silver') has silvery white flowers. ZONES 8–11.

Salvia farinacea 'Victoria' *(above)*

Salvia farinacea 'Argent' *(left)*

Salvia farinacea 'Strata' *(right)*

S

Salvia forsskaolii *(right)*
syn. *Salvia forskaohlei*

This highly variable perennial from southeastern Europe has slightly hairy basal leaves with small flowers on single 30 in (75 cm) long stems. The flower color will vary from violet to pinkish magenta with white or yellow markings on the lower lip. It is fully frost hardy but prefers drier winters. ZONES 7–10.

Salvia guaranitica *(below left)*

ANISE SCENTED SAGE

Plant this tall-growing perennial from Brazil, Uruguay and Argentina with care, as it has a tendency to 'gallop' in its second or third season, choking less valiant plants. Its deep violet-blue flowers are held aloft on strong 6 ft (1.8 m) stems from mid-summer to late autumn. **'Argentine Skies'** was selected for its pale blue flowers, and **'Purple Splendour'** for its intense blackish purple flowers. **ZONES 9–11.**

Salvia greggii *(above)*

FALL SAGE, CHERRY SAGE, AUTUMN SAGE

This species, which can reach 3–4 ft (1–1.2 m) in height, is native from Texas into Mexico and is a long-flowering addition to dryish gardens in California and southwestern USA. The leaves are small and aromatic; above the foliage rise slender stems with broad-lipped sage blossoms in red, orange, salmon, pink, pale yellow, white and blends. The flowers are produced from spring through autumn in coastal areas, and in autumn and winter in the desert. Many hybrids and named selections are available. **ZONES 9–10.**

Salvia gesneriiflora *(above)*

This erect Colombian and Mexican perennial usually grows to 24 in (60 cm) high, though reportedly can reach 25 ft (8 m). It has oval or heart-shaped leaves about 4 in (10 cm) long that are bright green and finely hairy. It produces its large orange-red flowers from spring to autumn. Each flower is 2 in (5 cm) long but presents no difficulty to nectar-seeking birds. A light pruning is necessary before winter. **ZONES 8–11.**

Salvia guaranitica 'Purple Splendour' *(left)*

Salvia multicaulis
(right)

This low-growing shrubby or mat perennial from southwestern Asia produces erect hairy stems to 18 in (45 cm) tall. The white-felted leaves are mainly basal, oval, 1½ in (35 mm) long and wavy. The hairy calyx can be lime green or purple, the flowers violet or white and up to ¾ in (18 mm) long. It is spring and summer flowering and needs full sun in cultivation. **ZONES 8–11.**

Salvia indica *(right)*

This plant from the Middle East forms an erect branched species to 5 ft (1.5 m) tall with heart-shaped hairy leaves to 12 in (30 cm). Masses of white and blue or lilac flowers are held by heel-shaped ½ in (12 mm) calyces during spring and summer. **ZONES 9–11.**

Salvia involucrata
ROSELEAF SAGE

This is a charming tall perennial that remains evergreen in mild climates but even so, is best cut back to the ground every year to promote flowering. From the highlands of central Mexico, it has erect cane-like stems to about 5 ft (1.5 m) high, and broad, long-stalked leaves that often develop red veining. The loose flower spikes terminate in groups of large mauve to magenta bracts, which are shed one by one to reveal a trio of developing flowers of the same or deeper color; each flower is up to 2 in (5 cm) long, tubular but swollen in the middle, and the small upper lip is covered in velvety hairs. It blooms over a long summer–autumn season, and appreciates sun and rich, well drained soil. In the UK, it has been known as **'Bethellii'**, a superior selection from the wild. **ZONES 9–10.**

Salvia involucrata **'Bethellii'** *(right)*

Salvia officinalis 'Purpurascens' and *Verbena tenuisecta* (red) *(left)*

Salvia pratensis *(below)*
MEADOW CLARY, MEADOW SAGE

This tough, reliable and fully frost-hardy sage from Europe and Morocco bears oval to oblong basal leaves and shorter leaves along its 3 ft (1 m) flowering stems; the flowers are rather sparsely distributed along these stems. The commonly grown form has violet-purple flowers but in the wild it is immensely variable, from the white and pale blue **'Haematodes'** through to deeper blues and darker purples and even **'Rosea'** with rose-pink flowers, and **'Rubicunda'** with rose-red flowers. ZONES 3–9.

Salvia nemorosa *(below)*
syn. *Salvia virgata* var. *nemorosa*

Many slender, erect spikes of pinkish purple or white flowers bloom in summer on this neat, clump-forming perennial. Growing 3 ft (1 m) high with an 18 in (45 cm) spread, this frost-hardy species has rough leaves of narrow elliptical shape. It is widespread from Europe to central Asia. ZONES 5–10.

Salvia officinalis 'Purpurascens' and *Verbena tenuisecta* (red) *(left)*

Salvia officinalis
(below)
COMMON SAGE, GARDEN SAGE

From Spain, the Balkans and North Africa, common sage is a decorative, frost-hardy, short-lived perennial that grows to 30 in (75 cm) high and wide, with downy gray-green oval leaves and short racemes of purple flowers in summer. Its culinary merits are well known, and it has entered folklore over the centuries for its real and supposed medicinal qualities. **'Purpurascens'** has gray-green leaves invested with a purplish hue and pale mauve flowers; **'Tricolor'** is a garish combination of green, cream and beet-root red leaves; **'Berggarten'** is a lower-growing form with larger leaves and blue flowers. ZONES 5–10.

Salvia sclarea (right)

BIENNIAL CLARY, CLARY SAGE

This native of southern Europe and Syria is a biennial and grows 3 ft (1 m) tall. Clary sage has been used medicinally and as a flavoring for beverages. Moderately fast growing and erect, it has long, loose, terminal spikes of tubular, greenish white tinged with purple flowers in summer, and velvety, heart-shaped leaves. **Salvia sclarea var. turkestanica** has pink stems and white, pink-flecked flowers. ZONES 5–10.

Salvia spathacea

(right)

PITCHER SAGE, HUMMINGBIRD SAGE, CRIMSON SAGE

This woody perennial with hairy stems up to 3 ft (1 m) tall has leaves which vary from oval to heart- or arrowhead-shaped with a white felt beneath. Many magenta flowers about 1¼ in (30 mm) long are held above the bush. It comes from California. ZONES 8–11.

Salvia puberula (right)

This species is closely allied to Salvia involucrata and comes from the same highland region of Mexico. It is a perennial of much the same size and growth habit, and the long-pointed leaves are somewhat more downy. The flowers also are very similar but a deeper magenta color and the inflorescence is shorter and has smaller bud bracts. It has been grown in southern USA and makes a fine ornamental, blooming mainly in autumn. ZONES 8–10.

S

Salvia splendens 'Salsa
Burgundy' *(above)*

Salvia splendens
'Van Houttei' *(below)*

Salvia splendens
SCARLET SAGE

This native of Brazil,
which is grown as an
annual, produces dense
terminal spikes of scar-
let flowers in summer
through early autumn.
The leaves are toothed
and elliptical. It grows
3–4 ft (1–1.2 m) tall and
wide. In hotter climates,
give some shade; it is
moderately frost hardy.
'Salsa Burgundy' has
deep burgundy flowers,
while **'Van Houttei'** has
a deep dull red calyx
with large lighter red
flowers; both prefer a
little shade. **ZONES 9–12.**

S

Salvia × sylvestris

This leafy perennial to
12–36 in (30–90 cm) high
is a hybrid between *Salvia
pratensis* and *S. nemorosa*.
It has hairy oblong heart-
shaped leaves 2–4 in
(5–10 cm) long. The sum-
mer flowers are purplish
violet in long-branched
heads. It comes from
western Asia and Europe
but is naturalized in North
America. There are many
cultivars, some of uncer-
tain origin. **'Blauhügel'**
('Blue Mound') is
compact with clear blue
flowers; **'Ostfriesland'**
('East Friesland') is deep
purple; **'Mainacht'** is
lower growing with black-
ish purple tones; and
'Wesuwe' is an early
bloomer with dark violet
flowers. **ZONES 5–10.**

Salvia × *sylvestris*
'Wesuwe' *(right)*
Salvia × *sylvestris*
'Mainacht' *(below left)*
Salvia × *sylvestris*
'Ostfriesland' *(below right)*

Salvia viridis (left)

This is an erect annual or biennial plant with oval or oblong leaves up to 2 in (5 cm) long. The green or purple calyx bears $\frac{1}{2}$ in (12 mm) flowers which may be white to lilac to purple. It occurs around the Mediterranean and flowers in summer. There are several named color forms available. ZONES 7–11.

Salvia taraxacifolia (above)

This perennial from Morocco with upright stems reaching only 18 in (45 cm) has ferny leaves that are white underneath and form rosettes. The flowers, which appear from spring to summer, may be white or pale pink with a yellowish blotch on the lower lip and purple specks on the upper. Each flower attains a length of $1\frac{1}{4}$ in (30 mm). ZONES 9–11.

Salvia uliginosa (left)
BOG SAGE

Long racemes of sky blue flowers appear in summer on this upright branching perennial from South America. The leaves are toothed, elliptical to lance-shaped and up to 3 in (8 cm) long, smooth or only slightly hairy. Growing to 3–6 ft (1–1.8 m), it has slender curving stems. In good or moist soil it sends out underground rooting shoots and may become invasive. ZONES 8–11.

S

SAMBUCUS
ELDERBERRY, ELDER

This genus includes about 25 species of perennials, deciduous shrubs and soft-wooded trees. Although most are rarely cultivated because of their tendency to be somewhat weedy and invasive, some species are useful for their edible flowers and berries, and are attractive in foliage and flower. Most have pinnate leaves and, in late spring and early summer, bear large radiating sprays of tiny white or creamy flowers followed by clusters of usually purple-black, blue or red berries.

CULTIVATION
Usually undemanding, *Sambucus* thrive in any reasonably well-drained, fertile soil in sun or shade. Prune out old shoots and cut young shoots by half. Propagate from seed in autumn, or cuttings in summer or winter.

Sambucus ebulus
(right)

DWARF ELDER, DANE'S ELDER,
DANEWORT, WALLWORT

From Europe, North Africa, Turkey and Iran, this is an herbaceous perennial growing up to 5 ft (1.5 m) high with strong creeping underground stems. The leaflets, usually 9 to 13, are elliptic, toothed and slightly hairy. It produces flat heads up to 4 in (10 cm) across of white-tinged pink flowers in summer, followed by black fruit. It is considered too invasive for a small garden. ZONES 5–10.

S

SANGUINARIA
BLOODROOT, RED PUCCOON

The single species of the genus is a widespread woodland plant from eastern North America, from Nova Scotia through to Florida. It is a low-growing perennial herb grown for its spring display of cup-shaped flowers.

CULTIVATION

It prefers sandy soil but will tolerate clay soil if not too wet. Bloodroot does well in sun or part-shade, and especially under deciduous trees. Propagation is by division in late summer when the leaves have died back.

Sanguinaria canadensis *(above)*

This perennial has a long stout horizontal rootstock. Each bud on the stock sends up a heart-shaped leaf with scalloped edges on stalks 6 in (15 cm) long. Each leaf is up to 12 in (30 cm) across. The solitary white or pink-tinged flowers are up to 3 in (8 cm) across, single, with 8 to 12 petals and many yellow central anthers. They appear in the folds of the leaves in spring before the gray leaves fully expand, and last for about 3 weeks. *Sanguinaria canadensis* var. *grandiflora* has larger flowers; the double form **'Flore Pleno'** has more but narrower petals. ZONES 3–9.

Sanguinaria canadensis 'Flore Pleno' *(left)*

Sanguisorba minor
(right)
syn. *Poterium sanguisorba*

GARDEN BURNET, SALAD BURNET

This perennial to 24 in (60 cm) has 6 to 10 rounded toothed leaflets on each leafstalk. The flowers occur in terminal oblong heads to 1 in (25 mm). They are white, the upper ones female, the lower ones male, with the middle section comprised of both. It occurs across Europe, western Asia and North Africa in dry rocky areas, often on limestone. It is often seen in herb gardens where fresh leaves are picked for soups and salads. It has a taste rather like cucumber and is excellent in cold drinks.
ZONES 5–9.

SANGUISORBA
syn. *Poterium*

BURNET

This is a genus of about 18 species found over the northern temperate zones. They may be rhizomatous perennials or small shrubs, and all have coarsely ferny leaves. The flowerheads resemble small bottlebrushes, and often only the lower half of the bottlebrush has male and female parts to the flowers.

CULTIVATION
They prefer full sun or part-shade and moderately fertile, moist but well-drained soil that should not be allowed to dry out in summer. Propagate from seed or by division.

Sanguisorba canadensis (above)
CANADIAN BURNET

A native of eastern North America, this vigorous perennial loves full sun and moist soil. The handsome, pinnate leaves form a clump around 18 in (45 cm) wide, above which are borne masses of white flowers in late summer. It grows to 6 ft (1.8 m) in height. ZONES 4–9.

S

Sanguisorba officinalis (above)

GREATER BURNET, BURNET BLOODWORT

The creeping rhizomes of this perennial carry erect stems, sometimes reddish, up to 4 ft (1.2 m) tall. The basal leaves are large with many leaflets up to 2 in (5 cm) long. The ¾ in (18 mm) long, dark reddish purple flowers appear in summer and autumn. It comes from China, Japan, North America and western Europe. ZONES 4–9.

Sanguisorba tenuifolia (below left)

This burnet, at 4 ft (1.2 m) one of the taller species, is found principally in Japan, but also occurs in China and Manchuria. It forms clumps of deeply serrated foliage composed of 11–21 leaflets up to 3 in (8 cm) long. The flowers, which open in summer, are carried in cylindrical 3 in (8 cm) long spikes and are usually white, though pink or purple flowers are not uncommon. Plant in partial shade. ZONES 4–9.

SANVITALIA
CREEPING ZINNIA

From southwestern USA and Mexico come
these 7 species of annuals or short-lived
perennials of the daisy family. The ovate
leaves come in pairs and the small white
or yellow flowers have a dark purplish
black or white center. They make good
ground covers, rock garden plants and
hanging basket specimens.

CULTIVATION
Plants do best in full sun in humus-rich,
well-drained soil. They are grown as
annuals, sown *in situ* or in small pots for
replanting with minimal root disturbance.
Propagate from seed.

Sanvitalia procumbens

A native of Mexico,
this summer-flowering,
fully frost-hardy annual
produces masses of
bright yellow flower-
heads like 1 in (25 mm)
daisies with blackish
centers. It is a prostrate
species with mid-green,
ovate leaves, growing
to 8 in (20 cm) high
and spreading at least
15 in (38 cm). Many
cultivars are available.
'Aztec Gold' is a good
example. ZONES 7–11.

Sanvitalia procumbens
'Aztec Gold' and
Gazania 'Orange Magic'
(right)

S

SAPONARIA
SOAPWORT

The common name of this genus of 20 species of annuals and perennials comes from the old custom of using the roots for washing clothes. They contain a glucoside called saponin, which is just as good as any detergent for dissolving grease and dirt and which, being edible, has been used as an additive to beer to ensure that it develops a good head when poured. These are good plants for rock gardens, banks and for trailing over walls.

CULTIVATION
Fully frost-hardy, they need sun and well-drained soil. Propagate from seed in spring or autumn or from cuttings in early summer.

Saponaria × olivana (above)

This soapwort forms a tight compact cushion to 3 in (8 cm) and bears profuse pale pink blooms in summer. It needs very good drainage. **ZONES 5–10.**

Saponaria ocymoides (left)
ROCK SOAPWORT

This alpine perennial from Europe forms a thick carpet from which profuse terminal clusters of small, flattish flowers, colored pink to deep red, bloom in late spring and early summer. It has sprawling mats of hairy oval leaves. **ZONES 4–10.**

SARMIENTA

The single species in this genus from southern Chile is a wiry stemmed, evergreen creeper or climber with smooth paired fleshy leaves. The flowers appear from the leaf axils on stalks; they are tubular with a central ballooning before narrowing again at the mouth with 5 small spreading lobes.

CULTIVATION

This plant needs well-drained, peaty soil in a protected shady place and abundant water. Propagate from seed in spring or cuttings in late summer.

Sarmienta scandens (above)
syn. *Sarmienta repens*

Smooth obovate to elliptic leaves 1 in (25 mm) long are toothed at the tip on this wiry clambering perennial. The numerous flowers on long fine stalks are bright scarlet and about ¾ in (18 mm) long. ZONES 5–9.

S

Sarracenia alata
(left)
YELLOW TRUMPETS

This species from southern USA produces erect, trumpet-like, yellowish green pitchers up to 30 in (75 cm) tall. The upper part of the trumpet and the adjacent part of its lid are often a dull red color. The nodding spring flowers are greenish yellow and up to 2½ in (6 cm) across. **ZONES 8–11.**

SARRACENIA
PITCHER PLANT

The *Sarracenia* genus consists of about 8 insectivorous evergreen or perennial species from the eastern part of North America; although they cover a wide area, they prefer to grow in peat bogs or in the sodden ground at the edges of pools. All the species have curious, many-petalled flowers whose styles develop into a sort of umbrella that shelters the stamens. The flowers are usually purple-red or greenish yellow or a blend of these colors, and the same tints are found in the modified leaves, called pitchers, which are nearly as decorative as the flowers. Insects are attracted to the foliage colors and slide down the slippery sides, drowning in the rainwater that accumulates at the bottom.

CULTIVATION
These moderately to fully frost-hardy plants need sun or part-shade and moist, peaty soil. Keep very wet during the growth period, and cool and moist in winter. Propagate from seed or by division in spring.

Sarracenia purpurea (right)

COMMON PITCHER PLANT, HUNTSMAN'S CUP, INDIAN CUP, SWEET PITCHER PLANT

This species is widespread in eastern North America, from New Jersey to the Arctic. It grows to 6 in (15 cm) in height. The pitchers are slender at the basal rosette, rapidly becoming swollen higher up. They are usually green with purple tints and the lid stands erect. The flowers appear in spring; they are purple or greenish purple and up to 2½ in (6 cm) wide. It has become naturalized in Europe, particularly Ireland. **ZONES 6–10.**

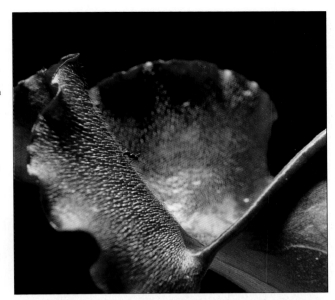

Sarracenia leucophylla (right)
syn. *Sarracenia drummondii*

This semi-evergreen perennial bears purpled-red flowers in spring and has erect, slender pitchers up to 4 ft (1.2 m) long with narrow wings and erect lids with wavy margins. These are usually white and have light purple-red netting, gradually merging into green bases. **ZONES 7–11.**

S

SAUSSUREA

This genus consists of 300 species of perennials from Europe, Asia and North America. Most are not particularly ornamental, but some species from the high Himalayas have adapted to the harsh conditions by covering themselves with downy hairs. The leaves are simple and alternate, and the flowerheads appear in rosettes but usually die down as the seeds are released.

CULTIVATION

They do best in full sun in humus-rich, moist but very well-drained soil in areas with cool, moist summers. Water well during growth, but protect them from winter wet. Propagate from seed or by division.

S

Saussurea stella
(above)

This plant is from damp grassland and bog tussocks up to 13,000 ft (4000 m) in the Himalayas. It is a flat rosette of dark green, 8 in (20 cm) long leaves with purple flowers in the center.
ZONES 7–9.

Saxifraga 'Glassel Crimson' *(above)*

SAXIFRAGA
SAXIFRAGE

Both the foliage and blooms on these perennials, biennials and annuals are equally appealing. The genus comprises some 440 species of evergreens and semi-evergreens. Their natural territory includes temperate, alpine and subarctic regions, mostly in the northern hemisphere, but many garden hybrids have been cultivated. They serve well in rock gardens and as ground cover. The flowers are mostly white, sometimes spotted with pink, but other colors are also available. The genus name combines two Latin terms, 'rock' and 'to break', suggestive of either the hardiness of their rooting system or their reputed medicinal effect on bladder stones. Many

Saxifraga 'Nona McGrory' *(below)*

cultivars are available. **'Glassel Crimson'** has two-tone crimson flowers with a yellow eye; **'Nona McGrory'** has beautiful pale pink spotted with deeper pink.

CULTIVATION
Soil and light requirements vary greatly depending on the species; they also vary from being very frost hardy to marginally frost hardy. Propagate from seed in autumn, by division or from rooted offsets in winter.

S

Saxifraga bronchialis

This plant forms a tuft to 8 in (20 cm) tall, with stiff linear leaves to ½ in (12 mm) long. The flowers are cream, spotted with red. It comes from North America and Asia. **Saxifraga bronchialis subsp.** *vespertina* is found in China, Mongolia and Siberia and bears greenish white flowers spotted with reddish pink. ZONES 4–9.

Saxifraga bronchialis **subsp.** *vespertina* (above)

Saxifraga × apiculata (right)

This perennial is a hybrid between **Saxifraga marginata** and **S. sancta**. It forms tight rosettes to 4 in (10 cm) high with small lance-shaped leaves and small yellow flowers of 10 to 12 per head. **'Alba'** has white flowers. **'Gregor Mendel'** has soft lemon flowers. Other hybrids are known and all, to various degrees, have a white encrustation to the leaves. They need some protection from heat and are intolerant of drying out. ZONES 6–9.

Saxifraga 'Apple Blossom' (left)

The parentage of this plant is unknown. It forms a rounded clump up to 3 in (8 cm) tall and spreads to 24 in (60 cm). The toothed oval green leaves make a dense wall, while the ½ in (12 mm) pale pink flowerbuds, opening to white, are held above the foliage; they appear from spring to early summer. ZONES 7–9.

S

Saxifraga burseriana
BURSER'S SAXIFRAGE

This is a slow-growing evergreen perennial from the eastern Alps that is woody at its base and forms a series of dense conical cushions rather than rosettes with grayish green to silver leaves. The crimson flowers are solitary on 2 in (5 cm) tall stems. Plant in full sun in moderately fertile, well-drained soil. **'Gloria'** is made distinctive by brilliant red flower stems and larger white flowers with deep yellow centers. **ZONES 6–9.**

Saxifraga burseriana 'Gloria' *(above)*

Saxifraga cotyledon
GREAT ALPINE ROCKFOIL

Found from Scandinavia and Iceland to the Pyrenees and the Alps, this rosette-forming species has central rosettes up to 5 in (12 cm) wide with smaller daughter rosettes around them. The leaves are finely toothed and secrete a chalky coating from the limestone on which they grow. The flower stems are branching and up to 28 in (70 cm) tall, carrying 8–40 tiny white flowers per branch. **'Southside Seedling'** has red flowers spotted and edged with white. **ZONES 6–9.**

Saxifraga cotyledon
'Southside Seedling' *(right)*

S

Saxifraga exarata subsp. *moschata*
(left)

syn. *Saxifraga moschata*

This is a delightful downy-leafed cushion-forming plant from central and southern Europe with many round-petalled flowers on 4 in (10 cm) stems. The colors range from white or creamy yellow to pink through to strong carmine pink or red. The tricky combination of full sun and moist soil with perfect drainage in winter will keep it robust and healthy. ZONES 6–9.

Saxifraga longifolia *(right)*
PYRENEAN SAXIFRAGE

This species forms a tight rosette of long narrow leaves with heavily lime encrusted margins. It bears a single panicle to 18 in (45 cm) long. This is multi-stemmed, each stem holding a ball-shaped head of tiny, round-petalled white flowers in spring. It is unfortunately mono-carpic, so must be grown from seed as it dies after flowering. **'Tumbling Waters'** is a particularly fine form. ZONES 6–9.

Saxifraga marginata

This species from southern Italy, Romania and the Balkans forms dense cushions of tiny lime-secreting leaves. The tiny white flowers are carried in panicles of up to 12 blooms on hairy, 1–5 in (25 mm–12 cm) high stems. *S. marginata* var. *rocheliana* has larger leaves on short stems. ZONES 7–10.

Saxifraga marginata var. *rocheliana* *(right)*

S

Saxifraga rotundifolia (right)
ROUND-LEAFED SAXIFRAGE

This species from southwest France to northern
Turkey grows from a stout rhizome and forms
loose clumps of open rosettes of scalloped
roundish leaves. It flowers on a sparsely leafed
stem 10 in (25 cm) tall, forming an open truss of
small white, often purple-spotted flowers shading
to yellow at the center. It is best grown in moist
soil in light shade. ZONES 6–9.

Saxifraga paniculata
'Rosea' (below right)

Saxifraga paniculata var. *baldensis* (right)

Saxifraga paniculata (bottom)
syn. *Saxifraga aizoon*
LIVELONG SAXIFRAGE

This summer-flowering
evergreen perennial
from central Europe
bears terminal clusters
of 5-petalled white,
pale pink or yellow
flowers, often with spots
of reddish purple. The
bluish green leaves form
a rosette below the
flower stems. *Saxifraga
paniculata* grows to a
height and spread of
8–10 in (20–25 cm).
Grow in full sun in
well-drained, alkaline
soil. Many forms
have variations in
flower size and color.
'Rosea' has bright pink
flowers. 'Minima'
has very small foliage
and flowers. *Saxifraga
paniculata* var.
baldensis has very
small rosettes of leaves
and red-tinged flower
stems. ZONES 3–9.

Saxifraga 'Ruth Draper' *(above)*

Ruth Draper was a British comedienne
of the 1930s, famous for her monologue,
'You should have seen my garden last
week'. Her namesake is a pretty example
of a mossy saxifrage, a group that likes a
moist and lightly shaded position. It bears
large, cup-shaped, purple-pink flowers in
early spring and grows to 2 in (5 cm) in
height. ZONES 6–9.

Saxifraga sempervivum *(left)*

An evergreen perennial with short leaves,
this species from the Balkans and northwestern Turkey forms open cushions with
minimal lime encrustations. It has tiny
reddish purple flowers, 15 to 20 per panicle
on a 4 in (10 cm) leafy purple flower stem.
Grow in full sun in well-drained soil.
ZONES 7–9.

Saxifraga stolonifera

syn. *Saxifraga sarmentosa*

MOTHER OF THOUSANDS, STRAWBERRY BEGONIA

Geranium-like leaves are a feature of this perennial, which has rounded, glossy leaves that are
olive green with silver veins, purplish pink on the
undersides. In spring through early summer,
oddly petalled white flowers are borne in delicate
panicles on thin, erect stalks. One petal on the
tiny flowers seems to outgrow its 4 companion
petals. Frost tender, it grows to a height of 6–8 in
(15–20 cm) and spreads to 12 in (30 cm) by
runners. **'Tricolor'** has deeply cut, green leaves
patterned with red and white. **ZONES 5–10.**

Saxifraga umbrosa (below)

This species from the Pyrenees forms a spreading
leafy rosette of gray-green foliage with small white
flowers on multiple 8 in (20 cm) stems. It is best
in humus-rich soil and, in full sun or part-shade
in hotter areas, it will flower freely from late
spring to early summer. Other forms with shell-
pink flowers are recorded. **ZONES 7–9.**

Saxifraga stolonifera
'Tricolor' *(above)*

SCABIOSA
SCABIOUS, PINCUSHION FLOWER

This genus of 80 annuals, biennials and perennials from temperate climates, bears tall-stemmed, honey-scented flowers ideal for cutting. The blooms, bearing multiple florets with protruding filaments giving a pincushion effect, range from white, yellow, red, blue and mauve to deep purple.

CULTIVATION
Best in full sun in well-drained, alkaline soil. Propagate annuals from seed in spring, and perennials from cuttings in summer, seed in autumn or by division in early spring.

Scabiosa caucasica (above)

This perennial bears summer flowerheads in many hues with centers often in a contrasting color. It reaches a height and spread of 18–24 in (45–60 cm). **'Clive Greaves'** has lilac-blue flowers; **'Miss Wilmott'** has white flowers; **'Staefa'** is a strong grower with blue flowers; and **'Mrs Isaac House'** has creamy white flowers. ZONES 4–10.

Scabiosa anthemifolia (below)

This is an annual or short-lived perennial with arching stems up to 30 in (75 cm) long bearing 2½ in (6 cm) flowers in shades of mauve, violet or rose. It comes from South Africa. ZONES 7–11.

Scabiosa columbaria 'Butterfly Blue' *(above)*

Scabiosa columbaria

This biennial or perennial grows to 24 in (60 cm) tall with a spread of 3 ft (1 m). Slender, erect, hairy stems produce globular heads of reddish purple to lilac-blue flowers in $1\frac{1}{2}$ in (35 mm) wide heads during summer and autumn. **'Butterfly Blue'** is a lower growing, dense, fuzzy leafed cultivar with lavender-blue pincushion flowers over a very long period. **ZONES 6–10.**

Scabiosa caucasica   *Scabiosa caucasica*
'Staefa' *(left)*   'Mrs Isaac House' *(above)*

S

Scaevola aemula 'Blue Wonder' *(left)*

Scaevola aemula
(below)
syn. *Scaevola humilis*

FAIRY FAN FLOWER

The thick, coarsely toothed, dark green leaves on this perennial herb grow along spreading stems to form ground-hugging cover not more than 18 in (45 cm) high with a similar spread. Spikes of large, purple-blue flowers with yellow throats continue to elongate as new flowers open, blooming from early spring to late summer. Native to the sandy coast and near coastal woodlands of Australia, it resists dry conditions, frost and salt spray. **'Blue Wonder'** bears lilac-blue flowers almost continuously in great profusion. Another similar cultivar is **'Diamond Head'**. ZONES 9–11.

SCAEVOLA
FAN FLOWER

This genus from Australia and the Pacific region contains 96 species of mainly temperate origin. Most are evergreen perennials, shrubs, subshrubs and small trees, with a number of ground-covering varieties that have proved adaptable to a wide range of garden conditions, including seaside gardens. Most have leaves that are fleshy, often hairy and occasionally succulent, borne on stout, sometimes brittle stems. Fan-shaped flowers, while generally fairly small at ½–1 in (12–25 mm) across, are profuse and are held on the plant for long periods. The flower color ranges from white to blue, mauve and deep purple.

CULTIVATION
Species of *Scaevola* tolerate a wide range of soils but prefer them light and well drained; they do best in sun or part-shade. Propagate from seed or cuttings in spring or summer.

S

Scaevola aemula 'Diamond Head' *(below)*

SCHIZANTHUS
POOR MAN'S ORCHID, BUTTERFLY FLOWER

This genus contains 12 to 15 species of annuals from the Chilean mountains. Although the blooms do look like miniature orchids, *Schizanthus* are in fact related to petunias. They come in shades of pink, mauve, red, purple and white, all with gold-speckled throats. They grow to about 3 ft (1 m) high and 12 in (30 cm) wide. Most of the flowers seen in gardens are hybrids, and give a colorful display over a short spring to summer season. '**Swingtime**' is a popular cultivar which flowers profusely in varying shades of red.

CULTIVATION
These subtropical mountain plants do not like extremes of heat or cold. They grow best outdoors in a mild, frost-free climate. In colder climates they need the controlled, even temperature of a greenhouse. Grow in full sun in fertile, well-drained soil and pinch out growing tips of young plants to ensure bushy growth. Propagate from seed in summer or autumn.

Schizanthus
'Swingtime' *(below)*

S

Schizanthus × *wisetonensis* (above)

This erect species bears tubular to flared, 2-lipped, white, blue, pink or reddish brown flowers often flushed with yellow from spring to summer. It has lance-shaped, light green leaves and grows to 18 in (45 cm) high with a spread of 12 in (30 cm). Most garden strains are derived from this species. **ZONES 7–11.**

Schizanthus hookeri (left)

This species grows to 18 in (45 cm) in height with divided leaves and large pink, violet or purple flowers, whose upper lips are yellow blotched. **ZONES 7–11.**

SCHIZOSTYLIS

A single species of grassy leafed rhizomatous perennial makes up this genus. It is widely distributed in South Africa where it grows beside streams. The long-flowering stems terminate in clusters of bowl-shaped 6-petalled flowers in deep scarlet and pink; it is an excellent cut flower.

CULTIVATION

Frost hardy, it prefers full sun and fertile, moist soil with shelter from the cold in cool-temperate climates. Divide every couple of years when it becomes crowded or propagate from seed in spring.

Schizostylis coccinea
CRIMSON FLAG

This variable species can fail in prolonged dry conditions. The sword-shaped leaves are green and are untidy unless pruned regularly and protected from thrips and slugs. It is valued for its late summer and autumn display which in some climates, conditions and seasons can extend into winter and beyond. The flowers are usually scarlet. It is a dainty plant reaching a height of 24 in (60 cm) and spread of 12 in (30 cm). Several named varieties are available in shades of pink, including the rose pink **'Mrs Hegarty'**, the salmon pink **'Sunrise'** and the crimson **'Grandiflora'** (syns 'Gigantea', 'Major'). **'Viscountess Byng'** has pale pink flowers with narrow petals. ZONES 6–10.

Schizostylis coccinea 'Grandiflora' *(left)*

Schizostylis coccinea 'Mrs Hegarty' *(above)*

Schizostylis coccinea 'Viscountess Byng' *(below left)*

Schizostylis coccinea 'Sunrise' *(below)*

S

SCUTELLARIA
SKULLCAP, HELMET FLOWER

The name of this genus comes from the Latin *scutella*, meaning a small shield or cup, which is a rough description of the pouch of the upper calyx. There are some 300 known species that consist mainly of summer-flowering perennials, most on a rhizomatous root system, though a few are annuals and rarely subshrubs. Most species occur in temperate regions throughout the northern hemisphere.

CULTIVATION
They are easily grown in full sun in most reasonable garden soil. None would be happy with parched soil in summer, but they are content with ordinary watering throughout dry weather. Propagation is by division in winter or from seed sown fresh in autumn. Cuttings may be taken in summer.

Scutellaria costaricana (left)

An erect perennial to 3 ft (1 m) tall with dark purple stems, this species has slender oval leaves and 2½ in (6 cm) tubular flowers that are bright orange-scarlet with a golden yellow lip. It comes from Costa Rica. **ZONES 9–12.**

Scutellaria austinae (below)

Found in rocky areas of the pine forests and chaparrals and coastal ranges of California, this spreading, rather sticky stemmed rhizomatous perennial grows to as much as 12 in (30 cm) high when in flower. Its stems are covered in short hairs and narrow lance-shaped leaves. The flowers, which open in early summer are violet-blue and around 1 in (25 mm) long. **ZONES 8–11.**

Scutellaria incana *(right)*

This is a rounded perennial to 4 ft (1.2 m) in height with lightly serrated oval leaves and large panicles of grayish blue flowers in summer. A light prune will sometimes produce a second flush of flowers in autumn. It is widespread throughout northeastern USA. **ZONES 5–9.**

Scutellaria orientalis 'Alpina' *(above)*

This is a quickly spreading perennial with slightly hairy, oval, light green leaves on gray-green stems. It has upright clusters of golden flowers with brownish lips, 4 to 6 flowers per stem. It is best used as a ground cover and comes from southern Europe to central Asia. **ZONES 7–10.**

Scutellaria indica var. *parvifolia* *(right)*

Scutellaria indica *(below right)*

This is an upright, slowly spreading perennial around 12 in (30 cm) high with light gray-green oval leaves and clumped heads of soft blue-gray, tubular flowers. *Scutellaria indica* var. *parvifolia* (syn. *S. i.* var. *japonica*) is lower growing to 4 in (10 cm) and clumps more rapidly. It has crowded heads of blue-mauve, shortish tubular flowers in late spring. If deadheaded immediately it will reflower in late summer. **ZONES 5–10.**

S

SEDUM
STONECROP

This large genus contains about 400 species of succulent annuals, biennials, perennials, subshrubs and shrubs native to the northern hemisphere. Quick-growing plants, they vary widely in habit from carpet forming to upright up to 3 ft (1 m) tall. Their lush, whole leaves may be tubular, lanceolate, egg-shaped or elliptical, and the 5-petalled flowers appear in terminal sprays. Excellent as hanging basket or pot plants.

CULTIVATION
They range from frost tender to fully frost hardy. Fertile, porous soil is preferred; some types, however, are extremely robust and will grow in most soil types. They need full sun. Propagate perennials, shrubs and subshrubs from seed in spring or autumn, or by division or from cuttings in spring through mid-summer. Propagate annuals and biennials from seed sown under glass in early spring or outdoors in mid-spring.

Sedum ewersii
(below)
syn. *Hylotelephium ewersii*

This plant from the northern Himalayas, Mongolia, central Asia and China has branching, spreading low stems up to 12 in (30 cm) high with oval gray-green leaves up to 1 in (25 mm) long. The pink flowers persist from late spring to early autumn. ZONES 4–9.

Sedum 'Herbstfreude' *(left)*
syn. *Hylotelephium* 'Autumn Joy',
Sedum 'Autumn Joy'

This plant forms a small clump which grows to 24 in (60 cm) tall. It has toothed fleshy leaves. Large heads of pink flowers appear in autumn. These fade to copper tones and then finally turn red. In cold climates it dies back to the ground in winter. ZONES 5–10.

S

Sedum
'Mohrchen' *(right)*

This ia an upright-
stemmed hybrid that
reaches about 18 in
(45 cm) tall in
flower. The stems are
purple-red with
brownish red leaves
with shallowly
toothed edges. The
flower clusters are
deep red and open
from late summer.
Valuable not just
for its show of late
flowers, but also
throughout the sum-
mer for its foliage.
ZONES 4–10.

Sedum spectabile
(above)
syn. *Hylotelephium
spectabile*
SHOWY SEDUM, ICE PLANT

Spoon-shaped, fleshy, gray-
green leaves grow in clusters on the erect branching
stems of this succulent
perennial from China and
Korea. Butterflies flock to
the flattish heads of small,
pink, star-like flowers,
which bloom in late sum-
mer. It grows to a height
and spread of 18 in (45 cm)
and is resistant to both
frost and dry conditions.
'Brilliant' bears profuse
heads of bright rose-pink
flowers. **'Stardust'** has rich
green leaves. ZONES 5–10.

S

Sedum telephium *(above)*
syn. *Hylotelephium telephium*
ORPINE, LIVE-FOREVER

Found from eastern Europe to Japan, this semi-succulent deciduous perennial is a very reliable plant for late season color. Its flowering stems are up to 24 in (60 cm) tall and carry heads of densely packed small reddish purple flowers that open from late summer until well into autumn. The leaves are oblong, 1–3 in (25 mm–8 cm) long with shallow teeth around the edges. **ZONES 4–10.**

Sedum spurium *(right)*

This summer-flowering, evergreen perennial from Turkey and northern Iran bears small blooms in big, rounded flowerheads; colors range from white to purple. Hairy stems carrying saw-edged, elliptical leaves spread widely into a carpet 4 in (10 cm) tall, suitable for covering banks and slopes. **'Schorbuser Blut'** ('Dragon's Blood') is a creeping cultivar with plum-toned leaves and magenta flowers; **'Sunset Cloud'** has deep pinkish orange flowers. *Sedum stoloniferum* is similar to *S. spurium* but its stems lie close to the ground and the flowers are pink. **ZONES 7–10.**

SELAGINELLA
LITTLE CLUB MOSS, SPIKE MOSS

There are about 700 species of evergreen, rhizomatous perennials in this genus, which occur mainly in tropical and warm-temperate zones. They are grown for their attractive branching foliage. Many are suitable for hanging baskets or for pots in greenhouses in cooler areas.

CULTIVATION
These frost-tender plants prefer part-shade and moderately fertile, moist but well-drained soil. Propagate from spores or by division.

Selaginella martensii
(below)

Overlapping bright green leaves on 6 in (15 cm) high stems trail and root from the nodes on this species. Some forms have a white variegation. It comes from Central America. ZONES 9–11.

Selaginella kraussiana *(above)*
SPREADING CLUB MOSS, TRAILING SPIKE MOSS, KRAUSS'S SPIKE MOSS

The trailing branched stems of this species form a bright green feathery mesh up to 1 in (25 mm) high. Dwarf plants are available, as well as the golden '**Aurea**' and the green and yellow '**Variegata**'. ZONES 9–11.

S

Sempervivum arachnoideum (left)
COBWEB HOUSELEEK

The web of white hairs covering the green, triangular-leafed rosettes of this species no doubt inspired its name. Through summer it produces pink to crimson flowers in loose terminal clusters. A native of the European Alps, it grows to a height of 3 in (8 cm) and spread of 12 in (30 cm). ZONES 5–10.

SEMPERVIVUM

This is a genus of about 40 evergreen, perennial succulents originating in Europe and western Asia. They almost all have small yellow, pink or white, star-shaped flowers in summer, but their chief beauty resides in the symmetry of their rosettes of leaves and the way they spread to form carpets of foliage. This makes them ideal for rock gardens, walls and banks, and like all succulents they do not mind dry conditions. They take their common name from a custom dating from Roman times, which was to grow them on the roofs of houses—it was said that no witch could land her broomstick on a roof on which houseleeks were growing.

CULTIVATION
Plant in full sun in gravelly, well-drained soil. Flowering does not begin for several years; the rosettes die after flowering leaving offsets, from which they can be propagated.

Sempervivum tectorum
'Purple Beauty' *(above)*

Sempervivum tectorum
COMMON HOUSELEEK, ROOF HOUSELEEK, HENS AND CHICKENS

The rosettes of this species are reddish tipped, sometimes red throughout. The flowers are purple to rosy red and appear in one-sided terminal clusters on 12 in (30 cm) high stems in summer. It reaches 4–6 in (10–15 cm) high and 18 in (45 cm) wide. Applying bruised leaves to the skin has a cooling effect and is said to relieve burns, insect bites, skin problems and fever; the juice is used on warts and freckles. **'Commander Hay'** from the UK has large rosettes of red and green; **'Purple Beauty'** has dark violet leaves; and **'Magnificum'** has large rosettes and pink flowers. ZONES 4–10.

SENECIO

This large genus of vigorous leafy plants includes some
1000 species from all over the world. Plants range from annuals,
biennials and perennials to evergreen tree-like shrubs and
climbers, some of the species being succulent. The daisy-like
flowers, usually yellow but sometimes red, orange, blue or
purple, are arranged in small to large clusters at the tops of the
plants. Some species contain alkaloids and are poisonous to
humans and animals.

CULTIVATION

Reasonably fertile, well-drained soil suits these frost-tender to
fully frost-hardy plants, as well as a sunny location. Regular tip
pruning encourages a bushy habit. Propagate shrubs from
cuttings in summer, annuals from seed in autumn and perennials
by division in spring.

Senecio elegans
(below)

WILD CINERARIA

This marginally frost-
hardy, hairy annual is
native to South Africa
and has an erect habit,
growing to 24 in (60 cm)
tall. Its branching
stems are covered with
variable dark green
leaves that range from
entire to pinnate, up to
3 in (8 cm) long. In
spring to summer
daisy-like purplish
pink flowers appear in
dome-shaped terminal
clusters. ZONES 9–11.

S

Shortia galacifolia
(left)

OCONEE BELLS

The rather round leaves of this perennial from eastern USA are 2 in (5 cm) in diameter, glossy green, toothed and becoming bronzed in winter. Single white or blue flowers occur on 4 in (10 cm) stalks, each flower reaching 1 in (25 mm) across. **ZONES 5–9.**

Shortia soldanelloides var. *ilicifolia* *(below)*

SHORTIA

There are 6 species of these evergreen stemless plants with creeping roots. They come from eastern Asia and North America. The long-stalked leaves form a rosette, each leaf being round or heart-shaped and rather glossy. The flowers may be white, blue or pink, either single or in small heads and rather nodding.

CULTIVATION

Species of *Shortia* need a deeply shady spot with humus-rich, moist but well-drained soil. Propagation is by division or from rooted runners.

Shortia soldanelloides

FRINGED GALAX, FRINGEBELL

This mat-forming perennial from Japan has rounded leaves 2 in (5 cm) in diameter and with coarse teeth. Deep pink, white or bluish flowers occur in groups of 4 to 6 on 3 in (8 cm) stalks; each flower is 1 in (25 mm) across with the petals fringed. It comes from Japan. **Shortia soldanelloides var. *ilicifolia*** has leaves which have only a few coarse teeth. **ZONES 7–9.**

Sidalcea malviflora (right)
CHECKERBLOOM

This erect perennial plant grows to 4 ft (1.2 m) tall with spreading fibrous roots. It has lobed leaves and loose heads of pink or white flowers resembling hollyhocks during spring and summer. Most cultivars included under this name are now believed to be hybrids with other species. ZONES 6–10.

SIDALCEA
PRAIRIE MALLOW, CHECKER MALLOW

These 20 to 25 species of upright annuals or perennials with lobed, rounded leaves are found in open grasslands and mountain forests of western USA. Pink, purple or white flowers have a silky appearance and feel, and last well when cut.

CULTIVATION
They prefer cool summers and mild winters in good, deep, moisture-retentive soil. They will tolerate a little shade in hot climates. If cut back after flowering they will produce a second flush of blooms. Propagate from seed or by division.

Sidalcea 'Rose Queen' *(below)*
syn. *Sidalcea malviflora* 'Rose Queen'

Large, deep pink, cupped flowers are borne in spikes in summer on this fully frost-hardy perennial. The divided leaves form a basal clump with a spread of 24 in (60 cm). The overall height of this plant is 4 ft (1.2 m) and tall plants may need staking. **'William Smith'** is similar but grows only 3 ft (1 m) tall and produces flowers in 2 tones of deep pink. ZONES 6–10.

Sidalcea campestris (left)
MEADOW SIDALCEA

This hairy stemmed perennial grows up to 6 ft (1.8 m) tall. The pale pink or white flowers are 3 in (8 cm) across. It comes from northwestern USA. ZONES 7–10.

S

SILENE
CAMPION, CATCHFLY

This genus contains over 500 species of annuals, biennials and deciduous or evergreen perennials. They all feature 5-petalled summer flowers, baggy calyces and a multitude of small, elliptical, often silky leaves. Some of the species do well potted and others make good ground covers, with numerous stems forming a mound. Many of the weedier species open their flowers only at night, when they can be quite pretty, though all that is seen during the day are shrivelled petals. Some exude gum from their stems; passing flies get stuck to this, hence the common name catchfly.

CULTIVATION

Widely distributed throughout temperate and cold climates of the northern hemisphere, these marginally to fully frost-hardy plants like fertile, well-drained soil and full or part-sun. Propagate from seed in spring or early autumn or from cuttings in spring.

Silene acaulis (above)
MOSS CAMPION

This is a mat-forming evergreen perennial with masses of small leaves and shortly stalked pink flowers in summer. It comes from subarctic regions of Europe, Asia and North America, but is often poorly flowering in cultivation. It reaches a height of only 2 in (5 cm) with an 8 in (20 cm) spread. ZONES 2–9.

Silene armeria (below)

This European annual or biennial has pink, bell-shaped flowers with 5 notched petals. Growing to a height of 12 in (30 cm) with a spread of 6 in (15 cm), it has slender, erect, branching stems and linear leaves. ZONES 6–10.

Silene coeli-rosa
(right)

syns *Agrostemma coeli-rosa, Lychnis coeli-rosa, Viscaria elegans*

ROSE OF HEAVEN

This upright annual from the Mediterranean bears pinkish purple flowers in summer. Its lance-shaped, green leaves have a grayish cast. It grows rapidly to 18 in (45 cm) high and 6 in (15 cm) wide. **'Blue Angel'** has bright mid-blue flowers with slightly darker centers. **ZONES 6–11.**

Silene coeli-rosa 'Blue Angel' *(below)*

Silene fimbriata *(above & left)*

This hairy perennial to 24 in (60 cm) tall with upright leafy stems has loose heads of large white flowers and a persistent light green inflated calyx. It comes from Turkey. **ZONES 6–10.**

Silene keiskei var. minor (below)

This evergreen perennial from Japan reaches 4 in (20 cm) tall and 8 in (20 cm) wide, on slender stems with hairy, dark green leaves. Sprays of dark rose-pink flowers appear in late summer. ZONES 6–10.

Silene laciniata (left)

INDIAN PINK, MEXICAN CAMPION

This 3 ft (1 m) tall perennial comes from California and northern Mexico. The flowers are held in small heads and are bright crimson in color. ZONES 7–11.

Silene pendula

NODDING CATCHFLY

This fast-growing, bushy annual from the Mediterranean bears clusters of pale pink flowers in summer and early autumn. It has oval, hairy, mid-green leaves and grows to 8 in (20 cm) high and wide. '**Compacta**' is dense and grows to just 4 in (10 cm). ZONES 7–11.

Silene pendula 'Compacta' (right)

Silene schafta 'Shell Pink'
(right)

Silene schafta

This is a hairy clump-forming, semi-evergreen perennial from western Asia. The deep purplish red flowers appear in late summer and autumn on stems 10 in (25 cm) high. **'Shell Pink'** has very pale pink, nearly white flowers. **ZONES 6–10.**

Silene vulgaris *(below)*

BLADDER CAMPION, MAIDEN'S TEARS

This perennial has stems up to 24 in (60 cm) tall, oval leaves and white flowers with 2-lobed petals; the flowers are either solitary or in heads. It is found throughout northern Africa, temperate Asia and Europe. However, most plants sold as *Silene vulgaris* are, in fact, *S. uniflora*. **ZONES 5–10.**

Silene uniflora *(above)*
syn. *Silene vulgaris* subsp. *maritima*

SEA CAMPION

This deep-rooted perennial bears a multitude of white flowers like pompons on branched stems in spring or summer. Its calyces are greenish and balloon like, and its lanceolate leaves have a grayish cast. Reaching about 8 in (20 cm) in height and spread, it can be grown on top of walls, in beds or containers and grows wild on cliffs along the European seaboard. **'Flore Pleno'** has double white flowers with deeply cut petals. **ZONES 3–10.**

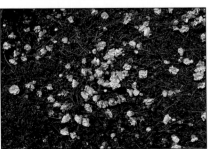

Silene uniflora 'Flore Pleno' *(left)*

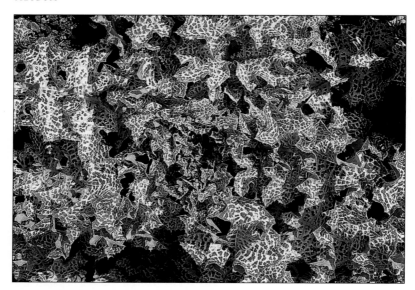

SILYBUM

Two erect annuals or biennials make up this genus from the Mediterranean, south-west Europe, central Asia and Africa. They are grown for their rosettes of intensely spiny, glossy dark green foliage, and the rounded, single, purple-pink flowerheads which are surrounded by thorny bracts.

CULTIVATION

Fully frost hardy, they prefer full sun and poor to moderately fertile, well-drained soil. Propagate from seed and watch out for slugs and snails.

Silybum marianum
(above)
BLESSED THISTLE, HOLY THISTLE

Viciously spiny dark green foliage marbled with white forms a rosette of dissected leaves on this biennial. Single stalks produce a head of flowers up to 4 ft (1.2 m) tall in the summer of the second year. It has become naturalized in California and the pampas of Argentina. ZONES 7–11.

SINNINGIA

This genus of about 40 species of tuberous perennials and deciduous or evergreen shrubs includes the flower-shop gloxinias.
The flowers can be as much as 4 in (10 cm) across and come in
the richest shades of blue, violet, pink or red, usually with
mottled throats and their petals edged in white or a pale color.
They make spectacular pot plants, each plant carrying as many
as 20 flowers at the center of a rosette of coarsely velvety leaves.
They are useless as garden plants because when rain fills the
trumpets they collapse.

CULTIVATION

They are best in a humid atmosphere with bright light and indirect sun, and moist, peaty soil. The leaves die down after flowering, when the tubers can be dried out and stored in a frost-free
area. Propagate from seed in spring or from stem cuttings in late
spring or summer.

Sinningia speciosa

(below)

FLORIST'S GLOXINIA, VELVET
SLIPPER PLANT

This perennial is valued
for its large, trumpet-
shaped, summer
flowers in white, red,
blue, purple and pas-
tels. Nearly stemless
with long, velvety
leaves, it grows to a
height and spread of
12 in (30 cm). The
Fyfiana Group has
large open flowers in
various colors; the
Maxima Group has
nodding flowers.
ZONES 11–12.

S

SISYRINCHIUM

The genus includes 90 marginally to fully frost-hardy species of annuals and rhizomatous perennials. They often self-destruct in seasons of prolific blooming, because the flower stem kills off the leaf stem from which it sprouts. *Sisyrinchium platense* was first collected in the River Plate region of Argentina.

CULTIVATION

Establish them in poor to moderately fertile, moist but well-drained soil. Although tolerant of part-shade, they prefer sun. They readily self-seed, otherwise they can be propagated by division in late summer.

Sisyrinchium 'Californian Skies' *(right)*

Often listed as a cultivar of *Sisyrinchium bellum*, but possibly a hybrid, 'California Skies' is a slowly spreading, grassy leafed perennial with branched stems of pale blue flowers in early summer. It is very like *S. bellum* but with flowers of a lighter, less mauve shade of blue. ZONES 8–11.

Sisyrinchium platense *(below)*

Sisyrinchium idahoense (below)

Winged unbranched stems grow to 18 in (45 cm) on this semi-evergreen perennial from western USA. The flowers are violet-blue with a yellow center, rarely white. **ZONES 3–9.**

Sisyrinchium graminoides (right)
syn. *Sisyrinchium angustifolium*

BLUE-EYED GRASS

This semi-evergreen perennial blooms in spring, producing terminal clusters of small pale to dark purple flowers like irises, with yellow throats. The stalks are flattened and winged. **ZONES 3–10.**

Sisyrinchium striatum (right)
syn. *Phaiophleps nigricans*

SATIN FLOWER

Long, narrow and sword-shaped, the leaves on this fully frost-hardy, evergreen perennial are gray-green. In summer it bears slender spikes of small cream flowers, striped purple. The species, which originates in Chile and Argentina, grows 18–24 in (45–60 cm) high with a 12 in (30 cm) spread. There is also an attractive variegated form. **ZONES 8–10.**

Smilacina racemosa (left)

FALSE SOLOMON'S SEAL, FALSE SPIKENARD

Red fleshy fruit appear on this North American and Mexican species after it blooms in spring through mid-summer, producing lemon-scented white flowers in feathery sprays above fresh green, elliptical leaves. It grows to 3 ft (1 m) high with a spread of 24 in (60 cm). **ZONES 4–9.**

Smilacina stellata (below)

STAR-FLOWERED LILY OF THE VALLEY, STARFLOWER

This species has stems up to 24 in (60 cm) long that produce lance-shaped 6 in (15 cm) long folded leaves which are finely hairy underneath. Up to 20 white flowers are crowded on a 2 in (5 cm) wide head. The berries are at first green with black stripes, later becoming dark red. It comes from North America and Mexico. **ZONES 3–9.**

SMILACINA

FALSE SOLOMON'S SEAL

The 25 species in this genus occur in North and Central America and over much of temperate and subtropical Asia. These very attractive perennials with their plumes of white flowers in early summer bear a genus name meaning 'like a *Smilax*', which is a closely related though mainly tropical genus from the roots of which sarsaparilla is made. The common name suggests that their rhizomes might be confused with those of another cousin, *Polygonatum multiflorum* (Solomon's seal). However, while both sarsaparilla and the 'true' Solomon's seal are used medicinally, *Smilacina* species are not. They colonize rapidly, adorning gardens with their luxuriant foliage and pretty flowers.

CULTIVATION

These fully frost-hardy plants prefer dappled or deep shade and humus-rich, moist but well-drained neutral to acid soil. Propagate from seed in autumn or by division in autumn or spring.

SOLANUM
syn. *Lycianthes*

*Solanum
pyracanthum*
(below)

This perennial from
tropical Africa grows to
5 ft (1.5 m) tall. The
lobed leaves are spiny
along the central vein.
The flowers are violet.
ZONES 10–12.

There are over 1400 species in this genus including trees, shrubs,
annuals, biennials, perennials and climbers from a range of habitats worldwide. Some are evergreen, others semi-evergreen or
deciduous. The genus includes important food plants like the
potato and eggplant (aubergine), though many species are
dangerously poisonous. Ornamental species are grown for their
flowers and fruits. The leaves are arranged alternately, while
the showy flowers are solitary or in clusters, star-shaped to bell-
shaped, ranging in color from white and yellow to blue and
purple. The fruits are berries that contain many seeds.

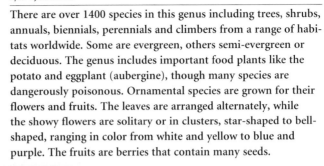

CULTIVATION
These warm-climate plants have a wide range
of requirements; most prefer full sun and rich,
well-drained soil. They are commonly grown
from seed in spring or cuttings in summer.
They are prone to attack by spider mite, white
fly and aphids.

*Solanum
pseudocapsicum* *(left)*

JERUSALEM CHERRY, WINTER CHERRY,
CHRISTMAS CHERRY

This frost-tender, evergreen
Mediterranean native produces
starry white flowers in summer,
followed by small scarlet
berries that are poisonous. It
grows sedately into a bushy,
velvety leafed shrub about 4 ft
(1.2 m) high and wide and is
perhaps best grown as an annual, even in wild areas, in
which case it should grow to
24 in (60 cm) tall. Several varieties with differently colored
fruit are available. The species
is related to the potato, eggplant and tomato, as well as to
some other less edible plants.
ZONES 9–11.

S

Soldanella caucasica
'Alba' *(left)*

SOLDANELLA
SNOWBELL

The soldanellas are elegant relatives of the primrose. They come from the mountains of Europe and flower at the end of spring. There are 10 species of evergreen perennials, all rather alike and interbreeding freely both in the wild and in gardens much to the irritation of those who like to be certain of their plants' names. They have nodding to pendent purple to white flowers and leathery leaves and are good plants for rock gardens and tubs. A good example is *Soldanella caucasica* 'Alba'.

CULTIVATION
These plants are mostly fully frost hardy, although the flower buds may be destroyed by frost. They need part-shade and humus-rich, well-drained, peaty soil. Propagate from seed in spring or by division in late summer. Watch out for slugs.

Soldanella hungarica (below)

Found on the Balkan Peninsula and the mountains of eastern central Europe, this delicate little alpine is a superb plant for a cool rockery. It has 1 in (25 mm) wide, rounded, kidney-shaped leaves that are deep green above, purplish below. The flowers, carried singly or in twos or threes, on hairy 4 in (10 cm) high stems, are ½ in (12 mm) long and lavender to pale purple in color with narrow petals. **ZONES 6–9.**

Soldanella montana (right)

Growing to about 12 in (30 cm) tall, this mound-forming species comes from the Alps but prefers the alpine woodlands to the bare rocks higher up. It flowers in early spring, often before the snows have not quite melted, producing long, pendent, bell-shaped, lavender-blue blossoms with fringed mouths. It has shallow-toothed, rounded leaves. **ZONES 6–9.**

S

SOLENOSTEMON
COLEUS, FLAME NETTLE, PAINTED NETTLE

This genus comprises 60 species of low shrubby perennials, often hairy and with variegated leaves from tropical Africa and Asia. The stems are 4-angled and the opposite leaves are often toothed. The flowers are small with an elongated lower lip.

CULTIVATION
These frost-tender plants are easily grown in milder climates with adequate summer moisture and protection from hot sun. They prefer humus-rich, moist but well-drained soil and need pinching back to promote bushiness. Propagate from seed or cuttings.

Solenostemon scutellarioides
(below)

syns *Coleus blumei* var. *verschaffeltii*, *C. scutellarioides*

Native to Southeast Asia, this bushy, fast-growing perennial is grown as an annual in more temperate climates. The leaves are a bright mixture of pink, green, red or yellow and are a pointed, oval shape with serrated edges. It grows 24 in (60 cm) high and 12 in (30 cm) wide. **ZONES 10–12.**

S

Solidago 'Baby Gold'
(right)
syn. *Solidago* 'Golden Baby'

Some garden hybrids are valuable for their bright color in early autumn. This one is an upright plant with feathery spikes of golden flowers. Reaching 3 ft (1 m) in height, it has lance-shaped, green leaves. **ZONES 5–10.**

SOLIDAGO
GOLDENROD

The goldenrods are a genus of about 100 species of woody based perennials, almost all indigenous to the meadows and prairies of North America, with a few species in South America and Eurasia. They are related to the asters and, like them, flower in autumn. Their effect is quite different, however, as the individual flowers are very much smaller and are bright yellow. Most of the species are too weedy to be allowed into even the wildest garden, but some are worth cultivating for their big flower clusters and there are some very attractive hybrids.

CULTIVATION
These fully frost-hardy plants grow well in sun or shade in any fertile, well-drained soil. Most species self-seed, or they can be propagated by dividing the clumps in autumn or spring.

S

Solidago 'Golden Wings' *(above)*

This perennial grows to 5 ft (1.5 m) high with a spread of 3 ft (1 m). It has downy, lance-shaped leaves with serrated margins, and produces small, bright yellow flowers in feathery panicles early in autumn. **ZONES 5–10.**

Solidago sphacelata *(below)*

FALSE GOLDENROD

This species grows 24–36 in (60–90 cm) tall and has serrated, heart-shaped leaves. It eventually forms a large clump but is not invasive. The yellow flowers are borne on narrow arching stems from late summer. **ZONES 4–9.**

Solidago virgaurea *(left)*

This 3 ft (1 m) tall plant from Europe blooms in summer and autumn, with dense heads of yellow flowers. **Solidago virgaurea** subsp. **minuta** only grows to 4 in (10 cm) high. **ZONES 5–10.**

SONERILA

These evergreen perennials and small shrubs come from Southeast Asia and southern China, and over 175 species are known. The leaves are oval, sometimes toothed with 3 to 5 veins, dark green, spotted, and bristly. The flowers appear in racemes or corymbs and are anything from star- to cup-shaped.

CULTIVATION

They are usually grown as greenhouse plants outside the tropics; outdoors they prefer dappled shade and humus-rich, moist but well-drained soil. Propagate from cuttings.

Sonerila margaritacea 'Argentea' *(left)*

Sonerila margaritacea var. *victoriae (below)*

Sonerila margaritacea

This 10 in (25 cm) high plant comes from Malaysia and Java. The arching or hanging stems are scarlet, and the leaves are dark polished green with white spots in lines in between the veins. Underneath the veins are purple. The rose-colored flowers are in heads of 8 to 10 and up to ¾ in (18 mm) across. **'Argentea'** has purple-red foliage with silver markings, a striking contrast. *Sonerila margaritacea* var. *victoriae* is similar but with wider leaves and wider petals.
ZONES 10–12.

S

SPATHIPHYLLUM

Most of the 36 species of this genus of evergreen, rhizomatous perennials come from tropical America, with some native to Malaysia. They are lush, with dark green, oval leaves that stand erect or arch slightly. The beautiful white, cream or green flowers resemble arum lilies and bloom reliably indoors. A NASA study of 'sick building syndrome' found spathiphyllums to be among the top 10 plants for their ability to 'clean' the air in offices.

CULTIVATION

Grow in loose, fibrous, porous potting soil in filtered light away from the sun. To simulate tropical conditions, increase the humidity by placing the plant on a tray of pebbles. Water or mist regularly and sponge any dust from the leaves. Keep the soil moist but not soggy, and allow it to dry out a little in winter. Feed every 4 to 6 weeks with half-strength soluble fertilizer in spring and summer. Propagate by division in spring or summer. They are generally pest free. Too much light may turn the foliage yellow.

S

Spathiphyllum
'Sensation' *(left)*

This is the largest of the *Spathiphyllum* cultivars. It has dark green foliage with prominent ribbing and large, well-shaped white flowers, ageing to green. It is a very attractive plant even when not in bloom.
ZONES 11–12.

Spathiphyllum 'Mauna Loa' *(right)*
PEACE LILY

The leathery, lance-shaped, glossy, mid-green leaves of this perennial reach lengths of 12 in (30 cm). Oval, white, papery spathes surrounding white spadices are borne intermittently, and turn green with age. It is the best known of a fairly numerous group of large-flowered cultivars. Others include **'Clevelandii'**, which is shorter, and **'Aztec'**. ZONES 11–12.

Spathiphyllum wallisii *(left)*
WHITE SAILS

This is a dwarf species that bears clusters of glossy green, lance-shaped leaves on reed-like stems, which grow to 12 in (30 cm). A white spathe encloses tiny, creamy white spadices of fragrant flowers tightly packed around an upright spike. The color changes to green with age. ZONES 11–12.

S

SPEIRANTHA

This genus consists of only one species, a perennial related to *Convallaria*. From thick spreading rhizomes, stemless leaves form a basal rosette. White flowers are followed by berries.

CULTIVATION

This plant prefers part-shade and moderately fertile, moist, humus-rich soil enriched with leafmold. Propagate from ripe seed or by division.

Speirantha convallarioides
(above)

This species has stemless leaves 6 in (15 cm) long and 1¼ in (30 mm) wide, tapering to a blunt point. The flower stalk is 4 in (10 cm) tall and carries a loose head of 25 white flowers in spring and summer. This plant for shady places comes from China. ZONES 8–10.

STACHYS

BETONY, WOUNDWORT, HEDGE NETTLE

This genus of the mint family contains about 300 species of annuals, perennials and evergreen shrubs. They have long been used in herb gardens and many of them have supposed medicinal value. They come from a range of habitats mostly in northern temperate regions. Many species are aromatic, and most are attractive to bees and butterflies. They bear tubular, 2-lipped, purple, red, pink, yellow or white flowers.

CULTIVATION

They all like well-drained, moderately fertile soil in full sun. Propagate from seed or cuttings or by division.

Stachys
albotomentosa
(below)

The specific name of this Mexican species means white felting, which is an apt description of the foliage as it is covered in a dense coating of fine white hairs. A perennial, it grows to around 18 in (45 cm) tall and produces salmon-pink flowers from early summer until cut back by cold. In its homeland the flowers are very attractive to hummingbirds. ZONES 9–11.

S

Stachys byzantina
'Cotton Boll' *(left)*

Stachys byzantina
'Silver Carpet' *(above)*

Stachys byzantina 'Big
Ears' *(below left)*

Stachys byzantina
'Primrose Heron' *(below)*

Stachys byzantina *(below right)*
syns *Stachys lanata, S. olympica*
LAMBS' EARS, LAMBS' TAILS, LAMBS' TONGUES

The leaves give this perennial its common names:
they are lance-shaped and have the same white,
downy feel of a lamb. Unfortunately, the leaves
turn to mush in very cold, humid or wet weather.
It makes a good ground cover or border plant,
growing 12–18 in (30–45 cm) high, with a 24 in
(60 cm) spread. Mauve-pink flowers appear in
summer. **'Silver Carpet'** seldom flowers, remaining more compact than the species; **'Cotton Boll'**
(syn. 'Sheila McQueen') has flowers that look like
cottonwool balls; **'Primrose Heron'** has yellowish
green leaves; and **'Big Ears'** (syn. 'Countess Helen
von Stein') is a large-growing cultivar that bears
tall spikes of purple flowers. ZONES 5–10.

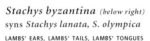

Stachys macrantha (right)

This perennial has erect stems up to 24 in (60 cm) tall bearing heads of hooded, purple-pink flowers from early summer to early autumn. The basal leaves are long and heart-shaped, wrinkled and rough with hairs. **ZONES 5–10.**

Stachys coccinea (below)
SCARLET HEDGE NETTLE

This long-flowering perennial native to southwest USA and Mexico bears red flowers, although pink and white forms are now available. The flowers are almost irresistible to hummingbirds. Flowering continues from spring through autumn on plants that grow 12–36 in (30–90 cm) tall and 18 in (45 cm) wide. **ZONES 6–10.**

S

STEIRODISCUS

This genus consists of 5 annuals from South Africa with spirally arranged, toothed, divided leaves. Yellow or orange daisy flowers appear in summer.

CULTIVATION

Frost tender, they prefer full sun and well-drained, humus-rich soil. Propagate from seed or cuttings.

Steirodiscus tagetes
(above)

This species grows to 12 in (30 cm) in height with wiry branching stems and 2 in (5 cm) long divided leaves. The bright yellow or orange flowers are $\frac{3}{4}$ in (18 mm) wide. **'Gold Rush'** is a larger yellow form. **ZONES 9–11.**

Steirodiscus tagetes
'Gold Rush' *(left)*

Stokesia laevis
(above)

syn. *Stokesia cyanea*

This fully frost-hardy perennial has evergreen rosettes of narrow, mid-green, basal and divided leaves. The blue-mauve or white blooms have a shaggy appearance reminiscent of corn-flowers, and are borne freely on erect stems.
ZONES 7–10.

STOKESIA
STOKES' ASTER

This genus of a single perennial species native to the southeastern states of the USA was named after Englishman Dr Jonathan Stokes (1755–1831). One of the most attractive late-flowering perennials, it grows to about 18 in (45 cm) high and flowers from late summer to autumn if the spent flower stems are promptly removed. It is very good for cutting.

CULTIVATION
Plant in full sun or part-shade and fertile, well-drained soil. Water well in summer. Propagate from seed in autumn or by division in spring.

S

STRELITZIA
BIRD OF PARADISE

These 5 species of clump-forming perennials have exotic flowers that resemble the head of a bird. Each bloom consists of several spiky flowers arising from a boat-like bract. The leaves are large and dramatic. Strelitzias form large clumps of evergreen banana-like foliage. They occur naturally in South Africa but are grown in warm climates around the world. In cool areas they are enjoyed as greenhouse specimens. The fruits are capsules.

CULTIVATION
They need full sun or part-shade and prefer well-drained soil enriched with organic matter and dryish conditions in cooler months. New plants can be produced by dividing a clump, but this is hard work as the clump and roots are very dense. They can also be propagated from seed or suckers in spring.

Strelitzia juncea
(above)
syn. *Strelitzia reginae*
var. *juncea*

Botanists have long disputed whether this should be treated as a species distinct from *Strelitzia reginae* or as a variety of that species. Its appearance is dramatically different with tall, rush-like, straight leaf stalks to 6 ft (1.8 m) high, lacking any leaf blade. The flowerheads are identical with those of *S. reginae*, but their stems are much shorter than the leaf stalks. ZONES 9–12.

Strelitzia nicolai (right)
WILD BANANA, GIANT BIRD OF PARADISE

The erect, woody, palm-like stems on this tree-sized species reach a height of 20 ft (6 m) and the clump spreads over 12 ft (3.5 m). It has large, dull green leaves over 5 ft (1.5 m) long on lengthy stalks. The flowers appear in summer near the top of the plant from the leaf axils. These striking flowers are greenish blue and white, and open a few at a time from a reddish brown bract. ZONES 10–12.

Strelitzia reginae
'Mandela's Gold'
(below)

Strelitzia reginae (below)
CRANE FLOWER, BIRD OF PARADISE

This shrub-sized species has blooms of bright orange and blue sitting in a pointed green bract edged with red. The main flowering season is spring to summer. It grows to 6 ft (1.8 m) high and spreads over 3 ft (1 m), forming an erect clump of leaves and smooth flower stalks arising from underground stems. The spoon-like leaves are grayish green. **'Mandela's Gold'** has yellow-orange and purplish blue blooms. ZONES 10–12.

S

STREPTOCARPUS

This genus consists of 130 species of annuals, perennials and rarely subshrubs from tropical Africa, Madagascar, Thailand, China and Indonesia. There are 3 main groups: shrubby bushy species with vigorous growth; rosetted plants; and single-leafed

species producing one very large leaf up to 3 ft (1 m) long. They all bear tubular flowers with 5 lobes and hairy, veined, crinkly leaves. An example of the rosette species is *Streptocarpus capensis.*

CULTIVATION
Frost tender, they prefer part-shade and leafy, humus-rich, moist but well-drained soil. Seeding will be prevented if flowers are deadheaded and stalks are removed. Propagate from seed or cuttings or by division.

Streptocarpus capensis (above)

Streptocarpus caulescens *(left)*

A native of Tanzania and Kenya, this upright fleshy stemmed perennial grows to around 24 in (60 cm) tall and has elliptical 2½ in (6 cm) long leaves that are covered in soft hairs. Its flowers, usually violet, are just under 1 in (25 mm) in diameter and are borne in sprays of 6–12 blooms. They open from autumn. ZONES 10–12.

Streptocarpus Hybrids

Most *Streptocarpus* hybrids have *S. rexii* as a major parent. They are generally plants with a rosette growth habit and large, showy, trumpet-shaped flowers in bright colors with a white throat. **'Bethan'** bears multitudes of lilac-purple flowers; **'Blue Heaven'** has flowers that are a strong mid-blue to pale purple; **'Falling Stars'** has many small sky-blue to lilac flowers; **'Gloria'** has pinkish flowers; **'Ruby'** has crimson-red flowers; and **'Susan'** has deep red flowers with yellow centers. ZONES 10–11.

Streptocarpus 'Falling Stars' *(left)*

Streptocarpus 'Gloria' *(center left)*

Streptocarpus 'Blue Heaven' *(bottom left)*

Streptocarpus 'Ruby' *(above)*

Streptocarpus 'Susan' *(below)*

Streptocarpus 'Bethan' *(bottom right)*

S

STROMANTHE

This genus of some 13 species of evergreen, rhizomatous perennials in the arrowroot family is found from Central America to southern Brazil. They often develop short trunks or sturdy, trunk-like stems. The leaves, enclosed in a petiole sheath before expanding, are oblong, heavily veined and 4–18 in (10–45 cm) long depending on the species. They are usually dark green above with purplish undersides. Inflorescences of small white, pink or mauve flowers appear in summer. Leafy bracts enclose the flowers and are occasionally brightly colored. Small, ridged fruits follow the flowers.

CULTIVATION
Plant in moist, humus-rich, well-drained soil in light to moderate shade. Principally tropical plants, they will not tolerate frosts and prefer a mild, humid climate. Propagate from seed or by division where possible, or by removing rooted basal offsets.

Stromanthe sanguinea (above)

This is an erect species from Brazil to 5 ft (1.5 m). The oblong 18 in (45 cm) leaves are dark green above and purple underneath. The stem-leaf sheaths are papery and broad and pink or red. White flowers occur in panicles and have red bracts and orange-red calyces. **ZONES 10–12.**

S

STYLIDIUM
TRIGGER PLANT

About 140 species of annuals, perennials and subshrubs make up this genus, most native to Australia, but some ranging as far as Southeast Asia. The leaves may be grass-like and basal, or short and narrow on wiry stems. Some species are clump forming, others shrubby, and at least one is a low-growing climber. All share a similar flowering habit with small, lobelia-like, white, pink or yellow flowers. Each flower has an irritable style that snaps over to deposit and receive pollen from visiting insects, hence the common name trigger plant.

CULTIVATION

These are tropical plants and few will tolerate anything other than very light frosts. Plant in well-drained, humus-rich soil with a sunny aspect or cultivate in a greenhouse. Propagate from seed or cuttings or by division.

Stylidium graminifolium
(right)

GRASS TRIGGER PLANT

This is a variable species from eastern Australia growing in habitats ranging from coastal to alpine. It forms a clump of grassy leaves, from which arise several stems 12–36 in (30–90 cm) tall; each stem bears a long, gradually opening spike of flowers ranging in color from palest pink to magenta, the latter color most often associated with the alpine forms. ZONES 9–11.

STYLOPHORUM
WOOD POPPY

This genus consists of 3 poppy-like perennials from eastern Asia and eastern North America. They form low rosettes of deeply lobed foliage: the basal leaves, which have long petioles, are about 18 in (45 cm) long, while the leaves higher in the rosette have shorter petioles and are correspondingly smaller. Simple 4-petalled, bright yellow flowers up to 2 in (5 cm) in diameter are carried in clusters at the top of leafy stems barely higher than the foliage rosette. They appear in spring and summer.

CULTIVATION
Woodland conditions with cool, moist, humus-rich soil in dappled shade are ideal. However, with occasional watering they can be grown in perennial borders with a sunny exposure. Propagate from seed or by dividing established clumps in late winter.

Stylophorum diphyllum (below)
CELANDINE POPPY

This hairy plant grows to 12 in (30 cm) in height and has deeply toothed leaves. The simple flower stalks give rise to a cluster of bracts holding yellow flowerheads up to 2 in (5 cm) across. It comes from eastern USA. ZONES 7–10.

SWAINSONA
PEA, DESERT PEA

This genus of around 50 species of perennials, annuals and subshrubs or trailing plants is endemic to Australia with one species from New Zealand. Most species are found in dry to arid areas, with some occupying moister sites in cooler regions. The leaflets are mostly gray to gray-green, with the pea-shaped flowers in extended racemes ranging in color from white to blue, mauve and dramatic scarlet.

CULTIVATION
Frost tender, they prefer full sun and moderately fertile, very well-drained soil. Propagate from seed or cuttings.

Swainsona formosa
(above)
syns *Clianthus dampieri, C. formosus*
STURT'S DESERT PEA

Native to the dry outback of Australia, this slow-growing, trailing annual has unusually large and showy, brilliant red, black-blotched spring flowers and small, grayish leaves. It grows to a height of 6 in (15 cm) and spread of 3 ft (1 m). ZONES 9–11.

S

Symphytum asperum (left)
PRICKLY COMFREY

This thick-rooted perennial from Europe, Turkey and Iran has oval, heart-shaped or oblong leaves covered with stiff prickly hairs. The flower stems grow up to 5 ft (1.5 m) tall and are openly branched with few hairs. There are many flowers in the head; they open a rose color, soon changing to lilac or blue, and are ½ in (12 mm) long. It has become naturalized in North America where it has been grown as a fodder plant.
ZONES 5–10.

SYMPHYTUM
COMFREY

This genus comprises 25 to 35 species of hairy perennials from damp and shaded places in Europe, North Africa and western Asia. They grow rapidly and may become invasive in the garden. The leaves are alternate and rather crowded at the base of the plant. The flowers are held in shortly branched heads of pink, blue, white or cream. Each flower consists of a tube terminating in 5 triangular lobes.

CULTIVATION
They are easily grown in sun or part-shade in moist, well-dug soil with added manure. Propagate from seed, cuttings, or by division.

Symphytum ×
uplandicum

RUSSIAN COMFREY

This coarse, hairy per-
ennial hybrid between
Symphytum asperum
and *S. officinale* grows
to 6 ft (1.8 m) tall.
Leaves are oblong and
run a short distance
down the stem. Flowers
are ¾ in (18 mm) long,
rosy at first then be-
coming purple or
blue. **'Variegatum'** has
attractive cream leaf
variegation, but flower
color is poor and flowers
are often removed.
ZONES 5–10.

Symphytum 5.5
uplandicum
'Variegatum' *(right)*

Symphytum
'Goldsmith' *(above)*
syn. *Symphytum*
'Jubilee'

'Goldsmith' grows to
12 in (30 cm) and has
leaves edged and
blotched with cream
and gold; the flowers
are blue, pink or white.
ZONES 5–10.

Symphytum
caucasicum *(right)*

This is a smaller, softly
hairy branched peren-
nial growing to 24 in
(60 cm). The leaves are
hairy on both sides and
oval to oblong up to
8 in (20 cm) long; they
run back a short way
down the stem. The
flowers are at first red-
purple, changing to
blue, and ¾ in (18 mm)
long in terminal paired
heads. It occurs natu-
rally in the Caucasus
and Iran. ZONES 5–10.

S

TACCA

This genus of 10 species of rhizomatous perennials is widespread throughout tropical Southeast Asia and Africa. They have basal leaves close to the ground, from which rise a scape with greenish yellow flowers surrounded by bracts. The strange, almost bizarre flowers have earned members of this genus names such as bat flowers, cats' whiskers and devil's tongue.

CULTIVATION

These frost-tender plants can be grown outdoors in the tropics and subtropics, but elsewhere require the protection of a greenhouse. They need a humid atmosphere, some shade and a peaty soil. Water amply in summer, but allow to dry out almost totally in winter. Propagate by division of the rhizomes or from seed, if available, in spring.

Tacca integrifolia (right)
BAT PLANT, BAT FLOWER

Found naturally in Southeast Asia and from eastern India to southern China, this upright species has lance-shaped leaves up to 24 in (60 cm) long. The flowers, which open in summer and are carried in racemes of up to 30 blooms, are purple-red to brown and are backed by 4 green to purple-tinted bracts. Filaments up to 8 in (20 cm) long hang from the flowers. ZONES 10–12.

T

Tagetes 'Disco Orange' *(right)*

Judging by the cultivar name, it's a safe bet that 'Disco Orange' first appeared sometime in the 1970s. It is a cheerful dwarf marigold suitable for the front of a summer border, and produces single, weather-resistant flowerheads from late spring to early autumn. ZONES 9–11.

TAGETES
MARIGOLD

These annuals were rare at the time of their discovery in the seventeenth century; today, they are among the most familiar of summer plants and are useful as bedding plants or for edging. The single or double flowers come in cheerful shades of orange, yellow, mahogany, brown and red and contrast brightly with the deep green leaves. Some of the 50 or so species have aromatic foliage, hence *Tagetes minuta*'s common name of stinking Roger. It is also said that the roots exude substances fatal to soil-borne pests, leading to their extensive use as companion plants.

CULTIVATION

These fast-growing plants thrive in warm, frost-free climates, but the young plants may need to be raised in a greenhouse in cooler climates. Grow in full sun in fertile, well-drained soil. Deadhead regularly to prolong flowering. Propagate from seed in spring after the danger of frost has passed. They may be prone to attack by slugs, snails and botrytis.

Tagetes lemmonii *(below)*
MOUNTAIN MARIGOLD

Native to Arizona and adjacent regions of Mexico, this species is unusual in being a shrub of 3–5 ft (1–1.5 m) in height, of somewhat sprawling habit. The leaves are light green and pinnately divided into narrow segments; they are very aromatic, giving off a smell like ripe passionfruit when brushed against. In autumn and winter it bears small golden yellow flowerheads, sometimes continuing through most of the year (encouraged by cutting back in early summer). A popular species in southwestern USA, it likes full sun and a sheltered position. ZONES 9–11.

T

Tagetes erecta and *Tagetes tenuifolia* (orange) *(above)*

Tagetes erecta
'Marvel Gold' *(below)*

Tagetes erecta
(above)

AFRICAN MARIGOLD, AMERICAN
MARIGOLD, AZTEC MARIGOLD

The aromatic, glossy dark green leaves of this bushy annual from Mexico have deeply incised margins. With its upstanding, branching stems, it grows to 18 in (45 cm) in height and spread. Orange or yellow daisy-like flowers bloom in summer and early autumn. The flowers can be as large as 4 in (10 cm) across. **'Crackerjack'** has double flowers and grows to a height of 24 in (60 cm). This species is used as a culinary and medicinal herb. **'Marvel Gold'** bears large pompons of golden yellow. ZONES 9–11.

Tagetes tenuifolia
SIGNET MARIGOLD

More delicate in its lacy foliage than other *Tagetes* species, the signet marigold grows to a height and spread of only 8 in (20 cm), making it suitable for edgings and bedding. The summer and early autumn flowers are also small and are soft yellow or orange. **'Tangerine Gem'** bears small, single, rich orange flowerheads. ZONES 9–11.

Tagetes patula *(below)*
FRENCH MARIGOLD

This fast-growing, bushy annual reaches 12 in (30 cm) in height and spread. It was introduced to European gardens from its native Mexico via France—hence its common name. The double flowerheads, produced in summer and early autumn, resemble carnations. They bloom in red, yellow and orange. The leaves are deep green and aromatic. **'Dainty Marietta'** is an all-yellow cultivar with single flowerheads; **'Naughty Marietta'** bears single, golden yellow flowerheads with dark red-brown markings on the petal bases; and **'Honeycomb'** has large, mahogany-red flowers edged with gold. ZONES 9–11.

Tagetes tenuifolia
'Tangerine Gem' *(above)*

Tagetes patula 'Dainty
Marietta' *(below)*

TANACETUM
syn. *Pyrethrum*

In classical Greek mythology, immortality came to Ganymede as a result of drinking tansy, a species of this genus of rhizomatous perennial daisies. Even in recent times, it has been used (despite being potentially quite poisonous even when applied externally) for promoting menstruation and treating hysteria, skin conditions, sprains, bruises and rheumatism. Confined mainly to temperate regions of the northern hemisphere, the 70 or so species of this genus, relatives of the chrysanthemum, are today more appreciated for their daisy-like flowers and their foliage, which is often white-hairy and in many cases finely dissected. The leaves of many of the perennials are also strongly aromatic.

CULTIVATION
Moderately to very frost hardy, they prefer full sun in well-drained, dryish soil; in fact, any soil that is not wet and heavy. Do not overwater. A second flowering may be encouraged if faded flowers are cut back. These plants spread readily and need to be kept under control. Propagate by division in spring or from seed in late winter or early spring.

Tanacetum argenteum *(above)*
syn. *Achillea argentea*

This usually evergreen perennial has a mat-forming habit. It reaches 10 in (25 cm) in height with a spread of 8 in (20 cm). Very frost hardy, it is prized for its fine, silvery green foliage. Masses of small, white, daisy-like flowers are produced in summer. ZONES 5–10.

Tanacetum balsamita
syns *Balsamita major*,
Chrysanthemum balsamita
CAMPHOR PLANT, ALECOST, COSTMARY

This tough, frost-hardy perennial with strong rhizomatous roots can become somewhat invasive. It grows to 5 ft (1.5 m) tall and produces heads of white flowers with bright yellow disc florets from late summer. The leaves can be used sparingly in salads and as a flavoring in meat and vegetable dishes. The name 'alecost' comes from its former use as a spicy additive to beer. It also has antiseptic properties. *Tanacetum balsamita* var. *tomentosum* has leaves densely covered with fine hairs on their undersides. It is commonly known as the camphor plant because of its strongly camphor-scented foliage, which the parent species lacks. ZONES 6–10.

Tanacetum balsamita var. *tomentosum* *(below)*

T

Tanacetum coccineum (right)

syns *Chrysanthemum coccineum, Pyrethrum roseum*

PAINTED DAISY, PYRETHRUM

This frost-hardy, erect perennial has dark green, feathery, scented leaves that are finely dissected. Its single, or sometimes double, long-stalked flower-heads may be pink, red, purple or white, and appear from late spring to early summer. The species grows 2–3 ft (60–90 cm) tall with a spread of 18 in (45 cm) or more. **'Brenda'** has striking magenta single flowers. **'Eileen May Robinson'** is one of the best single pinks. **'James Kelway'** has deep crimson-pink flowers. It is a native of western Asia. **ZONES 5–9.**

Tanacetum niveum (right)

SILVER TANSY

Growing to about 24 in (60 cm) with a spread of up to 3 ft (1 m), this attractive species has deeply divided gray-green leaves. In mid-summer it produces an abundant display of small white flower-heads with yellow centers. A fine orna-mental species, it will often self-seed when grown in a border. **ZONES 7–10.**

Tanacetum corymbosum (right)

This dense, clump-forming species from southern and central Europe and central Russia grows to a height of 3 ft (1 m) with a spread of 12 in (30 cm). The leaves are finely cut and the flowers white. **ZONES 2–10.**

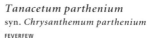

Tanacetum parthenium
syn. *Chrysanthemum parthenium*
FEVERFEW

Feverfew is one of those aromatic plants with a
long history of medicinal use. It was once used to
dispel fevers and agues, and as an antidote for
over-indulgence in opium. These days it is admired
for its pretty clusters of single or double, ½ in
(12 mm) wide, white-petalled, daisy-like flowers.
These are borne over a long period in summer.
Frost hardy, it has yellow-green leaves up to 3 in
(8 cm) long. This species reaches 24 in (60 cm) in
height with a spread of 18 in (45 cm). Although
perennial, it is short lived, and many gardeners
prefer to sow it afresh each spring. **'Aureum'** has
bright golden foliage. **'Golden Moss'** is a dwarf
cultivar with a height and spread of 6 in (15 cm).
It has golden, moss-like foliage and is often grown
as an edging or bedding plant. **'Snowball'** has
pompon flowers and grows to 12 in (30 cm) tall.
ZONES 6–10.

*Tanacetum
parthenium* 'Aureum'
(top)

*Tanacetum
parthenium* 'Golden
Moss' *(center)*

*Tanacetum
parthenium*
'Snowball' *(left)*

Tanacetum
ptarmiciflorum
(below left)
syn. *Chrysanthemum
ptarmiciflorum*
DUSTY MILLER, SILVER LACE

This bushy perennial
from the Canary Islands
spreads from a woody
tap root. Its silvery,
lanceolate leaves are
strongly divided. Mar-
ginally frost-hardy and
with a maximum height
and spread of 15 in
(38 cm), it is good for
the rock garden. White
flowerheads in terminal
clusters are borne in
summer. It is very use-
ful in floral arrange-
ments. ZONES 9–11.

T

TAPEINOCHILOS
INDONESIAN GINGER

Ranging in the wild from Southeast Asia to northern Australia, members of this genus are plants of the forest floor. There are some 15 tropical species in this genus and, like *Costus* and *Heliconia* species, they make their dramatic statement not so much from the insignificant flowers but from the brilliantly colored bracts that surround them. Unfortunately their splendor is often hidden beneath the handsome foliage. These evergreen perennials make excellent cut flowers, but their short stems and cultivation requirements have cost them popularity.

CULTIVATION

These frost-tender plants need heat and humidity to thrive. In cooler climates they are happy in a well-warmed greenhouse. Plant in part-shade in humus-rich soil. Propagate from seed or bulbils, or by division in spring.

Tapeinochilos ananassae (right) syn. *Tapeinochilos queenslandiae*

As the botanical name suggests, this species resembles a hard, scarlet pineapple (*Ananas*), but without the deep green fronds at the top. The flower spike rises about 15 in (38 cm) directly from the ground and is over-topped by the considerably taller stems, which carry the foliage. The scarlet bracts almost hide the small, tubular, yellow flowers. This species is native to eastern Indonesia, New Guinea and northeastern Australia. ZONES 11–12.

T

TELLIMA
FRINGECUPS

Native to North America, this genus consists of only one species. An evergreen perennial, it makes an ideal ground cover in
cool part-shaded woodland gardens or under shrubs in sunnier positions.

CULTIVATION
Very frost hardy, it does best in reasonably
well-drained soil. Propagate by division in
spring or from seed in autumn.

Tellima grandiflora *(above)*

This clump-forming perennial has heart-shaped,
purple-tinted green leaves. Semi-evergreen, they
form a neat clump around 24 in (60 cm) high.
Racemes of small, bell-shaped, creamy flowers are
borne in spring on 24 in (60 cm) stems, well
above the foliage. **'Rubra'** (syn. 'Purpurea') has
reddish purple leaves underlaid with dark green
and pink-tinged cream flowers. It can be grown as
a ground cover and in woodland gardens.
ZONES 6–9.

T

Thalia dealbata
(right)

This aquatic, deciduous perennial from the southeast of North America grows to 6 ft (1.8 m) in height with a spread of 24 in (60 cm) or more. It carries leaves that are broadly elliptical to lanceolate, and have a mealy whitish coating. Its stems are erect and unbranching. The flowers, which occur in tall spikes, are violet and waxy, their 6 petals forming a narrow tube; they are borne in summer and are followed by decorative seed heads. **ZONES 9–10.**

THALIA
WATER CANNA

The 7 species of this American genus honor a German botanist, Johann Thal, who lived from 1542 to 1583. Deciduous or perennial marginal water plants, they are grown for their spikes of tubular flowers and their oval, long-stalked, blue-green leaves.

CULTIVATION
Grow these frost-tender plants in baskets of fertile, loamy soil or in deep, humus-rich mud in up to 20 in (50 cm) of water and in full sun; some species tolerate cool water. Pick off spent foliage. Propagate from seed or by division in spring.

THALICTRUM
MEADOW RUE

Over 300 species make up this genus of perennials known for their fluffy, showy flowers. The branches of their slender, up-standing stems often intertwine. The leaves are finely divided. Blooming in spring and summer, the flowers have no petals, but instead have 4 or 5 sepals and conspicuous stamen tufts. They serve well in borders, particularly as a contrast to perennials with bolder blooms and foliage, and in the margins of bush gardens.

CULTIVATION
Grow these frost-hardy plants in sun or part-shade in any well-drained soil. Some species need cool conditions. Propagate from fresh seed in autumn or by division in spring.

Thalictrum aquilegiifolium
(above)
GREATER MEADOW RUE

This clump-forming Eurasian perennial grows to 3 ft (1 m) tall and has a spread of 18 in (45 cm). Pink, lilac or greenish white flowers in fluffy clusters on strong stems appear in summer. Each gray-green leaf comprises 3 to 7 small, elliptical, toothed leaflets in a feather-like arrangement, resembling the leaves of some *Aquilegia* species.
ZONES 6–10.

Thalictrum kiusianum (right)

This mat-forming perennial species from Japan grows to 6 in (15 cm) tall with a spread of 12 in (30 cm). It produces clusters of tiny purple flowers from spring to summer and has small, fern-like, 3-lobed leaves. There is also a white-flowered form. This species prefers shade and moist, sandy, peaty soil. It is particularly suitable for peat beds and rock gardens. **ZONES 8–10.**

Thalictrum delavayi (below)
syn. *Thalictrum dipterocarpum* of gardens
LAVENDER SHOWER

Rather than fluffy heads, this graceful, clump-forming perennial bears a multitude of nodding, lilac flowers in loose panicles, with prominent yellow stamens. The flowers are borne from the middle to the end of summer. The finely divided leaves give the mid-green foliage a dainty appearance. Reaching 4 ft (1.2 m) high, this species has a spread of 24 in (60 cm). **'Hewitt's Double'** has rounded, pompon-like, mauve flowers. **ZONES 7–10.**

T

THLADIANTHA

Related to the cucumbers, the 23 species in this East Asian and African genus are annual or perennial trailers or climbers. They have simple oval or trifoliate leaves and bell-shaped yellow flowers borne singly or in small clusters; these are followed by small, sometimes ribbed fruits.

CULTIVATION
Except for a few species, they are only moderately frost hardy. They prefer moist, humus-rich soil and a position in full sun. Propagate from seed or cuttings, or by layering.

T

Thladiantha dubia
(right)

Among the hardier species, this summer-flowering native of Korea and northeastern China climbs by means of tendrils and has 2–4 in (5–10 cm) heart-shaped leaves. ZONES 7–11.

THYMUS
THYME

This genus consists of over 300 evergreen species of herbaceous perennials and subshrubs, ranging from prostrate to 8 in (20 cm) high. Chosen for their aromatic leaves, these natives of southern Europe and Asia are frequently featured in rockeries, between stepping stones or for a display on banks. Some species are also used in cooking. The flowers are often tubular and vary from white through pink to mauve. Historically, thyme has been associated with courage, strength, happiness and well-being.

*Thymus ×
citriodorus* (left)
syn. *Thymus serpyllum*
var. *citriodorus*
LEMON-SCENTED THYME

This delightful rounded, frost-hardy shrub grows 12 in (30 cm) high and has tiny oval lemon-scented leaves and pale lilac flowers. The leaves are used fresh or dry in poultry stuffings or to add lemon flavor to fish, meat and vegetables. **'Anderson's Gold'** is a yellow-foliaged spreader that is inclined to revert to green; **'Argenteus'** has silver edges to the leaves; **'Aureus'** has golden variegated leaves; **'Doone Valley'** is prostrate with gold variegated leaves that develop red tints in winter; and **'Silver Queen'** has silvery white foliage.
ZONES 7–10.

Thymus species (below)

CULTIVATION
These plants are mostly frost hardy. For thick, dense plants, the flowerheads should be removed after flowering. Plant out from early autumn through to early spring in a sunny site with moist, well-drained soil. Propagate from cuttings in summer or by division.

T

Thymus caespititius *(left)*
syn. *Thymus micans*

This species is found naturally on dry, stony slopes in the Azores, northwestern Spain and Portugal. An evergreen, mat-forming subshrub, this moderately frost-hardy plant has slender woody stems and minute hairy, aromatic mid-green leaves. Small lilac or lilac-pink flowers are produced in late spring and summer. It grows to little more than 2 in (5 cm) high. ZONES 7–10.

Thymus camphoratus *(right)*

This Portuguese species has camphor-scented foliage, as its name suggests. It is a small, wiry stemmed shrub around 18 in (45 cm) high with slightly hairy leaves and purple flowers. ZONES 7–10.

Thymus pannonicus *(left)*

This species usually behaves as an herbaceous perennial, although in mild climates it may be evergreen. It is a low spreader or trailer with pink flowers and is native to southwestern and central Europe. ZONES 5–10.

Thymus polytrichus
syn. *Thymus praecox*
CREEPING THYME, WILD THYME

This evergreen creeping perennial grows to ½ in (12 mm) high, with prostrate woody stems covered in minute oval to oblong aromatic green leaves. The flowers are produced in clusters in summer; they are small, 2-lipped, and may be purple, mauve or white. This species is fully frost hardy. **'Porlock'** has rounded dark green leaves and fragrant pink flowers. **ZONES 5–10.**

Thymus polytrichus
'Porlock' *(above)*

Thymus serpyllum
'Annie Hall' *(right)*

Thymus serpyllum

WILD THYME, CREEPING THYME,
MOTHER OF THYME

This species grows to 10 in (25 cm) with a spread of 18 in (45 cm), forming a useful ground cover. Its creeping stem is woody and branching, and the scented, bright green leaves are elliptical to lanceolate. The bluish purple flowers are small and tubular with 2 lips, and are borne in spring and summer in dense terminal whorls. It is very frost hardy and will take moderate foot traffic. **'Annie Hall'** has rounded leaves and mauve flowers; **'Coccineus Minor'**, has crimson-pink flowers; and **'Pink Ripple'**, has bronze-pink flowers. **ZONES 3–9.**

Thymus serpyllum
'Pink Ripple' *(right)*

TIARELLA
FOAMFLOWER

The foamflowers are a genus of 5 species of forest-floor perennials, all of which are native to North America. They resemble their relatives, the heucheras, and can be hybridized with them. They all grow from thick rootstocks, with their decorative leaves growing close to the ground. The airy sprays of small white flowers are borne on bare stems about 12 in (30 cm) tall; pale pink forms occur rarely.

CULTIVATION
Very frost hardy, they are easy to grow in cool-temperate climates, and make good ground covers for a woodland-style garden. Plant in part- to deep shade in moist, well-drained soil. Propagate from seed or by division in early spring.

Tiarella cordifolia
(below)

FOAMFLOWER, COOLWORT

This vigorous spreading evergreen blooms profusely in early to late spring, producing terminal spikes of tiny, creamy white flowers with 5 petals. Its leaves are mostly pale green, lobed and toothed, with dark red marbling and spots; the basal leaves take on an orange-red hue in winter. When in flower, it has a height and spread of 12 in (30 cm) or more. ZONES 3–9.

Tiarella polyphylla (right)

This perennial species is native to China and the Himalayas. It grows to a height of 18 in (45 cm) with a similar spread. It has a stout, erect stem and heart-shaped leaves about 2 in (5 cm) in length. In late spring and summer, 5-petalled pink or white flowers are borne in terminal clusters. **ZONES 7–10.**

Tiarella wherryi (right)

An almost evergreen perennial, this slow-growing, clump-forming species reaches 8 in (20 cm) high and wide. The late spring flowers make a decorative mass of soft pink or white star shapes and last quite well when cut. The hairy, green leaves turn crimson in autumn. **ZONES 6–10.**

T

TILLANDSIA
AIR PLANT

This genus contains more than 350 species of evergreen, mainly epiphytic bromeliads from the Americas. They are grown for their foliage and unusual flowers, which are usually carried on spikes, heads or panicles and range in color from white to purple and green to red. Plants vary from 2½ in (6 cm) to more than 12 ft (3.5 m) high. The leaves may be gray, green or red-brown and are covered with microscopic silver scales.

CULTIVATION

All species are frost tender. Generally, the stiff, silver-leaved varieties are hardier and are grown in full sun, while the softer, green-leaved prefer part-shade. Plant in well-drained sphagnum moss or on slabs of bark or driftwood. Equal parts of bark and coarse sand can be used. They are often placed high up in hanging baskets to catch rising heat. Mist regularly and water moderately in summer, and sparingly at other times. Propagate from offsets or by division in spring to summer.

Tillandsia aeranthos
(left)

From the Latin meaning 'air blooming', this epiphyte is often confused with its close relative *Tillandsia bergeri*. It is a bromeliad with dark purple to red flowers. The plant is rosette-shaped and has a spread of 4–6 in (10–15 cm). The leaves are narrow and taper to a point. ZONES 9–11.

Tillandsia argentea
(below)

This small bromeliad grows 4–6 in (10–15 cm) wide, with a bulbous base and heavily scaled, silver, thread-like leaves. The leaves are arranged spirally around the short stem so that they resemble an onion. The red to violet flowers, held almost perpendicularly, are offset by red stems and red and green bracts. It grows best when mounted on trees or driftwood in filtered sunlight. Ensure good air circulation and a moderately humid atmosphere. ZONES 10–12.

Tillandsia bergeri *(left)*

Native to Argentina, this epiphyte grows in thick clumps with an average height of 4 in (10 cm) and a spread of 6 in (15 cm) and requires frequent watering. Its leaf blades are slightly channelled and thickly scaled. The flowers grow to $1\frac{1}{2}$ in (35 mm) long with blue petals that turn to pink as they fade. Both leaves and flowers are arranged spirally. **ZONES 9–11.**

Tillandsia caulescens *(below left)*

This species from Bolivia and Peru grows to 18 in (45 cm) high. It has compact, spiralled, gray-green foliage, red bracts and white to purple flowers; these are 1 in (25 mm) long with recurved tips to the petals. In its native habitat, it is epiphytic on trees or cliffs at high altitudes. It is easy to grow. **ZONES 10–12.**

Tillandsia cyanea *(right)*
PINK QUILL

The dense rosettes of grass-like, arching leaves on this species are usually deep green, but often reddish brown when young. In summer to autumn the spectacular, paddle-shaped flowerheads rise on tall stems from among the foliage. They consist of overlapping pink or red bracts with deep violet-blue flowers. It needs maximum humidity and is best in a compost of tree fern fiber, peat and sand. **ZONES 9–11.**

T

Tillandsia flabellata (right)

Native to the cloud forests of
Mexico and Guatemala, this is a
very decorative plant when in
flower. The foliage is rosette-
shaped and either red or green;
the bracts are pointed and bright
red. Its long, narrow bloom
spikes grow upright in a fan-like
arrangement to a height of 15 in
(38 cm). The flowers are blue
with petals up to 2 in (5 cm)
long, fused into a tube. It needs a
moderately humid atmosphere.
ZONES 10–12.

Tillandsia ionantha (right)

This small stemless bromeliad
from Mexico usually grows in
thick clumps. It has a tight, bulb-
like rosette with narrow, densely
scaly, triangular leaves. When in
flower, the inner rosette complements the white-tipped, violet
blooms by turning brilliant red.
It likes moderately damp conditions and its size makes it suitable
for terrariums; it can be grown
outdoors in summer. **ZONES 9–11.**

T

Tillandsia lindenii (left)

This species grows in a typical rosette. The arching leaves are thin,
smooth, pointed, and marked with
red-brown lines. In autumn, a large
flower spike of crimson or pink-
tinted bracts overlaps dense
clusters of pansy-shaped, deep blue
or purple-blue flowers rising just
above the leaves. **ZONES 10–12.**

Tillandsia stricta (right)
syns *Tillandsia krameri, T. meridionalis,*
T. stricta var. *krameri*

This epiphytic species may have a short stem or
be stemless, and usually grows in thick clumps.
The foliage is green and covered in silver-gray
scales on both sides. The flowers form a rigid,
upright, sometimes one-sided rosette; the bracts
are bright carmine and the petals blue with flared
tips. It prefers a moderately damp and shady position, but is easy to grow. When in flower, it is one
of the most beautiful species of the entire genus.
ZONES 9–11.

Tillandsia usneoides (right)
SPANISH MOSS, GRAY BEARD

This remarkable
epiphytic and rootless
plant hangs in pendu-
lous festoons from the
branches of other
plants. Inconspicuous
flowers in summer are
almost hidden by the
fine, curled leaves,
which are densely cov-
ered in silvery white
scales. It is widely dis-
tributed from the Deep
South of the USA to
northern South
America. ZONES 8–11.

T

TITHONIA
MEXICAN SUNFLOWER

This genus of 10 species consists mainly of tall, somewhat woody annuals, biennials and perennials. Originating in Central America and the West Indies, they are related to sunflowers and bear large, vivid yellow, orange or scarlet daisy-like flowerheads in summer and autumn. The leaves are often hairy on the undersides and sharply lobed.

CULTIVATION
Marginally frost hardy, these plants thrive in hot, dry conditions, but require a plentiful supply of water. They grow best in well-drained soil and need full sun. They may need staking. Deadhead regularly to promote a longer flowering season and prune hard after flowering to encourage new growth. Propagate from seed sown under glass in late winter or early spring.

Tithonia diversifolia (below)
TREE MARIGOLD

A very large, robust perennial or shrub growing to 15 ft (4.5 m) tall, this species has large, oval to oblong, hairy leaves with lobed margins. It is best suited to the rear of a shrub border where it can supply visual impact during the late summer months with its large, orange-yellow flowerheads. Dead flowers may be difficult to remove because of its height; the seed heads themselves are of interest. **ZONES 9–11.**

Tithonia rotundifolia *(above)*

This bulky annual needs plenty of room in the garden as it can easily grow to 5 ft (1.5 m) tall with a spread of 3 ft (1 m). Its leaves are heart-shaped. It is great for hot color schemes, both in the garden and as a cut flower, with its 4 in (10 cm) wide, zinnia-like flowers of orange or scarlet. **'Torch'** bears bright orange or red flowerheads and grows to 3 ft (1 m). ZONES 8–11.

Tithonia rotundifolia
'Torch' *(left)*

TOLMIEA
PIGGYBACK PLANT, YOUTH-ON-AGE, MOTHER-OF-THOUSANDS

A relative of *Heuchera* and *Saxifraga,* this genus consists of a single species of evergreen perennial from the west coast of North America. Its dark green leaves are very like those of some heucheras, heart-shaped and coarsely toothed, but the plant's most distinctive feature is the production, on some leaves, of a plantlet at the point where the leaf joins its stalk. As the leaves age and droop, these plantlets take root and grow, which allows the plant to spread quite extensively over the shaded forest floor of its normal habitat. The slender, erect flowering stems bear inconspicuous flowers, again very like those of some heucheras.

CULTIVATION
It is a popular indoor plant as well as being a useful ground cover for shade in regions of mild, moist climate. It adapts well to hanging baskets, making a ball of luxuriant foliage. Keep soil moist but not soggy and water sparingly in winter. Feed every 2 months in the warmer season with half-strength soluble fertilizer. Attacks by spider mites cause browning of the leaves, and require immediate treatment. It is easily propagated by detaching well-developed plantlets.

Tolmiea menziesii
(above)

The pale green leaves of this perennial are speckled with gold and somewhat hairy, 2–4 in (5–10 cm) long, and arise in dense clumps from short surface rhizomes. In late spring and early summer it produces sparse flowering stems 12–24 in (30–60 cm) tall bearing dull red-brown flowers with tiny narrow petals. ZONES 7–10.

TORENIA
WISHBONE FLOWER

This genus of 40 to 50 species of erect to spreading, bushy annuals and perennials comes from tropical African and Asian woodlands. They have oval to lance-shaped, entire or toothed, opposite leaves. In summer, they bear racemes of trumpet-shaped, 2-lipped flowers with 2-lobed upper lips and 3-lobed lower lips.

CULTIVATION

Torenias prefer a warm, frost-free climate. In cooler climates, they should not be planted out until the last frost. They make attractive pot plants and in cool climates are grown in greenhouses. Grow in fertile, well-drained soil in part-shade in a sheltered position.

Pinch out the growing shoots of young plants to encourage a bushy habit. Propagate from seed in spring.

Torenia fournieri
Summer Wave Series
'Large Blue' *(right)*

Torenia fournieri
(below)
BLUEWINGS

This branching annual has light to dark green, ovate or elliptical leaves with toothed edges. Frost tender, it grows fairly rapidly to a height of 12 in (30 cm) and a spread of 8 in (20 cm). Its flowers, borne in summer and early autumn, are pansy-like and a deep purplish blue with a touch of yellow, turning abruptly paler nearer the center. Red, pink and white varieties are also available. **Summer Wave** is a trailing, long-flowering strain with large light or dark blue flowers. **'Large Blue'** is an example. ZONES 9–12.

TOWNSENDIA

This North American genus comprises around 20 species of annual, biennial and perennial daisies. They form mats of narrow or spatula-shaped leaves, often silvery to gray-green in color. Most species are less than 6 in (15 cm) high and less than 18 in (45 cm) wide. The ½–1½ in (12–35 mm) diameter flowers, which open in spring and summer, resemble a single-flowered Michaelmas daisy. They are white, pink, mauve or purple, with a yellow central disc.

CULTIVATION

Most species are extremely hardy alpines that prefer to grow in well-drained soil that stays moist in summer. Plant in sun or morning shade. Despite their hardiness, they tend to be short lived and often do better in alpine houses, where they are protected from cold, wet conditions that may cause rotting. Propagate from seed.

Townsendia exscapa *(above)*

Probably the most widely cultivated species and a favorite of rockery enthusiasts, this little white-flowered, silver-leafed daisy occurs naturally from central Canada to Mexico. It demands perfectly drained soil and shelter from winter rain, protection it receives in the wild from a covering of snow. **ZONES 3–9.**

TRADESCANTIA
syns *Rhoeo, Setcreasea, Zebrina*
SPIDERWORT

This genus consists of 50 or more species
of perennials, some of them evergreen,
from North and South America. Some are
rather weedy, but the creeping species
(wandering Jew) make useful ground
covers and are grown for their attractive
foliage. Some of the upright species are
cherished for their pure blue flowers, a
color not easy to find for the late-summer
garden. Most of the trailing types are
rather frost tender and are usually grown
as greenhouse pot plants. In mild winter
climates they make good ground cover,
admired for their richly toned foliage.

CULTIVATION
Grow in full sun or part-shade in fertile,
moist to dry soil. Cut back ruthlessly
as they become straggly. Propagate by
division or from tip cuttings in spring,
summer or autumn.

Tradescantia, Andersoniana Group,
'J. C. Weguelin' *(above right)*

Tradescantia, Andersoniana Group, 'Jazz' *(right)*

Tradescantia, Andersoniana Group

This group covers a range of plants
formerly listed under *Tradescantia*
× *andersoniana* or *T. virginiana*.
They are mainly low-growing
perennials with fleshy, strap-like
leaves and heads of 3-petalled
flowers. Although the foliage
clump seldom exceeds 18 in
(45 cm) high, the flower stems
can reach 24 in (60 cm). There are
many hybrids in a range of white,
mauve, pink and purple flower
shades. Those of **'Alba'** are white;
'J. C. Weguelin' has lavender-
blue flowers; **'Jazz'** has magenta
flowers; and **'Red Cloud'** is cerise-
red. ZONES 7–10.

T

Tradescantia,
Andersoniana
Group, 'Red
Cloud' *(left)*

Tradescantia cerinthoides (left)
syn. *Tradescantia blossfeldiana*
FLOWERING INCH PLANT

Native to southeastern Brazil, this
species has glossy deep green, oval
leaves up to 6 in (15 cm) long that
are purple and hairy on the undersides. From spring to autumn it
bears heads of purple-pink flowers.
It is a sprawling plant of up to about
24 in (60 cm) in height. **ZONES 7–11.**

Tradescantia fluminensis
'Variegata' *(below)*

Tradescantia fluminensis
syn. *Tradescantia albiflora*
WANDERING JEW

This is a frost-tender, evergreen perennial with
trailing rooting stems and oval fleshy leaves about
1.5 in (35 mm) long that clasp the stem. The
leaves are a glossy green with purple undersides.
Tiny white flowers are produced intermittently,
enclosed in leaf-like bracts. It is invasive.
'Variegata' has glossy green leaves irregularly
striped with white, cream and yellow; they are
tinged with purple on the undersides. **ZONES 9–12.**

Tradescantia pallida
syn. *Setcreasea purpurea*

This species from eastern Mexico forms a dense clump of foliage and has small pink flowers in summer. The slightly succulent, lance-shaped, 3–6 in (8–15 cm) long leaves often develop red tints if grown in full sun. **'Purple Heart'** (syn. 'Purpurea') has purple foliage. ZONES 8–11.

Tradescantia pallida
'Purple Heart' *(above)*

Tradescantia spathacea
'Vittata' *(below)*

Tradescantia sillamontana
(above)
syns *Tradescantia pexata,* *T. velutina*

This evergreen erect perennial has oval, stem-clasping leaves that are densely covered in fine white hairs. It produces clusters of small purplish pink flowers in spring and summer. It has a height and spread of 12 in (30 cm) and is frost tender. ZONES 9–11.

Tradescantia spathacea
syns *Rhoeo discolor, R. spathacea*
BOAT LILY, MOSES-IN-THE-CRADLE

This evergreen, clump-forming, frost-tender species reaches 18 in (45 cm) high and 10 in (25 cm) wide. It bears rosettes of fleshy, lance-shaped, glossy leaves to 12 in (30 cm) long with purple undersides. Tiny white flowers, held in leaf-like bracts, appear throughout the year. **'Vittata'** has yellow-striped leaves. ZONES 9–11.

T

TRAGOPOGON

Widely distributed over Europe and temperate Asia, this genus consists of over 100 species of annuals, biennials and perennials belonging to the daisy family. They have solitary or sparsely branched stems, grass-like leaves and terminal, star-shaped flowerheads that are followed by large heads of thistle down.

CULTIVATION

Most species are frost hardy and adaptable to most soils. All prefer a sunny position. Propagate from seed sown in spring.

Tragopogon dubius
(below)

GOATSBEARD

This European species is an erect biennial herb that grows to 3 ft (1 m) tall. It has basal grass-like leaves that half sheathe the base of the stem. The lemon-yellow, star-shaped flowerheads open in the morning and close during the day.
ZONES 5–10.

Tricyrtis hirta *(above)*

This upright species bears 2 in (5 cm) wide, star-shaped white flowers spotted with purple from late summer to autumn. The branching stems are about 3 ft (1 m) long. ZONES 5–9.

TRICYRTIS
TOAD LILIES

The common name of this genus of about 20 species seems to have biased gardeners against the toad lilies—no one thinks of toads as attractive—but these clumping rhizomatous summer-flowering perennials from the woodlands of Asia are really quite attractive in their quiet colorings and markings. The flowers, which are star-, bell- or funnel-shaped, with opened-out tips, are held in the axils of the leaves. The leaves are pointed and pale to dark green, appearing on erect or arching, hairy stems.

Tricyrtis suzukii
(above)

The flowers in this species from Taiwan are white with purple spots, but otherwise it is similar to *Tricyrtis formosana*. It is seldom found in cultivation. ZONES 7–10.

CULTIVATION

Grow these very frost-hardy plants in part-shade in humus-rich, moist soil; in areas with cool summers, they need a warm spot. Propagate from seed in autumn or by division in spring.

Trifolium pratense (left)
RED CLOVER

This coarse, erect or decumbent perennial is up to 24 in (60 cm) tall. From late spring to early autumn it bears large, globose heads of pink to purple flowers . Native to Europe, it is a popular pasture clover. It is occasionally sold in cultivated forms and its flowers are popular with apiarists. ZONES 6–10.

Trifolium repens (below)
WHITE CLOVER

This European species has low creeping stems which root at the nodes. The trifoliate leaves have leaflets with serrated margins and a whitish mark at the base. The white or green flowers are produced in globular terminal clusters from spring to autumn and into winter in warmer climates. **'Purpurascens Quadrifolium'** is grown for its bronze-green 4-parted foliage that is variably edged with bright green. Although unwelcome in fine turf, white clover is an important pasture plant and honey source. ZONES 4–10.

TRIFOLIUM
CLOVER

This large genus of annuals, biennials or perennials consists of about 230 species, some of which are semi-evergreen. Widespread throughout temperate and subtropical regions, they are absent from Australia. Species have rounded, usually 3-parted leaves and heads of pea-like flowers. The individual blooms are often very small, making the head resemble a single bloom. Many species become invasive, but have agricultural uses; others are suitable for banks or in rock gardens.

CULTIVATION
All species are very frost hardy. Clovers will grow in sun or part-shade. Propagate from seed in autumn or by division in spring. Most species self-seed readily.

Trifolium repens
'Purpurascens
Quadrifolium' *(above)*

Trifolium uniflorum *(left)*

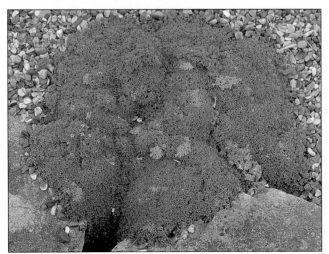

This is a low-growing
creeping and clump-
forming species from
the eastern Mediterra-
nean. It has trifoliate
leaves and the lilac
flowers are borne in
terminal clusters in
summer. **ZONES 7–10.**

TRILLIUM
WAKE ROBIN, WOOD LILY

Among North America's most beautiful wildflowers, this genus in the lily family contains 30 species of rhizomatous, deciduous perennials; they also occur naturally in northeastern Asia. Upright or nodding, solitary, funnel-shaped flowers with 3 simple petals are held just above a whorl of 3 leaves. The numerous species are found in woodland habitats, flowering in spring before the deciduous leaves which remain green until autumn. They make good ornamentals in wild gardens and shady borders.

CULTIVATION

Very frost hardy, they prefer a cool, moist soil with ample water and shade from the hot afternoon sun. Slow to propagate from seed in autumn or by division in summer, they are long lived once established.

Trillium albidum (above)

Native to western USA, this species has 8 in (20 cm) leaves, grows to over 18 in (45 cm) tall and is similar to *Trillium chloropetalum*. Its flowers are white flushed pink and are up to 4 in (10 cm) long. ZONES 6–9.

Trillium cernuum (below)
NODDING WOOD LILY, NODDING TRILLIUM

This species from eastern USA and Canada grows to no more than 2 in (5 cm) high and frequently less. It has almost stalkless foliage, 2–6 in (5–15 cm) long and narrower at the tips, and produces 2 or 3 stems in spring. These stems carry small, drooping white flowers, rarely pink, up to 1 in (25 mm) long and with the same diameter. ZONES 6–9.

T

Trillium chloropetalum *(above & right)*

GIANT TRILLIUM

The giant trillium is found from California to
Washington in western USA, in wooded or
streamside situations. Growing up to 24 in
(60 cm) tall, its flowers may be green, white,
pink or maroon, with the 3 petals held upright.
This species is more tolerant of dry shade than
others. **ZONES 6–9.**

Trillium cuneatum *(left)*

WHIPPORWILL FLOWER

Native to southern USA, this species bears reddish
brown to maroon flowers in early spring. It grows
to a height of 12–24 in (30–60 cm). It prefers a
soil that is slightly alkaline. **ZONES 6–9.**

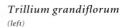

Trillium grandiflorum
(left)

SNOW TRILLIUM, WAKE-ROBIN

This showy, clump-forming trillium is the easiest to grow, reaching 12–18 in (30–45 cm) in height. The pure white flowers, borne in spring, fade to pink as they age. The double-flowered white form, **'Flore Pleno'**, is beautiful but rare, and has arching stems and oval, dark green leaves. **ZONES 3–9.**

Trillium luteum *(below)*
syns *Trillium sessile* var. *luteum, Trillium viride*

WOOD TRILLIUM

From Appalachian woodlands of eastern USA, this species is distinguished by its rather pointed leaves that are spotted and splashed with paler green, and small, stalkless yellow-green flowers that do not open very widely. **ZONES 6–9.**

Trillium grandiflorum
'Flore Pleno' *(below)*

T

Trillium sessile (left)
TOAD-SHADE, WAKE-ROBIN

This upright, clump-forming perennial reaches 12–15 in (30–38 cm) in height with a spread of 12–18 in (30–45 cm). It has deep green leaves marbled with pale green, gray and maroon. They bear stalkless, maroon flowers with lance-shaped petals in late spring. **Trillium sessile var. *californicum*** bears white flowers. ZONES 4–9.

Trillium rugelii
(below)

SOUTHERN NODDING TRILLIUM

Endemic to Tennessee, USA, this trillium is now regarded as rather rare and endangered in the wild. However, it is becoming more common in cultivation. ZONES 5–9.

Trillium sessile var. *californicum* (right)

Trollius chinensis
(left)
syn. *Trollius ledebourii*
CHINESE GLOBE FLOWER

This is one of the lesser known but still very desirable species. It grows 2–3 ft (60–90 cm) tall and bears its shining flowers in spring above handsomely slashed foliage. The flower color varies from light to deep yellow. It is a fast grower, but is not invasive. **ZONES 5–9.**

TROLLIUS
GLOBE FLOWER

The perennial globe flowers resemble their cousins the buttercups in their bright yellow flowers and their liking for wet ground, but they are much more sedate in their habits—no chance of the garden being taken over here. The flowers are also often bigger—to about 3 in (8 cm)—and their larger number of petals gives them the appearance of being double. From Europe and temperate Asia, any of the 30 species is worth growing. Spring is the main flowering season, but do not be surprised to see some autumn flowers, too.

CULTIVATION
Very frost hardy, they can be grown in regular flowerbeds in moist soil provided they are watered generously, but the boggy edge of a pond or stream suits them better. They are among the few water's edge plants that actually prefer a little shade. Propagate from seed in spring or autumn or by division in early autumn or early spring.

Trollius europaeus
(below left)
COMMON GLOBE FLOWER

The stem on this clump-forming perennial from northern and central Europe is smooth, hollow and upstanding, branching at the apex. Its spring flowers are yellow and terminal; the 5 to 15 petal-like sepals forming a rounded shape 2 in (5 cm) across. Each mid-green leaf has 3 to 5 lobes arranged palmately, with each lobe deeply incised. This species grows to a height of 24 in (60 cm) with an 18 in (45 cm) spread. **ZONES 5–9.**

TROPAEOLUM
NASTURTIUM

The 87 species of annuals, perennials and twining climbers in this genus from Chile to Mexico are admired for their brightly colored flowers. In warm areas, nasturtiums can survive for several years, self-sowing freely and flowering all year. The flowers can be single or double, about 2 in (5 cm) across, and come in red, orange, russet, yellow, cream and even blue. In the nineteenth century a white cultivar was bred, only to be lost.

CULTIVATION
Frost hardy to frost tender, most species prefer moist, well-drained soil in full sun or part-shade. Propagate from seed, basal stem cuttings or tubers in spring. Check for aphids and cabbage moth caterpillars.

Tropaeolum majus
GARDEN NASTURTIUM, INDIAN CRESS

The stem is trailing and climbing on this vigorous, bushy annual. Its leaves are rounded and marked with radial veins. It blooms in summer and autumn; its 5-petalled flowers are spurred, open and trumpet-shaped, and come in many shades from deep red to pale yellow. It grows to a spread of 3 ft (1 m) and a height of up to 18 in (45 cm). The hot-tasting leaves and flowers of this species are sometimes added to salads. There are several varieties with single or double flowers, and a compact or trailing habit. The **Alaska Hybrids** have single flowers in a range of colors and variegated leaves. **'Crimson Beauty'** has rich red flowers. ZONES 8–11.

Tropaeolum majus **Alaska Hybrids** *(left)*

Tropaeolum majus **cultivar** *(below left)*

Tropaeolum majus **'Crimson Beauty'** *(below)*

T

TUSSILAGO

This genus of about 15 species of perennials from cooler parts of the northern hemisphere is a rather humble relative of the more stately ligularias. Only one species is known in cultivation, and that is grown more for its medicinal uses than for any ornamental qualities—it has been renowned for centuries as a cough remedy, hence the genus name, from the Latin *tussis,* cough, and *-ago,* act upon. They are plants with long-running rhizomes that send up widely spaced tufts of often almost circular leaves. The flowerheads are borne on stems separate from the leafy shoots and often appearing before the leaves; they are daisy-like with numerous narrow ray-florets and a small central disc.

CULTIVATION

These plants are easily grown in a temperate climate, preferring heavy soils and damp ground, and where conditions suit them they may become invasive. They will thrive in full sun or part-shade. Propagate from seed or by division of rhizomes.

Tussilago farfara
(above & below left)
COLTSFOOT

Of wide occurrence in Europe, temperate Asia and North Africa, coltsfoot grows on moist banks, screes or river gravels. Its distinctively shaped leaves (hence the common name) are glossy green above and white-felted beneath, mostly 4–8 in (10–20 cm) across. From early spring onward tight groups of scaly flowering stems about 6 in (15 cm) high emerge from the ground, each stem bearing a gold flowerhead up to 1½ in (35 mm) across; the leaves emerge while later flowerheads are opening; they are commonly dried and then smoked like tobacco as a remedy for coughs and chest complaints. ZONES 3–9.

TWEEDIA

This genus of one species of straggling perennial is grown for its clear pale blue, star-shaped flowers, which are long lasting and cut well. White- and pink-flowered forms, usually sold as '**Alba**' and '**Rosea**' are occasionally offered. The seed pods are filled with seeds that have downy 'parachute' tufts.

CULTIVATION
Plant in full sun in a well-drained soil that is a little on the dry side. It is slightly frost hardy but otherwise undemanding. Propagate from seed.

Tweedia caerulea *(above)*
syn. *Oxypetalum caeruleum*

This perennial to 3 ft (1 m) has heart-shaped, gray-green, downy leaves. The summer flowers age to purple and are followed by 6 in (15 cm) long, boat-shaped, green seed pods. ZONES 9–11.

T

URSINIA

Native to southern Africa and Ethiopia, this genus contains up to 40 species of annuals, perennials, subshrubs and shrubs. The plants have pinnate, fern-like foliage. They bear open, terminal clusters of yellow, white, orange or occasionally red flowers with purple or yellow centers.

CULTIVATION

Ranging from marginally frost hardy to frost tender, they require warm, dry climates, full sun and well-drained, moderately fertile soil. Propagate from cuttings or seed in spring. Protect from aphids.

Ursinia calenduliflora (below)
SPRINGBOK ROCK URSINIA

This South African annual grows to 15 in (38 cm) tall. *Ursinia calenduliflora* has pinnate, 2½ in (6 cm) long leaves which consist of narrow to rounded leaflets. The daisy-like flowers, 2½ in (6 cm) in diameter, are yellow and are frequently marked with dark purple near the base. ZONES 9–11.

Ursinia cakilefolia *(above)*

Indigenous to the Cape Province area, this sun-loving annual grows to a height of 18 in (45 cm) and bears deep yellow or orange flowerheads, about 2 in (5 cm) across, with a darker central disc. The collar at the base of the flower is rigid and purple-tipped. The leaves are somewhat fleshy and coarsely divided and the stems are straw colored. **ZONES 9–11.**

Ursinia sericea
(right)

This species grows to about 30 in (75 cm) in height and bears large yellow flowers in summer. The leaves are tapered, hairy and about 3 in (8 cm) long. **ZONES 9–11.**

U

UTRICULARIA
BLADDERWORT

This large genus with worldwide distribution consists of more than 200 species of annual or perennial carnivorous plants including terrestrial, epiphytic and aquatic forms. A peculiarity of all species is that they do not possess any kind of root, but instead form long, occasionally branching stems or stolons. Most are found growing in water or wet places, some with submersed stems and leaves; some tropical species are epiphytic. The most remarkable feature of each plant are the stalked and bladder-like traps scattered on the stems or leaves of the plant, ingeniously adapted to catch tiny aquatic creatures. The 2-lipped, spurred flowers vary in size, form and color.

CULTIVATION
The diversity of these variably frost-hardy to frost-tender species necessitates different treatments. The aquatic species are best grown in aquaria or shallow pans of water with sphagnum moss; terrestrial species can be grown in pots of peat moss. They require full sun if grown outdoors. Propagate by division in spring and summer.

Utricularia reniformis (right)
Growing either in soil or as an epiphyte, this Brazilian perennial is notable for its large, heavily built, spreading stolons. Its insect traps are found on the branches of the stolons and are sometimes obscured from view by the 6 in (15 cm) long, leathery, kidney-shaped leaves. The flower scapes grows to as much as 3 ft (1 m) tall and have 1–1½ in (25–35 mm) wide, purple-edged violet flowers. ZONES 10–12.

Utricularia sandersonii (left)
RABBIT EARS

This small perennial species grows naturally among moss-covered rocks in the Cape Province to Natal area of South Africa. The leaves are light green to pale yellow and fan-shaped. The flowers, which appear throughout the year, are white with mauve veins and a yellow center. This terrestrial bladderwort is one of the prettiest and easiest to grow, and multiplies freely. ZONES 9–11.

U

UVULARIA
BELLWORT, MERRY-BELLS

The 5 species of rhizomatous perennials in this genus are native to eastern North America. These herbaceous woodland plants are usually found growing in moist but well-drained leafy soil in the shade of deciduous trees. The stems are either simple or branched, erect to arching and the leaves are perfoliate in some species. The pendulous, bell-shaped flowers are borne either solitary and terminal, or in axillary clusters. They usually come in shades of yellow and appear in spring.

CULTIVATION
Very frost hardy, they can be grown in rock gardens and beside water features provided they are in at least part-shade and the acidic soil contains plenty of organic matter. Propagate by division in late winter or early spring or from ripe seed.

Uvularia perfoliata
(above)

This species has markedly stem-clasping leaves, glabrous and paler underneath, and reaches a height of about 24 in (60 cm). The flowers are up to 2 in (5 cm) long, pale yellow with rather twisted, upturned segments and are carried conspicuously above the leaves in spring. It forms a clump that can be easily divided for propagation.
ZONES 4–9.

U

Valeriana officinalis *(left)*

CAT'S VALERIAN, COMMON VALERIAN, GARDEN HELIOTROPE

This clump-forming, fleshy perennial, which is attractive to cats, grows to 4 ft (1.2 m) tall with a spread of 3 ft (1 m). It occurs naturally throughout Europe and eastwards to Russia and western Asia. It bears rounded flowerheads of white to dark pink flowers in summer on erect, hollow, hairy stems. The leaves are opposite with serrated margins. ZONES 3–9.

VALERIANA
VALERIAN

This genus consists of more than 150 species of herbaceous perennials, herbs and subshrubs, but few of the plants are of any ornamental value. Those that are may be good border and rock garden plants. The name derives from the Latin *valere*, meaning 'keep well', in recognition of the medicinal properties of some species: before modern tranquilizers were introduced, the root from *Valeriana officinalis* was used to treat nervous conditions.

CULTIVATION
Very frost hardy, they will thrive in almost any soil, in sun or part-shade. Propagate from seed or by division of established plants in autumn.

Valeriana arizonica *(right)*

A low-growing plant with a creeping rhizome, this species is a native of Arizona and can grow up to 12 in (30 cm) in height. It has fleshy leaves and clusters of rounded flowerheads of tiny pink flowers appearing in late spring. ZONES 7–10.

V

VANCOUVERIA

There are 3 species in this genus of graceful, creeping, woodland plants with slender rhizomes. These perennial herbs and shrubs are native to western North America and are related to *Epimedium*. The leaves are rounded and often 3 lobed; the flowering stem, 8–16 in (20–40 cm) long, is normally leafless. The small pendulous flowers are white or yellow, and borne in spring or summer.

CULTIVATION

Useful as a ground cover in cool shaded areas, these frost- hardy plants usually prefer a cool position in peaty soil. Propagate by division, or from fresh ripe seed in spring.

Vancouveria hexandra (below)

This deciduous perennial reaches a height of 18 in (45 cm) and a spread of up to 3 ft (1 m). It is distributed from Washington to California, and is found in shady woods. The white flowers are tinged with pink and borne in pendent clusters in mid-summer. The leaves are divided into almost hexagonal leaflets and are thin but not leathery. ZONES 5–9.

Vancouveria planipetala (right)

REDWOOD IVY, INSIDE-OUT FLOWER

This plant is found growing in the redwood forests of North America in sunny or part-shaded positions which are sheltered in winter. It grows to 18 in (45 cm) in height with a 3 ft (1 m) spread. The stems are creeping, prostrate and branching. The evergreen leaves are thick and leathery with a wavy margin. The flower stem is leafless, up to 18 in (45 cm) tall, and the flowers are white, tinged with lavender and borne in spring. ZONES 7–9.

V

VERATRUM

This genus consists of about 45 species of perennial herbs found in Europe, Siberia and North America. They grow from a thick rhizome, which is poisonous, and from this arises erect, leafy stems which make arching mounds of foliage. The leaves are large, pleated and very decorative. The flowers, often on tall, leafless stalks, are broadly bell-shaped in terminal panicles. The powdered rhizome of *Veratrum album,* called hellebore powder, was once used to destroy caterpillars.

CULTIVATION

Very frost hardy, these are easy plants to grow given a rich, moist soil. When the plants need to be divided, this should be done in autumn as they start into growth very early in spring. They can also be propagated from seed in autumn. Protect from snails. All species are poisonous.

Veratrum nigrum (below)
BLACK FALSE HELLEBORE

This species is a rare perennial from southern Europe and Asia. It carries long, narrow, terminal spikes of small, purplish brown flowers with 6 petals that bloom from late summer. The large, pleated, elliptical leaves are arranged spirally into a sheath around the stout, erect stems. It grows to a height of 6 ft (1.8 m) and half as wide. ZONES 6–9.

Veratrum album (left)

WHITE FALSE HELLEBORE, EUROPEAN WHITE HELLEBORE

This clump-forming perennial grows to 6 ft (1.8 m) tall with a spread of 24 in (60 cm). The large, striking leaves are clear green and appear to be folded like a fan. The leafless flower stalk bears dense terminal panicles of pale green to almost white bell-shaped flowers in late summer. This species does best when grown in a shaded, protected position. ZONES 5–9.

V

Verbascum bombyciferum
(right)

This biennial from Asia Minor has silvery gray, furry, large leaves and grows 6 ft (1.8 m) tall. It bears golden yellow, cup-shaped flowers in summer, sometimes in terminal spikes. ZONES 6–10.

VERBASCUM
MULLEIN

This genus consists of semi-evergreen to ever-green perennials, biennials and shrubs from Europe and the more temperate zones of Asia. Including some very large and some very coarse species, the ge-nus offers much variety in the foliage with leaves ranging from glossy to velvety. They develop large, often complex, basal rosettes. Many of the 250 or so species are scarcely better than weeds. How-ever, several are desirable in the garden for their stately habit, gray foliage and long summer-flower-

ing season. The flowers do not open from the bottom up as, for example, delphiniums or foxgloves do, but a few at a time along the spike.

CULTIVATION
These plants are fully to moderately frost hardy but will not tolerate winter-wet conditions. Establish all species in well-drained soil and an open, sunny location, although they do tolerate shade. Propagate from seed in spring or late summer or by division in winter. Some species self-seed readily.

V

Verbascum dumulosum *(above)*

This evergreen, low-spreading perennial from southwest Turkey grows 6–12 in (15–30 cm) tall with a spread of about 18 in (45 cm). The gray-green leaves are felty in texture. In late spring is produces a succession of bright yellow flowers, each with 5 lobes, on short clusters. It will not tolerate wet soil. **ZONES 8–10.**

Verbascum chaixii *(left)*

This species from southern Europe can be relied on to live long enough to form clumps. The flowers, borne on 3 ft (1 m) tall stems in summer, are normally yellow. The white form **'Album'** is usually finer. **ZONES 5–10.**

Verbascum chaixii 'Album' *(left)*

Verbascum 'Letitia' *(right)*

This small-growing hybrid between *Verbascum dumulosum* and *V. spinosum* has slender, felted, silver-gray foliage. From mid-spring onwards, it produces masses of delicate lemon-yellow flowers on short, branched stems. It is ideal for a rock garden or as a container plant in a sunny position. The flowers are sterile, so propagation is by division. **ZONES 8–10.**

Verbascum nigrum
(right)

BLACK MULLEIN, HAG TAPER

Native to Morocco, this semi-evergreen, clump-forming perennial is very frost hardy and grows to a height and spread of about 3 ft (1 m). Long spikes of yellow flowers with purple centers appear from summer through to autumn. Its mid-green leaves taper to a point and carry a dense layer of hairs. Black mullein is used as a herbal remedy for colic, coughs and spitting blood. So-called witches of the Middle Ages were thought to use the plant in their love potions and brews, hence the common name hag taper. **ZONES 5–10.**

V

Verbascum phoeniceum
(left)

PURPLE MULLEIN

A native of Europe, this species forms basal rosettes of dark green, broad leaves from which rise branching stems bearing clusters of violet, pink or purple flowers. It is reliably perennial and self-sows quite prolifically when in a warm, well-drained situation. This species is one of the parents of the many beautiful garden hybrids. It grows to a height of 2–4 ft (0.6–1.2 m) and can make a strong focal point in a border. **ZONES 6–10.**

Verbascum thapsus
(left)

This species has soft, velvety, pale green leaves and yellow, stalkless flowers produced in dense, terminal spikes in summer. It grows on freely draining hillsides, often in very poor soil. The flowers, once dried, form an ingredient in herbal teas and cough mixtures. **ZONES 3–9.**

V

VERBENA

Originating in Europe, South America and North America, this genus of 250 or more species of biennials and perennials is characterized by small, dark, irregularly shaped and toothed leaves. They bloom in late spring, summer and autumn. An agreeably spicy aroma is associated with most verbenas.

CULTIVATION

Marginally frost hardy to frost tender, they do best where winters are not severe. Establish in medium, well-drained soil in full sun or at most part-shade. Propagate from seed in autumn or spring, stem cuttings in summer or autumn, or by division in late winter. They can also be propagated in spring by division of young shoots.

Verbena bonariensis *(left)*

This tall South American perennial is often grown as an annual, primarily for its deep purple flowers which top the sparsely foliaged 4–5 ft (1.2–1.5 m) stems from summer to autumn. The deeply toothed leaves cluster in a mounded rosette, which easily fits in the front or middle of a border; the floral stems give a vertical line without much mass. Frost hardy, it self-seeds readily and survives with only minimal water, even in dry areas. **ZONES 7–10.**

Verbena canadensis *(left)*
ROSE VERBENA, CREEPING VERVAIN

This native of eastern North America is a trailing or sprawling, short-lived perennial easily grown as an annual. It grows to 18 in (45 cm) in height with a spread of 24 in (60 cm). The dark purplish pink flowers appear from summer through autumn. **ZONES 5–10.**

V

Verbena × *hybrida* *(right & center)*

GARDEN VERBENA

This trailing perennial bears slightly hairy leaves and blooms from summer to autumn. Its fragrant flowers appear in dense clusters 1 in (25 mm) across, many showing off white centers among the hues of red, mauve, violet, white and pink. It is suitable for use in summer beds and containers. Avoid being heavy handed with fertilizers or the plants will yield more leaves than flowers. **'Homestead Purple'** is a sturdy cultivar with rich red-purple flowers. **'La France'** has bright pink flowerheads. **'Silver Ann'** has heads of light pink

flowers with darker blooms at the center. **'Sissinghurst'** has mid-green leaves and bears stems of brilliant pink flowerheads in summer, and it reaches a height of 6–8 in (15–20 cm). The **Tapien Series** verbenas are a seedling strain renowned for their depth and intensity of flower color. The are strong growing, heat- and disease-resistant trailers for hanging baskets. The **Temari Series** verbenas are a Japanese-raised strain with large flower clusters. The name means 'handful of flowers', which is exactly what you get with each head of bloom. Other cultivars include **'Patio Blue'** and **'Patio Purple'**. ZONES 9–10.

Verbena × *hybrida*
'Homestead Purple'
(right)

Verbena × *hybrida*
'La France' *(right)*

Verbena × *hybrida*
'Silver Ann' *(below)*

Verbena × *hybrida*
'Sissinghurst' *(below)*

V

Verbena ×
hybrida
'Patio Blue'
and 'Patio
Purple' *(left)*

Verbena × *hybrida*
'Tapien Blue' and
'Tapien Pink' *(left)*

V

Verbena × *hybrida*
'Temari Scarlet' *(right)*

Verbena laciniata *(below)*
syn. *Verbena erinoides*

This marginally frost-hardy, prostrate South American perennial grows to only 12–18 in (30–45 cm) tall, but spreads widely. It bears finely divided, gray-green leaves and abundant heads of blue, magenta or violet flowers. Trim back after flowering and avoid mildew by not over-watering. **ZONES 8–10.**

Verbena ×
hybrida, Temari
Series *(above)*

Verbena ×
hybrida 'Temari
Violet' *(right)*

Verbena tenuisecta
(below)

MOSS VERBENA

Native to Chile and Argentina, this evergreen perennial gets its common name from its dense, prostrate habit and minute, finely divided, vivid green foliage that forms a flat, moss-like ground covering. Through late spring and summer, it bears masses of flowers in shades of white, blue and purple in small, rounded inflorescences. It requires a hot, dry position and is frost tender. ZONES 9–11.

Verbena peruviana 'Red Cascade' *(below)*

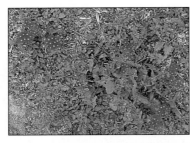

Verbena peruviana
syn. *Verbena chamaedrifolia*

This low, creeping perennial has stems rooting at the nodes and oval, toothed, mid-green leaves forming a carpet. Heads of small, tubular, intense scarlet flowers with spreading petals appear in summer and autumn. It reaches a height of 3 in (8 cm) with a spread of about 3 ft (1 m). Propagate from cuttings. **'Red Cascade'** has particularly bright flowers. ZONES 9–11.

Verbena rigida
(above right)
syn. *Verbena venosa*

A South American native, this tuberous-rooted perennial is an excellent species for seaside cultivation. It reaches a height of 18–24 in (45–60 cm) with a spread of 12 in (30 cm). The dense spikes of pale violet to magenta flowers are borne from mid-summer. **'Silver Jubilee'** bears a mass of red flowers right through the growing season. ZONES 8–10.

Verbena rigida
'Silver Jubilee' *(right)*

VERONICA
SPEEDWELL

Saint Veronica was the woman who, pious legend relates, wiped the face of Christ with her veil and was rewarded with having his image imprinted on it. Her connection with this flower is that the savants of the Middle Ages thought they could see a face in it. They must have peered rather closely, because veronica flowers are not exactly large—½ in (12 mm) wide is big for the genus. The shrubby species are now given a genus of their own, *Hebe*, and all the remaining 200 or so are herbaceous perennials. They range from prostrate, creeping plants suitable for the rock garden to 6 ft (1.8 m) high giants. Small as the flowers are, they make quite an impact, being gathered in clusters of various sizes and coming in great abundance in summer. Blue is the predominant color, although white and pink are also common. For example, '**Pretty in Pink**' bears spikes of deep pink flowers.

Veronica 'Pretty in Pink' *(below)*

CULTIVATION
Fully to moderately frost hardy, these plants are easy to grow in any temperate climate, and are not fussy about soil or position. Propagate from seed in autumn or spring, from cuttings in summer or by division in early spring or early autumn.

V

Veronica austriaca *(left)*
syn. *Veronica teucrium*

Distributed from southern Europe to northern Asia, this species grows in grassland and open woods. This clump-forming perennial grows to 10–18 in (25–45 cm) tall with long, slender stems bearing bright blue, saucer-shaped flowers in late spring. The leaves vary in shape from broadly oval to narrow and are either entire or deeply cut. Propagate by division in autumn or from softwood cuttings in summer. **'Crater Lake Blue'** is 12 in (30 cm) tall and has deep blue flowers; **'Royal Blue'** is taller with royal blue flowers. In late summer, *Veronica austriaca* **subsp**. *teucrium* bears 12 in (30 cm) high flower stems, comprising many tiny blooms in deep true blue; it prefers full sun and well-drained soil. ZONES 6–10.

Veronica austriaca 'Crater Lake Blue' *(left)*

Veronica austriaca 'Royal Blue' *(below)*

Veronica gentianoides *(right)*
GENTIAN SPEEDWELL

This mat-forming per-
ennial has wide, dark
green leaves from
which rise spikes of
pale blue or white
flowers in late spring.
It reaches 18 in (45 cm)
in height and spread.
ZONES 4–9.

Veronica cinerea *(left)*

This mat-forming,
many-branched peren-
nial from Turkey has
small, narrow or occa-
sionally oval leaves with
the margins inrolled and
silver gray in color. The
flowers are borne on
trailing stems in summer
and are purplish blue
with white eyes. Growing
to 6 in (15 cm) tall, it
makes a good plant for a
sunny rock garden.
ZONES 5–9.

V

Veronica longifolia
(left)

BEACH SPEEDWELL

From northern and central Europe and Asia, this perennial plant grows up to 3 ft (1 m) tall. Its narrow, tapering leaves are arranged in whorls and toothed on the edges. The flowers are lilac blue and closely packed on a long, erect infloresence. **'Rosea'** has pink flowers and branched stems. **ZONES 4–9.**

Veronica peduncularis

Ranging from the Ukraine and the Caucasus to western Asia, this spreading and mounding perennial has tiny oval leaves and 2–4 in (5–10 cm) sprays of pink-veined blue, white or pink flowers from late spring to early summer. **'Georgia Blue'** (syn. 'Oxford Blue') is a vigorous grower with bright blue flowers. **ZONES 6–9.**

Veronica longifolia
'Rosea' *(left)*

Veronica peduncularis
'Georgia Blue' *(below)*

V

Veronica prostrata
(right)

syn. *Veronica rupestris*

This perennial from Europe and parts of Asia has woody, branching stems and variable foliage, although all are tooth edged. The flowers are small and blue with widely flared petals, occurring in upright spikes in spring and early summer. This species spreads widely into a mat of indefinite coverage; however, it only reaches 12 in (30 cm) in height. **ZONES 5–9.**

Veronica spicata *(below)*

DIGGER'S SPEEDWELL, SPIKE SPEEDWELL

This very frost-hardy European perennial reaches a height of 24 in (60 cm) and a spread of up to 3 ft (1 m). Its stems are erect, hairy and branching. Spikes of small, star-shaped, blue flowers with purple stamens bloom in summer. The leaves are mid-green, linear to lanceolate. *Veronica spicata* subsp. *incana* is notable for its spreading clumps of silvery, felty leaves and deep violet-blue flowers; **'Floristan'** is similar. **'Blaufuchs'** is bright lavender blue; **'Blue Peter'** has dark blue flowers in very compact spikes; **'Heidekind'**, a compact form to 12–15 in (30–38 cm) tall, has hot pink flowers and silver-gray foliage; **'Red Fox'** has crimson flowers; and **'Rosea'** is a pink-flowered form. **ZONES 3–9.**

Veronica spicata subsp. *incana* *(below)*

V

Veronica spicata
'Blaufuchs' *(left)*

Veronica spicata
'Blue Peter' *(below)*

Veronica spicata
subsp. *incana*
'Floristan' *(left)*

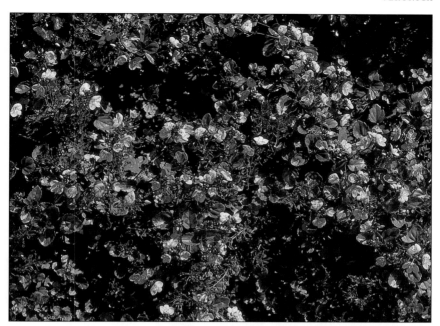

Veronica 'Waterperry'
(above)

The spreading 4 in (10 cm) high perennial has wiry reddish stems clothed with small, heart-shaped, deep green leaves rather like pansy foliage. The leaves develop purple tones in winter. From early summer, or year-round in mild areas, 'Waterperry' is covered in sprays of small lavender blue flowers. Provided it has good drainage and does not dry out in summer, it is easily grown in sun or partial shade. ZONES 8–11.

Veronica spuria *(above)*

This erect species from southeast Europe grows 12–36 in (30–90 cm) tall and has dense and downy foliage. The leaves are arranged in whorls and are slightly toothed. The flowers, produced in summer, are blue and in large terminal panicles. ZONES 3–9.

V

VERONICASTRUM
CULVER'S PHYSIC

This genus consists of 2 species of tall,
slender, perennial herbs closely related to
Veronica, found in eastern North America
and East Asia. Formerly used medicinally,
they are now grown as ornamentals only.
Pale blue or white flower spikes open
in summer.

CULTIVATION
Plant in a humus-rich, moist soil and do
not allow to dry out in summer. Any exposure from full sun to part-shade will do.
Propagate from seed or by division.

Veronicastrum virginicum *(below & below left)*
BLACK ROOT, CULVER'S ROOT, BOWMAN'S ROOT

Native to the USA, this perennial prefers moist,
swampy soils in a protected, shaded position.
Although frost hardy, it does not tolerate dry
conditions. This plant grows to about 5 ft (1.5 m),
and has slender, erect stems and lance-shaped,
finely serrated leaves. The tubular, purplish blue
or white flowers are produced in summer.
ZONES 3–9.

V

Victoria amazonica × *cruziana*
'Longwood Hybrid' *(above)*

VICTORIA
GIANT LILY, ROYAL WATERLILY

This genus of just 2 species of rhizomatous, deep-water aquatic annuals or perennials comes from tropical South America. Their strong rhizomes support huge floating leaves and bear nocturnal, waterlily-like flowers. Joseph Paxton (1801–65), gardener to the Duke of Devonshire, was the first to make them flower in Britain, and based his design for the Crystal Palace on the structure of its leaves—so strong they could bear the weight of his 7-year-old daughter.

CULTIVATION

These frost-tender plants need at least 3 ft (1 m) of water in which to grow and a position in full sun. Plant them in containers of rich loamy soil with added organic matter. Propagate from seed in early spring.

Victoria amazonica
syn. *Victoria regia*
AMAZON WATERLILY

This is the largest known waterlily, with leaves reaching to 6 ft (1.8 m) across. It grows quickly, achieving its huge size just 7 months after planting from seed. The flat, prickly leaves have upturned margins of 2–4 in (5–10 cm). Leaf size is determined by the depth of the water in which the plant is growing—the deeper the water, the bigger the leaves. The flowers, white outside and pink inside, have as many as 60 petals each; they are more than 12 in (30 cm) wide. Only one flower blooms at a time. '**Longwood Hybrid**', a hybrid between *Victoria amazonica* and *V. cruziana*, has white flowers that age to pink. ZONES 11–12.

V

VIOLA
VIOLET, HEARTSEASE, PANSY

This well-known and much-loved genus of annuals, perennials and subshrubs consists of as many as 500 species. They are found in most temperate regions of the world including high mountains of the tropics, though with the greatest concentrations of species in North America, the Andes and Japan. Most are creeping plants, either deciduous or evergreen, with slender to thick rhizomes and leaves most often kidney-shaped or heart-shaped, though in some species they are divided into narrow lobes. Flowers of the wild species are seldom more than 1 in (25 mm) across and characteristically have 3 spreading lower petals and 2 erect upper petals, with a short nectar spur projecting to the rear of the flower. Many species also produce *cleistogamous* flowers, with smaller petals that do not open properly, and are able to set seed without cross-pollination. A few Eurasian species have been hybridized extensively to produce the garden pansies, violas and violettas, with showy flowers in very bright or deep colors. These are nearly always grown as annuals, though potentially some are short-lived perennials.

CULTIVATION
Most of the cultivated *Viola* species will tolerate light frosts at least, and many are fully frost hardy. The more compact perennial species suit rock gardens where they do best in cooler, moister spots, while the more spreading species make effective ground covers beneath trees and taller shrubs, requiring little or no attention. Pansies and violas *(Viola × wittrockiana)* are grown as annuals or pot plants in full sun, but appreciate shelter from drying winds. Sow seed in late winter or early spring, under glass if necessary, planting out in late spring in soil that is well-drained but not too rich. Water well and feed sparingly as flowers develop. Propagate perennial species by division or from cuttings.

Viola cornuta
(opposite page)
HORNED VIOLET

Native to the Pyrenees, this is a broad-faced violet with a short spur at the back, in shades of pale blue to deeper violet and borne in spring and summer. The plants spread by rhizomes, sending up flowering stems to 6 in (15 cm) long. The horned violet is one of the major parent species of pansies and violas. **'Minor'** has smaller leaves and flowers. ZONES 6–9.

Viola cornuta 'Minor'
(right)

V

Viola cornuta
(right & below)

Viola elatior *(left)*

This species is found in the damp meadows and marshy areas of central and eastern Europe and northwest China. It has long, tapered leaves and grows up to 18 in (45 cm) tall. The stems are erect and tufted; the large flowers are lilac blue and appear in early summer. The plants grow well in leafy, peaty soil in sun or part-shade. **ZONES 5–9.**

Viola hederacea *(right)*

syns *Erpetion reniforme, Viola reniformis*

AUSTRALIAN NATIVE VIOLET

The small, scentless flowers borne on short stems on this creeping evergreen perennial from southeastern Australia are mostly white with a lilac blotch in the throat; they appear from spring to autumn. Its stems are prostrate, suckering and mat forming, spreading widely and growing 2–4 in (5–10 cm) in height. Its leaves are kidney-shaped with irregular edges. **ZONES 8–10.**

Viola labradorica *(left)*

LABRADOR VIOLET

Native to North America through to Greenland, this low-growing, spreading species has light purple flowers in spring. It does well in shady places, but can become invasive. **ZONES 2–9.**

Viola odorata (right)

SWEET VIOLET

A sweet perfume wafts from the flowers of this much-loved species, which are the well-known florists' violets. It is a spreading, rhizomatous perennial from Europe, which grows 3 in (8 cm) tall and may spread indefinitely on cool, moist ground. Its dark green leaves are a pointed kidney shape with shallowly toothed edges. Spurred, flat-faced flowers in violet, white or rose appear from late winter through early spring. It boasts many cultivars. **ZONES 6–10.**

Viola, Perennial Cultivars

Primarily of *Viola lutea*, *V. amoena* and *V. cornuta* parentage, these hardy perennial plants are long flowering, year round in mild climates. **'Hunter-combe Purple'** has creamy centered purple flowers; **'Jackanapes'** has brown upper petals and yellow lower petals; **'Maggie Mott'** has bright purple-blue flowers; **'Nellie Britten'** (syn. 'Haslemere') has lavender-pink flowers; and **'Magic'** is rich purple with a small eye of dark purple and yellow. **ZONES 6–10.**

Viola, Perennial Cultivar, 'Huntercombe Purple' *(right)*

V

Viola, Perennial Cultivar, 'Jackanapes' *(above)*   *Viola*, Perennial Cultivar, 'Magic' *(below)*

Viola
septentrionalis *(left)*
NORTHERN BLUE VIOLET

This spring-flowering perennial from North America bears large flowers with a spur, in hues usually of bluish purple but sometimes white. The hairy green leaves are pointed and oval to heart-shaped and have toothed edges. The plant has creeping and suckering stems and grows 6–8 in (15–20 cm) high and wide. **ZONES 7–10.**

Viola riviniana
DOG VIOLET

Found in Europe, Iceland, North Africa and Madeira, this tufted little violet produces colonies from sucker shoots. The flowers are blue-violet, scentless and are borne from spring through summer. The leaves are long-stemmed and rounded. **'Purpurea'** has purple-green leaves and purple flowers; it reaches 2–4 in (5–10 cm) in height, with a spread of 10 in (25 cm). **ZONES 5–10.**

Viola riviniana
'Purpurea' *(above)*

Viola sororia *(above)*
syn. *Viola papilionacea*
WOOLLY BLUE VIOLET

This stemless, herbaceous perennial
has scalloped, thickly hairy leaves 4 in
(10 cm) long. It bears short-spurred
white flowers heavily speckled with
violet blue from spring to summer; the
flowers are sometimes deep violet blue.
'**Freckles**' has white flowers speckled
with violet-purple. Both the species and
the cultivar reach 4–6 in (10–15 cm) in
height. *Viola sororia* var. *priceana* has
grayish white flowers with violet-blue
stems. **ZONES 4–10.**

Viola sororia
'Freckles' *(right)*

Viola tricolor 'Bowles' Black' *(right)*

Viola tricolor *(right)*

WILD PANSY, JOHNNY JUMP UP, LOVE-IN-IDLENESS

Of wide occurrence in Europe and temperate Asia, this annual, biennial or short-lived perennial produces neat flowers in autumn and winter in mild climates if cut back in late summer. They have appealing faces, in shades of yellow, blue, violet and white. It has lobed, oval to lance-shaped leaves. It grows to a height and spread of 6 in (15 cm) and self-seeds readily. *Viola tricolor* **'Bowles' Black'** is a striking cultivar with black velvety petals and a yellow center. **ZONES 4–10.**

V

Viola × *wittrockiana* *(below)*

PANSY, VIOLA

This hybrid group of compactly branched perennials are almost always grown as biennials or annuals. Offering flowers of a great many hues, the numerous cultivars bloom in late winter through spring and possibly into summer in cooler climates. The flowers are up to 4 in (10 cm) across and have 5 petals in a somewhat flat-faced arrangement. The mid-green leaves are elliptical, with bluntly toothed margins. The plants grow slowly, reaching about 8 in (20 cm) in height and spread. This is a complex hybrid group, including both pansies and violas, the latter traditionally distinguished by the flowers lacking dark blotches, but there are now intermediate types with pale-colored markings. Hybrids in the **Imperial Series** are large-flowered pansies. **'Gold Princess'** is a good example, producing bicolored flowers in golden yellow and red. The **Joker Series** are of an intermediate type, with a range of very bright contrasting colors such as orange and purple. The **Accord Series** of pansies covers most colors and has a very dark central blotch. **'Padparadja'** has vibrant orange flowers. **'Magic'** has purple flowers with a bright face. Other seedling strains include the **Universal, Princess** and **Sky Series**. ZONES 5–10.

Viola × wittrockiana
(above & right)

Viola × wittrockiana
'Jolly Joker' *(below)*

V

Viola × *wittrockiana*
'Accord Red Blotch'
(left)

Viola × *wittrockiana*
'Princess Deep
Purple' *(right)*

Viola × *wittrockiana*
'Universal Orange'
(below)

V

Viola × *wittrockiana*
'Sky Clear Purple' *(above)*

Viola × *wittrockiana*
'Universal True Blue'
(above)

Viola × *wittrockiana*
'Penny Azure Wing'
(right)

V

VRIESEA

Native to Central and South America, this genus consists of around 250 species of epiphytes. They are among the most popular bromeliads, and are closely related to *Tillandsia*. The smooth-margined leaves are often coated in mealy scales and have colored cross-bandings. The spectacular flower spikes vary in shape, with petals free or fused into a tube. They can be red, orange or yellow. Different species flower at different times of the year. Many hybrid cultivars have been developed, for example 'Christine'.

CULTIVATION

These plants are frost tender. Plant in part-shade in well-drained orchid medium. Water moderately during growth periods, always ensuring the rosette centers are filled with water. Propagate from offsets or seed from spring to summer.

Vriesea 'Christine'
(above)

Vriesea carinata (left)
LOBSTER CLAWS

The striking flattened spike of crimson and gold bracts gives this Brazilian bromeliad its common name. It grows to 10 in (25 cm) and has soft, arching, light green leaves. An excellent pot plant, be aware that this species needs a big pot as it has a larger root system than most bromeliads.
ZONES 11–12.

V

Vriesea splendens
(right)
syns *Tillandsia splendens, Vriesea speciosa*
FLAMING SWORD

This very striking bromeliad earned its common name from its sword-shaped flower spike of bright red or orange. It has medium-sized, soft green leaves with purple-black bands and a 18 in (45 cm) high inflorescence. **ZONES 11–12.**

WXYZ

WACHENDORFIA
RED ROOT

Only a couple of the 25 or so species of this genus of cormous perennials from South Africa are cultivated outside their own country. Wachendorfias have basal tufts of long, narrow, pleated leaves and bear erect spikes of starry, golden flowers in spring and summer. Their common name comes from the red sap of the corms, used as a dye, and the bright red-orange color of the roots themselves.

CULTIVATION
Only moderately frost hardy, they thrive when grown outdoors in warm, near frost-free climates. They require a moist but well-drained soil in a sunny position and are ideal for bog gardens. They spread readily throughout the garden by seed. Propagate from seed or by division in spring.

Wachendorfia thyrsiflora
(above & left)
RED ROOT

This is the best known species. It grows to 7 ft (2 m) and bears thick, straight spikes of bright yellow flower clusters in spring and early summer. The narrow, lance-shaped leaves are pleated, strong and strap-like, and up to 3 ft (1 m) long. It tolerates light frost. ZONES 8–11.

W

Wahlenbergia communis (right)
syn. *Wahlenbergia bicolor*

TUFTED BLUEBELL, GRASS-LEAF BLUEBELL

This tufted perennial is native to Australia where it occurs in all mainland states, sometimes in fairly arid areas. It grows up to 30 in (75 cm) high and has linear leaves to 3 in (8 cm) long, sometimes with small teeth. Masses of star-shaped, light blue flowers are borne in spring and summer. **ZONES 8–11.**

WAHLENBERGIA
BLUEBELLS

This is a genus of about 200 species of annuals or perennials with a wide distribution, mostly in the southern hemisphere. They have variable foliage and the flowers range from wide open stars to tubular bells, all with 5 prominent lobes, in shades of blue, purple or white. They are usually small in stature and are suitable for a rock garden or border.

CULTIVATION
Unless otherwise stated, the species described are fully frost hardy. Grow in a well-drained, humus-rich soil in full sun or light shade. Propagate from seed or by division in spring.

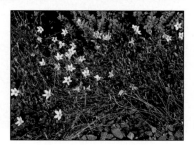

Wahlenbergia albomarginata (above)

NEW ZEALAND BLUEBELL

This tufted perennial to 8 in (20 cm) high forms basal rosettes of lance-shaped oval or spoon-shaped hairy leaves. Underground rhizomes spread to form new rosettes and these may develop into mat-like colonies. The nodding, usually solitary bell-shaped pale blue to white flowers with spreading lobes are borne on fine stems in summer. This marginally frost-hardy, short-lived plant grows best in part-shade. **ZONES 7–10.**

W

Wahlenbergia gloriosa *(left)*

ROYAL BLUEBELL, AUSTRALIAN BLUEBELL

This perennial with spreading rhizomes and erect stems to about 8 in (20 cm) high is a native of Australian alpine regions and is the floral emblem of the Australian Capital Territory. It has dark green, lance-shaped leaves to 1½ in (35 mm) long with wavy, toothed margins and bears a profusion of royal-blue or purple, bell-shaped flowers on separate fine stems in summer. **ZONES 8–10.**

Wahlenbergia stricta 'Tasmanian Sky' *(below left)*

Wahlenbergia stricta

syn. *Wahlenbergia consimilis*

TALL BLUEBELL

This tufted perennial herb to 3 ft (1 m) tall has a wide distribution throughout southern Australia and is quite common in open forests and grasslands. The basal obovate leaves with wavy margins become linear up the stem. Lower stems and leaves have spreading, long white hairs. Small, blue star-shaped flowers are borne in spring and summer. **'Tasmanian Sky'** has light purple flowers. **ZONES 9–10.**

W

WALDSTEINIA

Found over much of the northern temperate zone, the 6 species in this genus are clump-forming, rhizomatous perennials. They are semi-evergreen, creeping ground covers with 3-part leaves resembling those of their close allies, the strawberries. The hairy leaves are usually bright green with bronze tints if grown in the sun. In spring and summer, bright yellow 5-petalled flowers are borne singly or in clusters of up to 8 blooms.

CULTIVATION

Most species are quite frost hardy and easily grown in any well-drained soil in sun or part-shade. Propagate by division or by self-rooted offsets from the runners.

Waldsteinia ternata (right) syn. *Waldsteinia trifoliata*

Native to central Europe through Russia to China and Japan, this herbaceous or semi-evergreen creeping perennial grows to a height of about 6 in (15 cm). Golden yellow, buttercup-like flowers appear from late spring, mostly on the new growth. Each bloom is about ½ in (12 mm) across. It spreads quite fast and makes a thick ground cover in moist soil in part-shade beneath trees. In ideal conditions, *Waldsteinia ternata* can become invasive. **ZONES 3–9.**

W

WELWITSCHIA

This bizarre genus consists of a single species, native to the desert regions of southern Angola and Namibia. It is a gymnosperm, occasionally cultivated for its curiosity value. Its short, hollow, woody stems terminate in a 2-lobed disc-like apex. From opposite sides of the disc sprout 2 long strap-like leaves. These 2 leaves persist for the full lifetime of the plant, splitting length-wise with age. Male or female cones are borne on separate plants on branched stalks that arise from the center of the disc.

CULTIVATION

This is a very slow-growing frost-tender plant requiring dry, hot conditions and adequate soil depth for a long tap root. It needs full sun and perfect drainage. Water moderately during the growing season and keep completely dry during winter. Propagation is from seed.

Welwitschia mirabilis
(above & left)
syn. *Welwitschia bainesii*

This species' leaves are leathery and long, up to 8 ft (2.4 m), and 3 ft (1 m) wide, splitting with age into multiple strips. Scarlet cones are set in groups of up to 20 on stalks up to 12 in (30 cm) long, each female cone bearing many winged seeds under its scales. Male cones are smaller and insignificant. It is adapted to desert conditions. ZONES 9–10.

W

WITTROCKIA

This small genus of 7 species of bromeliads is found only in southern coastal mountains of Brazil. They are epiphytic, terrestrial or rock-dwelling plants that form stemless rosettes. Most species have colorful thinly textured linear leaves with a few marginal spines. Spikes of flowers nestled in the heart of the plant have colorful bracts and blue or white petals.

CULTIVATION

In warm, frost-free areas they may be grown outdoors in an open, well-drained soil in filtered shade. When grown as pot plants in a greenhouse, use an open, porous bromeliad potting mix. Indoors they need warm humid conditions and bright, filtered light. Propagation is from seed or offsets.

Wittrockia superba *(above)*
syns *Nidularium karatas, N. superbum, Canistrum cruentum*

In its natural habitat this rosette-forming bromeliad, to 3 ft (1 m) high and across, grows on trees, on rocks or in leaf litter on the ground. The long stiff leaves are a glossy green with red tips and sharp terminal spines. The flowers, arranged in a cone-shaped spike, are nestled in the heart of the plant. These are blue and white, surrounded by red bracts and are produced in summer. ZONES 11–12.

W

WULFENIA

This is a genus of about 6 species of small evergreen tufted perennials, native to southeastern Europe, western Asia and the Himalayas. Leaves are usually rough-textured with scalloped margins, set from a basal point on long stalks. Flowers are borne on spike-like racemes from the base of the plant—these are blue to purple, tubular in shape with 4 lobes. The fruits are capsules.

CULTIVATION

Fully frost hardy and suited to cold climates, plants resent high humidity and excessive moisture in winter. They prefer full sun and moist, but well-drained soil. Propagate from seed or by division in spring.

Wulfenia carinthiaca (above)

Native to the Alps and the Balkan Peninsula, this species has a height and spread of about 8 in (20 cm). Leaves are in a basal rosette and are lance-shaped to oval, about 7 in (18 cm) long, toothed, dark green and hairy underneath. The top quarter of the flower stem is a one-sided spike of tubular flowers; violet blue with rounded lobes, which are borne in summer. **ZONES 5–9.**

W

XERANTHEMUM
IMMORTELLE

The 5 or 6 annuals included in this genus are natives of the Mediterranean region, extending to Iran. They are known as immortelles or everlasting flowers because their dried flowerheads retain their color and form for many years. The upright, branching stems have narrow, hoary leaves. The flowerheads are solitary on long stems and the small fertile flowers are surrounded by papery bracts which may be white, purple or pink.

CULTIVATION
Moderately frost hardy, they grow best in a sunny position in fertile, well-drained soil. Propagate in spring from seed sown *in situ*.

Xeranthemum annuum
IMMORTELLE

A good source of dried flowers, this annual blooms in summer, producing heads of purple, daisy-like flowers; whites, pinks and mauves, some with a 'double' appearance are also available. The leaves are silvery and lance-shaped and the plants grow to around 24 in (60 cm) high and 18 in (45 cm) wide. **Mixed Hybrids** include singles and doubles in shades of pink, purple, mauve, red or white. ZONES 7–10.

Xeranthemum annuum
Mixed Hybrids *(below)*

X

XERONEMA

There are only 2 species in this genus and it has never been common, either in the wild or in gardens. Found naturally in New Caledonia and on the Poor Knights Islands northeast of New Zealand, they are striking plants that appeal to all who see them. There is nothing quite like their brilliant red flowers borne on one-sided racemes among iris-like, leathery, sword-shaped leaves.

CULTIVATION

Although able to be grown from seed or by careful division, tissue culture propagation has been the key to success and plants are now readily available to gardeners. It needs a frost-free climate and, even in a rich soil, can take a few years to settle down to flowering. Plant in a humus-rich soil with added pumice or scoria to ensure good drainage.

Xeronema
callistemon (below)
POOR KNIGHTS LILY

The unique and beautiful flowers of this perennial are a rare sight. A vivid red in color, their long stamens are massed to create a 6 in (15 cm) brush. They are held horizontally to provide a perch for the honey-eating birds that pollinate them. They are strictly greenhouse plants in areas with cool-temperate climates. ZONES 10–11.

X

YUCCA

The 40 or so species of unusual evergreen perennials, shrubs and trees in this genus are found in drier regions of North America. Often slow growing, they form rosettes of stiff, sword-like leaves usually tipped with a sharp spine; as the plants mature, some species develop an upright woody trunk, often branched. Yuccas bear showy, tall panicles of drooping, white or cream, bell- to cup-shaped flowers. The fruits are either fleshy or dry capsules, but in most species are rarely seen away from the plants' native lands as the flowers must be pollinated by the yucca moth.

CULTIVATION

Yuccas do best in areas of low humidity; they prefer full sun and sandy soil with good drainage. Depending on the species, they are frost hardy to frost tender. Propagate from seed (if available), cuttings or suckers in spring.

Yucca whipplei
(left)

OUR LORD'S CANDLE, CANDLE YUCCA

This is distinguished from most other yuccas by its very narrow, gray-green leaves which form a nearly perfect sphere. Native to the coastal lower ranges of California, in late summer and autumn it sends up a straight, flowering spike to 12 ft (3.5 m) high that is densely covered in creamy white flowers, some-times tinged with pur-ple. It is very tolerant of dry conditions. **ZONES 8–11.**

Yucca baccata *(above)*

BLUE YUCCA, BANANA YUCCA, DATIL YUCCA

Yucca baccata comes from southwestern USA and north-ern Mexico and grows to 5 ft (1.5 m) in height. Its twisted leaves are flexible near the base and are dark green tinged with yellow or blue. The pendent flowers are bell-shaped, white or cream and often tinged with purple. **ZONES 9–11.**

Y

Zantedeschia aethiopica (left)

WHITE ARUM LILY,
LILY OF THE NILE

Although normally deciduous, in summer and early autumn this species can stay evergreen if given enough moisture. It can also be grown in water up to 6–12 in (15–30 cm) deep. *Zantedeschia aethiopica* reaches 24–36 in (60–90 cm) in height and spread, with large clumps of broad, dark green leaves. The large flowers, produced in spring, summer and autumn, are pure white with a yellow spadix. **'Crowborough'** is more cold tolerant and better suited to cool climates such as the UK and the northwest USA. It grows to about 3 ft (1 m) tall. **'Green Goddess'** has interesting green markings on the spathes. ZONES 8–11.

ZANTEDESCHIA

ARUM LILY, CALLA LILY, PIG LILY

Indigenous to southern and eastern Africa, this well-known genus of the arum family consists of 6 species of tuberous perennials. The inflorescence consists of a showy white, yellow or pink spathe shaped like a funnel, with a central finger-like, yellow spadix. The leaves are glossy green and usually arrowhead-shaped.

Zantedeschia aethiopica 'Green Goddess' *(below)*

CULTIVATION

Consisting of both evergreen and deciduous species, this genus includes frost-tender to moderately frost-hardy plants. Most are intolerant of dry conditions, preferring well-drained soil in full sun or part-shade, although *Zantedeschia aethiopica* will grow as a semi-aquatic plant in boggy ground that is often inundated. Propagate from offsets in winter.

Z

Zantedeschia elliottiana
(left)

GOLDEN ARUM LILY

This summer-flowering species has a yellow spathe surrounding a yellow spadix, sometimes followed by a spike of bright yellow berries that are attractive to birds. It grows 24–36 in (60–90 cm) tall with a spread of 24 in (60 cm). The heart-shaped, semi-erect leaves have numerous white spots or streaks. **ZONES 8–11.**

Zantedeschia rehmannii *(right)*

PINK ARUM LILY, PINK CALLA

The spathe on this summer-flowering plant is mauve to rose-purple with paler margins, enclosing a yellow spadix. Its green, un-marked leaves are semi-erect and not ar-rowhead-shaped as in other species. It grows 15 in (38 cm) tall and 12 in (30 cm) wide. Marginally frost hardy, it likes well-composted soil, a protected loca-tion and part-shade. **ZONES 8–11.**

Z

Zantedeschia, New Zealand Mixed Hybrids

These hybrids of *Zantedeschia rehmannii* and *Z. elliottiana* have flowers in a range of colors from red, pink and bronze to orange. Some have spotted leaves. Although there are miniatures, most reach a height of 24 in (60 cm) or more with a spread of 8 in (20 cm). Not as easy to grow as their parents, they need warmth and very rich soil. The flowers of **'Brigadier'** are washed a reddish orange; and the orange-red tones of **'Mango'** varies with cultivation, a slightly alkaline soil giving richer color than an acid one. The 'flower' is about 6 in (15 cm) wide and the leaves are spotted. ZONES 8–11.

Zantedeschia, New Zealand Mixed Hybrid, 'Brigadier' *(left)*

Zantedeschia, New Zealand Mixed Hybrid, 'Mango' *(below)*

ZAUSCHNERIA

From southwestern USA and Mexico, this genus consists of about 4 species of shrubby perennials. Although very similar, for horticultural purposes they can be considered variations on *Zauschneria californica*. They are grown for their masses of orange to scarlet, tubular flowers. Some botanists now believe these species belong in the *Epilobium* genus.

CULTIVATION

These plants are marginally frost hardy. Grow in full sun in well-drained soil in a warm, sheltered position. Propagate from seed or by division in spring, or from side-shoot cuttings in summer.

Zauschneria septentrionalis *(below)*

syn. *Epilobium septentrionale*

HUMBOLDT COUNTY FUCHSIA

Native to western North America, this species is more or less mat-forming and grows to 8 in (20 cm) tall. The leaves are gray-white and felted; the flowers are bright orange-red. ZONES 8–10.

Zauschneria californica *(bottom)*

syn. *Epilobium canum* subsp. *canum*

CALIFORNIAN FUCHSIA

The common name refers both to the species' Californian origin and to its flowers, which are indeed like the related fuchsias. These are bright red, appearing in terminal spikes on erect, slender stems in late summer and early autumn. This evergreen shrub has lance-like, 1 in (25 mm) long leaves, is highly variable and grows 12–24 in (30–60 cm) tall and 3–6 ft (1–1.8 m) wide. It needs only occasional water and is hardy to around 15°F (–9°C). *Zauschneria californica* subsp. *cana* (syn. *Zauschneria cana*), a small suckering shrub, reaches 24 in (60 cm) high. It has felty gray foliage and its larger flowers are a brilliant vermilion red. *Z. c.* subsp. *canum* 'Dublin' (syn. 'Glasnevin'), more compact to 12 in (30 cm) tall with bright orange-red flowers, was selected at Glasnevin Gardens in Ireland. ZONES 8–10.

Z

ZINNIA
ZINNIA

This genus of 20 species of erect to spreading annuals, perennials and subshrubs has daisy-like, terminal flowerheads in many colors including white, yellow, orange, red, purple and lilac. Found throughout Mexico and Central and South America, some are grown for cut flowers and in mixed borders.

CULTIVATION

These plants are marginally frost hardy and are best in a sunny position in fertile soil that drains well. They need frequent deadheading. Propagate from seed sown under glass early in spring.

Zinnia elegans (right & below)
YOUTH-AND-OLD-AGE

This sturdy Mexican annual is the best known of the zinnias. The wild form has purple flowerheads, and blooms from summer to autumn. It grows fairly rapidly to 24–30 in (60–75 cm), with a smaller spread. Garden varieties offer hues of white, red, pink, yellow, violet, orange or crimson in flowers up to 6 in (15 cm) across. 'Envy' has pale green semi-double flowers. The **Dreamland Series** is compact and heavy flowering, which is typical of F1 Hybrid bedding zinnias. 'Dreamland Ivy' has pale greenish yellow flowers. The **Thumbelina Series** has 2 in (5 cm) wide flowerheads on plants that are only 6 in (15 cm) high. ZONES 8–11.

Z

Zinnia elegans 'Dreamland Ivy'
(above)

Zinnia elegans, Thumbelina
Series cultivar *(right)*

Zinnia elegans 'Envy' *(below)*

Z

Zinnia haageana
syns *Zinnia mexicana, Z. angustifolia*

This Mexican annual reaches 24 in (60 cm) in height with a spread of 8 in (20 cm). The small but profuse yellow, orange and bronze flowerheads, more than 1½ in (35 mm) wide, appear in summer and early autumn. **'Chippendale Daisy'** grows to 24 in (60 cm) tall and has simple, single, 2 in (5 cm) wide red flowers with gold petal tips. **'Old Mexico'** is an old but valuable cultivar that is drought resistant. **ZONES 8–11.**

Zinnia haageana 'Chippendale Daisy' *(above)*

Zinnia peruviana *(below)*

This species ranges in the wild from Arizona to Argentina. An erect-growing, summer-flowering annual, it reaches a height of 3 ft (1 m). The hairy stems are green, changing to yellow or purple. Its flowerheads are yellow to scarlet. **ZONES 8–11.**

Zinnia haageana cultivar *(above)*

Reference Table

This table provides information to help you choose annuals and perennials. Information on plant type, climate zones, color of flowers, planting time and flowering season will help you find the annuals and perennials best suited to your purposes.

Plant Type

The reference table uses the following symbols for plant type:

- A for annuals;
- B for biennials; and
- P for perennials.

As the classification of some plants is not clear cut, the following combinations are also used:

- A(P) or B(P), meaning annuals or biennials that can live on to become short-lived perennials;
- P(A) or B(A), meaning perennials or biennials that are usually treated as annuals;
- A(B), meaning annuals that can live on to become biennials; and
- P(B), meaning perennials that are usually treated as biennials

Climate Zones

These match the climate zones given in the main text for each plant. An explanation of climate zones can be found on pages 31–33.

NAME	TYPE	ZONES	COLOR	PLANTING TIME	FLOWERING SEASON
Abelmoschus moschatus	P	8–12	red, pink or white	spring	summer–autumn
Acaena argentea	P	7–10	purple	spring	summer
Acaena novae-zelandiae	P	5–10	red	spring	summer
Acanthus hungaricus	P	7–10	white	autumn–winter	summer–autumn
Acanthus mollis	P	7–10	white	autumn–winter	summer–autumn
Acanthus spinosus	P	7–10	white	autumn–winter	summer–autumn
Achillea 'Coronation Gold'	P	4–10	yellow	winter	summer–autumn
Achillea filipendulina & cultivars	P	3–10	yellow	winter	summer–autumn
Achillea 'Great Expectations'	P	2–10	yellow	winter	summer–autumn
Achillea × *kellereri*	P	5–10	white	winter	summer
Achillea 'Lachsschönheit'	P	3–10	salmon pink	winter	summer–autumn
Achillea millefolium & cultivars	P	3–10	white to pink & red tones	winter	summer
Achillea 'Moonshine'	P	3–10	yellow	winter	summer–autumn
Achillea ptarmica	P	3–10	white	winter	summer
Achillea 'Schwellenberg'	P	3–10	yellow	winter	summer–autumn
Achillea 'Taygetea'	P	4–10	yellow	winter	summer–autumn
Achillea tomentosa	P	4–10	yellow	winter	summer
Acinos alpinus	P	6–9	violet & white	spring	summer
Aciphylla aurea	P	7–9	yellow-green	spring	summer
Aciphylla hectori	P	7–9	pale yellow to white	spring	summer
Aciphylla montana	P	7–9	pale yellow	spring	summer
Aconitum carmichaelii	P	4–9	violet-blue	winter–spring	late summer–autumn
Aconitum 'Ivorine'	P	4–9	pale ivory yellow	winter–spring	autumn
Aconitum napellus	P	5–9	violet blue to purple	winter–spring	autumn
Aconitum vulparia	P	4–9	pale yellow	winter–spring	summer
Acorus gramineus	P	3–11	foliage plant	most of the year	summer
Acorus gramineus 'Ogon'	P	3–11	foliage plant	most of the year	summer
Actaea alba	P	3–9	white	late autumn–winter	late spring–early summer
Actaea rubra	P	3–9	white tinted mauve	late autumn–winter	late spring–early summer
Actinotus helianthi	B	9–10	pink & green, white bracts	spring–summer	late spring–summer
Adenophora uehatae	P	5–9	pale mauve-blue	winter–spring	summer
Adonis annua	A	6–9	red	autumn–spring	summer

NAME	TYPE	ZONES	COLOR	PLANTING TIME	FLOWERING SEASON
Adonis vernalis	P	3–9	yellow	late summer–autumn	spring
Aechmea chantinii	P	11–12	red & yellow	most of the year	summer
Aechmea chantinii 'Black'	P	11–12	red & yellow	most of the year	summer
Aechmea fasciata	P	10–12	mauve-blue, pink bracts	most of the year	summer
Aechmea nidularioides	P	10–12	yellow flowers, red bracts	most of the year	summer–autumn
Aechmea pineliana	P	10–12	yellow flowers, red bracts	most of the year	winter–spring
Aechmea 'Royal Wine'	P	11–12	dark blue	most of the year	variable
Aechmea 'Shining Light'	P	11–12	red flowers, red bracts	most of the year	summer
Aegopodium podagraria	P	3–9	white	winter	summer
Aethionema grandiflorum	P	7–9	pink	autumn–winter	spring
Aethionema 'Mavis Holmes'	P	7–9	pink	autumn–winter	spring
Agapanthus africanus	P	8–10	blue	autumn–spring	summer–autumn
Agapanthus campanulatus	P	7–11	light purple-blue	autumn–spring	summer
Agapanthus 'Irving Cantor'	P	8–11	purple-blue	autumn–spring	late spring–autumn
Agapanthus 'Loch Hope'	P	8–11	purple–blue	autumn–spring	late spring–autumn
Agapanthus praecox	P	9–11	lavender blue	autumn–spring	late spring–autumn
Agastache foeniculum	P	8–10	purple	late autumn–spring	summer
Agastache rugosa	P	8–10	pink or mauve & white	late autumn–spring	summer
Ageratina altissima	P	6–9	white	most of the year	late summer
Ageratina ligustrina	P	9–11	white flowers, pink bracts	most of the year	late summer–autumn
Ageratina occidentalis	P	6–9	white, pink or purple	most of the year	late summer
Ageratum houstonianum	A	9–12	dusky blue, pink or white	spring–summer	spring–autumn
Aglaonema 'Parrot Jungle'	P	10–12	foliage plant	most of the year	summer
Aglaonema 'Silver Queen'	P	10–12	foliage plant	most of the year	summer
Agrimonia eupatoria	P	6–10	yellow	winter	late spring
Agrostemma githago	A	8–10	deep pink	spring or autumn	summer
Ajania 'Bess', *A.* 'Benny'	P	4–10	yellow	winter–early spring	autumn
Ajania pacifica	P	4–10	yellow	winter–early spring	autumn
Ajania pacifica 'Silver and Gold'	P	4–10	yellow	winter–early spring	autumn
Ajuga pyramidalis	P	5–9	blue or mauve	most of the year	summer to autumn
Ajuga pyramidalis 'Metallica Crispa'	P	5–9	purple-blue	most of the year	summer to autumn
Ajuga reptans & cultivars	P	3–10	deep blue	most of the year	late spring to autumn
Alcea rosea	B	4–10	all except true blue	winter–spring	summer–autumn
Alchemilla conjuncta	P	5–9	yellow-green	late autumn–winter	late spring–summer

NAME	TYPE	ZONES	COLOR	PLANTING TIME	FLOWERING SEASON
Alchemilla mollis	P	4–9	yellow-green	late autumn–winter	late spring–summer
Alchemilla rohdii	P	6–9	yellow-green	late autumn–winter	late spring–summer
Alchemilla speciosa	P	4–9	yellow-green	late autumn–winter	late spring–summer
Alonsoa warscewiczii	P	9–11	pink, orange or red	spring	spring–autumn
Alpinia galanga	P	11–12	white & pink	winter	summer
Alpinia purpurata	P	11–12	white flowers, red bracts	winter	most of the year
Alpinia zerumbet	P	10–12	white, gold & red	winter	mainly spring–summer
Alstroemeria aurea	P	7–9	orange & bronze shades	early spring	spring–summer
Alstroemeria haemantha	P	7–9	orange to red	early spring	summer
Alstroemeria hybrids	P	7–10	all except true blue	early spring	summer–autumn
Alstroemeria psittacina	P	8–10	red & green	early spring	summer–early autumn
Alyssum chalcidicum	P	7–10	yellow	spring–early summer	spring
Alyssum murale	P	7–9	yellow	spring	spring
Amaranthus caudatus	A	8–11	red	spring	summer–autumn
Amaranthus tricolor & hybrids	A	8–11	red (mainly foliage plants)	spring	summer
Ammi majus	P	6–10	white	winter–early spring	summer–autumn
Amsonia tabernaemontana	P	3–9	pale blue	winter–early spring	late spring–summer
Anagallis monellii	P	7–10	blue or red	winter–early spring	summer
Anagallis tenella	P	8–10	pale pink or white	winter–early spring	summer
Anaphalis javanica	P	9–10	white	winter–early spring	summer
Anaphalis triplinervis	P	5–9	white	winter–early spring	summer
Anaphalis triplinervis 'Sommerschnee'	P	5–9	white	winter	summer
Anchusa azurea & cultivars	P	3–9	blue to purple tones	winter–early spring	spring–summer
Anchusa capensis	A(B)	8–10	blue	early spring	spring–summer
Anchusa capensis 'Blue Angel'	A(B)	8–10	blue	winter	spring–summer
Anchusa granatensis	P	6–9	reddish-purple	spring	spring–summer
Androsace sarmentosa	P	3–8	pink	spring	late spring–summer
Androsace sarmentosa 'Brilliant'	P	3–8	mauve-pink	spring	late spring–summer
Anemone appenina	P	6–9	blue	autumn–winter	spring
Anemone blanda	P	6–9	white, pink or blue	autumn–winter	late winter–spring
Anemone blanda 'Radar'	P	6–9	magenta with white center	autumn–winter	late winter–spring
Anemone b. 'White Splendour'	P	6–9	white	autumn–winter	late winter–spring
Anemone hupehensis	P	6–10	white, pink or mauve	winter–spring	late summer–autumn
Anemone × hybrida	P	6–10	white or pink shades	winter–spring	late summer–autumn

NAME	TYPE	ZONES	COLOR	PLANTING TIME	FLOWERING SEASON
Anemone × hybrida 'Honorine Jobert'	P	6–10	white	winter–spring	late summer–autumn
Anemone nemorosa	P	5–9	white	autumn–winter	spring
Anemone nemorosa 'Robinsoniana'	P	5–9	lavender blue	autumn–winter	spring
Anemone rivularis	P	6–9	white tinted blue	winter	spring–early summer
Anemone sylvestris	P	4–9	white	winter	spring–early summer
Anemone trullifolia	P	5–9	white, pale blue or yellow	winter–early spring	summer
Anemonella thalictroides	P	4–9	white to pale mauve	autumn	spring–early summer
Anemopsis californica	P	8–11	white	winter–spring	spring–autumn
Angelica pachycarpa	P	8–10	green	winter	summer
Angelica sylvestris	P	7–10	green	winter	summer
Anigozanthos, Bush Gems Series	P	9–11	yellow, orange, red & green	spring	spring–summer
Anigozanthos flavidus	P	9–11	greenish yellow	spring	spring–early summer
Anigozanthos humilis	P	9–11	cream to yellow & red	spring	late winter–spring
Anigozanthos manglesii	P	9–10	green & red	spring	spring–early summer
Anigozanthos 'Red Cross'	P	9–11	red	spring	spring–summer
Anigozanthos 'Regal Claw'	P	9–11	orange & red	spring	spring–summer
Antennaria dioica	P	5–9	white, pink or yellow	winter–early spring	summer
Antennaria dioica 'Australis'	P	5–9	white	winter–early spring	summer
Anthemis cretica	P	5–9	white & yellow	most of the year	spring–summer
Anthemis 'Moonlight'	P	5–10	yellow	most of the year	late spring–summer
Anthemis tinctoria	P	4–10	yellow	most of the year	spring–summer
Anthericum liliago	P	7–10	white	late winter–spring	summer
Anthericum liliago 'Major'	P	7–10	white	late winter–spring	summer
Anthurium andraeanum	P	11–12	red	spring	variable
Anthurium scherzerianum	P	10–12	red	spring	mainly summer–autumn
Anthyllis montana	P	7–9	pink & white	spring	late spring–summer
Anthyllis vulneraria	P	7–9	cream tinted purple	spring	late spring–summer
Antirrhinum hispanicum	P	7–10	mauve-pink	spring	late spring–summer
Antirrhinum majus seed strains	P(A)	6–10	all except true blue	most of the year	spring–summer
Aponogeton distachyos	P	8–10	white	winter–early spring	late spring–autumn
Aquilegia atrata	P	3–9	violet–purple	autumn–spring	spring–early summer
Aquilegia caerulea	P	3–9	dusky blue & white	spring	late spring–early summer
Aquilegia canadensis	P	3–9	red & yellow	late winter–spring	late spring–early summer

NAME	TYPE	ZONES	COLOR	PLANTING TIME	FLOWERING SEASON
Aquilegia chrysantha	P	3–10	yellow or white	late winter–spring	late spring–early summer
Aquilegia 'Crimson Star'	P	3–10	red & white	late winter– early spring	late spring– early summer
Aquilegia elegantula	P	5–9	pale orange or yellow	late winter–spring	late spring–early summer
Aquilegia flabellata	P	5–9	purple-blue & white	late winter–spring	late spring–early summer
Aquilegia formosa	P	5–9	orange-red	late winter–spring	late spring–early summer
Aquilegia, McKana Hybrids	P	3–10	most colors	late winter–spring	late spring–early summer
Aquilegia vulgaris	P	3–10	most colors	late winter–spring	late spring–early summer
Aquilegia vulgaris 'Nora Barlow'	P	3–10	pink & greenish-white	late winter–spring	late spring–early summer
Arabis blepharophylla	P	7–10	pink to purple	most of the year	spring
Arabis caucasica	P	4–10	white	most of the year	spring
Arctotheca calendula	P	8–11	light yellow	most of the year	spring–autumn
Arctotheca populifolia	P	9–11	yellow	most of the year	summer–autumn
Arctotis cumbletonii	P	9–11	golden yellow	most of the year	spring–summer
Arctotis fastuosa	P	9–11	orange & purple	most of the year	spring–summer
Arctotis hirsuta	P	9–11	orange, yellow or white	most of the year	spring–summer
Arctotis hybrids	P	9–11	most colors except blue	most of the year	spring–summer
Arenaria balearica	P	7–9	white & green	most of the year	spring–early summer
Arenaria montana	P	4–9	white & yellow-green	most of the year	spring–early summer
Arenaria tetraquetra	P	6–9	white	most of the year	spring
Argemone mexicana	A	8–11	yellow	spring	late spring–summer
Aristea ecklonii	P	9–11	purple–blue	autumn or spring	summer
Aristolochia clematitis	P	5–9	yellow	winter–spring	late spring–early summer
Armeria alliacea	P	5–9	purple-pink	autumn or spring	late spring–early summer
Armeria leucocephala	P	7–9	white, pink shades or red	autumn or spring	late spring–summer
Armeria maritima	P	4–9	pink shades or white	autumn or spring	spring–summer
Artemisia absinthium	P	4–10	yellow (foliage plant)	spring–summer	late summer
Artemisia arborescens	P	8–11	yellow (foliage plant)	spring–summer	late summer–autumn
Artemisia caucasica	P	5–9	yellow (foliage plant)	spring–summer	late summer
Artemisia dracunculus	P	6–9	insignificant	spring–summer	late summer
Artemisia ludoviciana	P	4–10	greyish cream (foliage plant)	spring–summer	summer
Arthropodium cirrhatum	P	8–10	white	autumn–early spring	summer–autumn
Arthropodium milleflorum	P	8–11	pale pink to lilac	autumn–early spring	late spring–summer
Aruncus dioicus	P	3–9	greenish white to cream	winter	summer
Aruncus dioicus 'Kneiffii'	P	3–9	cream	winter	summer

NAME	TYPE	ZONES	COLOR	PLANTING TIME	FLOWERING SEASON
Asarum arifolium	P	7–9	purple-brown (foliage plant)	late winter–early spring	late spring–early summer
Asarum canadense	P	3–8	purple-brown (foliage plant)	late winter–early spring	late spring–early summer
Asarum caudatum	P	6–9	purple-brown (foliage plant)	late winter–early spring	late spring–early summer
Asarum europaeum	P	6–9	purple-brown (foliage plant)	late winter–early spring	late spring–early summer
Asarum maximum	P	7–9	purple-brown (foliage plant)	late winter–early spring	late spring–early summer
Asarum muramatui	P	7–9	purple-brown (foliage plant)	late winter–early spring	late spring–early summer
Asclepias speciosa	P	2–9	pink & white	spring–summer	summer
Asperula arcadiensis	P	5–9	pink to pale purple	late winter–early summer	summer
Asperula setosa	A	5–9	lilac	late winter–spring	summer
Asphodeline lutea	P	6–10	yellow	winter–early spring	summer
Asphodelus aestivus	P	6–10	white to pale pink	summer	spring
Asphodelus albus	P	5–10	white striped pink	summer	spring
Astelia nervosa	P	9–10	creamy brown	winter	summer
Aster alpinus	P	3–9	white & pink or blue shades	autumn–winter	late spring–early summer
Aster amellus	P	4–9	pink or purple-blue	winter–early spring	late summer–autumn
Aster amellus cultivars	P	4–9	pink, mauve, blue or purple	winter–early spring	late summer–autumn
Aster 'Coombe's Violet'	P	4–9	light purple	winter–early spring	late summer–autumn
Aster divaricatus	P	3–9	white	winter–early spring	summer–autumn
Aster ericoides	P	4–10	white & pink or yellow	winter–early spring	summer–autumn
Aster ericoides 'White Heather'	P	4–10	white	winter–early spring	summer–autumn
Aster linosyris	P	4–10	yellow	winter–early spring	late summer
Aster novae-angliae	P	4–9	pink or mauve	winter–early spring	late summer–autumn
Aster novae-angliae cultivars	P	4–9	pink, mauve, blue or purple	winter–early spring	late summer–autumn
Aster novi-belgii	P	4–9	pink, mauve, blue or purple	winter–early spring	late summer–autumn
Aster sedifolius	P	5–9	pink, violet or purple	winter–early spring	late spring–autumn
Aster umbellatus	P	3–9	white	winter–early spring	summer
Astilbe, Arendsii Hybrids	P	6–10	white, cream, pink & red	winter–early spring	summer
Astilbe 'Betsy Cuperus'	P	6–10	pale peach pink	winter–early spring	summer
Astilbe chinensis	P	5–10	white flushed pink	winter–early spring	summer
Astilbe chinensis 'Pumila'	P	5–10	white flushed pink	winter–early spring	summer
Astilbe chinensis var. *davidii*	P	5–10	pinkish purple	winter–early spring	summer

NAME	TYPE	ZONES	COLOR	PLANTING TIME	FLOWERING SEASON
Astilbe 'Serenade'	P	5–10	pinkish red	winter–early spring	summer
Astilbe 'Straussenfeder'	P	6–10	rose pink	winter–early spring	summer
Astragalus angustifolius	P	7–9	light purple	spring–autumn	summer
Astrantia major	P	6–9	pink & white	winter–early spring	late spring–summer
Astrantia major 'Sunningdale Variegated'	P	6–9	pink & white	winter–early spring	late spring–summer
Aubrieta × cultorum	P	4–9	white & pink or purple shades	late winter–summer	spring
Aubrieta deltoidea	P	4–9	mauve-pink	late winter–summer	spring
Aubrieta gracilis	P	5–9	purple	late winter–summer	summer
Aurinia saxatilis	P	4–9	pale- to golden-yellow	spring–summer	spring–early summer
Baptisia alba	P	7–10	white	autumn–winter	summer
Baptisia australis	P	3–10	purple-blue	autumn–winter	summer
Begonia 'Cleopatra'	P	10–12	pale pink	winter	spring–summer
Begonia fuchsioides	P	10–12	pale pink to coral	summer	winter
Begonia × hiemalis	P	10–11	white, yellow, orange, red, pink	summer	winter
Begonia 'Pink Shasta'	P	10–12	salmon pink	winter	spring–autumn
Begonia, Semperflorens-cultorum Group	P(A)	9–11	white or pink & red shades	spring	summer–early autumn
Bellis perennis	P	3–10	white	most of the year	late winter–early summer
Bellis perennis 'Medicis White'	P	3–10	white	autumn–winter	late winter–early summer
Bellis perennis 'Pomponette Series'	P	3–10	white or pink & red shades	autumn–winter	late winter–early summer
Bergenia hybrids	P	4–9	white or pink to red shades	late spring	spring
Bergenia cordifolia	P	3–9	mauve-pink	late spring	spring
Bergenia purpurascens	P	5–9	pink to purple-red	late spring	spring
Bergenia × schmidtii	P	5–10	rose pink	late spring	spring
Bergenia stracheyi	P	6–9	white to deep pink	late spring	spring
Bidens aequisquamea	P	8–10	deep pink	most of the year	late spring–autumn
Bidens ferulifolia & hybrids	P	8–10	bright yellow	most of the year	late spring–autumn
Billbergia amoena	P	11–12	blue-green flowers, pink bracts	after flowering	variable
Billbergia nutans	P	10–12	green flowers, pink bracts	autumn–early winter	spring
Blandfordia grandiflora	P	9–11	pink to red & yellow	winter	early summer
Boltonia asteroides	P	4–9	white or pink & mauve tones	winter–early spring	late summer–autumn
Borago officinalis	A	5–10	purple-blue	spring	late spring–summer

NAME	TYPE	ZONES	COLOR	PLANTING TIME	FLOWERING SEASON
Boykinia jamesii	P	5–8	pink to purple-red	late winter	spring–summer
Brachycome hybrids	P	9–11	white & pink or purple	spring or autumn	late spring–summer
Brachycome iberidifolia	A	9–11	white, blue, pink or purple	spring	summer–early autumn
Brachycome multifida	P	9–11	mauve-pink	spring or autumn	late spring–summer
Bracteantha bracteata & strains	A(P)	8–11	cream, yellow, bronze, pink, red	spring–autumn	summer–early autumn
Bromelia balansae	P	10–12	purple flower, white bracts	spring	late summer
Brunnera macrophylla	P	3–9	light blue	autumn–winter	spring
Bulbinella floribunda	P	8–10	golden yellow	winter	late spring–summer
Bulbinella hookeri	P	8–10	golden yellow	winter	late spring–summer
Calamintha nepeta	P	7–10	pale mauve	winter–early spring	summer
Calathea burle-marxii	P	11–12	pale violet	early spring	variable
Calathea makoyana	P	11–12	white (foliage plant)	early spring	variable
Calathea veitchiana	P	11–12	white spotted violet	early spring	variable
Calathea zebrina	P	10–12	white & violet	winter	spring
Calceolaria, Herbeohybrida Group	B(A)	9–11	yellow, orange or red	most of the year	most of the year
Calceolaria tomentosa	P	9–10	yellow	late spring–summer	summer
Calendula arvensis	A	6–10	yellow	late winter–spring	spring–autumn
Calendula officinalis & cultivars	A	6–10	yellow, apricot or orange tones	autumn	winter–spring
Callistephus chinensis	A	6–10	white, pink, mauve, purple, red	spring	summer
Caltha palustris & cultivars	P	3–9	golden yellow	autumn–winter	spring
Campanula 'Birch Hybrid'	P	4–9	purple-blue	autumn–winter	late spring–summer
Campanula 'Burghaltii'	P	4–9	mauve–light purple	winter	summer
Campanula carpatica	P	3–9	white or blue to purple tones	winter	late spring–summer
Campanula glomerata	P	3–9	purple-blue	winter	early summer & autumn
Campanula isophylla & cultivars	P	8–10	white or purple-blue tones	winter–early spring	summer
Campanula lactiflora	P	5–9	lilac-blue, white or pink	winter–early spring	summer
Campanula latifolia	P	5–9	purple, lilac or white	winter–early spring	summer
Campanula medium	B	6–10	white or pink & blue tones	spring	spring–early summer
Campanula persicifolia	P	3–9	purple-blue or white	winter–early spring	summer
Campanula portenschlagiana	P	5–10	violet to purple	winter–early spring	late spring–summer
Campanula rapunculoides	P	4–10	violet blue	winter–early spring	summer
Campanula rotundifolia	P	3–9	lilac-blue or white	winter–early spring	early summer

NAME	TYPE	ZONES	COLOR	PLANTING TIME	FLOWERING SEASON
Campanula takesimana	P	5–9	lilac-pink to purple-red	winter–early spring	late spring–summer
Campanula takesimana 'Alba'	P	5–9	white	winter–early spring	late spring–summer
Campanula vidalii	P	9–11	pink shades or white	spring	early summer
Canistrum lindenii	P	11–12	white flowers, green bracts	autumn–winter	summer
Canna × *generalis* hybrids	P	9–12	yellow, orange or red tones	late winter–spring	summer–autumn
Canna indica	P	9–12	yellow or dark red	late winter–spring	summer
Cardamine raphanifolia	P	7–9	pinkish purple	winter–early spring	late spring–summer
Carthamus tinctorius	A	7–11	orange-yellow	spring	summer
Catharanthus roseus	P	9–12	white or pink & purple tones	most of the year	most of the year
Celmisia asteliifolia	P	6–9	white	autumn or spring	summer
Celmisia hookeri	P	7–9	white	autumn or spring	summer
Celmisia semicordata	P	7–9	white	autumn or spring	summer
Celosia argentea & seed strains	A	10–12	yellow, orange & red tones	spring	summer
Celosia spicata & seed strains	A	10–12	purple-pink	spring	summer
Cenia turbinata	P(A)	8–10	yellow	autumn	spring
Centaurea cineraria	P	7–10	lilac-pink	autumn or spring	summer
Centaurea cyanus	A	5–10	white or pink, blue, purple	spring	summer
Centaurea dealbata	P	4–9	white or pink to purple shades	autumn or spring	late spring–summer
Centaurea hypoleuca	P	5–9	pink shades	autumn or spring	early summer & autumn
Centaurea h. 'John Coutts'	P	5–9	deep rose pink	autumn or spring	early summer & autumn
Centaurea macrocephala	P	4–9	yellow	autumn or spring	summer
Centaurea montana	P	3–9	violet	late autumn–spring	summer
Centranthus ruber	P	5–10	white or pink to red shades	winter–early spring	late spring–autumn
Cerastium alpinum	P	2–8	white	winter–early spring	summer
Ceratostigma plumbaginoides	P	6–9	blue	winter–early summer	late summer–autumn
Chelidonium majus & 'Flore Pleno'	P	6–9	golden yellow	autumn	mid spring–mid autumn
Chelone lyonii	P	6–9	deep pink	autumn or early spring	summer
Chelone obliqua	P	6–9	rosy purple	autumn or early spring	late summer–autumn
Chiastophyllum oppositifolium	P	7–9	golden yellow	autumn or summer	late spring–early summer
Chrysanthemum carinatum	A	8–10	yellow, orange, red or white	spring	summer
Chrysanthemum coronarium	A	7–11	yellow shades	spring	summer
Chrysanthemum × *grandiflora* hybrids	P	8–11	white, yellow or pink shades	most of the year	most of the year

NAME	TYPE	ZONES	COLOR	PLANTING TIME	FLOWERING SEASON
Chrysanthemum segetum	A	7–10	yellow shades	spring	summer–autumn
Chrysocephalum apiculatum	P	8–11	golden yellow	most of the year	mainly spring & summer
Chrysocephalum baxteri	P	8–10	white, cream or pale pink	most of the year	most of the year
Chrysogonum virginianum	P	6–9	yellow	late winter–spring	summer–autumn
Chrysosplenium davidianum	P	5–9	yellow	late winter–spring	late spring–early summer
Cimicifuga japonica & var. *acerina*	P	5–9	white	autumn or spring	summer–autumn
Cimicifuga simplex	P	3–9	white	winter–spring	autumn
Cineraria saxifraga	P	9–11	yellow	most of the year	spring–autumn
Cirsium occidentale	B	9–11	red flowers, white bracts	spring	spring–summer
Clarkia amoena	A	7–11	white or pink & red tones	autumn or spring	summer
Clarkia unguiculata	A	7–11	white, pink, purple, orange, red	autumn or spring	summer
Clematis integrifolia	P	3–9	purple or lavender shades	winter	summer
Clematis mandshurica	P	7–9	white	winter	summer
Cleome hassleriana	A	9–11	pink & white	spring	summer–early autumn
Clintonia andrewsiana	P	7–9	carmine red	winter–spring	spring–early summer
Clintonia borealis	P	3–9	creamy white	winter–spring	spring–early summer
Clintonia umbellulata	P	4–9	white	winter–spring	spring–early summer
Clivia miniata	P	10–11	deep orange	summer	spring–early summer
Codonopsis clematidea	P	5–9	white to violet	winter–spring	summer
Codonopsis convolvulacea	P	5–9	pale lavender & purple	winter–spring	summer
Columnea arguta	P	11–12	bright red & yellow	spring–autumn	most of the year
Consolida ajacis	A	7–11	white or blue, pink & purple	autumn or spring	late spring–summer
Convallaria majalis	P	3–9	white or pale pink	winter	spring
Convolvulus althaeoides	P	8–10	bright pink	spring–autumn	late spring–summer
Convolvulus cneorum	P	8–10	white & yellow	spring–autumn	spring–summer
Convolvulus tricolor & cultivars	A	8–11	blue or purple & white	spring	summer
Coreopsis auriculata & cultivars	P	4–9	deep yellow	autumn or spring	summer
Coreopsis grandiflora	P	6–10	golden yellow	autumn or spring	late spring–summer
Coreopsis lanceolata & cultivars	P	3–11	golden yellow	autumn or spring	spring–early summer
Coreopsis tinctoria	A	4–10	bright yellow & red	autumn or spring	summer–autumn
Coreopsis verticillata	P	6–10	bright yellow	autumn or spring	late spring–early autumn
Coreopsis verticillata 'Moonbeam'	P	6–10	light lemon yellow	autumn or spring	late spring–early autumn

NAME	TYPE	ZONES	COLOR	PLANTING TIME	FLOWERING SEASON
Coronilla varia	P	6–10	pink to lilac-pink	most of the year	summer
Corydalis flexuosa	P	5–9	bright blue	winter	spring–early summer
Corydalis lutea	P	6–10	yellow	winter	spring–early summer
Corydalis solida	P	6–9	pink to purple-red	autumn–winter	spring
Corydalis wilsonii	P	7–9	yellow	autumn–winter	spring
Cosmos atrosanguineus	P	8–10	deep red-brown	early spring	summer–autumn
Cosmos bipinnatus seed strains	A	8–11	white, pink, purple or red tones	spring	summer–autumn
Costus speciosus	P	11–12	white to pale pink with yellow	spring	most of the year
Crambe cordifolia	P	6–9	white	autumn–spring	late spring–summer
Crambe maritima	P	5–9	white	autumn–spring	late spring–summer
Cryptanthus bivittatus	P	10–12	white (foliage plant)	most of the year	spring–early summer
Cryptanthus bivittatus 'Pink Starlight'	P	10–12	white (foliage plant)	most of the year	spring–early summer
Cryptanthus zonatus	P	10–12	white (foliage plant)	most of the year	spring–early summer
Ctenanthe lubbersiana	P	10–12	white (foliage plant)	early spring	variable
Ctenanthe oppenheimiana	P	10–12	white (foliage plant)	early spring	variable
Cynoglossum amabile	A(B)	5–9	blue, white or pink	autumn or spring	spring–early summer
Cynoglossum amabile 'Firmament'	A(B)	5–9	bright blue	autumn or spring	spring–early summer
Dahlia hybrids	P	7–11	all except true blue	early spring	summer–autumn
Darmera peltata	P	5–9	pale pink or white	winter	spring
Datura innoxia	P	9–11	white	spring	summer–autumn
Datura stramonium	A	7–11	white or purple	spring	summer–autumn
Delphinium, Belladonna Group	P	3–9	white or blue	late winter–spring	summer–autumn
Delphinium cardinale	P	8–9	orange-red & yellow	spring	summer
Delphinium, Elatum Hybrids	P	3–9	white, pink, blue, purple	late winter–spring	summer–autumn
Delphinium grandiflorum	P	3–9	bright blue	late winter–spring	summer
Delphinium grandiflorum 'Blue Butterfly'	P	3–9	bright blue	late winter–spring	summer
Delphinium, Pacific Hybrids	P(B)	7–9	white, pink, blue, purple	spring	summer–autumn
Delphinium semibarbatum	P	6–9	soft yellow	spring	spring–summer
Dianella caerulea	P	9–11	mauve-blue or white	autumn–spring	spring–early summer
Dianthus, Alpine Pinks	P	4–9	white, pink, red, mauve-purple	late winter–spring	late spring–summer
Dianthus barbatus	P(B)	4–10	white, pink, red or purple tones	autumn–spring	late spring–summer

NAME	TYPE	ZONES	COLOR	PLANTING TIME	FLOWERING SEASON
Dianthus caryophyllus	P	8–10	white, pink or mauve tones	late winter–spring	summer
Dianthus chinensis	A	7–10	white, pink, red or mauve tones	late winter–spring	late spring–summer
Dianthus erinaceus	P	7–9	pink	late winter–spring	summer
Dianthus giganteus	P	5–9	purple–pink	late winter–spring	summer
Dianthus gratianopolitanus	P	5–9	purple-pink	late winter–spring	late spring–autumn
Dianthus, Modern Pinks	P	5–10	white, pink, red, mauve-purple	late winter–spring	late spring–early autumn
Dianthus, Old Fashioned Pinks	P	5–9	white, pink, red, mauve-purple	late winter–spring	late spring–early summer
Dianthus pavonius	P	4–9	pale pink	late winter–spring	summer
Dianthus, Perpetual-flowering Carnations	P	8–11	all except true blue	spring	late spring–autumn
Dianthus plumarius	P	3–10	white, pink, red, mauve–purple	late winter–spring	summer
Dianthus, seedling strains	P(A)	5–9	white, pink, red, mauve-purple	spring	late spring–autumn
Dianthus superbus	P	4–10	purple-pink	late winter–spring	summer
Dianthus s. 'Rainbow Loveliness'	P	4–10	mauve & pink shades	late winter	spring
Diascia barberae	P	8–10	salmon pink	autumn or spring	late spring–autumn
Diascia barberae 'Ruby Fields'	P	8–10	deep salmon pink	autumn or spring	summer–autumn
Diascia 'Blackthorn Apricot'	P	8–10	apricot pink	autumn or spring	summer–autumn
Diascia fetcaniensis	P	8–10	rose pink	autumn or spring	summer–autumn
Diascia 'Rupert Lambert'	P	8–10	deep pink	autumn or spring	summer–autumn
Diascia stachyoidese	P	8–10	deep rose pink	autumn or spring	summer
Diascia vigilis	P	8–10	pink	autumn or spring	summer–early winter
Dicentra formosa	P	3–9	pink & red	winter	spring–summer
Dicentra formosa 'Alba'	P	3–9	white	winter	spring–summer
Dicentra spectabilis	P	2–9	pink & white	winter–early spring	late spring–early summer
Dicentra spectabilis 'Alba'	P	2–9	white	winter–early spring	late spring–early summer
Dichorisandra reginae	P	11–12	purple	early spring–summer	summer–autumn
Dichorisandra thyrsiflora	P	10–12	purple	early spring–summer	autumn
Dicliptera suberecta	P	8–11	orange-red	spring	summer–autumn
Dictamnus albus	P	3–9	white, pink or lilac	summer	early summer
Dierama pendulum	P	8–10	pink or magenta shades	early spring	summer
Dierama pendulum 'Album'	P	8–10	white	early spring	summer
Dietes bicolor	P	9–11	pale yellow & brown	early spring	spring–early autumn

NAME	TYPE	ZONES	COLOR	PLANTING TIME	FLOWERING SEASON
Dietes iridioides	P	8–11	white & golden yellow	early spring	spring–early autumn
Digitalis ferruginea	B(P)	7–10	golden brown	winter–early spring	late spring–summer
Digitalis grandiflora & cultivars	B(P)	4–9	pale yellow	winter–early spring	summer
Digitalis lanata	B(P)	4–9	cream & pale brown	winter–early spring	summer
Digitalis lutea	P	4–9	white to soft yellow	winter–early spring	summer
Digitalis × mertonensis	P	4–9	salmon- to deep pink	winter–early spring	late spring–summer
Digitalis purpurea	P	5–10	white, pale yellow, pink to purple	winter–early spring	late spring–summer
Digitalis purpurea f. *albiflora*	P	5–10	white	winter–early spring	late spring–summer
Dimorphotheca pluvialis	A	8–10	white & brownish purple	autumn or spring	late winter–early summer
Dionaea muscipula	P	8–10	white (foliage plant)	spring	late spring–summer
Dionysia involucrata	P	4–9	violet to violet-purple	spring	early summer
Dipsacus fullonum	B	4–10	mauve-pink	spring	summer
Dipsacus sativus	B	5–10	mauve-pink	spring	summer
Disporum flavens	P	5–9	light yellow	late winter–spring	spring
Disporum smilacinum	P	5–9	white	late winter–spring	spring
Dodecatheon jeffreyi	P	5–9	red-purple	autumn–winter	late spring–early summer
Dodecatheon meadia	P	3–9	white or rose pink	autumn–winter	late spring–early summer
Dodecatheon pulchellum	P	4–9	deep cerise to lilac	autumn–winter	late spring–early summer
Dodecatheon p. 'Red Wings'	P	4–9	magenta	autumn–winter	late spring–early summer
Doronicum columnae 'Miss Mason'	P	5–9	bright yellow	winter–early spring	spring
Doronicum orientale 'Magnificum'	P	4–9	bright yellow	winter–early spring	spring
Doronicum pardalianches	P	5–9	bright yellow	winter–early spring	spring
Dorotheanthus bellidiformis	A	9–11	white, yellow, pink or red	spring	summer
Doryanthes excelsa	P	9–11	deep red	winter–early spring	spring
Doryanthes palmeri	P	9–11	deep red	winter–early spring	spring
Draba aizoides	P	5–9	bright yellow	spring	late spring
Draba rigida var. *bryoides*	P	6–9	bright yellow	spring	late spring
Draba sachalinensis	P	5–9	white	spring	late spring
Dracocephalum forrestii	P	4–9	violet-blue to purple	late winter–spring	summer
Drosera aliciae	P	9–11	pink	most of the year	summer
Drosera binata	P	9–11	white or pink	most of the year	summer
Drosera capensis	P	9–11	purple	most of the year	summer
Drosera cuneifolia	P	9–11	purple	most of the year	summer

NAME	TYPE	ZONES	COLOR	PLANTING TIME	FLOWERING SEASON
Drosera regia	P	9–11	pale pink to purple	most of the year	summer
Drosophyllum lusitanicum	P	9–11	bright yellow	spring	spring–summer
Dryas octopetala & varieties	P	2–9	white	autumn or spring	spring–early summer
Duchesnea indica	P	5–11	yellow	late winter–early spring	spring–early summer
Dymondia margaretae	P	8–11	yellow	late winter–spring	spring
Echinacea pallida	P	5–9	mauve-pink, white or purple	winter–early spring	summer
Echinacea purpurea	P	3–10	purplish-pink	winter–early spring	summer
Echinops bannaticus	P	3–10	mauve-blue	winter–early spring	summer
Echinops bannaticus 'Taplow Blue'	P	3–10	bright blue	winter–early spring	summer
Echinops ritro	P	3–10	purple-blue	winter–early spring	summer
Echium pininana	B	9–10	lavender-blue	spring	late spring–early summer
Echium plantagineum	A(B)	9–10	purple-blue to pinkish-red	spring	late spring–summer
Echium vulgare	B	7–10	violet blue or white or pink	spring	late spring–summer
Echium wildpretii	B	9–10	coral red	spring	late spring–summer
Eichhornia crassipes	P	9–12	violet with blue & gold	most of the year	spring–autumn
Elegia capensis	P	9–10	brown (foliage plant)	late winter–early spring	summer
Elegia cuspidata	P	9–10	brown (foliage plant)	late winter–early spring	summer
Ensete ventricosum	P	10–12	red	spring	late spring
Epilobium angustifolium	P	2–9	deep rose pink	autumn or spring	late summer–autumn
Epimedium alpinum	P	5–9	yellow & crimson	autumn–winter	spring
Epimedium diphyllum	P	5–9	white or purple	autumn–winter	spring
Epimedium 'Enchantress'	P	5–9	pale pink	autumn–winter	spring
Epimedium grandiflorum	P	4–9	pink to reddish-purple	autumn–winter	spring
Epimedium g. 'Rose Queen'	P	4–9	rose pink	autumn–winter	spring
Epimedium g. 'White Queen'	P	4–9	white	autumn–winter	spring
Epimedium pinnatum	P	5–9	yellow	autumn–winter	spring
Epimedium pinnatum ssp. *colchicum*	P	5–9	yellow	autumn–winter	spring
Epimedium × *versicolor*	P	5–9	yellow & red	autumn–winter	spring
Epimedium × *versicolor* 'Sulphureum'	P	5–9	yellow	autumn–winter	spring
Epimedium × *youngianum*	P	5–9	white or mauve-pink	autumn–winter	spring
Epimedium × *youngianum* 'Niveum'	P	5–9	white	autumn–winter	spring

NAME	TYPE	ZONES	COLOR	PLANTING TIME	FLOWERING SEASON
Epimedium × youngianum 'Roseum'	P	5–9	mauve-pink	autumn–winter	spring
Episcia cupreata	P	10–12	red	spring	spring–autumn
Episcia cupreata 'Mosaica'	P	10–12	red	spring	spring–autumn
Episcia dianthiflora	P	10–12	white	spring	spring–autumn
Equisetum scirpoides	P	2–9	buff (foliage plant)	winter–early spring	early summer
Equisetum trachyodon	P	5–9	buff (foliage plant)	winter–early spring	early summer
Eremurus × isabellinus, Shelford Hybrids	P	5–9	white, pink, apricot, yellow tones	late summer–autumn	early summer
Eremurus robustus	P	6–9	pale peach pink	late summer–autumn	early summer
Eremurus spectabilis	P	5–9	bright yellow	late summer–autumn	early summer
Eremurus stenophyllus	P	5–9	bright yellow	late summer–autumn	early summer
Erigeron aureus	P	5–9	soft yellow	early spring	summer
Erigeron aureus 'Canary Bird'	P	5–9	soft to bright yellow	early spring	summer
Erigeron 'Charity'	P	5–9	pale lilac pink	early spring	summer
Erigeron compositus	P	5–9	white, pink, lilac or blue	early spring	summer
Erigeron 'Dunkelste Aller'	P	5–9	deep purple	early spring	summer
Erigeron foliosus	P	5–9	lavender-blue	early spring	summer
Erigeron formosissimus	P	6–9	blue, pink or white	early spring	summer
Erigeron glaucus & cultivars	P	3–10	lilac-pink	early spring	summer
Erigeron 'Wayne Roderick'	P	5–9	soft pink	early spring	summer
Erinus alpinus	P	6–9	rosy purple or white	autumn or spring	late spring–summer
Eriogonum nervulosum	P	8–10	pale yellow to red	most of the year	summer
Eriogonum umbellatum	P	6–9	bright yellow	most of the year	summer
Eriophyllum lanatum	P	5–9	bright yellow	late winter–spring	late spring–summer
Erodium cheilanthifolium	P	6–9	white to pink with deep pink	spring–early summer	summer
Erodium chrysanthum	P	6–9	cream to sulfur yellow	spring–early summer	summer
Erodium glandulosum	P	7–9	pale pink with purple	spring–early summer	summer
Erodium × kolbianum 'Natasha'	P	6–9	pink & purple-red	spring–early summer	summer
Erodium manescaui	P	6–9	bright magenta	spring–early summer	summer
Erodium pelargoniiflorum	P	6–9	white & purple	spring–early summer	late spring–autumn
Erodium trifolium var. *montanum*	P	7–9	pink & dark pink	spring–early summer	summer
Erodium × variabile 'Bishop's Form'	P	7–9	bright pink	spring–early summer	summer
Eryngium alpinum	P	3–9	purple-blue	winter–early spring	summer–autumn

NAME	TYPE	ZONES	COLOR	PLANTING TIME	FLOWERING SEASON
Eryngium amethystinum	P	7–10	purple & silver-blue	winter–early spring	summer–autumn
Eryngium bourgatii & cultivars	P	5–9	silver-blue to gray-green	winter–early spring	summer–autumn
Eryngium giganteum	P	6–9	pale silvery blue-green	winter–early spring	summer
Eryngium 'Jos Eijking'	P	7–9	silver-blue	winter–early spring	summer–autumn
Eryngium proteiflorum	P	8–11	silver-white	winter–early spring	summer–autumn
Eryngium × *tripartitum*	P	5–9	magenta	winter–early spring	summer–autumn
Eryngium variifolium	P	7–10	silver-blue	winter–early spring	summer–autumn
Erysimum × *allionii*	P	3–10	yellow or orange	autumn–spring	spring–early summer
Erysimum 'Bowles' Mauve'	P	6–11	rosy purple	most of the year	autumn–early summer
Erysimum cheiri	A(B)	7–10	most except true blue	autumn–spring	late winter–early summer
Erysimum cheiri 'Monarch Fair Lady'	A(B)	7–10	bright yellow to orange	autumn–spring	late winter–early summer
Erysimum 'Golden Bedder'	A(B)	8–10	yellow to orange	most of the year	winter–early summer
Erysimum 'Jubilee Gold'	P	7–10	golden yellow	autumn–winter	spring
Erysimum linifolium	P	6–10	deep mauve	most of the year	autumn–early summer
Erysimum 'Moonlight'	P	6–9	sulfur yellow	most of the year	spring–early summer
Erysimum mutabile	P	9–11	pale yellow to purple	most of the year	autumn–early summer
Erysimum ochroleucum	P	6–9	bright yellow	most of the year	spring–summer
Erysimum 'Orange Flame'	P	6–11	deep orange	most of the year	autumn–early summer
Erysimum perofskianum	B(P)	7–9	orange to orange-red	winter–spring	summer
Erysimum 'Winter Cheer'	P	6–11	cream, yellow & purple-pink	most of the year	autumn–early summer
Eschscholzia caespitosa	A	7–10	yellow	spring	summer–autumn
Eschscholzia californica	P	6–11	orange or yellow, pink, red tones	spring	summer–autumn
Espeletia schultzii	P	10–12	yellow	spring	spring–summer
Eupatorium fistulosum	P	7–10	mauve-pink	spring or late autumn	summer–autumn
Eupatorium maculatum	P	5–10	rose-purple	spring or late autumn	summer–autumn
Euphorbia amygdaloides	P	7–9	green	autumn–early spring	spring–early summer
Euphorbia characias	P	8–10	green	autumn–early spring	spring
Euphorbia glauca	P	9–11	blue-green	autumn or early spring	spring–early summer
Euphorbia griffithii	P	6–9	orange & yellow	autumn–early spring	summer
Euphorbia griffithii 'Fireglow'	P	6–9	orange-red & yellow	autumn–early spring	summer
Euphorbia marginata	A	4–10	green & white	early spring	summer

NAME	TYPE	ZONES	COLOR	PLANTING TIME	FLOWERING SEASON
Euphorbia palustris	P	5–9	yellow-green	autumn–early spring	late spring
Euphorbia polychroma	P	6–9	yellow	autumn–early spring	spring–early summer
Euphorbia polychroma 'Major'	P	6–9	yellow-green	autumn–early spring	spring–early summer
Euphorbia schillingii	P	5–9	green	autumn–early spring	summer–autumn
Euphorbia seguieriana ssp. *niciciana*	P	5–9	yellow to red	autumn–early spring	late summer
Euphorbia sikkimensis	P	6–9	yellow-green	autumn–early spring	summer–autumn
Eustoma grandiflorum	B	9–11	white, pink, blue or purple	spring	summer
Exacum affine	B(A)	10–12	purple-blue	spring	summer
Fagopyrum esculentum	A	3–9	white	spring–summer	summer
Farfugium 'Aureomaculatum'	P	7–10	bright yellow	early spring	autumn
Farfugium japonicum	P	7–10	bright yellow	early spring	autumn
Fascicularia bicolor	P	8–11	pale blue-green	spring–summer	late summer–autumn
Felicia amelloides	P	9–11	light sky blue	spring	spring–autumn
Felicia heterophylla	A	9–11	blue	spring	summer
Felicia petiolata	P	9–11	white to violet	spring	summer
Ferula communis	P	8–10	yellow	summer	early summer
Filipendula purpurea	P	6–9	purple-red	autumn–spring	summer
Filipendula ulmaria & cultivars	P	2–9	creamy white	autumn–spring	summer
Filipendula vulgaris	P	6–9	white	autumn–spring	summer
Fittonia verschaffeltii	P	11–12	greenish white (foliage plant)	summer	variable
Fragaria chiloensis	P	4–10	white	autumn–spring	spring–summer
Fragaria 'Pink Panda'	P	4–10	bright pink	autumn–spring	spring–autumn
Fragaria 'Red Ruby'	P	4–10	red	autumn–spring	spring–autumn
Francoa sonchifolia	P	7–10	pale pink	early spring	summer–early autumn
Gaillardia × *grandiflora*	A(P)	5–10	yellow, orange, red, burgundy	spring	summer–autumn
Gaillardia × *grandiflora* 'Dazzler'	A(P)	5–10	yellow-orange & maroon	spring	summer–autumn
Gaillardia × *grandiflora* 'Kobold'	A(P)	5–10	yellow & red	spring	summer–autumn
Galium odoratum	P	5–10	white	autumn or spring	late spring
Galium verum	P	3–10	yellow	autumn or spring	summer–early autumn
Gaura lindheimeri	P	5–10	white & pink	most of the year	spring–autumn
Gazania 'Flore Pleno'	P	9–11	bright yellow	autumn–spring	early spring–summer

NAME	TYPE	ZONES	COLOR	PLANTING TIME	FLOWERING SEASON
Gazania 'Gwen's Pink'	P	9–11	pink & red-brown	autumn–spring	early spring–summer
Gazania krebsiana	P	9–11	yellow to orange-red	autumn–spring	early spring–summer
Gazania rigens	P	9–11	orange & brown-black	autumn–spring	early spring–summer
Gazania, Sunshine Hybrids	P	9–11	cream, yellow, orange, pink	autumn–spring	summer
Gentiana acaulis	P	3–9	deep blue	early spring	spring–early summer
Gentiana asclepiadea	P	6–9	violet blue	early spring	autumn
Gentiana bellidifolia	P	7–9	white to cream	early spring	summer–early autumn
Gentiana dinarica	P	6–9	deep blue	early spring	summer
Gentiana farreri	P	5–9	sky blue & white	early spring	autumn
Gentiana 'Inverleith'	P	5–9	light blue & dark blue	early spring	autumn
Gentiana lutea	P	5–9	yellow	early spring	summer
Gentiana paradoxa	P	6–9	deep blue, white & purple	early spring	late summer
Gentiana septemfida	P	3–9	dark blue to purple-blue	early spring	late summer–early autumn
Gentiana sino-ornata	P	6–9	dark blue	early spring	autumn
Gentiana sino-ornata 'Alba'	P	6–9	white	early spring	autumn
Gentiana verna	P	5–9	bright deep blue	early spring	spring
Gentiana verna 'Angulosa'	P	5–9	bright deep blue	early spring	spring
Geranium 'Brookside'	P	4–9	bright purple	most of the year	spring
Geranium × *cantabrigiense*	P	5–9	purplish pink	most of the year	spring–summer
Geranium cinereum	P	5–9	white or pink with purple	most of the year	late spring–early summer
Geranium cinereum 'Ballerina'	P	5–9	pink with purple veins	most of the year	late spring–early summer
Geranium clarkei	P	7–9	white or violet with pink	most of the year	summer
Geranium endressii	P	5–9	pale pink	most of the year	early summer–early autumn
Geranium erianthum	P	3–9	violet	most of the year	early summer
Geranium himalayense	P	4–9	violet-blue & white	most of the year	late spring–summer
Geranium himalayense 'Gravetye'	P	4–9	lavender blue & purple-red	most of the year	late spring–summer
Geranium himalayense 'Plenum'	P	4–9	purplish pink	most of the year	late spring–summer
Geranium ibericum	P	6–9	violet	most of the year	early summer
Geranium incanum	P	8–10	deep pink	spring	summer–autumn
Geranium 'Johnson's Blue'	P	5–9	purplish blue	most of the year	late spring–summer
Geranium macrorrhizum	P	4–9	pink, purple or white	most of the year	spring–early summer
Geranium m. 'Ingwersen's Variety'	P	4–9	pale pink	most of the year	spring–early summer
Geranium maculatum	P	6–9	lilac-pink & white	most of the year	late spring–summer

NAME	TYPE	ZONES	COLOR	PLANTING TIME	FLOWERING SEASON
Geranium maderense	P	9–10	magenta pink	late winter–early spring	spring–summer
Geranium malviflorum	P	9–10	violet-blue & purple-red	spring	spring
Geranium × oxonianum	P	5–9	pink with dark veins	most of the year	late spring–autumn
Geranium × oxonianum 'Claridge Druce'	P	5–9	mauve-pink with dark veins	most of the year	late spring–autumn
Geranium × oxonianum 'Wargrave Pink'	P	5–9	bright pink	most of the year	late spring–autumn
Geranium phaeum & varieties	P	5–10	brownish purple, pink or white	most of the year	late spring–early summer
Geranium pratense & cultivars	P	5–9	violet-blue	most of the year	summer
Geranium psilostemon	P	6–9	magenta	most of the year	summer
Geranium renardii	P	6–9	white with purple veins	most of the year	early summer
Geranium robertianum	P	6–10	pink shades	most of the year	summer–autumn
Geranium sanguineum & varieties	P	5–9	pink to magenta	most of the year	summer
Geranium sylvaticum & varieties	P	4–9	white to purple & white	most of the year	late spring–summer
Geranium traversii & varieties	P	8–9	white to pale pink	most of the year	summer–autumn
Gerbera jamesonii cultivars	P	8–11	white, yellow, orange, pink, red	most of the year	spring–summer
Geum chiloense	P	5–9	bright red	autumn or spring	late spring–summer
Geum chiloense 'Lady Stratheden'	P	5–9	golden yellow	autumn or spring	late spring–summer
Geum chiloense 'Mrs Bradshaw'	P	5–9	bright red	autumn or spring	late spring–summer
Geum montanum	P	6–9	golden yellow	autumn or spring	summer
Geum triflorum	P	5–9	white to pale pink	autumn or spring	summer
Gilia capitata	A	7–9	lavender blue	spring	summer–early autumn
Gillenia trifoliata	P	3–9	white to pale pink	spring	summer
Glaucidium palmatum	P	6–9	lilac to mauve	early spring	late spring–early summer
Glaucidium palmatum var. leucanthum	P	6–9	white	early spring	late spring–early summer
Glechoma hederacea	P	6–10	mauve (foliage plant)	autumn–spring	late spring–early summer
Glechoma hederacea 'Variegata'	P	6–10	mauve (foliage plant)	autumn–spring	late spring–early summer
Globularia cordifolia	P	6–9	blue to mauve	spring	late spring–early summer
Globularia gracilis	P	7–9	lavender blue	spring	summer
Globularia × indubia	P	5–9	mauve	spring	spring–early summer
Globularia punctata	P	5–9	purple-blue	spring	summer
Globularia sarcophylla	P	6–9	mauve	spring	spring–early summer
Gunnera manicata	P	7–9	greenish-red (foliage plant)	winter–early spring	summer

NAME	TYPE	ZONES	COLOR	PLANTING TIME	FLOWERING SEASON
Gunnera tinctoria	P	7–9	red-brown (foliage plant)	winter–early spring	late spring–early summer
Guzmania lingulata	P	11–12	white to yellow flowers, red bracts	spring–summer	summer
Guzmania lingulata 'Indiana'	P	11–12	white to yellow flowers, orange-red bracts	spring–summer	summer
Guzmania 'Squarrosa'	P	11–12	white flowers, red bracts	spring–summer	summer
Gypsophila paniculata	P	4–10	white	spring–autumn	late spring–summer
Gypsophila paniculata 'Compacta Plena'	P	4–10	white to pale pink	spring–autumn	late spring–summer
Gypsophila repens	P	4–9	white, lilac or pale purple	spring–autumn	summer
Haberlea rhodopensis	P	6–9	lilac or white	most of the year	spring–early summer
Hacquetia epipactis	P	6–9	yellow flowers, green bracts	winter	early spring
Hedychium coccineum	P	9–11	coral to red	winter–early spring	mainly summer
Hedychium gardnerianum	P	9–11	red & pale yellow	winter–early spring	mainly summer
Helenium autumnale	P	3–9	yellow & red to maroon	winter–early spring	late summer–autumn
Helenium 'Moerheim Beauty'	P	5–9	brownish orange-red	winter–early spring	summer–autumn
Heliamphora heterodoxa	P	11–12	white to pink	spring	early winter
Heliamphora nutans	P	11–12	white to pink	spring	early winter
Helianthemum nummularium	P	5–10	cream, yellow, pink, orange	spring–summer	late spring–summer
Helianthus annuus	A	4–11	cream, yellow, russet red	spring	summer–autumn
Helianthus maximilianii	P	4–9	bright yellow	autumn–spring	summer–autumn
Helianthus × multiflorus & cultivars	P	5–9	bright yellow	autumn–spring	late summer–autumn
Helichrysum argyrophyllum	P	9–11	yellow	most of the year	summer–early winter
Helichrysum petiolare	P	9–10	cream (foliage plant)	spring–summer	late winter–spring
Helichrysum retortum	P	9–11	white	most of the year	spring
Heliconia bihai	P	11–12	white flowers, red bracts	spring	variable, mainly summer
Heliconia collinsiana	P	11–12	yellow flowers, red bracts	spring	variable, mainly summer
Heliconia latispatha	P	11–12	yellow flowers, red & yellow bracts	spring	variable, mainly summer
Heliconia psittacorum	P	11–12	yellow flowers, orange bracts	spring	summer
Heliconia rostrata	P	11–12	cream flowers, red & yellow bracts	spring	variable, mainly summer
Heliconia wagneriana	P	11–12	cream flowers, cream & red bracts	spring	spring
Heliopsis helianthoides	P	4–9	golden yellow	autumn–spring	summer
Heliopsis h. 'Light of Loddon'	P	4–9	bright yellow	autumn–spring	summer
Heliotropium arborescens	P	9–11	lavender to purple-blue	spring	late spring–autumn

NAME	TYPE	ZONES	COLOR	PLANTING TIME	FLOWERING SEASON
Helleborus argutifolius	P	6–9	green	autumn	late winter–early spring
Helleborus foetidus	P	6–10	green	autumn	winter–early spring
Helleborus lividus	P	7–9	creamy green	autumn	winter–early spring
Helleborus niger	P	3–9	white tinted pink	autumn	winter–early spring
Helleborus orientalis	P	6–10	white, green, pink to purple	autumn	late winter–early spring
Helleborus purpurascens	P	6–19	pink & green	autumn	winter–early spring
Helleborus 'Queen of the Night'	P	6–10	deep brownish purple	autumn	winter–early spring
Hemerocallis forrestii	P	5–10	yellow	autumn–spring	summer
Hemerocallis fulva	P	4–11	orange-red	autumn–spring	summer
Hemerocallis fulva 'Flore Pleno'	P	4–11	orange-red	autumn–spring	summer
Hemerocallis hybrids	P	5–11	cream, yellow, pink, orange, red	autumn–spring	summer–autumn
Hemerocallis lilioasphodelus	P	4–9	bright yellow	autumn–spring	summer
Hepatica nobilis	P	5–9	blue, pink or white	autumn	spring
Hesperis matronalis	B(P)	3–9	white to lilac	spring	summer
Heterocentron elegans	P	10–11	carmine-purple	spring	summer
Heterotheca villosa	P	5–9	yellow	spring	summer–autumn
Heuchera × brizoides	P	3–10	white, pink or red	autumn or spring	spring–summer
Heuchera × brizoides 'June Bride'	P	3–10	white	autumn or spring	spring–summer
Heuchera maxima	P	9–10	pinkish white	autumn or spring	spring–summer
Heuchera 'Palace Purple'	P	5–10	white	autumn or spring	summer
Heuchera 'Pewter Veil'	P	5–10	pinkish red	autumn or spring	spring–summer
Heuchera pilosissima	P	6–10	pink or white	autumn or spring	late spring
Heuchera sanguinea	P	6–10	coral to scarlet	autumn or spring	spring–summer
Heuchera villosa	P	5–10	white or pink	autumn or spring	spring–summer
× *Heucherella tiarelloides*	P	5–9	bright pink	autumn–spring	spring–summer
× *Heucherella t.* 'Bridget Bloom'	P	5–9	light pink	autumn–spring	spring–summer
Hibiscus moscheutos	P	5–9	white to pink	spring	summer–autumn
Hosta 'Birchwood Parky's Gold'	P	6–10	mauve (foliage plant)	late winter–spring	late spring–summer
Hosta crispula	P	6–10	lavender (foliage plant)	late winter–spring	early summer
Hosta 'Eric Smith'	P	6–10	lavender (foliage plant)	late winter–spring	early summer
Hosta fluctuans & cultivars	P	6–10	pale violet (foliage plant)	late winter–spring	summer
Hosta fortunei & cultivars	P	6–10	lavender (foliage plant)	late winter–spring	summer
Hosta 'Frances Williams'	P	6–10	white (foliage plant)	late winter–spring	early summer

NAME	TYPE	ZONES	COLOR	PLANTING TIME	FLOWERING SEASON
Hosta 'Gold Edger'	P	6–10	white to lavender (foliage plant)	late winter–spring	summer
Hosta 'Golden Sculpture'	P	6–10	lavender (foliage plant)	late winter–spring	early summer
Hosta 'Golden Tiara'	P	6–10	purple (foliage plant)	late winter–spring	summer
Hosta 'Halcyon'	P	6–10	dusky mauve (foliage plant)	late winter–spring	summer
Hosta 'Honeybells'	P	6–10	white & mauve (foliage plant)	late winter–spring	late summer
Hosta 'Hydon Sunset'	P	6–10	lavender-purple (foliage plant)	late winter–spring	summer
Hosta 'June'	P	6–10	dusky mauve (foliage plant)	late winter–spring	summer
Hosta 'Krossa Regal'	P	6–10	lavender (foliage plant)	late winter–spring	summer
Hosta lancifolia	P	6–10	pale lilac (foliage plant)	late winter–spring	late summer–autumn
Hosta 'Pearl Lake'	P	6–10	lavender-blue (foliage plant)	late winter–spring	summer
Hosta plantaginea	P	3–10	white (foliage plant)	late winter–spring	late summer–early autumn
Hosta 'Royal Standard'	P	3–10	white (foliage plant)	late winter–spring	early summer
Hosta sieboldiana	P	6–10	white (foliage plant)	late winter–spring	early summer
Hosta tokudama & cultivars	P	6–10	pale mauve (foliage plant)	late winter–spring	summer
Hosta undulata	P	6–10	mauve (foliage plant)	late winter–spring	summer
Hosta 'Wide Brim'	P	6–10	mauve (foliage plant)	late winter–spring	summer
Houttuynia cordata	P	5–11	yellow & white (foliage plant)	spring–summer	summer
Hunnemannia fumariifolia	P	8–10	yellow	spring	summer–autumn
Hypericum cerastoides	P	6–9	bright yellow	spring–summer	late spring–early summer
Hyssopus officinalis	P	3–11	violet-blue, white or pink	spring–summer	late summer
Iberis amara	A	7–11	white or pink	spring	spring–summer
Iberis pruitii	A(P)	7–11	white to lilac	spring	summer
Iberis sempervirens	P	4–11	white	late winter–spring	spring–early summer
Iberis umbellata	A	7–11	white, mauve, pink to carmine	spring	late spring–summer
Impatiens glandulifera	A	6–10	lilac to purple or white	spring	summer
Impatiens, New Guinea Hybrids	P(A)	10–12	pink, orange, red or cerise	spring	late spring–autumn
Impatiens pseudoviola	P	10–12	rose-pink & violet	spring	late spring–autumn
Impatiens p. 'Woodcote'	P	10–12	pale lilac-pink	spring	late spring–autumn
Impatiens repens	P	10–12	golden yellow	spring	late spring–autumn
Impatiens usambarensis	P(A)	10–12	vermilion to deep red	spring	late spring–autumn

NAME	TYPE	ZONES	COLOR	PLANTING TIME	FLOWERING SEASON
Impatiens usambarensis × *walleriana*	P(A)	10–12	most except true blue	spring	late spring–autumn
Incarvillea arguta	P	8–10	deep pink or white	spring	summer
Incarvillea delavayi	P	6–10	purplish pink	spring	summer
Inula helenium	P	5–10	yellow	autumn–spring	summer
Ipomoea × *multifida*	A	9–12	crimson & white	spring	summer
Ipomoea nil	P(A)	9–12	white, pink, mauve to crimson	spring	summer–autumn
Ipomoea tricolor	P(A)	9–12	mauve to blue	spring	summer–autumn
Iresine herbstii & cultivars	P(A)	10–12	cream (foliage plant)	spring	late spring–summer
Iris, Bearded Hybrids	P	5–10	most except true red	early summer	late spring–early summer
Iris bracteata	P	7–9	cream to yellow, red veining	spring	early summer
Iris cristata	P	6–9	lavender to purple	spring	early summer
Iris cristata 'Alba'	P	6–9	white	spring	early summer
Iris douglasiana	P	8–10	white to deep purple-blue	spring	spring–early summer
Iris ensata	P	4–10	white, lavender, blue, purple	winter–spring	late spring–early summer
Iris ensata 'Exception'	P	4–10	deep purple	winter–spring	late spring–early summer
Iris germanica	P	4–10	violet to purple-blue	early summer	late spring–early summer
Iris germanica 'Florentina'	P	4–10	white flushed blue	early summer	late spring–early summer
Iris germanica var. *biliottii*	P	4–10	purple & reddish purple	early summer	late spring–early summer
Iris innominata	P	8–10	cream, gold, lavender or purple	winter–spring	late spring–early summer
Iris japonica	P	8–11	white or pale blue with violet	winter	late winter–early spring
Iris lactea	P	4–9	pale lavender or white	early summer	late spring–early summer
Iris, Louisiana Hybrids	P	7–10	most except true red	late winter–spring	late spring–early summer
Iris lutescens	P	5–9	yellow, violet-blue or white	winter	early spring
Iris maackii	P	4–9	light yellow	early summer	spring–early summer
Iris missouriensis	P	3–9	violet to purple-blue	winter	spring
Iris munzii	P	8–10	pale blue, lavender, purple-red	winter–early spring	summer
Iris orientalis	P	6–9	white & golden yellow	winter	early summer
Iris pallida & cultivars	P	4–10	pale blue to violet	early summer	late spring–early summer
Iris pseudacorus & cultivars	P	5–9	yellow	autumn	late spring–early summer
Iris pumila	P	4–9	white, yellow violet or purple	early summer	spring
Iris pumila 'Purpurea'	P	4–9	deep purple	early summer	spring

NAME	TYPE	ZONES	COLOR	PLANTING TIME	FLOWERING SEASON
Iris 'Roy Davidson'	P	5–9	golden yellow	autumn	late spring–early summer
Iris setosa ssp. *canadensis*	P	3–9	lavender-blue	autumn–winter	late spring–early summer
Iris sibirica & cultivars	P	4–9	white, violet to purple-blue	winter	late spring–early summer
Iris, Spuria Hybrids	P	4–9	white, yellow, blue to	late winter–spring	summer
Iris tectorum	P	5–10	lilac blue & white, dark veins	late autumn–winter	spring–early summer
Iris tenax	P	8–10	white, yellow, lavender to blue	late autumn–winter	spring–summer
Iris unguicularis	P	7–10	violet, purple-blue or white	late summer–early winter	autumn–spring
			purple		
Jeffersonia diphylla	P	5–9	white	late winter–spring	late spring–early summer
Jovibarba hirta	P	7–10	brown (foliage plant)	late spring–summer	summer
Keckiella antirrhinoides var. *anti.*	P	9–11	yellow & orange-red	spring	spring
Keckiella corymbosa	P	8–11	bright scarlet	spring	summer
Kirengeshoma palmata	P	5–10	pale yellow	winter–early spring	late summer–autumn
Knautia macedonica	P	6–10	reddish purple	winter–early spring	summer–auutmn
Kniphofia caulescens	P	7–10	coral pink to yellow	spring	summer–autumn
Kniphofia ensifolia	P	8–10	yellow	spring	autumn–winter
Kniphofia hybrids	P	7–10	cream, yellow & orange tones	spring	late spring–autumn
Kniphofia × *praecox*	P	7–10	orange and/or yellow	spring	summer
Kniphofia triangularis	P	7–10	orange to yellow	late winter–spring	summer
Kniphofia tuckii	P	7–10	pale yellow & red	spring	autumn–winter
Kniphofia uvaria	P	7–10	orange-red & yellow	spring	late summer–autumn
Kohleria eriantha	P	10–11	orange to orange-red	spring	summer–autumn
Lamium album	P	4–10	white	early spring	late spring–early autumn
Lamium galeobdolon	P	6–10	yellow (foliage plant)	early spring	summer
Lamium garganicum	P	6–10	pink, purple or white	early spring	early summer
Lamium maculatum	P	4–10	pink shades	early spring	spring–summer
Lamium maculatum cultivars	P	4–10	white or pink to purple shades	early spring	spring–summer
Lathraea clandestina	P	6–10	purple pink	autumn	summer
Lathyrus nervosus	P	8–10	purple-blue	autumn or spring	summer
Lathyrus odoratus & cultivars	A	4–10	most except true yellow	autumn or spring	summer
Lathyrus vernus	P	4–10	reddish-purple to blue	autumn	late winter–spring
Lavatera trimestris	A	8–11	white or pink shades	spring	late spring–autumn
Lavatera trimestris 'Mont Blanc'	A	8–11	white	spring	late spring–autumn

NAME	TYPE	ZONES	COLOR	PLANTING TIME	FLOWERING SEASON
Lavatera trimestris 'Silver Cup'	A	8–11	deep pink	spring	late spring–autumn
Leontopodium alpinum	P	5–9	silvery white	spring	spring–early summer
L. ochroleucum var. *campestre*	P	4–9	cream to pale yellow	spring	spring–early summer
Leucanthemum paludosum	A	7–11	pale yellow or cream	spring	summer
Leucanthemum p. 'Show Star'	A	7–11	bright yellow	spring	summer
Leucanthemum × superbum	P	5–10	white	late winter–spring	summer–autumn
Leucanthemum × superbum cultivars	P	5–10	white to creamy yellow	late winter–spring	summer–autumn
Leucanthemum vulgare	P	3–10	white	late winter–spring	early summer
Lewisia 'Ben Chace'	P	5–9	pink	spring	summer
Lewisia columbiana	P	5–9	white to pale pink	spring	summer
Lewisia cotyledon	P	6–10	white, yellow, pink, purple tones	spring	summer
Lewisia cotyledon var. *howellii*	P	6–10	pinkish purple	spring	early summer
Lewisia cotyledon 'Pinkie'	P	6–10	pink	spring	summer
Lewisia tweedyi	P	5–9	pale to peach pink	spring	spring–summer
Liatris punctata	P	3–10	purple or white	winter–early spring	autumn
Liatris spicata	P	3–10	purple, pink or white	winter–early spring	late summer–autumn
Liatris spicata 'Floristan Violett'	P	3–10	deep violet	winter–early spring	late summer–autumn
Liatris spicata 'Kobold'	P	3–10	bright purple	winter–early spring	late summer–autumn
Libertia peregrinans	P	8–10	white	winter–early spring	spring–early summer
Ligularia dentata	P	4–9	orange-yellow	late winter–spring	summer
Ligularia stenocephala	P	5–10	yellow	late winter–spring	summer
Limonium gmelinii	P	4–10	lilac	winter–early spring	late spring–summer
Limonium latifolium	P	5–10	lavender-blue or white	winter–early spring	summer
Limonium minutum	P	8–10	lilac	winter–early spring	late spring–summer
Limonium perezii	P	9–11	mauve to purple & white	winter–early spring	summer
Limonium sinuatum	P(A)	9–10	lilac to purple	early spring	summer–early autumn
Limonium s. Petite Bouquet Series	P(A)	9–10	most except true red	early spring	summer–early autumn
Linaria alpina	P	4–10	white, yellow, violet or pink	autumn or spring	spring–summer
Linaria purpurea	P	6–10	violet tinged purple	autumn or spring	summer
Linaria purpurea 'Canon J. Went'	P	6–10	pale pink	autumn or spring	summer
Linaria vulgaris	P	4–10	yellow	autumn or spring	summer–autumn
Lindernia americana	P	9–11	purple & white	spring	spring–summer

NAME	TYPE	ZONES	COLOR	PLANTING TIME	FLOWERING SEASON
Lindheimera texana	A	6–10	yellow	spring	late summer–early autumn
Linum campanulatum	P	7–10	yellow–orange	autumn–spring	summer
Linum capitatum	P	7–10	deep golden yellow	autumn–spring	summer
Linum flavum	P	5–10	golden yellow	autumn–spring	summer
Linum narbonense	P	5–10	violet	autumn–spring	summer
Linum perenne & varieties	P	7–10	light blue, blue or white	autumn–spring	summer
Liriope muscari & varieties	P	6–10	violet-blue to purple	early spring	late summer
Lithodora 'Star'	P	7–10	lilac striped purple	spring	spring–early summer
Lobelia cardinalis	P	3–10	bright red	autumn–spring	late summer–autumn
Lobelia erinus	A	7–11	white, pink, blue or purple	spring	spring–autumn
Lobelia erinus 'Crystal Palace'	A	7–11	deep violet-blue	spring	spring–autumn
Lobelia erinus 'Tim Riece'	A	7–11	pale violet-blue	spring	spring–autumn
Lobelia × *gerardii*	P	7–10	pink, violet or purple	autumn–spring	late summer
Lobelia × *speciosa*	P	4–10	pink, mauve, red or purple	autumn–spring	late summer–autumn
Lobelia splendens	P	8–10	bright red	late winter–spring	late summer
Lobelia tupa	P	8–10	scarlet to brick red	late winter–spring	late summer–autumn
Lobularia maritima	A	7–10	white	spring	spring–autumn
Lobularia maritima cultivars	A	7–10	white, cream, pink to purple	spring	spring–autumn
Lotus berthelotii	P	10–11	red	spring–early summer	spring–early summer
Lotus maculatus	P	10–11	brownish yellow	spring–early summer	spring–early summer
Lotus maculatus 'Gold Flame'	P	10–11	golden yellow to orange	spring–early summer	spring–early summer
Lunaria annua	B	8–10	white or magenta to purple	autumn or spring	spring–early summer
Lunaria rediviva	P	8–10	pale violet	autumn or spring	spring–early summer
Lupinus hartwegii	A	7–11	blue, white or pink	late summer–autumn	late winter–early summer
Lupinus hybrids	P	3–9	most colors	autumn–early spring	late spring–summer
Lupinus texensis	A	8–10	blue & white	autumn or spring	late spring–early summer
Lychnis × *arkwrightii* 'Vesuvius'	P	6–10	deep orange	late winter–spring	summer
Lychnis chalcedonica	P	4–10	orange-red	late winter–spring	summer
Lychnis coronaria	P(B)	4–10	pink to scarlet	late winter–spring	summer
Lychnis coronaria 'Alba'	P(B)	4–10	white	late winter–spring	summer
Lychnis flos-jovis	P	5–9	bright pink	late winter–spring	summer
Lychnis viscaria	P	4–9	mauve to magenta	late winter–spring	summer
Lychnis viscosa 'Splendens Plena'	P	4–9	bright magenta	late winter–spring	summer
Lycopodium phlegmaria	P	11–12	foliage plant	most of the year	not applicable

NAME	TYPE	ZONES	COLOR	PLANTING TIME	FLOWERING SEASON
Lysichiton americanus	P	5–9	soft yellow	winter–early spring	spring–early summer
Lysichiton camtschatcensis	P	5–9	white	winter–early spring	spring
Lysimachia clethroides	P	4–10	white	late winter–early spring	summer
Lysimachia congestiflora	P	7–10	golden yellow	spring	late summer
Lysimachia ephemerum	P	6–10	white	late winter–early spring	summer
Lysimachia nummularia & cultivars	P	4–10	bright yellow	late winter–early spring	late spring–early autumn
Lysimachia punctata	P	5–10	golden yellow	late winter–early spring	summer–early autumn
Lysimachia vulgaris	P	5–10	bright to golden yellow	late winter–early spring	summer–early autumn
Lythrum salicaria	P	3–10	pink to magenta	winter–early spring	summer–autumn
Lythrum virgatum	P	4–10	pink, mauve, crimson	winter–early spring	summer–autumn
Malva moschata	P	3–10	pink	spring	summer
Malva moschata 'Alba'	P	3–10	white	spring	summer
Malva moschata 'Husker's Red'	P	3–10	crimson	spring	summer
Maranta leuconeura & cultivars	P	11–12	white (foliage plant)	spring	summer
Marrubium kotschyi	P	7–10	reddish-purple	spring	summer
Marrubium supinum	P	7–10	pink or lilac	spring	summer
Matricaria recutita	A	6–10	white & golden yellow	spring	summer–autumn
Matthiola incana strains	B	6–10	white, pink, mauve to purple	autumn–spring	mid-winter–early summer
Meconopsis betonicifolia	P(B)	7–9	sky blue	spring	late spring–early summer
Meconopsis cambrica	A, B or P	6–10	bright yellow	spring	spring–autumn
Meconopsis grandis	P	5–9	deep sky blue	spring	late spring–early summer
Meconopsis pseudointegrifolia	P	7–9	soft yellow	spring	late spring–early summer
Meconopsis × *sheldonii*	P	6–9	sky blue	spring	late spring–early summer
Melissa officinalis	P	4–10	white	late winter–spring	late summer
Mentha arvensis	P	4–10	lilac	autumn or spring	summer–autumn
Mentha × *piperita*	P	3–10	purple	autumn or spring	spring
Mentha pulegium	P	7–10	white, pale lilac to purple	autumn or spring	summer–autumn
Menyanthes trifoliata	P	3–10	white	spring	summer
Mertensia ciliata	P	4–10	blue	autumn–spring	late spring–summer
Mertensia ciliata 'Blue Drops'	P	4–10	bright blue	autumn–spring	late spring–summer
Mertensia pulmonarioides	P	3–9	bright blue	autumn–spring	spring

NAME	TYPE	ZONES	COLOR	PLANTING TIME	FLOWERING SEASON
Meum athamanticum	P	4–9	white or purple-pink	spring	summer
Mimulus cardinalis	P	7–11	yellow & red	spring	summer–autumn
Mimulus × hybridus hybrids	P(A)	6–10	cream, yellow, orange or red	spring	late spring–summer
Mimulus × hybridus 'Ruiter's Hybrid'	P(A)	6–10	orange	spring	late spring–summer
Mimulus luteus	P	7–10	bright yellow	spring	summer
Mimulus moschatus	P	7–10	yellow spotted red-brown	spring	summer–autumn
Mirabilis jalapa	P	8–11	white, yellow, pink to crimson	spring	summer
Moltkia doerfleri	P	6–10	deep purple	spring	late spring–summer
Moluccella laevis	A(B)	7–10	white flowers, green calyces	spring	summer
Monarda citriodora	A	5–11	white or pink to purple	spring	summer–autumn
Monarda didyma	P	4–10	white, pink, mauve or red	late winter–spring	summer–autumn
Monarda didyma 'Aquarius'	P	4–10	lilac-purple	late winter–spring	summer–autumn
Monarda 'Mahogany'	P	4–10	lilac to wine red	late winter–spring	summer–autumn
Monardella villosa	P	8–11	pale pink to rose purple	most of the year	summer
Monopsis lutea	A	10–11	bright yellow	spring	spring–summer
Morina longifolia	P	6–10	white to cerise	spring	summer
Musa velutina	P	9–12	yellow flowers, red bracts	spring	summer
Myosotidium hortensia	P	9–11	purple-blue or white	late winter–spring	spring–early summer
Myosotis alpestris	P(A)	4–10	blue, pink or white	autumn–spring	late spring–early summer
Myosotis sylvatica	B(P)	5–10	blue, pink or white	autumn–spring	spring–early summer
Myosotis sylvatica 'Blue Ball'	B(P)	5–10	blue	autumn–spring	spring–early summer
Myriophyllum aquaticum	P	10–12	yellow	most of the year	summer
Myrrhis odorata	P	5–10	white	autumn or spring	early summer
Nelumbo lutea	P	6–11	pale yellow	spring	summer
Nelumbo nucifera	P	8–12	pink or white	spring	summer
Nemesia caerulea	P	8–10	pink, lavender or blue	spring	summer
Nemesia caerulea 'Elliot's Variety'	P	8–10	mauve-blue	spring	summer
Nemesia strumosa & seed strains	A	9–11	white, yellow, red or orange	spring–summer	spring–autumn
Nemophila maculata	A	7–11	white & purple	autumn or spring	summer
Nemophila menziesii	A	7–11	blue & white	autumn or spring	summer
Neomarica northiana	P	10–11	creamy white, crimson, violet	autumn–spring	spring–summer
Neoregelia carolinae & cultivars	P	10–12	blue-purple (foliage plant)	spring–autumn	summer

NAME	TYPE	ZONES	COLOR	PLANTING TIME	FLOWERING SEASON
Neoregelia chlorosticta	P	10–12	white (foliage plant)	spring–autumn	summer
Neoregelia concentrica & cultivars	P	10–12	blue (foliage plant)	spring–autumn	summer
Nepenthes bicalcarata	P	11–12	brownish purple (foliage plant)	spring–summer	summer
Nepenthes × coccinea	P	11–12	brownish purple (foliage plant)	spring–summer	summer
Nepenthes maxima	P	11–12	brownish purple (foliage plant)	spring–summer	summer
Nepeta cataria	P	3–10	white	spring–summer	spring–autumn
Nepeta clarkei	P	3–9	lilac & white	spring–summer	summer
Nepeta × faassenii & cultivars	P	3–10	lavender-blue	spring–summer	summer
Nepeta nervosa	P	5–9	purplish-blue or yellow	spring–summer	summer
Nepeta racemosa	P	3–10	lavender-blue	spring–summer	summer
Nepeta racemosa 'Blue Wonder'	P	3–10	deep violet-blue	spring–summer	summer
Nepeta racemosa 'Snowflake'	P	3–10	white	spring–summer	summer
Nertera granadensis	P	8–11	greenish-white	spring	early summer
Nicotiana alata	P(A)	7–11	white, pink or red	spring	summer–autumn
Nicotiana langsdorfii	A	9–11	lime green	spring	summer
Nicotiana × sanderae	A	8–11	white, pink, crimson to red	spring	summer–autumn
Nicotiana × sanderae 'Falling Star'	A	8–11	white or pale to deep pink	spring	summer–autumn
Nicotiana sylvestris	P	8–11	white	spring	summer
Nicotiana tabacum	A(B)	8–11	greenish white to rose red	spring	summer
Nidularium innocentii	P	10–12	white or red	spring to early summer	variable
Nigella damascena	A	6–10	white, blue or purple tones	autumn or spring	spring–early summer
Nigella damascena 'Miss Jekyll'	A	6–10	blue	autumn or spring	spring–early summer
Nolana paradoxa	A	8–11	purple-blue & white	spring	summer
Nuphar lutea	P	4–11	deep yellow-orange	spring	summer
Nuphar polysepala	P	4–11	greenish yellow tinted purple	spring	summer
Nymphaea capensis	P	9–11	bright blue	spring	summer–autumn
Nymphaea gigantea	P	10–12	sky blue to purple-blue	spring	summer–autumn
Nymphaea, Hardy Hybrids	P	5–10	all except true red	spring	late spring–autumn
Nymphaea nouchali	P	11–12	blue, pink or white	spring	summer–autumn
Nymphaea odorata	P	3–11	white	spring	summer–autumn
Nymphaea tetragona 'Helvola'	P	7–10	soft yellow	spring	summer–autumn

NAME	TYPE	ZONES	COLOR	PLANTING TIME	FLOWERING SEASON
Nymphaea, Tropical Day Hybrids	P	10–12	all except true red	spring	summer–autumn
Nymphaea, Tropical Night Hybrids	P	10–12	all except true red	spring	summer–autumn
Nymphoides indica	P	10–12	white & yellow	late winter–early spring	summer
Nymphoides peltata	P	6–10	golden yellow	late winter–early spring	summer
Ocimum tenuiflorum	P(A)	10–12	pale mauve	spring	summer
Oenanthe crocata	P	5–10	white	late winter–spring	summer
Oenothera biennis	B	4–10	bright yellow	spring	summer
Oenothera elata ssp. *hookeri*	B(P)	7–9	yellow to orange-red	spring	summer
Oenothera fruticosa & forms	B(P)	4–10	bright to deep yellow	spring	summer
Oenothera macrocarpa	P	5–9	bright yellow	spring	summer
Oenothera odorata	P	7–10	yellow to orange-red	spring	summer
Oenothera speciosa & cultivars	P	5–10	white to pink shades	spring	summer
Omphalodes cappadocica	P	6–9	purple-blue	autumn–spring	spring
Omphalodes c. 'Cherry Ingram'	P	6–9	purple-blue	autumn–spring	spring
Omphalodes c. 'Starry Eyes'	P	6–9	purple-blue edged white	autumn–spring	spring
Omphalodes verna	P	6–9	blue & white	autumn–spring	spring
Onopordum acanthium	B	6–10	light purple	spring	late summer–autumn
Onosma alborosea	P	7–9	white to pink	summer–autumn	summer
Onosma tauricum	P	6–9	pale yellow	summer–autumn	summer
Ophiopogon japonicus	P	8–11	pale purple	autumn	summer
Origanum 'Barbara Tingey'	P	7–9	pink flowers, purple-pink bracts	autumn or spring	summer
Origanum laevigatum	P	7–9	lavender flowers, purple bracts	autumn or spring	summer
Origanum libanoticum	P	8–10	pink flowers, pink bracts	autumn or spring	summer
Origanum vulgare & cultivars	P	7–10	white flowers	autumn or spring	summer
Orontium aquaticum	P	7–9	cream to yellow	late winter	summer
Orthophytum gurkenii	P	9–11	green flowers, green bracts	summer	variable
Orthophytum navioides	P	9–12	white flowers, red-purple bracts	summer	variable
Orthrosanthus multiflorus	P	9–10	blue to purple	late winter	spring
Osteospermum fruticosum & cultivars	P	8–10	white. pink, burgundy to purple	spring	winter–spring
Osteospermum 'Pink Whirls'	P	8–10	pink	spring	summer
Osteospermum 'Whirligig'	P	8–10	white & purplish gray	spring	summer

NAME	TYPE	ZONES	COLOR	PLANTING TIME	FLOWERING SEASON
Oxalis articulata	P	8–11	rose pink	autumn–early winter	summer–autumn
Oxalis massoniana	P	9-10	soft orange	autumn–early winter	late summer–autumn
Oxalis oregana	P	7–10	rose pink or white	autumn–early winter	spring–autumn
Paeonia bakeri	P	5–9	bright purple-red	late winter–spring	late spring
Paeonia lactiflora hybrids	P	6–9	white, cream, pink, mauve, red	late winter–spring	late spring–summer
Paeonia mascula & subspecies	P	8–10	pink, white or red	late winter–spring	late spring
Paeonia mlokosewitschii	P	6–9	pale to bright yellow	late winter–spring	late spring–early summer
Paeonia mollis	P	6–9	deep pink or white	late winter–spring	early summer
Paeonia officinalis & cultivars	P	5–9	white, cream, pink, mauve, red	late winter–spring	late spring–summer
Paeonia peregrina	P	8–10	deep red	late winter–spring	late spring
Papaver alpinum	P(A)	5–10	white or yellow	spring	summer
Papaver atlanticum & cultivars	P	6–10	pale orange to red	spring	summer
Papaver bracteatum	P	5–10	red	autumn or spring	summer
Papaver commutatum	A	8–10	bright red	spring	summer
Papaver nudicaule	A	2–10	white, yellow, orange, pink, red	spring	summer
Papaver orientale & cultivars	P	3–9	white, yellow, orange, pink, red	spring	summer
Papaver rhoeas & seed strains	A	5–9	white, pink, red to purple	spring	summer
Papaver somniferum & seed strains	A	7–10	white, pink, red or purple	spring	summer
Paris japonica	P	8–10	white flushed pink	late winter–early spring	spring–summer
Paris lanceolata	P	7–10	golden anthers, green sepals	late winter–early spring	spring–summer
Paris polyphylla	P	7–10	yellow-green	late winter–early spring	spring–summer
Paris polyphylla var. *yunnanensis*	P	7–10	white	late winter–early spring	spring–summer
Paris tetraphylla	P	8–10	green & white	late winter–early spring	late spring
Parnassia grandifolia	P	6–10	white	late winter–spring	late spring–summer
Parochetus communis	P	9–11	bright blue	spring	late summer–autumn
Paronychia argentea	P	7–11	yellow	spring	summer
Paronychia capitata	P	5–10	yellow	spring	summer
Pelargonium crispum	P	9–11	pink (foliage plant)	spring–summer	summer
Pelargonium cucullatum	P	9–11	reddish-mauve	spring	spring–summer

NAME	TYPE	ZONES	COLOR	PLANTING TIME	FLOWERING SEASON
Pelargonium, Ivy-leaved Hybrids	P	9–11	white, pink, mauve, purple, red	spring–summer	spring–autumn
Pelargonium odoratissimum	P	10–11	white (foliage plant)	spring	summer
Pelargonium peltatum	P	9–11	pink	spring–summer	spring–autumn
Pelargonium, Scented-leafed Hybrids	P	9–11	white, pink or purple	spring–summer	summer
Pelargonium 'Splendide'	P	9–11	red & white	spring	spring–autumn
Pelargonium tricolor	P	9–11	white & red	spring	summer
Pelargonium, Zonal Hybrids	P	9–11	white, pink, mauve, purple, red	spring–summer	spring–autumn
Pelargonium zonale	P	9–11	red	spring	summer
Penstemon barbatus	P	3–10	purple-pink	spring–summer	summer–autumn
Penstemon campanulatus	P	9–11	reddish purple to violet	spring–summer	summer–autumn
Penstemon cardwellii	P	8–10	bright purple	spring–summer	summer
Penstemon cultivars	P	7–10	white, pink, mauve, purple, red	spring–summer	summer–autumn
Penstemon digitalis	P	3–9	white or pale lavender	spring–summer	summer–autumn
Penstemon glaber	P	3–10	purple-red & white	spring–summer	late summer–autumn
Penstemon × gloxinioides	P	7–9	pink or red with white	spring–summer	summer–autumn
Penstemon heterophyllus	P	8–10	violet-pink to blue	spring–summer	summer
Penstemon hirsutus	P	3–9	pale purple	spring–summer	summer
Penstemon pinifolius	P	8–11	orange-red	spring–summer	summer–autumn
Penstemon serrulatus	P	5–10	deep blue to purple	spring–summer	late summer–autumn
Pentaphragma horsfieldii	P	11–12	cream to green	summer	summer
Pentas lanceolata	P(A)	10–12	pink, lilac, white or red	spring	spring–summer
Peperomia argyreia	P	11–12	creamy white (foliage plant)	spring–summer	variable
Peperomia caperata & cultivars	P	11–12	creamy white (foliage plant)	spring–summer	variable
Pericallis × hybrida	P(A)	9–11	most except yellow shades	autumn–spring	winter–early summer
Pericallis lanata	P	9–11	purple & white	spring	spring
Perovskia atriplicifolia	P	6–9	lavender-blue	late winter–spring	late summer–autumn
Persicaria amplexicaulis & cultivars	P	5–9	red & crimson shades	autumn–spring	summer–autumn
Persicaria bistorta	P	4–9	white or pink	autumn–spring	summer
Persicaria bistorta 'Superba'	P	4–9	soft pink	autumn–spring	summer
Persicaria campanulata	P	8–10	white or pink	autumn–spring	late summer–autumn
Persicaria campanulata 'Rosenrot'	P	8–10	deep pink	autumn–spring	late summer–autumn

NAME	TYPE	ZONES	COLOR	PLANTING TIME	FLOWERING SEASON
Persicaria filiformis	P	5–10	greenish white to pale pink	autumn–spring	summer–autumn
Persicaria macrophylla	P	5–9	pink or red	autumn–spring	summer
Persicaria orientale	P	8–11	pink, purple-pink or white	autumn–spring	late summer–autumn
Petunia × *hybrida*	P(A)	9–11	most colors	spring–summer	late spring–autumn
Petunia integrifolia & seed strains	P	9–11	crimson to purple tones	spring–summer	late spring–early winter
Phacelia grandiflora	A	8–11	mauve to white	spring–early summer	summer–autumn
Phlomis russeliana	P	7–10	yellow	late winter–spring	summer
Phlomis tuberosa	P	7–10	pink to light purple	late winter–spring	summer
Phlox adsurgens & cultivars	P	6–10	bright pink	late winter–early spring	late spring–early summer
Phlox douglasii	P	5–10	lavender, pink to crimson or white	late winter–early spring	late spring–early summer
Phlox drummondii & seed strains	A	6–10	most colors except true yellow	spring	summer
Phlox maculata & cultivars	P	5–10	white, pink or purple	late winter–early spring	summer
Phlox paniculata & cultivars	P	5–10	pink, purple, red shades or white	late winter–early spring	summer–autumn
Phlox pilosa ssp. *ozarkana*	P	5–10	white, pink or purple	late winter–early spring	spring
Phlox subulata & cultivars	P	3–10	pink, purple, red shades or white	late winter–early spring	spring–early summer
Phormium cookianum cultivars	P	8–11	red-brown to yellow (foliage plant)	late winter–spring	summer
Phormium cultivars	P	8–11	red-brown to yellow (foliage plant)	late winter–spring	summer
Phormium tenax cultivars	P	8–11	red-brown to yellow (foliage plant)	late winter–spring	summer
Phuopsis stylosa	P	7–9	pink	spring	summer–autumn
Physalis alkekengi	P	6–10	white	spring	summer–early autumn
Physalis alkekengi var. *franchetii*	P	6–10	creamy white	spring	summer–early autumn
Physalis peruviana	P(A)	8–11	purple & yellow	spring	summer–early autumn
Physostegia virginiana	P	3–10	pink, magenta or white	spring	late summer–autumn
Physostegia v. 'Summer Spire'	P	3–10	deep pink	spring	late summer–autumn
Phyteuma comosum	P	6–9	violet-blue	late winter–early spring	summer
Phyteuma spicatum	P	6–10	white, cream or blue	late winter–early spring	summer
Phytolacca americana	P	2–11	white	winter–early spring	summer
Pilea involucrata	P	10–12	greenish white (foliage plant)	spring–summer	summer

NAME	TYPE	ZONES	COLOR	PLANTING TIME	FLOWERING SEASON
Pilea nummulariifolia	P	10–12	cream (foliage plant)	spring–summer	summer
Pilosella laticeps	P	8–10	yellow	spring–early summer	summer
Pinguicula gypsicola	P	10–12	violet & purple shades	spring–summer	variable
Pinguicula moranensis	P	10–11	crimson or pink with red	spring–summer	variable
Pistia stratiotes	P	10–12	cream (foliage plant)	spring–summer	summer
Pitcairnia ringens	P	10–12	scarlet	spring–summer	summer
Platycodon grandiflorus & cultivars	P	4–10	blue, pink, purple shades or white	late winter–spring	summer
Plectranthus neochilus	P	10–12	pale lavender, purple bracts	spring	summer
Podophyllum peltatum	P	3–9	cream	late winter–spring	spring
Pogostemon cablin	P	11–12	pale lavender (foliage plant)	spring–summer	summer
Pogostemon heyneanus	P	11–12	pale lavender	spring–summer	summer
Polemonium boreale	P	3–9	blue to purple	winter–early spring	late spring–summer
Polemonium 'Brise d'Anjou'	P	3–9	lavender (foliage plant)	winter–early spring	late spring–summer
Polemonium caeruleum	P	2–9	blue to purple	winter–early spring	summer
Polemonium delicatum	P	6–9	blue to lavender	winter–early spring	summer
Polemonium reptans & cultivars	P	4–9	lavender to blue	winter–early spring	late spring–summer
Polemonium 'Sapphire'	P	4–9	light blue	winter–early spring	late spring–summer
Polygonatum falcatum	P	6–9	white	late winter–spring	spring
Polygonatum × hybridum	P	6–9	white	late winter–spring	spring
Polygonatum multiflorum	P	4–9	cream & green	late winter–spring	spring
Polygonatum odoratum	P	4–9	white & green	late winter–spring	spring–early summer
Pontederia cordata	P	3–10	blue	late winter–spring	summer
Portea petropolitana	P	9–12	violet-blue flowers, red-brown bracts	spring–summer	summer
Portulaca grandiflora	A	10–11	yellow, orange, pink or red	spring–early summer	summer–autumn
Potentilla alba	P	5–9	white	autumn or spring	summer
Potentilla cuneata	P	5–9	bright yellow	autumn or spring	summer
Potentilla megalantha	P	5–9	bright yellow	autumn or spring	summer
Potentilla nepalensis	P	5–9	pink to apricot & red	autumn or spring	summer
Potentilla nepalensis 'Miss Willmott'	P	5–9	cerise-red	autumn or spring	summer
Potentilla neumanniana	P	5–9	bright yellow	autumn or spring	spring–summer
Potentilla × tonguei	P	5–9	orange & red	autumn or spring	summer
Pratia perpusilla	P	8–10	white	spring	summer

NAME	TYPE	ZONES	COLOR	PLANTING TIME	FLOWERING SEASON
Primula allionii	P	7–9	pink to light rose-red	spring	winter–early spring
Primula auricula & cultivars	P	3–9	pale yellow, green, pink, maroon	late winter spring	spring
Primula beesiana	P	5–9	purple-red & yellow	late winter–spring	spring
Primula bulleyana	P	6–9	bright yellow	late winter–spring	spring
Primula capitata ssp. *mooreana*	P	5–9	violet to purple	late winter–spring	spring
Primula cockburniana	P	5–9	orange-red	late winter–spring	spring
Primula denticulata	P	6–9	purple, lilac or pink	late winter–spring	spring
Primula denticulata ssp. *alba*	P	6–9	white	late winter–spring	spring
Primula elatior	P	5–9	yellow to orange	late winter–spring	spring
Primula florindae	P	6–9	bright yellow	late winter–spring	spring
Primula forrestii	P	6–9	bright yellow	late winter–spring	spring
Primula frondosa	P	5–9	lilac to purple with yellow	late winter–spring	spring
Primula 'Garryarde Guinevere'	P	5–9	pink	late winter–spring	spring
Primula japonica	P	5–10	white, pink, crimson or purple	late winter–spring	spring
Primula juliae	P	5–9	purple & yellow	winter–spring	late winter–spring
Primula malacoides	P(A)	8–11	white, pink or magenta	autumn–early spring	winter–spring
Primula obconica	P(A)	8–11	white, pink or purplish tones	autumn–winter	winter–early spring
Primula poissonii	P	6–9	pink to crimson with yellow	late winter–spring	spring–early summer
Primula, Polyanthus Group	P(A)	6–10	all colors	autumn–spring	winter–spring
Primula polyneura	P	5–9	pink to purple-red	late winter–spring	spring
Primula pulverulenta	P	6–9	white, pink or red	late winter–spring	spring
Primula sieboldii	P	5–9	white, pink or purple	late winter–spring	spring
Primula sinopurpurea	P	5–9	purple-pink	late winter–spring	spring
Primula veris	P	5–9	soft yellow to light orange	late winter–spring	spring
Primula vialii	P	5–9	purple flowers, crimson buds	late winter–spring	spring
Primula vulgaris & seed strains	P	6–9	all colors	autumn–spring	winter–spring
Primula vulgaris 'Gigha White'	P	6–9	white & yellow	autumn–spring	winter–spring
Primula 'Wanda'	P	6–9	purple & yellow	winter–spring	late winter–spring
Protasparagus densiflorus	P	9–11	white (foliage plant)	spring	summer
Prunella grandiflora	P	5–9	pink to deep purple	most of the year	spring–early autumn
Prunella grandiflora 'Loveliness'	P	5–9	soft mauve	most of the year	spring–early autumn
Psylliostachys suworowii	A	6–10	pink to carmine	spring	summer

NAME	TYPE	ZONES	COLOR	PLANTING TIME	FLOWERING SEASON
Ptilotus manglesii	P(A)	9–11	pink to purple	summer–autumn	late winter–early summer
Pulmonaria longifolia	P	6–9	violet to blue-violet	winter–early spring	spring
Pulmonaria longifolia 'Lewis Palmer'	P	6–9	soft blue tinted pink	winter–early spring	spring
Pulmonaria 'Mawson's Blue'	P	5–9	deep blue	winter–early spring	spring
Pulmonaria officinalis	P	6–9	deep blue	winter–early spring	spring
Pulmonaria rubra	P	6–9	blue, purple-blue, pink or white	winter–early spring	spring
Pulmonaria rubra 'Redstart'	P	6–9	deep pinkish red	winter–early spring	spring
Pulmonaria saccharata	P	3–9	white, pink or blue	winter–early spring	spring
Pulmonaria saccharata 'Highdown'	P	3–9	deep blue	winter–early spring	spring
Pulsatilla alpina ssp. *apiifolia*	P	5–9	yellow	late winter–early spring	spring
Pulsatilla bungeana	P	4–9	light violet-blue	late winter–early spring	spring
Pulsatilla halleri	P	5–9	purple-pink to purple	late winter–early spring	spring
Pulsatilla halleri ssp. *slavica*	P	5–9	dark violet	late winter–early spring	spring
Pulsatilla montana	P	6–9	deep blue to purple	late winter–early spring	spring
Pulsatilla vulgaris & cultivars	P	5–9	purple, pink, red or white	late winter–early spring	spring
Puya alpestris	P	8–9	deep greenish blue	late winter–spring	summer–early autumn
Puya berteroniana	P	9–10	deep greenish blue	late winter–spring	summer–early autumn
Puya mirabilis	P	9–10	green to white	late winter–spring	summer
Quesnelia liboniana	P	11–12	blue flowers, orange-red bracts	spring	summer
Ramonda nathaliae	P	6–9	purple & yellow	early spring	late spring–early summer
Ranunculus acris & cultivars	P	5–9	bright yellow	winter–early spring	summer
Ranunculus cortusifolius	P	9–10	bright yellow	winter–early spring	summer
Ranunculus ficaria	P	5–10	bright yellow or cream to bronze	winter–early spring	spring
Ranunculus gramineus	P	7–10	bright yellow	winter–early spring	spring–summer
Ranunculus lyallii	P	7–9	white	early spring	late spring–early summer
Raoulia australis	P	7–9	yellow (foliage plant)	spring	summer
Raoulia eximia	P	7–9	cream (foliage plant)	spring	summer
Raoulia haastii	P	7–9	yellow (foliage plant)	spring	late spring
Rehmannia elata	P(B)	9–10	deep pink	late winter–spring	summer–autumn

NAME	TYPE	ZONES	COLOR	PLANTING TIME	FLOWERING SEASON
Reineckea carnea	P	7–10	white or pink	winter–early spring	late spring
Reseda luteola	B(P)	6–10	pale yellow to yellow-green	winter–early spring	summer
Reseda odorata	A	6–10	green tinted red	spring	summer–autumn
Rheum officinale	P	7–10	white to greenish white	winter–early spring	summer
Rheum palmatum	P	6–10	cream to pink or red	winter–early spring	summer
Rheum palmatum 'Atrosanguineum'	P	7–10	dark pinkish red	winter–early spring	summer
Rhodanthe chlorocephala ssp. rosea	A	9–11	white to deep pink	spring	late spring–summer
Rhodanthe 'Paper Star'	P	7–11	white	most of the year	most of the year
Rhodiola heterodonta	P	5–10	yellow to orange-red or greenish	late winter–early spring	spring–early summer
Rhodiola kirilowii	P	5–10	yellow-green to rusty red	late winter–early spring	summer
Rhodiola purpureoviridis	P	6–10	light greenish yellow	late winter–early spring	early summer
Rhodiola rosea	P	2–9	pale purple, green or yellow	late winter–early spring	spring–early summer
Rhodiola stephanii	P	5–10	creamy white	late winter–early spring	summer
Rodgersia aesculifolia	P	5–9	cream to pale pink	winter–early spring	late spring–summer
Rodgersia pinnata & cultivars	P	6–9	cream, pink or red	winter–early spring	summer
Rodgersia podophylla	P	5–9	cream	winter–early spring	late spring–summer
Rodgersia sambucifolia	P	6–10	cream to very pale pink	winter–early spring	summer
Romneya coulteri	P	7–10	white	late winter–spring	summer
Roscoea cautleoides	P	6–9	yellow to orange	late winter–early spring	late spring–summer
Rosmarinus officinalis & cultivars	P	6–11	lavender to deep blue	most of the year	autumn to early summer
Rudbeckia fulgida & varieties	P	3–10	golden yellow & brown	late winter–spring	summer
Rudbeckia hirta	B(P)	3–10	bright yellow & purplish brown	late winter–spring	summer
Rudbeckia hirta 'Toto'	B(P)	3–10	golden yellow	late winter–spring	summer
Rudbeckia laciniata & cultivars	P	3–10	bright yellow	late winter–spring	summer–early autumn
Rudbeckia subtomentosa	P	5–10	yellow & purple-brown	late winter–spring	late summer–autumn
Rumex patienta	P	6–10	green flushed pinkish red	late winter–spring	summer
Sagittaria lancifolia & cultivars	P	9–12	white	spring	summer
Saintpaulia ionantha cultivars	P	11–12	white or mauve, purple, pink shades	spring–summer	most of the year

NAME	TYPE	ZONES	COLOR	PLANTING TIME	FLOWERING SEASON
Saintpaulia ionantha hybrids	P	11–12	white or mauve, purple, pink shades	spring–summer	most of the year
Saintpaulia magungensis	P	10–12	purple	spring–summer	most of the year
Salpiglossis sinuata	A	8–11	white, gold, orange, purple, red	spring–early summer	summer–autumn
Salvia argentea	B(P)	6–9	white (foliage plant)	spring	spring–summer
Salvia austriaca	P	6–10	pale yellow	late winter–spring	summer
Salvia blepharophylla	P	8–11	red suffused orange or pink	spring	summer–autumn
Salvia cacaliifolia	P	8–10	deep blue	spring	summer–autumn
Salvia chamaedryoides	P	8–11	deep violet-blue	late winter–spring	summer
Salvia coccinea	P(A)	8–11	white or salmon pink to red	spring	early summer–late autumn
Salvia coccinea 'Coral Nymph'	P(A)	8–11	coral pink	spring	early summer–late autumn
Salvia confertiflora	P	9–11	deep brownish red	spring	late summer–autumn
Salvia darcyi	P	8–10	rich scarlet	late winter–spring	summer–early autumn
Salvia dolomitica	P	9–11	dusky lavender pink	late winter–spring	spring
Salvia elegans & cultivars	P	8–11	bright red	late winter–spring	summer–autumn
Salvia farinacea & cultivars	P(A)	8–11	white, pink & blue to purple tones	spring–early summer	summer–autumn
Salvia forsskaolii	P	7–10	violet to pinkish magenta and white	late winter–spring	summer
Salvia gesneriiflora	P	8–11	orange-red	spring	spring–autumn
Salvia greggii	P	9–10	red, orange, pink, yellow or white	spring	spring–autumn
Salvia guaranitica	P	9–11	deep violet blue	late winter–spring	summer–late autumn
Salvia guaranitica 'Purple Splendour'	P	9–11	deep purple	late winter–spring	summer–late autumn
Salvia indica	P	9–11	white & blue or lilac	spring	spring–summer
Salvia involucrata & cultivars	P	9–10	deep pink	spring	summer–autumn
Salvia multicaulis	P	8–11	violet or white	spring	spring–summer
Salvia nemorosa	P	5–10	pinkish purple or white	winter–spring	summer
Salvia officinalis & cultivars	P	5–10	bluish mauve (foliage plant)	late winter–spring	summer
Salvia pratensis	P	3–9	violet-purple or white to pale blue	winter–spring	spring–summer
Salvia puberula	P	8–10	magenta	spring	late summer–autumn
Salvia sclarea	B	5–10	greenish white tinged purple	late winter–spring	summer
Salvia spathacea	P	8–11	magenta	spring	summer

NAME	TYPE	ZONES	COLOR	PLANTING TIME	FLOWERING SEASON
Salvia splendens & cultivars	P	9–12	red to scarlet tones	spring	summer–autumn
Salvia × *sylvestris* & cultivars	P	5–10	blue to deep purple tones	late winter–spring	late spring–summer
Salvia taraxacifolia	P	9–11	white to pale pink with yellow	spring	spring–summer
Salvia uliginosa	P	8–11	sky blue	late winter–spring	summer–early autumn
Salvia viridis	A(B)	7–11	white to lilac or purple	spring	summer
Sambucus ebulus	P	5–10	white tinged pink	winter–early spring	summer
Sanguinaria canadensis & cultivars	P	3–9	white or white tinted pink	late summer–autumn	spring
Sanguisorba canadensis	P	4–9	white	late winter–spring	summer
Sanguisorba minor	P	5–9	white	late winter–spring	summer
Sanguisorba officinalis	P	4–9	reddish purple	late winter–spring	summer–autumn
Sanguisorba tenuifolia	P	4–9	white to purple	late winter–spring	summer
Sanvitalia procumbens & cultivars	A	7–11	bright yellow	spring	summer
Saponaria × *olivana*	P	5–10	pale pink	spring	summer
Saponaria ocymoides	P	4–10	pink to deep red	late winter–spring	late spring–early summer
Sarmienta scandens	P	5–9	bright red	late winter–spring	summer
Sarracenia alata	P	8–11	light yellow tinted pink	spring	spring
Sarracenia leucophylla	P	7–11	purple	late winter–spring	spring
Sarracenia purpurea	P	6–10	purple or greenish purple	late winter–spring	spring
Saussurea stella	P	7–9	purple	spring	summer
Saxifraga × *apiculata*	P	6–9	yellow	winter–spring	spring
Saxifraga 'Apple Blossom'	P	7–9	pale pink to white	winter–spring	spring–summer
Saxifraga bronchialis	P	4–9	cream spotted red	winter–spring	spring–early summer
Saxifraga bronchialis ssp. *vespertina*	P	4–9	greenish white spotted deep pink	winter–spring	spring–early summer
Saxifraga burseriana	P	6–9	crimson	winter–spring	spring–early summer
Saxifraga cotyledon	P	6–9	white sometimes spotted red	winter–spring	spring–early summer
Saxifraga exarata ssp. *moschata*	P	6–9	white or cream to pink & red	early spring	spring–early summer
Saxifraga longifolia	P	6–9	white	autumn	spring
Saxifraga marginata	P	7–9	white	winter–spring	spring–early summer
Saxifraga paniculata	P	3–9	white to cream or yellow	winter–spring	summer
Saxifraga paniculata 'Rosea'	P	3–9	bright pink	winter–spring	summer
Saxifraga paniculata var. *baldensis*	P	3–9	white tinged red	winter–spring	summer

NAME	TYPE	ZONES	COLOR	PLANTING TIME	FLOWERING SEASON
Saxifraga rotundifolia	P	6–9	white, often spotted purple	winter–spring	spring–early summer
Saxifraga 'Ruth Draper'	P	6–9	purple-pink	winter–early spring	spring
Saxifraga sempervivum	P	7–9	reddish purple	winter–spring	spring
Saxifraga stolonifera & cultivars	P	5–10	white	winter–spring	spring–early summer
Saxifraga umbrosa	P	7–9	white	winter–spring	spring–early summer
Scabiosa anthemifolia	A(P)	7–11	mauve, violet or rose	spring	summer
Scabiosa caucasica	P	4–10	mauve-blue, pink, to reddish purple	late winter–spring	summer
Scabiosa caucasica 'Staefa'	P	4–10	blue	late winter–spring	summer
Scabiosa columbaria	B(P)	6–10	reddish purple to lilac-blue	late winter–spring	summer–autumn
Scaevola aemula & cultivars	P	9–11	mauve-blue to purple with yellow	late winter–spring	early spring–late summer
Schizanthus hookeri	A	7–11	pink or violet to purple with yellow	spring	spring–summer
Schizanthus × *wisetonensis* strains	A	7–11	white, pink, blue to red with yellow	spring	spring–summer
Schizostylis coccinea	P	6–10	bright red	late winter–spring	late summer–autumn
Schizostylis coccinea cultivars	P	6–10	white or pink to red shades	late winter–spring	late summer–autumn
Scutellaria austinae	P	8–11	violet-blue	late winter–spring	summer
Scutellaria costaricana	P	9–12	orange-red & gold	spring	summer
Scutellaria incana	P	5–9	grayish blue	late winter–spring	summer–autumn
Scutellaria indica	P	5–10	blue–gray	late winter–spring	late spring–late summer
Scutellaria indica var. *parvifolia*	P	5–10	blue–gray & white	late winter–spring	late spring–late summer
Scutellaria orientalis 'Alpina'	P	7–10	golden yellow	spring	summer
Sedum ewersii	P	4–9	pink	winter–early spring	late spring–early autumn
Sedum 'Herbstfreude'	P	5–10	pink to brick red	winter–early spring	autumn
Sedum 'Mohrchen'	P	4–10	deep red	winter–early spring	late summer–early autumn
Sedum spectabile	P	5–10	pink	winter–early spring	late summer–early autumn
Sedum spurium	P	7–10	white, pink or red to purple	winter–early spring	summer
Sedum telephium	P	6–10	purple-red	winter–early spring	late summer–early autumn
Selaginella kraussiana	P	9–11	foliage plant	most of the year	not applicable
Selaginella martensii	P	9–11	foliage plant	most of the year	not applicable
Sempervivum arachnoideum	P	5–10	deep pink to crimson	late winter–spring	summer
Sempervivum tectorum	P	4–10	purple to rosy red	late winter–spring	summer

NAME	TYPE	ZONES	COLOR	PLANTING TIME	FLOWERING SEASON
Senecio elegans	A	9–11	bright purple-pink	spring	spring–summer
Shortia galacifolia	P	5–9	white, pink or blue	late winter–spring	spring–early summer
Shortia soldanelloides	P	7–9	white, pink or blue	late winter–spring	spring–early summer
Sidalcea campestris	P	6–10	pale pink or white	late winter–spring	summer
Sidalcea malviflora	P	6–10	pink or white	late winter–spring	late spring–summer
Sidalcea 'Rose Queen'	P	7–10	deep pink	late winter–spring	summer
Silene acaulis	P	2–9	pink	spring–early summer	summer
Silene armeria	A(B)	6–10	pink	spring–early summer	summer
Silene coeli-rosa	A	6–11	pinkish purple	spring–early summer	summer
Silene coeli-rosa 'Blue Angel'	A	6–11	light sky blue	spring–early summer	summer
Silene fimbriata	P	6–10	white	spring–early summer	summer
Silene keiskei var. *minor*	P	6–10	deep rose pink	spring–early summer	late summer–autumn
Silene laciniata	P	7–11	bright crimson	spring–early summer	summer–early autumn
Silene pendula	P	7–11	pale pink	spring–early summer	summer
Silene schafta	P	6–10	purple-red	spring–early summer	late summer–autumn
Silene schafta 'Shell Pink'	P	6–10	soft pink	spring–early summer	late summer–autumn
Silene uniflora & cultivars	P	3–10	white	spring–early summer	spring–summer
Silene vulgaris	P	5–10	white	spring–early summer	spring–summer
Silybum marianum	A(B)	7–11	purple-pink	spring	spring–summer
Sinningia speciosa	P	11–12	white, pink, blue, purple, red	spring–summer	summer
Sisyrinchium 'California Skies'	P	5–10	violet blue	autumn–spring	late spring–summer
Sisyrinchium graminoides	P	3–10	purple shades with yellow	autumn–spring	late spring–summer
Sisyrinchium idahoense	P	3–9	violet-blue with yellow	autumn–spring	late spring–summer
Sisyrinchium striatum	P	8–10	cream to pale yellow	late winter–spring	summer
Smilacina racemosa	P	4–9	white	autumn–early spring	summer
Smilacina stellata	P	3–9	white	autumn–early spring	summer
Solanum pseudocapsicum	P(A)	9–11	white	spring	summer
Solanum pyracanthum	P	10–12	violet	spring–early summer	summer
Soldanella hungarica	P	6–9	lavender to pale purple	early spring	spring
Soldanella montana	P	6–9	lavender	autumn or early spring	spring
Solenostemon scutellarioides	P(A)	10–12	white-cream (foliage plant)	spring–early summer	summer
Solidago 'Baby Gold'	P	5–10	golden yellow	winter–early spring	autumn
Solidago 'Golden Wings'	P	5–10	bright yellow	winter–early spring	autumn

NAME	TYPE	ZONES	COLOR	PLANTING TIME	FLOWERING SEASON
Solidago sphacelata	P	4–9	golden yellow	winter–early spring	late summer–autumn
Solidago virgaurea	P	5–10	bright yellow	winter–early spring	summer–autumn
Sonerila margaritacea & cultivars	P	10–12	pink to rose shades	spring	summer
Spathiphyllum cultivars	P	11–12	cream flowers, white spathes	spring–summer	most of the year
Spathiphyllum wallisii	P	11–12	cream flowers, white spathes	spring–summer	most of the year
Speirantha convallarioides	P	8–10	white	autumn–early spring	late spring–early summer
Stachys albotomentosa	P	9–11	salmon pink	spring	summer–autumn
Stachys byzantina	P	5–10	mauve-pink	late winter–spring	summer
Stachys byzantina cultivars	P	5–10	pink to purple shades	late winter–spring	summer
Stachys coccinea	P	6–10	red, pink or white	late winter–spring	spring–autumn
Stachys macrantha	P	5–10	purple-pink	late winter–spring	summer–early autumn
Steirodiscus tagetes & cultivars	A	9–11	yellow to orange	spring	summer
Stokesia laevis	P	7–10	white, lilac to blue	spring	late spring–summer
Strelitzia juncea	P	9–12	orange & blue	late winter–spring	spring–summer
Strelitzia nicolai	P	10–12	greenish blue & white	late winter–spring	summer
Strelitzia reginae	P	10–12	orange & blue	late winter–spring	spring–summer
Strelitzia reginae 'Mandela's Gold'	P	10–12	yellow-orange & purple-blue	late winter–spring	spring–summer
Streptocarpus caulescens	P	10–11	violet	spring–early summer	autumn
Streptocarpus hybrids	P	10–11	white, pink, mauve, purple, crimson	spring–early summer	variable, mainly spring–summer
Stromanthe sanguinea	P	10–12	white flowers, red bracts	spring	summer
Stylidium graminifolium	P	9–11	pale pink to magenta	spring	summer
Stylophorum diphyllum	P	7–10	yellow	late winter–earlyspring	spring–summer
Swainsona formosa	A	9–11	bright red with black	winter–spring	late winter–summer
Symphytum 'Goldsmith'	P	5–10	blue, pink or white	winter–early spring	summer
Symphytum asperum	P	5–10	rose to lilac	winter–early spring	summer
Symphytum caucasicum	P	5–10	red-purple to blue	winter–early spring	summer
Symphytum × *uplandicum*	P	5–10	rose to purple or blue	winter–early spring	summer
Tacca integrifolia	P	10–12	purple-red	spring	summer
Tagetes erecta seed strains	A	9–11	yellow or orange	spring–summer	summer–autumn
Tagetes lemmonii	A(P)	9–11	golden yellow	spring–summer	variable, mainly summer
Tagetes patula seed strains	A	9–11	yellow, orange or red	spring–summer	summer–autumn
Tagetes tenuifolia seed strains	A	9–11	yellow or orange	spring–summer	summer–autumn

NAME	TYPE	ZONES	COLOR	PLANTING TIME	FLOWERING SEASON
Tanacetum argenteum	P	5–10	white	late winter–early spring	summer
Tanacetum balsamita & varieties	P	6–10	white	late winter–early spring	summer
Tanacetum coccineum	P	5–9	pink, red, purple or white	late winter–early spring	late spring–early summer
Tanacetum corymbosum	P	2–10	white	late winter–early spring	summer
Tanacetum niveum	P	7–10	white	late winter–early spring	summer
Tanacetum parthenium & cultivars	P	6–10	white (also foliage plant)	late winter–early spring	summer
Tanacetum ptarmiciflorum	P	9–11	white	late winter–early spring	summer
Tapeinochilos ananassae	P	11–12	yellow flowers, scarlet bracts	spring	summer
Tellima grandiflora	P	6–9	cream	late autumn–early spring	spring
Thalia dealbata	P	9–10	violet	late winter–spring	summer
Thalictrum aquilegiifolium	P	6–10	pink, lilac or greenish white	winter–early spring	summer
Thalictrum delavayi	P	7–10	lilac	winter–early spring	summer
Thalictrum kiusianum	P	8–10	purple or white	winter–early spring	late spring–summer
Thladiantha dubia	P	7–11	yellow	spring	summer
Thymus caespititius	P	7–10	lilac to lilac-pink	late winter–spring	late spring–summer
Thymus camphoratus	P	7–10	purple	late winter–spring	summer
Thymus × citriodorus	P	7–10	lilac	late winter–spring	summer
Thymus pannonicus	P	5–10	pink	late winter–spring	summer
Thymus polytrichus	P	5–10	purple, mauve or white	late winter–spring	summer
Thymus polytrichus 'Porlock'	P	5–10	pink	late winter–spring	summer
Thymus serpyllum & cultivars	P	7–10	pink to purple shades	late winter–spring	spring–summer
Tiarella cordifolia	P	3–9	creamy white	late winter–early spring	spring
Tiarella polyphylla	P	7–10	pink or white	late winter–early spring	late spring–summer
Tiarella wherryi	P	6–10	soft pink or white	late winter–early spring	late spring
Tillandsia aeranthos	P	9–11	purple flowers, red bracts	spring–summer	summer–autumn
Tillandsia argentea	P	10–12	red or violet fls, red & green bracts	spring–summer	summer–autumn
Tillandsia bergeri	P	9–11	blue flowers, red bracts	spring–summer	summer–autumn

NAME	TYPE	ZONES	COLOR	PLANTING TIME	FLOWERING SEASON
Tillandsia caulescens	P	10–12	white to purple flowers, red bracts	spring–summer	summer–autumn
Tillandsia cyanea	P	9–11	violet-blue flowers, pink bracts	spring–summer	summer–autumn
Tillandsia flabellata	P	10–12	blue flowers, red bracts	spring–summer	summer–autumn
Tillandsia ionantha	P	9–11	white & violet flowers, red bracts	spring–summer	summer–autumn
Tillandsia lindenii	P	10–12	blue or purple flowers, red bracts	spring–summer	autumn
Tillandsia stricta	P	9–11	blue flowers, carmine bracts	spring–summer	summer–autumn
Tillandsia usneoides	P	8–11	greenish yellow (foliage plant)	spring–summer	summer
Tithonia diversifolia	P	9–11	yellow to orange-yellow	spring	late summer–autumn
Tithonia rotundifolia & seed strains	A	8–11	orange to orange–red	spring–early summer	late summer–autumn
Tolmiea menziesii	P	7–10	red-brown (foliage plant)	late winter–spring	summer
Torenia fournieri & seed strains	A	9–12	blue, purple pink, red, white	spring–early summer	summer–early autumn
Townsendia exscapa	P	3–9	white	spring	spring–early summer
Tradescantia, Andersoniana Group	P	7–10	white, mauve, pink to purple	late winter–spring	spring–autumn
Tradescantia cerinthoides	P	7–11	purple-pink	late winter–spring	spring–autumn
Tradescantia fluminensis & cultivars	P	9–12	white (foliage plant)	spring	late spring–summer
Tradescantia pallida & cultivars	P	8–11	pink (foliage plant)	late winter–spring	summer
Tradescantia sillamontana	P	9–11	purple-pink	late winter–spring	spring–autumn
Tradescantia spathacea & cultivars	P	9–11	white	late winter–spring	variable
Tragopogon dubius	B	5–10	yellow	spring	summer
Tricyrtis hirta	P	5–9	white spotted purple	late winter–spring	late summer–autumn
Tricyrtis suzukii	P	7–10	white spotted purple	late winter–spring	late summer–autumn
Trifolium pratense	P	6–10	pink to purple	autumn or spring	spring–autumn
Trifolium repens & cultivars	P	4–10	white or green	autumn or spring	spring–autumn
Trifolium uniflorum	P	7–10	lilac	autumn or spring	summer
Trillium albidum	P	6–9	white flushed pink	autumn, late winter–spring	spring
Trillium cernuum	P	6–9	white or pink	autumn, late winter–spring	spring
Trillium chloropetalum	P	6–9	green, white, pink or maroon	autumn, late winter–spring	spring

NAME	TYPE	ZONES	COLOR	PLANTING TIME	FLOWERING SEASON
Trillium cuneatum	P	6–9	red-brown to maroon	autumn, late winter–spring	early spring
Trillium grandiflorum & cultivars	P	3–9	white to pink	autumn, late winter–spring	spring
Trillium luteum	P	6–9	yellow-green	autumn, late winter–spring	spring
Trillium rugelii	P	5–9	white	autumn, late winter–spring	spring
Trillium sessile	P	4–9	maroon	autumn, late winter–spring	spring
Trillium sessile var. *californicum*	P	4–9	white	autumn, late winter–spring	spring
Trollius chinensis	P	5–9	golden yellow	autumn or spring	spring–early summer
Trollius europaeus	P	5–9	golden yellow	autumn or spring	spring–early summer
Tropaeolum majus & cultivars	A	8–11	cream, yellow, orange & red	spring	summer–autumn
Tussilago farfara	P	3–9	golden yellow	winter	spring–early summer
Tweedia caerulea	P	9–11	blue, also white or pink	spring	summer–autumn
Ursinia cakilefolia	A	9–11	deep yellow–orange	spring	summer
Ursinia calenduliflora	A	9–11	golden yellow with purple	spring	summer
Ursinia sericea	P	9–11	yellow	spring	summer
Utricularia reniformis	P	10–12	purple edged violet	spring–early summer	summer
Utricularia sandersonii	P	9–11	mauve & yellow	spring–early summer	most of the year
Uvularia perfoliata	P	4–9	pale yellow	late winter–early spring	spring
Valeriana arizonica	P	7–10	pink	autumn or spring	late spring
Valeriana officinalis	P	3–9	white to deep pink	autumn or spring	summer
Vancouveria hexandra	P	5–9	white tinged pink	late winter–early spring	summer
Vancouveria planipetala	P	7–9	white tinged lavender	late winter–early spring	spring
Veratrum album	P	5–9	pale green to white	late winter–spring	late summer
Veratrum nigrum	P	6-9	purplish brown	late winter–spring	late summer
Verbascum bombyciferum	P	6–10	golden yellow	early spring	summer
Verbascum chaixii	P	5–10	bright yellow	early spring	summer
Verbascum chaixii 'Album'	P	5–10	white	early spring	summer
Verbascum dumulosum	P	8–10	bright yellow	early spring	late spring–early summer
Verbascum 'Letitia'	P	8–10	bright yellow	early spring	spring–summer
Verbascum nigrum	P	5–10	bright yellow with purple	early spring	summer–autumn

NAME	TYPE	ZONES	COLOR	PLANTING TIME	FLOWERING SEASON
Verbascum phoeniceum	P	6–10	violet, pink or purple	early spring	spring–summer
Verbascum thapsus	B	3–9	bright yellow	early spring	summer
Verbena bonariensis	P	7–10	deep purple	spring–early summer	summer–autumn
Verbena canadensis	P(A)	5–10	purplish pink	spring–early summer	summer–autumn
Verbena × *hybrida*	P	9–10	red, purple, pink, mauve, white	spring–early summer	summer–autumn
Verbena laciniata	P	8–10	blue, magenta or violet	spring–early summer	summer–autumn
Verbena peruviana & cultivars	P	9–11	vivid red	spring–early summer	summer–autumn
Verbena rigida	P	8–10	pale violet to magenta	spring–early summer	summer–autumn
Verbena rigida 'Silver Jubilee'	P	8–10	red	spring–early summer	spring–autumn
Verbena tenuisecta	P	9–11	purple-pink edged white	spring–early summer	late spring–summer
Veronica austriaca	P	6–10	bright blue	late winter–early spring	late spring
Veronica austriaca cultivars	P	6–10	blue shades	late winter–early spring	late spring
Veronica cinerea	P	5–9	purplish blue & white	late winter–early spring	summer
Veronica gentianoides	P	5–9	pale blue or white	late winter–early spring	late spring
Veronica longifolia	P	4–9	lilac blue	late winter–early spring	late spring
Veronica longifolia 'Rosea'	P	4–9	pink	late winter–early spring	late spring
Veronica peduncularis	P	6–9	pink & blue, white or pink	late winter–early spring	late spring–early summer
Veronica peduncularis 'Georgia Blue'	P	6–9	bright blue	late winter–early spring	late spring–early summer
Veronica prostrata	P	5–9	blue	late winter–early spring	spring–early summer
Veronica spicata	P	3–9	blue	late winter–early spring	summer
Veronica spicata varieties	P	3–9	lavender, blue, pink or white	late winter–early spring	summer
Veronica spuria	P	3–9	blue	late winter–early spring	summer
Veronica 'Waterperry'	P	8–11	lavender blue	spring	variable, mainly summer
Veronicastrum virginicum	P	3–9	purplish blue or white	late winter–early spring	summer
Victoria amazonica	P	11–12	pink & white	spring–early summer	summer
Victoria amazonica × *cruziana* 'Longwood Hybrid'	P	11–12	white turning pink	spring–early summer	summer

NAME	TYPE	ZONES	COLOR	PLANTING TIME	FLOWERING SEASON
Viola cornuta & cultivars	P	6–9	pale blue to deep violet	late winter–early spring	spring–summer
Viola elatior	P	5–9	lilac blue	late winter–early spring	early summer
Viola hederacea	P	8–10	pale blue to deep violet	late winter–early spring	spring–summer
Viola labradorica	P	6–9	white & lilac	winter–early spring	spring–autumn
Viola odorata	P	6–10	violet, white or rose pink	autumn–early spring	late winter–early spring
Viola, Perennial Cultivars	P	6–10	all colors	most of the year	most of the year
Viola riviniana	P	5–10	violet-blue	late winter–early spring	spring–summer
Viola riviniana 'Purpurea'	P	5–10	purple	late winter–early spring	spring–summer
Viola septentrionalis	P	7–10	bluish purple or white	late winter–early spring	spring–summer
Viola sororia	P	4–10	white to deep violet blue	late winter–early spring	spring–summer
Viola sororia 'Freckles'	P	4–10	white flecked violet-purple	late winter–early spring	spring–summer
Viola tricolor	B(P)	4–10	yellow, blue, violet or white	most of the year	late summer–early winter
Viola tricolor 'Bowles' Black'	P	4–10	black with yellow	most of the year	late summer–early winter
Viola × *wittrockiana* hybrid seedlings	P(A)	5–10	all colors	all except midsummer	all except midsummer
Vriesea carinata	P	11–12	golden yellow flowers, red bracts	spring–summer	late autumn
Vriesea 'Christine'	P	11–12	orange-yellow flowers, red bracts	spring–summer	mainly summer
Vriesea splendens	P	11–12	yellow flowers, purple-green bracts	spring–summer	mainly summer
Wachendorfia thyrsiflora	P	8–11	bright yellow	late winter–early spring	spring–early summer
Wahlenbergia albomarginata	P	7–10	pale blue to white	spring	summer
Wahlenbergia communis	P	8–11	light blue	spring	spring–summer
Wahlenbergia gloriosa	P	8–10	deep blue to purple-blue	spring	summer
Wahlenbergia stricta	P	9–10	blue to light purple	spring	spring–summer
Waldsteinia ternata	P	3–9	golden yellow	late winter–early spring	late spring–summer
Welwitschia mirabilis	P	9–10	scarlet cones	spring	variable
Wittrockia superba	P	11–12	blue flowers, red bracts	spring–summer	summer
Wulfenia carinthiaca	P	5–9	deep violet-blue	spring	summer

NAME	TYPE	ZONES	COLOR	PLANTING TIME	FLOWERING SEASON
Xeranthemum annuum	A	7–10	white, pink or mauve	spring	summer
Xeranthemum annuum, Mixed Hybrids	A	7–10	pink, purple, mauve, red or white	spring	summer
Xeronema callistemon	P	10–11	bright red	spring	spring
Yucca baccata	P	9–11	white or cream tinged purple	late winter–spring	late summer
Yucca whipplei	P	8–11	cream, sometimes tinged purple	late winter–spring	late summer–autumn
Zantedeschia aethiopica	P	8–11	yellow flowers, white spathe	winter–early spring	late spring–early winter
Zantedeschia a. 'Green Goddess'	P	8–11	yellow flowers, green spathe	winter–early spring	late spring–autumn
Zantedeschia elliottiana	P	8–11	yellow flowers, yellow spathe	winter–early spring	summer–autumn
Zantedeschia, New Zealand Hybrids	P	8–11	yellow, orange, pink, red spathes	winter–early spring	summer
Zantedeschia rehmannii	P	8–11	yellow flowers, deep pink spathes	winter–early spring	summer–autumn
Zauschneria californica	P	8–10	bright red	late winter–early summer	late summer–early autumn
Zauschneria septentrionalis	P	8–10	orange-red	late winter–early summer	late summer–early autumn
Zinnia elegans seed strains	A	8–11	all except true blue	spring	summer–autumn
Zinnia haageana seed strains	A	8–11	yellow, orange & bronze	spring	summer–autumn
Zinnia peruviana	A	8–11	yellow to orange or scarlet	spring	summer–early autumn

Index to Common Names and Synonyms